D1250742

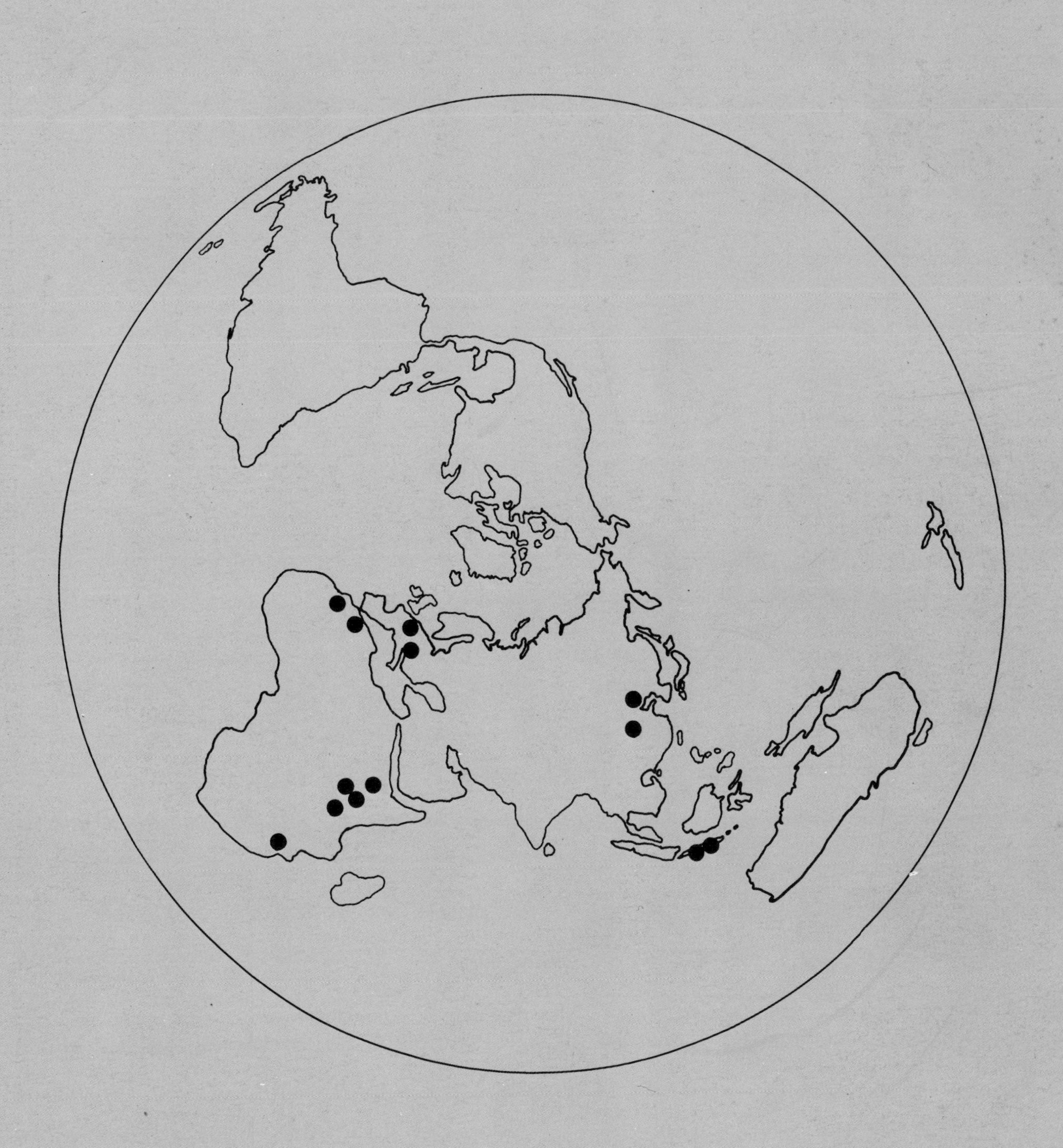

FOSSILS, TEETH AND SEX
New Perspectives on Human Evolution

FOSSILS, TEETH AND SEX
New Perspectives on Human Evolution

CHARLES E. OXNARD

UNIVERSITY OF WASHINGTON PRESS
Seattle and London

University of Washington Press edition first published in 1987
Printed in Hong Kong

Library of Congress Cataloging in Publication Data

Oxnard, Charles E., 1933-
Fossils, teeth and sex.

1. Human evolution. 2. Sex differences. 3. Teeth, Fossil. I. Title.
GN282.096 1987 573.2 87-1328
ISBN 0-295-96389-1

End papers
1 A map of China showing now known fossil human sites.
2 World distribution of fossil *Homo*.
3 World distribution of ramapithecines.
4 World distribution of dryopithecines.

Liang Yu Printing Factory Ltd.
9-11 Sai Wan Ho Street,
Shau Kei Wan, Hong Kong.

feo

Contents

Preface

This book presents a new picture of human evolution. It is one that stems, in part, from treating fossils more as we generally treat living forms. But it is also one that comes, in part, from what we learn by studying the living forms as though they were fossils.

Thinking of fossils as living forms is the reverse of what is usually done in studies of fossil primates. It means thinking of fossils as populations and as two sexes, even although we cannot actually know which individual specimens are in which populations, nor of which sex. Such a procedure better helps display the varieties of structures that exist, than when only one or a very few fossil specimens or subjects, are available for study. As a result of adopting such a strategy, this book is forced to concentrate on dimensions of teeth, because these are the only remains that are numerous enough to allow it.

Thinking of living forms as fossils is also the reverse of what we usually do. Living forms, are of course, usually studied in situations where we know the populations and the sexes from information independent of the data. Thinking of living forms as though they were fossils, means examining living forms as though we did not know population and sex for each specimen. The comparison between these two sides of the coin helps powerfully in understanding the situation in fossils where only the one side is available.

Treating the fossils more as though they were living forms also means looking at comparisons, without making the assumption that any particular fossils are on the same lineages as others. This is also different from that usually done in studies of primate fossils where, in contrast to paleontological studies of other organisms, it seems that investigators of human evolution are mainly trying to establish ancestors. Even although different species have existed at different times, this is a 'holy grail' of a task. It is generally most unlikely that fossils separated by any great amount of time one from another are ever in actual ancestral-descendent relationships to one another. Not assuming lineages allows us far more freedom to follow where our data lead, prevents us from posing the kinds of evolutionary speculations that are untestable, and takes us into a more objective assessment of individual fossils, and their relationship to our own evolution.

It is in these ways that this book differs from many others. Yet it has not been written in a vacuum. It follows from a great deal of work on human evolution that has been carried out over the centuries.

This is the fourth book in a series. The first two are an initial pair. *Form and Pattern in Human Evolution: Some Mathematical, Physical and Engineering Approaches*, and *Uniqueness and Diversity in Human Evolution: Morphometric Studies of Australopithecines*. *Form And Pattern* describes some modern methods available for the study of biological structure, with resulting implications for understanding biological function. *Uniqueness and Diversity* then applies these methods to particular supposed human ancestors, the australopithecinae. The results are interesting. On the one hand a series of general analytical methods are explained and used in ways that meet with wide approval from many scientific colleagues in biology. These methods are now applied in the study of form throughout the life sciences. On the other hand, specific results about australopithecines are anathema to many anthropologists, suggesting as they do that the australopithecines may not be as close to humans as is generally thought.

Since those books were published early in the seventies, my investigations have expanded. They now include a wider range of methods for studying biological form and pattern that are based in mathematics, physics and engineering. And they now span a far wider range of anatomical regions and animals: most parts of the body and most of the members of the Order Primates.

Thus a second pair of volumes, *The Order of Man: A Biomathematical Anatomy of The Primates*, and this book, *Fossils, Teeth and Sex: New Perspectives on Human Evolution* naturally came about. *The Order of Man* is an attempt to expand the use of morphometric methods, widely defined. In contrast, however, to the earlier *Form And Pattern* its chief aim is to apply the most well worked out of the methods, multivariate morphometrics, to as many of the living members of the Order Primates as possible. It is, as the title indicates, mainly about the living primates. In the part of that book, that deals with primate fossils, I was unable to take into account the full diversity of the fossils believed relevant to human evolution. Indeed, at that time, very few data on any fossils were available.

The present book, *Fossils, Teeth and Sex*, is an extension of the fossil part of *The Order of Man*. In contrast to the second book of the first pair, *Uniqueness And Diversity*, this one is aimed at a wide range of different fossils, because substantial new data have become available to me.

Fossils, Teeth and Sex is also due to both a logical development and a fortuitous encounter.

The fortuitous encounter occurred as a result of Professor F. Peter Lisowski, previously of Hong Kong University and now of the University of Tasmania, introducing me to Professor Wu Rukang of Beijing, China. That meeting has produced a collaboration, wherein data collected by Professor Wu Rukang and his colleagues in the Institute of Vertebrate Paleontology and Paleoanthropology of the Academia Sinica, are analysed using techniques available in our laboratory in the School of Medicine at the University of Southern California. First, the studies examined measures of over one thousand fossil teeth of ramapithecines found in excavations in Yunnan Province. Later, the investigations included the dimensions of over one thousand teeth of *Gigantopithecus* from caves in Guangxi Province. These have lead, most recently of all, to a series of studies of equivalent data from many other fossils from all over the world believed pertinent to human evolution. The total body of fossil data thus now available is as voluminous, perhaps even more so, than those already known from the living species. Analyses of all these data, and the assessments and discussions that flow from them form the basis for this book.

The logical development is also clear. All the prior studies of fossils with which I have been associated, depended upon measurements of only a few australopithecine post-cranial bones. They resulted in controversial conclusions about this group of fossils. The new studies of teeth present a totally independent way of testing these conclusions and redefining these controversies.

The conclusions are of three orders.

The **first** is that whenever we look at australopithecine post-cranial parts (*Australopithecus africanus* and *A. robustus*) using multivariate statistical tools we conclude that they are not like humans in their structure. They are not even intermediate between humans and modern African apes. Indeed, they are more different from humans and African apes than humans and African apes are from each other.

This conclusion was disputed for many years, it being generally asserted that the fragments were closest to humans in their form. There is now abundant evidence from many laboratories that this is not so. This first order conclusion is now generally accepted. Attention has been drawn to it by all reviewers of *The Order of Man* although it is true that the enthusiasm with which this is done varies enormously. Thus, Fleagle, 1984, in a review entitled 'The Master of Multiple Dimensions' in the *American Journal of Primatology*, 7:151-153, Stern, 1984, in the *American Journal of Physical Anthropology*, 65:329-331, Moore, 1984, in the *Journal of Anatomy*, 139:584-585, and Ashton, in the *Annals of Human Biology*, 11:590-592, are infectiously enthusiastic in their agreement with this point. Shea, 1984, in a review entitled 'Primate Morphometrics' in *Science*, 224:148-149, is grudgingly appreciative. Wood, 1984, in a review entitled 'Primatology by Numbers' in *Nature*, 309:289-290 is in quite disparaging agreement.

The **second** order conclusion speaks to the functions implied by the structures of those fossil fragments. The earlier view was that bony structures similar to humans implied bipedality 'in the human manner'. Given that the bones are now recognized as being of a uniquely different structure than is found in either humans or African apes, it seems that these particular fossils may have possessed an equivalently unique set of functions. These may have included a form of bipedality biomechanically quite different from that of humans today, together with abilities for climbing in trees different from those of any living ape. Each of these abilities and their combination in a single species would certainly supply a unique set of functions to go with the unique structures that we now know existed.

This conclusion was also largely disputed for several years, and to some degree still is. But there is now a large and rapidly increasing volume of results, from many independent workers, suggesting that some assessment like this may be closer to the truth than the idea that these fossils were simply human bipeds. Again, even the aforementioned reviewers have come easily (Fleagle, Stern, Moore, Ashton) or been forced, unwillingly, it seems (Shea, Wood) to this conclusion. The recent discovery of even earlier fossils (*A. afarensis*) makes it easier for the later species to be evaluated in this way. Whether it will also take as long for the earlier species to be so evaluated, is an interesting question. It appears, however, as though it will not be long before acceptance of such a new functional description for australopithecines will become the norm.

The **third** order conclusion that comes from all this speaks to a phylogenetic position. Thus, a unique morphology implying a unique behaviour denies the view that has existed for many years: that the australopithecines were pre-human ancestors that were intermediate between us and some non-human, probably African ape-like ancestor. A unique morphology implying a unique behaviour may mean either (**a**) that the australopithecines were indeed on the human lineage, but as some unique mosaic form or (**b**), that the australopithecines were on some parallel lineage, a third branch in a radiation of forms that included also both humans and, separately, the African apes.

Mosaic evolution is a perfectly good biological idea. It is quite old. And it must be reckoned to be a real possibility. But parallel evolution is yet a better biological idea, is even older, and perhaps even more likely.

There are still some workers who hold to the older view of the australopithecines as intermediate in a human lineage. Other workers have been willing to change to include australopithecines as mosaic forms close to the human lineage. Scarcely anyone at all is willing to even look at the parallel possibility. *I do not know which of these is the way things were. But I insist upon the right to test all. And I suspect that the last is the most likely.*

If a different form (or even several different forms) of bipedalism did exist in one or more australopithecines, then it is not unlikely that bipedalism has arisen more than once in the radiation of species with which humans and African apes are associated. Multiple appearances of new developments in new evolutionary radiations are a relatively frequent feature of evolution. This leads to the suggestion that, perhaps the australopithecines themselves were not so close to the human lineage, that one or more of them were direct human ancestors. Perhaps they were far enough distant from the human lineage to be a sister group (or even several sister groups) to both the African apes and, separately, humans.

This third conclusion is, of course, less certain than either of the others. But it does follow logically and therefore must be examined and not swept under the carpet. The evidence of the reviews of Moore and Ashton indicates that this is no problem for them; but then these are individuals with whom I have worked in the past. Fleagle and Stern view this suggestion more critically in their reviews but they do not shrink from discussing it. So far, however, even just voicing the possibility has been almost totally unacceptable to some anthropologists. The great majority of discussions on this third conclusion are, at least at the present time, as negative as were the initial reactions to the first two conclusions. Thus the review by Shea, mentioned above, categorically rejects the idea, while the review by Wood refuses, almost hysterically, to accept that it should even be discussed. It is an interesting commentary on the history of ideas that, within nine months of his negative reactions, Wood (1985) presents a major paper indicating that his own new data show that no australopithecine currently known could have been a human ancestor!

But the discovery of *Australopithecus afarensis* has started a small crack in the idea that *A. africanus* was simply and unequivocally a human ancestor. From a time when it seemed that almost everyone was quite certain that *Australopithecus africanus* was that ancestor (it was even named *Homo africanus* by one exuberant investigator) we have moved to a time when there is argument as to which of *A. africanus* or *A. afarensis* is that ancestor. It is not yet fashionable to suggest that it might have been neither.

What this book therefore attempts to do is to look, using both univariate and multivariate morphometric techniques, at a wide range of hominid and hominoid fossils. As with my previous books, this is done without involving the general reader in the complexities of the statistical analyses. Those remain in original scientific papers for the scrutiny of peer investigators. Yet the reader is encouraged to understand what statistical analysis can do for us. The studies of primate post-cranial bones depend upon information from large numbers of dissections of primate cadavers that I have carried out. Dissection is merely a way of studying the form of soft tissues through observation and using scalpel and forceps. The studies of bones and teeth, likewise, depend upon information from very large numbers of measurements analysed using statistical techniques. In this sense these statistical techniques are merely a way of dissecting the form of bones defined by numbers and using calculators and computers.

What this book further attempts to do, bearing in mind that results from studies of small numbers of post-cranial fossils have not been overly persuasive within the profession, is to carry out these studies using large samples. This means that we can better know populations through averages and variations, and be less dependent upon the vagaries of single, possibly far from average, specimens. Such studies have to be based upon teeth, because these are the only anatomical parts that are available in such large samples. Using teeth means we lose the functional inferences that can be readily derived from post-cranial bones. But we gain from the marked improvements in the sample sizes.

This book attempts to see to what extent data from teeth also corroborate, or deny, or modify the controversial questions raised by the earlier studies. And as this book examines patterns due to the differences between females and males, the effects of many features taken together as well as individual characteristics, and fossil data from Asia as well as Africa, it has the capacity to introduce new elements into the human evolutionary story.

Perhaps the most exciting part of the results is the quite unexpected glimpse that we are given of the evolution of sexual dimorphism in humans and apes. The implications that stem from it may be of fundamental importance in understanding both the process of hominisation and our current human condition.

Acknowledgements

As I have explained this book naturally follows from the earlier ones. But it also depends upon a number of other factors.

A series of speaking invitations have been especially important in its development. These include three keynote lectures that I have given to the most recent biennial meetings of the Chinese Medical Association (Anatomy Section) at the invitation of Professor Wu Rukang. They also include two series of lectures on the evolution of hominids and hominoids, first in the Department of Anatomy, Hong Kong University, under successive heads, Professors Peter Lisowski and Brian Weatherhead, and second in the Department of Anatomy, St Andrews University, Scotland, under the headship of Professor David Brynmor Thomas. And they include, finally and most recently, the first Distinguished Faculty Lecture in the Graduate School at the University of Southern California.

These ideas also owe much of their development to a series of invited papers that have been part of the thinking process. These include a contribution entitled 'Hominoids and Hominids, Lineages and Radiations' published in the volume *Past Present and Future of Hominid Evolution* edited by Professor Philip Tobias, and arising from the Taung Diamond Jubilee International Scientific Symposium. They also include a chapter entitled 'Comparative Anatomy of the Primates: Old and New' in *Comparative Primate Biology, Volume I: Systematics, Evolution and Anatomy* edited by Professor Daris R. Swindler. And they include, most recently, a chapter entitled 'Evolutionary Radiations in Humans and Great Apes: Some Quantitative Evidence' in *Perspectives in Primate Biology*, edited by Professors P. K. Seth and S. Seth.

Because I am not myself a statistician, I must especially acknowledge the help and collaboration that I have received from a number of statisticians over the years who have especial expertise in this area (Professors Michael Healy, Roger Flinn, Peter Neeley, Paul Meier, David Wallace and William Kruskal). In addition to such personal discussion and help in the statistical area, I have also felt it most important to 'put my head in the lion's mouth' by accepting every invitation to present these studies in departments of statistics. In this regard, the Department of Statistics at the University of Chicago has been especially important through its invitations to me over the years. In more recent times, the Department of Statistics and its head, Professor John Aitchison of the University of Hong Kong, and the Department of Statistics and its head, Professor Michael Healy of the London School of Hygiene and Tropical Medicine, have likewise provided critical comment. Most recently of all have been invitations to speak, by mathematicians Professors Michael Waterman and Robert Guralnick, both at the University of Southern California, and by statistician Professor Paul Sampson of the University of Washington (who invited me to participate in a symposium on morphometrics at the joint meeting of the Institute of Mathematical Statistics and the Biometric Society at Utah State University, Logan, in 1984).

Another kind of lecture participation has also been especially helpful. Those undergraduate, graduate, and medical students and faculty at the Universities of Chicago and Southern California who have suffered my lectures on *The Analysis of Biological Form and Pattern*, *The Order of the Primates*, *Animal Mechanics*, and *The Human Place in Primate Evolution* have contributed to this book in a manner that continually emphasizes to me the very close relationship and interaction that there is between teaching and research. These participations have been further augmented by invitations from individuals such as Professors Michael Waterman (in a course on *Evolutionary Biology*, Department of Biological Sciences), Joan Walker (in courses on *Biomechanics* in the Department of Physical Therapy), Suzanne Engler (in a course on *An Introduction to Human Evolution*, Department of Anthropology) and Walter Williams in a course on the study of women and men in society, all at the University of Southern California. These have allowed me to make contributions to teaching courses that emphasized new research results and directions as well as the broad general picture.

This interplay between research and teaching has, in recent years, been central in my enjoyment of academic life. In particular, the teaching has facilitated, rather than the reverse, the research and writing upon which this book so heavily depends.

The Universities of Chicago and Southern California have made it possible for me to continue my research work while I held administrative posts as Dean of the College and the Graduate School respectively. More recently the University of Southern California has supported my work generously through the provision of a Research Fund for my position as University Professor, through a Faculty Research and Innovation Fund Grant of the Graduate School, and through a Biomedical Research Support Grant of the School of Medicine.

My work has been much aided by honorary appointments that I now hold: Overseas Associate in Anatomy, University of Birmingham, U.K., Research Associate in Vertebrate Anatomy, Field Museum of Natural History, Chicago, U.S.A., Research Associate in Life Sciences, Natural History Museum, Los Angeles, and sometime Honorary Professor of Anatomy, University of Hong Kong. The collegiality engendered by these appointments has contributed greatly to this book. The Field Museum of Natural History, Chicago, and the Natural History Museum, Los Angeles have also been most helpful through allowing me to examine materials in their care.

Especial thanks go to a group of individuals who have provided direct support in the production of this book. Dr. Susan Lieberman has been my Research Associate for two years now, and has carried out many of the multivariate statistical analyses that form the background for this book. She has been especially valuable in discussion of matters to do with the biology of sexual differences. Professor Bruce Gelvin, of California State University, Northridge, has also participated strongly in these discussions and has supplied much of the original data on extant primates considered here. Professor Wu Rukang has especially provided the data on the Chinese ramapithecines and on *Gigantopithecus* and has been the source of many fruitful suggestions and collegial hospitality in China. Dr. Clifford Willcox, Orthodontist, Pasadena, has given me access to materials and records in his care that allow study of the human sexes in a carefully chosen population, and has tutored me in many aspects of the human dentition. Professor Gene H. Albrecht, Department of Anatomy, University of Southern California must be mentioned as one who participated in many of my earlier investigations and who has helped in discussions of the most recent studies on teeth.

It is an especial delight to acknowledge the work of Erika Oller who has contributed all the drawings and many of the diagrams in this book. She has not only pictured what I could not myself, but she has also contributed ideas to the artistic and scientific expression that are beyond what I had any right to expect.

I am particularly indebted to my wife, Eleanor Oxnard, whose skills in librarianship have contributed so very much to my work for many years and especially, of course, to this book.

My investigations have always been stimulated by colleagues in the Science of Biological Form. Among these mention must be made of my first colleagues at the University of Birmingham, U.K. where I received my start in research and was on the Faculty for four years: Professors F. Peter Lisowski (now of the University of Tasmania) and James W. Moore, (now of the University of Leeds), Dr. Roger M. Flinn and Mr. Thomas F. Spence. Mention must also be made of colleagues at the University of Chicago where for twelve seminal years I was involved with Professor Jack T. Stern, Jr., (now of the Department of Anatomy, State University of New York at Stony Brook), and Professors James Hopson, R. Eric Lombard, the late Leonard Radinsky, and Ronald Singer.

Although my main work has been carried out in the United States I am especially indebted to one person who guided my earliest research and with whom I have collaborated at intervals throughout my entire career: Professor Eric H. Ashton, Department of Anatomy, University of Birmingham, U.K. His sudden death has broken our career-long collaboration.

Professor A. J. E Cave, scholar, morphologist and friend has influenced me in more ways than he will ever realize.

And, finally, it is always appropriate to recognize the initial research stimulus, and the continuing interest, collaboration and support over many years now, of my own Professor, Lord Zuckerman, O.M., K.C.B., M.D., D.Sc., F.R.S., previously Sands Cox Professor of Anatomy, University of Birmingham, England, and President, Zoological Society of London, and now Honorary Professor, University of East Anglia. Many years ago he started me on the idea that the quantification of biological structure might yield new insights into function and evolution.

CHAPTER 1

Sexual Dimorphism as a Problem in Human Evolution

Abstract: There are, of course, many differences between the sexes that are directly related to the reproductive act and process. But there are also many other anatomical differences between the sexes that are only indirectly related to reproduction and are manifest all over the body. The sum total of these differences is called sexual dimorphism. Though relatively small in humans, sexual dimorphism is quite enormous in some of our closest living relatives, gorillas and orang-utans.

The current picture of this sexual dimorphism is that it is a single, unidimensional phenomenon that is displayed to greater (e.g. gorillas, orang-utans) or lesser (e.g. humans) degrees in the different primate species. It is, moreover, generally believed to be primarily related to differences in overall bodily size between the sexes. The evolutionary implication is, that in the past human sexual dimorphism must have been very much greater than it is today, perhaps more like that in the living apes.

With this in mind we examine the results of new anatomical studies of the overall form of the body in primates, using various morphometric tools (especially those of canonical variates analyses and high-dimensional displays). These studies show that sexual dimorphism is more complex than a single unidimensional spectrum. They suggest that several different sexual dimorphisms exist in the living primates. They imply that there must have been a number of different evolutionary directions in which sexual dimorphisms evolved. And this means that current views of sexual dimorphism in human ancestors are to be questioned.

The general problem of ancestors in studies of human evolution

Understanding the human lineage is one of the main problems in studying human evolution. But many fossil hunters seem to believe that this means that their task is to find the fragments of the precise human ancestor in the field. Likewise, many laboratory workers seem to believe that this means that their task is showing that a particular fossil remnant is that ancestor. Even in the public mind, studying human evolution seems to be this matter of going from 'missing' to 'found' links.

The problem seems to be the
discovery of ancestors.

But what is the reality of such an endeavour? Even from a population as large and concentrated as that of any major metropolitan area, and over as many as hundreds of generations, the statistical chances of any particular individual ever becoming fossilised and found by a palaeontologist millions of years later must be almost infinitesimal. How much less must be the chances of finding representatives of populations of perhaps only a few thousand, scattered over an area of the world as large as Africa or Asia, during periods of time measured in hundreds of thousands, even millions of years. Once we are a few thousand years beyond a death, perhaps a few tens of thousands of years at the outside, the chances of ever finding anything fossilised that can be said to be a direct ancestor of anything in our time, are small indeed.

If finding ancestors is not our main aim,
what then is?

Our aims are multiple. One aim is to compare the structures of living forms one with another and with such fossils as by chance have come to light. Such comparisons allow us to evaluate the amounts and kinds of morphological differences that have existed among related biological organisms. From these structural contrasts, a second aim is to estimate differences in function in fossil species, more widely, in behaviour, most widely of all, in environment and ecology. These estimations allow us to understand what kinds of changes may have occurred during the evolutionary process, even though we do not have direct information about what those changes were. A third aim is to attempt to understand those evolutionary mechanisms and processes specific to the group of organisms under examination. And this leads on to an understanding of those mechanisms and processes that, through extension, may apply more widely in biology. This aim includes, at the deepest level, a search for those portions of evolutionary mechanism and process that are yet hidden from us, for they surely do exist. Current theory is far from providing the total picture. Finally, our aim is to incorporate into our conclusions such information as may become available from a wide range of other disciplines: information from studies of growth and development of organisms, from the new geological dating methods, from direct studies of ecology and the environment, from the revolutionary investigations of biological molecules of recent decades, and from comparative studies of behaviour. These, all these, are the aims of evolutionary investigations of the structure of organisms in general, and of studies of living primates and primate fossils in particular.

One major implication of all this is that our studies should be producing new knowledge that adds to what we already know. Proving (testing) hypotheses and then improving them is the heart of the business of science. This applies as much to the study of human evolution as to any other study.

But the 'search for ancestors' does not, on the whole, work in this way. If finding an ancestor stood some reasonable statistical chance of success then on occasion a new find should indeed produce a new ancestor. But in a situation where the chances of anything being an ancestor of something known today are almost infinitesimal, then each find, if treated as an ancestor, takes us along the blind alley of yet another non-existent lineage, until the next 'ancestor' turns up.

We can reiterate once again that there is either no such thing as a missing link (we can never find them) or that there are thousands of missing links (and no particular one is especially more significant than any other). This problem has bedevilled the study of human evolution. So many new finds have been made. Each one is believed newly important as the human ancestor. Each is ever more shrillily lauded by its discoverers. Each new 'ancestor' (or rather the finder of each new ancestor) tries to displace the previous 'ancestor' (or its finder). It is almost as if there were a 'law of discovery of ancestors' that says 'that the degree of importance of a fossil as an ancestor is correlated with the newness of its discovery'!

In fact, the study of mechanism and process in evolution depends very little upon direct knowledge of individual fossil ancestors in particular lineages. It depends mainly on indirect inference from groups of related fossils about radiations and parallels, about convergences and divergences, and about extinctions, always, always extinctions. Such comparisons inevitably provide us, not with just one, but several different hypotheses about history, mechanism and process. And we should be able to juggle these alternative hypotheses, pending better data, without developing scientific schizophrenia. The evolutionary systems that arise from such studies should not especially be denied just because a new fossil is discovered. They should, in general, be capable of accepting most new fossils as they come to light. If, indeed, such systems cannot accommodate most new finds, then how can we say that our findings ever have any scientific validity.

Of course, the possibility of a totally new and unexpected fossil find is always present. Complete denial of hypotheses is not, and must not be excluded. It must be possible for occasional fossils to suggest new evolutionary vistas to us. Such finds must sometimes be capable of implying that certain types of structure, believed to have existed only early in time, are also represented by basically similar forms much later in time. Such finds must sometimes be able to show us that a given set of structures extends much further back in time than we may have previously believed. Such finds must sometimes be able to demonstrate to us that some utterly unsuspected structure existed. And such new fossil discoveries must sometimes provide for us new relationships between known structures, that we previously thought unlikely or even impossible. We must retain the ability to completely overturn old ideas, after due consideration. This comparative procedure, thus, uses fossils in evolutionary studies in a way somewhat similar to the way in which it uses extant forms.

Everyone knows that extant forms cannot be ancestors of one another. It is less clearly understood that this is also generally true of fossils, certainly of hominoid fossils, once we are past a million years or so. True ancestors should be found on so few occasions that we could be pardoned for not recognising them. Indeed, it is most likely that they would only rarely provide us with the information that could tell us that they were ancestors. Though fossils do indeed give us information about difference over time it must be only infrequently that they provide information about change over time. The main information that they provide is basically similar to that given by living forms, that is: information about the products of radiations. It must be rarely, indeed, that fossils ever provide us with direct information about lineages.

The sex of ancestors as a special problem in human evolution

Alongside the problem of ancestors is the problem of sex. Whether we choose to ignore it, decry it, or applaud it, we cannot deny that males and females are not the same. Primary sex differences are related to the essentially different roles played by the sexes in reproduction. This can usually be ascertained unequivocally in living species.

But many other differences are apparent, secondarily between the sexes. These give rise to the phenomenon of sexual dimorphism. In mammals this is most often associated with size: large males, small females. But it is also generally associated with the type of mating system: polygyny in species where the difference in size between the sexes is large, monogamy where it is small (Trivers, 1972; Alexander, 1977). In most primates, however, these differences are smaller than is evident in a species like the southern elephant seal (the males of which may weigh as much as three tons, as much as five times more than the females). Even in the most dimorphic primates there is usually considerable overlap between males and females.

In such a situation, just as we can only rarely know if a given fossil is an ancestor or not, so we can only rarely know if a given fossil is female or male. Even in living specimens determination of sex may not be easy. If the anatomical region examined is not part of the reproductive apparatus it may be quite difficult to say, even through measurement, whether or not the part comes from a male or a female.

There is however, one special difference between extant forms and fossils. Even though, in living species we may not know the sex of a particular specimen for certain, we can decide for certain when a particular anatomical feature or measure presents a difference between known samples of males and females. For fossils we do not have known samples of males and females. This renders even more difficult the problem of understanding sexual dimorphism in fossils.

This is an especial problem in studying the evolution of those groups of animals where there is great variation in sexual dimorphism. Differences between the sexes in a species that shows large sexual dimorphism may be mistaken for a difference between two species. Differences between species in which there is only small sexual dimorphism may, equally, be mistaken for differences between the sexes. Obviously, because of the overlap, often enormous, that exists between all females and all males in most non-reproductive features, it is only rarely possible to decide from which sex a given fragment (especially if that fragment be a piece of jaw or a tooth – which is what most fossils are) may have derived. This is an especially vexing problem for hominoid evolution because, among the hominoids, ourselves and our closest living relatives, the great apes, great variation in the amount of sexual dimorphism is the rule. Gorillas and orang-utans show enormous sexual dimorphism. Chimpanzees and humans show very little.

It is clear that this problem can only be studied at the population level. We just cannot examine sexual dimorphism from individual specimens. Such studies as attempt to do so (e.g. Zihlman, 1985) are invalid.

There are two kinds of population studies. For a living species where we can know the sex of every individual specimen from independent information about it, it is truly possible to investigate the nature of population differences and overlaps in sexually dimorphic characteristics. We can obtain sure and certain estimates about the forms of each of the two sex sub-populations, and we can know, with a certain probability, the chances of an unknown (test) specimen coming from each sub-population. Many biological statisticians have a great interest in this problem (e.g. van Vark and Howells 1984).

But for fossil fragments for which we have no independent evidence about sex, all that we can do is look at the single overarching species population (if we even know that) to see if there is any evidence of the existence of two sub-populations within it. In this second case, though we can expect to obtain some assessments about the form of each of the two sub-populations, we can almost never obtain sure and certain definitions of each individual within them. The sexes of the actual specimens composing the two sub-populations will usually remain completely uncertain, being inseparably linked in the overarching total population. In particular we must almost never try to decide the sex of any individual specimen (unless from some absolute characteristic like genitalia or Y chromosomes).

Indeed, the problem of the determination of sex in fossils is similar to the problem of the determination of ancestors. It is always possible to discuss the likelihood of sex differences within a single fossil cluster just as it is always possible to discuss the probability of ancestral-descendent relationships between fossil groups. Just as, however, it is generally meaningless to discuss individual fossils as ancestors, so it is generally meaningless to assess the sex of individual fossils. The population overlaps that underly both such comparisons (except in the most banal of situations such as the dimensions of the canines in a few species) require the probabilistic evaluation and deny the more specific diagnosis.

In other words, the main task is not to decide upon the sex of an individual specimen, but upon the existence of similarities and differences, and if so of what kinds, between samples of specimens. This is an impossible task for rare fossils. But the diligence of the fossil finders has now provided us with enough specimens for many of the fossils, that population studies of a sort can sometimes be carried out.

It likewise follows, that such studies are almost impossible to prosecute using observational data. The eye just cannot readily assess differences between closely similar samples. The problem is really only amenable to mensuration and analysis of one kind or another. Mensuration is especially important because it is a truism that females in most populations tend to be physically smaller than males, and this holds for most, but not all parts of their anatomy. Indeed, most studies of sexual dimorphism relate it primarily to size difference (e.g. Brace and Ryan, 1980). And this is not without good reason. Size exerts physical constraints on form. Form places limits on size. Both are related as the products of development and evolution.

There have been, as we shall see, many studies of sexual dimorphism over the years that show that most structural differences between the sexes in primates are strongly related to sexual differences in overall bodily size (e.g. see the review volume edited by Hall, 1982). More recently however, there have been other studies that demonstrate that many factors in addition to overall bodily size have implications for sexual dimorphism (e.g. Leutenegger and Kelly, 1977). There is, especially, a newly awakened interest in the matter of resemblances and differences of all kinds between the human sexes. This is, then, a topic and a time that has re-emerged as important in the human evolutionary story.

Once we become interested in sexual dimorphism, many provocative questions can be raised. What evolutionary forces are related to the level of sexual dimorphism that we presently see in *Homo sapiens*? Has it changed during hominoid history, or perhaps, how has it changed? How does sexual dimorphism in fossils believed related to the human line compare with, differ from, that in other primate fossils? What part may sexual dimorphism have played in the evolution of the hominoids?

There are also other far-reaching questions, the reasons for which will be evident later on. Are all these first questions wrong because they beg further questions? More specifically: Is there really only one kind of sexual dimorphism? Is that one kind of sexual dimorphism really so simple that it is dependent mainly upon overall size differences between the sexes? More specifically still: Is the use of data from males (commonplace in evolutionary studies) or data from females (rare but becoming increasingly common) as the standard for evolutionary comparison really appropriate? What is the place of the sexless phantom in such investigations?

Some of the difficulties in prosecuting such studies are rather easily explicated by forgetting about real fossils for a moment or two, and considering some actual specimens, gorillas and orang-utans, for which we have field records of sex.

Sexual dimorphism in living primates

There seems little doubt that if the skulls of male and female gorillas and orang-utans were known only as a handful of fragmentary fossils we would assess them as belonging to two species far removed one from another. Certainly there would not be unanimity on the matter.

Thus, we can see major visual differences (sexual dimorphism) between the skulls shown in the rows in Figure 1:1 (upper row: males, lower row: females). This sexual dimorphism is clearly evident in features like the large skull crests and the large dagger-like

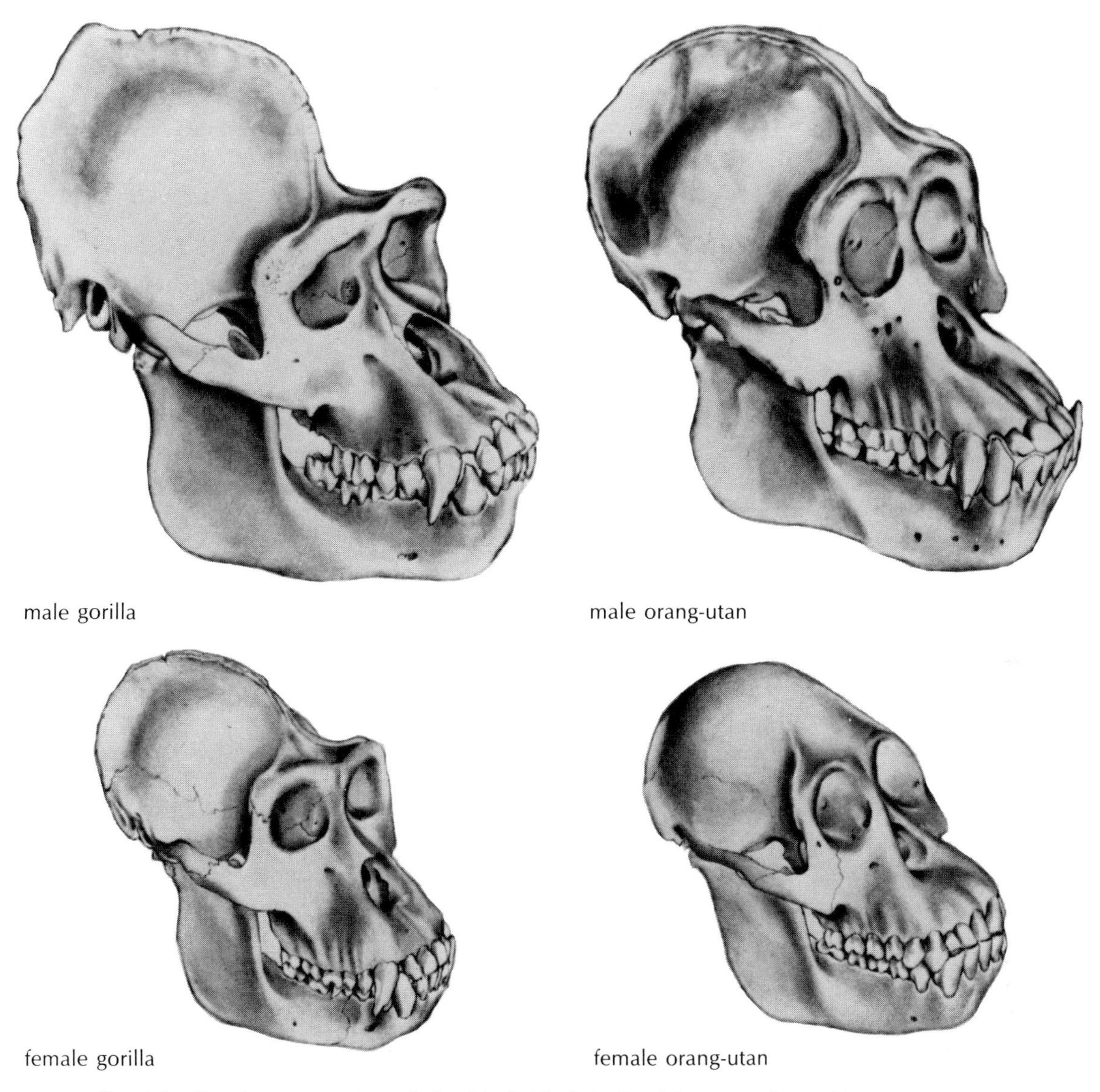

Fig. 1:1 Sketches, correctly scaled, of individual skulls of the most dimorphic great apes.

canines that characterize more strongly each of the adult males rather than the adult females. Such features seem to outweigh greatly other differences (species differentiations) that exist between the skulls in the columns in Figure 1:1 (first column: gorillas, second column: orang-utans). An example of the species differentiations is the brow ridge which is continuous across the midline in both male and female gorillas when compared with the divided brow ridge in both male and female orang-utans.

Only our more complete knowledge (more complete because they are alive today) of populations of gorillas and orang-utans, and of males and females of each, allows us to make the unequivocal distinction between the sex and the species differences. Only full information prevents us from suggesting that complete brow ridges are robust male characteristics and that incomplete brow ridges are less robust female features. Only full information prevents us from assuming that the larger specimens (male gorillas and male orang-utans) are the males and females of a giant species, the smaller specimens (female gorillas and female orang-utans) the males and females of a dwarf species.

The problem is further compounded if we add into this picture the skull shown in Figure 1:2 drawn to the same scale. This skull is similar in size and robustness to the female skulls of the lower row of Figure 1:1. If it, too, were a fossil we might judge it

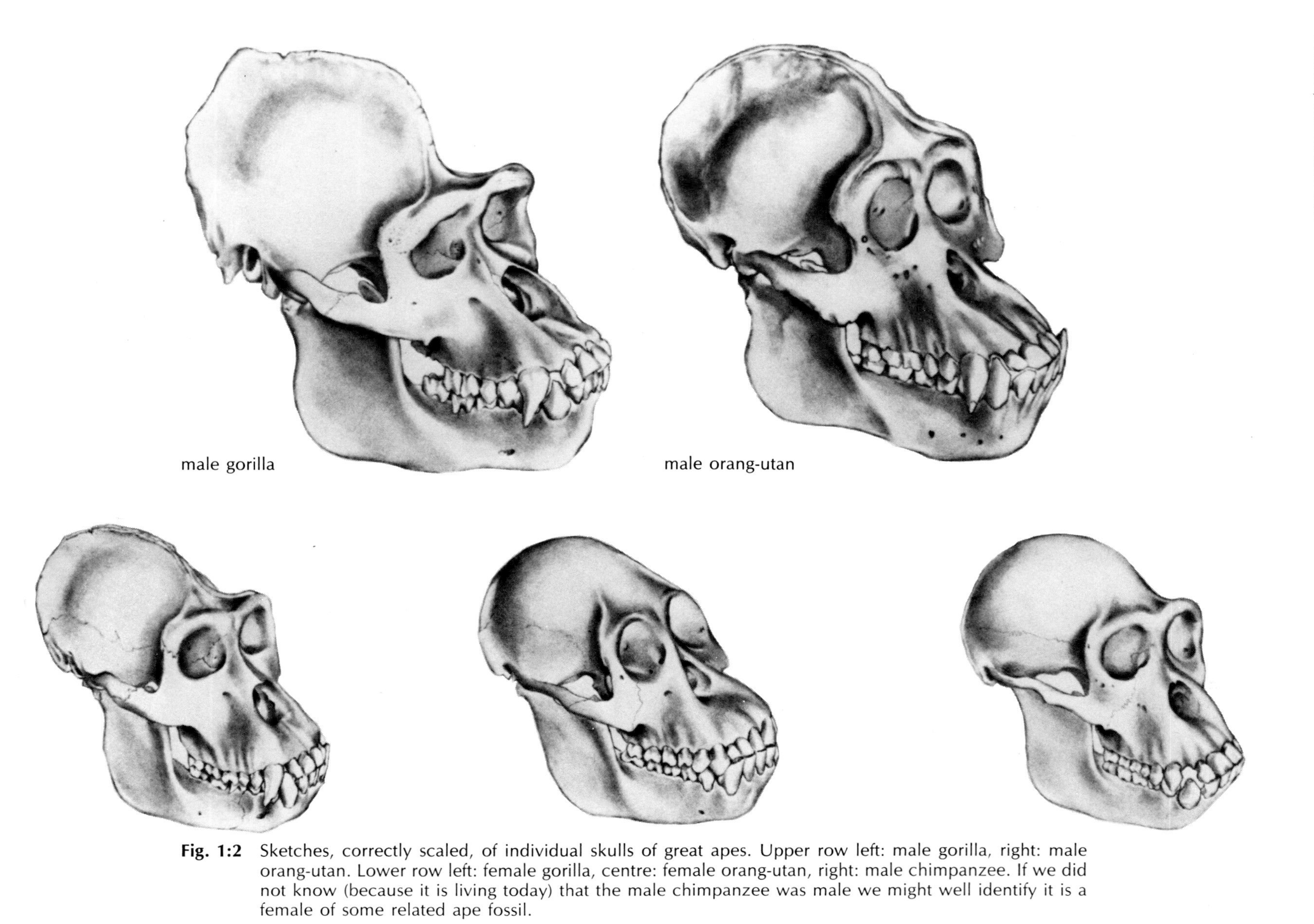

Fig. 1:2 Sketches, correctly scaled, of individual skulls of great apes. Upper row left: male gorilla, right: male orang-utan. Lower row left: female gorilla, centre: female orang-utan, right: male chimpanzee. If we did not know (because it is living today) that the male chimpanzee was male we might well identify it is a female of some related ape fossil.

to be yet another female. It is our recognition of current-day female chimpanzees (Figure 1:3, also drawn to the same scale) that tells us that this is a male of yet a third ape species.

The final compounding of this problem is shown in Figure 1:4. The first frame compares a male ape, an australopithecine and an early human. This overemphasizes the similarity between australopithecines and humans and is frequently figured in the literature. The second frame is the reverse comparison with a female ape and a late human. This overemphasizes the difference between australopithecines and humans. Obviously, neither comparison is correct; both are biased.

Such differences between the sexes are not related directly to reproductive structures and processes. Yet they exist in the living great apes as differences that are so enormous that mistaking them for species differences could be (and has been) pardoned many times over. The equivalent difference between male and female humans, in contrast, is very small. This has lead to the assumption that at some time in the past the differences between the sexes in human ancestors must have been much greater and possibly much more like that in the heavily dimorphic living apes. The assumption has always been that great ape-like sexual dimorphism was the ancestral condition. With this went the idea that the life histories of these groups included exuberant but reasonably limited periods of sexual activity in which a small number of large dominant males did most of the effective copulation with a larger number of small sexually receptive females.

The cartoon depiction of this situation: the huge brutal cave-man with the large club dragging the small and fragile cave-woman by the hair across the cave floor, forms the public stereotype of this situation (Fig. 1:5). And the scientific stereotype is almost as crass. Brace and Ryan (1980) put it thus: 'as some philosophers and many women have realized, there remains a bit of the baboon in every human male' (Fig. 1:6).

Paleoanthropologists have always looked most carefully for evidences of marked sexual dimorphism in prehuman fossils. They have tried to identify just when it was large, and just how long ago and in what species the reduction towards the modern condition commenced.

The study of sexual dimorphism has thus played a most important part in our assessment of human and prehuman fossils, and in our estimates of the evolution of sexual patterns. But sexual dimorphism has also, been a source of error in our evaluations of fossils. It can suggest two species when only one actually exists. It can imply one species with two very different sexes, when in fact, two species are truly present.

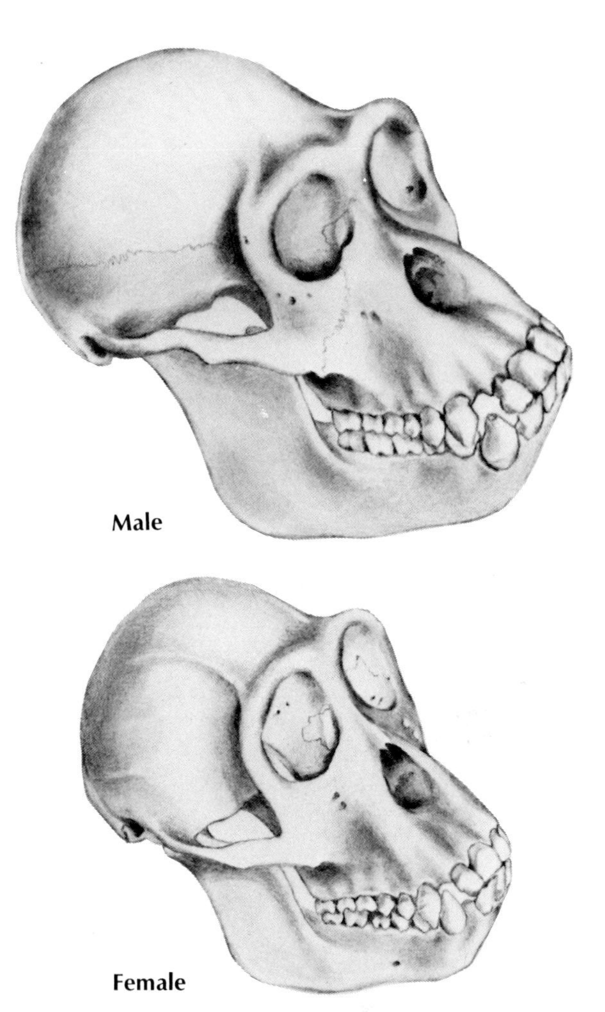

Fig. 1:3 Sketches of skulls of chimpanzees: male, above and female below. This is the knowledge that allows us to correct the misimpression (of Fig. 1:2) that the male chimpanzee seems to have relationships with the females of the other great apes. Seen purely from such sketches, the problem seems to be one of size.

Twenty years ago this problem surfaced in Brace's (1967) view that the australopithecines were one species. The slender *Australopithecus* was the female and the robust *Paranthropus* the male. This view was never strongly supported because of the unlikely chance of all males being found at Swartkrans and Kromdraai and all females at Sterkfontein, Makapansgat and Taung. It is now refuted.

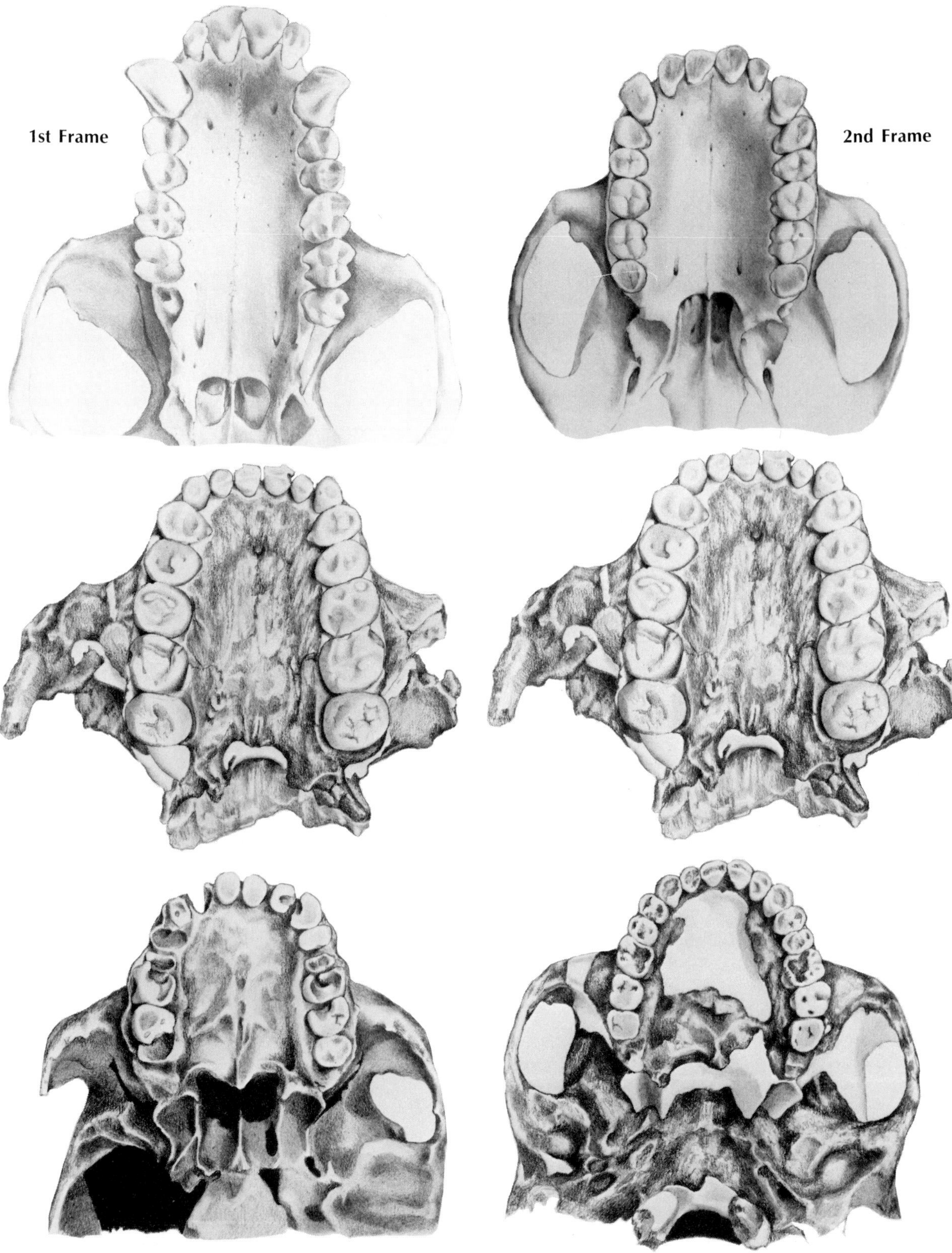

Fig. 1:4 Sketches, scaled to the same size, of skulls of highly dimorphic male and female great apes, of a fossil human, and of an australopithecine.

1st Frame: it is not uncommon to make the comparison between male apes, australopithecines and early humans. This over-emphasizes the similarity between australopithecines and humans. It is a view frequently seen in scientific and popular articles about these fossils.

2nd Frame: the comparison can also be made between female apes, australopithecines and late humans. This over-emphasizes the similarity between australopithecines and apes.

Obviously the most correct picture takes account of both these views. This is why differences between the sexes loom so large in the study of these fossils.

Fig. 1:5 "My wives don't understand me!"

Fig. 1:6 She could not resist the sound but also was not certain that he was a lion and not a baboon.

At the present time a similar view (e.g. Pilbeam and colleagues, 1980, 1982, 1984) suggests that the various ramapithecines are one species. The smaller *Ramapithecus* is the female and the larger *Sivapithecus* the male. The differences are, apparently, so great that sex can be decided from looking at individual specimens of individual teeth. How likely is it that this is correct?

Finally, however, the assumption, that we really know what sexual dimorphism is because of the peculiarities of the few species that are alive today, may have already channelled us away from discovering quite different sexual dimorphisms that may have existed in times past. It is hard to escape from such situations.

These, all these, are the problems
for this book.

Yet the only place to start is the study of the living forms. Only here do we know the sexes and the species. And because the study of fossils at the population level can only be undertaken where we have rather large numbers of specimens, comparisons are best made through studies of teeth. For although sex differences are more clearly evident in complete skulls and pelves, we possess only a handful of broken skulls for each fossil species and not a single pelvis for most of them. But we do have available hundreds of teeth for many of the fossils critical to human and ape evolution. And we have, especially, thousands of fossil teeth due to the new diligence of a generation of investigators in China.

All this leads us unerringly to our primary title:

FOSSILS, TEETH AND SEX

It is for the rest of this book to define whether or not our subtitle is equally apt.

Anatomical sexual dimorphism in the living primates: the current picture

Among the many anatomical characters that differentiate the sexes in animals, one set of features relates directly to the reproductive process and apparatus. Some of these features become most marked after the onset of sexual maturity: the enlargement of mammary glands in the human female, the growth of the testes in the males of chimpanzees. Others are manifest at other times and in other ways during growth and development: the development of external genitalia during foetal life, the physiological cycles of gonadal function in relation to oestrous and pregnancy, even the dissolution and atrophy of some anatomical parts as reproductive life wanes and dies.

There is, however, a second set of structural differences between the sexes that is related less directly to the primary reproductive process. This includes those differences that are meant when we speak of sexual dimorphism. Because many of these differences can be observed in the bones they are also evident in fossil materials. Some of these characteristics become more and more obvious in late maturity, skull crests in great ape males for instance. Others, for example, enlarged canines in many primate males, may become prominent at earlier times during development and growth.

This second set of differences, generally known as sexual dimorphism, has been widely studied, especially in humans. It encompasses many different phenomena, not only structural, as in the examples above, but also functional, not only biological but also behavioral, not only social but also psychological, cultural, intellectual and so on (see reviews in Campbell, 1972; Montagu, 1974; Friedman et al, 1974; Hall, 1982).

From the viewpoint of living and fossil primates, however, sexual dimorphism of structure is most easily studied. Let us review what is generally believed about it.

First, among the various members of the Order Primates (prosimians, New World monkeys, Old World monkeys, and apes and humans), the most obvious sexually dimorphic feature is overall bodily size. Males may be as much as twice the size of females in baboons, proboscis monkeys, orang-utans and gorillas. Outside of the Primates, differences in bodily size between the sexes can reach tremendous proportions (as in aquatic mammals such as elephant seals).

This does not, however, apply to all primates. Thus, within the Primates, in species such as squirrel monkeys, some langurs, colobus monkeys and gibbons, males and females are rather similar in size. And in some primates, for example, in some lemurs, some marmosets and in spider monkeys differences in size may even be reversed so that females may be larger than males (e.g. Schultz, 1969, in a study that reviews many of his own earlier investigations; see also Napier and Napier, 1967, and Leutenegger and Kelly, 1977). Again, elsewhere in the animal kingdom females may be very much larger than males (as outside the mammals, e.g. in many of the social insects).

A second, very obvious structural sexual dimorphism in primates involves shape: overall form and proportions. This, too, is well documented. There are differences in proportions between males and females of various species (again see Schultz, 1969; Napier and Napier, 1967). For instance, chest circumference and shoulder breadth are relatively larger in males of many primates than in females. The differences are most pronounced in those species with the greatest size differences between the sexes. Thus, in the orang-utan, chest girth is over 200 per cent of trunk length in males, but only about 170 per cent of trunk length in females. In howler monkeys the proportional differences in chest girth are even greater, 150 per cent of trunk length in males as compared with 90 per cent in females. Even greater shape differences between the sexes exist in many non-primate animals as the size examples mentioned above testify.

However, this finding is not ubiquitous. There are many primates, for example, squirrel monkeys and gibbons, where differences in proportions between the sexes seem to be minimal. And there are, similarly, many non-primate animals where the sexes can scarcely be differentiated at all without examination of the external genitalia.

Although, among primates and other mammals, these variations in size and shape between the sexes differ, the nature of the variations has generally been assumed to be similar in each species. Structural sexual dimorphism is usually thought of as a single descriptive idea. Smaller size differences between the sexes go with smaller differences in proportions. Larger size differences go with larger differences in proportions. Both are related to differences in robusticity. Even in those few species in which the size difference is reversed, it is generally assumed that the proportional differences are equivalently reversed. Size is declared to be the key factor.

Certainly, within the primates, this idea of sexual dimorphism as a single, primarily size-related, phenomenon with differential expression seems to be confirmed by the studies of Schultz (1969) as he examines, one by one, the proportions of various major segments of the body of many representative genera of the Order. And this is also the specific finding of the only other study (Wood, 1975, 1976) of more than a single pair of genera that examines variables taken together using somewhat more complex statistical methods. Thus, Wood employed correlation, regression and Penrose's size and shape statistics for studying several measurements of the body of five genera (*Homo*, *Pan*, *Gorilla*, *Papio*, and *Colobus*). In addition, Wood reviewed many other results for species representing the primates rather widely. He proposed that the idea 'that considerable differences in shape exist between males and females must be rejected'. He suggested, that such shape differences as appear to exist are simply those effects that are the result of differential size.

Some attempts have been made to evaluate the possible underlying causal agent of this type of sexual dimorphism. In earlier studies (reviewed in Schultz, 1969) the phenomenon was seen as having greater expression in terrestrial primates than in arboreal species. Though this idea might appear reasonable in the largely ground living baboons, macaques and gorillas, all showing heavy sexual dimorphism, it is certainly not applicable to the extremely arboreal proboscis monkeys and orang-utans, also heavily sexually dimorphic. Another early attempt to assess causal mechanisms suggested that sexual dimorphism had greater expression in savannah species and less in forest forms (also noted in Schultz, 1969, in reviewing an earlier literature). Again, it is easy to think of particular genera, e.g. orang-utans, gorillas, heavily dimorphic forest forms, to which this suggestion does not apply.

More recently, however, more complex views have arisen as to the nature of sexual dimorphism and its associations. Thus Geist (1974) and Leutenegger and Kelly (1977) showed that sexual dimorphism in overall body size is not correlated closely with sexual dimorphism in other dimorphic characters. For instance, sexual dimorphism in overall bodily size does not correlate highly with canine dimorphism. When there is a relationship between these two features, it is not the same across several genera. Thus different sexual dimorphisms may be both species specific and character specific. This is consistent with the idea that there is no single gene or group of genes coding for the entire range of sexually dimorphic characters. The heritability of each quantitative sexually dimorphic trait (such as body size, tooth length and breadth, and body weight) is separate, and often largely independent.

Many other authors have started to recognize the role of multiple factors in the evolution of sexual dimorphism. For instance, differences in the social organization of the sexes (e.g. Crook, 1972; Gautier-Hion, 1975; Clutton-Brock *et al*, 1978; Leutenegger and Kelly, 1977; Harvey *et al*, 1978; Leutenegger, 1982; Leutenegger and Cheverud, 1982; Fedigan and Baxter, 1984) have been strongly implicated in the evolution of structural sexual dimorphism. This concept follows much earlier work in many vertebrates (especially birds — e.g. as reviewed in Selander, 1966). Thus, among those primates that live in more complex polygynous groups, in which it might be supposed that there might be overt competition between members of one sex for access to the other, greater degrees of sexual dimorphism are expected. In contrast, among those primates that live in nuclear families or small groups with approximately equal numbers of adult males and females, such competition may be less with consequently smaller degrees of sexual dimorphism.

In each of the foregoing examples, troop protection or defence might be additionally implicated as a causal factor. In species in which there are more adult females than males, the larger males are often more involved in protective roles against predators or rival groups. In non-human species with a social structure embodying equal numbers of males and females, there is a tendency for defence to be relatively equally carried out by equal sized males and females.

At least in human species, and there is certainly a possibility that this might also apply to non-human species, nutritional status has been suggested as a factor in the degree of sexual dimorphism. It seems clear that the realization of the maximum limit of growth is more easily thwarted by nutritional deprivation in human males than in human females (Stini, 1969; Tobias, 1972). It may be that reduced dimorphism may sometimes be due to such a mechanism.

And in turn, many other causal explanations have been suggested: the combination of diet and locomotion, of habitat and locomotion, and so on (reviewed in Leutenegger and Kelly, 1977).

My own general survey of the primates suggests that even more factors may be involved. For instance, sexual dimorphism seems most pronounced in species that change most during the period of growth. Thus, those species that apparently display neoteny — retention of immature-looking forms into sexually mature stages of life — are often less conspicuous in their sexual dimorphism. Such a possibility is supported by the smaller sex differences obtaining in many prosimians, in certain New World monkeys, and of course, among the hominoids, in the lesser apes and humans.

A second example revolves around what may be intra-generic (or even on occasion, intra-specific) differences in sexual dimorphism. For example, gibbons, *Hylobates*, are usually thought of as displaying very little sexual dimorphism and this is correlated with their monogamous sexual-social structure. In fact, however, on occasions gibbons will show polygynous sexual-social groups and it is possible that this relates to local superabundances of food or territory. Some gibbons are, in fact, quite markedly sexually dimorphic (e.g. *Hylobates concolor*) and this group is reported to be often polygynous in its sexual-social arrangements (Elliot Haimoff, personal communication).

Yet other factors may be involved. For example, sexual dimorphism may relate to physiological, or social, or psychological, (or even other) 'costs' of the differential reproductive mechanisms of each sex.

Is it possible to test these various ideas through examinations of animal anatomies?

The existence of Professor A. H. Schultz' meticulously obtained data on the proportions of the limbs, trunk, and head and neck of a wide range of primates allows us to examine anatomical sexual dimorphism in a way not previously attempted. Thus, differences in body proportions can be studied using methods that provide a summation of information from many features. These methods include new information due to the interactions between the features. They are capable, further, of subtracting such redundant information as is shared among the features. They can visualize, finally, information in complex, many-dimensional situations. Accordingly, these data on the overall bodily proportions of primates — kindly made available to me during Professor Schultz' lifetime — have been studied (Oxnard, 1983a, 1984) using multiple discriminant functions (canonical variates analyses) and high-dimensional displays (sine-cosine functions).

If there truly is a common form of sexual dimorphism among the primates, a single sexually dimorphic spectrum with greater or lesser degrees of expression in different species, such methods should allow (**a**) a more complete recognition of its existence, and (**b**) a further description of its precise nature.

Or, if sexual dimorphisms are truly plural, perhaps the result of a number of different causal agents, such studies might recognize (**a**) a multiplicity of anatomical patterns, and (**b**) the nature of the differences among them from one species to another.

Anatomical sexual dimorphisms in the living primates — new views

The data and its preliminary examination: The data used in this study are from 455 primates representing 18 genera as given in Schultz (1929, 1936) and listed in Oxnard (1983a, 1984). The sexes of specimens are known from field records. They are all adult individuals with full permanent dentitions. The subset of the materials used is given in Table 1:1.

Table 1:1

Numbers of Specimens in Each Sex Subgroup of Each Genus*

Genera	Females	Males
Nycticebus	4	5
Galago	3	7
Tarsius	9	2
Aotus	6	6
Alouatta[a]	2	2
Cebus	11	14
Saimiri	23	26
Ateles	47	27
Leontocebus	10	14
Macaca	17	10
Cercocebus[a]	2	1
Presbytis	7	7
Nasalis	15	10
Hylobates	37	41
Pongo	8	5
Pan	17	9
Gorilla	6	5
Homo	20	20
Total 18	Total 244	Total 211

*The total number of genera from which selection was made was 34 representing 59 sex subgroups (both sexes were not always represented in Schultz's data). Thus there were 472 specimens in Schultz's original study.
[a]The numbers of specimens in these two genera are very small. The genera were included in the study because the differences between their sexes are very large.

There are 23 dimensions available for study. They were all measured uniformly by Professor A. H. Schultz employing the techniques described by him in 1929 and in some cases as modified by him later in 1956. They provide an overall description of the shape of the various bodily regions through the compounding, by Professor Schultz, of his original measurements into a series of ratios (Table 1:2). Unfortunately, the original measures are no longer available, and the particular way in which they were transformed into ratios (e.g. with trunk height as the denominator in many of them) does not allow the original measurements to be regenerated. We are, therefore, forced to use the ratios.

To some degree overall size is reflected in trunk height. Thus, using this quantity as the denominator in many of the ratios provides some indication of contrasts emerging from differences in proportion rather than size. It allows, for instance, shoulder breadth to be compared in animals where trunk length is as different as in hapalemurs and humans. But using a ratio in this way does not eliminate the total effect of difference in size. Such ratios only do this fully if the relationships between the pairs of measurements are similar and linear in all the animals studied. This is not, of course, the case. But such ratios do eliminate the biggest component of size and are, therefore, of value in a study covering an entire Order containing contrasts in size as marked as those between, say, spectral tarsiers and spectacled langurs.

Indeed, the more complex elements of size should specifically not be removed in studies like this that purport to investigate differences in form and proportions. The existence of such non-linear relationships is part of what it is desired to investigate in such studies. They should, therefore, be retained by avoiding the use of 'size-removing techniques' such as allometric, multiple regression or principal components' methods.

Care must also be taken with Schultz' data because trunk height, as he measured it, is a particularly precarious variable. This measure was defined as the distance from the upper border of the sternum to the upper margin of the pubis. The precise definition of this length is clearly affected by the different shapes of the sternal notch and the pubic symphysis in the different primates. Likewise this measure is affected by the different orientations of the trunk during measurement and by different degrees of shrinkage of cadavers prior to measurement. McArdle (1978) has shown, however, that even such an ill-defined measure as this can, with care, be reasonably replicated by two investigators. Replicability by a single careful worker over time is thus highly likely to be achievable. That it was Professor Schultz who was that single careful researcher lends yet more credence to the data.

Another problem with Schultz' data is that we are forced to group the specimens into genera. Despite his lifetime's collection of primate materials, specimens are still not sufficient to allow

Table 1:2

Dimensions Used in Morphometrics of Overall Bodily Proportions*

Anatomical features

Schultz's data on upper limbs	Schultz's data on lower limbs	Schultz's data on head, neck, and trunk
Relative chest circumference	Relative hip breadth	Relative chest circumference
Relative shoulder breadth	Relative lower limb length	Relative shoulder breadth
Relative upper limb length	Intermembral index	Relative hip breadth
Intermembral index	Crural index	Chest index: chest breadth as per cent of saggital chest diameter
Brachial index	Length of foot relative to limb	Relative head size
Relative hand length	Length of foot relative to trunk	Relative face height
Relative hand breadth	Relative foot breadth	Relative upper face height: as per cent of average head diameter
Relative thumb length		Cephalic index: head breadth as per cent of head height
		Interocular index: inner eye breadth as per cent of face breadth
		Relative ear size: ear height × ear breadth as per cent of head length × total head height

*Subanalyses performed without duplication of variables
†All dimensions relative to trunk height unless otherwise indicated

the examination of data for individual species. Thus, in our use of his data, special care was taken to eliminate those genera, the sex subgroups of which derived from different species within the genus. For the remainder, the sex subgroups represent more or less equal balances of species within each genus, and this, combined with the fact that differences between the species within a genus are generally a good deal smaller than differences between the sexes within a species, is the best that can be done with this problem in these data.

The precision of the data is discussed by Professor Schultz and he indicates the level of inaccuracy due to mensurational difficulties. Further studies on these data (Ashton, Flinn and Oxnard, 1975) confirm that the scale of these inaccuracies is, in general, small enough to render it unlikely that the results of comparisons among groups of animals and between the sexes of each group would be affected.

In the 36 sex subgroups (from 18 genera) for each of which reasonable samples of specimens are available, basic statistical data (e.g. means, variances, standard deviations, coefficients of variation, skewness and kurtosis, standard errors and confidence intervals of the mean, when possible) are computed for each variable. A variety of univariate and bivariate techniques are used, both to test assumptions in the data, and to display more clearly the simpler statistical results. Thus, univariate distribution plots, bivariate and trivariate scatter plots, multivariate normal plotting, statistical tests of distributions (in those genera with samples large enough to allow them to be undertaken), investigations of large groups separately from small groups (to eliminate the possibility that small groups might be unduly biasing the results), indeed, the entire battery of tests outlined in Oxnard (1983b) are performed. These studies confirm that features liable to perturb subsequent multivariate statistical examinations are not present in the data.

The question of the statistical normality of the data is especially interesting. Only a small number of the groups have a sufficient number of specimens to actually decide whether or not the data in those groups are normally distributed. Because it is worth knowing as much about this as is possible those few variables were studied for normality. As seems usual in studies of this type, normality or near normality do generally characterize these data (Oxnard, 1983a, b, 1984).

The notion, however, that normality of the data is a condition necessary before canonical analysis (the multivariate statistical technique that we used on these data) can be applied is spurious with our particular usage. Canonical analysis can be used in situations where it is not known for certain if there are differences between the groups (i.e. in the study of geographic differences among humans, or of subspecific variants of species of non-human primates). Under such a circumstance, non-normality in the data may truly have disturbing effects (although the methods are robust enough that even this is not common). But the technique can also be used in a descriptive sense, to define the patterns of differences among groups which are already known to be clearly and statistically significantly different. Under this circumstance normality in the data is not a requirement. In fact the need for normality in the data is inversely proportional to the distances between the groups. As, in our studies, the distances between the groups are large (gorillas are clearly different from gibbons) the need for normality is small. There has been considerable confusion in the literature between the two applications of these methods. They are explicated by Oxnard, (1978a), and Albrecht, (1980).

A series of multivariate studies are available from these data (Oxnard, 1983c). They are somewhat similar to the computations carried out by Ashton, Flinn and Oxnard (1975). But, in that study the issues related to understanding the differences among genera and therefore, sex subgroups were pooled. In this present study, in contrast, the analyses are carried out with the sex subgroups separate. And there is necessarily a reduced number of groups in the present study reflecting only those genera with appreciable samples for each sex.

The current study investigates, using canonical variates analysis, sex differences in several different sub-studies. **One** is the entire suite of dimensions representing every region of the body. A **second** comprises those dimensions of anatomically localized subunits of the body (e.g. all upper limb dimensions, all trunk dimensions). A **third** consists of those dimensions containing only length measures of the body. A **fourth** and most critical study is of those dimensions containing only breadth measures of the body. The dimensions are divided into suites in this way because of the findings from the univariate investigations. It is in differences of bodily breadths in relation to lengths, that males differ most from females (wider shoulders in males, for instance, wider hips in females, for example).

The methods — canonical variates and high-dimensional analyses

The principle of canonical variates analysis is now well understood. It produces a partitioning of the information about the separations of given groups into a series of independent axes (canonical variates). Most generic groups, and all sex subgroups, are real groups whose definition is based upon information already known about the animals. These new axes (or variates) are chosen in such a way that the first axis includes the linear separation between the groups that is of greatest degree. The second axis contains the next greatest set of separations that is independent (uncorrelated) with the information in the first. The third includes the next greatest amount of information independent of both the first and the second axes, and so on. The total number of such axes is the same as the number of variables, or one less than the number of groups, whichever is the smaller. Figure 1:7 outlines some of the different methods to which canonical variates analysis is related.

Most information, however, is generally contained within a much smaller number of axes. Thus, the first two or three axes often describe as much as 95% of the information in the variables responsible for separating the groups. In the case of the current studies, the main separations are those between genera and they are, indeed, contained within the first three axes.

The separations between the sexes, in contrast, are generally subordinate to those between the genera and apparently not highly correlated with them. They, therefore, influence the statistical choice of the axes much less. Separations due to differences between the sex subgroups though clearly evident in the early axes, are also spread into additional (higher) axes.

Accordingly then, though the first three axes are studied using bivariate and trivariate plots of canonical axes against one another, the entire substructure of the canonical axes is best examined using high-dimensional displays.

The technical details of the high-dimensional display is given in Andrews (1972, 1973). A more general description is provided by Oxnard (1983a, 1984). The technique has been used fairly extensively in studying the anatomy of the living non-human primates (Oxnard, 1973a, 1975a, 1981a, 1983d), in examining human anatomy (Oxnard, 1975a; Howells, 1976), and in investigating the anatomy of fossils (Oxnard, 1975a, 1983a, 1984; Feldesman, 1979). It has recently been further described as a statistical display mechanism (Wilson, 1984; Lieberman, work in progress).

The method involves embedding the first, second, third, and so on, values for the mean of a sex-subgroup in each canonical axis within the first, second, third and so on, terms of a sine-cosine function. The remaining terms of the sine-cosine function are then deleted. This truncated function can then be used to draw a sine-cosine plot. The curvature of this plot represents the position, within the several axes of the original canonical analysis, of the mean of that particular sex-subgroup. Another sex-subgroup with different values in each canonical axis generates another plot with a different curvature.

The actual multi-dimensional relationships of these two sex-subgroups cannot be visualized because they are in more than three dimensions (more than three canonical variates). The new sine-cosine plots, however, allow us to see when three such groups lie close together (i.e. three groups with similar values in the canonical axes have three similar curvatures of their plots). These plots allow us, furthermore, to see when a fourth group lies far distant from the first three (i.e. a fourth group with a different pattern of canonical axes has a radically different curvature of its plot). They allow us, even further, to see when a fifth group lies intermediate between the first three and the fourth (i.e. a group with intermediacy in canonical values displays intermediacy in curvature of its plot).

The high-dimensional display is an especially valuable way of studying multi-dimensional situations, which cannot be modelled within the three dimensions of the real world (Fig. 1:8).

This technique is particularly appropriate in the display of canonical axes which, because they are independent of one another, produce curvatures in the high-dimensional plots that retain statistical properties of the original canonical axes. Thus, the concept of the standard deviation still exists. At any one point along two plots, the vertical distance between them can be given in standard deviation units. Similarly, the concept of (Mahalanobis') generalized distance is kept. The squared generalized distance between two groups is the area between the two plots representing them. Though statistical parameters are determined by the original multivariate analyses, it is useful for interpretation that they are maintained in these high-dimensional displays. Figure 1:9 shows some of the

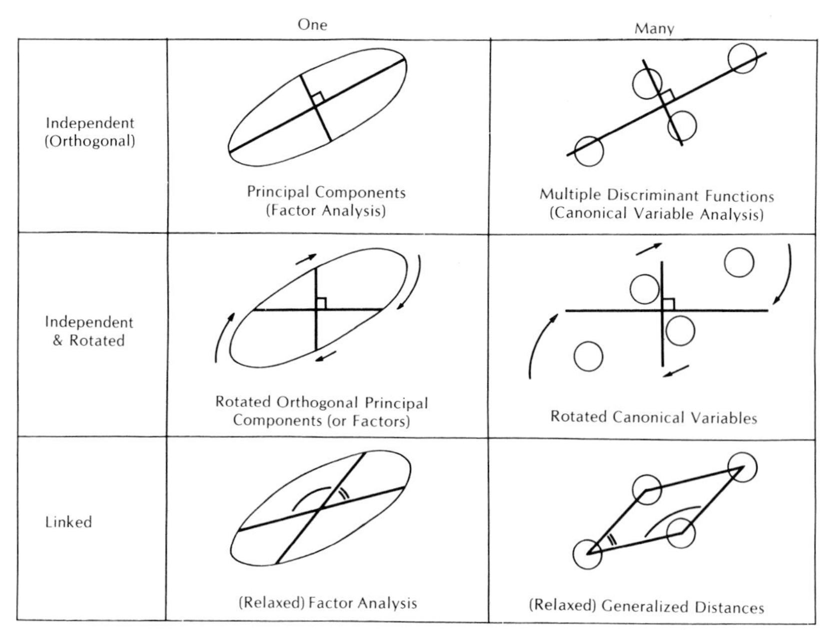

Fig. 1:7 1st Frame: geometric representations of some multivariate statistical methods available for the study of morphometric data.

If the specimens form a single group — or are not known to form more than a single group, then the structure of that group can be studied by the methods shown in the first column. In principal components analysis (upper sketch) — often known as the 'factor analysis' in the USA, the statistical descriptors are both uncorrelated and start with maximum separations among the specimens. The middle and lower sketches demonstrate that rotated descriptors (middle sketch — rotated orthogonal principal components, or factors), and relaxed descriptors (lower sketch — relaxed components, factor analysis in U.K.) can also be obtained. There may be some uses for these latter techniques if independent information provides some indication of importance of these rotations and relaxations.

If the specimens are known (from information independent of the data) to form several groups, then the structure between those groups can be studied by the methods shown in the second column. In canonical variates analysis (multiple discriminant functions — upper sketch) the statistical descriptors are both uncorrelated and start with maximum separations among the groups. The middle and lower sketches in this column demonstrate that rotated descriptors and relaxed descriptors can also be obtained. There are uses for the rotated canonical variates if independent information from the specimens provides some indication of the necessary rotation. There are most important uses for the relaxed descriptors (generalized distances) because these give the full separations between groups.

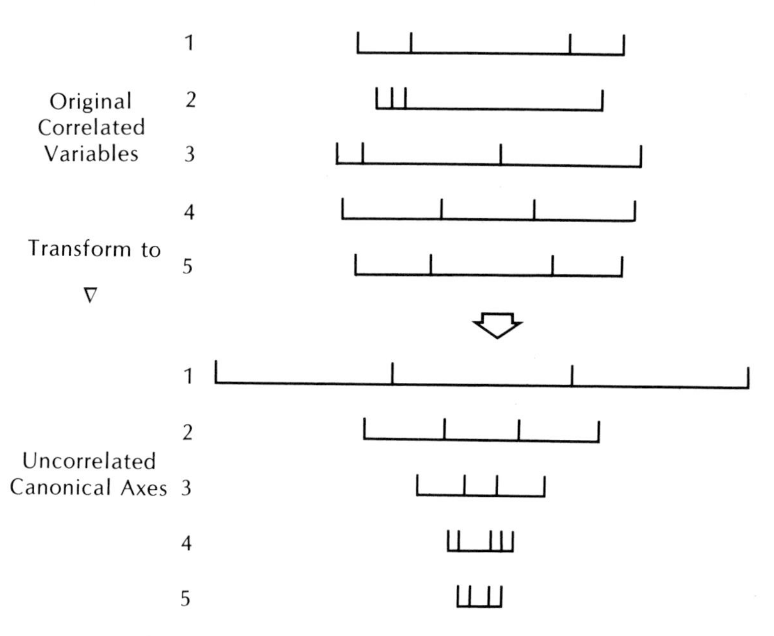

2nd Frame: a diagram of the transformation of original variables in canonical variates analysis. The first few canonical variates axes may well contain almost all the information.

3rd, 4th and 5th Frames: differences between principal components analysis and canonical variates analysis with different arrangements of original data (after Albrecht). Because it treats the data as a single group, principal components analysis always chooses as it's first axis, the overall diameter of the raw data. Thus, in each case, the principal components result is a rotation of the raw data.

Canonical variates analysis treats the data as three (in this example) groups after their transformation to make them the same size (same variance) and circular (equal variance in all directions). Thus the canonical variates result is not necessarily the same as the principal component result. Nor are the different results the same depending upon the arrangements of the original data.

When relationships between already known groups are to be examined, principal components analysis is wrong and canonical variates analysis correct.

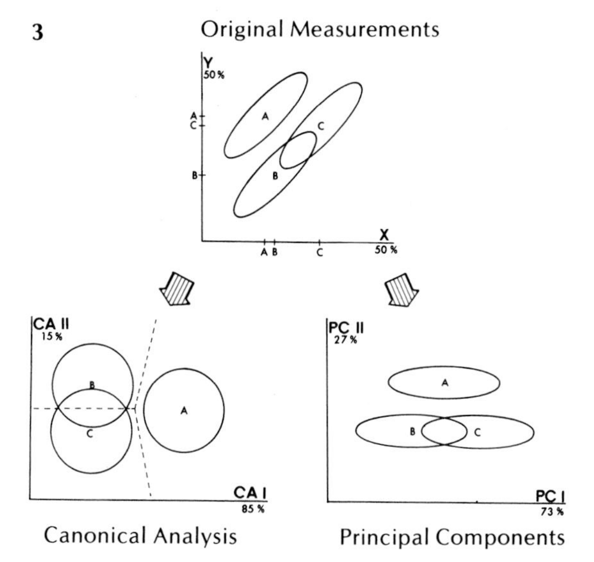

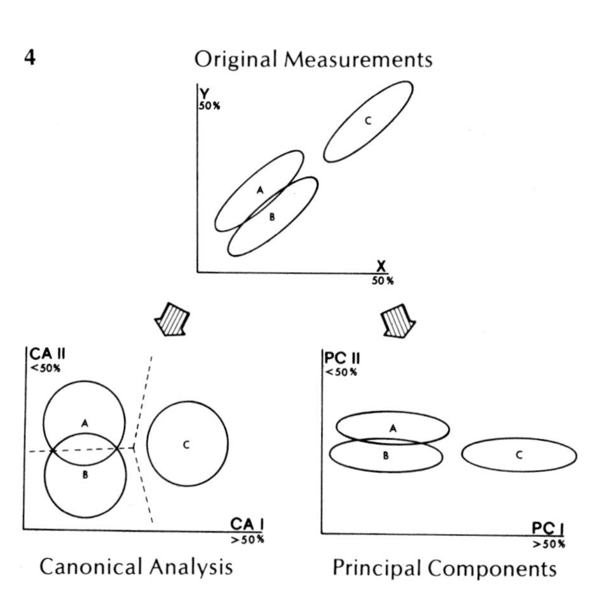

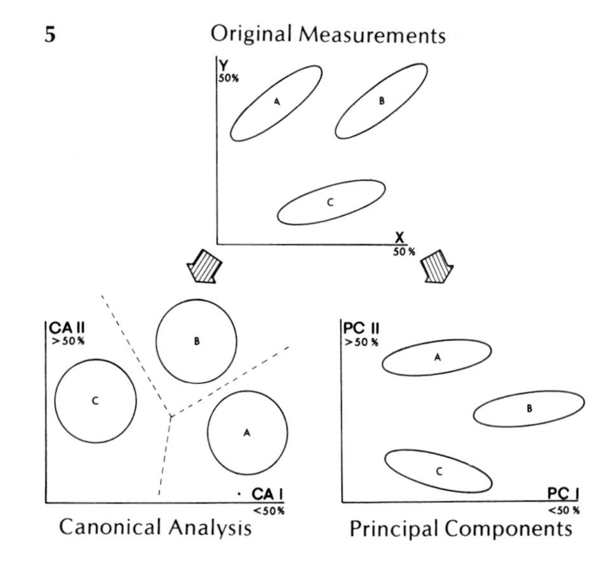

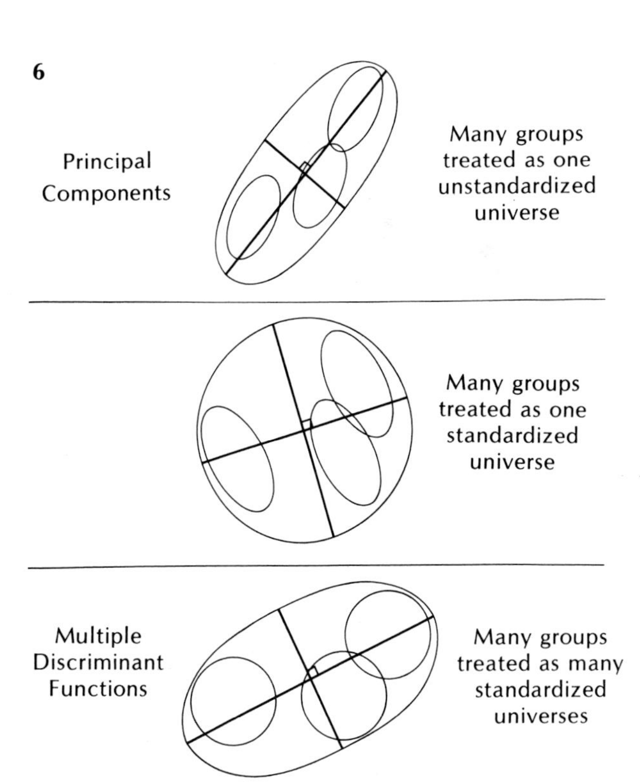

6th Frame: different ways of standardizing the data of the upper diagram. These differ according to whether the entire group is standardized (middle diagram — inappropriate) or whether the individual groups are standardized (lower diagram — appropriate).

Fig. 1:8 **1st Frame:** shows one of the sine/cosine formulae which can be used for the calculation of the high-dimensional displays, and the results for five groups in a high-dimensional space. It demonstrates that when three groups have similar positions in an uncorrelated high-dimensional space (i.e. form a cluster in a canonical variates space) then those three groups are represented by a cluster of sine/cosine curves. When a fourth group is completely different from those three in the high-dimensional space (i.e. an outlier) then, though the high-dimensional space cannot be visualized, the complete difference of that outlier is seen in the complete difference of the sine/cosine curve for that group. Likewise, when a fifth group is intermediate between the cluster of three and the fourth outlier, then that fact, too, is displayed even though it is impossible to see the actual high-dimensional space concerned.

Multidimensional Group Detection

$f_x(t) = x_1/\sqrt{2} + X_2\sin t + x_3\cos t + x_4 \sin 2t + x_5 \cos 2t + \ldots$

The standard deviation unit markers imply that, when uncorrelated canonical variates are the 'dimensions' that are used in the calculations, the concept of variance is retained. Likewise, the area between any two curves is the generalized distance between the two groups. Retention of these statistical descriptors in the high-dimensional display is one of its most useful features.

2nd Frame: the effects of differences between groups in single canonical variates. Differences in a first canonical axis are expressed as differences upwards or downwards on the graph; curvatures are unchanged. Differences in a second canonical axis alone (as can be seen from consideration of the formula) rotates the plots around the pi and zero positions. Differences in a third canonical axis alone (as can be seen from consideration of the formula) rotates the plots around the half pi positions. Similar differences exist for yet higher canonical axes. Obviously, in any real case differences exist in many axes together. This helps us to obtain a 'feel' for how the method works.

Effect of Reducing x
Multidimensional Data

$f_x(t) = \mathbf{x_1/\sqrt{2}} + x_2\sin t + x_3\cos t + x_4 \sin 2t + x_5 \cos 2t + \ldots$

Effect of Reducing x_2
Multidimensional Data

$f_x(t) = x_1/\sqrt{2} + \mathbf{x_2\sin t} + x_3 \cos t + x_4 \sin 2t + x_5 \cos 2t + \ldots$

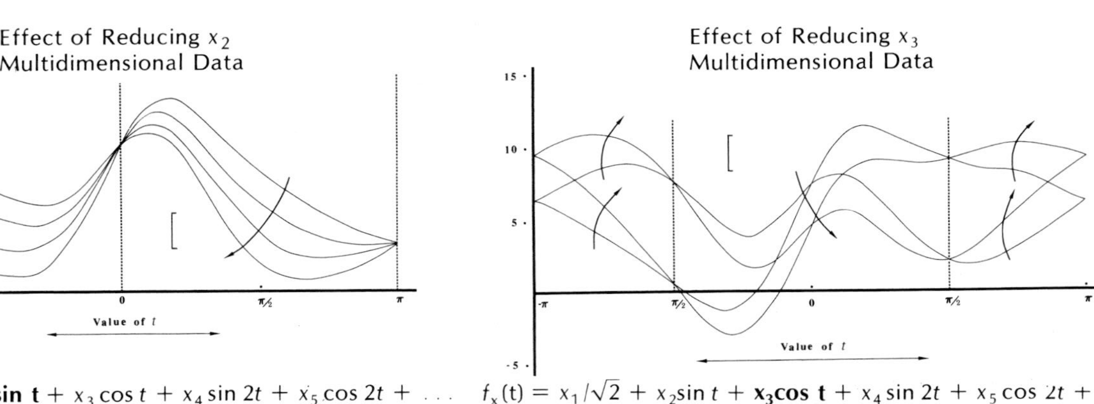

Effect of Reducing x_3
Multidimensional Data

$f_x(t) = x_1/\sqrt{2} + x_2\sin t + \mathbf{x_3\cos t} + x_4 \sin 2t + x_5 \cos 2t +$

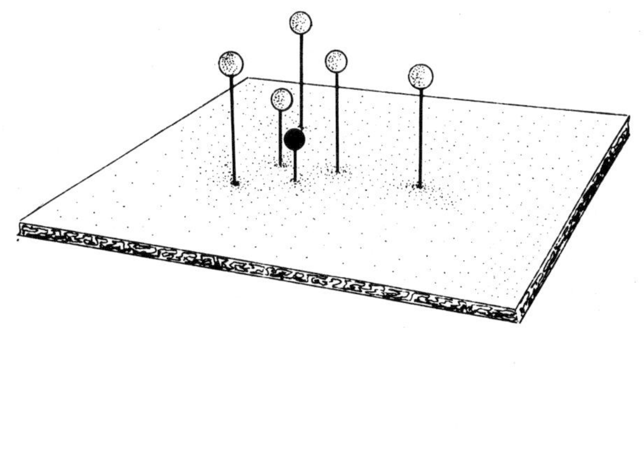

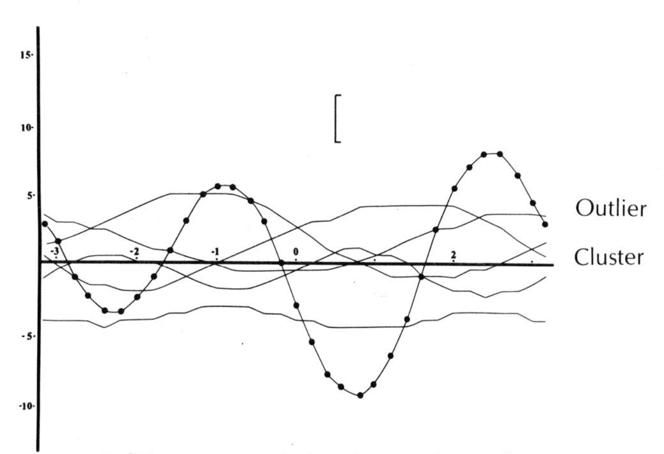

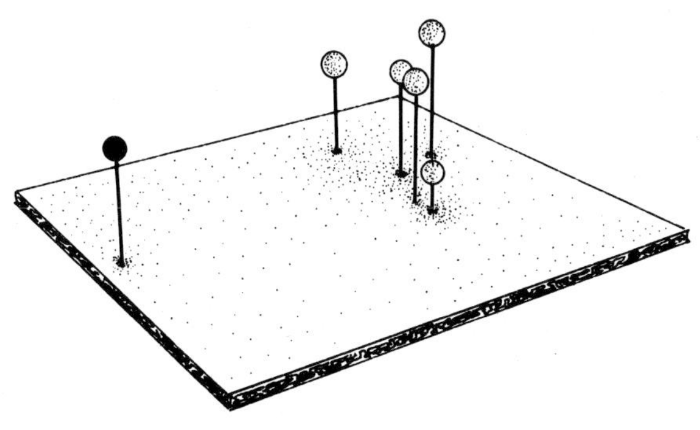

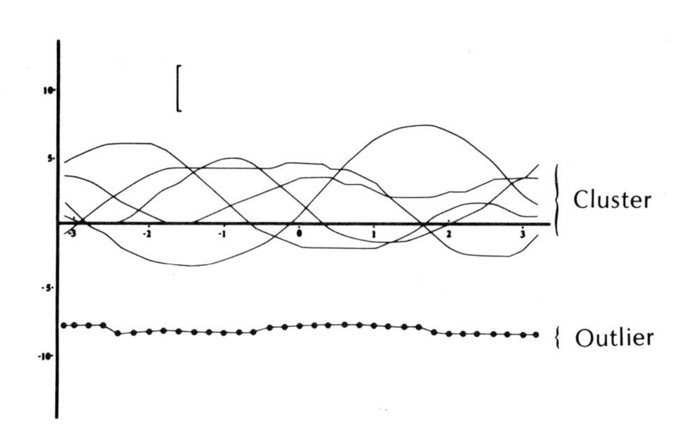

3rd Frame: canonical variates analyses of a real situation with five closely related groups and one outlier. In the first three-dimensional diagram the fact that the group, represented by the dark ball, is markedly different from the others is hidden because that group was interpolated into the analysis without its own patterns of variances and covariances being included in the analysis. In the second three-dimensional model the dark group was included in the analysis. Its complete difference from the other groups is evident as a large separation in the first canonical axis.

The first sine/cosine plot shows the high-dimensional technique applied to the study of the second three-dimensional model. The separation of the dark group is as evident in the high-dimensional display as in the canonical variates analysis.

The second sine/cosine plot shows the high dimensional technique applied to the study of the first three-dimensional model. Though the three-dimensional model does not tell us about the separation of the outlier, the sine/cosine plot does.

Thus, although the two ways of doing canonical analysis seem to give different pictures, the two high-dimensional displays show that they do not. The additional information is hidden in axes that are higher than those normally displayed in canonical variates analysis.

questions for which these displays may be useful. An outlier can be readily separated from a cluster. Groups can be readily separated from one another even though this may require comparisons of pairs of plots. Differences between pairs of subgroups (obviously, in these studies, between sex-subgroups for given species) can be readily distinguished.

The results, and their implications

Examination of dimensions one by one: Studies of the various individual length dimensions (ratios of lengths against lengths) show only a few statistically significant differences between the sexes, and even these are very small in scale. Knowing, as we do, that differences in overall lengths are one of the major size differences between the sexes, it is apparent that Schultz' use of ratios, crude though it may be, has indeed removed the major portion of simple size difference among the genera and between the sexes of each genus.

In contrast, however, studies of the six breadth measures (ratios of breadths against lengths) show

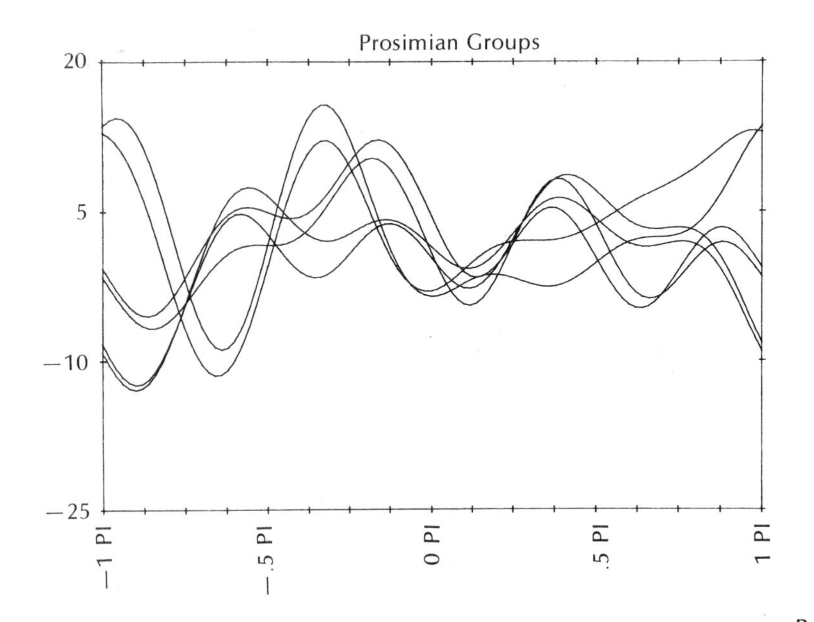

Fig. 1:9 Examples of the use of the high-dimensional display for demonstrating groups and outliers. The **first frame** shows a cluster of three pairs of genera that are related because they are all types of lemur.

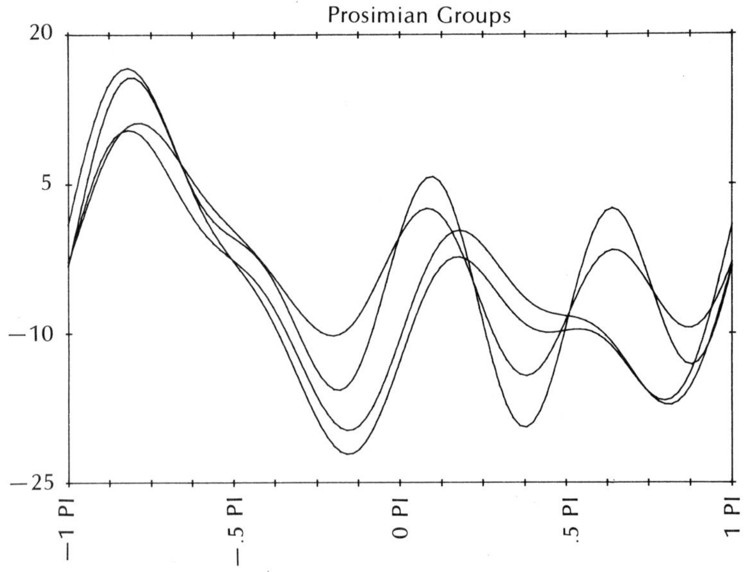

The **second frame** shows two pairs of genera that are related because they are all lorisines. They are, however, quite different from the lemurs, and the high-dimensional plot shows this.

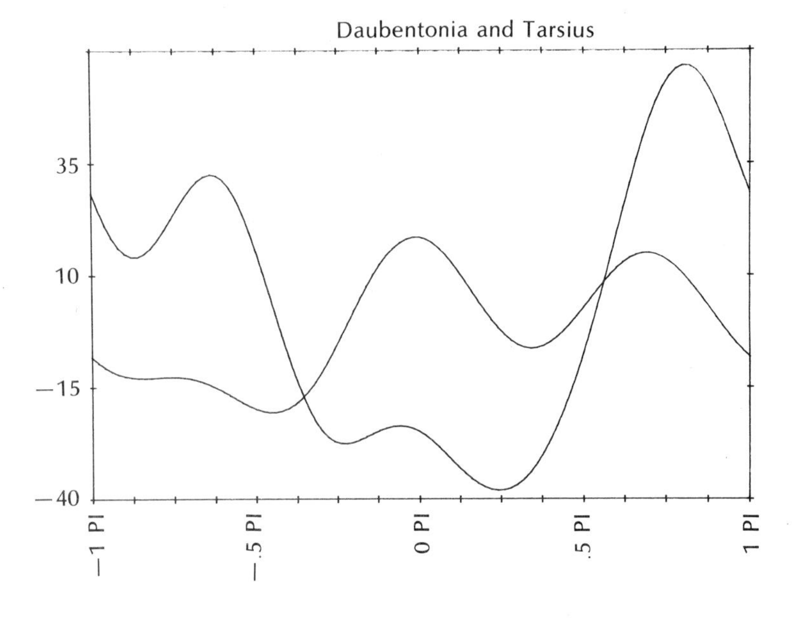

The **third frame** shows two individual genera that are not only different from each other, but that are also, each, different from the first two clusters. One of these is the tarsier which is neither lemur nor lorisine. The other is the aye-aye, which, though generally believed to a be a lemur, is actually totally different from any other living lemur. Similarities and differences are sometimes easily displayed with this technique.

All Andrews Plots

that many differences in proportions between the sexes are both statistically significant and biologically big. Though these differences represent primarily shape, they undoubtedly also contain some remaining (allometric) components associated with overall size.

As we expect, the major differences between the sexes prove to be in shoulder breadth and hip breadth. In 16 of the 18 genera examined, relative shoulder breadth is statistically greater in males than in females. In only two genera in the multivariate study, douroucoulis (*Aotus*) and tamarins (*Leontocebus*), is this not so.

Relative hip breadth shows even greater differences. In all genera except tamarins (*Leontocebus*) relative hip breadth is relatively larger in females than in males.

The chest index also has values that are higher generally in males than in females, but the degree of difference is generally smaller than for shoulder and hip ratios. Relative foot breadth is even less informative, being only slightly greater in females than males in as few as four genera, slightly greater in males than in females in five genera, and showing little difference indeed in the remainder.

Finally, studies of the two ratios of head breadths (cephalic index and relative facial breadth) are the least informative of all. In 3 genera, males are considerably greater than females in cephalic index, and in 2 genera females are considerably greater than males, with most differences rather small. Likewise, in the relative facial breadth, two groups of females are larger than equivalent males to a considerable degree and in two cases males largely outstrip females; but in general there are only small differences between the two sexes in these dimensions.

The overall result of looking at these individual ratios of body breadths confirms the commonly held notions (**a**) that males generally have relatively wider shoulders and chests than females, (**b**) that females generally have relatively wider hips than males, (**c**) that these sexual differences are greater in species such as baboons, orang-utans and gorillas, and less in species such as bushbabies, douroucoulis and spider monkeys, and (**d**) that little else that is consistent is visible. Similar results have also been noted many times in these genera and in others not included in this study (e.g. as reviewed in Schultz, 1969, and Wood 1975, 1976).

Examination of dimensions taken together: Study of the results of canonical variates analyses of these data is carried out first by viewing plots of the first against the second, and the first against the third canonical axes; these are the ones containing the major portion of the differences between the groups.

In the study of all dimensions of the limbs, trunk, head and neck combined, these plots show separations among the genera that resemble, broadly, the main systematic subdivisions of the primates (as described in Oxnard, 1983a, 1984). Separations between the sexes are negligibly small.

In the same way, study of suites of ratios in subsets relating to anatomical regions of the body (e.g. upper limb dimensions alone, lower limb dimensions alone) shows separations between the genera that resemble the main functional differences in those anatomical regions in these primates (also as described in Oxnard, 1983a, 1984). Again, separations between the sexes are extremely small indeed.

Examination yet again of the subset of length dimensions demonstrates, also yet again, very little difference between the sexes (Fig. 1:10).

In complete contrast, is the result of the analysis, by themselves of the full series of breadth dimensions (breadths of hand and feet, upper and lower limb girdles, thorax and abdomen, cranium and face) from wherever they are taken on the body. Of course, fairly big differences are found between the genera. But the primary finding (Fig. 1:11) is that the sex sub-groups of the genera are markedly separated in each of the first three axes. For most genera, the length of the line joining males with females is quite large relative to the standard deviation unit scale, and larger by far than the equivalent separations between the sexes in the study of length dimensions (compare with Fig. 1:10).

This indicates something we already know from univariate analysis, that the differences between the sexes is much bigger in these breadth dimensions than in any of the others.

But closer inspection of the degrees of these differences reveals other results considerably more surprising and not suggested by univariate investigations. Thus the lines joining the sexes are indeed very long in baboons, gorillas and orang-utans, three genera that we know have heavy sexual dimorphism. But the lines joining the sexes for bush-babies, slender lorises and tarsiers are also very long. This indicates that sexual dimorphism is also big in these species *even though we already know, from prior work, that there are no great differences in size between the sexes within these genera*.

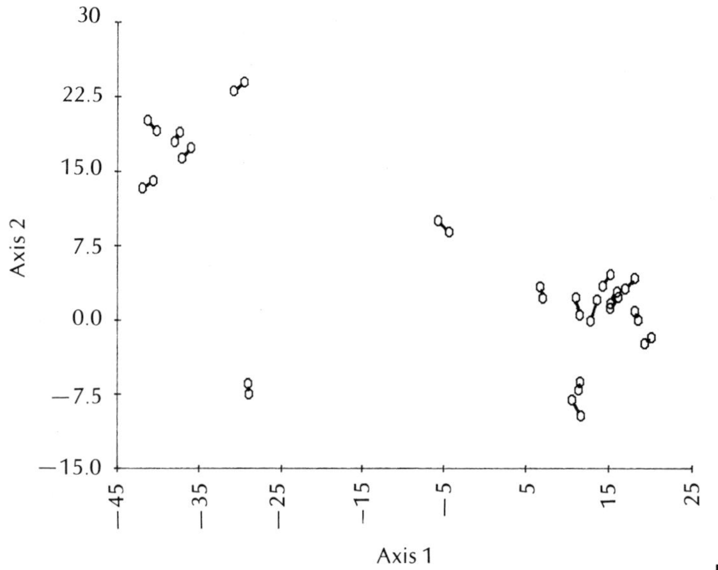

Fig. 1:10 Plot of the first two canonical variates in the study of longitudinal proportions of primates. The circles joined by short lines represented females and males. The short distance between male and female for each group (group not identified) indicates that there is little sexual dimorphism in this analysis.

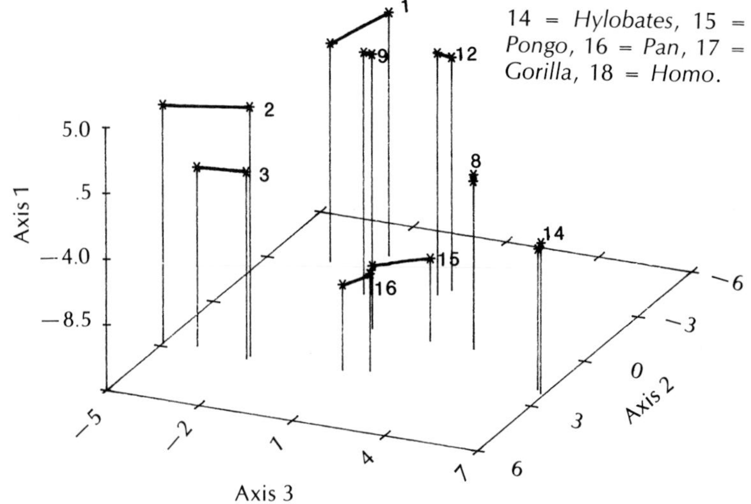

Fig. 1:11 Three dimensional canonical variates plots for the study of breadth dimensions of primates. Sexes of individual genera are joined by straight lines. In each case the identifying numeral for each genus is placed at the position for the female. The genera are named according to the following key:
1 = *Nycticebus*, 2 = *Galago*, 3 = *Tarsius*, 4 = *Aotus*, 5 = *Alouatta*, 6 = *Cebus*, 7 = *Saimiri*, 8 = *Ateles*, 9 = *Leontocebus*, 10 = *Macaca*, 11 = *Cercocebus*, 12 = *Presbytis*, 13 = *Nasalis*, 14 = *Hylobates*, 15 = *Pongo*, 16 = *Pan*, 17 = *Gorilla*, 18 = *Homo*.

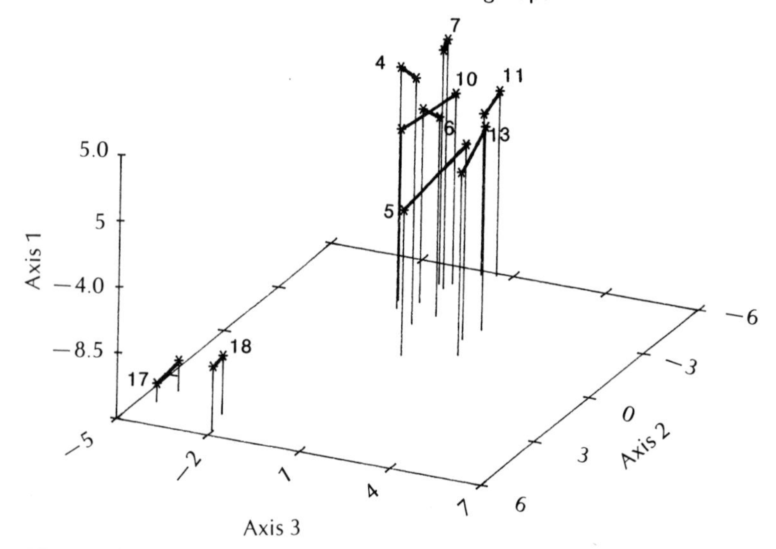

Two plots are shown because the number of genera is too great to be seen on a single plot. The **upper plot** shows mainly genera with horizontal trends in sexual dimorphism. The **lower plot** shows mainly genera with oblique trends in sexual dimorphism. Some genera are reversed compared with others. It is evident that sexual dimorphism is more complex than usually imagined.

Figure 1:11 also shows that the differences between the sexes do not all fit a single pattern. It is true that several primate genera show sexual separations that are parallel one with another; that is, whatever is the position of the females of a given group, the males differ in each direction of the first three canonical axes in the same way, so that lines joining females and males are approximately parallel. But it is also true that, in each plot, a number of genera show angulations of the lines joining the two sexes that are quite different. These particular genera thus have multivariate patterns of sexual dimorphism that are different from those found in the majority of species. In douroucoulis (*Aotus*) and proboscis monkeys (*Nasalis*), the differences between the sexes are represented by lines angulated obliquely to the general pattern. In capuchins (*Cebus*) and humans (*Homo*), the differences between the sexes are represented by lines actually at right angles to the general pattern. In gorillas (*Gorilla*) the directions of the lines representing the differences between the sexes are actually in the reverse direction.

These are the results of scanning the first three canonical axes. Visual examination of the fourth and higher canonical axes shows that though each successively higher axis contains a proportionately reducing amount of the total difference among the genera, each still contains a considerable amount of the differentiation between each sex, though this is much less for the canonical variates analysis of lengths than of breadths.

We can, therefore, re-examine the totality of the significant canonical axes from each of the studies using high dimensional displays. Before we interpret these results, however, it is helpful to look at a series of high-dimensional plots to see how they work with simple theoretical data. The first frame of Figure 1:12 shows differences between plots which differ by regular amounts (two standard deviation units) in a single (the first) canonical axis. The second frame shows the same theoretical analysis for similar variations in a second canonical axis, the third frame in a third and the fourth frame in a fourth. In contrast, the fifth frame of Figure 1:12 shows separations of the same amounts expressed in all four axes at once. These plots provide us with a feel both for the scale of differences between similar plots, and for the nature of the effect of separations that are in separate individual axes or several shared together.

In the light of differences between the curves in this theoretical example, it is obvious that the study of length dimensions does not provide any marked differences between the sexes (Fig. 1:13). In total contrast, it is equally obvious that the study of breadth dimensions does (Figures 1:14, 1:15 and 1:16).

Thus, the result for the study of length dimensions (Fig. 1:13) shows that the finding that the sexes are scarcely differentiated by the first three canonical axes of that study is further confirmed when all canonical axes are viewed at once. The narrowness of the envelopes defined by the sine/cosine plots for each sex of each representative genus indicates clearly that there is very little

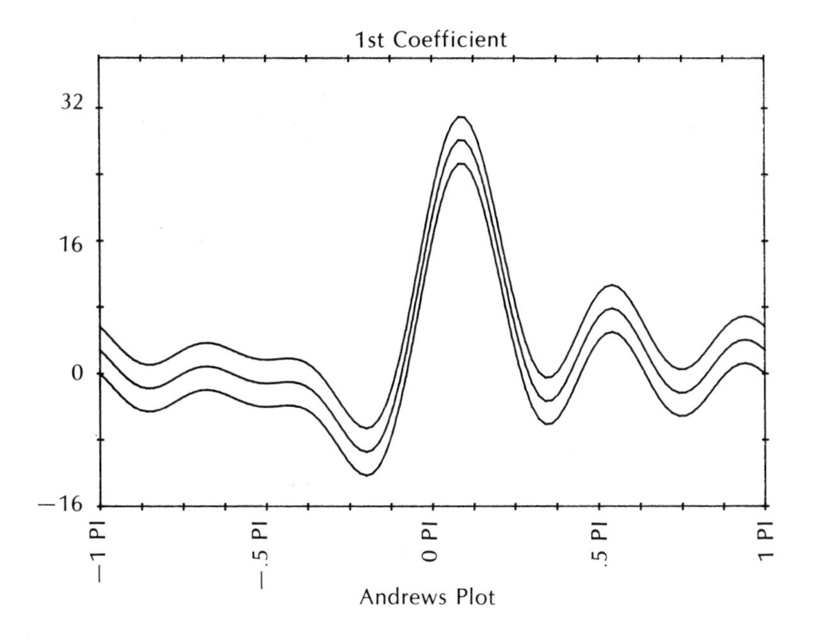

Fig. 1:12 Following the explanations of the high-dimensional display evident from figure 1:9, this figure shows the effects of varying the amount of difference between three groups by two standard deviation units in, successively, the first, second, third and fourth canonical variates and then in all four together. Again, it gives us a 'feel' for the interpretation of similarity in the plots. It also provides a rather precise calibration of two distance units in this method of display. Following pages.

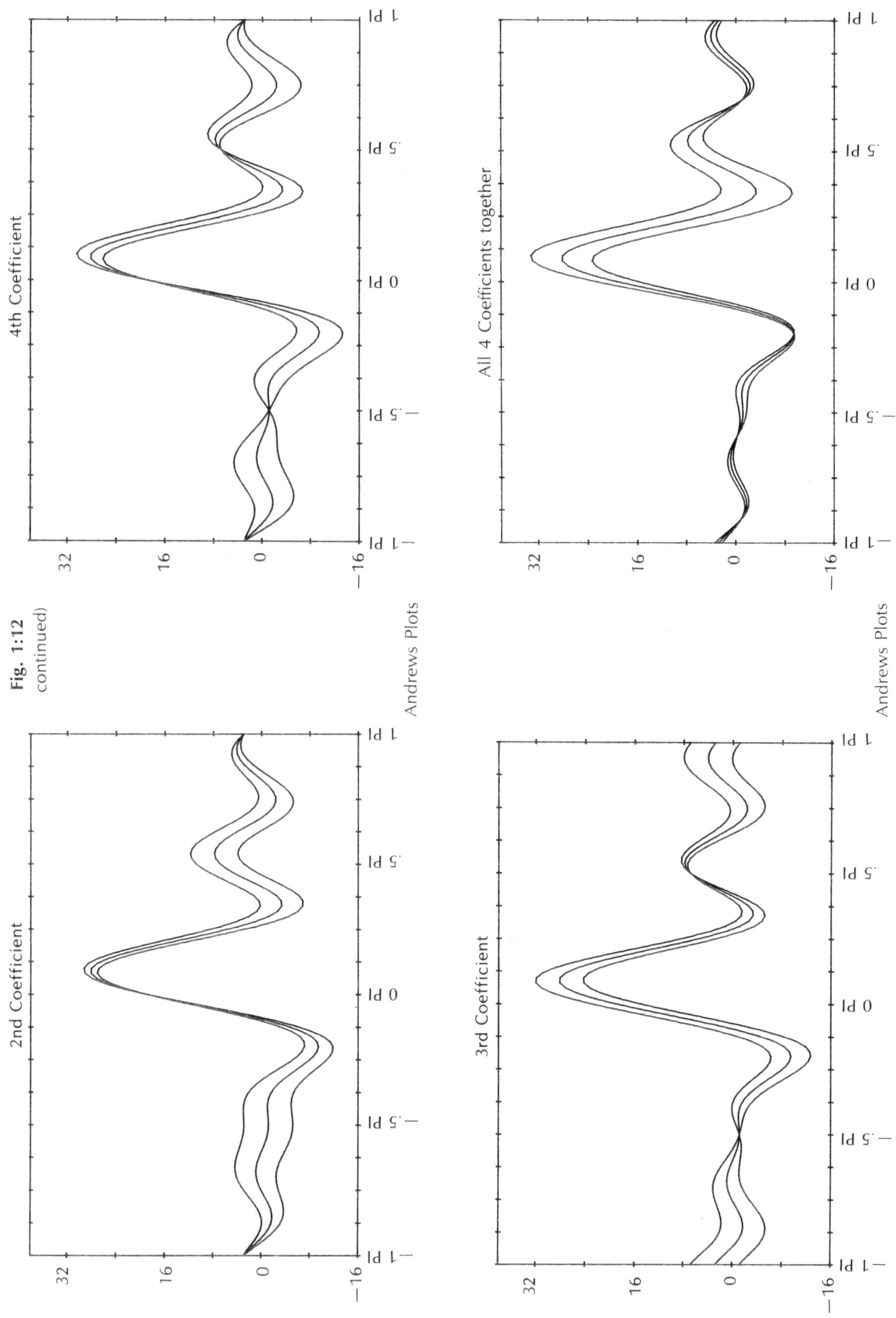

Fig. 1:12 continued)

difference between the sexes even in the totality of the canonical space. The differences are so small, indeed, that it cannot be judged whether or not any coherent differences exist across all genera.

The picture (Figs. 1:14, 1:15 and 1:16) seen in the examination of all canonical axes in the study of breadth dimensions show big differences between the sexes. In every case, the width of the envelope between the plots for each sex for each genus as described through breadths, is far greater than is the case for the high-dimensional display of the analysis of lengths (Fig. 1:13).

Types of sexual dimorphism: Further information is apparent, however. The separations between the sexes are now seen to fall into three categories. One of these is a pattern of separations (Fig. 1:14) for each sex such that, whatever the specific curvature of the sine-cosine plots for any given genus, they display similar differences between the sexes. Thus for each genus in this category the difference between the plots for each sex is similar. The sets of curves are parallel for about three-quarters of the plot, and then cross twice in the last 0.5 pi units near the right hand end of the plot. This pattern is shared by several genera representing every major taxonomic group of the primates except hominoids: slow lorises (*Nycticebus*), howlers (*Alouatta*), macaques (*Macaca*), proboscis monkeys (*Nasalis*), and with a slight variation, mangabeys (*Cercocebus*).

A second category is reflected in a series of pairs of sine-cosine curves for respective sex subgroups that cross four times, two on the left hand side of the plot and two on the right (Fig. 1:15). This pattern is a little more variable than the first but is also shared by several genera, squirrel monkeys (*Saimiri*), capuchins (*Cebus*), spider monkeys (*Ateles*), langurs (*Presbytis*), gibbons (*Hylobates*), and, again with a slight variation, certain marmosets (*Leontocebus*).

Finally, there remains a category of genera which do not share any common pattern. Each of these is quite different from the two patterns just enumerated. And, in addition, each is also different from each of the others. This category includes several prosimians (bush-babies and tarsiers), but, in particular, it includes ourselves (*Homo*), and our closest living relatives, gorillas (*Gorilla*), chimpanzees (*Pan*) and orang-utans (*Pongo*) (Fig. 1:16).

'Dissection' of 'mathematical' anatomies.

With the hindsight of these results it is now possible to reverse our steps and discover what are the internal arrangements in the original data that provide these several patterns of sexual dimorphism.

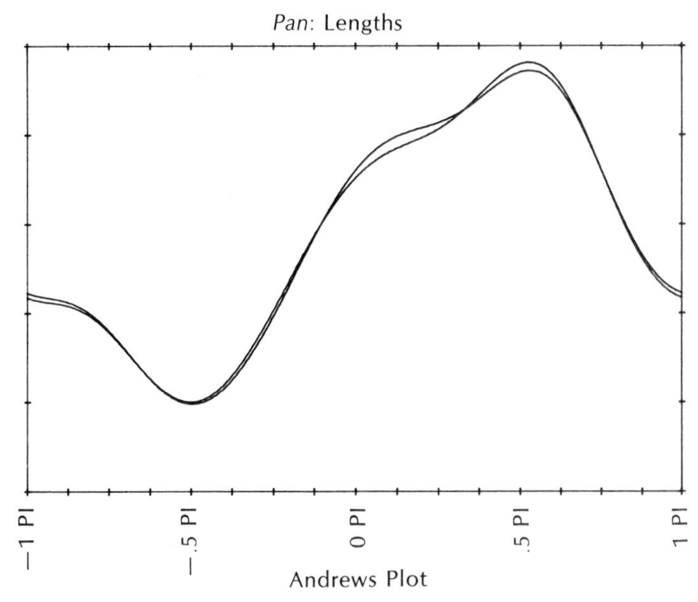

Fig. 1:13 High dimensional curves for the differences between the sexes in a series of representative genera for the study of longitudinal dimensions. The plot for each sex in each case is enormously similar. It is clear that very little sexual dimorphism is evident in these data even when high dimensional information is included. This supports entirely the information provided from viewing the first two canonical axes alone — Fig. 1:10, and following page.

Fig. 1:13
(continued)

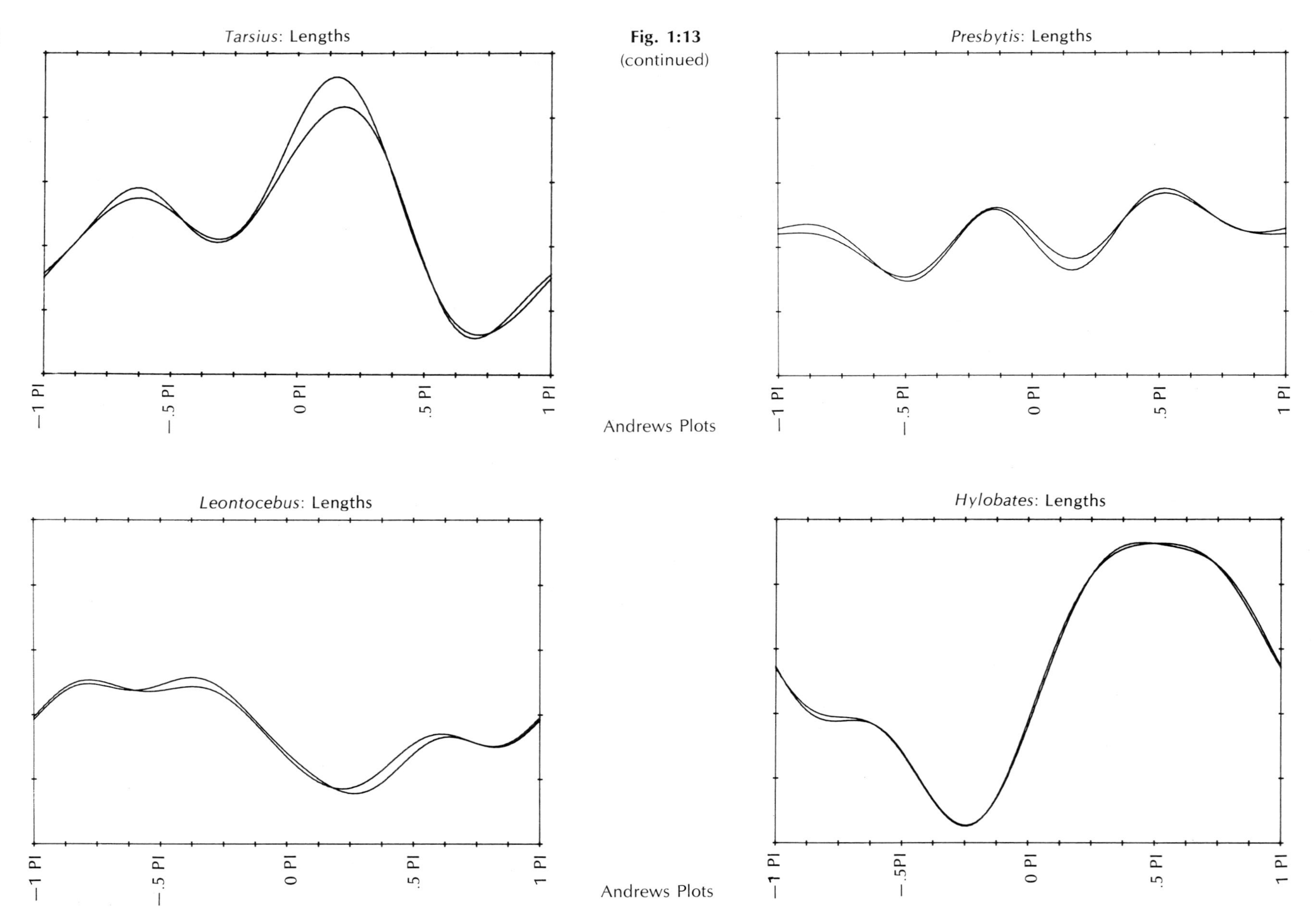

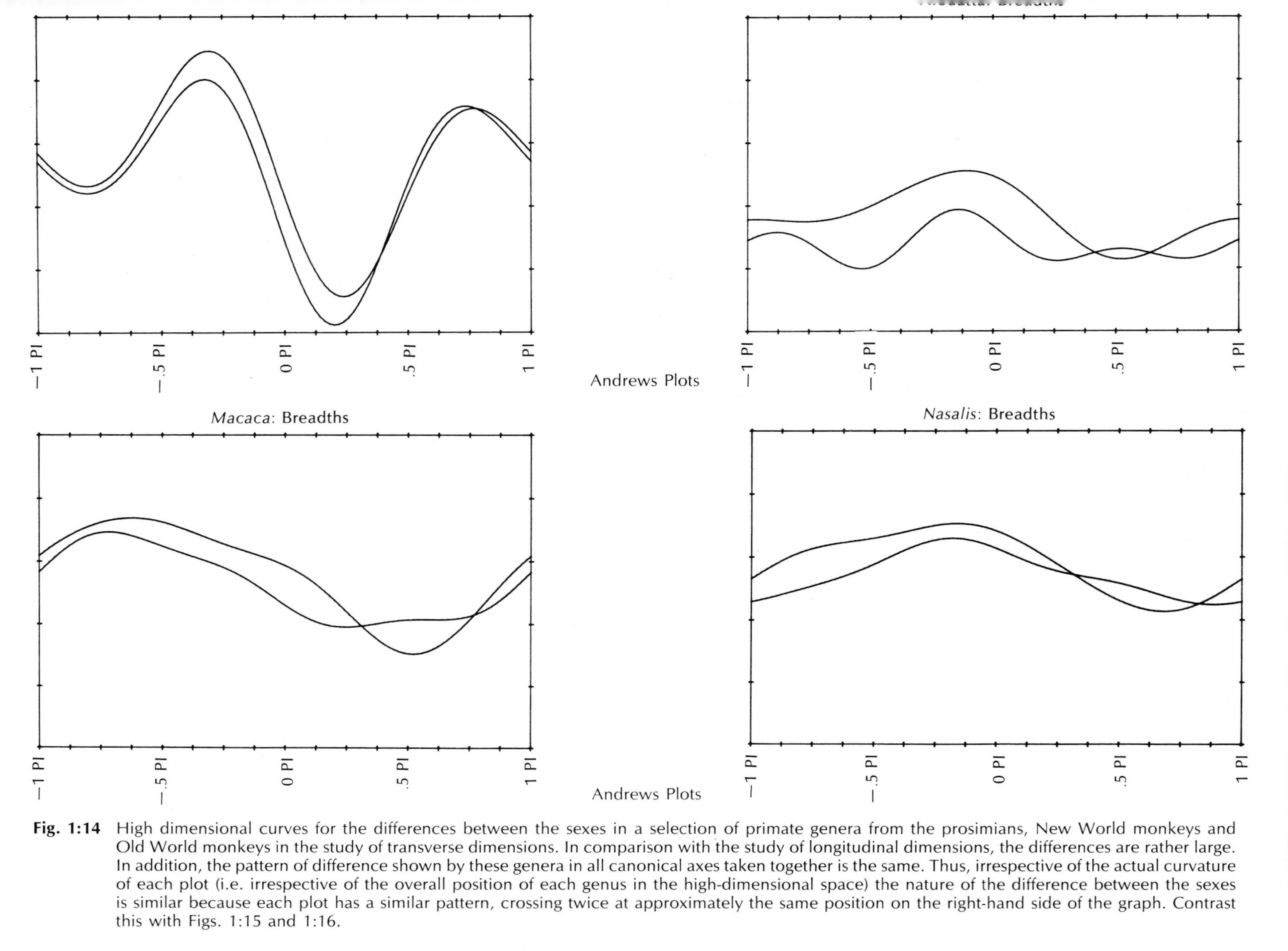

Fig. 1:14 High dimensional curves for the differences between the sexes in a selection of primate genera from the prosimians, New World monkeys and Old World monkeys in the study of transverse dimensions. In comparison with the study of longitudinal dimensions, the differences are rather large. In addition, the pattern of difference shown by these genera in all canonical axes taken together is the same. Thus, irrespective of the actual curvature of each plot (i.e. irrespective of the overall position of each genus in the high-dimensional space) the nature of the difference between the sexes is similar because each plot has a similar pattern, crossing twice at approximately the same position on the right-hand side of the graph. Contrast this with Figs. 1:15 and 1:16.

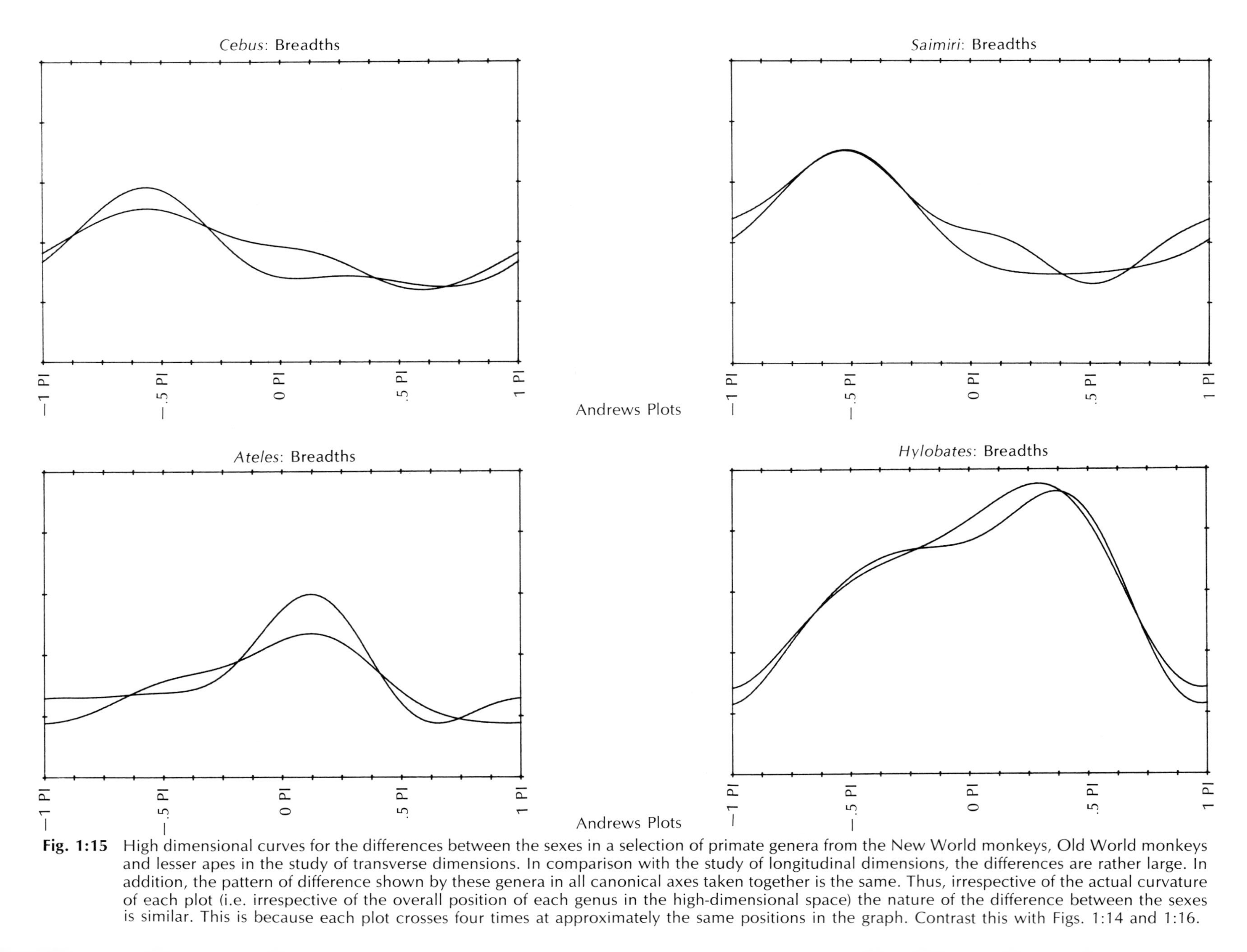

Fig. 1:15 High dimensional curves for the differences between the sexes in a selection of primate genera from the New World monkeys, Old World monkeys and lesser apes in the study of transverse dimensions. In comparison with the study of longitudinal dimensions, the differences are rather large. In addition, the pattern of difference shown by these genera in all canonical axes taken together is the same. Thus, irrespective of the actual curvature of each plot (i.e. irrespective of the overall position of each genus in the high-dimensional space) the nature of the difference between the sexes is similar. This is because each plot crosses four times at approximately the same positions in the graph. Contrast this with Figs. 1:14 and 1:16.

The first step in this process is to see if these same three categories can be seen in the pattern of differences between the sexes in each individual canonical axis. This, indeed, turns out to be the case.

The first part of Table 1:3 shows the genera that have a similarity of plots for the first category of high-dimensional curves (those in Fig. 1:14). It shows that this group of similar plots does indeed result from similar patterns of differences between the sexes in each canonical axis for each genus.

In the same way, the second part of Table 1:3 shows the genera that have a similarity of plots for the second category of high-dimensional curves (those in Fig. 1:15). Table 1:3 also shows that this group of similar plots results from a second group of common patterns of difference between the appropriate sex subgroups in each canonical axis.

The third part of Table 1:3 shows the opposite situation. Here, each genus in this part of the table has a different arrangement of high-dimensional plots. The table shows that this is paralleled by separate patterns of difference between the canonical values for each sex subgroup in each genus.

Although these findings are easily seen with the hindsight of the high-dimensional displays, they were not clearly evident before the sine/cosine plots were computed and drafted.

The second step in this process is to reach even further back and discover what the patterns are of original variables contributing to each canonical variate separating the sexes. This can be done easily, in this case, because there are only six variables and six canonical axes. Thus, the first group of genera is characterized by a similar pattern of variables for each genus, but in an arrangement that contrasts with that for the second group of genera. In both cases, relative shoulder breadth and chest index are among the chief determining variables, as would be expected from looking at the raw data. But the differences between these two groups of genera relate to differences in the way that these variables interact. Table 1:4 shows that the effect of the chest index is the opposite in the first axis in the first category of genera than in the second category. In addition, Table 1:4 shows that each of the other variables also has its part to play, both in the similar patterns within each group and, in the differential separations between them.

In the case of each of the unique patterns existing in the African apes and humans, differences, rather than similarities, are apparent. Table 1:5 shows a different pattern of differential contributions for each variable to the differentiation between each sex in pairwise comparisons for each genus.

Table 1:3

Direction of Difference in Canonical Variates Values From Male to Female for Selected Genera

	Canonical variates values in each axis[a]					
Genera	1	2	3	4	5	6
Nycticebus	+	—	+	=	+	+
Alouatta	=	—	+	=	+	+
Macaca	+	—	+	=	+	+
Cercocebus	+	=	+	—	+	—
Nasalis	+	—	—	—	+	=
Saimiri	+	+	+	+	+	+
Cebus	+	+	+	+	+	=
Ateles	+	+	+	+	+	+
Presbytis	+	+	—	+	+	—
Hylobates	+	+	=	+	+	—
Pongo	+	+	+	+	+	—
Pan	+	=	+	—	+	=
Gorilla	—	+	—	+	+	—
Homo	+	+	=	—	+	=

[a] A more positive value for the mean of a female group as compared with a male group is indicately by + in the table.

Table 1:4

Principal Contributions of Variables to Each Canonical Axis

Axes	Major contributions of variables					
	Shoulder	Chest	Hip	Foot	Face	Head breadth
First group of genera[a]						
1	−	−			−	
2		−	+		−	
3			+	−		
4						
5	−	−				−
6						
Second group of genera						
1	−	+			+	
2		+	−		+	
3			−	−		
4			−			
5	−	+				
6						−

[a] + = larger in female.

Table 1:5

Principal Differences Between Contributions of Variables to Canonical Axes in Three Unique Genera

	Major contributions of variables[a]					
	Shoulder	Chest	Hip	Foot	Face	Head breadth
Human vs gorilla						
Axis 1	−	−			+	
Axis 3			+	−		
Human vs chimp						
Axis 2		+	−		+	
Axis 5	−	+				
Axis 6						+
Gorilla vs chimp						
Axis 1	+	+			−	
Axis 2		−	+		−	
Axis 3			−	+		
Axis 4			−			

[a] + = larger in first genus.

Fig. 1:16 ▷ High dimensional curves for the differences between the sexes in the four large hominoids in the study of transverse dimensions. In comparison with the study of longitudinal dimensions, the differences are very large. In this case however, in contrast to those in Figs. 1:14 and 1:15, the patterns of difference shown by these four genera in all canonical axes taken together are quite different. Thus, irrespective of the actual curvature of each plot (i.e. irrespective of the overall position of each genus in the high-dimensional space) the nature of the difference between the sexes is different. The curves for the orang-utan sexes cross twice on the left side of the plot and once on the right. The curves for the gorilla sexes cross six times. The difference between the chimpanzee sexes is different again with only two regularly spaced crossing points. And the differences between the human sexes displays four regularly spaced crossing points. In this case, sexual dimorphism in each large hominoid is different from each of the others, contrasting, thus, with Figs. 1:14 and 1:15.

Fig. 1:16

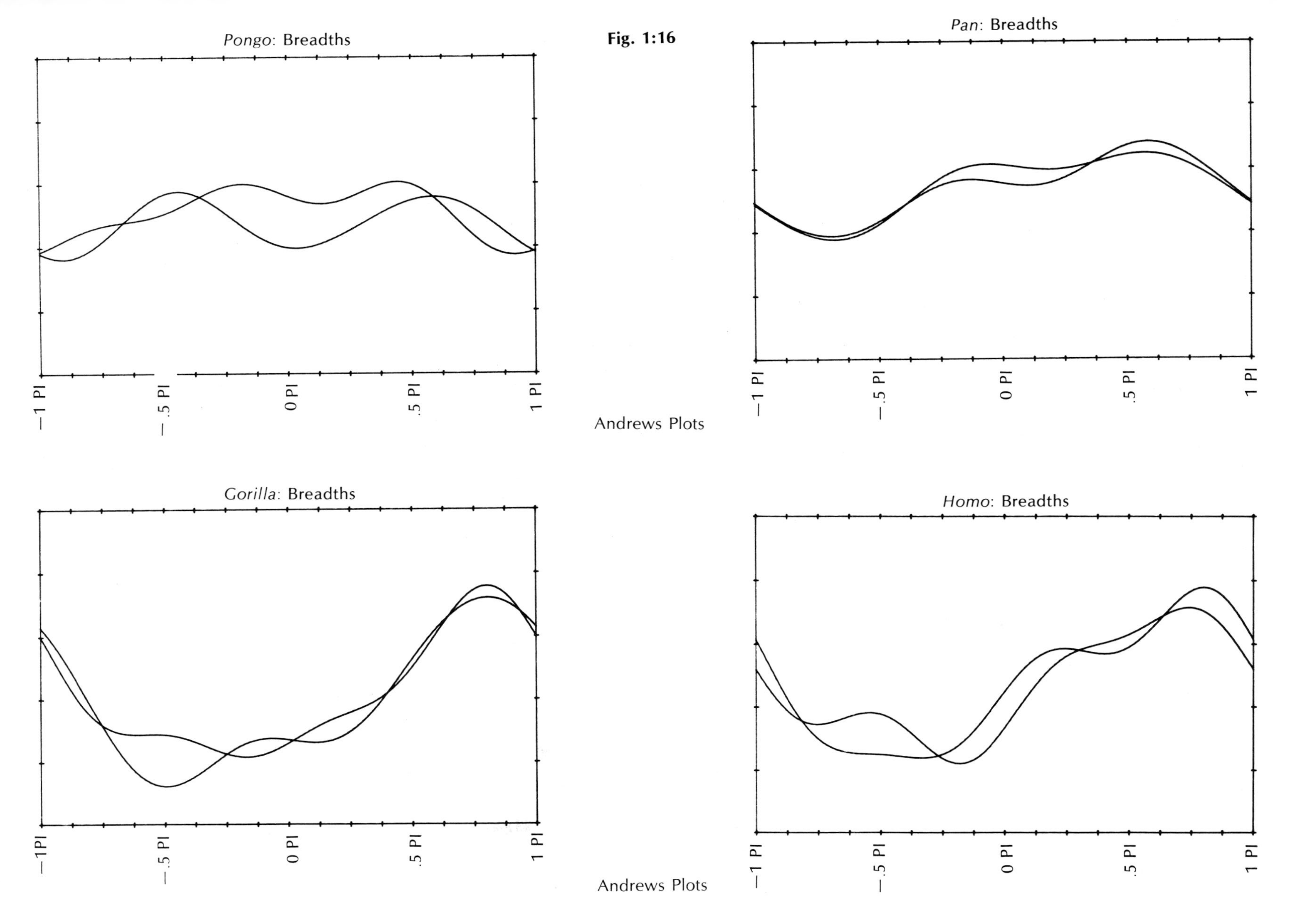
Pongo: Breadths
Pan: Breadths
Gorilla: Breadths
Homo: Breadths
−1 PI
−.5 PI
0 PI
.5 PI
1 PI
Andrews Plots
Andrews Plots

Implications for the evolution of great apes and humans

In summary, there is an infra-structure of canonical values, for each sex for each genus, that gives rise to two separate consistent patterns of difference in two groups of genera (Figs. 1:14 and 1:15), and a further number of genera showing, each, unique differences (Fig. 1:16).

These findings have implications, **first**, for the very description of the phenomenon of sexual dimorphism. No longer can we describe structural sexual dimorphism, at least as viewed through the overall proportions of the body, as a single phenomenon with differential expression. There are clearly a number of different sexual dimorphisms. Two of these patterns are each spread among several major taxonomic groups of the primates: prosimians, New World monkeys and Old World monkeys. For this reason neither pattern can be especially thought to be primitive although additional data might show that one of them was. Presumably, therefore, at least one of these patterns (and at this point most likely both) must have arisen in parallel a number of times.

This leads inevitably, **second**, to the denial of the idea that differences between the sexes are simply a result of the differences in overall size (e.g. Wood, 1975, 1976). For if that were the case, then the biggest dimorphisms would be found in those animals which have the biggest overall size differences between the sexes. The large size of the differences between the sexes for bushbabies (*Galago*), tarsiers (*Tarsius*), douroucoulis (*Aotus*), spider monkeys (*Ateles*) and gibbons (*Hylobates*), for example, some among the genera that display the smallest differences in size between the sexes is directly contrary. Indeed, this finding suggests that there may be major sexual dimorphisms in overall body proportions that are scarcely related to size at all. It would obviously be false to claim that size is not implicated in at least a part of the sexual dimorphisms that have been discovered here; but the data clearly demonstrate that there must also be many other parts of the sexual dimorphisms that are associated with other factors.

And this leads, **third**, to different views of the causality of sexual dimorphisms. Because many different sexual dimorphisms exist it would seem unreliable for us to lean upon a single causal explanation. Thus the simpler notions such as terrestrial-arboreal or savannah-forest differences (e.g. Pilbeam, 1972), or the more complex ones such as harem organization (e.g. Gautier-Hion, 1975) are, by themselves, unlikely causal factors. Multifactorial explanations are far more likely.

And there have been a number of multifactorial suggestions. Crook (1972) suggests that the amount of sexual dimorphism is related to a spectrum in primate behavior running from least dimorphism in solitary, arboreal, nocturnal species to most dimorphism in gregarious, terrestrial, diurnal species. Gautier-Hion (1975) implies that sexual dimorphism is related to both harem structure and terrestriality. Leutenegger and Kelly (1977) provide as many as seven possible factors for what they term body size dimorphism.

But the existence of several different anatomical sexual dimorphisms suggests not only that they are multifactorially determined, but also that the interplay of the multiple factors is different in each case. Thus, though there is no single consistent arrangement of social organization, of ecological niche, of territorial availability, of feeding pattern, of locomotion, of troop defence, of reproductive efficiency, or even of developmental transformation that fits the results here, it is possible that some or all of these taken together, in different weightings for each genus, might be truly implicated. It is also not impossible that other, hitherto unconsidered, factors may be involved.

The findings also lead on to yet more speculative ideas. **Fourth**, it is possible to say something about the evolution of these sexual dimorphisms. At least some sexual differences in the primates (additional to those initially present as a result of a much older sexual dimorphism, presumably shared with mammalian progenitors of primates) must have evolved more than once within the group. In prosimians, monkeys and apes the two major patterns that we have found must, in each case, have evolved in parallel several times. And the various individual patterns must, likewise, represent a series of independent evolutionary radiations.

Fifth, it is possible to say something about associated phenomena. As far as can be judged from the somewhat restricted representation of primate genera in Schultz' data, it might be suggested that one of these major groups indeed represents the 'polygynous social structure/male troop defence grouping' of several authors, containing, as it does, howler monkeys (*Alouatta*), macaques (*Macaca*), mangabeys (*Cercocebus*) and proboscis monkeys (*Nasalis*). On the other hand, the inclusion of the monogamous slow loris (*Nycticebus*), and the exclusion of some polygynous cebids, langurs and great apes from this group tends to deny such an idea. The second major group, containing, as it does, douroucoulis (*Aotus*), tamarins (*Leontocebus*) and gibbons (*Hylobates*) may represent principally the 'monogamous/equal male and female troop defence grouping' of these same authors. Again, however, the inclusion of spider monkeys (*Ateles*) and langurs (*Presbytis*) within this group, and the exclusion from it of tarsiers (*Tarsius*) reduces the likelihood of that idea. And in the various genera of prosimians and hominoids that each have their own unique sexually dimorphic patterns there must have been other evolutionary factors perhaps unrelated to the concepts involving the monogamous-polygynous social structure alternatives and the equal/unequal troop defence options.

Finally, these findings mean that when we attempt to view differences between the sexes in pre-human, pre-hominid, or even pre-hominoid fossils, we can no longer assume (as do Fleagle, Kay and Simons, 1980; Johanson, 1980; Gingerich, 1981; Gingerich and Martin, 1981) that a single form of sexual dimorphism with differential expression covers all genera. Now we must be prepared to ask: are the sexual dimorphisms of, for instance, *Home sapiens neandertalensis*, *Homo erectus*, *Gigantopithecus*, the various australopithecines and the various ramapithecines, like those of humans, or of gorillas, or of chimpanzees, or even of orangutans (species presumably very far removed from human ancestry)? Are any of them even like one of the two general patterns that exist more widely among the primates? Indeed, it would be entirely appropriate that we might even ask: are the sexual dimorphisms of any of these fossil creatures like those of no extant Primate at all, but presenting yet other patterns unique unto themselves? Presumably, now, whenever we attempt to assess sexual dimorphism in any fossil species, we enter into this more complex realm.

Before we can be certain about the suggestions stemming from study of extant forms, we need a far larger study than is allowed by Schultz' data (big though his lifetime's collection is). Such a new study, or studies, requires (**a**) much larger samples of each primate group, (**b**) greater representation of the different groups of primates, (**c**) primate groups represented at the species grade (even the geographic locality level) rather than the generic, (**d**) more detailed morphometric definitions of the anatomical structure of each animal, and (**e**) far more detailed correlations with functional, ecological, social, developmental and systematic data. Such extensive investigations will not be quickly or easily carried out; but they at least now appear far more interesting than merely certifying the existence of a single pattern of sexual dimorphism with differential expression in each genus.

But the existence of these new suggestions also has implications for the study of fossils, even if we can never directly know these factors for any given fossil. An equivalent series of more detailed studies is required for those fossils believed to be associated with the evolution of living apes and humans. In this case what is needed are studies of much greater numbers of fossils than have hitherto been published, with the idea of understanding population differences, and with the concepts of multiple sexual dimorphisms and multiple interacting causalities in mind. Because of the sizes of samples necessary for such studies, this will be achieved first and most easily with data from teeth. It is to this that the rest of this book is addressed. And because sexual dimorphism in the teeth of extant apes and humans necessarily forms the background for any such studies of hominoid fossils it is to the study of the teeth of extant forms to which we must apply ourselves in the next chapter.

Summary: In this chapter we have seen that in terms of overall bodily proportions, sexual dimorphism in primates is a far more complex phenomenon than we have hitherto been lead to believe.

The sexes of each species do not possess greater or lesser degrees of expression of a single sexual dimorphism, along some unidimensional axis heavily dependent upon differences in overall bodily size in each sex. Rather they possess, in addition, a complexity of structural form, such that at least two major and several smaller qualitatively different patterns of sexual dimorphism are evident within the Order.

The distribution of these is such, as to suggest that the various sexual dimorphisms have arisen independently a number of times during the last 70 million or more years, the span of evolution of the Order. And the distribution of the unique patterns of sexual dimorphism found within each of the large hominoids suggests, in its turn, that sexual dimorphisms within this group have been able to change within only the last few million years of their divergence.

One way of testing this is to study sexual dimorphisms in the teeth of living species. This is carried out in the next chapter.

CHAPTER 2

The Present Day: Sexual Dimorphisms in the Teeth of Living Apes and Humans

Sexual Dimorphism or Sexual Dimorphisms?
The Dimensions of Ape and Human Teeth — Canines — Incisors
Premolars — Molars — Measures taken one by one
Sexual Dimorphism in Multivariate Studies of Ape and Human Teeth
Canonical Variates Analyses — High Dimensional Displays
Some Implications for Evolution

Abstract: In this chapter we study sexual dimorphism in the teeth of the living large hominoids: humans, chimpanzees, gorillas and orang-utans. The discussion of Chapter 1 suggests that we must look for many sexual dimorphisms not one, for complex sexually dimorphic patterns rather than simple, and for arrangements evident in studies of measures taken altogether as well as studies of measures taken individually.

In this chapter we examine the measures of the teeth using simple statistical tools, such as means and variances, and frequency histograms and normal distributions. We also study them using the multivariate statistical methods of canonical variates analysis and high-dimensional displays.

It turns out that there is not a single sexual dimorphism common to all these species. There are many, and they are certainly highly complex. The findings have implications not only for the evolution of the species but also for the evolution of their sexual differences. And they have especial significance for the study of the fossils examined in comparable ways in later chapters.

Sexual dimorphism or sexual dimorphisms?

The larger problem of the nature and meaning of sexual dimorphism in general can be elucidated through study of the smaller problem of sexual differences in tooth dimensions. But we should consider first two very obvious possibilities.

First, since the teeth are primarily a food processing device we must ask: could differences in tooth sizes be specifically adaptive to diet? More specifically, could sexual dimorphisms in tooth sizes be related to differences in diet in males and females? Certainly this is the case in food processing apparatuses in some species — bird bills, for example (Selander, 1966). But there is no compelling case from present evidence that this is a major factor for any ape or monkey group (where the greatest differences between the sexes are to be found).

There are well-known sex differences in canine size and form in many non-human primates. But these seem to be unrelated to diet and have no parallels in the human dentition. Nevertheless there are some differences in diet between the sexes and this is a matter to which we shall return.

Second, many studies imply, both directly and by default, that sexual differences in tooth size are reflections of differences in body size. This has never been fully studied in the non-human primates, for the necessary basic data from large enough populations do not exist. Here we have to be careful for many studies have shown that this relationship only holds within a particular population (Brace and Ryan, 1980). In the one instance within humans where body size and tooth size are available within known family groups 'taller parents do have children with systematically larger... dental dimensions' (Garn, Lewis and Walenga, 1968). And genetic links of jaw shape with sexual dimorphism are known (e.g. in rats: Bailey, 1984).

How do these ideas stand up against the data presented in the last chapter?

The studies of chapter one on overall bodily proportions (see also Oxnard, 1983a, c, 1984) must have already raised doubts in our minds about such conventional concepts of sexual dimorphism in primates, especially in apes and humans. The examination, first, of body variables taken one by one in those studies show what is well known: that there are considerable statistical differences between the sexes, especially in measures of breadth, and that these can be described as greater or lesser degrees of dimorphism along a uni-dimensional scale closely allied with size.

But the examination, second, of those many body variables taken all together using multivariate statistical methods, shows a completely different picture. At least two major patterns of sexual difference exist among the primates studied. Each of these patterns is shared by genera representing every main taxonomic grade. In addition, there are seven unique patterns of sexual difference specific to individual genera, including one for each species of large hominoid.

The degree of these sexual dimorphisms seems to be related to more than just size differences between the sexes. Sexual dimorphism, by these measures, is almost as large, proportionately, in orang-utans as in bushbabies; two genera at opposite ends of the scales of difference, both in absolute size between the species and relative size between the sexes.

In addition, the unique patterns of sexual dimorphism seem related as much to the interactions of the variables as to their individual variation. They were not discovered until we applied an appropriate multivariate statistical technique (canonical variates analysis). It seems inevitable that yet other complexities will be found as a wider range of genera, species, even of geographically separated groups, and a better selection of osteological and perhaps other variables are included in such studies.

Table 2:1

Numbers of specimens per sex and per genus

Maxillary teeth

Genus	Females	Males	Total
Gorilla	42	42	84
Pan	42	44	86
Pongo	38	41	79
Homo: sexes unknown			59
			308

Mandibular teeth

Genus	Females	Males	Total
Gorilla	39	40	79
Pan	44	39	86
Pongo	43	38	81
Homo: sexes unknown			56
			299

These findings clearly mean that it is also important to try to discover if they exist in other structural components of the body. One such component that has frequently been examined is the dentition. It is happily the case that data for the form of the dentition are already available for reasonably large samples of higher primates.

The teeth, moreover, show a special sexual dimorphism that is particularly obvious in the canines of many species. So marked is that canine dimorphism that we investigate it first. Study of the canines is followed, however, by equivalent investigations of the other teeth of both upper and lower jaws; they, too, show evidence of sexual dimorphism. A visual impression of sexual dimorphism in the jaws of living hominoids is provided in Figures 2:1 and 2:2.

The dimensions of ape and human teeth: measures taken one by one

The dimensions of ape and human teeth include their lengths and breadths. These measures are available from each tooth in both upper and lower jaws for reasonably large samples. Measures to better define the form of these teeth have certainly been devised (e.g. Ashton and Zuckerman, 1950a,b) But lengths and breadths, though merely defining overall shape, are especially important because they allow comparisons with equivalent data that are all that are available for many of the fossils.

The data (Table 2:1) used in this study represent all three genera of great apes and humans. Data on 308 specimens are culled from the studies of Gregory and Hellman (1926), Pilbeam (1969), Wolpoff (1971), Frayer (1973) and Mahler (1973). Only individuals with permanent dentitions were measured. The sexes of the specimens of apes are obvious from independent information available, either from the rest of the specimen (e.g. skull or pelvis) or from field records. Because samples with sexes known are not available for the human part of these data, a separate suite of measures are taken from an additional 60 specimens, the sexes of which were known from clinical records kindly made available to me by Orthodontist, Dr. Clifford Willcox.

The verbal descriptions of the measurements and the similarities in their mean values for respective samples from the same taxa suggest that Pilbeam's (1969) and Mahler's (1973) measurement techniques are truly comparable. Frayer's (1973) measures were also taken by Mahler. The descriptions of measures taken from Gregory and Hellman (1926; see also Gregory, Hellman and Lewis, 1938) are comparable with those of Pilbeam and Mahler. One change made in these data is because the maxillary third premolar length measurements from Pilbeam (1969) are not compatible with those of Mahler (1973); in this case Pilbeam's 'maximum projected length' is more comparable with Mahler's 'maximum morphological length'. Statistical tests confirm that in only three dimensions out of 32, and in only a single sex subgroup, can differences be associated with the different sources of the data. This indicates, without reservation, that it is legitimate to compare data from these particular investigators.

Tests of technique made on the additional 60 human specimens (30 of each sex), made available by Dr. Clifford Willcox, confirm that the scale of inaccuracy in measurement of individual teeth, is, in general, insufficiently large to render it likely that the results of comparisons among the genera and between the sexes would be affected. But the absolute values for these additional human data cannot be directly compared with those for the other humans and apes mentioned above because the technique of measurement differs. These additional data do allow the examination of distributions within each human sex subgroup. And this separate comparison leads to a better understanding of the main set of human data for which sex is not known.

In each sex subgroup, from each genus, basic statistical data for each measurement are calculated (means, variances, standard deviations, and coefficients of skewness, kurtosis, variance and correlation). These allow searches for outliers and non-normal distributions, and provide standards for comparisons of the data. The significance of differences between means and dispersions for each sex are assessed by 't' and 'F' tests.

The detailed distributions of the data are examined through calculation of frequency distribution histograms, and through their comparison with fitted normal curves using standard 'chi square' tests.

Differences between the means are essentially similar to those already reported in the literature (e.g. humans: Lavelle, 1968; apes: Ashton and Zuckerman, 1950a,b; Swindler, 1976). Differences between dispersions and distributions do not appear to have been previously assessed for these dimensions in the sex subgroups of these genera.

Particular attention is paid to avoiding the methodological problems shown by Jacklin (1981) to be ubiquitous in studies of sex-related differences in humans. Jacklin reminds us of these errors.

One includes use of the concept of a difference between sex sub-groups to misleadingly suggest differences between individuals. This is especially wrong in cases (like those examined here) where overlap between the sex sub-groups is so great that individual differences are much greater than differences attributable to sex. We have a particularly blatant example in Chapter 6. A second includes failure to distinguish between the significance of an effect and the size of that effect, both relative to other differences and relative to possible biological implications. A significant (especially if significant because samples are very large) but very small difference may be biologically unimportant (see differences between lengths and breadths, Chapter 1). A third involves the bias towards the acceptance of positive information alone. Variables that show only very small differences, even differences so small as to be essentially non-existent, may be important indicators of lack of difference. Yet they may be neglected when such a bias exists (see later this chapter). A fourth is assuming that the cause of an established sex-related difference must be a single simple major factor (a point fundamental to this entire book). A fifth and very important one is not recognising the large number of variables that can be confounded with sex (see discussion in the final chapter).

Specific attempts have been made in these investigations to be conscious of, and to avoid, these and the other problems noted by Jacklin.

Canine sexual dimorphisms in humans and apes

The lengths and breadths of both upper and lower canines show the well-known difference that we expect (males larger than females). They also show the expected quantitative variation (smaller dimorphism in humans and chimpanzees, larger dimorphism in orang-utans and gorillas). These are the major elements of sexual dimorphism in primate canines that have long been recognized.

Even in these univariate studies, however, the lengths and breadths of the canines show further differences between the sexes to which attention has not been previously drawn in each of the four genera.

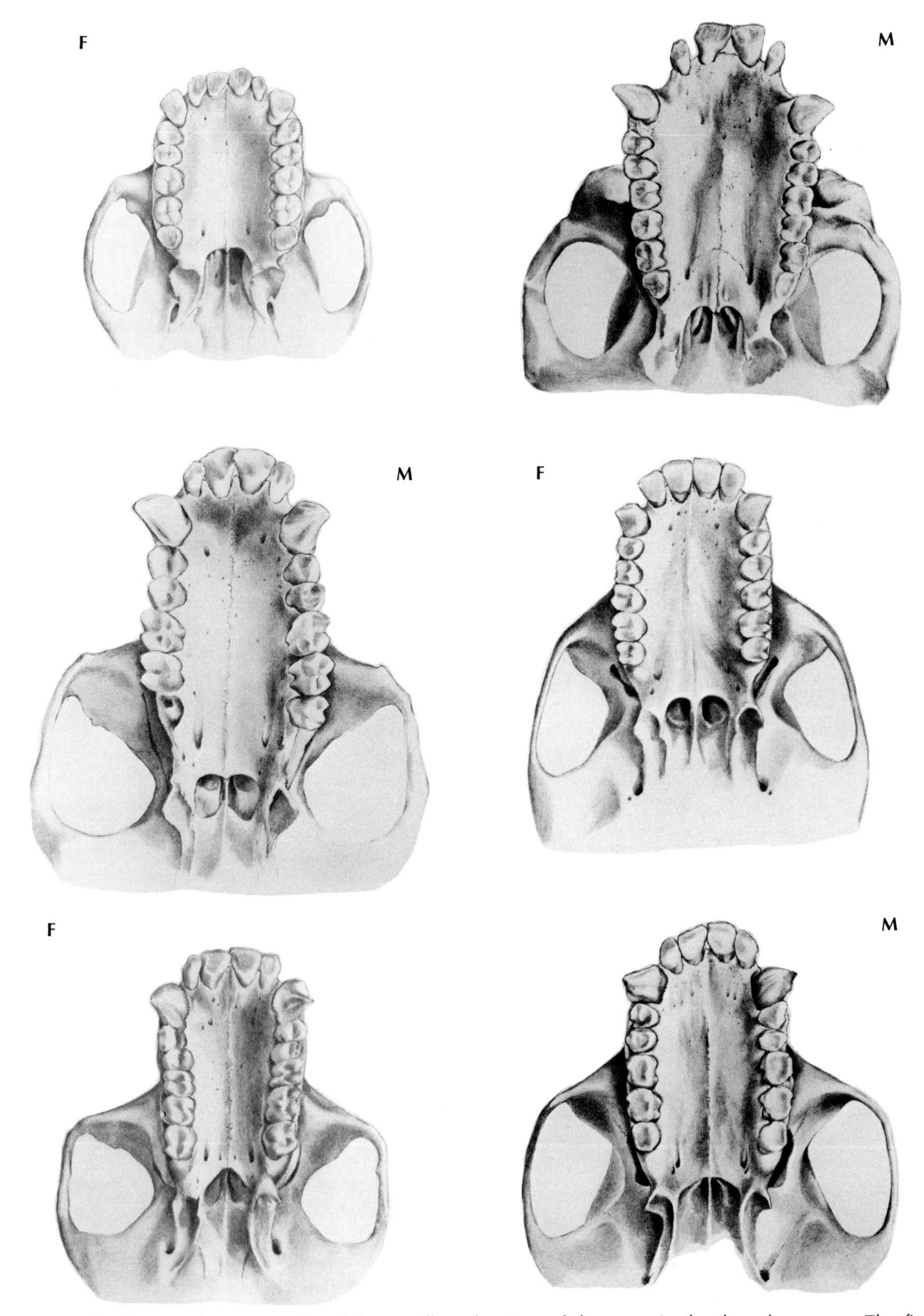

Fig. 2:1 Sketches, to the same scale, of the maxillary dentition of the sexes in the three large apes. The first two are of orang-utan females and males, the second pair of gorilla males and females, the third chimpanzee females and males. There are no easily observable differences between the human sexes.

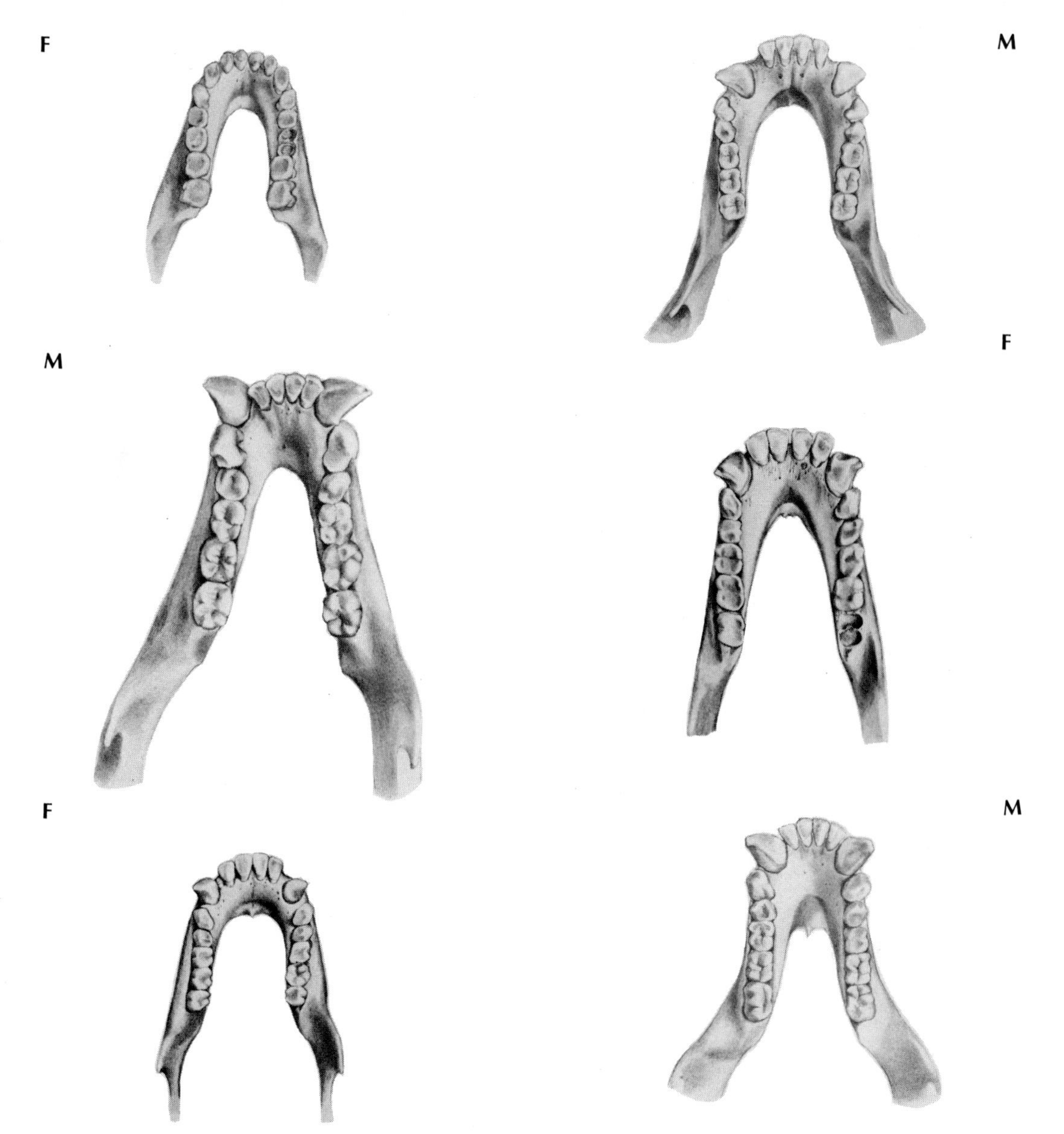

Fig. 2:2 Sketches, to the same scale, of the mandibular dentition of the sexes in the three large apes. The first two are of orang-utan females and males, the second pair of gorilla males and females, the third chimpanzee females and males. There are no easily observable differences between human females and males.

Homo: In humans, as is well known, the canines are smaller than in any of the other species. The basic statistical data confirm that the differences between the means for each sex for each measure are much less than in any ape. This also fits the conventional view. It is nevertheless somewhat surprizing that this sexual dimorphism of means is as large as is shown by the histograms for sexes defined as shown in Figure 2:3.

The histograms for each individual sex (for the subset of the data for which sex is known from clinical records) fit normal curves very closely and overlap to considerable degrees. These individual histograms also show similar dispersions for each sex. Thus, canine sexual dimorphism in humans not only shows very small (indeed, almost zero) differences in mean values for each sex (sexual dimorphism of means), but also demonstrates very small (essentially zero) differences in dispersion between each sex (sexual dimorphism of dispersion). There truly is only small sexual dimorphism in the genus *Homo*.

Yet, when we come to examine histograms for the entire sample (sexes not defined) we find that

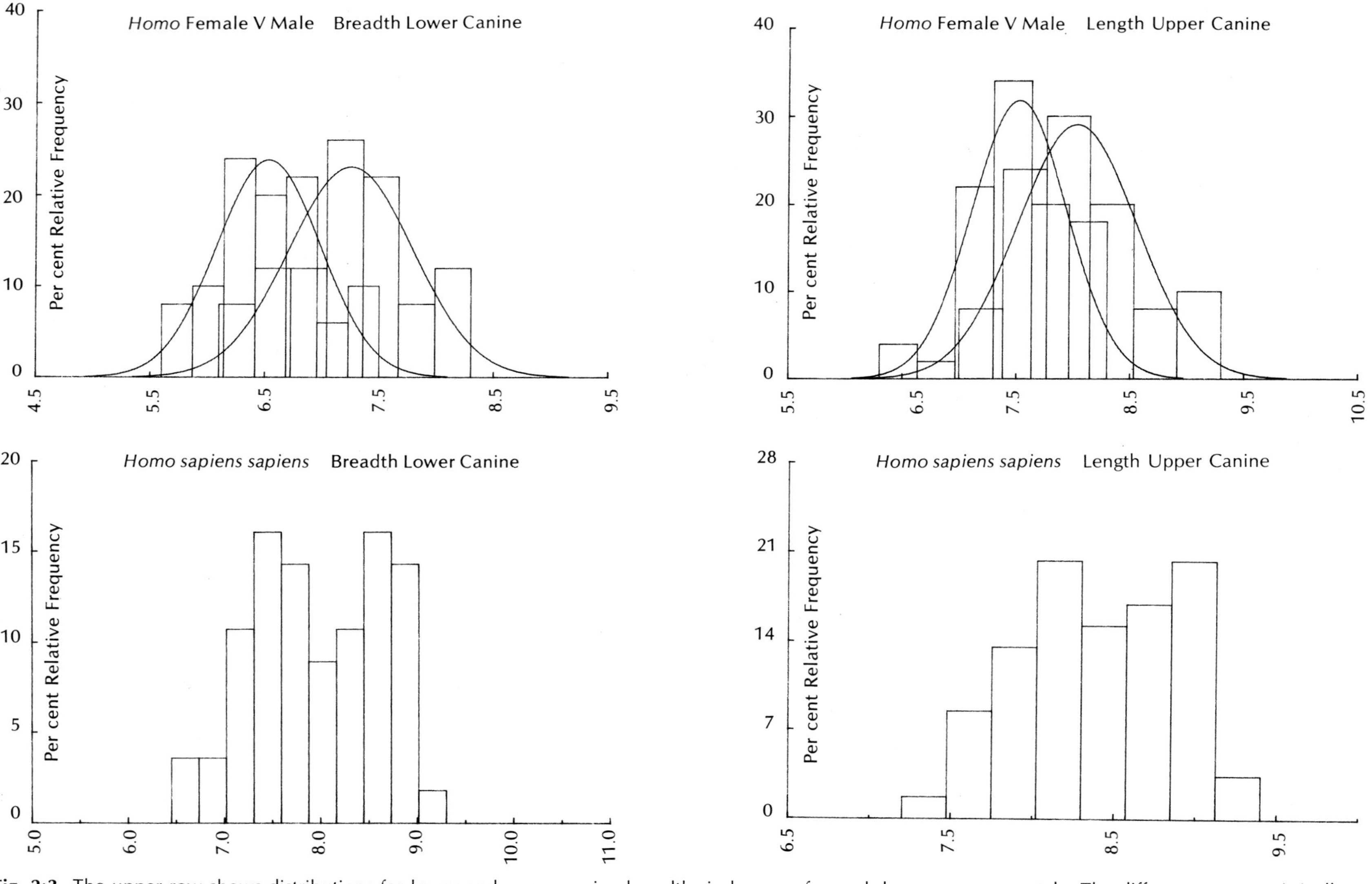

Fig. 2:3 The upper row shows distributions for lower and upper canine breadths in humans for each known sex separately. The differences are statistically significant. The distance between the means of each sex is rather small, there is very much overlap, and the spreads for each sex are the same.
The lower row shows the distributions for the same data for humans when we ignore the information about the sex of each specimen. In spite of the enormous overlap, the presence of two sexes can be clearly seen from the bimodality of the plot. And the fact that there are equal numbers of each sex in the sample can be seen from the equal sizes of the two peaks in the bimodal plot. Yet, of course, these two peaks each include many specimens from each sex. Thus, though this can provide an estimate of the sex ratio, it cannot be a basis for deciding on the sex of any individual specimen.

they do not always show a single peak as befits a situation where there is only a small difference between heavily overlapping normal distributions for two groups. It is already known that the addition of two very close normal distributions gives a normal distribution (Wu and Oxnard, 1983a,b). This is not what we have found. In three of the four canine measures there is a bimodal histogram showing that the differences between the sexes are somewhat more extensive than we may have thought.

The bimodal form of the histograms for the data, sexes undefined, possesses two equally large peaks. This implies that there are approximately equal numbers of specimens for each sex. This finding is related, surely, to the equal numbers of males and females that we might expect to find in any reasonably large sample of human materials.

This does not mean, of course, that only males occupy the upper peak and females the lower. Both sexes are clearly found in both peaks. But because of the displacement of the means the overall display is bimodal. The modes approximate to the means for each sex. And the equality in size of each mode implies that the entire sample is made up of approximately equal numbers of each sex.

Taken by itself there is little that is novel here. It is in the subsequent comparison of humans with extant apes and fossils, that new information is recorded.

Pongo: In contrast to humans the canines in *Pongo* are very big. *Pongo* is also opposite to *Homo* in having marked canine sexual dimorphism of means, the basic statistical data showing that there are only small absolute overlaps between the sexes (from 2 to 3 mm, Fig. 2:4).

The distributions for each sex separately (sexes are known for these data) are, as in *Homo*, not significantly different from their fitted normal curves. And the patterns of each distribution resemble markedly those in *Homo* because the dispersions are virtually identical in each sex in both genera (Figs. 2:3 and 2:4). This new measure, sexual dimorphism of dispersion, thus shows no difference at all between the sexes in both *Pongo* and *Homo*. This is a negative finding that looms important as we make comparisons with other genera. To my knowledge, it has not been previously realized.

The numbers of specimens of each sex for *Pongo* have been artificially adjusted in these studies so that the ratio between females and males is 2:1 (a random numbers table was used to reduce the numbers of males to half those of females). This has been done not because we know that this is the actual ratio in field situations, but rather because we know that orang-utans have a social structure whereby there are fewer solitary males occupying larger territories and more females in smaller territories in the local areas occupied by this genus.

The existence of the artificial ratio that we have introduced is revealed in the bimodal histogram for the sample, sexes not identified, because the peaks for the smaller teeth contain twice as many specimens as the peaks for the larger teeth. Again, this does not mean that the lower peak contains only teeth from females nor the upper only teeth from males; there is overlap. But with an unbalanced sex ratio of this degree, a bimodal histogram with such unequal peaks results. And this is exactly what we would expect to find if the samples were representative of a 2:1 abundance of adult females to males in a sample representative of the field situation. (Only adult materials, of course, are examined here).

If, instead of an artificially chosen sample with a 2:1 female to male ratio, we had a random sample from a field situation where 2:1 was indeed the sex ratio, this type of histogram is exactly what we would find. Though not important for the orang-utan *per se* this point is very important for our later examination of fossils where we do not know the sexes in the available samples.

Gorilla: The largest canines and the largest canine sexual dimorphism of means in extant hominoids are evident in *Gorilla*.

The degree of sexual dimorphism in *Gorilla* is so great that the frequency distribution histograms for each sex do not overlap at all for three of the four canine dimensions. Overlap exists only in the case of the length of the lower canine. Yet the hiatus between the sexes (when it exists) is quite small, the largest gap being 0.9mm for the length of the upper canine. It is perhaps of interest that even this great degree of dimorphism, in this most dimorphic of characters, in this most dimorphic of primates, yields only a very small absolute gap between the sexes.

The normal curves that can be fitted to the distributions for each sex are not significantly different from them. What is a big surprise, however, is the fact that the distributions for females, in each case, differ markedly and significantly from those for males, not only in means, which we expect, but also in dispersions. Females show very much smaller dispersions than males (Fig. 2:5). This is true for all

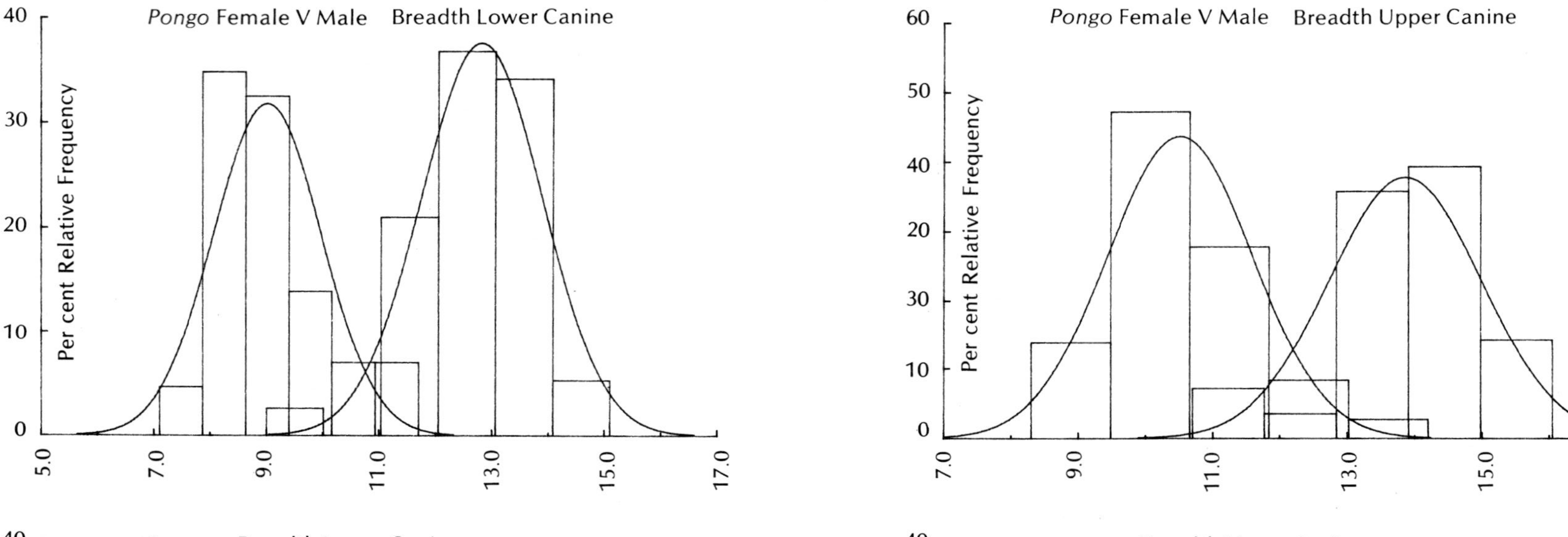

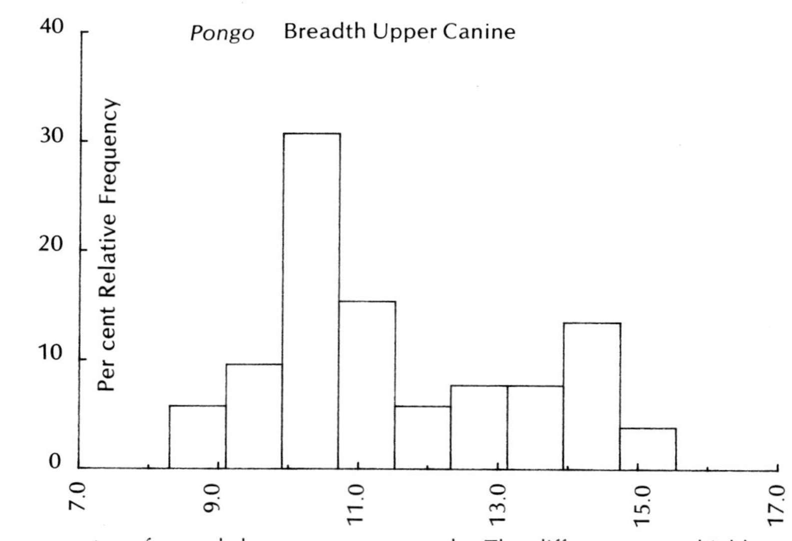

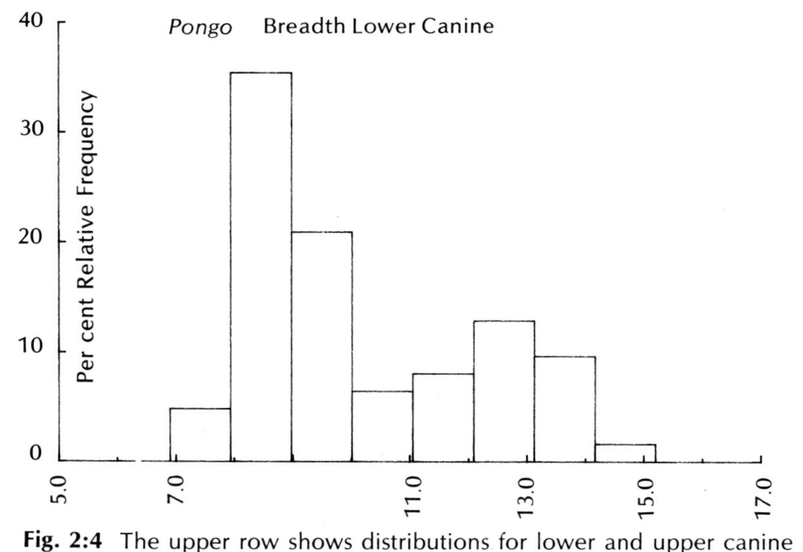

Fig. 2:4 The upper row shows distributions for lower and upper canine breadths in orang-utans for each known sex separately. The differences are highly statistically significant. In contrast to humans, the distances between the means of each sex are rather large with very little overlap. As with humans, the spreads for each sex are the same.

The lower row shows the distributions for the same data for orang-utans when we ignore the information about the sex of each specimen and when we artificially set the sex ratio at two females to each male. The presence of two sexes can be clearly seen from the bimodality of the plot. And the fact that there is a 2:1 sex ratio in the sample can be seen from the unequal sizes of the two peaks in the bimodal plot. Yet, of course, these two peaks each include specimens from each sex. Though this can provide an estimate of the sex ratio, it cannot be a basis for deciding on the sex of any individual specimen.

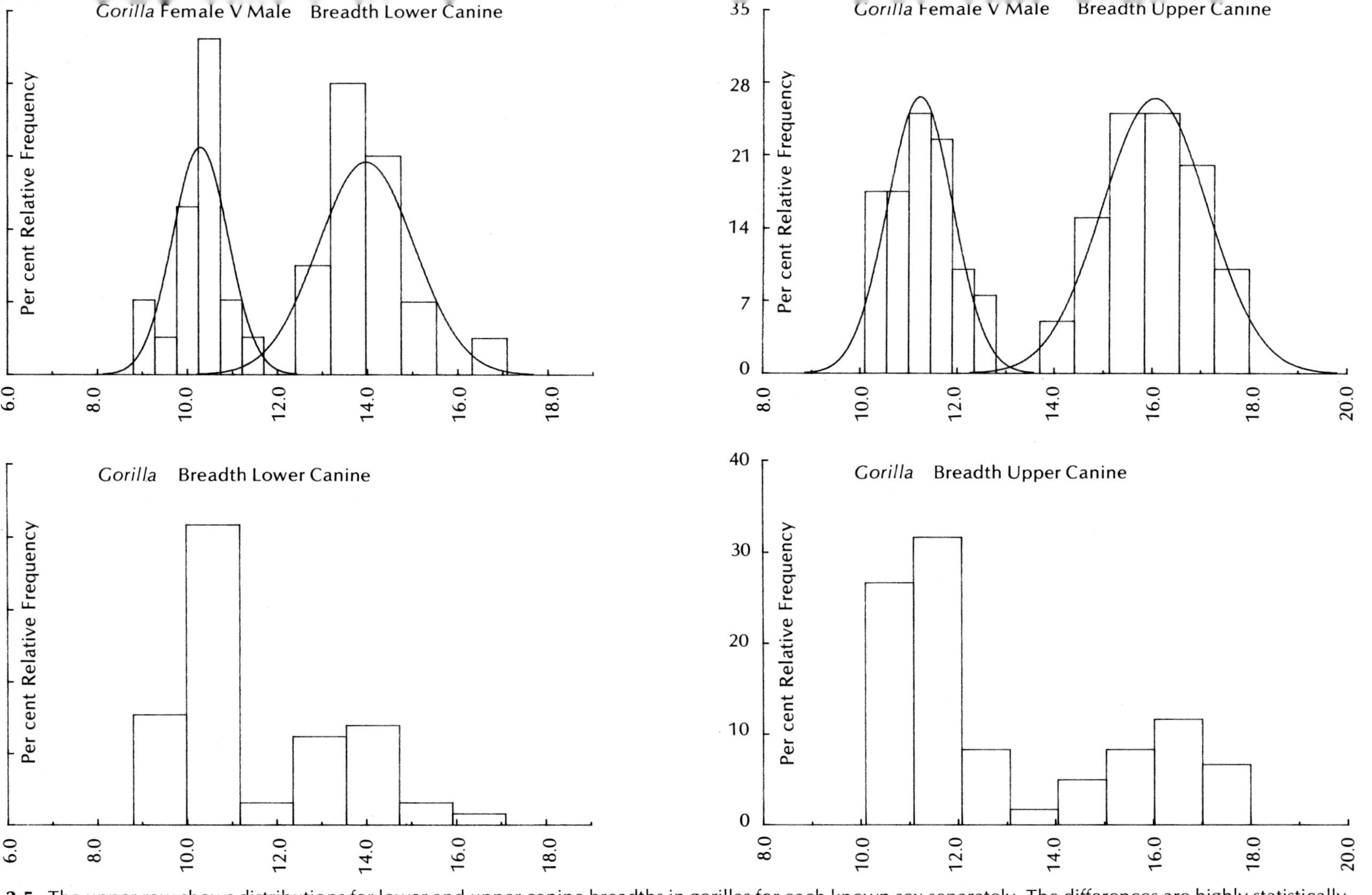

Fig. 2:5 The upper row shows distributions for lower and upper canine breadths in gorillas for each known sex separately. The differences are highly statistically significant. In contrast to the case for humans, the distances between the means of each sex are large and there is no overlap at all. And in contrast to both humans and orang-utans, the spreads for each sex are significantly different (in this case the spreads for males being much greater than those for females).

The lower row shows the distributions for the same data for gorillas when we ignore the information about the sex of each specimen and when we artificially set the sex ratio at two females to each male. The presence of two sexes can be clearly seen from the bimodality of the plot. And the fact that there is a 2:1 sex ratio in the sample can be seen from the unequal sizes of the two peaks in the bimodal plot.

canine measures. It is, perhaps, of even greater interest, that, in this dimorphic species, this sexual dimorphism of dispersion is, perhaps, an even bigger differentiator between the sexes than is the sexual dimorphism of mean size difference itself. This is in complete contrast to the situation in that other highly dimorphic primate *Pongo*, and quite different, of course, to *Homo*.

As with *Pongo*, the numbers of specimens of each sex have been artificially adjusted to a ratio of 2 females to 1 male. This, again, is not to suggest that we think that 2:1 is the actual ratio that exists between the adult sexes. Rather is it to take some account of the known social structure of gorilla groups which do have usually one breeding male and two or three breeding females in each 'family' group. (The reason for this ratio amongst adults is not the same as the orang-utan. Both sexes of *Gorilla* share the same living territory. It is merely the case that various social and competitive factors result in the eventual adult female to male ratio in the family group being something like 2:1 or 3:1).

But the artifical selection that we have carried out results, when we examine the total data sexes undefined, in bimodal histograms that have unequal peaks as in *Pongo* (Fig. 2:5). In this case the unequal dispersions for each sex are also clear in the histogram where the sexes are undefined because they are so completely separated. The exercise has again its value when we come to study distributions in samples of fossils where we do not know the sexes.

Pan: In *Pan* the canines are also large in contrast to humans, but canine sexual dimorphism of means as measured by the difference in mean size in each sex is quantitatively considerably less than in *Gorilla*.

Normal curves fit the distributions for each individual sex (sex known from other data) well. But the histograms for each sex overlap very considerably, indicating that the sexual dimorphism of means is less than in *Gorilla* or *Pongo* just considered.

But the forms of the distributions for each sex are such that the dispersions of males are seen to be enormously larger than those of females. Thus, the lesser sexual dimorphism of means in *Pan* is combined with sexual dimorphisms of dispersions that are greater even than in *Gorilla* (compare Fig. 2:5 and 2:6). In this particular sense, *Pan*, not *Gorilla*, is the most highly dimorphic of the great apes. This finding flies completely in the face of conventional views about sexual dimorphism in these two species. But it does exist, and is immediate evidence of new complexity in this phenomenon.

Again, we can study histograms for sexes undefined using artificially adjusted samples with a ratio of females to males of 2:1, mimicking, to some degree, the approximate adult sex ratio in adult social groups in the field. Again, this is not to suggest that we 'know' that this is the ratio in the field, nor to imply that the unbalanced sex ratio in the field is due to similar situations as in either *Gorilla* or *Pongo*. In fact, we know that this is not the case. Chimpanzee family groups do not have the territorial arrangements of orang-utans, and they are considerably larger than gorilla groups. Each chimpanzee family group includes several adult males and females. Nevertheless, within this third type of social structure in the great apes, a ratio of more females and fewer males obtains.

As a result of this procedure we might expect to see bimodal distributions with unequal peaks as in *Gorilla* and *Pongo*. But, though there is a clear hint of bimodality in these distributions (Fig. 2:6), the combination of the smaller absolute differences in means between the sexes together with major differences in dispersions between the sexes mutes the bimodality somewhat. Thus, the upper peak contains fewer male specimens than it otherwise would because more of the widely dispersed male specimens fall with the females. This peak thus approximates to the extended tail of a heavily skewed distribution. The main peak clearly represents all the female specimens together with some of the male specimens. The smaller peak when present (or the extended upper tail when the distribution is extra-heavily skewed) represents the rest of the male specimens. That the sex ratio is not one-to-one can nevertheless be clearly discerned even in this more complicated situation.

Summary of canine dimensions: In summary, *Homo* and *Pan* are similar in having smaller differences between the mean dimensions for the canines for each sex, *Gorilla* and *Pongo* in having greater. But *Homo* and *Pongo* are similar in having small differences in dispersion in each sex, *Gorilla* and *Pan* in having much greater. Thus canine size and canine dispersion taken together present qualitatively different patterns of sexual difference in each of the four species. Only *Homo* has small sexual dimorphism in all parameters; each ape, (even the allegedly lesser dimorphic *Pan*) has, in its own special way, very large sexual dimorphism. In addition, should any natural population display a major difference in numbers of males and females, then this would be observable, even although we

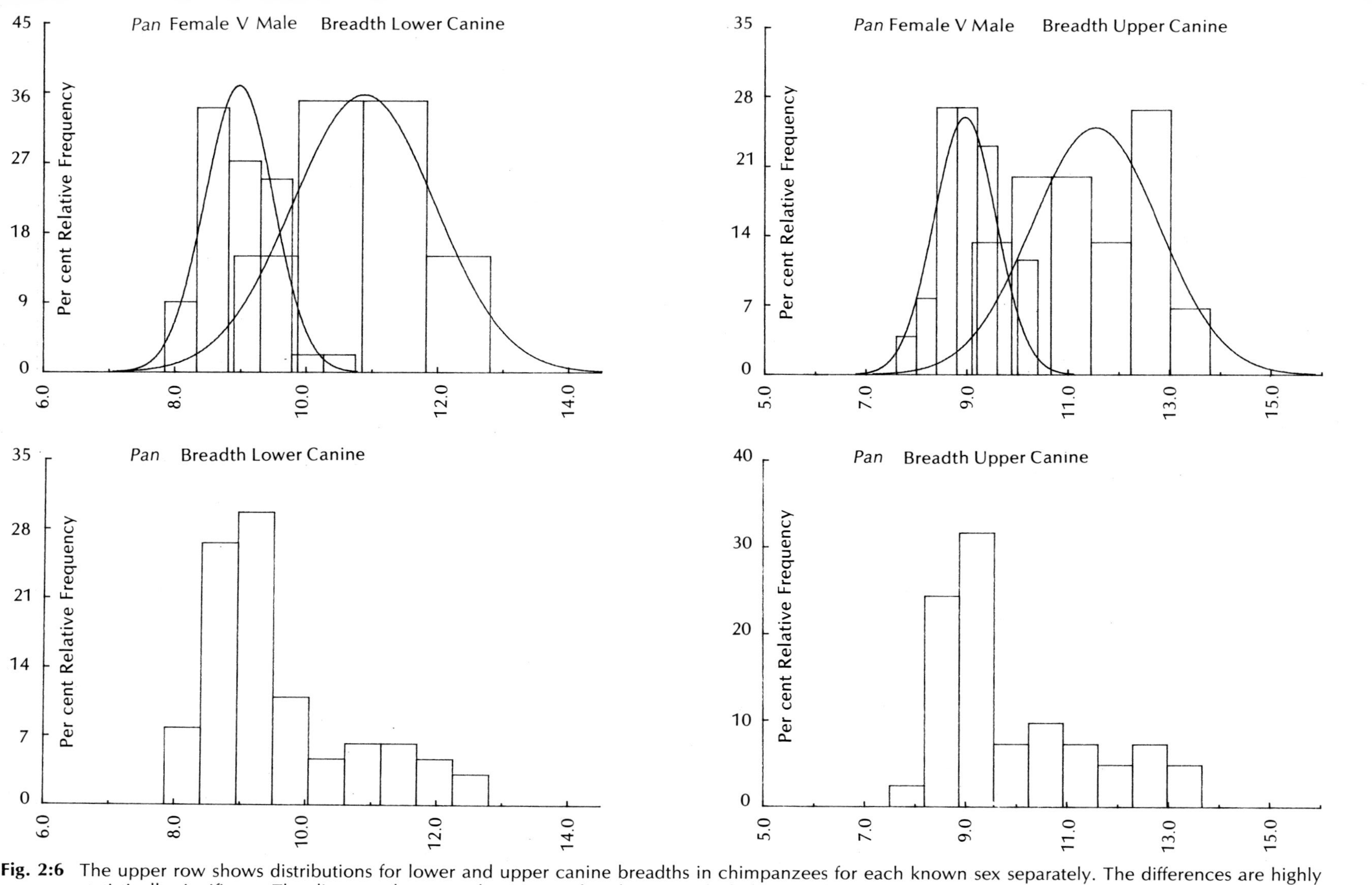

Fig. 2:6 The upper row shows distributions for lower and upper canine breadths in chimpanzees for each known sex separately. The differences are highly statistically significant. The distances between the means of each sex are fairly large and the overlaps quite small. In contrast to both humans and orang-utans, but as in gorillas, the spreads for each sex are significantly different.

Again, in this case, the spreads for males are much greater than those for females but, rather remarkably, this difference is actually larger in chimpanzees than even in gorillas. In this aspect of sexual dimorphism, chimpanzees show the greatest dimorphism among the large hominoids, not gorillas.

The lower row shows the distributions for the same data for chimpanzees when we ignore the information about the sex of each specimen and when we artificially set the sex ratio at two females to each male. The presence of two sexes can be seen, though less clearly than in gorillas from the bimodality of the plot. And the fact that there is a 2:1 sex ratio in the sample can be seen from the unequal sizes of the two peaks in the bimodal plot. Yet, of course, these two peaks each include many specimens from each sex.

did not know which specimens were female and which male.

Sexual dimorphisms in incisors and premolars

Homo: In *Homo* the great majority of the measures of the incisor and premolar teeth show, when sexes are known, distributions for each sex that are normal and markedly similar. They also show frequency distributions, sexes undefined, that are totally unimodal.

The normal curves for each sex are, as for the canines, not significantly different in dispersion (and in this regard reflect the majority of the distributions in *Pongo*). Again, therefore we have a genus in which there is virtually no sexual dimorphism between means, and no detectable sexual dimorphism at all between dispersions.

But in a few measures, and among the anterior teeth this includes the length of the lower first incisor, the breadth of the upper first incisor and the breadth of the upper fourth premolar, examinations of the samples, sexes undefined, show bimodal distributions. In these cases there are significant separations between the means for each sex even though there is a good deal of overlap between them (e.g. Fig. 2:7).

The bimodal distributions show equally large

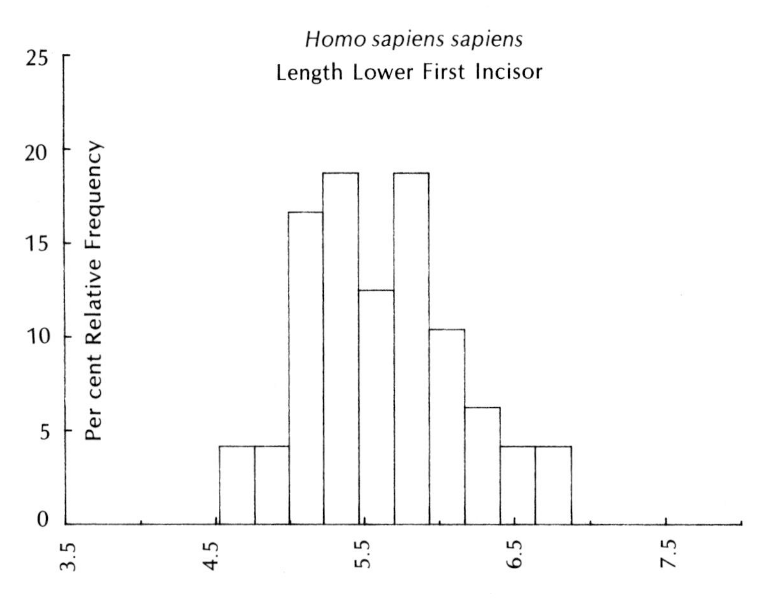

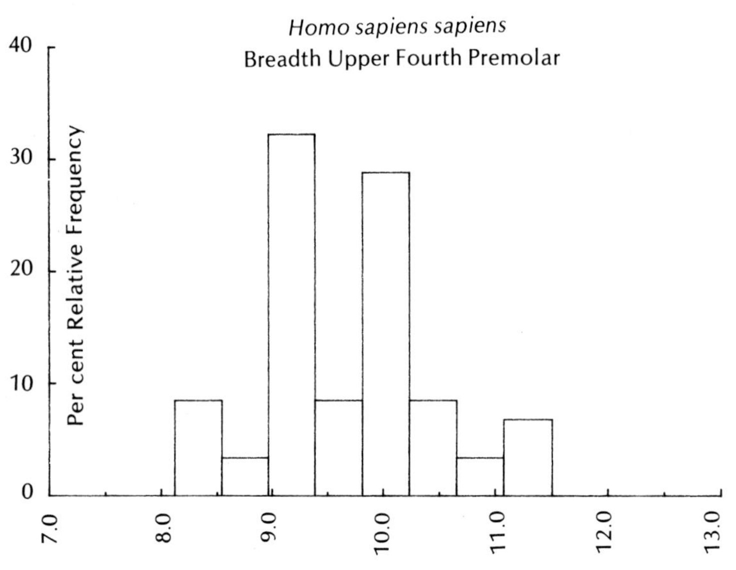

Fig. 2:7 Examination of dental dimensions of incisors and premolars in humans when the sexes are not defined. In each case, though obviously less clearly than in the canines, the facts of bimodal distributions and the equal sizes of their two peaks are evident. These distributions result from small sexual dimorphism between means with heavy overlap, zero sexual dimorphism between variances, and a one-to-one sex ratio in the samples.

peaks and thus in these data, sexes undefined, we are justified in assuming that approximately equal numbers of dimensions come from teeth of each sex.

Pongo: There is a completely different pattern in the anterior dentition of *Pongo*.

Examination of the distributions for each sex separately shows that *Pongo* differs markedly from *Homo* in having large sexual dimorphism of means. It resembles *Homo*, however, in having no sexual dimorphism of dispersion to speak of. *Pongo*, thus, shows less dimorphism in dispersion than does even the so-called lesser dimorphic genus *Pan* (see later).

Almost all measures of both incisors and premolars show bimodal distributions indicating further that large sexual dimorphisms of means (Fig. 2:8) exist. The bimodal distributions also show that peaks for smaller measures contain more specimens whilst peaks for larger measures show fewer specimens. This is indicative of the artificial 2:1 sex ratio that was entered into the analyses.

Gorilla: As for *Pongo*, *Gorilla* also shows distributions that indicate large sexual dimorphisms for many dimensions (Fig. 2:9). Some of these sexual dimorphisms are to do with difference in mean values for each sex and, of course, these differences are always what would be expected: larger means in males, smaller in females.

Others are, however, to do with dispersions. They are not random in their pattern. In incisors, the normal curves that closely fit the histograms for incisor dimensions in females are broad and encompass, at their upper end, the entire curves for males. This is the opposite of what we found for canines. The equivalent normal curves fitting the histograms for premolar dimensions in females are small and are encompassed by the lower ends of the far broader curves for males. This is the same as for canines.

As was the case for *Pongo* those dimensions that show bimodal distributions also show that the peaks for smaller measures contain more specimens, and the peaks for larger measures fewer. This is indicative of the artificial 2:1 sex ratio that was entered into the analyses.

Pan: The pattern evident in the anterior teeth in *Pan* differs even from that in *Gorilla*.

Thus, there is sexual dimorphism of means such that males show somewhat greater values than females, than is the case in humans. This dimorphism is, nevertheless, considerably less than in *Gorilla*.

In contrast, however, the relationships between the dispersions for each sex are quite different from those in *Gorilla*. Like the canines, and in marked contrast to the incisors in *Gorilla*, most incisor measures in *Pan* (Fig. 2:10) show a pattern in which the lower end of the broad curve for males encompasses, or almost so, the much narrower curve for females. Also like the canines, but in this case in marked similarity with the premolars in *Gorilla*, this pattern of dispersion difference is repeated in the premolar measures in *Pan*.

Though the distributions for the whole genus, sexes undefined, show some evidence of bimodality in the upper first incisor, in the great majority of the anterior dental measures, the relationships between the two sexes are such that their separate normal distributions coalesce into heavily skewed distributions. This is due to the combination of a smaller difference between the means for each sex together with a large difference in dispersion between each sex than in *Gorilla*. It resembles what was seen in one of the canine dimensions. It is apparent, then, that these skewed distributions, though unimodal, are indicative of the 2:1 sex ratios that were entered into the analysis.

As was the case for *Pongo* and *Gorilla* those dimensions, where the differences between the sexes are large enough that bimodal distributions exist, show peaks for smaller measures that contain more specimens and peaks for larger measures containing fewer. This is also indicative of the artificial 2:1 sex ratio that was entered into the analyses.

Sexual dimorphisms in molars

Homo: In *Homo* the great majority of the measures (there are no data for third molars) show normal distributions that overlap almost completely when sexes are defined and examined separately, and unimodal normal frequency distributions when the sexes are undefined. There are no significant differences in dispersion anywhere along the tooth row.

But in the single case of the length and breadth of the lower second molar (e.g. Fig. 2:11) the normal curves for each sex have significantly different means. And for this tooth when sex is undefined, there are bimodal distributions that are significantly different from the fitted normal curves. These bimodal distributions have approximately equal peaks and are thus indicative of the 1:1 sex ratio that should exist in any randomly selected sample of human materials.

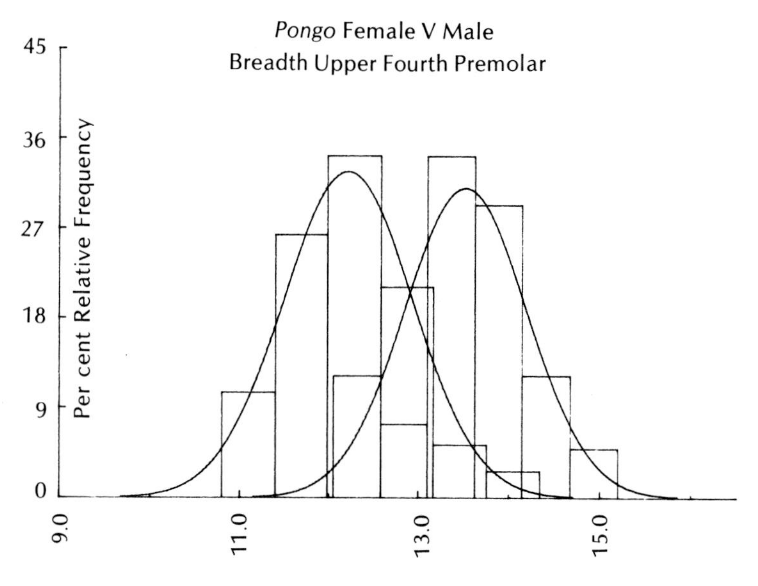

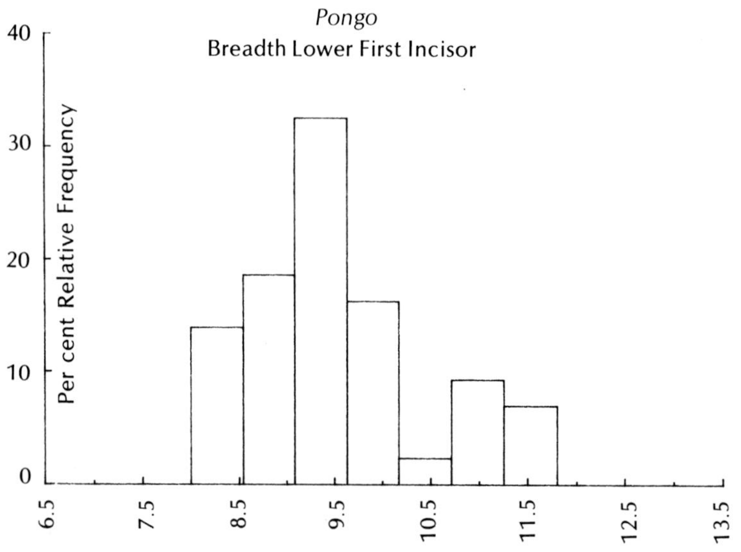

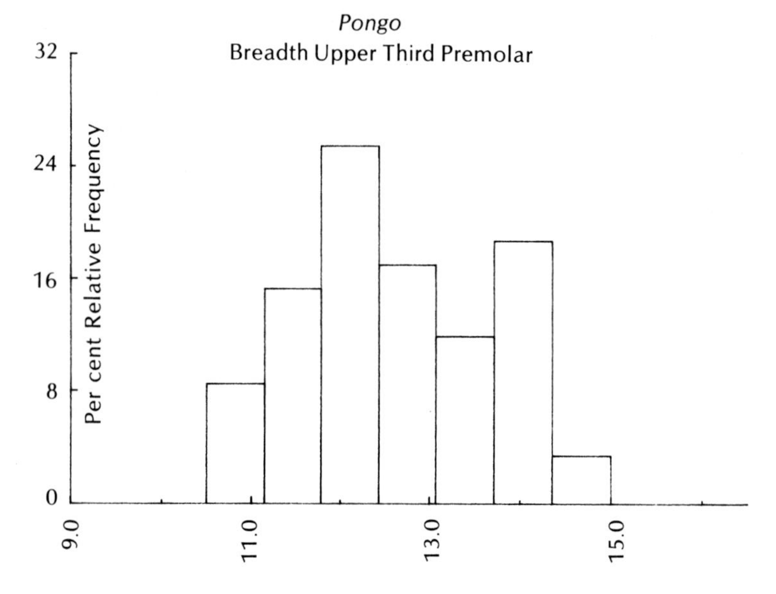

Fig. 2:8 Examination of dental dimensions of incisors and premolars in orang-utans. The upper frame shows an example where the sexes are defined. In contrast with humans, considerably greater sexual dimorphism of mean difference with much less overlap between the sexes is evident. But in similarity with humans there is zero sexual dimorphism of variance.

The middle and lower frames show two examples of distributions in the orang-utan when sex is undefined and the sex ratio is artificially set at 2:1. In each case, though obviously less clearly than in the canines, and in contrast to humans, the facts of bimodal distributions and the unequal sizes of their two peaks are evident. These distributions result from large sexual dimorphism of means with less overlap, zero sexual dimorphism between variances, and two-to-one sex ratios in the samples.

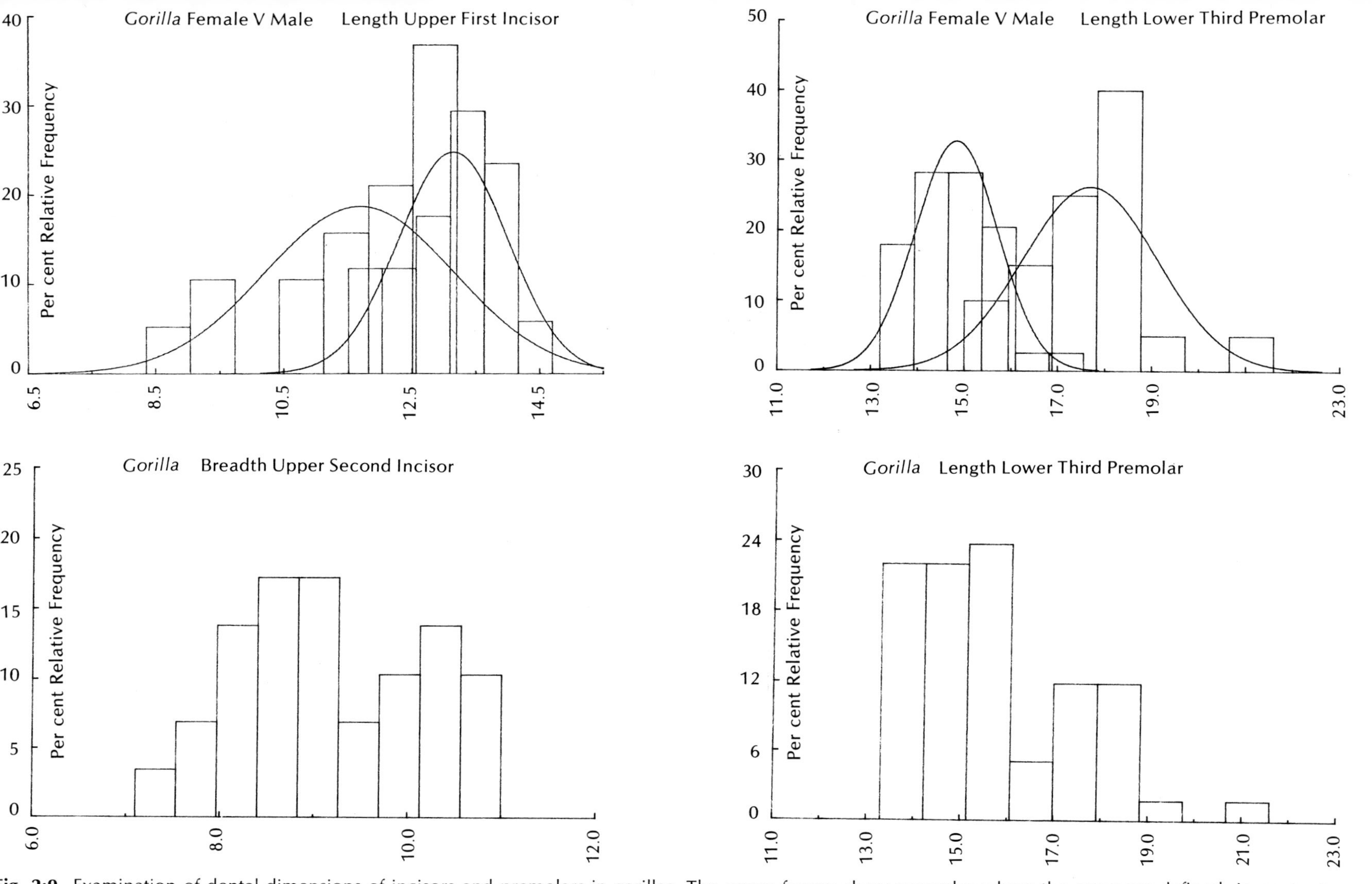

Fig. 2:9 Examination of dental dimensions of incisors and premolars in gorillas. The upper frames show examples where the sexes are defined. In contrast with humans, considerably greater sexual dimorphism of mean difference with much less overlap between the sexes is evident. In contrast with both humans and orang-utans there is marked sexual dimorphism of variance that can be exhibited either as larger variance in males (lower third premolar) or, most surprisingly, as larger variance in females (upper first incisor).

The lower two frames show two examples of distributions in the gorilla when sex is undefined and the sex ratio is artificially set at 2:1. In each case, though obviously less clearly than in the canines, and in contrast to humans, the facts of bimodal distributions and the unequal sizes of their two peaks are evident. These distributions result from large sexual dimorphism between means with less overlap, large sexual dimorphism between variances, and two-to-one sex ratios in the samples.

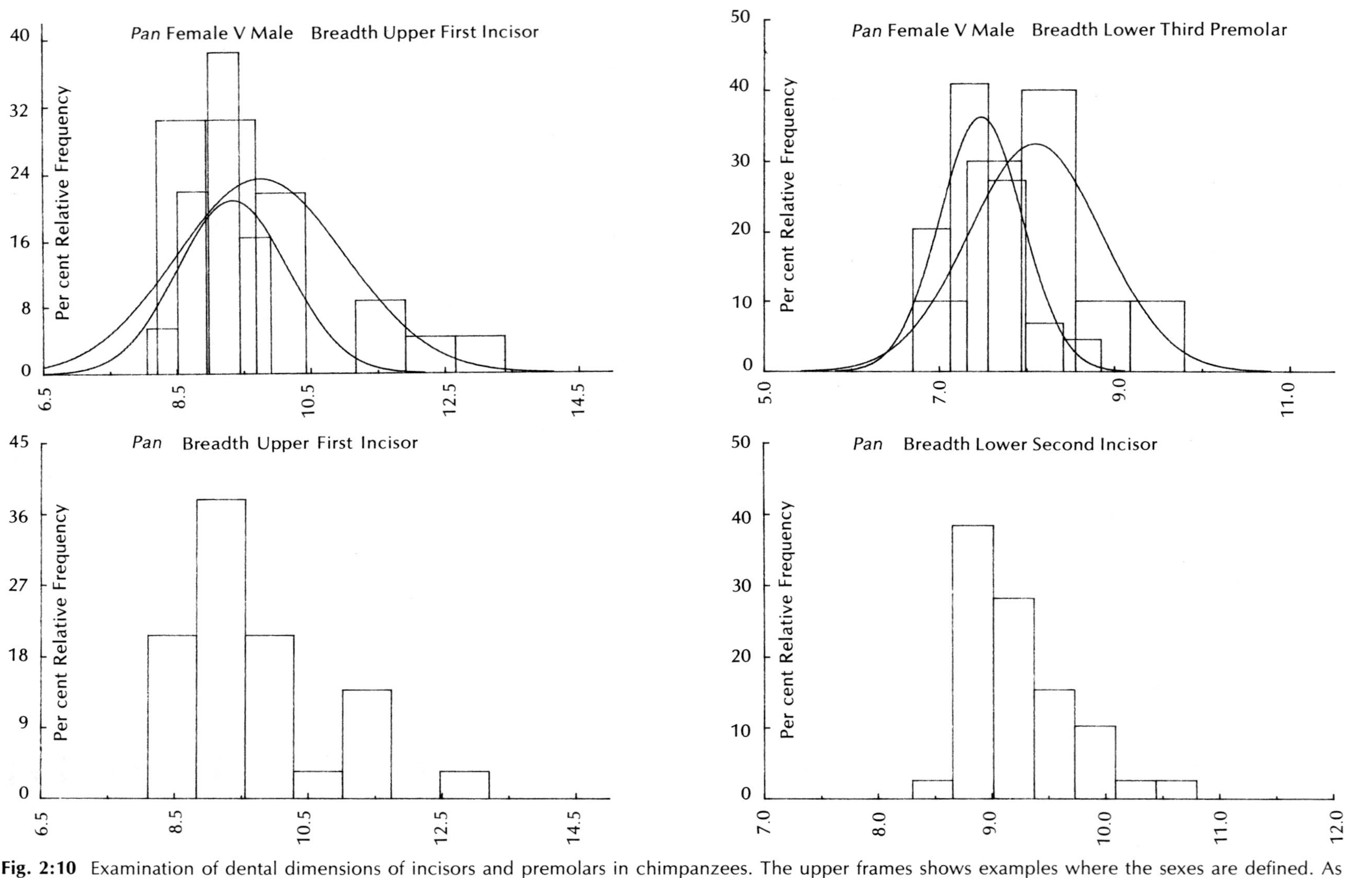

Fig. 2:10 Examination of dental dimensions of incisors and premolars in chimpanzees. The upper frames shows examples where the sexes are defined. As in gorillas, though to lesser degrees there is considerable sexual dimorphism of mean difference. The amount of overlap is considerably greater than in gorillas. Again, as with canines, there is marked sexual dimorphism of variance but in these teeth, in contrast with gorillas, it seems to be always the males that have the larger variances.

The lower two frames show two examples of distributions in chimpanzees when sex is undefined and the sex ratio is artificially set at 2:1. In these cases bimodal distributions are not easy to see. Though there is some tendency towards bimodality, the closer relationship between the means for each sex together with the even more marked difference between the variances and the 2:1 sex ratio results in the combined distributions tending towards unimodal form with heavy skewing. Even unimodal distributions may not, therefore, rule out significant sexual dimorphisms in a given species. And heavy skewing may point towards both unbalanced sex ratios and large differences in variances for each sex.

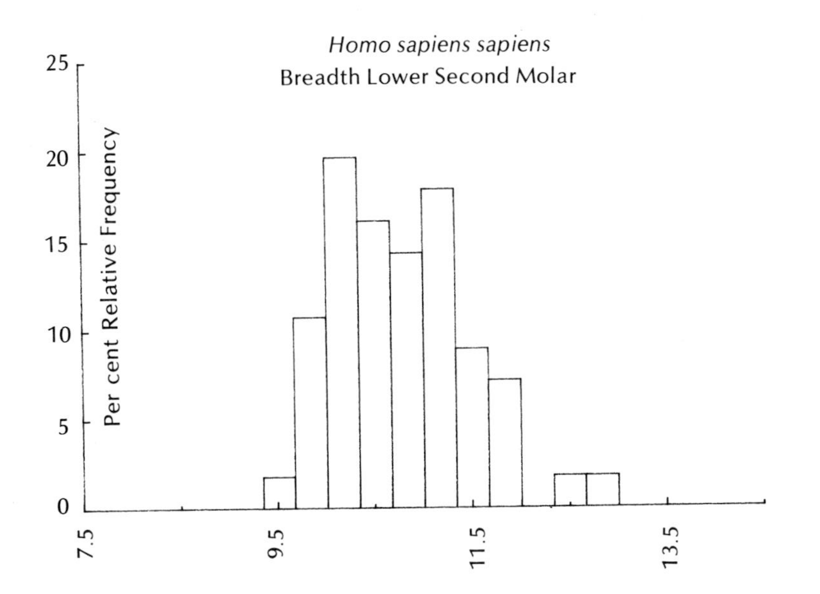

Fig. 2:11 Examination of a dental dimension in a molar tooth in humans when the sexes are not defined. The picture is similar to each of those other teeth of humans that show bimodality and significant differences between the sexes. Though obviously less clearly than in the canines, the fact of a bimodal distribution and the equal size of the two peaks is evident. This distribution results from small sexual dimorphism between means with heavy overlap, zero sexual dimorphism between variances, and a one-to-one sex ratio in the sample.

Pongo: Most measures of molars possess significantly different means for each sex. But they show essentially no sexual differences in dispersion. This reflects what exists in the canines and the anterior teeth in *Pongo*.

However, examinations of the samples sexes undefined show bimodal distributions that reflect the fairly large differences that exist between each sex (Fig. 2:12). This is similar to the picture shown by the canines and other anterior teeth in *Pongo*.

These bimodal distributions have peaks for smaller measures that contain more specimens and peaks for larger measures containing fewer. This is indicative of the artificial 2:1 sex ratio that was entered into the analyses.

Gorilla: The overall pattern that characterizes the molars is the reverse arrangement of that seen in the incisors and similar to that in canines and premolars. Broad normal curves for males encompass at their lower ends the entire very narrow curves for females. There is clearly therefore, both marked dimorphisms of means and marked dimorphisms of dispersions.

As for the anterior teeth, although the differences in both means and dispersions for males and females are not as great as in canines (Fig. 2:13) bimodal distributions nevertheless exist when the teeth are examined, sexes undefined.

As was the case for *Pongo*, those dimensions that show bimodal distributions particularly show peaks for smaller measures that contain more specimens and peaks for larger measures containing fewer. This is indicative of the artificial 2:1 sex ratio that was entered into the analyses.

Pan: The pattern of non-canine sexual dimorphism in the molar teeth in *Pan* differs from that in any other genus (Fig. 2:14). Both means and dispersions for females and males separately are essentially similar with complete overlap.

Distributions, sexes undefined, are totally normal.

Sexual dimorphism in *Pan* is, thus, virtually absent in the posterior teeth. In this dental region *Pan* has not only less sexual dimorphism than *Gorilla* and *Pongo*, but also less dimorphism than the genus conventionally described as least dimorphic of all, *Homo*.

And in contradistinction to the cases of *Pongo* and *Gorilla* the artificial 2:1 sex ratio that was entered into the analysis is not revealed as unequal bimodal distributions. This is, of course, because there are no differences in sexual dimorphisms of means or dispersions in these particular teeth in this genus.

Summary for individual dimensions of non-canine teeth

The situation in the non-canine teeth is, thus, considerably more complicated than is the case for the canines.

Sexual differences between mean values for non-canine dimensions seem to be related both to the overall size differential between the sexes and to

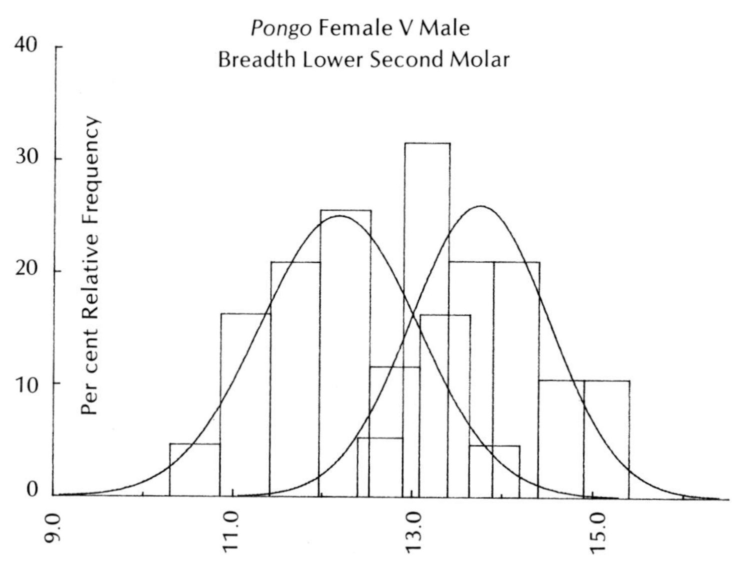

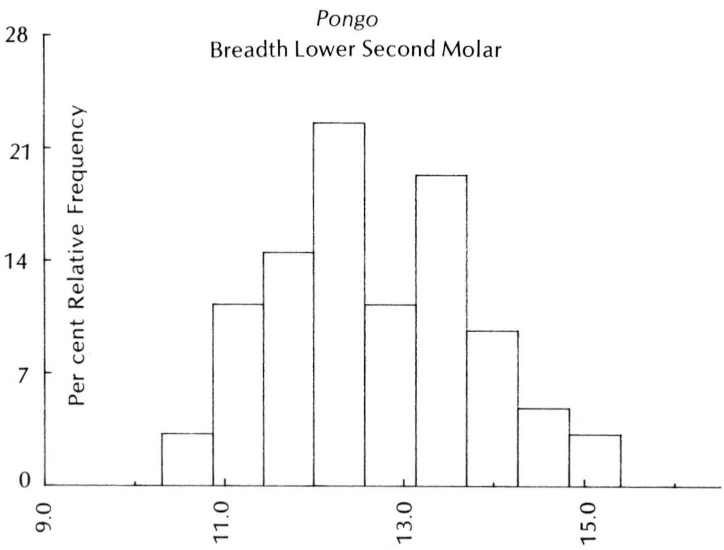

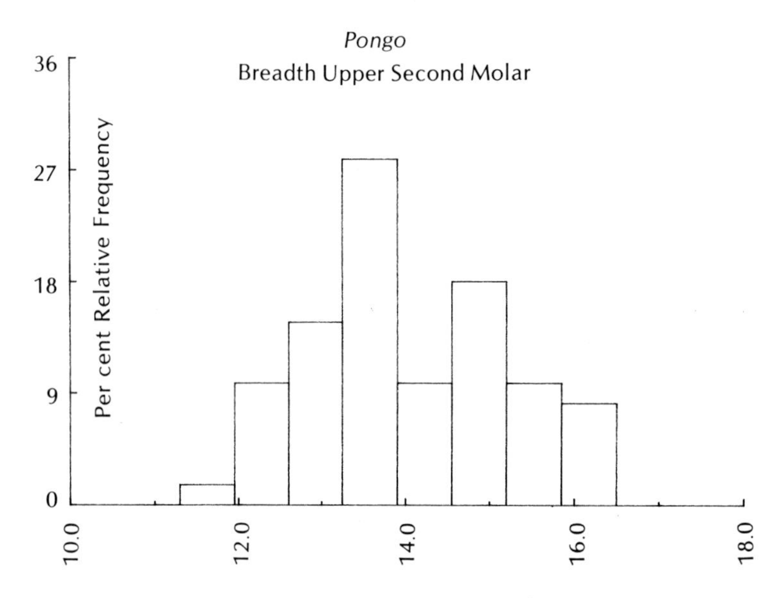

Fig. 2:12 Examination of dental dimensions of molars in orang-utans. The upper frame shows an example where the sexes are defined. In contrast with humans, considerably greater sexual dimorphism of mean difference with much less overlap between the sexes is evident. But in similarity with humans there is zero sexual dimorphism of variance.

The middle and lower frames show two examples of distributions in the orang-utan when sex is undefined and the sex ratio is artificially set at 2:1. In each case, though obviously less clearly than in the canines, and in contrast to humans, the facts of bimodal distributions and the unequal sizes of their two peaks are evident. These distributions result from large sexual dimorphism between means with less overlap, zero sexual dimorphism between variances, and two-to-one sex ratios in the samples.

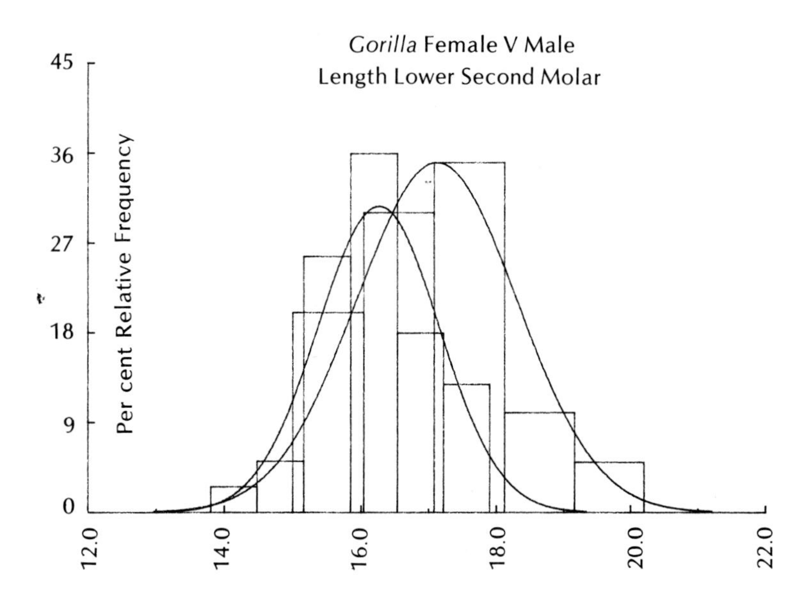

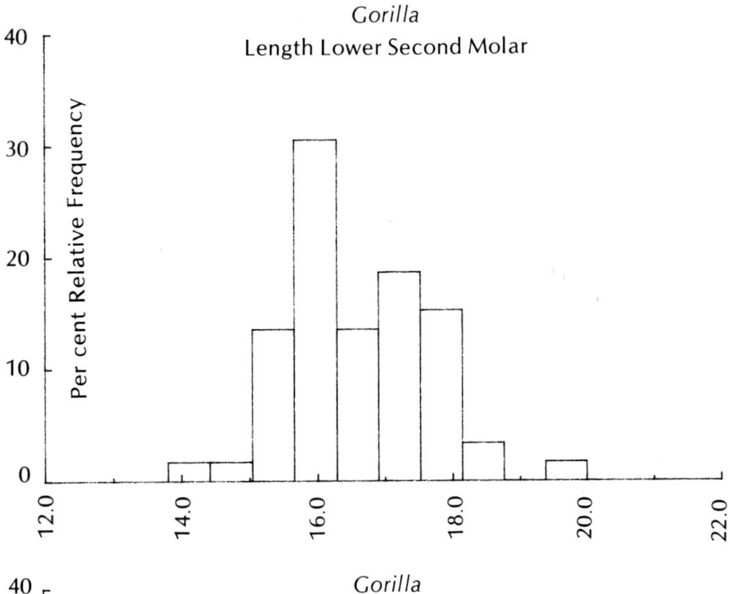

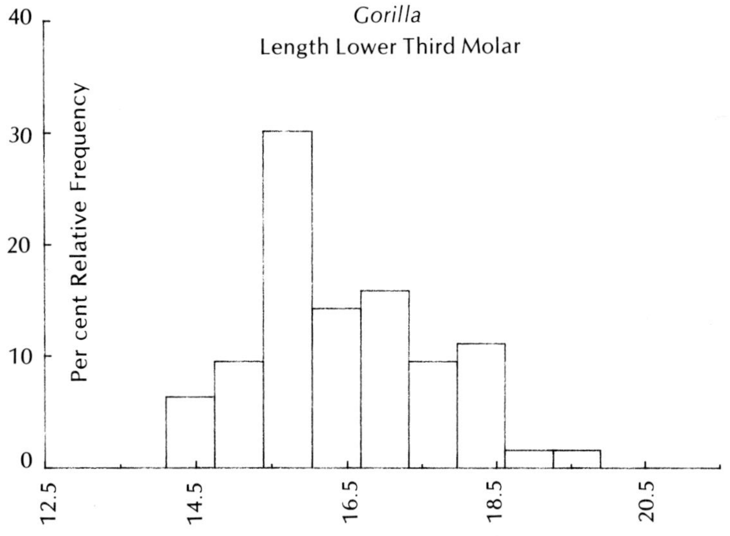

Fig. 2:13 Examination of dental dimensions of molars in gorillas. The upper frame shows an example where the sexes are defined. In this tooth, and this is replicated in other molars, there is considerably less sexual dimorphism of mean difference with much more overlap between the sexes than in canines. In contrast with both humans and orang-utans there is marked sexual dimorphism of variance exhibited as a larger variance in males.

The lower two frames show examples of distributions in the gorilla when sex is undefined and the sex ratio is artificially set at 2:1. There is a tendency to an unequal bimodality, but also to heavy skewing in contrast to the case in humans and orang-utans. Such distributions result from the combination of only intermediately large (in comparison with that in canines) sexual dimorphism between means with considerable overlap, rather large sexual dimorphism between variances, and two-to-one sex ratios in the samples. Again, therefore, even unimodal distributions may not rule out significant sexual dimorphisms in a given species. And heavy skewing may point towards both unbalanced sex ratios and large differences in variances for each sex.

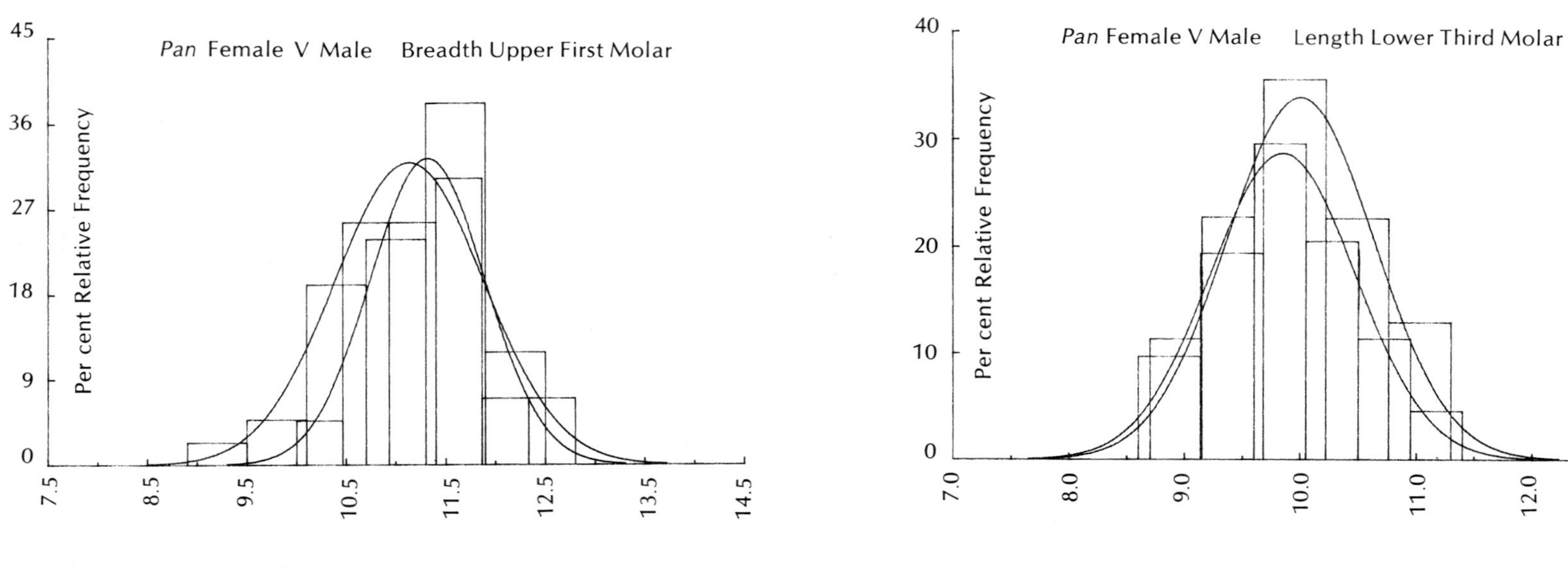

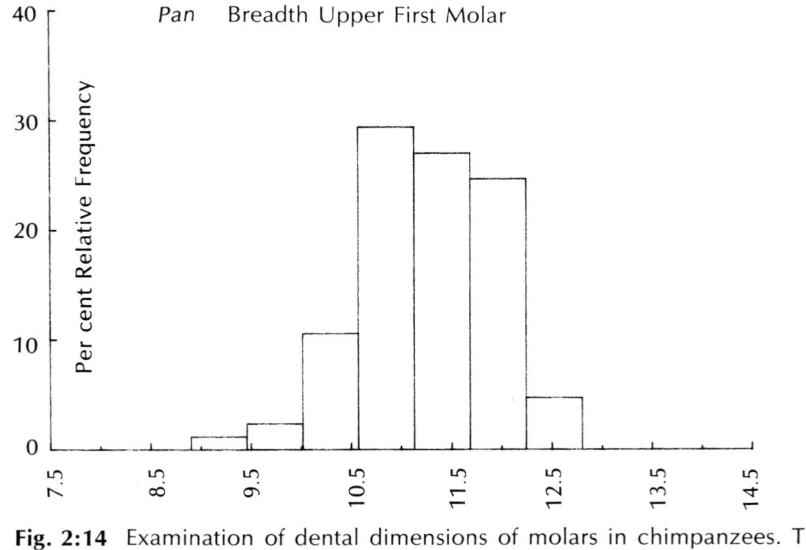

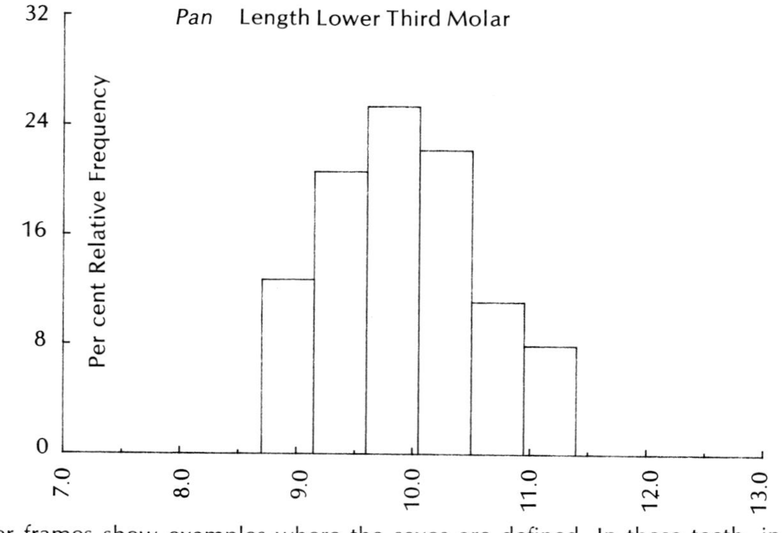

Fig. 2:14 Examination of dental dimensions of molars in chimpanzees. The upper frames show examples where the sexes are defined. In these teeth, in contrast with the case in all other large hominoids, and this is replicated in every other molar, there is no determinable sexual dimorphism of mean difference or variance differences.

The lower two frames show the natural concomitants of the upper: that in the molar teeth in the chimpanzee, when sex is undefined all distributions are unimodal and non-skewed. Though not shown here they fit a normal distribution very well. There is no evidence, from these sex undefined distributions, of the sex ratio that was used in their determination.

specifically canine sexual dimorphism of mean dimensions. Sexual dimorphisms in dispersions for non-canine dimensions seem to be related to sexual dimorphisms in dispersions of canine dimensions.

Thus the two genera, *Gorilla* and *Pongo*, that have large overall sexual dimorphisms of bodily size between the sexes, show large sexual dimorphisms of mean dimensions of the teeth at almost every dental locus. The other two genera, *Pan* and *Homo* that have only small overall sexual dimorphism of bodily size, have, likewise, only small sexual dimorphisms of mean dental dimensions.

The two genera, *Gorilla* and *Pan*, that have large sexual dimorphisms of dispersions of dimensions of the canines for each sex, show (irrespective of the size of the sexual dimorphism of means for the canines, big in *Gorilla* and small in *Pan*) major and highly significant sexual dimorphisms in dispersions of dimensions of teeth neighbouring on the canines.

In contrast, the two genera that have no significant sexual dimorphism in dispersion in canine dimensions, also show no significant sexual dimorphisms in dispersions for all (*Homo*) or most (*Pongo*) of the other dental dimensions.

In final summary, then, values of means and dispersions present two qualitatively different kinds of sexual dimorphisms for each individual dental measure in each of the four genera (Table 2:2 and 2:3). This is a degree of complexity of sexual dimorphism of which we have not previously been fully aware.

Table 2:2

Regional Differences in Sexual Dimorphism of Means: Extant Species

	I1	I2	C	P3	P4	M1	M2	M3
Homo								
Lower Jaw	*		*				*	
Upper Jaw				*	*			
Pan								
Lower Jaw	*	*	*	*	*			
Upper Jaw	*	*	*					*
Gorilla								
Lower Jaw	*	*	*	*	*	*	*	*
Upper Jaw	*	*	*	*	*	*	*	*
Pongo								
Lower Jaw	*	*	*	*	*	*	*	
Upper Jaw	*	*	*	*				

Table 2:3

Regional Differences in Sexual Dimorphism of Spreads: Extant Species

	I1	I2	C	P3	P4	M1	M2	M3
Homo								
Lower Jaw	=		=				=	
Upper Jaw				=	=			
Pan								
Lower Jaw	≠	≠	≠	≠	≠	=	=	=
Upper Jaw	≠	≠	≠	=	=	=	=	=
Gorilla								
Lower Jaw	≠	≠	≠	≠	≠	≠	≠	≠
Upper Jaw	≠	≠	≠	≠	≠	≠	≠	=
Pongo								
Lower Jaw	=	=	=	=	≠	=	=	
Upper Jaw	=	=	=	=	=	=	=	=

We also recognize that sex ratio can be documented in samples where the sexes are undefined as long as there are reasonable differences between the sexes. This is the case even when we act as though we did not know which specimens were from males and which from females.

As we shall see in the next section, however, these more complex dimorphisms are still not the entire story. The sexually dimorphic differences in individual dental measures also show different overall arrangements from genus to genus.

Sexual dimorphisms in dental patterns as revealed in univariate studies

Sexual dimorphisms within the dental arcade are even more complex than is revealed by looking at individual measures of individual teeth. For the arrangements of the sexually dimorphic features for each measure at each tooth obviously form patterns along the tooth row and between the jaws.

In *Homo* there are very few dental loci that show sexually dimorphic features of whatever kind. As a result, for this genus, we can summarize overall patterns by suggesting that such differences are merely sporadically located along the dental arcade and between each jaw. This finding may be because such differences genuinely do not exist in this species. It is also possible that they do exist but that the number of dental positions at which the small sexual dimorphism of humans is evident is too small to allow us to recognize anything other than eclectic situations.

In the apes, however, the arrangements at different tooth positions are more complex. First, they involve the question of the existence or otherwise of patterns along the tooth row.

In *Pongo* and *Gorilla* the great majority of tooth dimensions along the tooth row show sexual dimorphisms of one kind or the other. But in *Pongo* these are confined, of course, to sexual dimorphisms of means, and they are not evident in the mandibular posterior dentition (the last premolar and the molars). In *Gorilla*, in contrast, it is the anteriormost dentition (incisors) that shows the fewest sexually dimorphic features, and this in both jaws. In *Pan* there is a yet another pattern in that there are few significant sexually dimorphic features in premolars and none at all in molars in either jaw.

Second is the question of the existence or otherwise, of different sexually dimorphic patterns for each jaw.

In the great apes which have many sexually dimorphic differences along the dental arcade in each jaw, differences in their arrangement can be assessed in two ways. The first is the number of significantly different measures along the maxillary arcade as compared with that along the mandibular. The second is the size of the differences as judged by the actual values of the means for each sex along the dental arcade in each jaw.

In *Pongo* there are a smaller number of significant differences in the lower jaw than the upper because of their relative absence in lower molars but not in uppers. But there are greater differences between the sexes in the lower jaw than in the upper in the sizes of the differences between the mean values for each sex.

In *Gorilla* the number of significant differences in each jaw is approximately similar, those loci at which the numbers are least being in the anterior dentition of both jaws, the incisor teeth. In this sense *Gorilla* is quite different from *Pongo*. In terms of the sizes of differences between means for each sex, however, *Gorilla* resembles *Pongo* in that these are considerably greater in the lower jaw as compared with the upper.

Pan, again, differs from each of the other great apes. The numbers of significant differences are slightly greater in the mandible than the maxilla. They are, however, totally confined to the incisors, canines and first premolars. The sizes of the differences at each tooth locus again coincide with the situation in the other three apes in that they are greater for the mandible than for the maxilla.

We can thus conclude this summary of the univariate studies by pointing to two further characterizations of sexual dimorphisms in these large hominoids. One is to do with the pattern of location of sexually dimorphic differences along the tooth row. The second is related to differences in the patterns of sexual dimorphisms between the two jaws. Both show differences in each of the species that we have studied.

Measures of teeth of apes and humans: examination in combination

We can now attempt to expand these univariate studies by using an appropriate multivariate statistical method. Several questions are addressed.

What is the overall nature of sexual dimorphism in the dentition of extant higher primates?

What patterns are apparent, from multivariate analyses, which take account of correlations among measures that might not have appeared in univariate studies, in which correlations are ignored?

Are these patterns the same in all genera?

There are two multivariate analyses for these data because measurements are not available from the same suite of specimens for both upper and lower jaws. Thus, for these extant primates mandibular and maxillary data are analyzed separately using canonical variates analyses. Canonical variates analysis is the method of choice because it is our desire to know the relationships between groups that are already known to be different one from another. In both cases we have seven groups: *Gorilla* females, *Gorilla* males, *Pan* females, *Pan* males, *Pongo* females, *Pongo* males, and *Homo*, sex unknown. In each case, therefore, six canonical axes are generated.

Canonical variates analysis: Let us first examine information from the studies of the upper teeth. There are fourteen variables used, the lengths and breadths, each, of the incisors, canines, premolars and the first two molars. The first four axes only are statistically significant and comprise more than 95% of the information within the data. The first canonical axis is mainly due to canine length, with some involvement of third premolar breadth. The second axis contains primarily information contributed by the breadth of the first incisor and by canine breadth. With the exception of canine length all important variables in the first four axes are breadths and this is consistent with the notion that most of primate sexual dimorphism is in breadth dimensions rather than lengths, whether of bodily dimensions (Chapter 2; also Oxnard, 1983a, c, 1984) or of the dimensions of teeth (Wu and Oxnard, 1983a, b; Oxnard, Lieberman and Gelvin, 1985). That sexual dimorphism is most obvious in breadths of teeth had been noted much earlier for humans by Garn, Lewis, Swindler and Karevsky (1967).

Figure 2:15 presents the scores on the first four canonical axes for all seven of the extant groups in the maxillary analysis. For the first two axes, the greatest separation between males and females, representing the greatest degree of sexual dimorphism, is in *Gorilla*. The greatest female/male overlap in canonical space, representing the smallest sexual dimorphism, is in *Pan*. But although the sexes are not known for *Homo*, the close association of all human specimens implies that sexual dimorphism is considerably less in *Homo* than in *Pan*. Certainly, *Homo*, though closer to female *Pan* than to any other ape group is yet completely separate from it.

The first axis separates *Homo* from all apes, and males from females for all non-human genera. This suggests that the contributing factors to this axis, canine length and premolar breadth have similar contributions to both the difference between ape females and males, and the difference between humans and apes. *Homo*, in this axis, then, resembles a much more feminized form of an ape than does any female ape.

The second axis separates *Pongo* from each of the other forms: *Gorilla*, *Pan*, and *Homo*, and male from female *Pongo*. The variables that make up the second axis are the breadths of the first incisor and canine, and this makes it is immediately clear that this aspect of sexual dimorphism in *Pongo* differs from that in the other apes.

The third and fourth axes also contribute to the separations of the sexes of each genus. This ranges from least in *Pan* (in which genus they overlap), through more in *Pongo* (in which the peripheries of

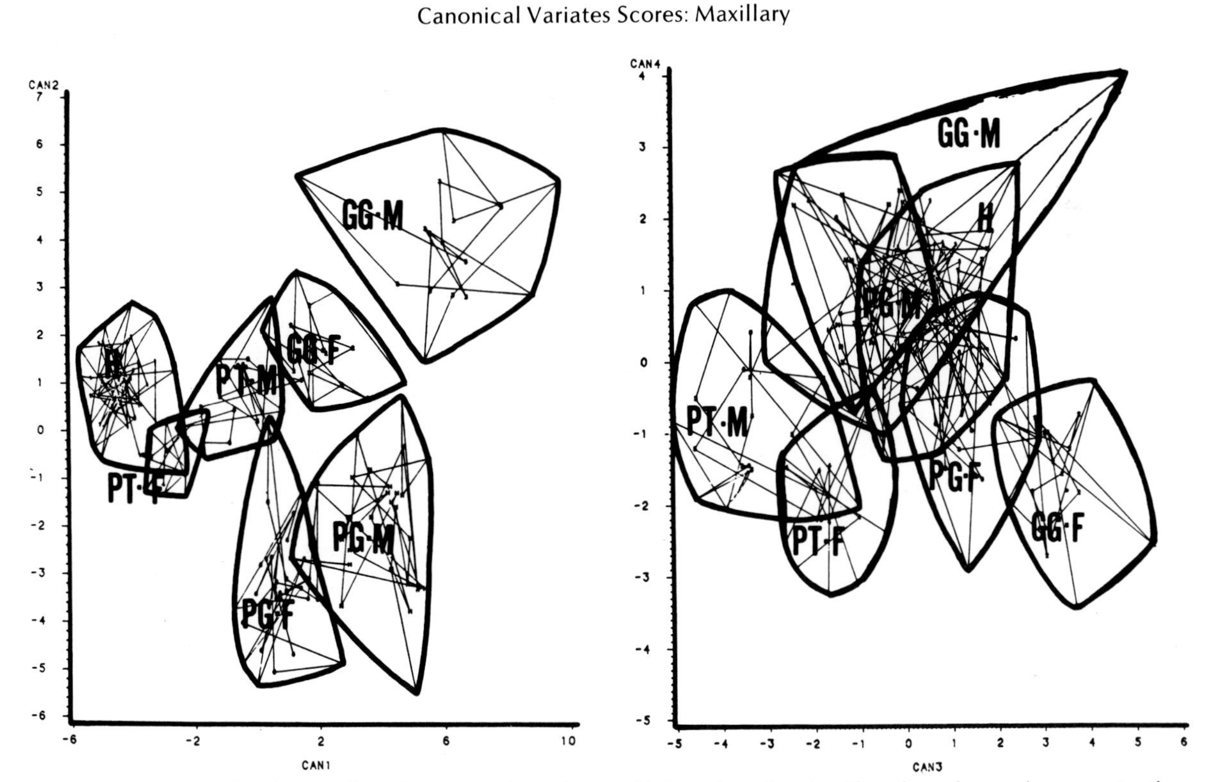

Fig. 2:15 Plots of the first against the second, and the third against the fourth values for each genus in the canonical variates analysis of the maxillary teeth data. PT.F and PT.M = respective females and males of chimpanzees; PG.F and PG.M = females and males respectively of orang-utans; GG.F and GG.M = females and males of gorillas. H = humans, sexes undefined. The scale is in standard deviation units.

each sex scarcely touch) to *Gorilla* in which further additional absolute separation between the sexes is achieved. This axis, thus, specifically defines sexual dimorphism in *Gorilla* as different from that in *Pan*.

These two axes place *Homo* squarely between the sexes in *Pongo* and, therefore, achieve additional separation of *Homo* from *Pan* which was the closest genus to us in axes one and two.

Sexual dimorphism is greater in the mandible. In this case the first five axes are significant, containing over 95% of the information. The first axis represents mainly canine length and the length of the third premolar, the same two teeth as were represented in the first axis of the maxillary study. There are also contributions from canine breadth and the breadth of the first molar. The length of the first molar is the predominant variable in the second axis. Indeed, the lengths of the teeth are as important as the breadths in separating the groups in the mandibular analysis, and this contrasts with the situation in the upper jaw.

Figure 2:16 shows the positions of each sex-subgroup of each genus within the first four canonical axes of the mandibular analysis. The within group variability is much lower for every genus and sex subgroup than is the case for the maxilla. *Homo* is especially more distinct from the other genera in the mandibular analysis than in the maxillary.

In this case the first axis achieves major separation between females and males of each ape (with the separation for the sexes in *Gorilla* being absolute). And in this plot, in contrast with the upper jaw, no particular ape is any closer to *Homo* than any other, female *Gorilla*, female *Pongo* and female *Pan* being all equidistant from *Homo*.

The second axis separates *Gorilla* positively and *Pan* negatively from all other forms.

The third and fourth axes provide considerably fewer separations overall, but continue to add to the separations of the sexes in *Gorilla* (further very large absolute separation) and in both *Pan* and *Pongo* (in both of which, the sexes only just touch

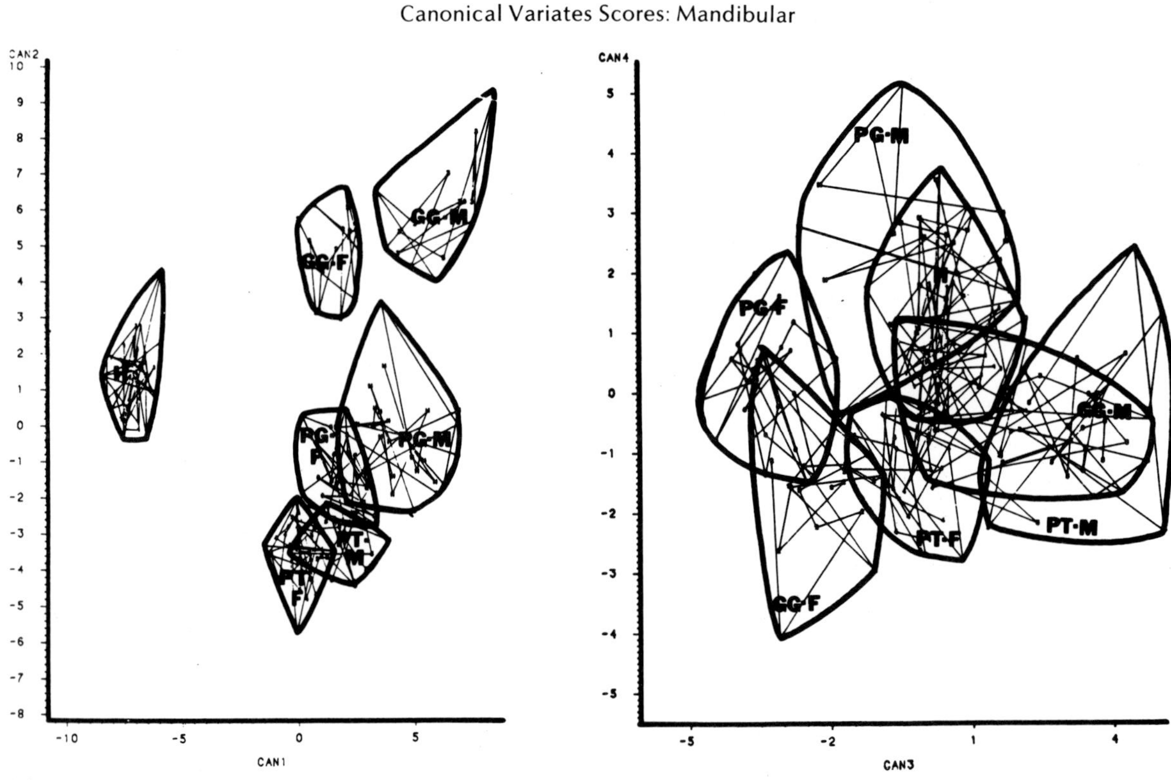

Fig. 2:16 Plots of the first against the second, and the third against the fourth values for each genus in the canonical variates analysis of the mandibular teeth data. PT.F and PT.M = females and males respectively of chimpanzees; PG.F and PG.M = females and males respectively of orang-utans; GG.F and GG.M = females and males respectively of gorillas. H = humans, sexes undefined. The scale is in standard deviation units.

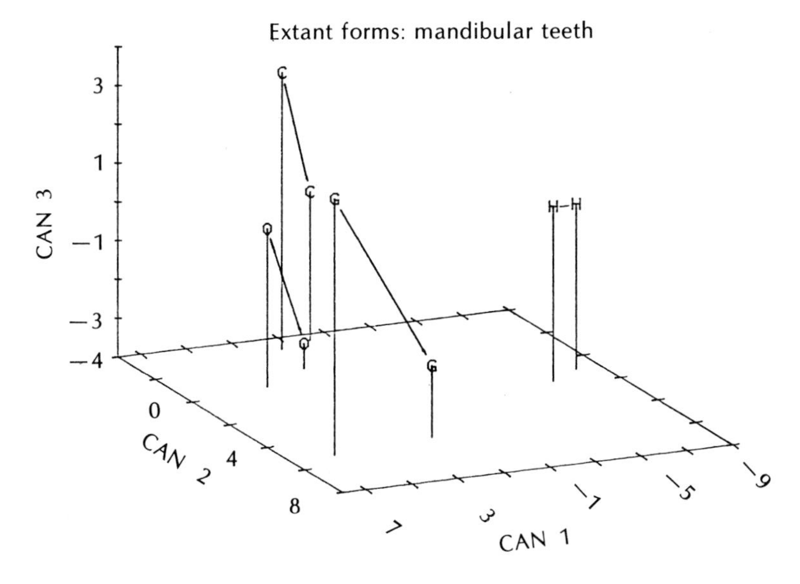

Fig. 2:17 Three-dimensional plot of the first three canonical axes. H = humans, C = chimpanzees, O = orangutans and G = gorillas. The female, in each case, is on the right. The pattern of difference between female and male is similar in the three apes and quite different in humans.

one another). *Homo* is not separated by these axes, being centrally located in this plot.

It is in the plot of the first three axes together that the patterns of sexual dimorphisms are most evident. Figure 2:17 shows that all three apes share a similar direction from female to male that is quite different from that in *Homo*.

High-dimensional displays. For both the maxilla and the mandible, information in higher axes, though real and statistically significant, is difficult to interpret, given the graphical and conceptual limitations that preclude ready visualisation in more than two or three dimensions simultaneously. The data are therefore represented graphically using high-dimensional plots as described in Chapter 1.

Figures 2:18 to 2:20 are the high-dimensional displays of the canonical variates means for the seven extant groups for both maxillary and mandibular analyses. As seen from figure 2:18, male and female *Gorilla* are more similar in their lower than

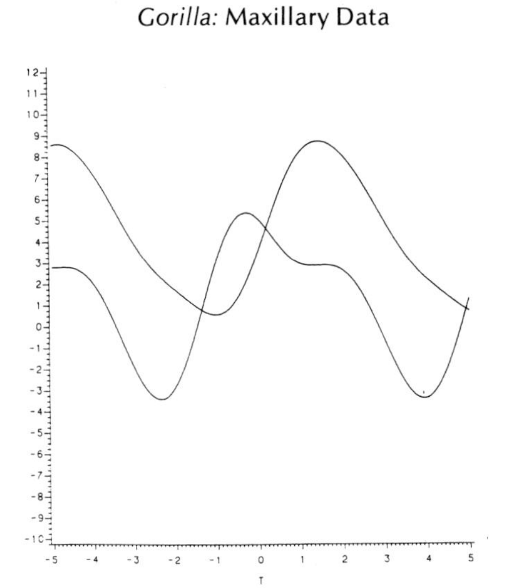

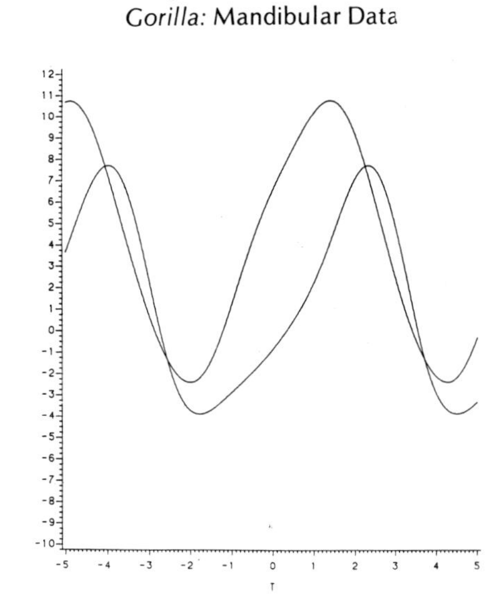

Fig. 2:18 High-dimensional plots for each sex of gorillas for the maxillary and mandibular analyses. The upper curve in each case is the curve for the male. The large difference between the sexes is evident in the large area between the two curves. As can be seen from the greater similarity between the curves for each sex in the mandibular analysis, the pattern for each sex is more similar in the mandible than in the maxilla.

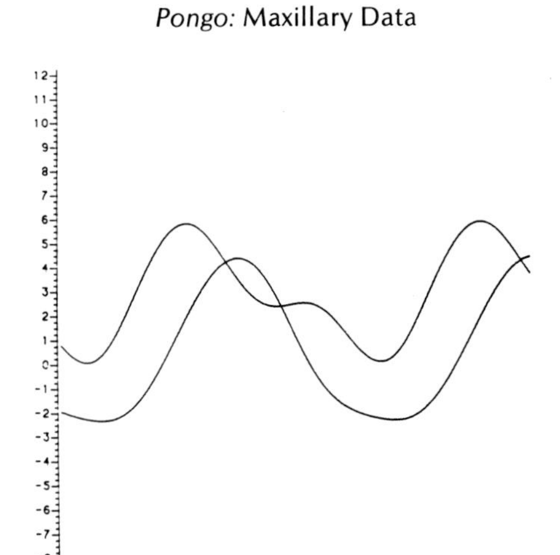

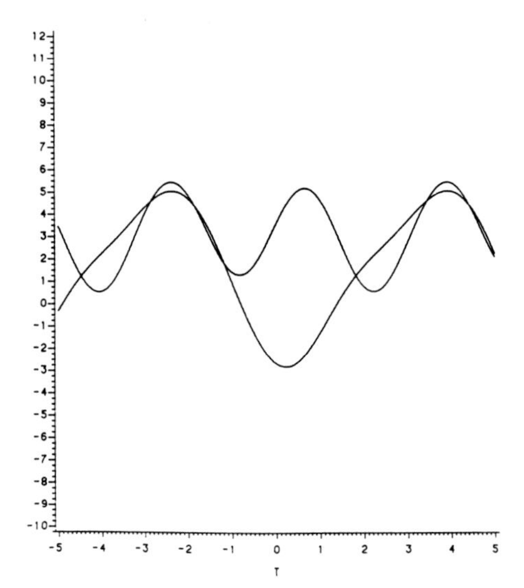

Fig. 2:19 High-dimensional plots for each sex of orang-utans for the maxillary and mandibular analyses. The upper curve in each case is the curve for the male. As with the gorilla, the fact that there is a large difference between the sexes is evident from the large area between the two curves. In orang-utans, however, in contrast with gorillas, the pattern of difference between the sexes is more complex in the mandible than the maxilla.

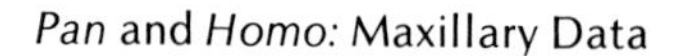

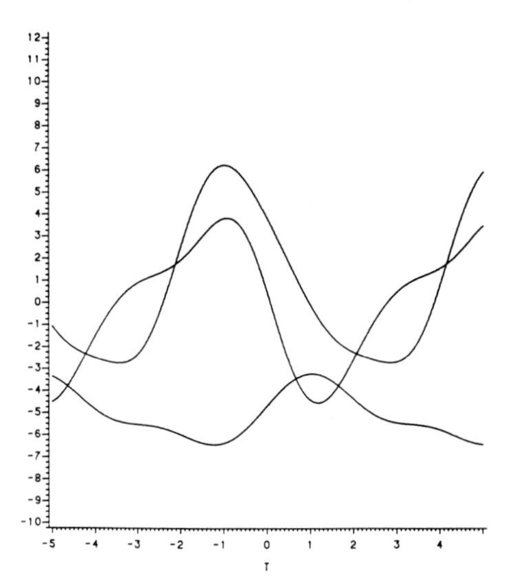

Fig. 2:20 High-dimensional plots for each sex of chimpanzees (the upper pair of heavily curved plots) and for humans, sexes undefined (the single lower almost horizontal plot). That chimpanzees are somewhat closer to humans is evident from the fact that their high-dimensional curves do actually overlap at some points with the human curve. But the total high-dimensional dissimilarity in pattern between humans and chimpanzees is evident from the form of the curves. As with both gorillas and orang-utans, the patterns for the chimpanzee result in plots with extremely marked maxima and minima; this differentiates chimpanzees completely from the human pattern. For chimpanzees, as with gorillas, the fact that there is a considerable difference between the sexes is evident from the large area between the curves for each sex. And the nature of the interrelationship between the two curves in chimpanzees is similar to those in gorillas (Fig. 2:18) rather than in orang-utans (Fig. 2:19).

in their upper jaws, although the absolute generalized distances between them are not that different (6.34 for the maxilla, 6.83 for the mandible). This greater dissimilarity between the mandibular and maxillary patterns in *Gorilla* may be a reflection of the unique pattern of canine dimorphism found in *Gorilla* as seen from univariate analyses (see earlier this chapter, and Oxnard, Lieberman and Gelvin, 1985).

The high-dimensional plots for *Pongo* show a completely different pattern of dimorphism than that in *Gorilla*, as well as more marked maxillomandibular differences (Fig. 2:19).

For *Pan*, as seen from figure 2:20, there is much less sexual dimorphism than for the other apes. And *Homo*, though somewhat closer to *Pan*, is shown to possess a totally different curvature to either sex in *Pan*.

Evolutionary Implications. The original idea that sexual dimorphism is mainly related to overall bodily size differences (e.g. most recently Wood, 1976) has been modified by newer findings suggesting that greater or lesser degrees of sexual dimorphism in primates have a multifactorial basis (e.g. Leutenegger, 1982). In turn, however, even that thesis has been further developed by the concept that sexual dimorphism is not just a matter of greater or lesser degree but includes several qualitatively different patterns. This has been shown by the multivariate statistical studies of overall bodily proportions of twenty genera representing most primate groups (chapter two and Oxnard, 1983a, c, 1984). It is now confirmed (in the more restricted group of hominoids examined here) by these various studies of dental dimensions.

Univariate Studies: This new complexity is most obvious in consideration of canine sexual dimorphism. Prior studies of canine sexual dimorphism have leant heavily upon the degree of its expression. Thus Leutenegger (1982) emphasizes a spectrum of canine sexual dimorphism that ranges from that in species (such as geladas, *Theropithecus*) in which males have canines twice the size of those in females, to that in species (such as night monkeys, *Aotus*) in which canine size is virtually the same in the two sexes. Leutenegger goes on to show the degree to which this canine size differential is influenced by body size differentials between the sexes. The present studies demonstrate that, in addition to these size differentials, qualitatively different patterns of canine dimorphism exist between the sexes in each large hominoid (Figs. 2:3 to 2:6; Table 2:2 to 2:3).

Thus, *Pan* and *Homo* are somewhat similar in both having smaller degrees of canine dimorphism of means (smaller differences between the mean values for each sex). *Gorilla* and *Pongo* are similar in both having large degrees of canine dimorphism of means (larger differences between the mean values for each sex). Yet *Pan* and *Homo* themselves differ. *Pan* possesses very much larger (and, of course, statistically significantly different) dispersions for males than females for canines (as well as most other anterior teeth). In contrast *Homo* possesses dispersions for the dimensions of canines (as well as all other teeth) that do not show significant differences between the sexes. A similar finding is evident for the other pair of genera, *Gorilla* having unequal dispersions for the sexes, *Pongo* having equal dispersions for each sex.

It is therefore possible that at least two factors enter into the results for canines. One may be based simply on the overall differences in size between the sexes in each group. A small difference in overall bodily size between the sexes (as in *Pan* and *Homo*) may be related to a small difference in mean size of canines. A big difference in overall bodily size between the sexes (as in *Gorilla* and *Pongo*) may be related to a big difference in mean size of canines.

The second may be a specifically canine dimorphism that is unrelated to body size dimorphism whether that be small or big. It may be expressed as small differences in dispersions (essentially equal) for each sex in *Pongo* and *Homo*, and big differences in dispersions for each sex in *Gorilla* and *Pan*, irrespective, in each case, of the degree of overall bodily size dimorphism.

Much less attention has been paid to sexual differences in non-canine teeth. Such data as have been recorded (e.g. Ashton and Zuckerman, 1950a,b; Swindler, 1976) emphasize quantitative differences between means of measurements. Though confirmation of such quantitative difference is one finding in the present study, of far greater interest are the quantitative sexual dimorphisms in dispersion and the qualitative dimorphisms in patterns of sexual dimorphisms in tooth locations in the non-canine teeth (Figs. 2:7 to 2:14; Tables 2:2 to 2:3).

These patterns are more complex than in the canines. They include the same significant sexual dimorphisms in mean values and in dispersions for each sex in each genus as in the canines. But they also include different patterns of placement of all of these sexual dimorphisms along the tooth row together with different patterns of placement for sexual dimorphisms between the upper and lower jaws. Let us first discuss the teeth that border upon the canines: the incisors and premolars.

The two genera, *Pan* and *Gorilla*, that should, on all biological grounds, be remarkably similar except in degree of dimorphism, actually show markedly different patterns in the teeth bordering on the canines. In *Gorilla* the dispersions for males are generally narrow, and are encompassed by the upper end of broad distributions for females; the reverse is the case for *Pan*. Such a reversed difference would not seem to be related directly to the fact that overall size dimorphism is greater in *Gorilla* than *Pan*. Nor would it seem related to the fact that canine mean dimorphism is greater in *Gorilla* than *Pan*. But the interaction of overall size dimorphism and specifically canine mean dimorphism (which is different in each species) together with canine dispersion dimorphism (which is the same in both species) could, through developmental field phenomena, have different effects upon the teeth bordering upon the canines.

In the other pair of genera, *Pongo* and *Homo*, the absolute values of the means of non-canine dimensions show sexual dimorphisms of means to be big in *Pongo* but small in *Homo*. This could be related mostly to differences in overall bodily size dimorphism and its related canine mean size dimorphism. But the similar dispersions for each sex in both genera could be related to absent (or much reduced) specifically canine dispersion dimorphism with, consequently, little effect upon neighboring teeth through developmental fields.

In the case of those teeth (molars and last premolars) more distantly removed from the canines (and therefore, presumably, less influenced by developmental effects associated with canines) yet other patterns are found. For these teeth the primary similarity is between *Gorilla* and *Pongo* where there are large differences in sexual dimorphisms of means. This could be simply related to large overall bodily size dimorphism between the sexes affecting all teeth in these two genera. The fact that the dispersions are different for *Gorilla* as compared with *Pongo* could be due to the different developmental effects of canine dispersion dimorphism on the teeth more distant from the canines (canine dimorphism in dispersion is large in *Gorilla* and small in *Pongo*).

The posterior teeth in *Pan* show no significant differences between males and females and this could well result from the fact that there is only a small overall size dimorphism and small canine mean size dimorphism in this creature. As with the other genera, the large specifically canine dispersion that exists by itself in this genus may not spread its effects so far along the tooth row.

In *Homo* the patterns of distributions may stem from a yet different combination of factors. Most human teeth, whether close to the canines or not, show fairly complete overlap of the distributions for males and females. This could be related to the combination of small overall bodily size dimorphism, small canine mean dimorphism and small canine dispersion dimorphism. In those tooth loci where some mean differences do exist, they are of the equal dispersion type and are located sporadically along the entire tooth row. This may reflect the possibility of a small aliquot of overall bodily size dimorphism in *Homo* which affects the canines as well as some other teeth even though there seems to be almost no specifically canine dimorphism.

Finally there are the findings of the increased degrees and complexities of sexual dimorphisms in mandibles as compared with maxillae in those species with larger sexual dimorphisms of various kinds (all apes). It seems at least possible that sexual dimorphisms are more constrained in upper jaws because of their connections with other functional and structural parts (such as the face, the cranial base, and the nasal and orbital regions). These regions may, for functional and developmental reasons, undergo less marked sexual dimorphism. The mandible, being regionally and structurally more distant from these areas, may be less constrained by such factors.

As in the case of the prior study of overall proportions, it therefore behooves us to reject the idea of a single phenomenon of sexual dimorphism in the dentition, and, likewise, a single causal explanation.

Multivariate Studies: The hypothesis that sexual dimorphism in the great apes can be represented along a single dimension, or by a single number, and is a function only of size (e.g. Wood, 1975, 1976) is yet further rejected, this time by the multivariate studies. Canonical variates analysis shows that there are four significant axes for the maxilla and five for the mandible. From the separations given by these axes three different patterns of sexual dimorphism for each ape emerge from both the mandibular and maxillary studies.

These are multivariate differences in **(a)** the positions of each extant genus, **(b)** the patterns between the sexes for each genus, and **(c)** the patterns for each jaw for the sexes of each genus. These three pattern differences are additional to those evident from the univariate studies because they are due in part to information (correlations among measures) that are not examined in the univariate investigations. They are further strong evidence in support of the hypothesis of multiple causality of sexual dimorphism even in as limited an anatomical region as the dentition. No single hypothesis or mechanism is a likely source of such a multiplicity of pattern.

Sexual dimorphism in each genus may thus relate to a complex series of factors. These may include genetic and developmental associations along the tooth row (Butler first spoke about developmental fields in 1939 and Biggerstaff reviews genetic effects in 1979). They may also include, however, functional differences related to diet (dietary differences do exist between the sexes as well as between the species), ecological differences (clearly present between sexes as well as between species, and particularly in the case of *Pongo*), and differential sexual selection. It is more likely that a complex interaction between some or all of the above mechanisms accounts for the different patterns of sexual dimorphisms in the extant apes. Further research into these problem is of the utmost importance for our understanding of the complexity of sexual dimorphism.

Pongo has in the past been thought to be highly specialized as compared with the African apes. But the univariate data suggest that the large specific canine dimorphism of the African apes today was probably not the general hominoid situation. Rather, the large canine dimorphisms, especially the large dispersion differences, are probably recently evolved features in African apes that are not typical of either earlier hominid or hominoid ancestors. Indeed, some orang-utan characters may be shared with humans because they are more general for hominoids.

The multivariate information seems to tell the same story. Comparison of the maxillary and mandibular plots for *Homo* and *Pongo* show that these genera clearly share similar patterns in each jaw. Given the very long time since there was a close phylogenetic relationship between humans and orang-utans it is possible that this may represent an ancient condition. In contrast, the maxillary and mandibular plots for *Pan* and *Gorilla* are quite different from them and from each other. This demonstrates that there is a major difference between each jaw in both these species. Given the relatively short time that must have existed since the evolutionary divergence of the African apes, this finding supports the idea that increased differences between upper and lower jaw may be more recently evolved states.

All this is consistent with anatomical views of the orang-utan as a 'living fossil' (Walker as reported by Lewin, 1983). Since a 'living fossil' is a species that has undergone little change over a period of evolutionary time, further studies of the orang-utan should have important implications for hominid evolution. Many characters found in the orang-utan can be assumed to be more similar to early hominids than are characters found in other extant apes, such as *Gorilla* and *Pan*, genera that may have undergone considerably more evolutionary divergence (in these characteristics) from the main stock from which they sprang. The study of yet further characteristics also supports the idea of the African apes as being more derived hominoids (Ward and Kimbel, 1983; Templeton, 1983; Ettler, 1983).

It is true that Schwartz (1984) interprets the raw data, through vigorous application of the cladistic method, as supporting the view that orang-utans and humans are more closely related to each other than are either to the African apes. But this last opinion is denied by both the molecular and morphometric approaches (see comparisons in Oxnard, 1983a, 1984). It seems to stem from a naive cladistic approach that is forced to group each 'character' as 'primitive' or 'derived'

This approach is not able to recognize that assessments of 'observable features' (especially when quantitative in form) as 'purely primitive' or 'purely derived' are almost certain to be totally wrong. The complexities of organismal structure are such that the great majority of 'observable features' are bound to comprise a blend of information. Some of this will stem from 'underlying characters' that are truly primitive and others from 'underlying characters' that are truly derived. In that sense any 'observable feature' available for study by evolutionary biologists will be a combination of primitive and derived portions.

At the present stage in our knowledge we do not know how to partition those contributions. We do not even know if they sum to 100% or if there are other elements within them (e.g. redundancies) that may further complicate the problem. But their expression in quantitative form makes it more likely that eventually we will be able to make these separations. What is clear at this time, however, is that 'observable features' will almost never be purely 'primitive' or 'derived' even though this may indeed be true of the underlying characters of which they are comprised (but which we can normally never see). We can confidently assert that assessments of 'observable features' as '100% primitive' or '100% derived' are almost certain to be wrong.

Let us return to the overall picture. Of equally great interest are other relationships among the genera. There is some tendency to believe that the least dimorphic genus *Homo* is closest to the lesser dimorphic genus *Pan* rather than to the other two much more heavily dimorphic species, *Pongo* and *Gorilla*. But considerable information now supports the thesis developed from the univariate studies, that this is not a simple matter. In the maxillary analyses *Homo* is only slightly closer to *Pan* than to *Pongo*. In the more discriminating mandibular analyses, there is very little to choose between the two. And female gorillas are also almost the same distance from *Homo*. It is true, however, that male orang-utans and gorillas are most distant from *Homo* by any count. A final conclusion on the significance of such similarities and differences requires intercalation of information from studies of the various fossil species in later chapters.

Summary: This review of sexual dimorphisms in dental dimensions of extant humans and great apes shows just how complex this entire problem is.

Study of individual measures demonstrates that there are sexual dimorphisms not only of means (which we all knew) but also of dispersions, of patterns of individual dimensions along the tooth row, and of differences between the mandible and maxilla. Study of measures taken together using multivariate morphometrics further shows that there are multivariate position differences between the species, different multivariate sexual dimorphisms in each species, and multivariate sexual dimorphism differences between the jaws.

All this lies against a background of a sex ratio for apes that is artificially set at 2:1. This is done not because we believe that this is the exact ratio for any given ape, but rather to allow us to understand better what we find in studies of the fossils in later chapters. In the fossils, clear differences in the numbers of specimens in bimodal distributions sometimes exist.

The conclusions at this point relate to the idea that the complexity of sexual dimorphisms in the teeth of humans and apes must be related to great complexity in evolutionary and other causal mechanisms. In particular, the idea that something simple, such as a difference in overall size and robusticity, can account for the findings must be dismissed.

The complexity is not so great, however, that it is not possible to estimate what some of the causal factors might be. They include, among others, the effects of overall bodily size dimorphism, of specifically canine size dimorphism, of spread of canine dimorphisms to neighbouring teeth along the tooth row through developmental (field) phenomena, and of the existence of phylogenetically ancient features in species extant today. It is indeed also likely that they include other functional features, such as diet and more broadly ecology. But the evidence here is less clear because of the restricted nature of the original data with which we have had to work.

All this supplies a fascinating background to the question of sexual dimorphism or dimorphisms, and to questions about the interrelationships of species as we move on to study the various fossil data that have become available.

CHAPTER 3

Zero to Two Million Years Ago: Sexual Dimorphisms in Very Early Humans

Abstract: We first review briefly the current evidence of sexual dimorphism in *Homo sapiens neandertalensis* and *Homo erectus*. In the remainder of the first half of this chapter we then examine, one by one, individual lengths and breadths for such samples of teeth of these two species as are available. In comparison with the situation in the extant apes and humans of the last chapter, we do not know here which specimens of which fossil belong to which sex. Accordingly, therefore, the data are examined as a whole. The distributions that are obtained are used to reveal to us what, if any, evidence there may be of sexual dimorphism. Again, in contrast to the living forms, instead of assuming that we know the ratios of the number of each sex in the fossil species, we examine the distributions obtained to see if they suggest any specific sex ratios to us.

Although most investigators believe that the fossil, *Homo habilis*, despite its designation, is generally closer to australopithecines than to *Homo* we have here anticipated the chapter on the australopithecines by describing briefly the results for that group.

In the second half of this chapter we study the fossils multivariately by intercalating them within the morphometric studies of Chapter 2 on the living forms. However, this cannot be done in the same way as for the living forms; we just do not know which specimens are from which sex. Accordingly, therefore, we estimate the modes for each sex for each dimension using information from the univariate studies, that suggests when marked sexual differences may be present. This process allows us to see clearly the relationships of the fossils to the living forms, especially, of course, to modern *Homo* to which, naturally, they are most close. It also allows us to see, if somewhat more mistily, the nature of such multivariate sexual dimorphisms as may exist.

We again anticipate some of the results of Chapter 5 by reviewing briefly the place of *Homo habilis* within these studies.

Both the univariate and multivariate steps in this analysis show an obvious relationship between the two groups of fossil *Homo* and the modern species. They also show how completely different they are from the various apes. The place of *Homo habilis* in these studies is especially interesting.

Human Sexual Dimorphism — the Current View

Most of the enquiries into sexual dimorphism in fossil groups of humans have depended upon the notion that to study this, it is essential to know the sex of each individual specimen. Yet the materials that are most abundant are teeth and these do not bear recognizable gonads. Accordingly most of the definitive investigations have been confined to study of samples of teeth that are associated with other skeletal materials for which adequate sexual determinations can be made: i.e. where the remains include especially, for instance, the pelvis.

Thus Brace and Ryan (1980) have presented extensive studies of sexual dimorphism in human teeth back as far as the last 40,000 years. However, it becomes increasingly difficult to assign fragments to identifiable individuals. Thus, the number of remains for which accurate sexual determinations can be made becomes vanishingly small. Brace and Ryan (1980) note that assessments of sex of individuals in neanderthal, *erectus* and even earlier hominid populations can be little more than exercises in informed speculation.

But Brace and Ryan do present convincing evidence of sexual dimorphism in more recent times. They are able to do this, partly because there probably really were more people alive at any one time during these later stages, and partly because there has actually been very much less time, for weathering and other natural processes of dissolution, to have produced their deleterious consequences upon the materials.

Again most of the enquiries into sexual dimorphism have been biased, a priori, by the idea that sexual dimorphism is a size related uni-dimensional phenomenon that can be measured as smaller or greater percentages of sexual dimorphism. The smallest average sexual dimorphism of teeth in Brace's and Ryan's studies (using their convention of that measure), is less than 5% and is apparent in Hong Kong Chinese, Thai, and Late Woodland Amerindians from northeast Ohio (for this last see Lovejoy *et al.*, 1977). These figures are compared with 15% to 20% sexual dimorphism for gorillas and baboons (by the same measure). Sexual dimorphism is intermediate, as much as 12% by this measure, in the oldest human group that was studied, from the Upper Paleolithic (Frayer, 1978). Brace and Ryan found various other groups lying between these two figures for humans and, discussed the degree to which changes in both male and female body bulk, changes in level of nutrition, and changes in preparation of the food may have contributed to the complex sexual dimorphisms that they see. With these changes, they thought, might also be associated differences in activity patterns and social arrangements between females and males.

These views do indeed represent good possibilities. But Brace and Ryan are more concerned to present them as challenges, rather than conclusions. Their solid data do show that human dental sexual dimorphism was greater during the Upper Paleolithic than at any subsequent time, and that it is at its least in some modern human populations. But they point out that they are unable to control for other complexities. That other complexities do exist, however, is not for them in doubt. As they noted, such studies cannot be performed on older human or pre-human remains. But the methodology that we are adopting in this book can be applied on older remains. We can therefore go on to look at older fossils such as neanderthalers and *Homo erectus*.

Homo sapiens neandertalensis: current evidence of sexual dimorphism?

Neanderthalers have always been a problem. Although the first specimen was the Gibraltar cranium found in 1848, the group takes its name from the skeleton found in 1856 in the Neander valley. They are usually defined as a morphologically characteristic population represented by fossil material dating from as long ago as the Wurm glacial complex and scattered widely throughout Europe, Asia and the Near East (though there are even controversies with this definition, e.g. see Brose and Wolpoff, 1971, and Howells, 1973).

Their crania are generally long and low, with a characteristic bulge in the parietal region. The occiput projects in a manner that resembles a 'chignon' or 'bun'. Brow ridges arch over the large orbits. The face is high with forwardly projecting nose and teeth. The cheeks are swept back and the mastoid processes are small. Cranial capacities are large, larger on average than in modern human populations.

The few postcranial bones that are known are also very large, in particular with large weight bearing surfaces. But the form of various postcranial bones (e.g. the foot – Rhoads and Trinkhaus, 1977) demonstrate unequivocally that posture and gait resemble the condition in modern humans.

Were 'neanderthals' simply one end of a spectrum of hominid variation existing at that time? Or were they a separate breeding group? Is there any evidence of a population obviously ancestral to them? Are they exclusively European? What was their eventual fate?

In spite of all these questions there is a wide measure of agreement that the classic neanderthals arose from an earlier common gene pool in Europe, Asia, the Near East and Africa. From this stemmed several discernable groups, one with an essentially modern morphology, another forming the classical neanderthalers, and a third separate Mid Eastern group. This scheme forms the basis of the so-called 'spectrum' hypothesis (Weiner and Campbell, 1964) in which these groups are seen as extremes of what may have been essentially continuous morphological gradients.

There is less agreement about their fate. More

recently, Brose and Wolpoff (1971) and Bilsborough (1973) have suggested that the differences among the neanderthalers have been exaggerated and that gradual change to *Homo sapiens* was the most likely course of events. The countervailing view was already represented in the work of Howell (1951). This suggests that the Western European neanderthals were quite suddenly replaced by modern-looking populations of *Homo sapiens* (Fig. 3:1). Certainly, metrical evidence of a discontinuity has been presented by Howells (1973) and modern views of evolution could interpret this as either sudden replacement or sudden change. Whatever it was that occurred, however, the one thing that we do know is the discontinuity in the morphology shown by Howells (1973).

All this notwithstanding there have been a few minor attempts to estimate sexual dimorphism in the group: *Homo sapiens neandertalensis*. It is believed that they display some evidence of sexual dimorphism. But the morphological features that in general, distinguish populations of the sexes in modern humans, do not seem to apply as well in this group. Projecting brow ridges and retreating foreheads do not seem especially diagnostic of males; female neanderthalers seem just as extreme in these features. In contrast, increased occipital projection does appear to distinguish the slightly larger (male ?) skulls in a manner not noted in modern humans.

Overall bodily proportions may likewise have been somewhat different in *Homo sapiens neandertalensis* than in present day humans. Wolpoff (1980), for instance, estimates their body-size dimorphism as being slightly less than in modern humans. He believes that the stature of females was about 94% of the stature of males. Thus, though skeletal robusticity and presumed hyper-muscularity are far more marked in neanderthalers as a group than in modern humans, it is possible that differences in skeletal robusticity and presumed muscularity between the sexes are actually somewhat less than in modern humans. These are general bodily features that might tally with the findings for the brow ridge and forehead features of the skull. What precise bodily differences there might have been have not yet been explicated. But the notion that there might have been very little division of labour in this group, together with the possibility that both males and females may have had to withstand rigorous environmental conditions, may possibly mean that there was a smaller difference between males and females than in modern humans.

How do these possibilities, tentative in the extreme, compare with dimorphism in the teeth? In all the years that neanderthalers have been known, a rather large number of skulls and jaws with teeth have been found (Fig. 3:2). The total number of teeth available for study here ranges from as few as 17 lower incisors to as many as 57 lower first molars

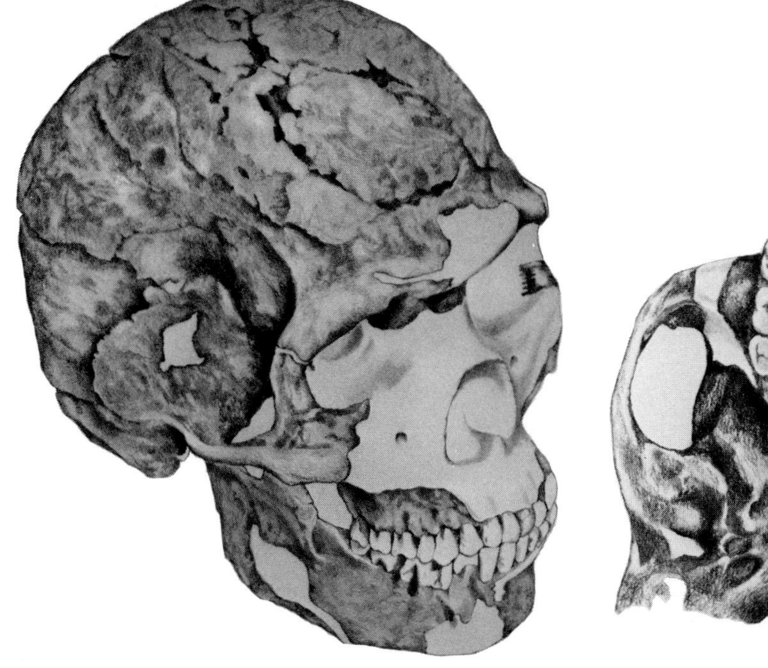

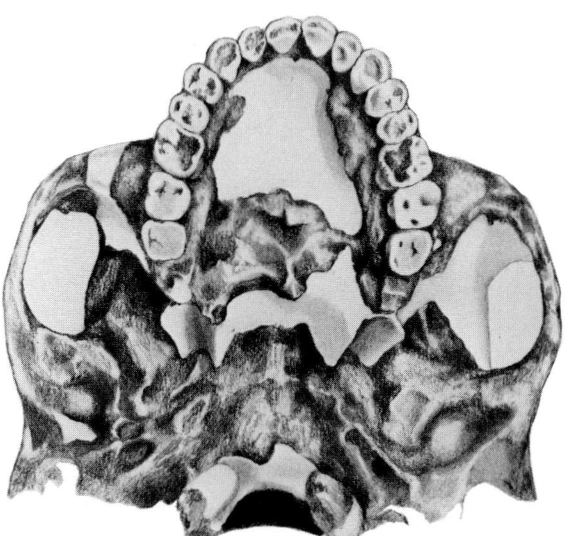

Fig. 3:1 Sketches of skull and dentition of fossil *Homo sapien sapiens*.

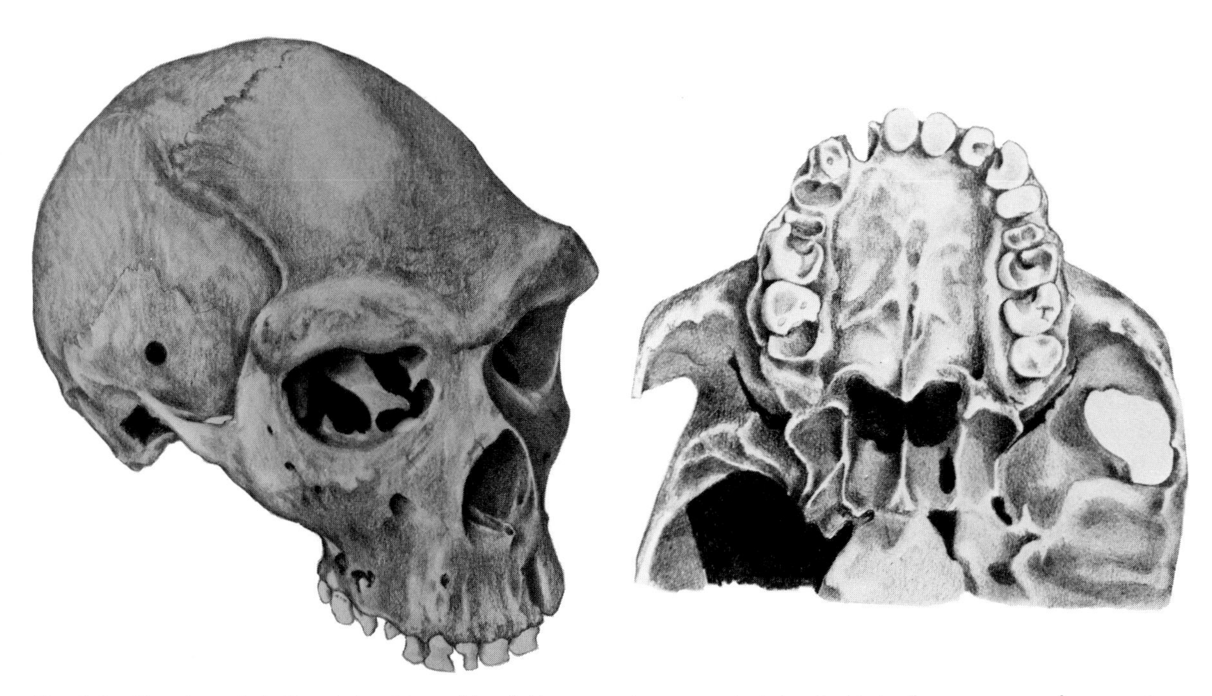

Fig. 3:2 Sketches of skull and dentition of fossil *Homo sapiens neandertalensis*. Note, for purposes of comparison and because the original specimen is incomplete, this sketch is of the more complete left side. It has been reversed to make it comparable with the other sketches.

(Table 3:1). Although the sizes of the samples are somewhat small for a few teeth positions (e.g. one tooth has a sample of below 20 and six teeth have sample sizes below 30) yet samples are large enough in many cases (between 30 and 40 for seven teeth and even above 50 for two) to allow study of the distributions of the dimensions of the teeth in the same way that we have just carried out for extant apes and humans. But before we study the results of the new analyses, let us also look at an even older relative *Homo erectus*.

Table 3:1

Numbers of specimens available for study in neanderthalers

	Lower teeth	Upper teeth
First incisor	17	27
Second incisor	22	27
Canine	32	33
Third premolar	40	27
Fourth premolar	36	28
First molar	57	53
Second molar	47	38
Third molar	41	28

Homo erectus: current evidence of sexual dimorphism?

For a long time now scientific and popular attention has been focussed on the presumed early stages of hominid evolution and one of the results has been some neglect of studies relating to *Homo erectus*. The original definition of *Homo erectus* has now been expanded to include remains widely distributed in Asia, Africa and Europe, and dating from the Middle and Lower Pleistocene.

Homo erectus had a considerably smaller brain than modern humans or neanderthalers. The average was just under 1,000 cc, only a little more than halfway between ape and modern human sizes. The cranial shape is distinctive. There is a prominent brow ridge separated from a receding forehead. The vault of the skull is low with the widest part at the base rather than high up in the vault as in modern humans. The bones of the skull are unusually thick. The skeleton of the face is strong with a broad cheek. The mandible is more robust than in modern humans, less so than in australopithecines. Little is known of the post-cranial skeleton, but such bones as there are, including a single pelvic fragment, show all the features of an upright posture and bipedal gait.

As with neanderthalers, the problems relating to *Homo erectus* concern first its phylogenetic links with earlier taxa. *Homo erectus* is widely spread throughout the Old World. Did *Homo erectus* originate in some limited part of this range and then spread? Or did *Homo erectus* have a multifocal origin?

Problems relating to this group also involve discussion of its presumed descendents. Do the remains of *Homo erectus* provide any clues as to the later populations of *Homo sapiens*? Can we see in *Homo erectus* any beginnings of the regional variations that we see in *Homo sapiens* today?

We are even interested if their remains provide any evidence of social and cultural adaptations similar or different from what we know for modern humans.

Much research makes it clear that these fossils were spread widely over Asia, Africa, and Europe between 1.5 and just under 0.5 million years ago. Recent finds even suggest that 2 million years, or more, is not an exaggerated upper limit (Walker, 1984). There are still too few data to determine the extent of genetic interchange among all the various subpopulations of *Homo erectus* that must have existed. Some meagre cultural evidence suggests that hunting and fire were regular attainments at least in some populations.

As to origins of the group, some evidence suggests that *Homo erectus*, like the robust australopithecines, was an evolutionary sideline, with the main pathway being from *Homo habilis* directly on to *Homo sapiens* (Leakey, 1966, but, it should be noted, Leakey is one of the co-definers of the *Homo habilis* species). Most workers believe, however, that this group was a *bona fide* intermediate between *Homo habilis* and *Homo sapiens*. Certainly the newest work demonstrates three important findings. **First**, *Homo erectus* was truly more widespread and extended further back in time than previously thought. **Second**, there are fossils from earlier formations that may represent a transition from *Homo habilis*. **Third**, at the later end of the time scale there is now some evidence of a change to an appearance more like *Homo sapiens* of yesterday and today.

What of sexual dimorphism in this widespread group. The form of the cranium and its superstructures indicate, possibly, a sexual dimorphism that is greater than that found in neanderthals or modern humans. It does seem, for instance, as though projecting brow ridges and retreating foreheads that are not good sexual markers in neanderthalers, also do not distinguish the sexes of *Homo erectus*. But facial sizes, sizes of mastoid processes, and occipital projections do seem to distinguish two groups of individual skulls (the sexes ?). At the same time, however, the uncertainty in sexing many of the individuals indicates a great amount of individual variation within one or possibly both sexes. In fact, it is rather likely that *Homo erectus* is not, itself, a single form but several different creatures each with its own overlap in sexual dimorphism.

In terms of body size and skeletal and muscular robusticity it is generally believed that the sexual dimorphism of *Homo erectus* was also probably somewhat greater than that in neanderthalers or modern humans. Indeed, Wolpoff (1980) thinks that sexual dimorphism in *Homo erectus* may have been as great as in australopithecines which, in turn, he thinks to have been very large indeed.

Again, how do these possibilities compare with sexual dimorphisms in the teeth? In all the time that *Homo erectus* has been known, a fairly large number of skulls and jaws with teeth have been found (Fig. 3:3). Blumenberg (Blumenberg and Lloyd, 1983; Blumenberg, 1985) in studies that actually try to assess the width of dispersion of the dimensions of the teeth in the different species (through study of the coefficient of variation, and using that coefficient as a measure of sexual dimorphism) believes that sexual dimorphism was high in *Homo erectus*. But the whole matter is controversial. Brace and Ryan (1980) see a marked decrease in sexual dimorphism between what they regard as the transition from higher sexual dimorphism in *Australopithecus* to lower sexual dimorphism in *Homo erectus*.

Materials are available providing data that we can study here to examine these ideas. The total number of teeth ranges from as few as 5 upper second incisors (a number far too small for the type of study presented in this book) to as many as 25 upper first molars (a number that is still small, yet large enough to allow distributions to be examined, Table 3:2). In fact, the samples are impossibly small (below 10) for all lower incisors and canines, and are marginal (between 10 and 20) for all upper teeth. It is only for lower premolars and molars that there are more than twenty specimens available at each tooth position. The final answer for sizes of these samples depends, of course, upon the amount of dimorphism. If dimorphism proves to be as great as in the canines of large apes, then even a sample as small as 10 may be capable of divulging information about sexual dimorphism. If sexual dimor-

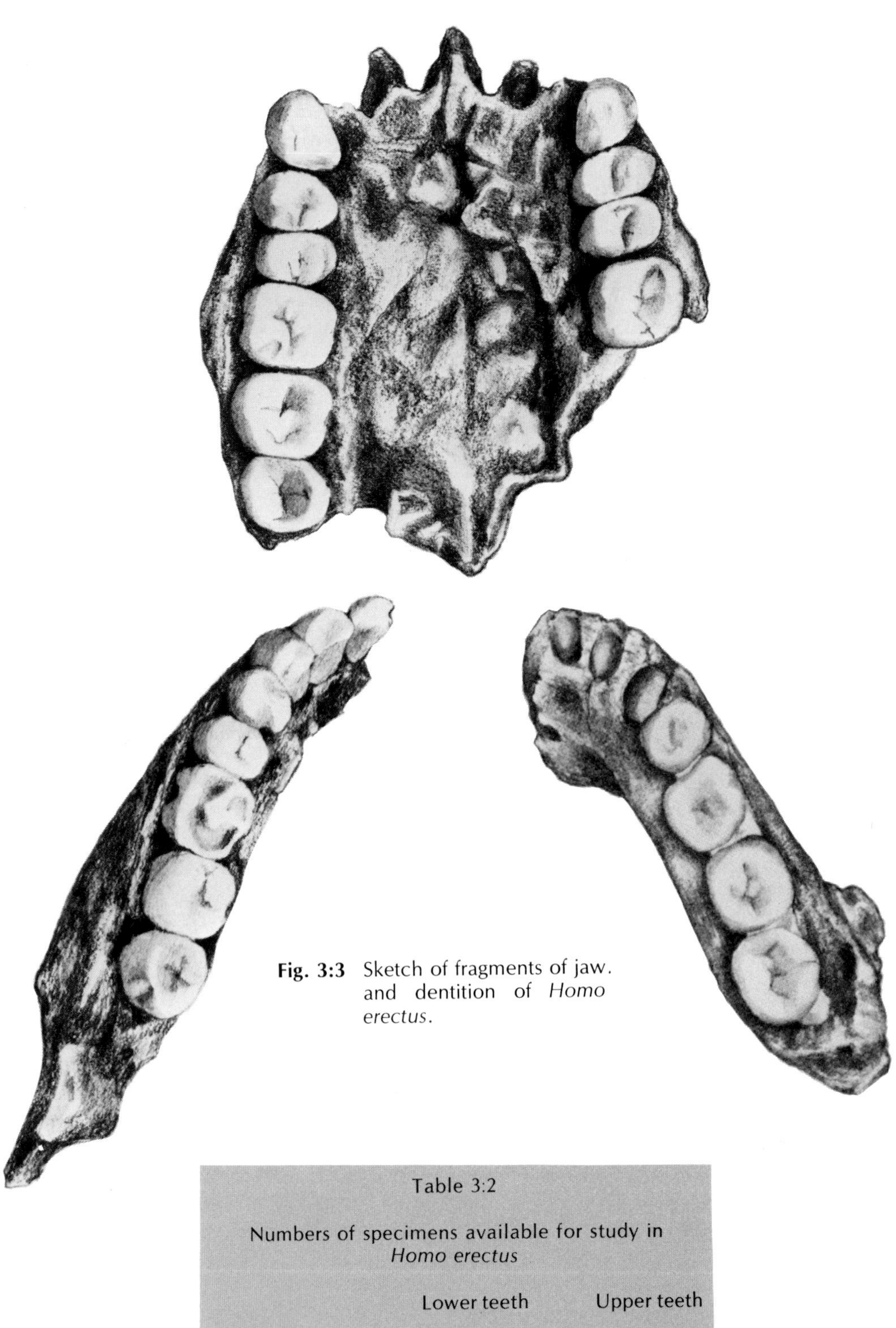

Fig. 3:3 Sketch of fragments of jaw. and dentition of *Homo erectus*.

Table 3:2

Numbers of specimens available for study in *Homo erectus*

	Lower teeth	Upper teeth
First incisor	10	6
Second incisor	11	5
Canine	15	9
Third premolar	24	10
Fourth premolar	20	14
First molar	25	13
Second molar	22	12
Third molar	20	15

phism turns out to be as small as in most modern human teeth, then samples of about 20 would be the minimum. All that we can do is investigate the data that we have.

New studies: individual dimensions of teeth

The same univariate statistical methods, including histograms and fitted normal curves, that are applied to extant humans and apes in Chapter 2 are here applied to these fossil data. The measures that are available are the same, lengths and breadths, as for the extant apes and humans studied in the last chapter. They are not, of course, the result of measurement by the same investigators. The data are from Billy and Vallois (1977), Blumenberg and Lloyd (1983), Coon (1967), Jacob (1973), Murrill (1975), Rightmire (1980), Sartono (1973), Sausse (1975), von Koenigswald (1968) and Wolpoff (1971); (Tables 3:1 and 3:2). Blumenberg and Lloyd (1983) and Wolpoff (1971) have provided most useful compendia and summaries. It is entirely possible that there are elements of the data that derive from inter-observer differences. However, it is rather likely that such differences are small and relatively random, as compared with the coherent results that stem from the large differences we found in making these analyses. Of course, we do not know which teeth are from females and which from males; our studies depend upon our being able to detect evidence of sexual dimorphism even when we do not know the sexes.

Canine sexual dimorphisms.

Homo sapiens neandertalensis: The breadths of both upper and lower canines demonstrate unequivocal and statistically significant bimodal distributions (Fig. 3:4). The lengths show less obvious dimorphism, though the length of the upper canine is still significantly bimodal and the length of the lower canine though unimodal is yet significantly different from normal.

The distances between the values that represent the peaks of the two bimodal distributions is more than 2 mm and this represents a slightly greater difference than in modern humans. This, together with the fact that three of the four canine measures are bimodal, whereas in modern humans only one such measure is clearly bimodal, suggests that in the canines at least, *Homo sapiens neandertalensis* actually shows somewhat greater sexual dimorphism than does modern *Homo sapiens*. This sexual dimorphism is still rather small, however, compared with that in any ape.

The approximately equal widths of each peak in those measures that have bimodal distributions suggest, again like modern humans (but also like orang-utans) that the element of sexual dimorphism, that seems to be measured by a difference between the dispersions of each measurement, is absent. This is, perhaps, an additional major difference of all of these species from the extant African apes.

And the fact that the two peaks of the distributions (in each dimension that is bimodal) show, approximately, the same numbers of specimens suggests that, like modern humans, the female/male ratio was 1:1.

Homo erectus: The numbers of upper and lower canines available for *Homo erectus* are so small that it is almost impossible to do any definitive statistical tests. Nevertheless it turns out that there are two 'groups' of *Homo erectus* so separate that, even with these small samples, they seem to be defined in bimodal distributions for the dimensions of the lower canine (Fig. 3:5). It is likely that this represents canine sexual dimorphism.

The distances between the values that represent the peaks of the two modes is more than 1.5 mm. In comparison with modern humans, given the small samples of erectus that we have, this could represent a greater degree of sexual dimorphism of means. This, together with the fact that two of the four canine measures are bimodal (even with these small samples, whereas in modern humans only one such measure is clearly bimodal even with samples of about 60) suggests that in the canines at least, *Homo erectus* actually shows somewhat greater sexual dimorphism than do modern humans. These data even suggest a degree of sexual dimorphism that is greater than in neanderthalers just examined.

The approximately equal width of each peak in those measures that have bimodal distributions suggests that, like modern humans and neanderthalers (but also like orang-utans), the element of sexual dimorphism that seems to be measured by a difference between the dispersions of each measurement for each sex, is absent. This is a major difference of humans and orang-utans from extant African apes.

The fact that each peak in the distributions that are bimodal shows an approximately equal number of specimens, suggests also that, like modern humans and neanderthalers the female to male ratio was 1:1.

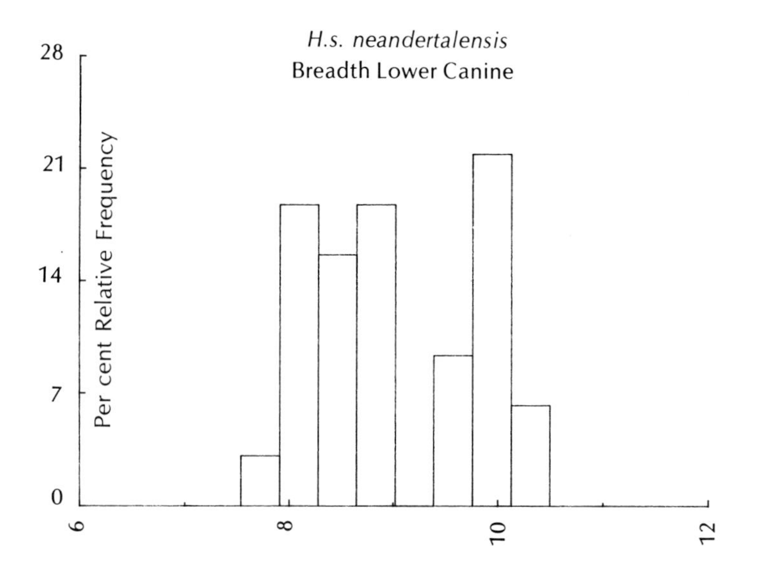

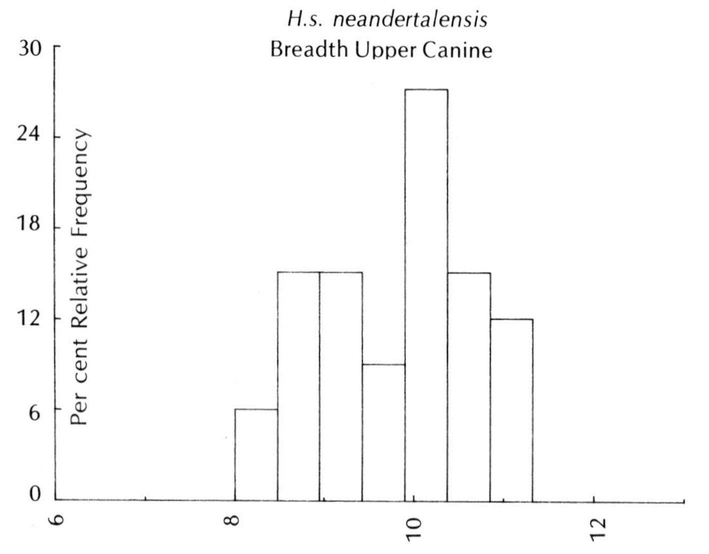

Fig. 3:4 Distribution for breadths of canines, sexes, of course, undefined, for *Homo sapiens neandertalensis*. Though the numbers of specimens are somewhat marginal, the fact of bimodality is clear. The size of the difference between modes is quite small suggesting small sexual dimorphism of means. There is no evidence of differences in variance in each sex (which would be suggested by skewed distributions). And there is a relative equality (equal area) to each peak that speaks of a 1:1 sex ratio. This is a picture quite similar to that in modern *Homo sapiens* (see Chapter Two).

Sexual dimorphisms in incisors and premolars.

Homo sapiens neandertalensis: The incisors and premolars also show a considerable number of statistically significant bimodal departures from normal distributions (Fig. 3:6) in *Homo sapiens neandertalensis*. This is most marked in the incisors, especially the breadth of the first lower incisor and the length of the second lower incisor, and in both length and breadth of the upper first incisor. Several of the premolar measures, however, have unimodal distributions that do not differ significantly from normal curves (Fig. 3:7).

The distances between the peaks in each bimodal dimension is 1 mm or greater. This, together with the fact that such differences exist in several more measures than is the case in modern humans, suggests that sexual dimorphism of means in these teeth in *Homo sapiens neandertalensis*, though still small compared with all apes, is somewhat greater than in modern humans. It is certainly evident in a different mix of tooth positions.

The equal dispersions of the two peaks in such bimodal distributions as exist again confirm the concept that, unlike the African apes, females and males show no sexual dimorphism in dispersions of measurements. They thus, again, resemble modern humans (and orang-utans).

Finally, the approximately equal sizes of the two peaks in the bimodal distributions suggest, also again, that there are equal numbers of females and males in the available samples. This is the same situation as in modern humans, and is in contradistinction to that in all extant great apes.

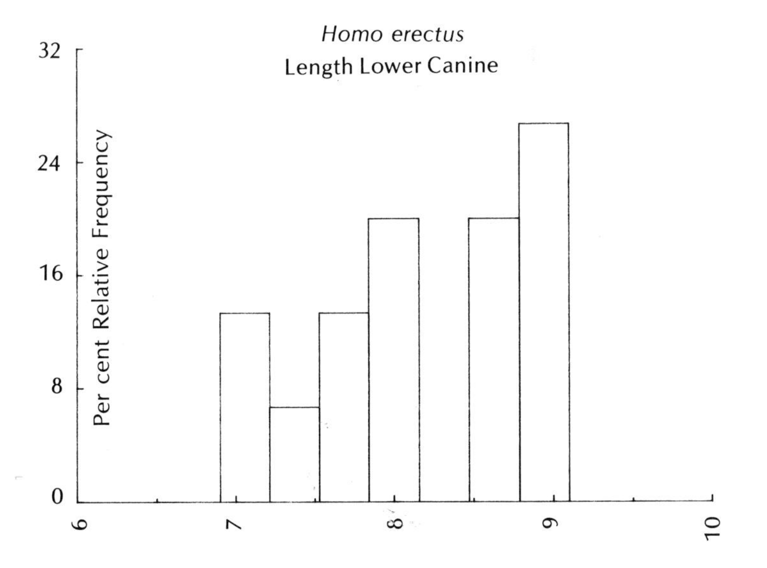

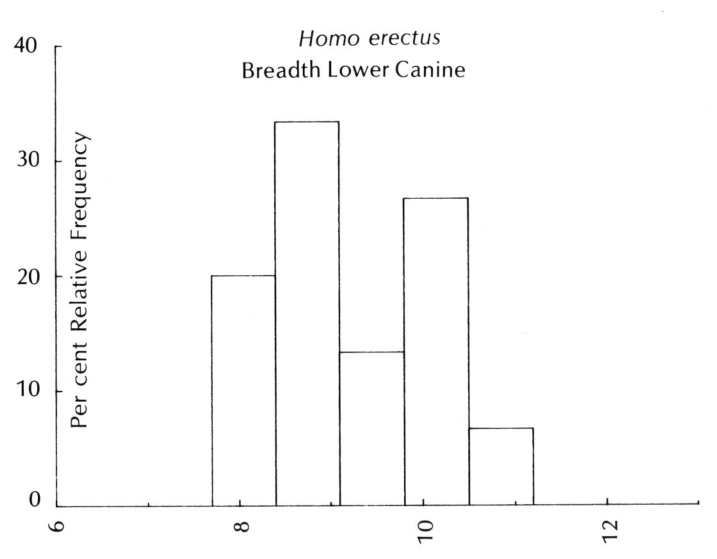

Fig. 3:5 Distribution for dimensions of canines, sexes, of course, undefined, for *Homo erectus*. The numbers of specimens are even smaller than for neanderthalers yet the fact of bimodality is clear. The size of the difference between the modes is quite small suggesting small sexual dimorphism of means. There is no evidence of differences in variance in each sex (which would be suggested by skewed distributions). And there is a relative equality (equal area) to each peak that speaks of a 1:1 sex ratio. This is a picture quite similar to that in modern *Homo sapiens* (see Chapter Two).

Homo erectus: There are too few lower incisor teeth for any significant information to be divulged for *Homo erectus* although it is of interest that the very small number of measures that we do have show, for the lengths of the lower incisors, two approximately equal clusterings. There are even fewer upper incisors yet one of their dimensions, the breadth of the upper first incisor, also shows two clear equal groups. There are slightly larger samples of premolars and three dimensions, the length of the upper fourth premolar, the length of the lower third premolar and the breadth of the lower fourth premolar show very distinct bimodal distributions. Of these three dimensions, samples are large enough for the last two that we can be certain that these bimodal distributions represent significant departures from normal distributions (Fig. 3:8).

The distances between the peaks in each of the significant bimodal dimensions is greater than 1 mm for the length of the lower third premolar and almost 2 mm for the breadth of the lower fourth premolar. This, together with the fact that, once again, such differences exist in several more measures than is the case in modern humans and neanderthalers, even though only smaller samples are available, suggests that sexual dimorphism, if this is what these bimodal distributions represent in *Homo erectus*, is actually considerably greater than in both modern humans and neanderthalers. It is

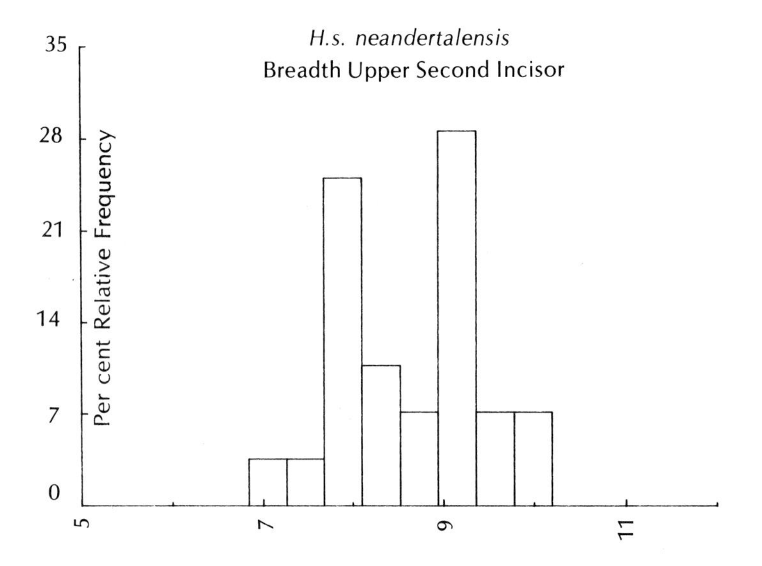

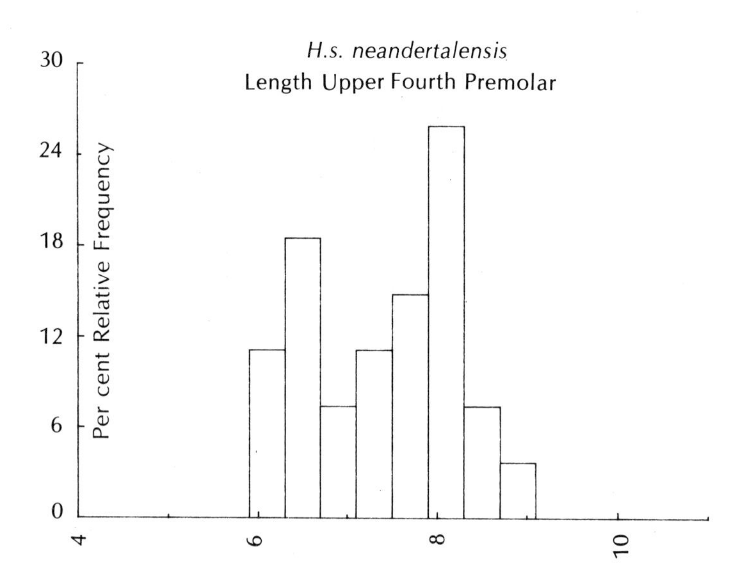

Fig. 3:6 Sample distributions for incisor and premolar dimensions, sexes, of course, undefined, for *Homo sapiens neandertalensis*. The numbers of specimens are here considerably larger so that the picture is clearer and statistically much sounder. The distribution shows the kind of bimodality that is entirely representative of that in *Homo sapiens sapiens* of the present day (see Chapter Two). The size of the difference between the modes is quite small suggesting small sexual dimorphism of means. There is no evidence of differences in variance in each sex (which would be suggested by skewed distributions). And there is a relative equality (equal area) to each peak that speaks of a 1:1 sex ratio.

still rather small, of course, compared with extant apes. It is again evident at a different mix of tooth positions than in those later groups.

The equal dispersions of the two peaks in those distributions that show bimodality suggest, again, that there is no sexual dimorphism of dispersion such as exists in the African great apes. In this regard, *Homo erectus* resembles other members of the genus *Homo* (but also, it should be noted, the orang-utan).

Finally the equal sizes of the two peaks in those distributions that exhibit bimodality suggest that, as in the case of neanderthalers and modern humans, there are equal numbers of each sex represented in the total sample.

Sexual dimorphisms in molars.

Homo sapiens neandertalensis: Only for the upper third molar is there any evidence of a bimodal distribution in *Homo sapiens neandertalensis*. In that tooth, however, the bimodality is unequivocal and large for both length and breadth (Fig. 3:9). The distances between the crests of each mode are between 1 and 2 mm and are quite large compared with that for the single measure, length of upper second molar, that is significantly bimodal in modern humans. Once again, therefore, such dimorphism as is present in the posterior teeth of neanderthalers is greater than that in modern humans, though much less than in apes.

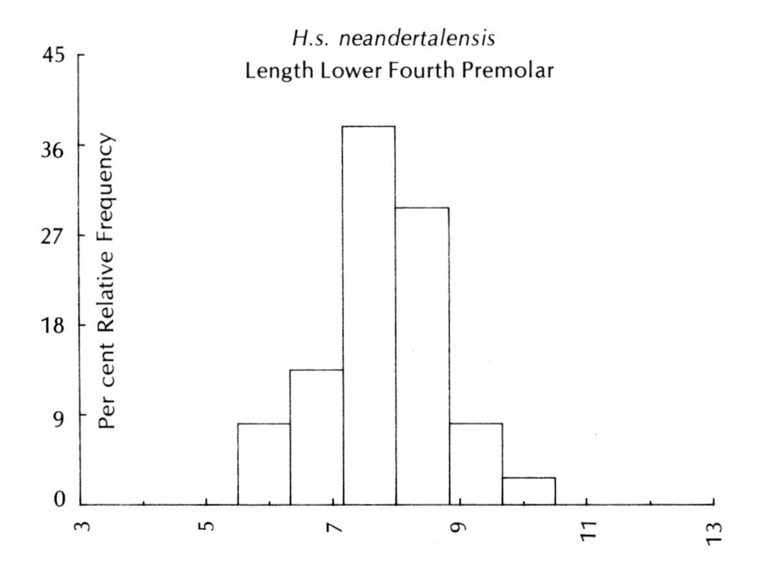

Fig. 3:7 A premolar dimension for *Homo sapiens neandertalensis* shows a unimodal distribution that fits the normal curve very well. This, too, is a picture that is frequently found in modern *Homo*.

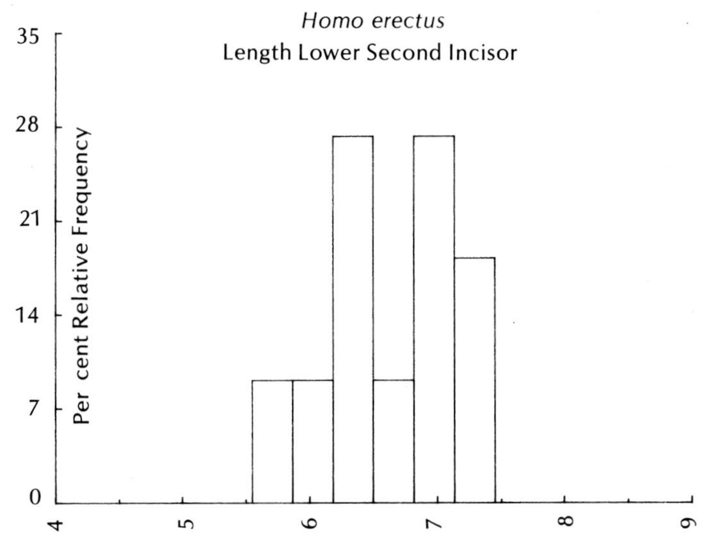

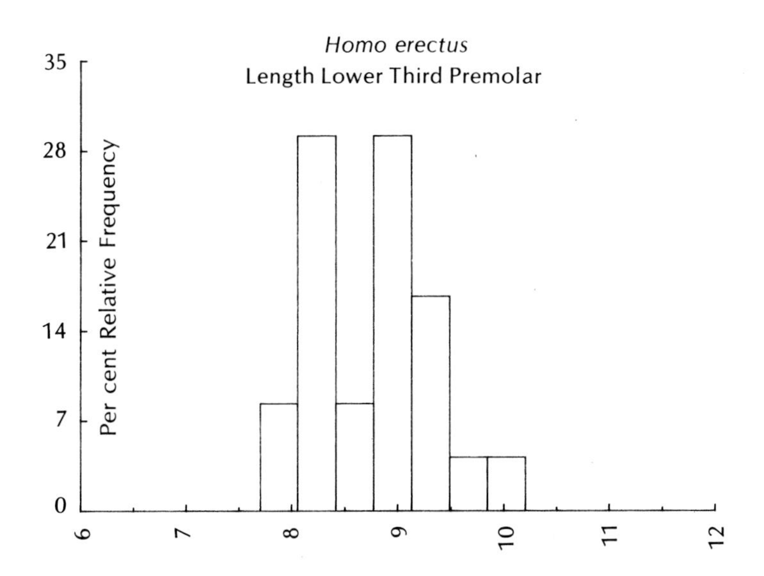

Fig. 3:8 Distributions for dimensions of incisors and premolars in *Homo erectus*, sexes undefined, show the same features as for those dimensions of modern *Homo sapiens sapiens* (see Chapter Two). They are indicative of small but significant sexual dimorphism of means, no sexual dimorphism of variance, and a 1:1 sex ratio. Again, the samples here are considerably larger than for the canine teeth.

The dispersions of each mode in each of the bimodal distributions appear to be similar for each sex as in modern humans and orang-utans, and in decided contradistinction to the African apes.

The numbers of specimens in each peak in the bimodal distributions suggest, as is also suggested by the data on the other teeth, that there is an approximately 1:1 female/male sex ratio in *Homo sapiens neandertalensis*.

Homo erectus: It is in the posterior dentition that samples of *Homo erectus* are largest. Although the lengths of the lower molars do not diverge statistically from a normal distribution, the breadths of the lower second and third molars are significantly and markedly bimodal and, though not statistically significant, the distribution for the breadth of the lower first molar shows, visually, a bimodal form. This is mirrored in both dimensions of the upper first molar but not in either of the upper second or third molars. It is thus evident that two subgroups can be easily defined by the posterior teeth, but by different teeth in each jaw (Fig. 3:10).

The distances between the peaks in the case of each bimodal distribution is 2 mm or even slightly more. It is therefore larger than that for any single measure in either neanderthalers or modern humans and it is found, despite small sample sizes, in a larger number of dimensions. This bimodality is greater in breadths than in lengths even in these incomplete samples and is further evidence, therefore, that we are dealing with bimodal distributions that genuinely represent sexual dimorphism. Once again, such dimorphism as may be present in the posterior teeth of *Homo erectus* is greater than that in neanderthalers and modern humans.

The equal widths of each peak in the bimodal distributions that exist imply that sexual dimorphism of dispersion is zero, resembling that in modern humans, neanderthalers and orang-utans, rather than extant African apes.

The equal sizes of the peaks in the distributions that are bimodal suggest that, as with the anterior teeth, there is a 1:1 female to male sex ratio as in modern humans and neanderthalers, and in contradistinction to the situation in all apes.

Summary: univariate sexual dimorphisms in fossil *Homo*

Both *Homo sapiens neandertalensis* and *Homo erectus* show increased sexual dimorphism in tooth size along the tooth row (and *Homo erectus*, perhaps, the greater) as compared with modern humans. This sexual dimorphism of means is, however, still rather small compared with that typical of apes. Both human fossil species show the same, zero, dispersion difference between males and females as in modern humans (and therefore they also share this feature with orang-utans alone among other living species). Finally both show evidence of a female/male ratio of approximately 1:1. This also coincides with the situation in modern humans but contrasts, of course, with that in any extant great ape.

More detailed visual inspections of plotted histograms (Fig. 3:4 through to 3:10) suggest that the number of males is actually somewhat greater (by some small amount) than the number of females in both *Homo sapiens neandertalensis* and *Homo erectus*. This difference is small and there is no statistical test that we can apply to corroborate it; but it is consistent in almost every dimension where a bimodal distribution can be discerned!

The patterns of differences along the tooth row in both fossil forms also differ quite markedly from that in modern humans (Tables 3:3, 3:4 and 3:5). As with all extant forms examined so far, sexual dimorphism is considerably greater in the lower jaw than in the upper.

Table 3:3

Pattern of differences in sexual dimorphism in neanderthalers along the tooth row.

Lower teeth	length	breadth
I_1	*B* =	B =
I_2	*B* =	N
C,	N	B = *
P_3	N	B =
P_4	N	N
M_1	N	N
M_2	N	N
M_3	S *	P *P
Upper teeth		
I^1	N	N
I^2	*B* = *	*B* = *
C′	*B* = *	*B* = *
P^3	*B* = *	B = *
P^4	*B* = *	*B* = *
M^1	N	N
M^2	B =	N
M^3	*B* = *	*B* = *

Notes: N = unimodal distribution; S = unimodal distribution skewed to the left; P = plateau-like distribution; B = bimodal distribution; "=" = approximately equal peaks in bimidal distribution; italics = slightly larger number of male specimens than females; * = statistically significantly different from normal.

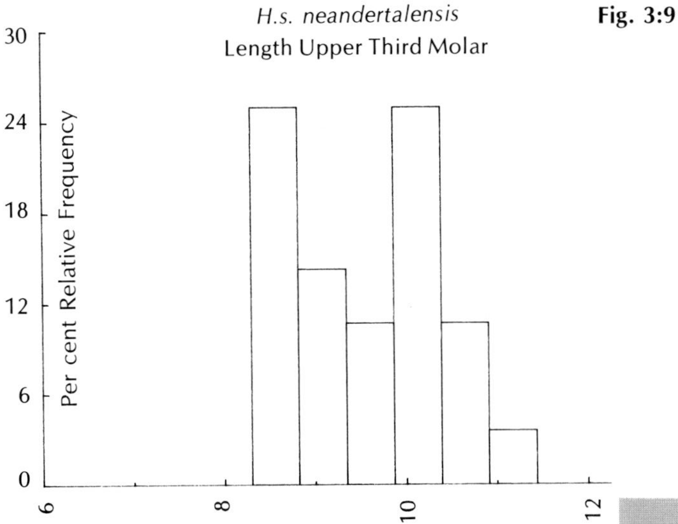

Fig. 3:9 The only distribution for a molar dimension, sexes, of course, undefined, that is available for *Homo sapiens neandertalensis*. The numbers of specimens are quite large so that the picture is clearer and statistically much sounder than for the canines. The distribution shows the kind of bimodality that is entirely representative of that in *Homo sapiens sapiens* of the present day (see Chapter Two). The size of the difference between the modes is quite small suggesting small sexual dimorphism of means. There is no evidence of differences in variance in each sex (which would be suggested be skewed distributions). And there is a relative equality (equal area) to each peak that speaks of a 1:1 sex ratio.

Table 3:4

Pattern of differences in sexual dimorphism in *Homo erectus* along the tooth row.

Lower teeth	length	breadth
I_1	*B*	N
I_2	*B* =	B
C,	B = *	Irregular
P_3	*B* = *	Irregular
P_4	N	B = *
M_1	N	*B* =
M_2	B	*B* = *
M_3	Irregular	B = *
Upper teeth		
I^1	—	—
I^2	—	—
C′	N	—
P^3	N	S *
P^4	Irregular	B
M^1	*B* = *	B = *
M^2	S *	S *
M^3	S *	B

Notes: N = unimodal distribution; S = unimodal distribution skewed to the left; P = plateau-like distribution; B = bimodal distribution; "=" = approximately equal peaks in bimodal distribution; italics = slightly larger number of male specimens than females; * = statistically significantly different from normal.

Table 3:5

Regional Differences in Sexual Dimorphism of Means: *Homo*

	I1	I2	C	P3	P4	M1	M2	M3
sapiens sapiens								
lower jaw	*		*				*	
upper jaw				*	*			
s. neandertalensis								
lower jaw	*	*	*	*				
upper jaw		*	*	*	*			*
erectus								
lower jaw		*	*	*	*		*	*
upper jaw				*		*		
habilis								
lower jaw				*	*	*	*	*
upper jaw				*		*		

Regional Differences in Sizes of Sex Peaks: *Homo*

	I1	I2	C	P3	P4	M1	M2	M3
sapiens sapiens								
lower jaw	=		=				=	
upper jaw				=	=			
s. neandertalensis								
lower jaw	=	=	=	=				
upper jaw		=	=	=	≠			=
erectus								
lower jaw		=	=	=	=	=	=	=
upper jaw				=		=		
habilis								
lower jaw				=	=	=	=	
upper jaw				=		=		

The case of a special australopithecine

In this study we have, in general, started our investigations by treating the fossil *Homo habilis* as though it were an australopithecine. We have done this because it would appear that, though the

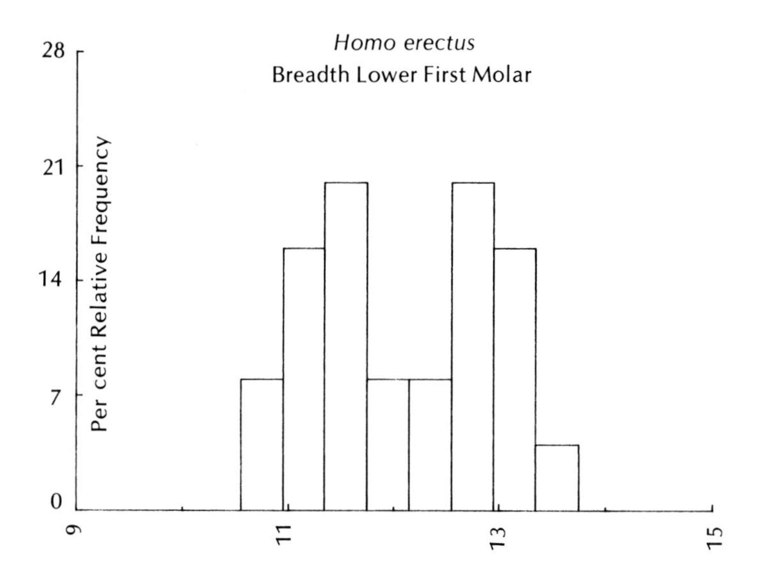

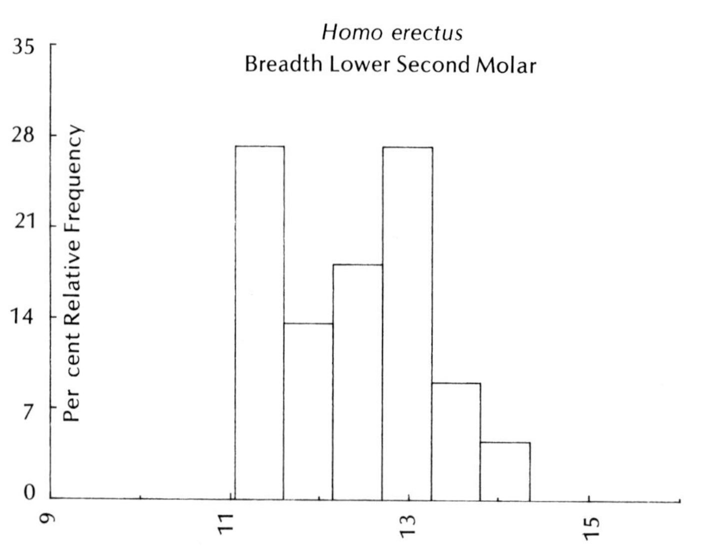

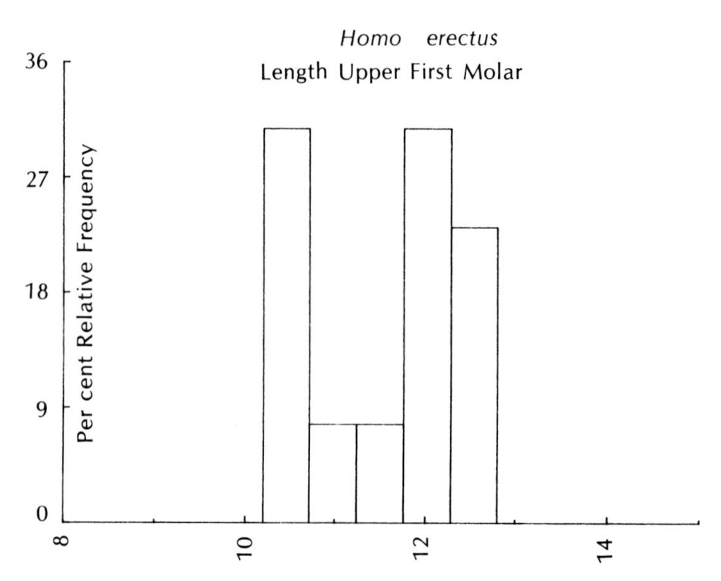

Fig. 3:10 Examples of distributions for molar dimensions, sexes, of course, undefined for *Homo erectus*. The numbers of specimens are quite large so that the picture is much clearer and statistically much sounder than for the canines. The distribution shows the kind of bimodality that is entirely representative of that in *Homo sapiens sapiens* of the present day (see Chapter Two). The size of the difference between the modes is quite small suggesting small sexual dimorphism of means (though a little larger than in modern humans). There is no evidence of differences in variance in each sex (which would be suggested by skewed distributions). And there is a relative equality (equal area) to each peak that speaks of a 1:1 sex ratio.

generic nomen *Homo* has been generally accepted for it, the current consensus is that it is morphologically, temporally and perhaps even phylogenetically closer to one or other of the various australopithecines than to *Homo*. However, in order to understand an additional and unanticipated aspect of our results, we must anticipate the findings of Chapter 5 on australopithecines.

As is more fully discussed there, we have discovered that *Homo habilis* has relatively small sexual dimorphism of means, small or zero differences in dispersions for each sex, and equal peaks in bimodal distributions that imply equal numbers of each sex in the samples that are available (e.g. Fig. 3:11 and Table 3:5). These are all features in which *Homo habilis* differs from other australopithecines. They are all features in which *Homo habilis* resembles every group so far labelled with the generic designation *Homo*.

Current views suggest that we should expect evidence of a separation between all *Homo* and all *Australopithecus* species. But two species have equivocal histories. *Australopithecus africanus* has been thought close enough to the human lineage by some to be designated *'Homo africanus'* (Robinson, 1973). And *Homo habilis* has been thought to be close enough to australopithecine lineages to be discussed as though it were *'Australopithecus habilis'*. It is interesting that assessment of individual dimensions of teeth giving information about sexual dimorphisms and sex ratios unequivocally supports the idea of *Homo habilis* but not *Homo africanus*. Clearly, for *Homo habilis*, close comparisons with the genus *Homo* are valid, for *Austrolopithecus africanus* they are not.

New studies: dimensions of teeth in combination

Of course, the foregoing data come from individual teeth from many different and incomplete fossils. It is not therefore possible to say, except to a limited degree, which particular tooth at one tooth locus is from the same individual as another tooth at another locus. For this reason it is not possible to carry out a multivariate statistical study which incorporates the data from the neanderthalers and erectus specimens in the same manner as for the humans and extant apes examined in the last chapter.

But it is possible to obtain the mean values for each dimension for each tooth. Each unimodal dimension provides only a single mean value for the species. And although the means for each sex might well be different from this mean, we have no basis for any better estimation of the mean of the sex subgroups. However, for those distributions that are bimodal, the modes for each of the peaks are measures of the mean values for the sex subgroups. This allows a better estimation of mean values for each sex subgroup. The entire suite of values for each sex are, then, a compound of measurements from these two procedures. These estimates can be interpolated into the previously determined multivariate statistical analyses in order to provide an estimate of how sexual differences are arranged in the fossil forms.

We should notice that this procedure underestimates sexual dimorphism rather than the reverse, because the values for each sex are the same in those dimensions which have unimodal distributions; distributions in which, undoubtedly, if we knew the sexes, we would still sometimes be able to discern a significant difference. However, underestimation is to be preferred to overestimation in this situation; it plays against our ideas rather than for them. Any differences that appear following such underestimations are the more likely to be real.

We should also notice that, again because of limitations in the original extant data, this procedure can only be done for the upper and lower jaws separately. And though this, too, loses us a considerable amount of discriminating power, given the limitations in the data from the original extant species, it is the best that we can do. It does at least allow us to see if sexual dimorphism in the upper jaw is the same phenomenon as that in the lower jaw.

The goal of the multivariate part of this investigation, is to expand the univariate studies of the data from extant hominoids using a particular multivariate statistical approach: canonical variates analysis. Several questions are addressed. What is the multivariate nature of sexual dimorphism in the dentition of fossil humans? What patterns are apparent in multivariate analyses of neanderthalers and erectus that have not appeared in the univariate studies? Which of the extant species do neanderthalers and erectus most resemble? What, if any, are the implications of the results for primate and more specifically human phylogeny?

Materials and Methods: The data on extant

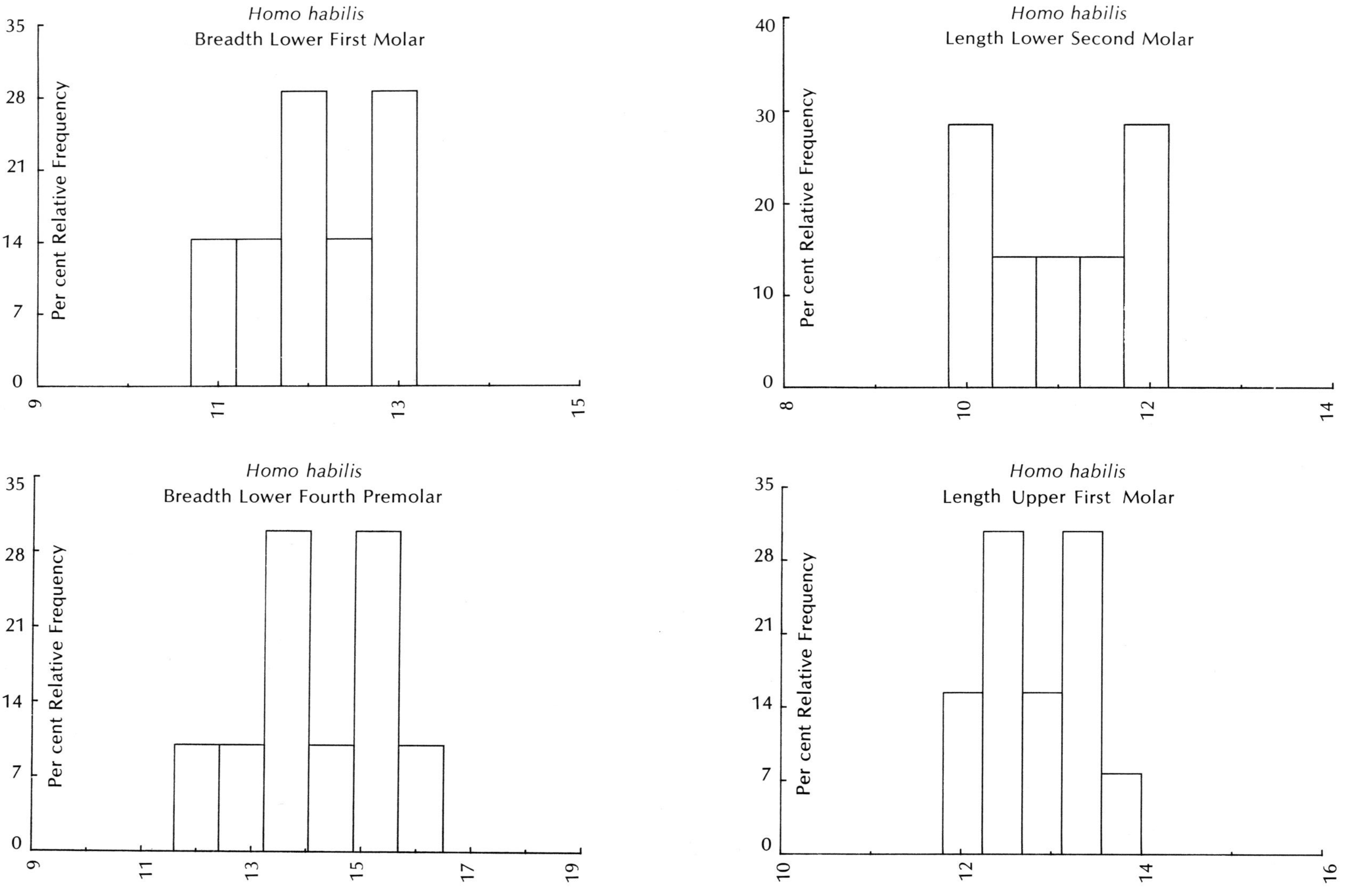

Fig. 3:11 Examples of distributions for dimensions of teeth, sexes, of course, undefined for *Homo habilis*. The numbers of specimens are marginal. However, the same picture obtains for each distribution. They demonstrate the same kind of bimodality that is entirely representative of that in various other modern and fossil *Homo*. The size of the difference between the modes is small suggesting small sexual dimorphism of means. There is no evidence of differences in variance in each sex (which would be suggested by skewed distributions). And there are relative equalities (equal areas) to each peak in the bimodal distributions that speak of 1:1 sex ratio.

primates used in this study are outlined in the last chapter. The fossil data used in this study are mean lengths and breadths estimated as just described (Tables 3.6 and 3.7) from those measurements of neanderthal and erectus specimens provided in various publications (e.g. Wolpoff, 1971; Blumenberg and Lloyd, 1983) and others previously cited.

There are 555 *Homo sapiens neandertalensis* teeth suitable for study in this way (adult, unbroken, undistorted and not too badly worn). They include representatives from every tooth position in both maxilla and mandible, with from 17 to 53 teeth per locus. There are considerably fewer, 232 teeth, including representative teeth from every tooth position in each jaw and with from 5 to 25 teeth per locus, that are similarly suitable for study in *Homo erectus*.

Two separate multivariate analyses were performed on the data coinciding with the same studies of extant forms alone. For the extant primates, mandibular and maxillary data came from seven groups: *Gorilla* females, *Gorilla* males, *Pan* females, *Pan* males, *Pongo* females, *Pongo* males, and *Homo*, sex unknown. In each case, therefore, six canonical axes were generated.

The values for females and males in the two fossil groups and in modern humans (using new data culled from the records of Orthodontist, Dr Clifford Willcox) were then interpolated into the canonical variates analyses previously made on the extant species, using the previously generated eigenvectors. This allows us to examine the relative positions of the fossils against not only the extant forms initially involved in the analyses but also sex subgroups for humans (not known in the group of data for humans used in the initial analysis).

Table 3:6

Mean lengths and breadths of teeth for sex subgroups of neanderthalers

Lower teeth	Length		Breadth	
	f	m	f	m
I_1	5.0	6.2	7.0	8.0
I_2	6.2	7.5	8.1	8.1
$C_,$	7.8	7.8	8.5	10.0
P_3	7.8	7.8	9.0	9.0
P_4	7.6	7.6	9.1	9.1
M_1	11.7	11.7	11.1	11.1
M_2	11.8	11.8	11.2	11.2
M_3	11.6	11.6	10.4	10.4
Upper teeth				
I^1	9.9	9.9	8.6	8.6
I^2	7.2	8.4	8.0	9.2
C'	8.2	9.0	9.0	10.3
P^3	7.3	8.2	10.5	11.0
P^4	6.6	8.0	9.8	10.8
M^1	11.3	11.3	12.0	12.0
M^2	10.0	11.3	12.5	12.5
M^3	8.8	10.1	10.8	12.1

Table 3:7

Mean lengths and breadths of teeth for sex subgroups of *Homo erectus*

Lower teeth	Length		Breadth	
	f	m	f	m
I_1	6.1	6.7	6.5	6.5
I_2	6.3	7.2	7.1	7.6
$C_,$	7.8	8.8	9.3	9.3
P_3	8.1	9.2	9.8	9.8
P_4	8.8	8.8	9.1	11.7
M_1	12.7	12.7	11.5	13.0
M_2	12.9	14.0	11.3	13.0
M_3	11.4	11.4	11.0	12.5
Upper teeth				
I^1	9.6	9.6	7.9	7.9
I^2	7.8	7.8	8.6	8.6
C'	9.5	9.5	10.3	10.3
P^3	8.2	8.2	11.4	11.4
P^4	7.9	7.9	11.2	12.4
M^1	10.5	12.2	12.0	13.8
M^2	11.3	11.3	13.0	13.0
M^3	9.9	9.9	12.0	13.5

Results: canonical variates analyses: Figures 3:12 and 3:13 are plots of canonical variates means for the seven extant groups described in Chapter 2 for the mandibular analysis. The fossils are, additionally, interpolated into these diagrams.

Homo sapiens neandertalensis: For the first three axes in the mandibular analysis the means of neanderthaler putative females and males are intermediate between *Homo* and *Pan* (Figs. 3:12 and 3:13). The direction of difference between female and male neanderthalers is similar to that for *Homo* and markedly different from any ape. This is mirrored in the maxillary analysis. However, the separations achieved in the mandibular analysis are considerably greater than in the maxillary study, and this reflects the finding from the univariate studies, that sexual dimorphism seems to be greater in lower as compared with upper jaws.

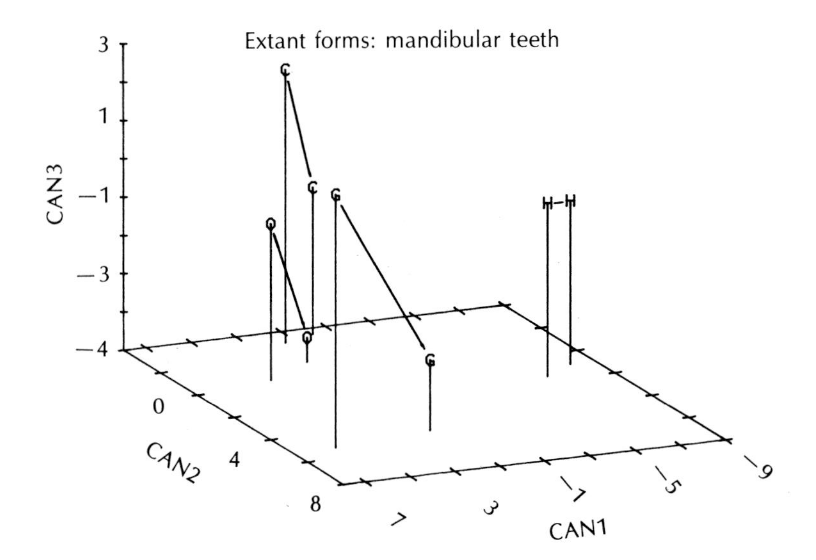

Fig. 3:12 This is the three-dimensional plot of the extant species for the canonical variates analysis of the extant forms. For this plot H-H = females and males of modern humans, C-C of chimpanzees, O-O of orang-utans and G-G of gorillas. The left hand symbol in each case represents the male. Sexual dimorphism in humans is expressed solely as a difference in axes one and two. Sexual dimorphism in the great apes is additionally represented by differences in axis three so that the male is placed higher on the graph than the female.

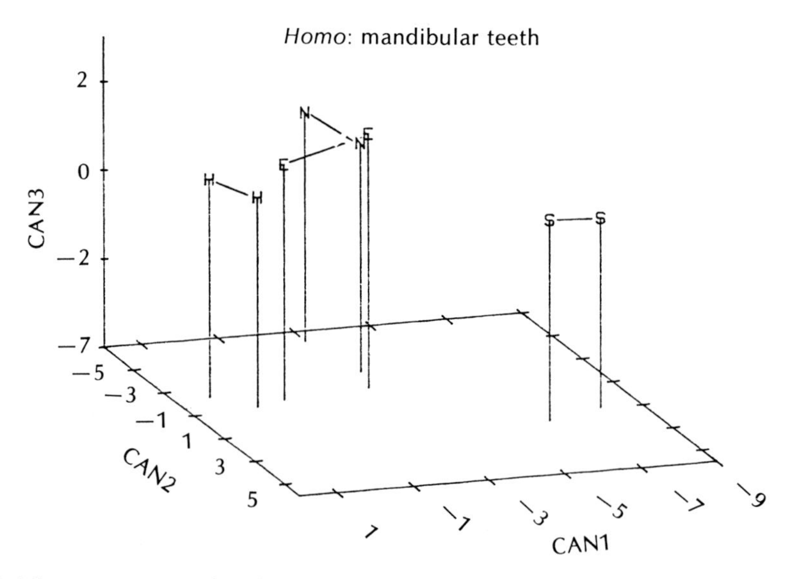

Fig. 3:13 This is a three-dimensional plot, drawn from the same perspective but covering a more restricted part of the scale, for extant humans and the various *Homo* fossils. In this plot S-S = females (right) and males of modern humans, and the intercalation of the various *Homo* fossils, N-N being neanderthalers, E-E erectus, and H-H habilis, is indicated. The females are also on the right of the plot in each case. It can be seen that, though the fossil *Homo* lie somewhat towards the chimpanzee and orang-utan (see Fig. 3:12) the nature of the sexual difference expressed multivariately is such that it is entirely within the first two axes as is the case for modern humans. In this sense then, sexual dimorphism in all these *Homo* species differs absolutely from that in modern apes.

For both maxilla and mandible there is a somewhat greater overall sexual dimorphism in neanderthalers than in *Homo sapiens*. However, neanderthalers have much less dimorphism than in any extant ape, even *Pan*, that least dimorphic of the living apes.

Homo erectus: Figures 3:12 and 3:13 also show the interpolation of *Homo erectus* in the mandibular analysis. For both maxillary and mandibular analyses *Homo erectus* putative females and males are between *Pan* and *Homo*. The direction of difference between female and male *Homo erectus* is similar to that between females and males for *Homo sapiens*. It is, therefore, completely different from any ape including *Pan* but also somewhat different from neanderthalers.

Again, for both maxilla and mandible there is a greater overall sexual dimorphism in *Homo erectus* than in *Homo sapiens* but a less overall sexual dimorphism than for any extant ape, even *Pan*.

In the mandibular analysis, which provides the

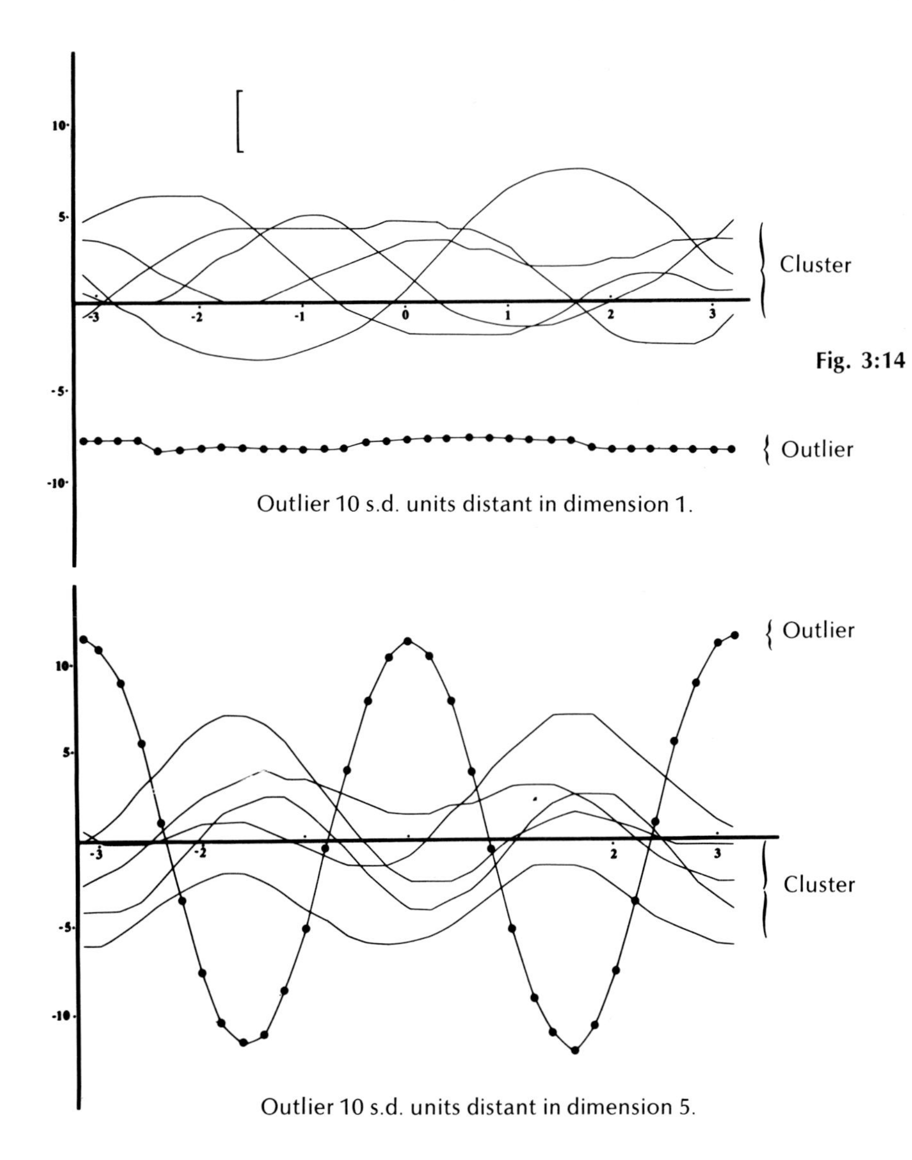

Fig. 3:14 This study shows high-dimensional displays for groups that are outliers by 10 standard deviation units whether in the first axis (upper diagram) or the fifth axis (lower diagram). That they are both outliers is clear whatever the axis in which they are distinct.

greatest discrimination presumably because sexual dimorphism is greater in lower than upper jaws (as in the univariate studies), the nature of the difference between the sexes is similar in modern humans and *Homo erectus*. The differences in the apes are also all similar to one another as judged by the nature of the separations between the sexes. The difference between male and female neanderthalers is considerably different from that in the other humans (living or fossil) and is not mirrored in any extant form.

High-dimensional plots: As was the case with the extant genera, high-dimensional plots were generated in order to include information in higher axes. The importance of this procedure is twofold. First, as for the extant species, it allows us to view multi-dimensional information in a way denied us by the more usual two or three-dimensional plots of individual canonical axes. Second, however, because the fossils are interpolated into the analyses, using statistics to which their variances and covariances have not contributed, even although the higher axes may contain little or no significant information for the extant forms, it is not at all unlikely that big, important, and statistically significant information may be parlayed into these axes for the interpolated (fossil) groups. This matter has been explored in Oxnard (1972a, 1975a, 1978a, 1983a, and 1984). High dimensional analyses allow ready recognition of this situation (Fig. 3:14).

Figure 3:15 shows the high-dimensional plot of the mandibular analyses for putative female and male fossil means. Total sexual dimorphism

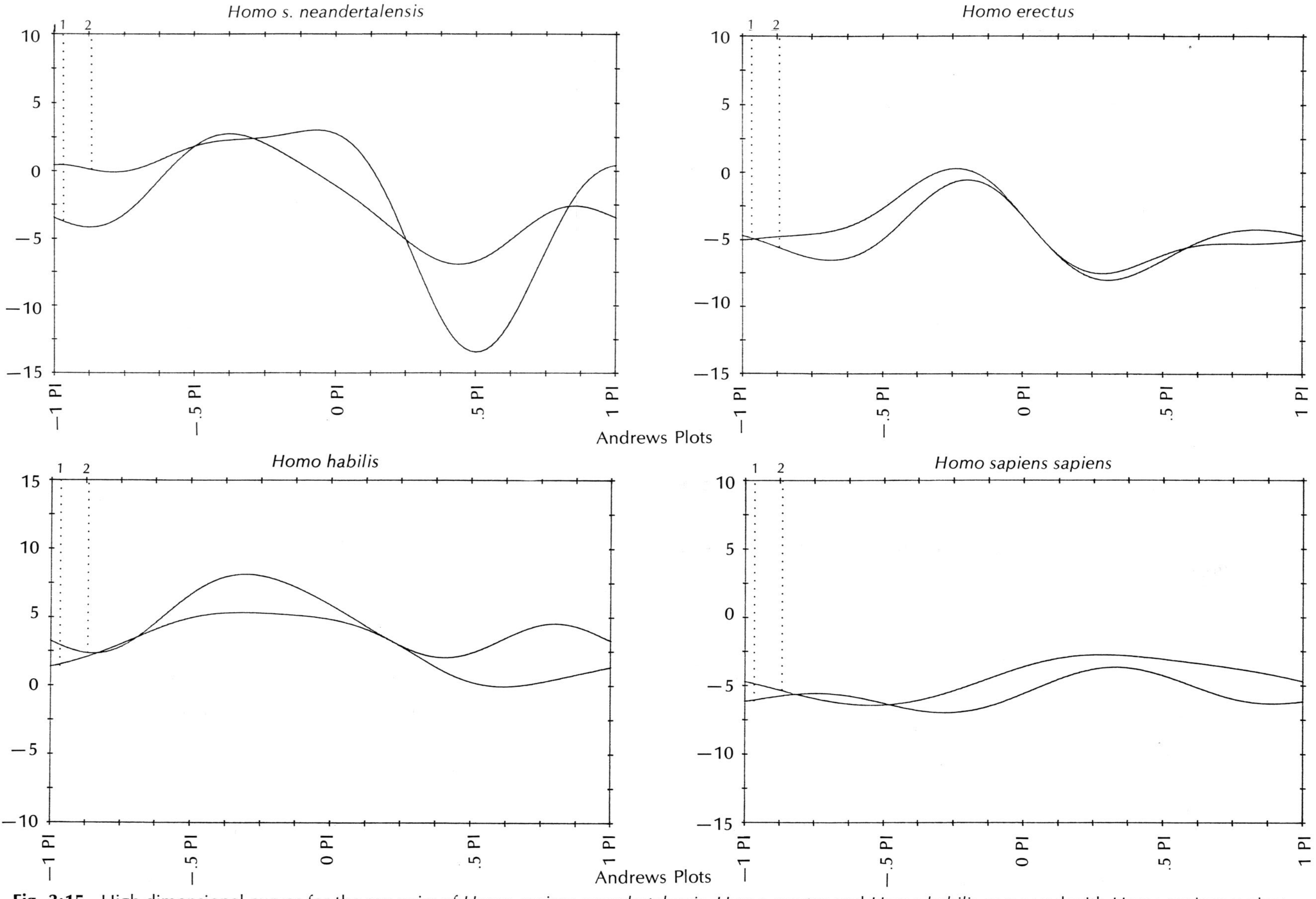

Fig. 3:15 High-dimensional curves for the sex pairs of *Homo sapiens neandertalensis*, *Homo erectus* and *Homo habilis* compared with *Homo sapiens sapiens*. Male curves (= 2) are highest in the plot in each case. The differences between the sex pairs is small compared with the apes. All genera occupy a closely similar part of the graph.

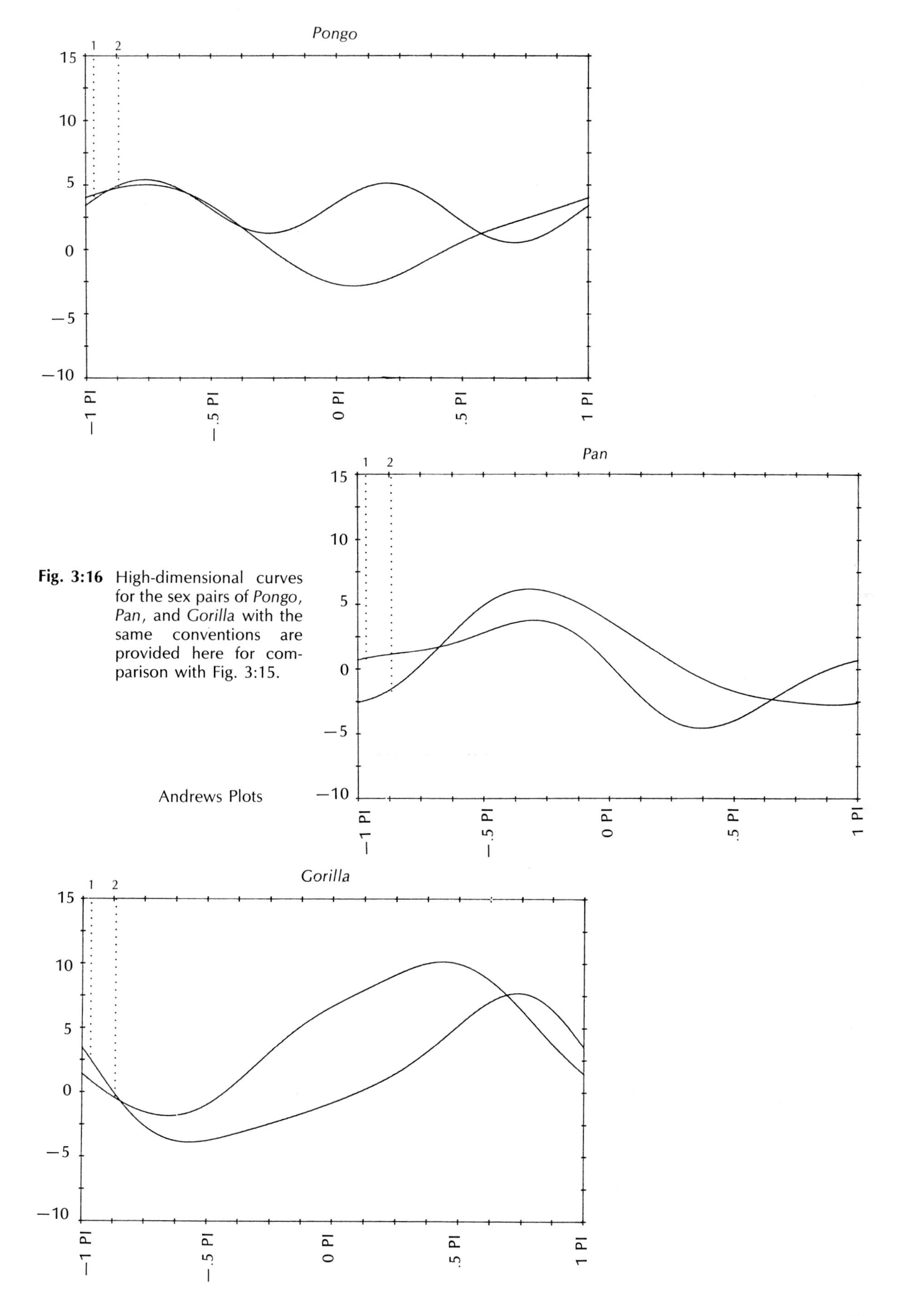

Fig. 3:16 High-dimensional curves for the sex pairs of *Pongo*, *Pan*, and *Gorilla* with the same conventions are provided here for comparison with Fig. 3:15.

Andrews Plots

(represented by the area between the high dimensional plots and by how different the curvatures of the plots are one from another) is slightly more in both neanderthalers and erectus in the maxilla than in modern humans.

Comparison of this figure with the high dimensional plots for the apes (Figures 3:16) shows that both are, in fact, completely different from them.

***Homo habilis* again**: At this point, in order to understand an additional aspect of the results, we must once more anticipate the findings of Chapter 5. Just as in the individual dimensions of the teeth, *Homo habilis* displays all the features of the genus *Homo*, so, too, in its multivariate arrangements, *Homo habilis* coincides more with the genus *Homo*. (Figures 3:13 and 3:15). All this information shows three particularly fascinating facts.

One is that the females for each fossil species of *Homo* are much more similar one to another and more similar to modern humans (Fig. 3:11) than to the next nearest extant form *Pan*. The males are more disparate in different ways in each subgroup from the females (see also Fig. 3:17).

The second is that the multivariate form of the sexual dimorphism — the relationship between

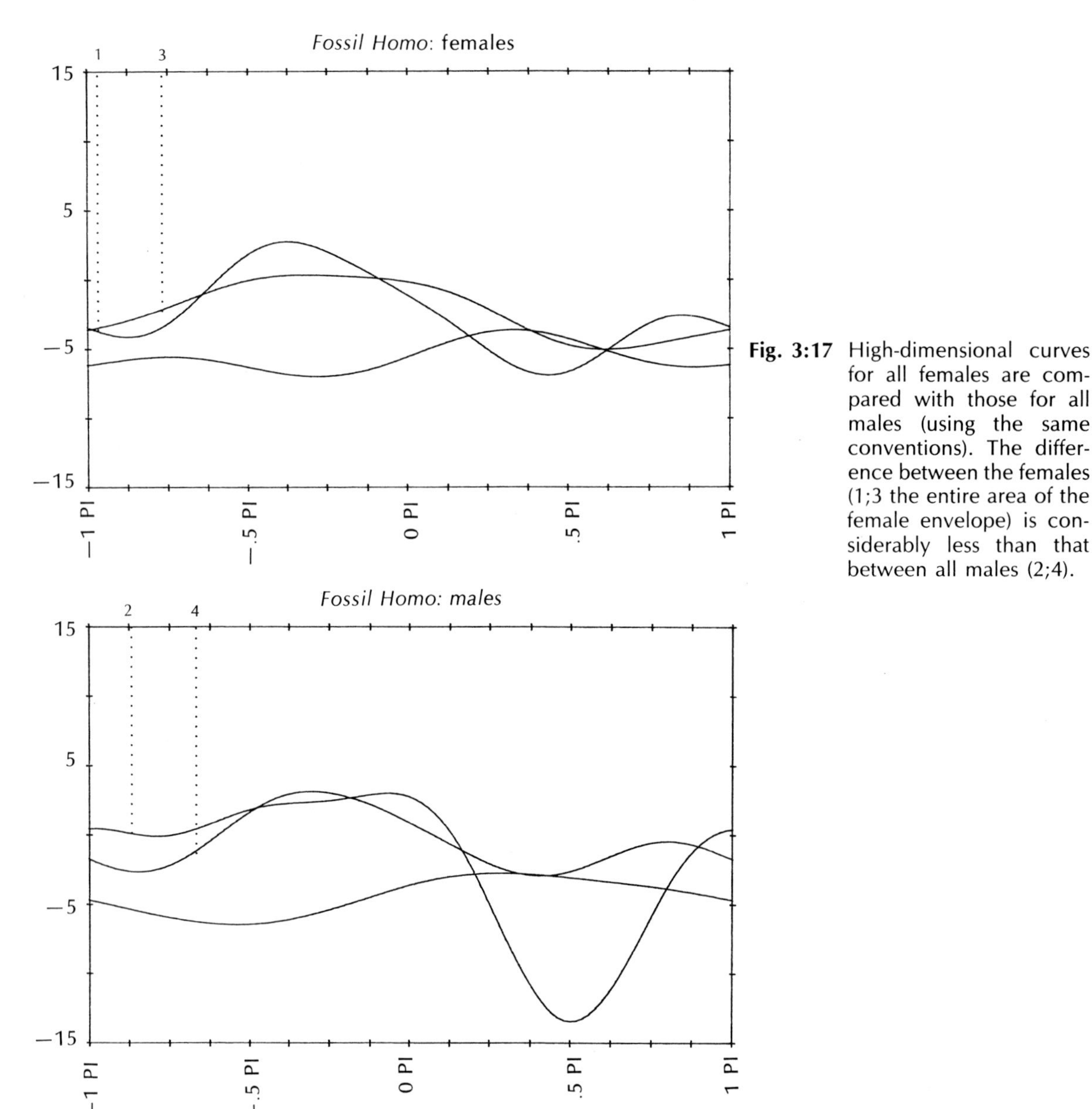

Fig. 3:17 High-dimensional curves for all females are compared with those for all males (using the same conventions). The difference between the females (1;3 the entire area of the female envelope) is considerably less than that between all males (2;4).

Andrews Plots

female and male for each group in the plot – is similar in all members of the genus *Homo* (though least so for the aberrant group *H. s. neandertalensis* (Fig. 3:13). It is quite different from that in the apes. And it is different also from those in the various other australopithecines, although it is true that this is clearest when data for australopithecines are also examined (hence the anticipation of Chapter 5).

The third is that all three species link with *Homo sapiens sapiens* in ways that make sense in the light of the dating information. The most recent form, *H. s. neandertalensis*, is closest to modern humans, though neanderthalers show evidences of being somewhat aberrant in the nature of the offset separation of males. The intermediate *Homo erectus* lies intermediately and has a difference between the sexes that parallels that of *Homo s. s.* The earliest form, *Homo habilis*, lies furthest away towards the genus *Pan*. But even *Homo habilis*, though a little closer to *Pan*, displays a direction of sexual difference that links it with the other human species rather than with the markedly different African ape.

Conclusions Sexual dimorphisms in fossil humans: Univariate analyses indicate clearly that all three fossil genera of the genus *Homo* have small (though gradually increasing) sexual dimorphism of means, as compared with the small dimorphism of means in modern humans, the rather large dimorphism of means in extant *Pan*, and the very large dimorphism in the other great apes.

These analyses also show – to the degree that this can be estimated – that sexual dimorphism of dispersion is negligible in these fossil species. Again this resembles the situation in modern humans. It is quite different from that in the African great apes (in which it is *Pan* that has the greatest dimorphism of dispersion). It does mirror the zero sexual dimorphism of dispersion that exists in *Pongo*.

Finally, these analyses show that in each of the many samples of specimens available for each tooth locus in each fossil species, the numbers of putative females and males are in a ratio of 1:1. This is a ratio that is found among extant large hominoids only in modern humans. In modern humans it is related to pair bonding and the existence of nuclear family social sexual structures.

Multivariate analyses show that the three fossil groups lie between *Homo sapiens sapiens* and *Pan* with the most recent form, *Homo s. neandertalensis* being closest to modern humans and the oldest form, *Homo habilis*, furthest away.

These analyses further show the closer relationships among the females of each of the species. It is as though the males represented wider and different departures from the stem female form in each case. It is, nevertheless, in the somewhat aberrant neanderthalers that this multivariate expression of sexual dimorphism is different from that for the other members of the genus *Homo*. The multivariate sexual dimorphism in the closest ape genus, *Pan*, indeed in all the extant apes, is quite different and clearly unrelated.

We must recognize, at this point, that there is a fundamental difference between the living and fossil forms in these analyses. The multivariate analyses for all the extant forms contain, of course, all the information provided in their prior univariate analyses, together with the addition of the information about the interactions between the individual variables. But this is not the case for the fossils. For the fossils, it is only the estimated mean values that are interpolated. Therefore for the fossils, all the information that comes from studying the distributions in a univariate manner is additional to that provided by the multivariate interpolations. This markedly strengthens all the arguments about the fossils. The multivariate results for the fossils are information that we can add to their univariate results.

The fact that both the univariate and multivariate analyses, for the fossils, confirm that sexual dimorphism is different in mandibles as compared with maxillae, is further evidence of the complexity of sexual dimorphism.

All the foregoing information has marked implications for possible evolutionary links of these fossil specimens with the extant species. It seems immediately obvious that their relationships (including the more problematical *Homo habilis*) are with modern humans. However, the full impact of this cannot be understood until the investigations of the fossils in other chapters are included.

Summary: This review of sexual dimorphism in the dental dimensions of *Homo sapiens neandertalensis* and *Homo erectus* suggests to us that within at least the last two million years, sexual dimorphism has not been excessively large. It does appear to have been larger than in modern humans, but it does not approach that of any extant ape.

More than that we learn that, though there are different patterns of sexual dimorphism in modern humans than in apes, as we discovered in the last chapter, the features of dental sexual dimorphism in neanderthalers and *Homo erectus* are similar to those in modern humans. Both these fossil forms have similar sexual dimorphisms of means, of variances and of univariate patterns, similar multivariate positions and multivariate sexual dimorphisms, and, perhaps most significantly of all, sex ratios in each that are approximately one-to-one. In not one of these features do any of these fossils resemble the African apes. And in only one feature, equal dispersions between the sexes (as far as can be judged in a situation where one cannot provide a significance test for this characteristic) do they show a resemblance to orang-utans.

Finally, the rather older fossil, *Homo habilis*, that is often said to be linked with the australopithecines, likewise shows univariate and multivariate features and one-to-one sex ratios that place it with fossil humans. This may well indicate somewhat close relationships with these species. However, this finding awaits study of equivalent features of australopithecines. But if it can be confirmed, it would imply that sexual dimorphism of a human type had been around for even longer than the two million years indicated by the above *Homo erectus* findings. It would place this phenomenon as being perhaps three million years old or even older.

CHAPTER 4

Eight to Eighteen Million Years Ago: Sexual Dimorphisms in Early Relatives

Abstract: We first review briefly the current consensus about the ramapithecines. This is the idea that they are merely ape ancestors, probably more closely related to orang-utans than to anything else alive today. What had earlier been assessed as two separate species, are currently believed to be merely the males and females of an extremely dimorphic 'ape'.

We next examine information about new ramapithecines from China, especially the fact that there have been found over one thousand teeth for this group. Such data clearly allow us to prosecute studies on these fossils in a way usually denied to studies of primate fossils: that is, in a population mode.

Dental dimensions, lengths and breadths, are investigated, separately, for each tooth position: canines, incisors, premolars and molars. When the data are grouped as ramapithecines, a single species or species group, then the results make it very obvious that if ramapithecines truly form only a single cluster of 'apes', their sexual dimorphism must have been enormously greater than anything else known from the entire span of the living or fossil primates.

In contrast, however, examination of each 'sex' of each of these 'apes' demonstrates a new phenomenon. Each 'sex' has, itself, evidence of two subgroups within it!

It is evident that the Chinese ramapithecines actually comprise two species or species groups, each showing evidence of two subgroups. Special features of these two subgroups (for example, that they are more obvious in the examination of breadth dimensions than of lengths) imply that it is not inappropriate for us to designate them the two sexes of each group.

The evidences of this sexual dimorphism in each ramapithecine, which at this point we designate: *Ramapithecus* and *Sivapithecus*, are then studied separately. Their sexual dimorphism is clearly complex and is not only different in each, but also shows differences from, and similarities to, the extant species already studied in Chapter 2 and the human fossils of Chapter 3.

This is further evident when the dimensions of the teeth are examined altogether using multivariate morphometrics. These studies allow additional comparisons with the extant apes and extant and fossil humans. The findings have major implications for human and ape evolution, although for a full discussion, we must also await the results of examining other fossils (such as the australopithecines) in later chapters.

Ramapithecines, the current consensus: ape ancestors?

A fragment of upper jaw described by Pilgrim in 1910 and 1915 was the first ramapithecine to be recognized as such. It was described by G. Edward Lewis (1934) as human-like. Following this, remains of similar fossils have been recovered in Africa, Europe and Asia (e.g. Leakey, 1962; Simons, 1964; Von Koenigswald, 1972, Simons, 1974; Kretzoi, 1975; Andrews and Tobien. 1977; Simons, 1978). The processes of discovery of these fragments goes on even today, Walker and Leakey (1984) having recently found further fragments in Africa. These fragments are mostly limited to small pieces of jaw bones and isolated teeth, and all are believed to be between approximately ten and eighteen million years old. They have been assumed to represent many different groups at different times. At first they were given many different names representing Hindu deities (e.g. *Bramapithecus*, *Ramapithecus* and *Sivapithecus*) or geographic sites of discovery (e.g. *Kenyapithecus*, *Graecopithecus* and *Rudapithecus*).

In a major revision of the entire group of early fossil apes in 1965, Simons and Pilbeam thought they had recognized, among the earlier fragments, two major subgroups of species, *Ramapithecus* and *Sivapithecus*. Since then the number of individual finds has gradually increased so that, by 1977, as many as two dozen fragments of jaws and teeth had been found. At that time the view that they could be assigned to two species groups (*Ramapithecus* and *Sivapithecus*) was reaffirmed, and the concept that one of them (*Ramapithecus*) was ancestral to hominids was put forward (e.g. Simons, 1977).

Even more recently, however, examination of new fossil finds and acceptance of new biomolecular evidence have meant that the specific affinities of the entire assemblage of these fossils could be reassessed. Some workers continue to believe that hidden within this assortment are creatures ancestral or close to the human lineage (Kay, 1981, 1982a,b; Wolpoff, 1982). Other investigators believe that the relationships are not clearly understood (see discussants in Wolpoff, 1982).

Yet other investigators, however, have re-evaluated the old evidence and provided new information, and as a result they now suggest that this entire cluster of fossils comprises only a single group. It is a single group, moreover, that they aver is more closely related to apes, and in particular, to a specific ape (the orang-utan). Relationships with humans are denied (e.g. Smith and Pilbeam, 1980; Lipson and Pilbeam, 1982; Andrews and Cronin, 1982; Todd, 1982). This is the picture that is current today.

There has been increased 'lumping' over the years, from many genera at the beginning, through two main species groups in the 1960's and 1970's, to now, only a single assemblage. This relates, at least in part, to the increased numbers of specimens available for study and the lack of quantitative information about them. With only a few specimens and only qualitative data it is relatively easy to support the notion of many separate types. With the apparently more continuous anatomical variation that appears when more specimens are available, it is less easy to see differences in qualitative characteristics. Hence as more materials have been found, they have been coalesced into fewer and fewer groups.

But it would also appear that the new interpretations have been forced upon us, in part, by acceptance (after a delay of about a decade) of molecular viewpoints about the relationships of the extant higher primates. Of course, the biomolecular studies cannot, in our present phase of understanding, be applied to these very old fossils directly. But they now provide substantial indirect evidence that stems from many different techniques including immunodiffusion, radioimmunoassay, electrophoresis, microcomplement fixation, aminoacid sequencing, nucleic acid hybridization, nucleotide sequencing, restriction endonuclease mapping and cytogenetics. The results imply a close relationship between humans and African apes and only a distant linkage with Asian apes (e.g. as reviewed in Gribbin and Cherfas, 1982).

This biomolecular result is, for the first time, supported by organismal level evidence from two different sets of studies. One of these is based upon a morphometric study of overall bodily proportions of primates. It shows fairly clearly the separation between humans and African apes on the one hand, and the Asian apes on the other (Oxnard, 1981a). The second is based upon a summation of morphometric studies of many different localized anatomical regions. This shows even more clearly the separation between the gibbon and orang-utan on the one hand, and the African apes and humans on the other (Oxnard, 1983a, d, 1984). This molecular/morphometric pattern of clustering of the living primates can scarcely now be challenged.

In addition, however, the biomolecular evidence can also be interpreted in another way. It may give evidence about time. Hypotheses about 'molecular clocks' suggest that times of divergence can be precisely estimated (e.g. also reviewed in Gribbin and Cherfas, 1982). Thus, a recent time of divergence between humans and African apes 4 to 5 million years ago, has been postulated. And the divergence of orang-utans from the (at that point) conjoint human-African ape lineage, has been assessed as having taken place as long ago as 9 to 12 million years. Gibbons may be even more distantly removed in time from this entire group: on this basis perhaps 18 to 20 million years. (These estimates are not, however, the only divergence times that can be obtained; they are merely those estimates that most investigators seem to favour at this time — see later this chapter and especially Chapter 8).

It is these particular estimates of divergence times that have major implications for our views of the ramapithecines. Anything that existed prior to the postulated 4 or 5 million year link between African great apes and humans, cannot have been an ancestor of humans without also being an ancestor of African apes. It is thus easy to see why, in the new studies of the morphology of the ramapithecines, emphasis should have changed towards their more ape-like features, and why, furthermore, their relationships to orang-utans should now loom so large.

If eventually shown to be correct, these separation times would indeed locate the various ramapithecine fossils as outside any involvement in a human lineage that was distinct from African apes. But it is entirely possible, indeed even likely, that further advances in our understanding of biomolecular evolution will show that the simple 'molecular clock' idea as used at present is not correct. We must, therefore, still hold as tentative, even this idea. In any case, none of this necessarily denies or confirms, for ten to eighteen million year old ramapithecines, places on a lineage leading to both humans and modern apes.

New ramapithecines from China

During the time that all these older ramapithecine fossils were being studied in the West a series of similar fossils, but somewhat younger in time, were being unearthed in China. The earliest of these discoveries was made in 1956. The fragments, (mainly isolated teeth) together with a few other remnants found in later years, begin to give us some insight into the group (e.g. Wu, [Woo] 1957, 1962).

In the last few years a larger and larger number of these fossils have been recovered, so that the great bulk of ramapithecine materials in the world are now known from China. These include nine almost complete jaws (e.g. Fig. 4:1) and five partial skulls much more complete than any others so far known. Most of all, however, they include more than 1,000 identifiable teeth (Xu and Lu, 1979, 1980; Wu *et al.*, 1981, 1982 and 1983; Wu, 1982; Yip, 1983). An extensive bibliography of the Chinese literature is presented by Lisowski (1984).

The more complete specimens indicate (Wu *et al.*, 1981, 1982, 1983) that one set of skulls and jaws, designated by Professor Wu Rukang on morphological grounds as *Ramapithecus*, has smoother, and more round and bulging crania than have modern apes. The nuchal crest is not marked and the nuchal area is not excessively rough. The face is rather short and the foramen magnum situated in a more forward position when compared with modern apes. The dental arch is divergent with small vertically oriented front teeth. The canines are also small and do not project beyond the other teeth. Among the three molars the second is the biggest and all have thick enamel.

The skulls and jaws of the second type were named, on morphological grounds, *Sivapithecus* by

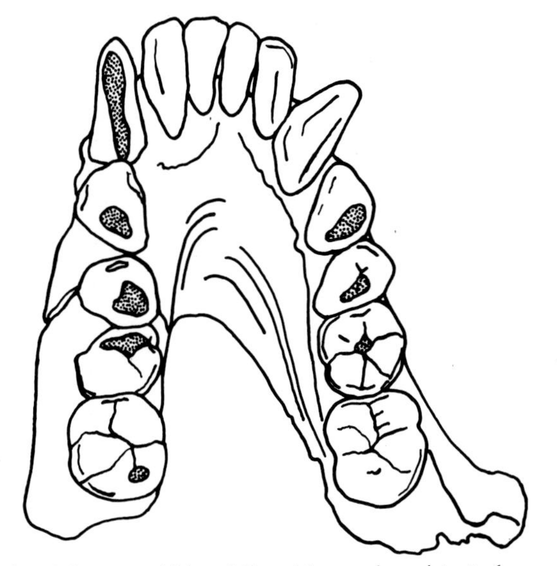

Fig. 4:1a Mandible of *Sivapithecus* found in Lufeng County in 1975.

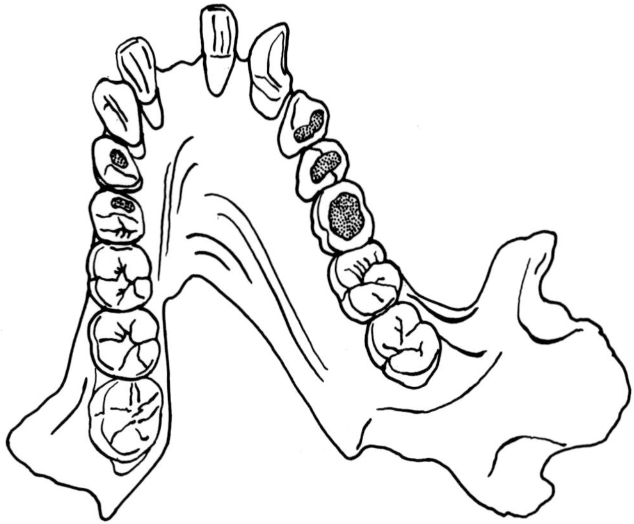

Fig. 4:1b Mandible of *Ramapithecus* found in Lufeng County in 1976.

Professor Wu. They contrast considerably with the others. They have generally more ape-like configurations in each anatomical feature, being generally larger and especially possessing orang-utan-like form of the brow ridges and concave facial profile (although both sets of specimens seem to have these last features to some degree).

It should be emphasized that these original attributions were not made upon the basis of size but morphology. Indeed, all these attributions had been provided by Professor Wu and his colleagues before metrical data became available for quantitative analysis. These scientists have now examined more than a thousand such teeth (Wu *et al.*, 1981, 1982 and 1983) and are thus far more experienced with this particular group of ramapithecines than workers anywhere else in the world.

Certain specimens of these ramapithecines, especially the more complete jaws and skulls, have been studied by visitors to Beijing. Some of the visitors have agreed with the separation of these specimens into the two groups: *Ramapithecus* and *Sivapithecus*. Others, however, have demurred. The latter believe that the two sets of specimens represent the males and females of a single ape-like (orang-utan-like) species, displaying marked sexual dimorphism. Their assessment has been supported by the enumeration of a number of apparently orang-utan-like features of the skulls. These include the absence of brow ridges extending across the face above the root of the nose, and the generally concave profile of the face. Following these observations together with more recent study of all the more complete remains (five crania, nine mandibles and other assorted large fragments) some support for this position was reported (Wu, Xu and Lu, 1983). [It must be recorded, in parenthesis, however, that an even more recent evaluation by this same laboratory suggests a reverse position (Wu and Wu, 1983).]

Though the teeth have been examined visually and identified through their morphology, they have not yet been studied with the full panoply of modern methods. It is clear that a great deal could be learned (**a**) through dental biomechanics about the functional nature of the dentition, (**b**) through morphometrics about changes in size and complexity along the tooth row, (**c**) through stereometrics and pattern recognition about the relationships in the patterns of cusps, and even (**d**) through scanning electron microscopy about specific dietary components such as may be revealed from studies of microwear of the tooth surfaces.

It should also be emphasized that the differences between *Ramapithecus* and *Sivapithecus* so defined are so great that even differences in size are clear cut. It is only in the case of the upper second and first molars that differences based upon size might result in confusion (second molars of the smaller animal being possibly hard to distinguish, on the basis of size alone, from first molars of the larger).

Ramapithecus and *Sivapithecus*: dental measures taken one by one

The teeth were discovered in Late Miocene aged coalfields of Shihuiba near Lufeng in Yunnan province. The different but contiguous areas that were examined in each of the different years' excavations and the details of the local stratigraphy are given in considerable detail in English in the original publications (Wu *et al*, 1981, 1982 and 1983; see also: Wu and Olsen, 1985; Ettler, 1983).

Each tooth position in both upper and lower jaws is represented. The sizes of the samples for each range from as few as 17 for the lower first incisor to as many as 44 each for the lower third molar and lower canine of *Ramapithecus*, and from as few as 16 for the lower second incisor to as many as 49 for the lower second molar for *Sivapithecus*. There are a total of 955 teeth shared approximately equally between these two groups.

The same series of dimensions as are available for extant species (Chapter 2: maximum length and maximum breadth) are available for these teeth (kindly provided by Professor Wu Rukang). Though most of the specimens have both measurements, there are a few with only the one or the other. In order to increase the sizes of the smaller samples, measures are included for each dimension even when the other is missing. As long as the analyses of length and breadth are kept separate, this is appropriate and accounts for the different sample sizes that are sometimes given for lengths as compared with breadths at particular tooth positions (Table 4:1). In studies in which lengths and breadths for the same teeth are examined together (for instance to examine relative tooth areas) the additional measures are ignored. Estimated measurements were supplied for some individual teeth because of damage. In other teeth, measurements are suspect because of heavy wear. Neither of these latter types of measure are included in the current study. Table 4:1 indicates the full range of specimens and basic statistical data.

TABLE 4:1

Basic Statistical Data for Tooth Dimensions

Tooth	No.	$\bar{X}$ length	SD length	$\bar{X}$ breadth	SD breadth
Ramapithecus					
I^1	31	8.84	0.40	8.15	0.29
I^2	21	5.55	0.42	6.33	0.38
C′	27/24	10.25	0.48	9.15	0.33
P^3	24	7.50	0.46	10.39	0.60
P^4	28	7.00	0.43	10.97	0.61
M^1	32	10.11	0.43	11.25	0.54
M^2	24	10.99	0.69	12.18	0.57
M^3	24	10.58	0.61	11.83	0.63
I_1	17/20	5.09	0.21	6.78	0.35
I_2	21	5.39	0.21	7.91	0.45
C,	44	9.40	0.43	6.42	0.33
P_3	32	10.62	0.41	6.74	0.23
P_4	35/34	7.89	0.65	9.08	0.52
M_1	35	10.57	0.48	9.63	0.37
M_2	40	12.12	0.56	11.30	0.36
M_3	44/43	12.69	0.67	11.14	0.54
Sivapithecus					
I^1	48/46	10.07	0.56	9.46	0.38
I^2	18	6.57	0.45	7.71	0.71
C′	19	14.64	1.19	11.57	0.81
P^3	28	12.41	0.62	12.41	0.69
P^4	34/31	9.46	0.61	12.80	0.47
M^1	31/30	11.79	0.58	13.03	0.46
M^2	36	13.38	0.84	14.77	0.82
M^3	22/24	12.75	1.08	14.36	0.53
I_1	24/22	5.86	0.34	8.35	0.76
I_2	16	6.06	0.24	9.64	0.65
C,	28	12.04	0.91	9.54	0.87
P_3	27	13.13	0.82	8.23	0.19
P_4	32/33	9.49	0.62	10.48	0.37
M_1	33	12.20	0.53	11.18	0.48
M_2	49	14.51	0.59	13.23	0.60
M_3	25	15.03	0.77	12.90	0.64

The univariate studies include examination of the same suite of basic statistical data as for the other forms studied in this book. This includes, of course, means and standard deviations, and computed frequency distribution histograms and fitted normal curves. The distributions of the histograms in comparison with their fitted normal curves are tested using standard chi square statistics.

The means and standard deviations for length and breadth measures for each tooth within both upper and lower jaws for each fossil group are given in Table 4:1. The marked difference between *Ramapithecus* which is always smaller and *Sivapithecus* is clear (Wu and Oxnard, 1983a and b). These differences are far greater than those generally found between the sexes of extant forms, even between the sexes of such markedly dimorphic species as gorillas and orang-utans.

The first frame of Fig. 4:2 provides the example of canine breadth. That figure shows that when the entire sample is treated as a single group (i.e. as the '*Sivapithecus*' of the most recent investigations) then two completely separate histograms are evident. Unless sexual dimorphism in *Sivapithecus* is something totally outside the ken of anthropologists, unless we can characterize these measurements as though they were tiny gonads attached to individual teeth, then it is utterly unlikely that these two histograms are evidence of females and males. This separation is so great that not only is there no overlap at all of the two parts but the fitted normal curve is visually totally unrelated to the histogram and statistically different from it at a probability of less than 1 in 10,000.

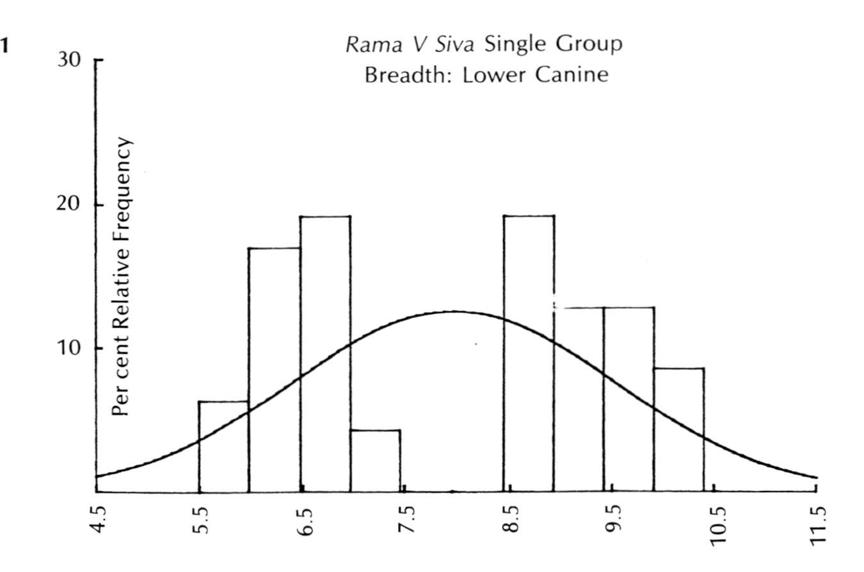
1
Rama V Siva Single Group
Breadth: Lower Canine
Per cent Relative Frequency
30
20
10
4.5
5.5
6.5
7.5
8.5
9.5
10.5
11.5

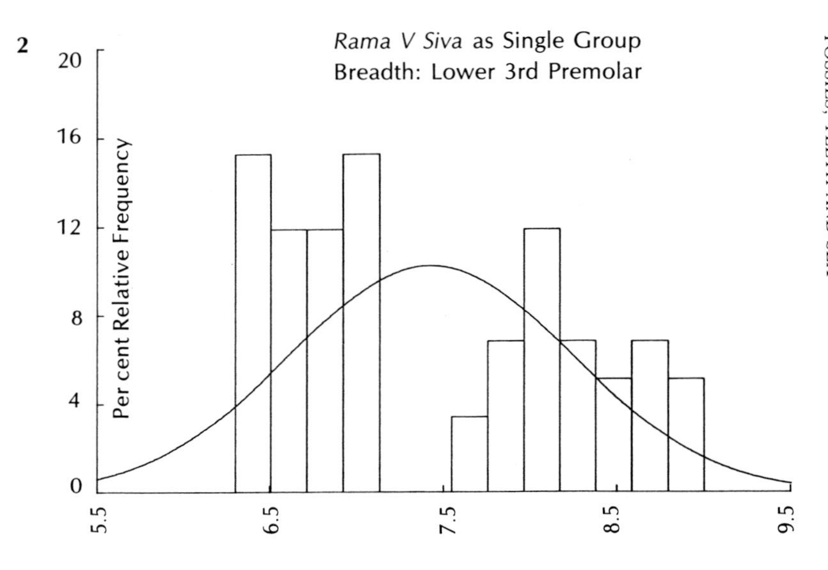
2
Rama V Siva as Single Group
Breadth: Lower 3rd Premolar
Per cent Relative Frequency
20
16
12
8
4
0
5.5
6.5
7.5
8.5
9.5

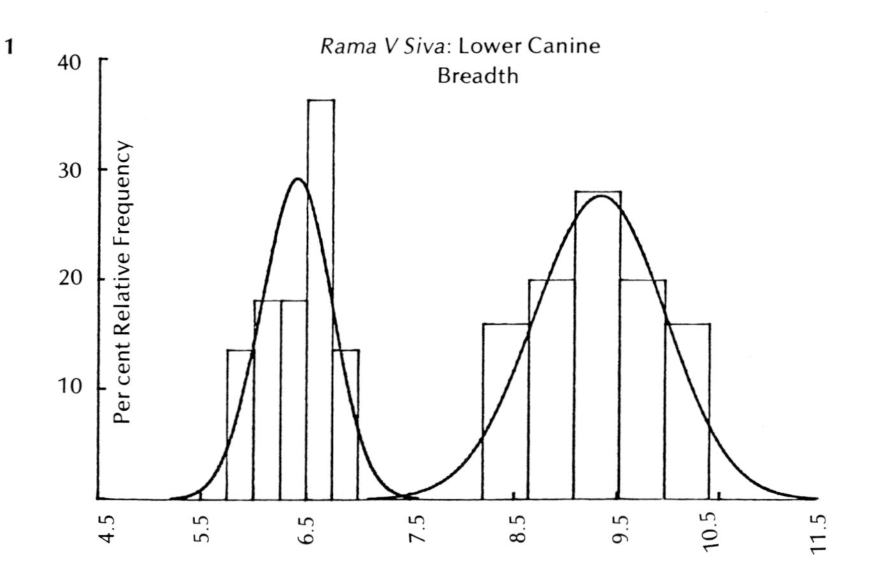
1
Rama V Siva: Lower Canine
Breadth
Per cent Relative Frequency
40
30
20
10
4.5
5.5
6.5
7.5
8.5
9.5
10.5
11.5

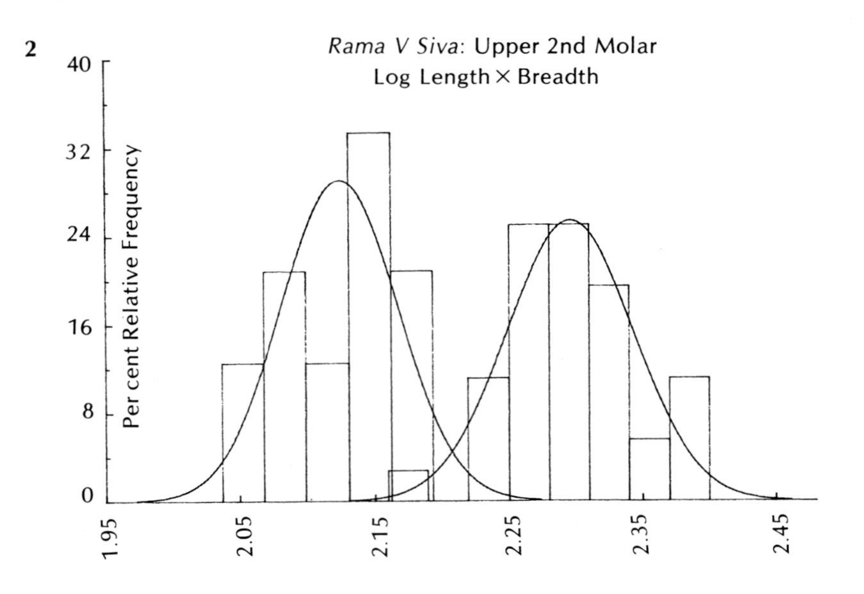
2
Rama V Siva: Upper 2nd Molar
Log Length × Breadth
Per cent Relative Frequency
40
32
24
16
8
0
1.95
2.05
2.15
2.25
2.35
2.45

When the two groups for this same tooth measure are treated separately, i.e. as the *Ramapithecus* and *Sivapithecus* originally defined on morphological grounds by Professor Wu Rukang, not only are the two histograms completely separate as before, but even the two fitted normal curves for each scarcely overlap (Figure 4:2). Similar findings exist to greater or lesser degree for each of the other tooth dimensions (see lower third premolar breadth and upper second molar log breadth times length, second frame, Fig. 4:2, and means and standard deviations for each dimension, Table 4:1). It is therefore necessary to assume that the separation of these ramapithecines into two groups is not one between two sexes, but truly one between two species or species groups.

It is true, however, that if sexual dimorphism could be seen within each of these groups it would strengthen that idea enormously. Accordingly, then, in subsequent analyses, we shall treat each as a separate group and seek evidence of internal sexual dimorphism.

Ramapithecus and *Sivapithecus* — canine sexual dimorphisms?

Sivapithecus: Bimodal distributions exist for both dimensions of the upper canine in *Sivapithecus* (and that for the breadth is statistically significant). Computed histograms for each of the lower canine dimensions are not bimodal, but the breadth displays a unimodal, plateau-like, distribution that is significantly different from a normal distribution. It could well have arisen from two separate but overlapping normal curves, one for each sex. The distribution of the product of length and breadth for each canine gives especially markedly (and statistically significant) bimodal curves (Wu and Oxnard, 1983b).

As can be seen from Figure 4:3 and Table 4:2, the bimodality is such that the dispersion of the upper peak is considerably larger than the dispersion of the lower peak. If this were also found in the other teeth, then it would resemble the type of sexual dimorphism of dispersion that exists in living African apes. However, results that follow indicate that this is not the case for any other tooth and it thus has to be treated as a quirk in the results. There is no way at this time of testing this observation statistically.

As can also be seen from Figure 4:3, the number of specimens in the peak representing the smaller specimens is about twice the number of specimens in the peak representing the larger ones. Again, if the numbers of males and females in the original living populations, before fossilisation, are even approximately represented in the numbers of fossils, then this may indicate a female to male ratio of 2:1, a ratio not unlike, of course, that in both African apes and *Pongo*.

Ramapithecus: Bimodal distributions are also found for both dimensions of the upper canine of *Ramapithecus*. That for the length is statistically significant. Computed histograms for each of the lower canine dimensions are not bimodal, but the length displays a unimodal, plateau-like, distribution that is significantly different from normal. It could well have arisen from two separate but overlapping normal curves, one for each sex (again, see Wu and Oxnard, 1983b).

Fig. 4:2 ◁ **1st Frame:** distribution (upper diagram) for the breadth of the lower canine for all ramapithecine specimens from Lufeng. The histogram separates itself into two parts separated by a very large interval. It does not fit a normal curve at all. In no other known primate is sexual dimorphism as large as this. The proposition must arise that this is not sexual dimorphism.

Distribution (lower diagram) of each part of the histogram for the canine calculated separately. Each of these fits the normal curve quite well. There is no overlap in the histograms and even when fitted normal curves are calculated, the overlap that they exhibit is extremely small. This further suggests that we have here two species (which Professor Wu Rukang called *Ramapithecus* and *Sivapithecus*) rather than two sexes.

2nd Frame: distribution (upper diagram) for the breadth of the lower third premolar for all ramapithecines from Lufeng. Like the canine, this also shows two completely separate parts. The smaller part shows, itself, an equal bimodal distribution, the upper part shows an unequal bimodal distribution. If ever an information shows that the two main parts of this histogram cannot be females and males of a single species, this does. Not in *Gorilla*, not even in *Gigantopithecus* with its absolutely enormous sexual dimorphism, do we have total separation between the sexes for the breadth of a premolar.

Distribution (lower diagram) of log length × breadth for the upper second molar shows that this process is even carried into the cheek teeth. Treating the two groups at Lufeng separately gives histograms and fitted normal curves that scarcely overlap at all. This just cannot be sexual dimorphism.

TABLE 4:2

Nature and Statistical Significance of Distribution at Each Tooth Locus

	Ramapithecus			*Sivapithecus*		
Tooth	Length	Breadth	Log area	Length	Breadth	Log area
I^1	N	B*	N	B*	B*	N
I^2	F*	F*	N	B	B*	B*
C′	B*	B	N	B	B*	B
P^3	B*	B	N	N	B*	B*
P^4	N	B	B*	B	B*	B
M^1	N	F	N	B	F	N
M^2	B*	N	B*	B	B*	B
M^3	B	B*	B*	B*	B*	B
I_1	B	B*	F	B*	B*	B*
I_2	N	N	B	B	B*	B*
$C_,$	N	F*	N	N	F	B*
P_3	B	B	B*	B	B*	B*
P_4	N	N	N	B	B	B
M_1	B*	B*	B*	F	B*	B*
M_2	N	N	N	F*	N	B*
M_3	N	B*	N	B	B*	B

Form of distribution: B = bimodal distribution; N = normal; F = plateau-like. *Distributions significantly different from normal (less than 0.10).

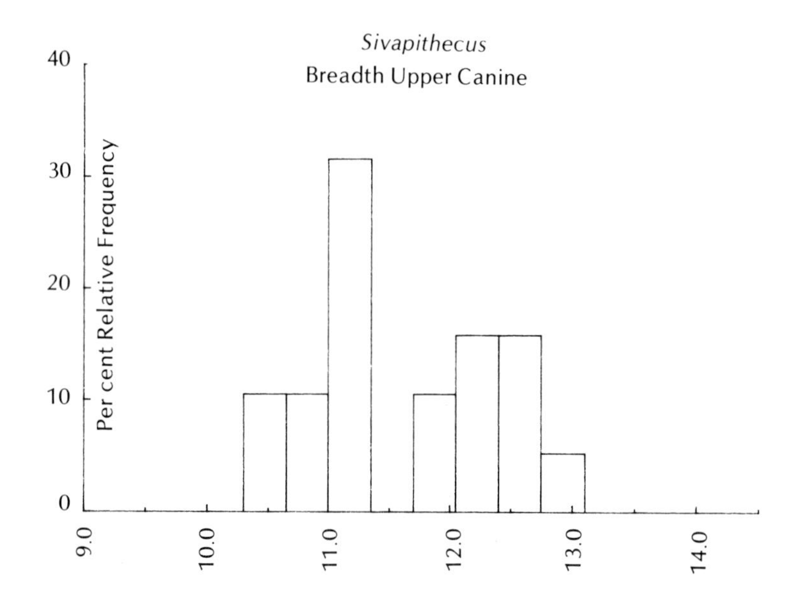

Fig. 4:3 Distribution for the breadth of the upper canine for *Sivapithecus*. The plot is bimodal suggesting that two sexes are present with an intermediate degree of dimorphism. The spreads of the two peaks seem to be similar, suggesting that, like orang-utans, *Sivapithecus* has zero differences in variance between the sexes. There are more specimens in the lower peak than in the upper, as in orang-utans in which the sex ratio has been artificially set at two females to each male. An approximately 2:1 ratio may have existed in this sample of canines of *Sivapithecus*.

As can be seen from Figure 4:4 and Table 4:2, the bimodality is such that the dispersion of the peak of larger specimens is the same as the dispersion of the peak of smaller specimens. If this is also found in the other teeth, then it resembles the picture that is produced by the type of sexual dimorphism that exists in humans and the Asian ape, *Pongo*. It is the opposite of what is found in the living African apes. Again, however, there is no way at this time to test this statistically.

As can also be seen from Figure 4:4, the number of specimens in the peak representing the smaller specimens is the same as the number of specimens in the peak representing the larger ones. Again, if

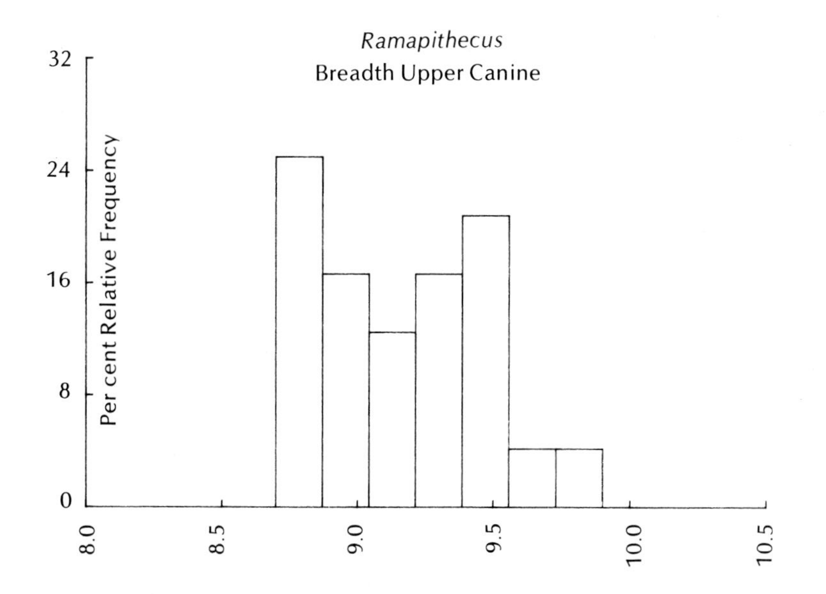

Fig. 4:4 Distribution for the breadth of the upper canine for *Ramapithecus*. The plot is bimodal suggesting that two sexes are present with a small degree of dimorphism. The spreads of the two peaks seem to be similar, suggesting that, like humans and orang-utans, *Ramapithecus* has zero differences in variance. The numbers of specimens in the two peaks are approximately the same, similar to all living and fossil *Homo*. This suggests that a 1:1 ratio may have existed in this sample of canines of *Ramapithecus*.

the numbers of males and females in the original living populations before fossilisation are even approximately represented in the numbers of fossils (see Chapter 7), then this indicates a female-to-male ratio of 1:1, similar only, among the living large hominoids, to humans.

Ramapithecus and *Sivapithecus* — sexual dimorphisms in anterior teeth?

Sivapithecus: The lengths and breadths of the incisors and premolars show bimodal distributions at 15 of a total of 16 dimensions. Of these as many as 9 are statistically different from their fitted normal curves. This is a degree of dimorphism, as measured by number of dimorphic tooth positions, that is every bit as great as that in gorillas and orang-utans. The size of this dimorphism (of means) as judged by the distance between the modes, is probably somewhat less than that in gorillas and orang-utans, although it is certainly greater than in *Pan*. Figure 4:5 shows three typical examples: breadths of the upper first incisor and of the lower third premolar, and length of the lower fourth premolar (see also Table 4:2).

In each of these dimensions the dispersions of the two modes appear to be very similar although there is no statistic that can be applied to test this. The number of cells in the two peaks are approximately equal. This resembles the type of sexual dimorphism of dispersion that we now know is typical of both *Homo* and *Pongo*. It is quite different from the large dimorphism of dispersion that characterizes *Gorilla* and the especially large dimorphism of dispersion that defines *Pan* (given the lesser dimorphism of means between the sexes in that species).

Each bimodal distribution shows, however, a peak for the smaller specimens that contains twice or more the number of specimens represented in the peak for the larger specimens. With, once again, the caveat that the distribution in the fossil sample be not too far removed from the distribution in the prior sample of adults when they were alive, this information suggests that the female/male sex ratio is 2:1 or thereabouts. This is similar to what we found in the African apes and in orang-utans.

But the combination of zero sexual dimorphism of dispersion and a 2:1 sex ratio is found only in orang-utans, among living species.

Ramapithecus: The lengths and breadths of the incisors and premolars show bimodal distributions at 8 of the total of 16 dimensions. Of these as few as 5 are statistically significantly different from the fitted normal curve. This is a degree of dimorphism, as measured by number of dimorphic tooth positions, that is a good deal less than is found in the great apes. But it is still considerably more than exists in *Homo*. The size of the dimorphism as judged by the distance between the modes (sexual dimorphism of means) is also less than that in the apes but greater than that in humans. Figure 4:6 shows four typical examples: breadths of the upper first incisor and of the upper fourth premolar, and lengths of the upper and lower fourth premolars (see also Table 4:2).

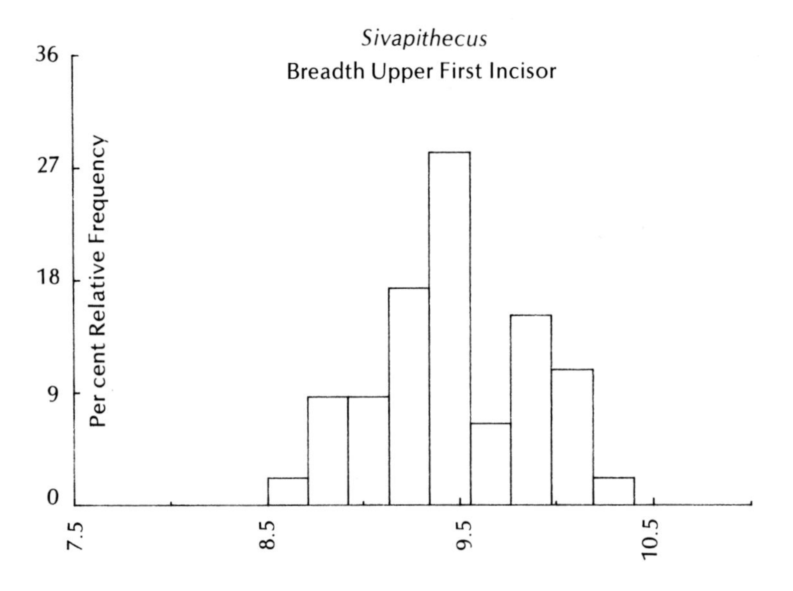

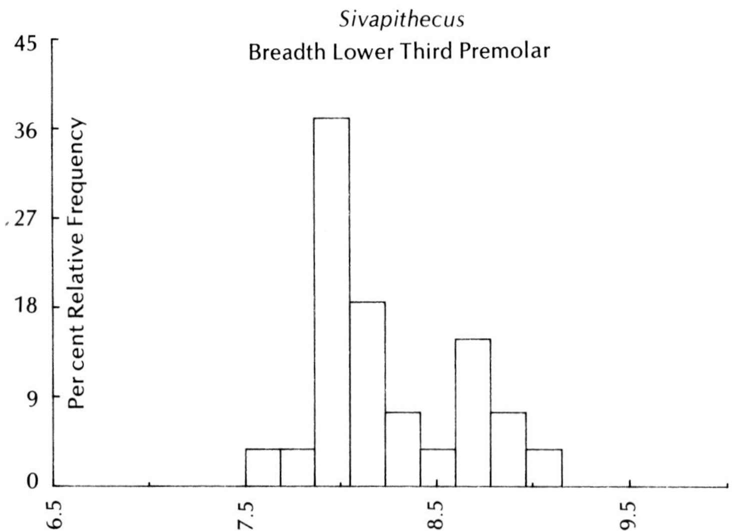

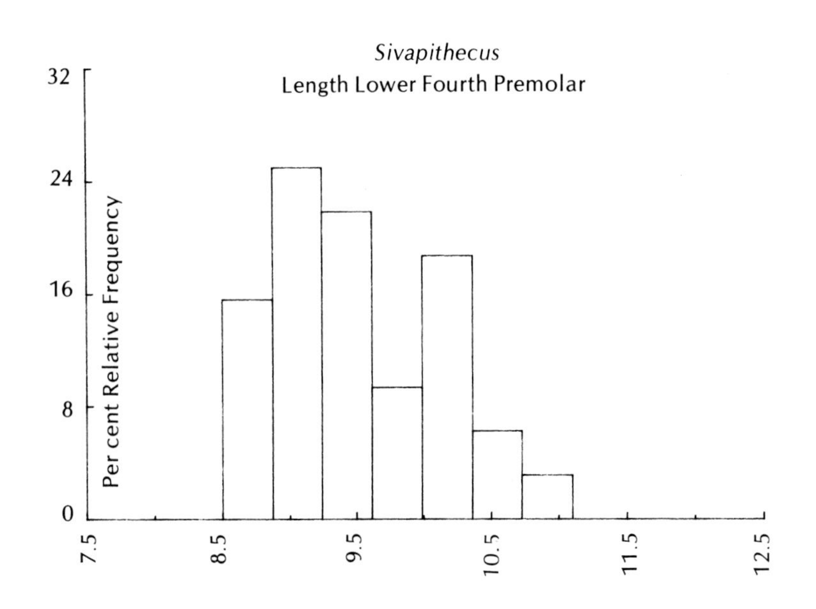

Fig. 4:5 Distributions for several dimensions of incisor and premolar teeth for *Sivapithecus*. Each plot is bimodal suggesting that two sexes are present. The amount of dimorphism of means as judged by the separation of the modes is less than in the canines. The spreads of the two peaks seem to be similar, suggesting that, like orang-utans, *Sivapithecus* has zero differences in variance between the sexes. However, one dimension, that in the lowest position in the figure, possibly suggests that the female variance is greater than the male. That only one dimension shows this feature makes it unlikely to be due to more than a chance distribution for this particular tooth. In every case there are more specimens in the lower peak than in the upper, a situation entirely similar to that presenting in orang-utans in which the sex ratio has been artificially set at two females to each male. This suggests that an approximately 2:1 or even greater ratio may have existed in these sample of teeth of *Sivapithecus*.

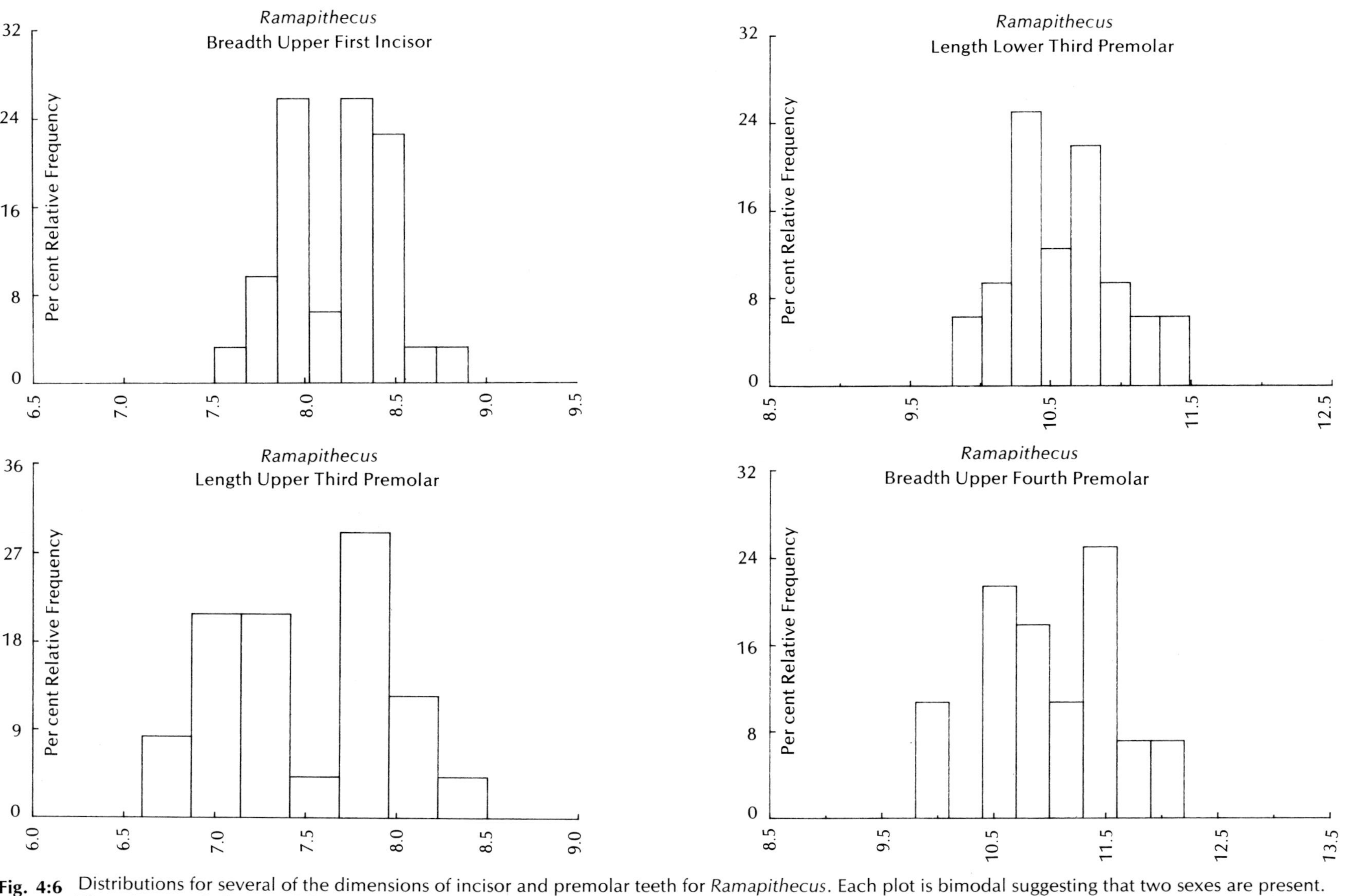

Fig. 4:6 Distributions for several of the dimensions of incisor and premolar teeth for *Ramapithecus*. Each plot is bimodal suggesting that two sexes are present. There is a small degree of dimorphism as based upon the small separations between the modes. The spreads of the two peaks in each distribution seem to be the same, suggesting that, like humans and orang-utans, *Ramapithecus* has zero differences in variance between the sexes. The numbers of specimens in the two peaks are approximately the same, a situation entirely similar to that presenting in all living and fossil *Homo*. This suggests that a 1:1 ratio may have existed in these samples of anterior teeth of *Ramapithecus*.

In each of these dimensions the dispersions of the two modes appear to be very similar. The number of cells in the two peaks are approximately equal in each case. Again, however, there is no statistical test that can be applied with samples of these sizes. This resembles the type of sexual dimorphism of dispersion that we now know is typical of both *Homo* and *Pongo*. It is quite different from the large dimorphism of dispersion that characterizes *Gorilla* and the especially large dimorphism of dispersion that defines *Pan* (given the lesser dimorphism of means between the sexes in that species).

Each bimodal distribution shows peaks for the smaller and larger specimens that contain approximately the same numbers. With the same caveat as above, this suggests that the female/male ratio is 1:1 or thereabouts.

The combination of these two features, zero sexual dimorphism of dispersion and a 1:1 sex ratio, characterizes only the various living and fossil members of the genus *Homo*.

Ramapithecus and *Sivapithecus* — sexual dimorphisms in molars?

Sivapithecus: The lengths and breadths of the molars show bimodal distributions at 8 of a total of 12 dimensions. Of these as many as 6 are statistically different from the fitted normal curve. This is a degree of dimorphism, as measured by number of tooth positions at which bimodality can be discerned, that is every bit as great as that in gorillas and orang-utans. The size of the dimorphism as judged by the distance between the modes is also at least as great as that in the two largest apes. Figure 4:7 shows two typical examples: breadths of the upper second and lower third molars (see also Table 4:2).

In each of these dimensions the dispersions of the two modes appear to be very similar. The number of cells in the two peaks are approximately equal. This resembles the type of sexual dimorphism of dispersion typical of both *Homo* and *Pongo*. It is quite different from the large dimorphism of dispersion that characterizes *Gorilla*, and it is, of course, totally different from the situation in *Pan* in which there is no dimorphism of note in any posterior teeth.

Each bimodal distribution shows, however, the same unequal (2:1) ratio between the numbers of specimens in the smaller peaks and those in the larger peaks. This again suggests that the female/male sex ratio is 2:1 or thereabouts. It is similar to what we find in the African apes and in orang-utans.

But the combination of zero sexual dimorphism of dispersion and a 2:1 sex ratio is found only in the orang-utan, among living species.

Ramapithecus: The lengths and breadths of the molars show bimodal distributions at 6 of a total of 12 dimensions. Of these as many as 5 are statistically different from their fitted normal curves. This is, once again, an amount of dimorphism that is greater than that in *Homo*, which has only one such difference in the molar series, and certainly greater than in *Pan* which has none. The size of the dimorphism is, however, considerably less than that in *Gorilla* and *Pongo*. Figure 4:8 shows two typical examples: lengths of the upper second and lower first molars (see also Table 4:2).

In each of these dimensions the dispersions of the two modes appear similar. This resembles the type of sexual dimorphism of dispersion typical of both *Homo* and *Pongo*. It is quite different from the large dimorphism of dispersion that characterizes *Gorilla*. It is quite different also from that defining *Pan* but for a different reason: that there is no dimorphism of any kind in the posterior teeth of that genus.

Each bimodal distribution shows the 1:1 ratio between the numbers of specimens in the smaller peaks and larger peaks. This implies a 1:1 ratio between females and males and exists, of course, only in *Homo* among the extant species.

Additional univariate results for ramapithecines.

The data assembled in Chapter 2 and the new information discussed here for the ramapithecines indicate that there are additional contrasts in these dental patterns. Thus, humans display only a few significant sex differences in dimensions within the permanent dentition. Most of these are in breadth measures, e.g. of lower second incisors, of lower canines, of upper first and second premolars and of upper second molars. The extant apes display many differences in both lengths and breadths at almost every tooth locus (summarized in the first eight columns of Table 4:3).

For the two fossil groups, it is not, of course, possible to carry out such tests of males against

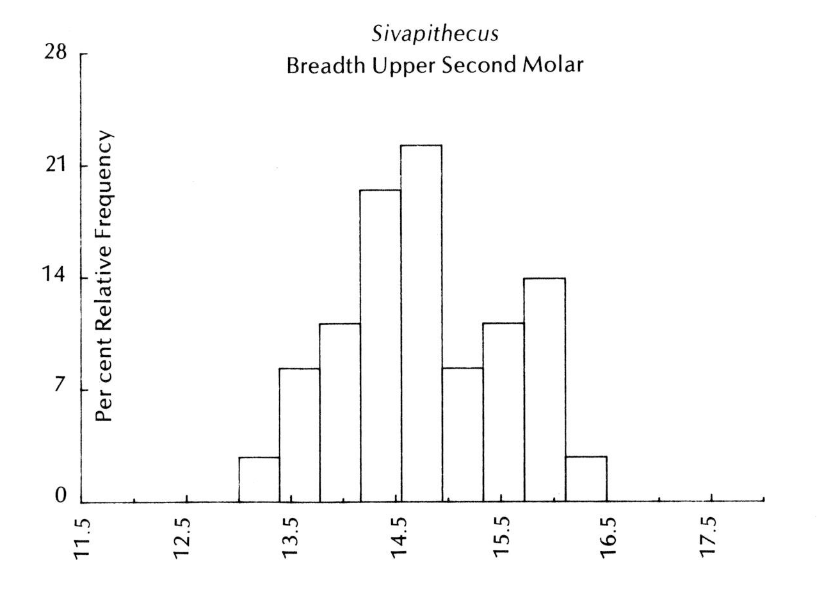

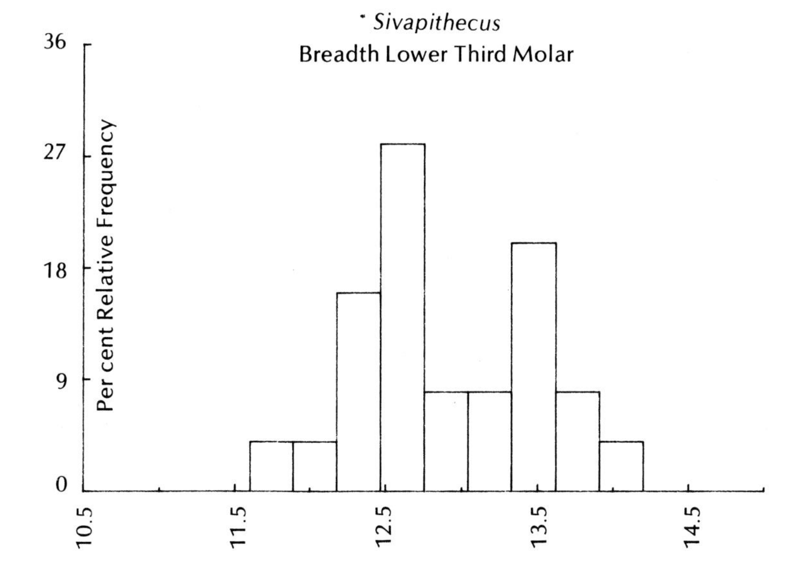

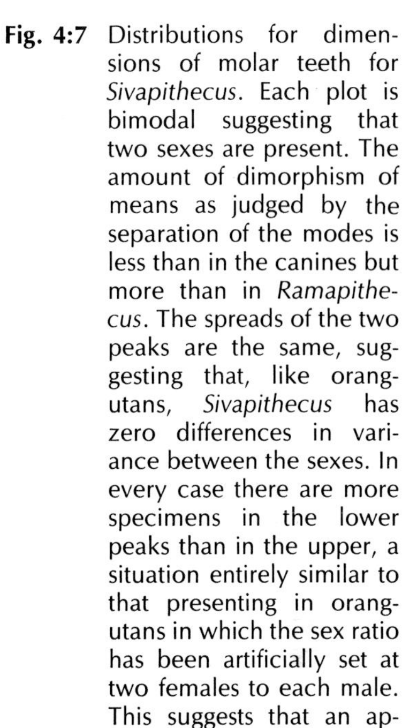
Fig. 4:7 Distributions for dimensions of molar teeth for *Sivapithecus*. Each plot is bimodal suggesting that two sexes are present. The amount of dimorphism of means as judged by the separation of the modes is less than in the canines but more than in *Ramapithecus*. The spreads of the two peaks are the same, suggesting that, like orang-utans, *Sivapithecus* has zero differences in variance between the sexes. In every case there are more specimens in the lower peaks than in the upper, a situation entirely similar to that presenting in orang-utans in which the sex ratio has been artificially set at two females to each male. This suggests that an approximately 2:1 or even greater ratio may have existed in these samples of teeth of *Sivapithecus*.

females because the sexes are not known. But, based upon the degree to which the various distributions found here are bimodal and significantly different from normal, it is possible to say that *Ramapithecus* is less dimorphic than the extant apes (significant differences at 11 positions) although considerably more bimodal than humans. In contrast *Sivapithecus* is bimodal at 20 positions, and is as bimodal, therefore, as gorillas (20), chimpanzees (20) and orang-utans (21). Finally, Table 4:3 shows that the pattern of bimodal differences along the tooth row in *Ramapithecus* is generally closer to the pattern of sexual dimorphism in humans. That table likewise shows that the bimodal pattern in *Sivapithecus* contrasts in being generally closer to the sex differences in the various apes.

These data clearly also allow us to study the product of length and breadth (for each tooth for which both dimensions are available). These areas are compared at each tooth position and the computed histograms and fitted normal curves examined as before. In general the areas (logged) show the same distributions as the individual lengths and breadths. When the individual measures are normal, the log areas tend to be normal. When the individual measures are bimodal, the log areas tend

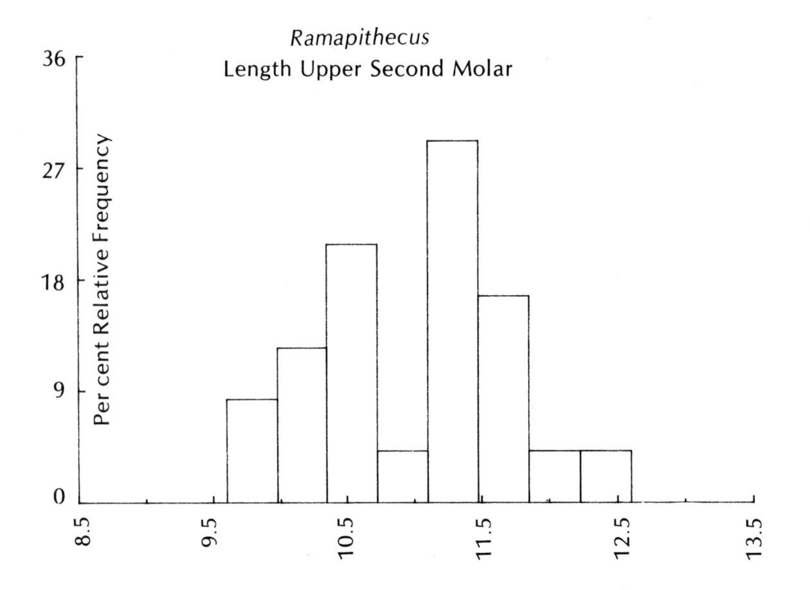

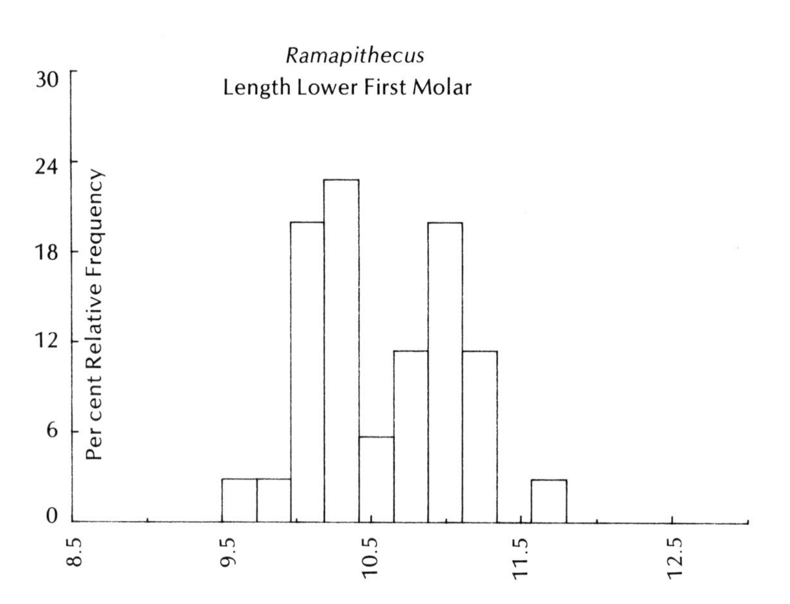

Fig. 4:8 Distributions for the dimensions of molar teeth for *Ramapithecus*. Each plot is bimodal suggesting that two sexes are present and with a small degree of dimorphism as based upon the small separations between the modes. The spreads of the two peaks in each distribution are similar, suggesting that, like humans and orang-utans, *Ramapithecus* has zero differences in variance between the sexes. The numbers of specimens in the two peaks are approximately the same, a situation entirely similar to that presenting in all living and fossil *Homo*. This suggests that a 1:1 ratio may have existed in these samples of posterior teeth of *Ramapithecus*.

to be bimodal. In this latter case the areas are usually more significantly bimodal because correlated information from both length and breadth are included in them (see Figure 4:9 for examples). These findings corroborate what we have learnt from individual dimensions of the teeth.

Dimensions of ramapithecine teeth: all variables taken together

Of course, the aforementioned data come from individual teeth from many different and incomplete fossils. It is not therefore possible to say, except to some limited degree, which particular tooth at one tooth locus is from the same individual as another tooth at another locus. For this reason it is not possible to carry out a multivariate statistical study which incorporates the data from ramapithecines in the same manner as for the humans and extant apes as examined in Chapter 2.

But it is possible to obtain the mean values for each dimension for each tooth. Each unimodal dimension provides only a single mean value for the species. And although the means for each sex might well be different from this species mean, we

Table 4:3

Sizes and Statistical Differences between Measures in Each Sex for Extant Great Apes and Humans Compared With Sizes and Statistical Differences Between Peaks of Bimodal Distributions of Measures in *Ramapithecus* and *Sivapithecus*

	Homo		*Gorilla*		*Pan*		*Pongo*		*Ramapithecus*		*Sivapithecus*	
	L	B	L	B	L	B	L	B	L	B	L	B
I^1	0.3	0.2	0.7*	1.3*	0.5*	0.5*	0.9	1.0	0.0	0.5*	0.9*	0.8*
I_1	0.7*	0.2	0.1	0.9*	0.3	0.6*	1.2*	0.7	0.4	0.5*	0.8*	1.8*
I^2	1.2	0.1	0.9	0.7	0.5	0.3	0.4	0.1	0.0	0.0	0.7*	1.4*
I_2	0.2	0.5*	0.0	0.6	0.5*	0.5	1.3*	1.3*	0.0	0.0	0.4	1.4*
C'	0.3	0.4	6.4*	4.7*	3.3*	2.5*	3.9*	2.4*	0.7	0.6	2.5*	1.4*
C_1	0.2	0.3	4.1*	5.1*	2.3*	2.8*	2.3*	2.9*	0.0	0.0	0.0	0.0
P^3	0.4	1.3*	0.8	1.0	0.1	0.6*	0.7	1.4*	0.9*	1.0*	0.0	1.0*
P_3	0.3	0.3	2.1	0.7*	0.3	1.0*	1.8	1.7*	0.5	0.0	0.8	0.7*
P^4	0.5	0.8*	0.2*	0.8*	0.0	0.7*	0.7	1.2*	0.0	0.9*	0.5*	0.8*
P_4	0.5	0.3	0.5	1.3*	0.3	0.6*	0.8	1.5*	0.0	0.0	1.0	0.8
M^1	0.1	0.1	0.9*	0.4	0.2	0.8*	0.9*	1.9*	0.0	0.0	1.2*	0.0
M_1	0.1	0.1	0.8	0.2	0.2	0.6*	2.0*	0.8*	0.8*	0.7*	0.0	1.0*
M^2	0.8	0.9*	1.5*	1.2*	0.3	0.9*	0.8	1.2*	1.2*	0.0	1.7*	1.6*
M_2	0.0	0.6	1.3*	1.4*	0.4*	0.7*	0.9*	1.6*	0.0	0.0	0.0	0.0
M^3	?	?	1.5*	0.8*	0.5*	1.0*	0.9*	1.5*	0.9*	0.8*	1.7*	1.0*
M_3	?	?	2.8*	1.9*	0.4	0.9*	0.6	1.1*	0.0	0.9*	0.8	1.1*

B = breadths; L = lengths. Difference in mm.
*Statistically significant differences between sexes for extant forms, and from normal distributions for fossils.

have no basis for any better estimation of the means of the sex subgroups. However, for those distributions that are bimodal, and this includes many of the teeth, the modes for each of the peaks are estimates of the means for the sex subgroups. An entire suite of means for each sex can, thus, be formed from a compound of data from these two procedures. These estimates can be interpolated into the previously determined multivariate statistical analyses in order that we can evaluate how sexual differences are arranged in the fossil forms.

We should remember that this procedure underestimates sexual dimorphism rather than the reverse, because the values for each sex are the same in those dimensions which have unimodal distributions. Yet these are distributions in which, undoubtedly, if we knew the sexes, we would still sometimes be able to discern significant differences. However, underestimation is to be preferred to overestimation in such situations. Underestimations play against our ideas rather than for them. This prevents our exuberance from running away with us. Any differences that appear following such underestimations are all the more likely to be real.

We should also remember, as in the previous chapter, that because of limitations in the original data for extant species, this procedure can only be done for the upper and lower jaws separately. Although this, too, loses us a considerable amount of discriminating power, given the limitations in the data from the original extant species, it is the best that we can do. It does at least allow us to see if sexual dimorphism in the upper jaw is the same phenomenon as that in the lower jaw.

The goal of the multivariate part of this investigation is to expand the univariate studies of the data from extant hominoids, to include the ramapithecines from China using a particular multivariate statistical approach: canonical variates analysis. Several questions are addressed.

What is the multivariate nature of sexual dimorphism in the dentition of the ramapithecines?

In particular, what patterns are apparent in multivariate analyses of *Ramapithecus* and *Sivapithecus* that have not appeared in the univariate studies?

Which of the extant species do these ramapithecines most resemble?

What, if any, are the implications of the results for primate and more specifically human phylogeny?

The data on extant primates used in this study are outlined in Chapter 2. The fossil data used in this study are the mean lengths and breadths, estimated as just described from those measurements provided by Professor Wu Rukang, that are the basis for the above univariate studies.

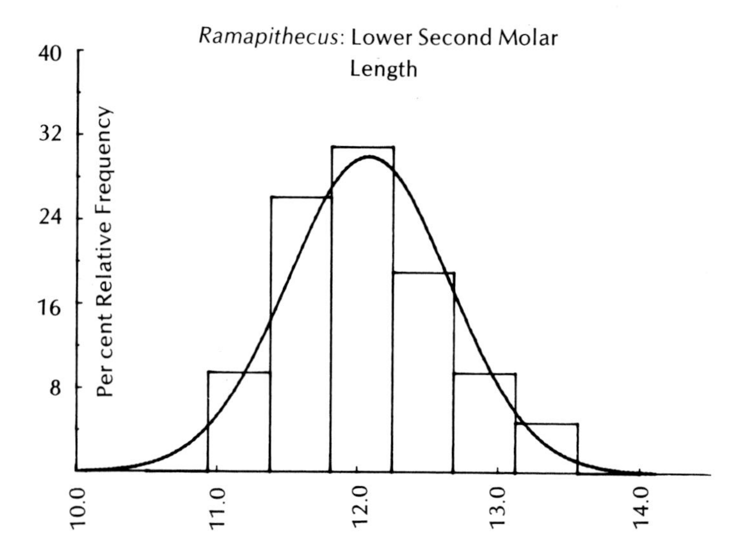

1st Frame

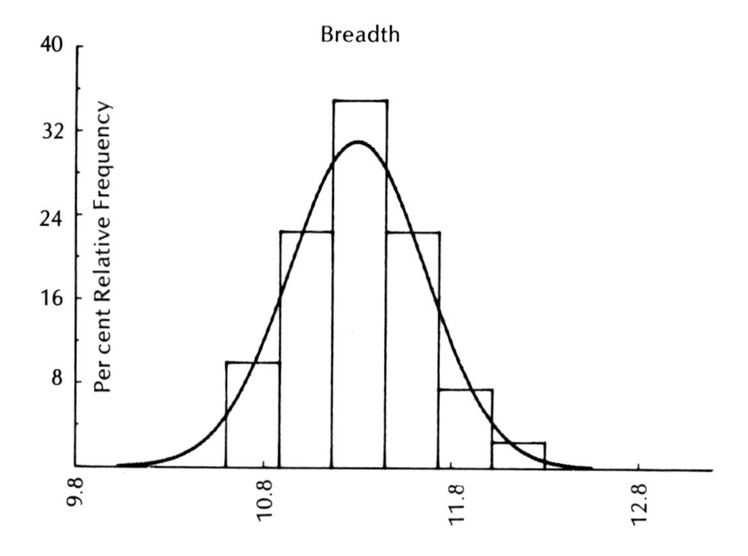

Fig. 4:9 The first two frames of this figure demonstrate that when distributions for individual lengths and breadths in both *Ramapithecus* and *Sivapithecus* are normal, then the distribution for the corresponding areas (logged) are also normal.

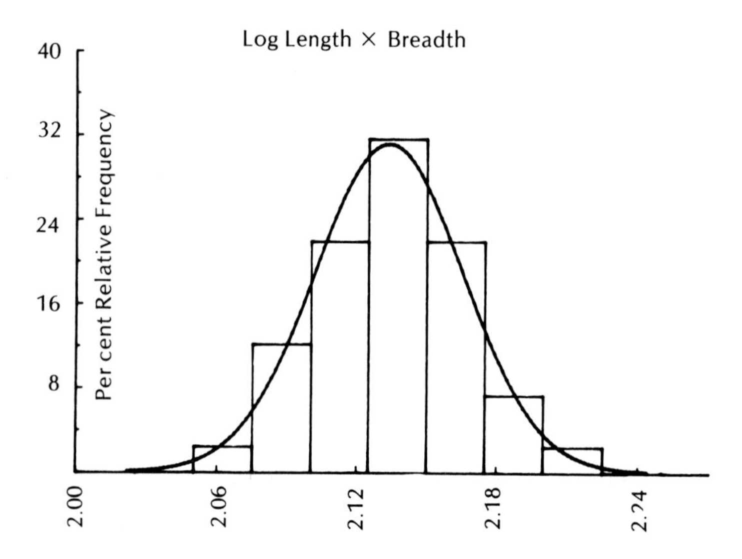

2nd Frame

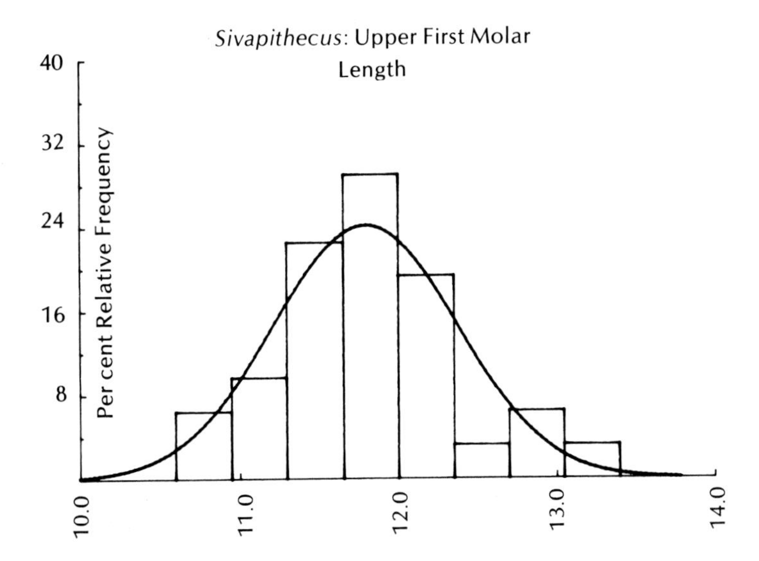
Sivapithecus: Upper First Molar
Length
Per cent Relative Frequency
40
32
24
16
8
10.0
11.0
12.0
13.0
14.0

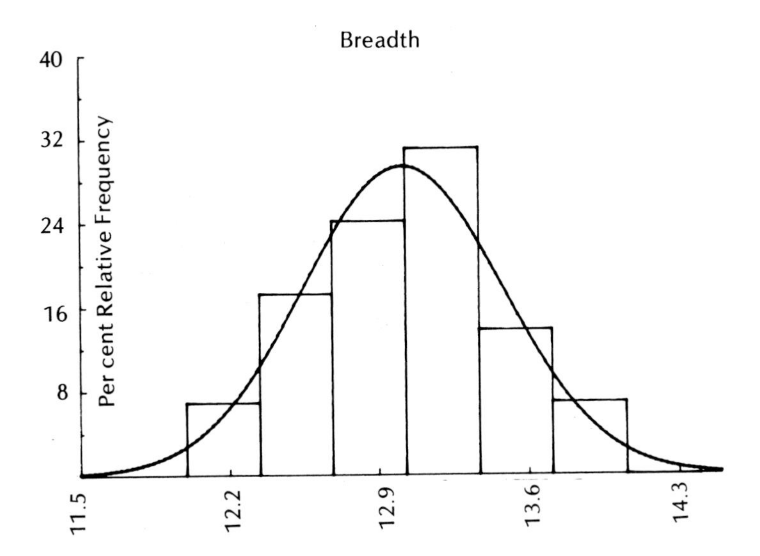
Breadth
Per cent Relative Frequency
40
32
24
16
8
11.5
12.2
12.9
13.6
14.3

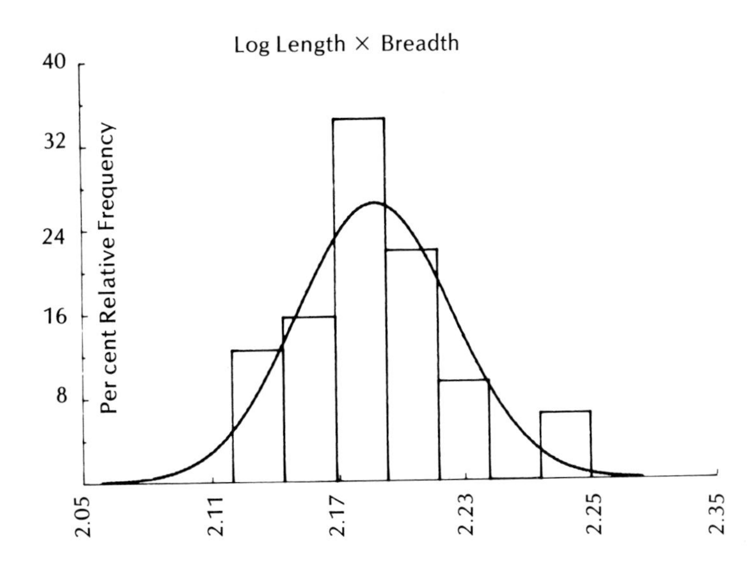
Log Length × Breadth
Per cent Relative Frequency
40
32
24
16
8
2.05
2.11
2.17
2.23
2.25
2.35

3rd Frame

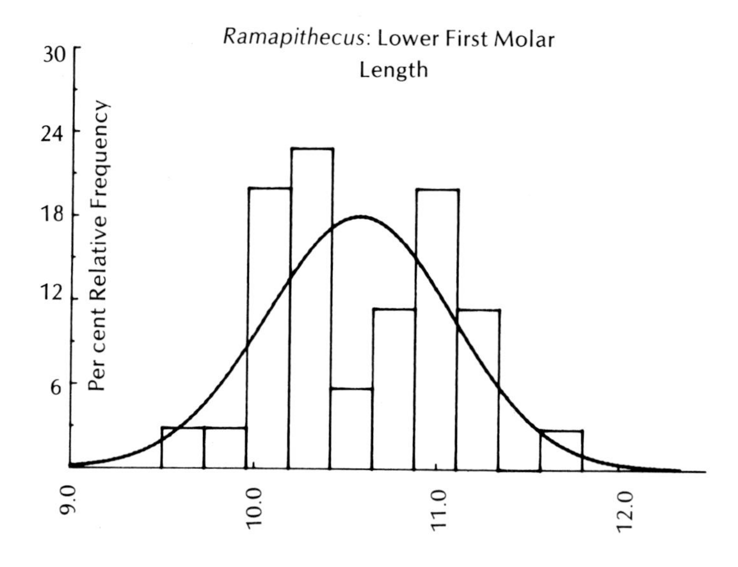

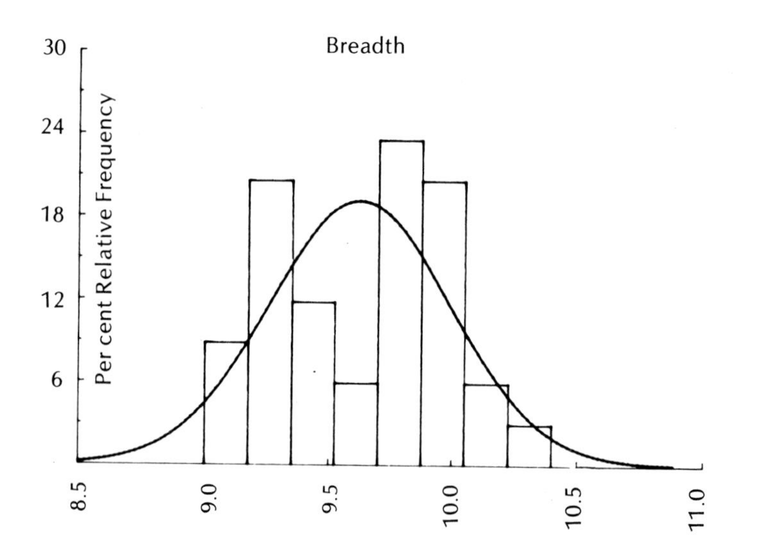

The third and fourth frames demonstrate that when lengths and breadths are bimodal whether equal, *Ramapithecus*, or unequal, *Sivapithecus*, then the areas (logged) are also bimodal in the appropriate manner.

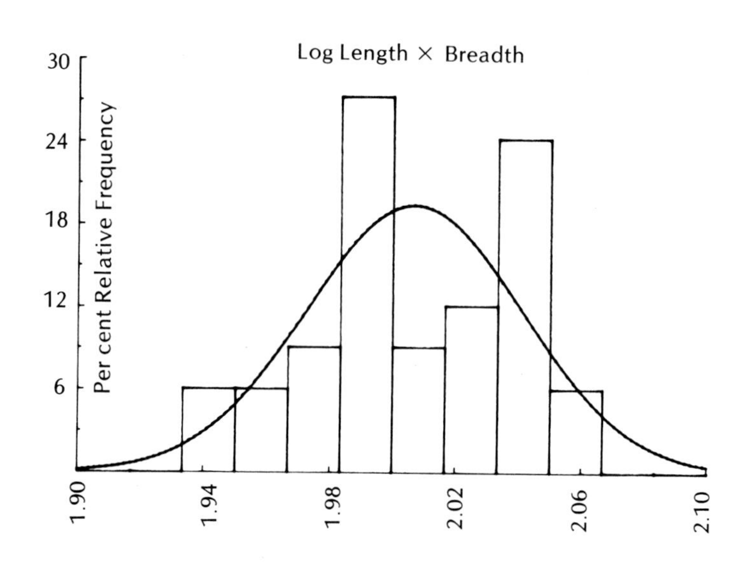

4th Frame

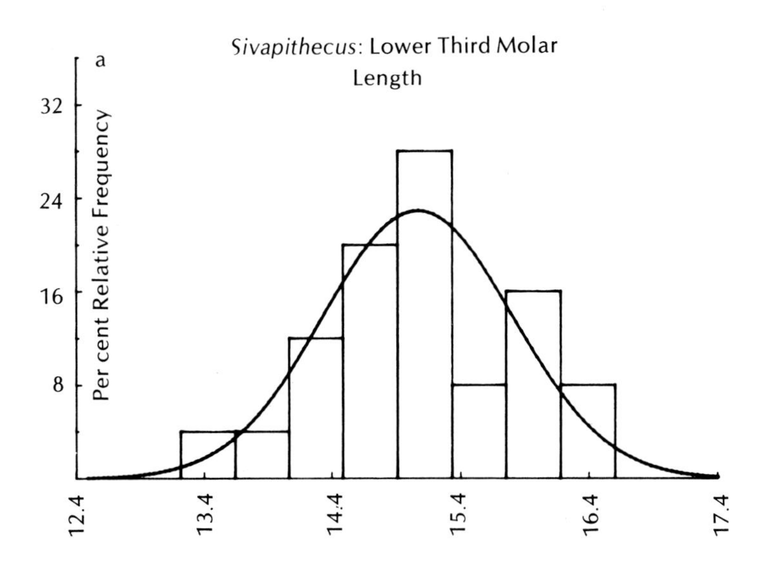
Sivapithecus: Lower Third Molar
Length
a
Per cent Relative Frequency
32
24
16
8
12.4
13.4
14.4
15.4
16.4
17.4

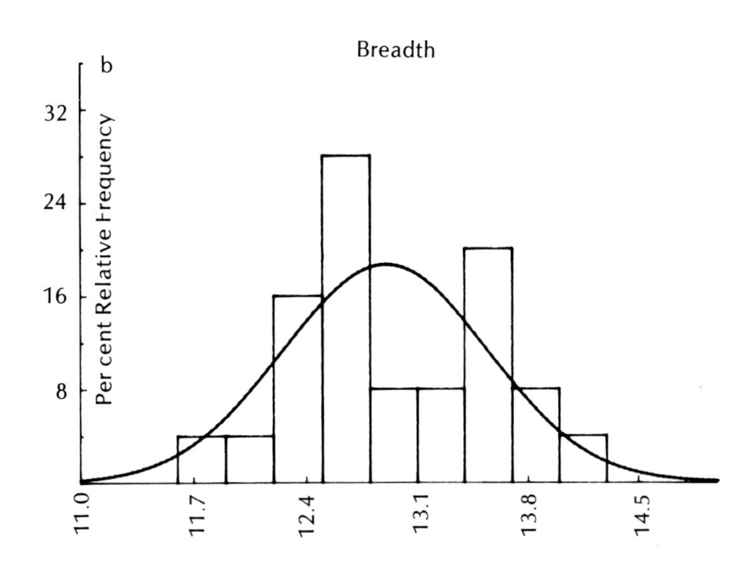
Breadth
b
Per cent Relative Frequency
32
24
16
8
11.0
11.7
12.4
13.1
13.8
14.5

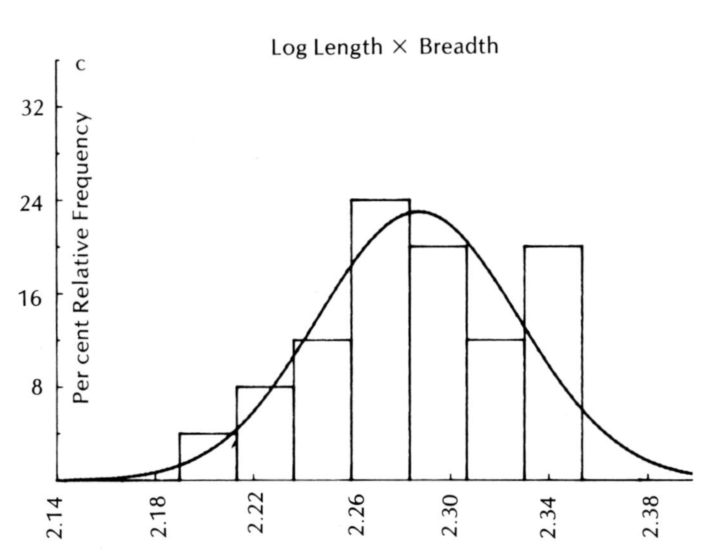
Log Length × Breadth
c
Per cent Relative Frequency
32
24
16
8
2.14
2.18
2.22
2.26
2.30
2.34
2.38

The same two separate multivariate analyses were performed on the data coinciding with the same studies of extant forms alone. For the extant primates, mandibular and maxillary data came from seven groups: *Gorilla* females, *Gorilla* males, *Pan* females, *Pan* males, *Pongo* females, *Pongo* males, and *Homo*, sex unknown. In each case, therefore, six canonical axes were generated.

The values for females and males in the two fossil groups (and for known males and females of modern *Homo*, Willcox' materials) are then interpolated into the canonical variates analyses on the extant species, using the previously generated eigenvectors. This allows us to examine the relative positions of the fossils against the extant forms initially involved in the analyses.

Canonical variates analyses

Figures 4:10 and 4:11 are plots of canonical variate means for the seven extant groups described in Chapter 2 for the mandibular analysis. The fossils are, additionally, interpolated into these diagrams.

***Sivapithecus*:** For the first four axes in the maxillary analysis *Sivapithecus* putative females and males are closer to the two large apes than to *Pan* or *Homo*. The direction of difference between female and male *Sivapithecus* is different to that between females and males for each extant form. This picture is mirrored for the first four axes in the mandibular analysis (Fig. 4:10). However, in this case, the separations achieved in the maxillary analysis for *Sivapithecus* are considerably greater than in the mandibular study. This is the reverse of the position for the extant forms. It reflects the finding from the univariate studies, that sexual dimorphism in *Sivapithecus* seems to be greater in upper as compared with lower jaws. To this degree then, *Sivapithecus* is different from all extant forms. But the primary finding is an overall pattern in *Sivapithecus* similar to that in *Pongo* (Fig. 4:11).

Sivapithecus also differs from all extant forms in another way. Consideration of the higher axes (five and six) in this study (Fig. 4:10) shows that large separations also exist here for this group. This indicates that there are additional elements of form in *Sivapithecus* that are not captured in the analysis based only on living species. Were it possible to include *Sivapithecus* in the analysis from the beginning (and future studies may allow this) the analyses would undoubtedly move separations for this group into one of the first three or four axes. What that would do to the arrangement of the extant forms cannot be predicted until such a study can be carried out. It awaits the recovery of a greater number of more complete specimens where we know which particular teeth belong with each other.

***Ramapithecus*:** Figures 4:10 and 4:11 show interpolation of *Ramapithecus*. For both maxillary and mandibular analyses *Ramapithecus* putative females and males are closer to *Homo* than to any other of the extant forms. The direction of difference between female and male *Ramapithecus* is quite small indicative of the lesser degree of sexual dimorphism of means indicated by the univariate studies.

The position of this fossil in the first two axes seems also to tend towards the genus *Pan* among the extant apes. But consideration of differences in axes three and four shows that this is not so.

And consideration of those higher axes (five and six, also Fig. 4:10) which scarcely separate the extant forms at all, shows that there are significant separations even for *Ramapithecus* from all living forms, including *Homo*. Indeed, were only early axes to be studied (early axes are all that should be studied when examining the living forms alone) we would obtain a spurious extra similarity between *Ramapithecus* and *Homo*. That such a spurious similarity between interpolated forms and original forms sometimes occurs and can be most misleading, has now been shown many times (e.g. for toe bones, ankle bones, metacarpals, reviewed in Oxnard, 1983a, 1984). Yet again however, the primary finding is an overall similarity of *Ramapithecus* to *Homo* (Fig. 4:11).

High-dimensional displays

As was the case with the extant genera, high-dimensional plots are generated in order to display information in higher axes that we have just discussed. Let us remind ourselves of the importance of this procedure. First, as for the extant species, it allows us to view multi-dimensional information in a way denied us by the more usual two- or three-dimensional plots of individual canonical axes. Second, however, because the fossils are interpolated into the analyses using eigenvectors to which their variances and co-variances have not contributed, then, even though higher axes may

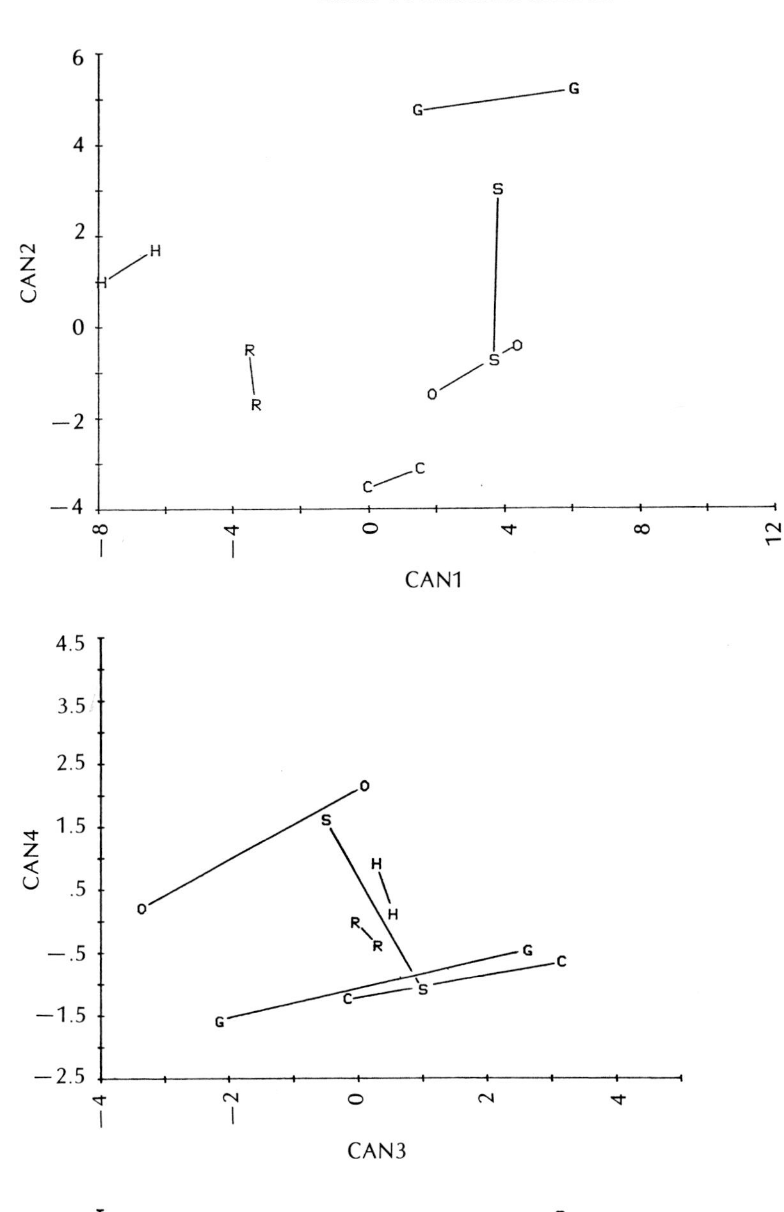

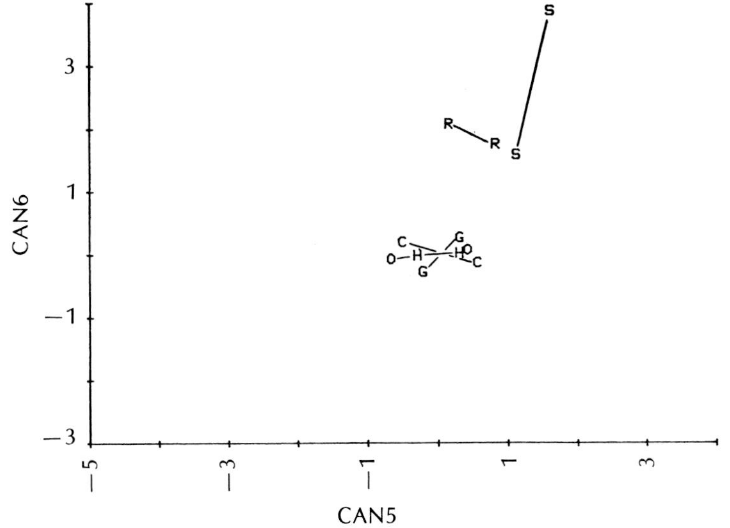

Fig. 4:10 This figure provides the three two-dimensional plots of the first against the second, the third against the fourth and the fifth against the sixth, for the canonical analysis of the mandibular data from extant forms with the ramapithecines interpolated. H-H, C-C, O-O and G-G are the positions of the extant forms, modern *Homo*, *Pan*, *Pongo* and *Gorilla* respectively. In the first plot the females are, in each case, the symbol most towards the left. *Sivapithecus* (S-S) falls between orang-utans and gorillas though closest to orang-utans. However, the form of its sexual dimorphism is clearly rather different from each. *Ramapithecus* (R-R) falls almost halfway between *Homo* and chimpanzees.

In the second plot it is evident that *Sivapithecus* has further elements of its sexual dimorphism that distinguish it from the living apes. *Ramapithecus* has elements of its sexual dimorphism that are very little different from those of humans.

In the third plot, there are seen to be no additional higher dimensional differences among the extant species. *Sivapithecus* has yet additional differences in these axes. *Ramapithecus*, though not totally similar to *Homo*, remains fairly close to it. The net result emphasizes the similarity between *Sivapithecus* and the orang-utan. It also emphasizes the similarity between *Ramapithecus* and *Homo*. The axes are in standard deviation units.

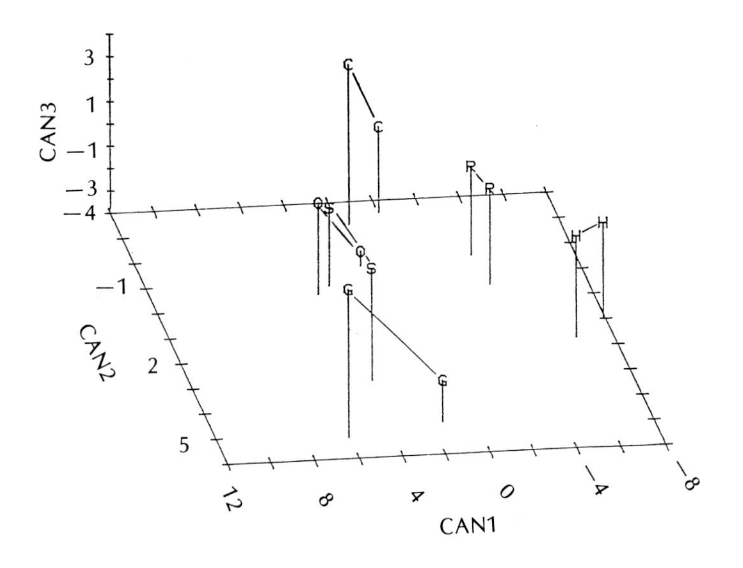

Fig. 4:11 This figure presents a three-dimensional model of the first three axes of the same analysis. It especially emphasizes the similarity between *Ramapithecus* and *Homo*, and between *Sivapithecus* and *Pongo*. The axes are in standard deviation units. Key as last figure.

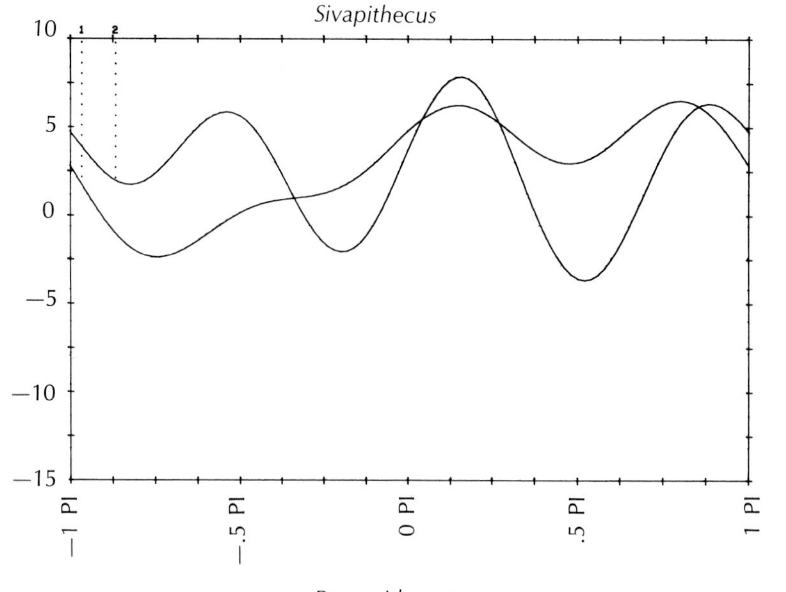

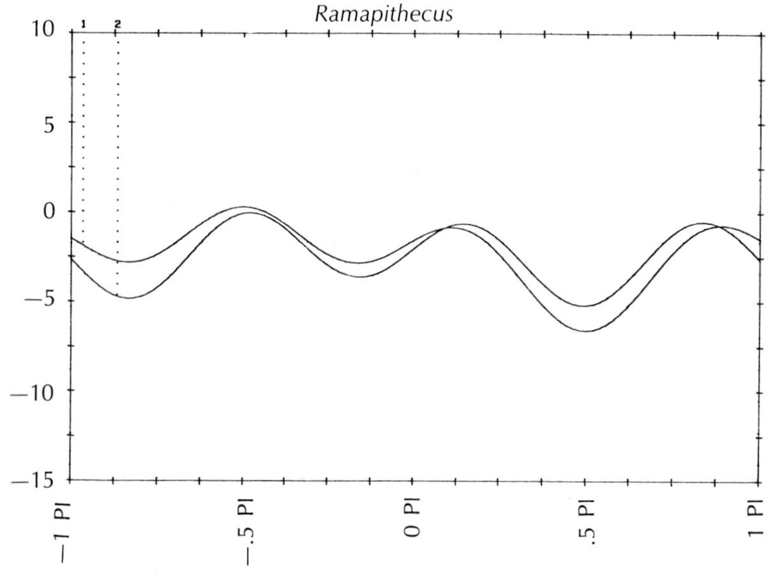

Fig. 4:12 This figure shows the high-dimensional displays for *Sivapithecus* and *Ramapithecus* for the analysis of the mandibular data. The area between the two groups is clearly far greater than could possibly be associated with sexual dimorphism in primates thus further displaying the unlikelihood that these two groups are the males and females of some ape-like form. The area within each group displays that sexual dimorphism is greater in *Sivapithecus* than *Ramapithecus*.

Andrews Plots.

contain no significant information for extant forms, they may well contain big, important, and statistically significant information for the fossils. High dimensional analyses allow ready recognition of this situation (see Chapter 3).

Figures 4:12 to 4:14 show the high-dimensional displays for the mandibular analyses. Total sexual dimorphism (represented by the area between the high dimensional plots for sex-subgroups and by differences in curvature for the high dimensional plots for sex-subgroups) is less in *Ramapithecus* and greater in *Sivapithecus*.

But the chief and immediately obvious information is that *Ramapithecus* is more like *Homo* than anything else. *Sivapithecus* is more similar to both of the large dimorphic apes but is not identical to either though nearest *Pongo*. Though *Ramapithecus* is not too far distant from *Pan*, it is still vastly different from it compared with *Homo*. The finding that both of the fossils are different from all extant species in higher axes is clearly displayed by the high frequency elements in their high dimensional plots.

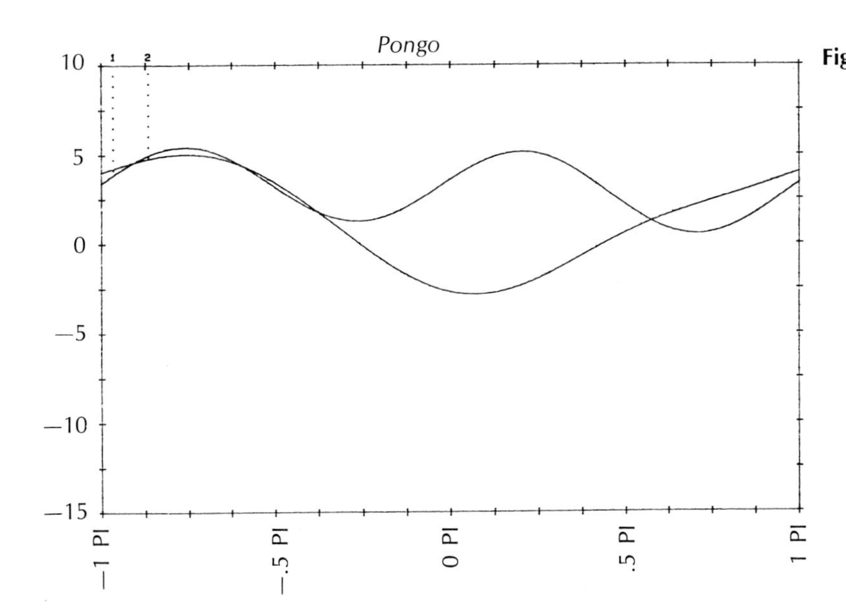

Fig. 4:13 This figure repeats the result (from Chapter Two) for *Pongo* for the mandibular analysis. It shows how close *Sivapithecus* is to *Pongo* even though it is not totally identical with *Pongo*.

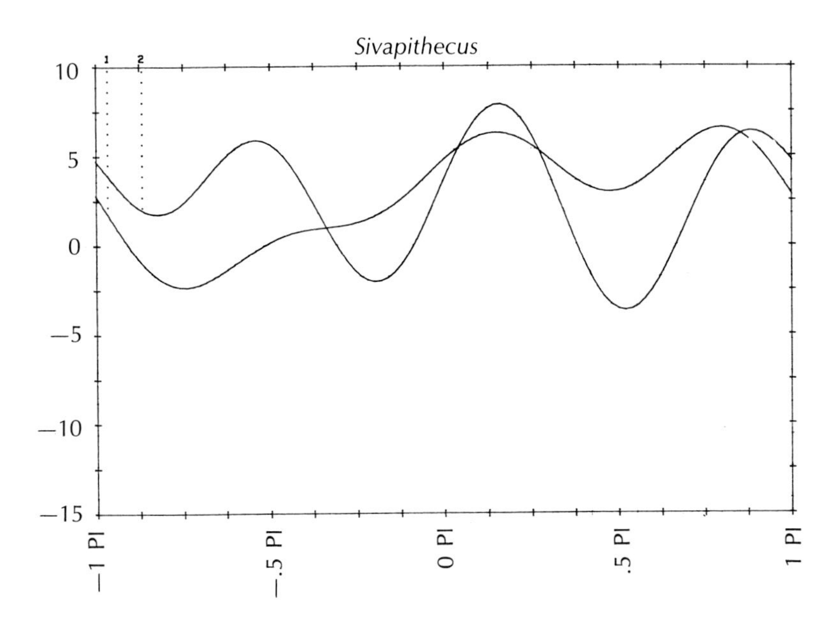

Andrews Plots

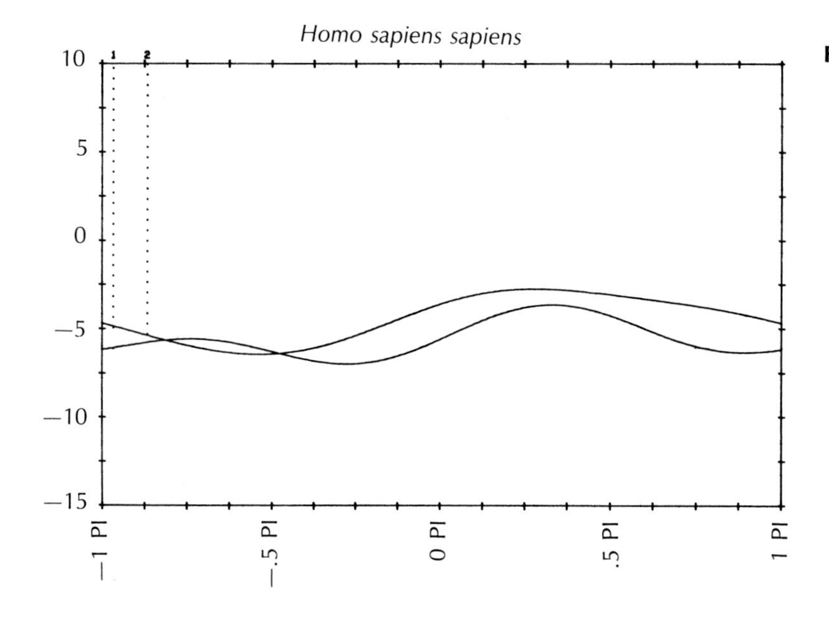

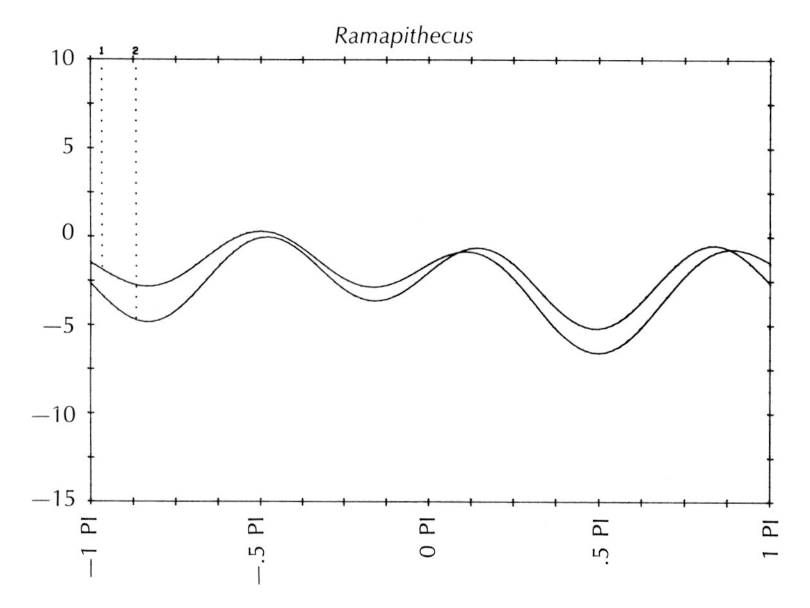

Fig. 4:14 This figure repeats the result (from Chapter Two) for *Homo* for the mandibular analysis. It shows that though *Ramapithecus* is not totally similar to *Homo* (modern), it possesses considerable similarity with it.

Andrews Plots

Conclusions: sexual dimorphism in the Chinese ramapithecines

Univariate analysis indicates clearly that *Sivapithecus* and *Ramapithecus* are quite different from one another. They cannot be the sexes of a highly dimorphic form.

The generally bimodal distributions for each tooth locus for each ramapithecine separately are likely to be reflecting true sexual dimorphisms in these data. It is strengthened by the fact that the discreteness between the peaks is greater for breadths than for lengths. This is a well-known phenomenon for the teeth of extant primates (Swindler, 1976) and is now confirmed for other bodily measures in Chapter 2.

A tentative case for this viewpoint, that both *Ramapithecus* and *Sivapithecus* display, each, their own sexual dimorphism was made for the Siwalik ramapithecines by Kay (1982a). But, though that study resulted in the same conclusion as here, the sizes of the samples that were available to Kay (in no case greater than twelve and mostly about seven) were not big enough to do more than hint at the possibility. Our studies here demonstrate that even when samples are as great as sixteen (the smallest of our samples, but more than twice the size of the average samples in Kay's study) individual measures are still found where this sample size is too small to permit statistical estimation. The best results are clearly obtained where samples are in the thirties and forties.

Univariate study of *Sivapithecus* shows large dimorphism of means, zero dimorphism of dispersions, and a 2:1 or greater sex ratio in the available samples. This combination is mirrored among extant forms only in *Pongo*. Multivariate analyses indicate clearly that *Sivapithecus* is close to both *Gorilla* and *Pongo* having large multivariate sexual dimorphism. When we remember that the method of interpolation means that, the multivariate information for the fossils is largely additional to the univariate information (because the method of interpolation does not allow the dispersions and sex ratios of the fossils to be included), then our overall assessment must be that it is with *Pongo* that *Sivapithecus* is most similar. Even this however, must not be taken too far; *Sivapithecus* has major ways, only shown by the high-dimensional displays, in which it differs even from *Pongo*.

Univariate study of *Ramapithecus* shows small dimorphism of means, zero dimorphism of dispersions, and a 1:1 sex ratio in the available samples. This combination is mirrored among extant forms only in *Homo*. Multivariate analyses also indicate clearly that *Ramapithecus* is closer to *Homo*, being relatively largely separated even from *Pan* the next nearest extant species. Again, the method of interpolation means that the multivariate information is largely additional to the univariate information. Thus our overall assessment is even more strongly that it is indeed to *Homo* that *Ramapithecus* is most closely similar. Even this however, must not be taken too far; *Ramapithecus* has some features, shown by higher axes, in which it differs even from *Homo*.

Both the univariate and multivariate analyses confirm that sexual dimorphism is different, in mandibles as compared with maxillae, especially between the extant and the fossil forms. This is further evidence of the complexity of this phenomenon of sexual dimorphism.

Implications for evolution

The idea that the Chinese ramapithecines are only a single species or species group displaying marked sexual dimorphism (e.g. Pilbeam and colleagues, Smith and Pilbeam, 1980; Lipson and Pilbeam, 1982; Andrews and Cronin, 1982; Todd, 1982; Pilbeam, 1984) is rendered completely untenable by these studies. There is no doubt that there exist two quite different samples of specimens with virtually non-overlapping differences. And there is little doubt that each of these exhibits evidence of sexual dimorphism and, to whit, a different sexual dimorphism in each (Wu and Oxnard, 1983a, b, Oxnard, 1983a, 1984, and earlier this chapter).

If these sexual dimorphisms mirror in any way what is known for the living primates then the social structure of *Ramapithecus* includes approximately equal numbers of adult males and females. This implies troupes with equal numbers of males and females: monogamy or (as is discussed in Chapter 8) the mildly polygynous situation that is found in some monogamous species. Both of these last are characteristic among extant large hominoids, only of humans.

Again, if these findings relate at all to what is known among living apes, then the situation in *Sivapithecus* is consistent with a few-male/multi-female, or even a single-male/multi-female social structure. This implies a 'forced' polygynous social structure (see Chapter 8) such as is found in many monkeys and all great apes.

Because, in these patterns of sexual dimorphism, *Ramapithecus* resembles only modern humans, and *Sivapithecus* all the modern great apes (especially orang-utans) it is tempting to draw the obvious evolutionary implications. Such implications could certainly be made immediately, for instance, if we relied upon the conventional views **(a)** that structural sexual dimorphism is basically a single phenomenon within the primates, mainly associated with size (e.g. Wood, 1975, 1976), and **(b)** that it is displayed to greater degrees in species with polygynous social organizations, and to lesser degrees in those that are monogamous (e.g. Fleagle, Kay and Simons, 1980; Gingerich, 1981; Kay, 1982a).

But we now know that dental sexual dimorphism may include many different phenomena (dimorphism of means, dimorphism of dispersions, canine dimorphism, different dimorphisms in the various dental regions, different dimorphisms in each jaw, complex multivariate dimorphisms and so on). We also now know that sexual dental dimorphisms may exist in as many as five different patterns among the living hominoids alone and several other patterns for many of the prosimians and monkeys. Sexual dimorphisms must be clearly related to more than a simple small-to-large size difference and monogamous-to-polygynous sexual structure axis (Oxnard, 1983a, c, 1984, and Chapters 1, 2 and 8). We must be far more circumspect in interpreting the data for the Chinese ramapithecines.

The patterns described above are not the only differences between the sexes in these two fossils. For instance, it is possible to view the relationships between the sexes by looking at the patterns of differences for each sex at each tooth position.

Table 4:3 outlines these data and it demonstrates that humans differ from all apes in having most of their large sexual differences confined to breadths: lower second incisors, upper first and second premolars, and upper second molars. Only one length difference is large, that for the lower first incisor. Among the apes, a majority of the largest differences are indeed breadths at many different loci, but an appreciable number of length differences are also large. This befits the notion of greater sexual dimorphism in the great apes. However, from one ape to another there are differences. For instance, Table 4:3 shows that chimpanzees differ from gorillas in having larger differences in the lower second incisors and upper first premolars. Orang-utans differ markedly from both the African great apes in having larger differences in both upper and lower premolars and both first molars. And the table shows that other differences also exist.

It is not, of course, possible to insert values of the same parameters for each of the fossils into this table because, although we know on morphological grounds which teeth belong to *Ramapithecus* and which to *Sivapithecus*, we do not know for certain which teeth are from males and which from females of each. We can use the information from each peak of the bimodal distributions to obtain approximate mean values, presumed due to the existence of sexual dimorphism. The results of performing these computations are given in the last two columns of Table 4:3. They demonstrate fairly clearly that not only does the small form, *Ramapithecus*, exhibit a lesser bimodality than the larger *Sivapithecus*, but also each group exhibits patterns of sexual dimorphism (if this is the cause of the bimodality) that differ from each of the extant genera (which, however, differ among themselves in equivalent ways).

Thus, *Ramapithecus* resembles the human pattern somewhat more than *Sivapithecus* or any living great ape. There are 11 positions in which *Ramapithecus* resembles humans. But *Ramapithecus* does also possess six positions in which it resembles apes, three the gorilla and three the orang-utan. *Sivapithecus*, in contrast, shares a human pattern at only five positions. Of the more ape-like patterns existing at the majority of the other tooth positions, seven are more similar to those in gorillas, three to those in orang-utans.

Special note must be taken of the human-like relative areas of the canine in the smaller form, *Ramapithecus*, and the ape-like relative canine areas in the larger *Sivapithecus*. It is likely that in *Sivapithecus* alone this is related to the special canine difference (much larger canines than other teeth) that is shown by many other primates. It is further support for the suggestions noted above (Table 4:4).

And this finding should be noted in relation to canine heights in the two forms. Table 4:5 and Figure 4:15 show that *Sivapithecus* has canine teeth that project well above the tooth row like many apes. The opposite is the case in *Ramapithecus* in which the canines are the same height as the other teeth (as in humans).

Of course, this may also be the difference between the sexes of a dimorphic animal so that we must read this together with the distributions for canine heights in the two animals (Fig. 4:16). These show quite marked canine bimodality of the unequal ratio type of both upper and lower canines in *Sivapithecus*. In contrast, in *Ramapithecus*, there is a normal appearing distribution for the upper canine and an equal ratio bimodal distribution for the lower. For the upper canine the number of specimens is so small that a normal curve cannot be fitted. Thus, in this dimension we have reached the level of sensitivity due to the reduced size of the sample. The samples of heights are reduced more than other measures, due to the fact that many more heights than other measures have to be eliminated because of heavy wear or damaged specimens. The examination of canine heights corroborates the ideas about sexual dimorphism obtained from the other dimensions.

It is not surprising that eight million year old creatures should not display sex differences identical to any living form. But it is of major interest that what we can discern of these many patterns of sexual dimorphism, should fall into the dichotomy of one fossil that is somewhat more human-like, and one that is somewhat more ape-like (orang-utan-like). Presumably, our continued investigation of these teeth may provide further evidence about the phylogenetic relationships that have been sampled here. What can they suggest at

Table 4:4

Ratios Between Area of Canine and Area of Each Other Dental Region

Ratio	*Homo*	*Gorilla*	*Pan*	*Pongo*	*Ramapithecus*	*Sivapithecus*
C'/I^{1+2}	0.72	1.29	0.84	0.79	0.78 (ALL)	1.352 (G)
C'/P^{3+4}	0.38	0.67	0.88	0.54	0.42 (H)	0.56 (O)
C'/M^{1+2+3}	0.13	0.31	0.40	0.30	0.15 (H)	0.22 (O)
$C_{,}/I_{1+2}$	0.70	0.98	0.74	0.69	0.87 (ALL)	1.12 (G)
$C_{,}/P_{3+4}$	0.40	0.74	0.90	0.71	0.61 (H-G)	0.7 (G-O)
$C_{,}/M_{1+2+3}$	0.14	0.35	0.42	0.36	0.25 (H)	0.31 (G-O)

H = *Homo*-like; O = *Pongo*-like; G = *Gorilla*-like.

Ratios Between Areas of Various other Dental Regions

Ratio	*Homo*	*Gorilla*	*Pan*	*Pongo*	*Ramapithecus*	*Sivapithecus*
$I^{1+2}+C'/P^{3+4}+M^{1+2+3}$	0.65	1.00	1.35	1.22	0.73 (H)	1.17 (O)
$I_{1+2}+C_{,}/P_{3+4}+M_{1+2+3}$	0.69	1.01	1.48	1.22	0.95 (H-G)	1.02 (G)
P^{3+4}/M^{1+2+3}	0.34	0.45	0.46	0.55	0.37 (H)	0.39 (least distant G)
P_{3+4}/M_{1+2+3}	0.35	0.47	0.47	0.51	0.41 (H-G)	0.43 (least distant G)

H = *Homo*-like; O = *Pongo*-like; G = *Gorilla*-like.

Table 4:5

Ratios Between Heights of Canines and Incisors

Ratio	*Homo*	*Gorilla*	*Pan*	*Pongo*	*Ramapithecus*	*Sivapithecus*
C'/I^1	0.96	1.92	1.47	1.30	1.13 (H)	1.42 (O-G)
$C_{,}/I_1$	1.05	1.67	1.45	1.72	1.10 (H)	1.39 (C)
C'/I^2	1.20	2.29	1.63	1.45	1.68 (C)	2.09 (G)
$C_{,}/I_2$	1.07	1.67	1.36	1.38	1.05 (H)	1.30 (O-C)

H = *Homo*-like; O = *Pongo*-like; G = *Gorilla*-like; C = *Pan*-like. Sexes for extant forms averaged.

this time for our understanding of higher primate evolution?

The biomolecular information (reviewed in Gribbin and Cherfas, 1982) and now the morphometric evidence (Oxnard, 1981a, 1983b) about the relationships of the living forms are unequivocal. The African great apes and humans are closely linked and have only distant associations with orang-utans.

If we also accept the more tentative information that the time of this linking between the African apes and humans was about 4 to 6 million years (from molecular clock hypotheses) then we are forced into the notion that none of these fossils can have been ancestral to humans without also being ancestral to African great apes. This would still allow, however, that at least some ramapithecines could have been ancestral to both modern African great apes and humans, i.e. hominoid ancestors rather than hominid ancestors.

If, however, this were so, then we would have to accept the following sequence of changes: from (**a**) prior ancestors of *Ramapithecus*, through (**b**) *Ramapithecus* itself, to (**c**) two groups of extant forms, African great apes and humans. This would be a sequence of changes from (**a**) prior ancestors of *Ramapithecus* that had large overall sexual dimorphisms, large canines relative to other teeth

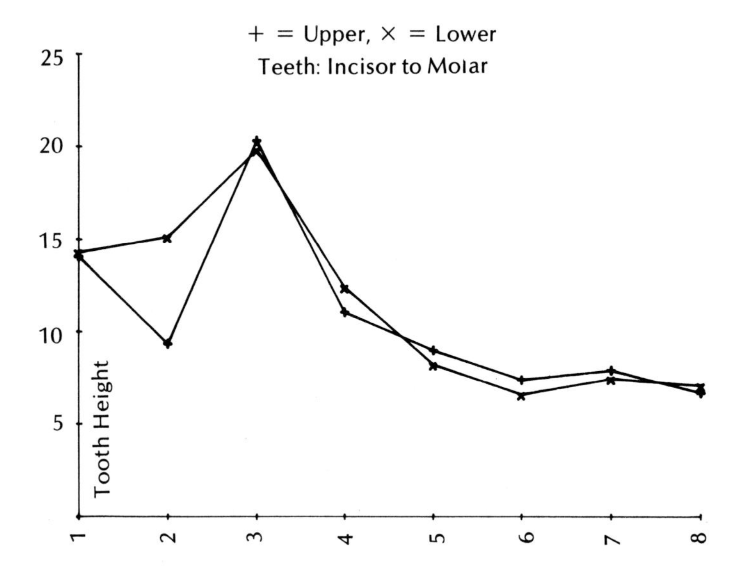

Fig. 4:15 Canine heights are available from sufficient specimens to make comparisons with the heights of the other teeth. The upper plot shows how the canines (tooth position number 3) project above the tooth row in *Sivapithecus* in both upper and lower jaws somewhat as in apes. The lower plot shows that the canines do not project above the anterior part of the tooth row in *Ramapithecus*. This is a further similarity of *Ramapithecus* to *Homo*.

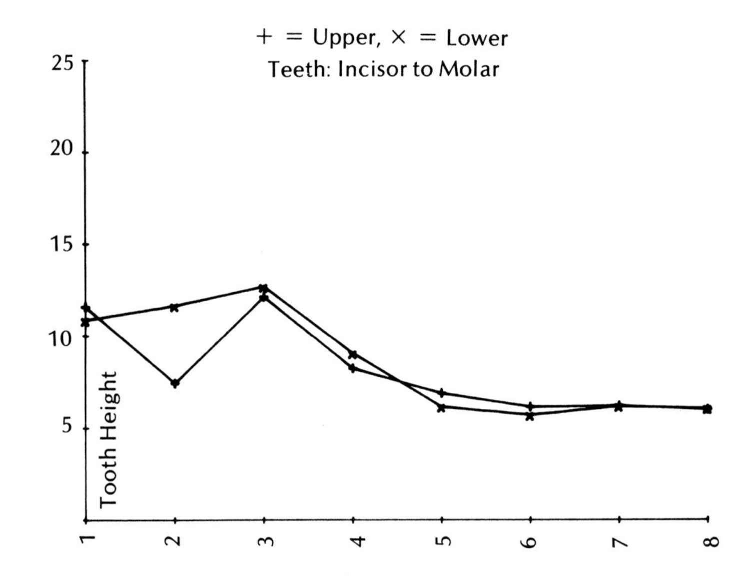

and large canine sexual dimorphism, polygynous social structures, more vegetarian diets, and more ape-like (in general terms) teeth, to **(b)** *Ramapithecus* itself showing small overall sexual dimorphism, small canines relative to other teeth and small canine dimorphism, approximately equal numbers of females and males and possibly, therefore, a monogamous family social structure, more omnivorous diet, and more human-like general features of the teeth. This would then have to be followed by re-evolving **(c)** large overall sexual dimorphisms, large canines relative to other teeth and large canine sexual dimorphism, female to male ratios considerably greater than 1:1 and, presumably, related polygynous social structures, mainly vegetarian diets, and generally ape-like features of the teeth as in the extant African great apes. Such a series of complexities and reversals seems unlikely.

In such a scheme, the more sexually dimorphic, increased canine size and dimorphism, 2:1 female to male ratio, polygynous social structure, vegetarian diet, and other ape-like features of *Sivapithecus* would appear to have had little place save, perhaps, as a possible ancestor to a more distant pathway related to an older link of all of these forms with orang-utans.

It is also possible to accept another idea that is not defeated by the molecular clock hypothesis. That is, of course, the idea that none of the

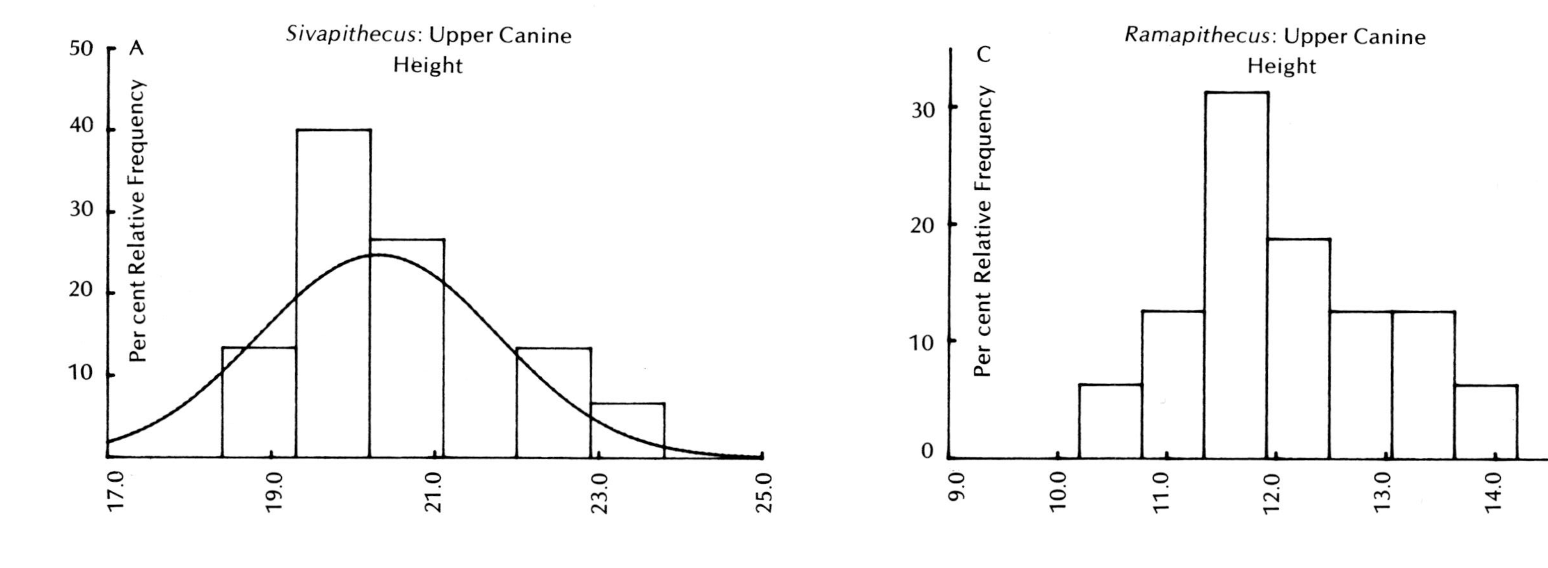

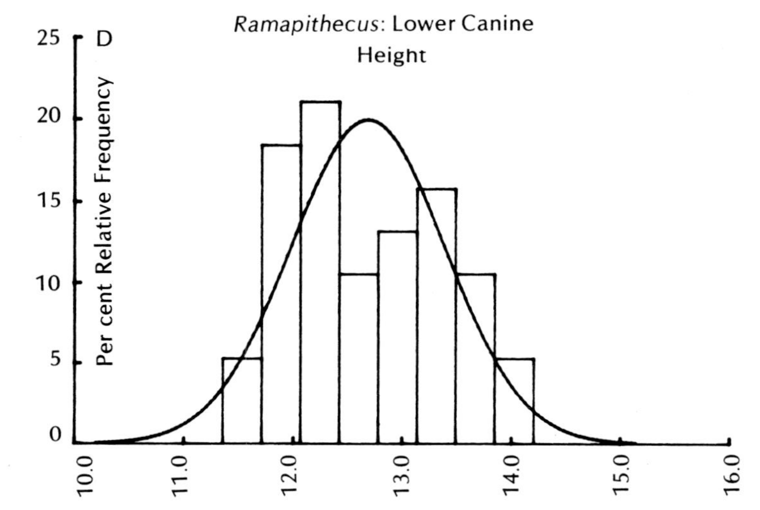

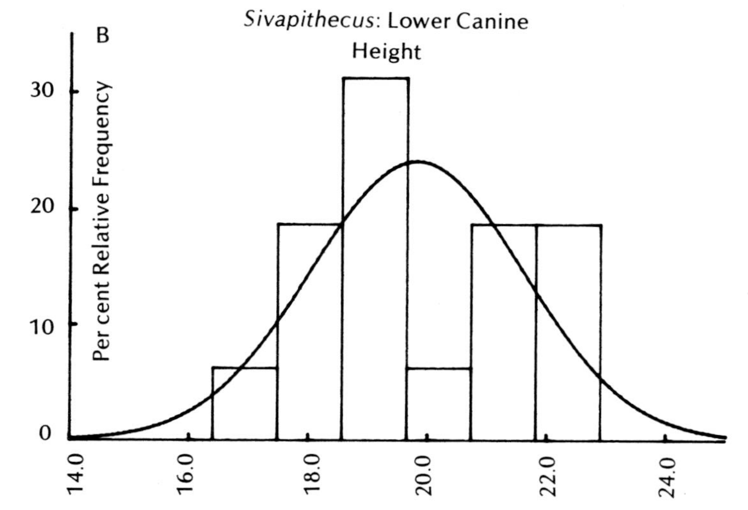

Fig.4:16 The canine heights for each genus are distributed in the same way as the other dimensions of the teeth: two unequal bimodal distributions in *Sivapithecus* as in apes, a normal distribution and an equal bimodal distribution in *Ramapithecus* as in *Homo*.

ramapithecines are ancestral to any of the modern African apes or humans.

This would imply that large and small overall sexual dimorphisms, large and small canines relative to other teeth and large and small specifically canine sexual dimorphism, 1:1 and 2:1 female to male ratios, monogamous and polygynous social structures, omnivorous and vegetarian diets, and human-like and ape-like features *in these paired combinations* must have arisen in parallel a number of times. This is possibly a little less unlikely than may appear at first sight, because parallel evolutionary trends in closely related groups with extinctions are far more common in biology, and far more parisimonious for our thinking therefore, than single evolutions of unique forms. But it still seems rather unlikely.

It is possible, however, that we need not accept the precise times of the molecular clock hypotheses while yet accepting the unequivocal molecular evidence of patterns of relationship. This would allow us to see the lesser sexually dimorphic, smaller canine size (relative to other teeth) and lesser canine dimorphic, 1:1 sexually distributed, monogamous, omnivorous, and more human-like *Ramapithecus* as nearer to a human lineage. It would also allow us to see the more sexually dimorphic, larger canine size, more canine dimorphic, 2:1 sexually distributed, polygynous, vegetarian and more ape-like *Sivapithecus* as nearer to lineages leading to orang-utans.

These are certainly not impossible ideas because ramapithecines broadly defined do, after all, cover a time frame of some eight million years, a period as long as the entire time that has elapsed since the last of the known ramapithecines became extinct. These are simpler ideas, and new developments and more critical thinking about alternative possibilities in molecular clock concepts, could easily accommodate them. Whether or not it makes any sense to modify these molecular dates is discussed in the final chapter.

At least all this discussion is now based, thanks to major efforts by many Chinese palaeoanthropologists, upon almost two orders of magnitude more morphological data, and upon a much more complete statistical study of overall dental dimensions, than have been all prior speculations about this group of fossils. Whatever the ancestor/descendent relationships may have been, we do now have a far more concrete description of at least two groups, each comprising two sub-groups existing in China millions of years ago.

The full impact of these findings cannot be clear until the investigations of the fossils of other chapters are also included. For this we must await the examination and discussion, in the next two chapters, of the fossils intermediate in time between the ramapithecines and the genus *Homo*. Those intermediate fossils include the mainstream (as it is believed to be) group of australopithecines and the side issue (as it is believed to be) species of *Gigantopithecus*. By mainstream we mean: a part of, or very close to, the main human lineage. By side issue we mean: an aberrant form generally thought to be more closely related to apes than to anything else.

Summary: This review of sexual dimorphism in the dental dimensions of the Chinese ramapithecines *denies absolutely* the idea that we have here only a single species, or species group, displaying marked sexual dimorphism. Because these results arise from a total sample of almost one thousand, and samples for many individual tooth dimensions that are close to one hundred, the evidence for this is at least an order of magnitude greater than is usual in studies of fossils. Indeed, these samples are greater than those often examined in studies of extant species.

What we learn, both from the univariate and multivariate investigations, is that there are two species or species groups here which we can designate *Ramapithecus* and *Sivapithecus*.

Sivapithecus has all the characteristics of a form showing marked dimorphism. As with other species examined in prior chapters, this dimorphism is complex. It involves, of course, (**a**) a dimorphism of size: larger teeth in putative males and smaller in putative females (sexual dimorphism of means). But it also shows (**b**) differences in the particular dental sites at which the dimorphism occurs, (**c**) differences between the two jaws in the pattern of dimorphism, and (**d**) differences in the multivariate form of the dimorphism. In addition, *Sivapithecus* as an overall group shows (**e**) a special multivariate placement quite different from *Ramapithecus*. Finally, it is especially evident that (**f**) the sex ratio (ratio between females and males) in *Sivapithecus* is between two-to-one and four-to-one.

These are all characteristics of ape-like creatures. And of the extant apes with which *Sivapithecus* is compared it is to orang-utans that it is most close. Even here, we must be careful, however. There are multivariate features of the *Sivapithecus* results that separate this group markedly, even from orang-utans.

In complete contrast are our findings for *Ramapithecus*. *Ramapithecus* has all the characteristics of a form showing little dimorphism between the sexes. Again, however, this small dimorphism is not just a matter of degree.

Though small, its sexual dimorphism is every bit as complex as in other forms examined in prior chapters. It involves, as always, of course, (**a**) one group with larger teeth (putative males) and one with smaller teeth (putative females) as seen from dimorphism of means. As with *Sivapithecus* (but at different loci) it also includes (**b**) differences in the particular dental sites at which the dimorphisms occur, (**c**) differences in the pattern of dimorphism between the two jaws, and (**d**) differences in the multivariate form of the dimorphism. In addition, *Ramapithecus* as an overall group shows (**e**) a special multivariate placement quite close to *Homo*. Finally, it is especially evident that (**f**) the ratio between females and males in *Ramapithecus* is like that in modern humans, approximately one-to-one.

None of these characteristics are found in extant apes. All are such as we have already found in modern and fossil humans. Again, even here, we must be careful. There are multivariate features of the *Ramapithecus* results that separate this group somewhat, even from modern humans.

There are clear implications for the discussion of human and ape evolution. But we again await the studies of later chapters to see to what degree they are influenced by the findings for australopithecines and *Gigantopithecus*.

CHAPTER 5

The Intervening Period: African Ancestors?

Abstract: We first review briefly current ideas about the evolutionary relationships of the australopithecines. These ideas imply that one or another, or even more, of the australopithecines are indeed human ancestors; and that the remainder are either also on that lineage or closely related to it.

We also review some of the challenges to those views. One of these — now fully confirmed — states that australopithecines are quite different morphologically from the genus *Homo*. A second, now largely agreed, implies that they were probably arboreal as well as being bipedal in a manner different from humans. A third suggests that as a result of these first two, we cannot say whether the australopithecines form a curious mosaic on the human lineage (accepted, reluctantly, by some) or a radiation that lies alongside the human lineage (scarcely accepted by anyone). The earlier view, that they were obviously direct human ancestors, is under fire.

We next test these ideas through new studies of sexual dimorphism. We examine what little is known about general sexual dimorphism in australopithecines and then go on to study the dimensions of their teeth, using the methods generally adopted in this book.

Univariate studies demonstrate once again, the general complexity of the phenomenon of sexual dimorphism. They show that bimodal distributions are ubiquitous in the various australopithecine groups. The nature of that bimodality is such that it was almost certainly sexual dimorphism. It is likely that a dimorphism in variance also exists, at least in some of the species or species groups. Different patterns of dimorphism along the tooth row can be discerned. And the distributions allow us, generally, to make assessments of sex ratios in the different subgroups of these fossils.

Multivariate studies of these same dimensions are next presented. They allow us to assess the size of the multivariate sexual dimorphisms, to study multivariate sexually dimorphic patterns both between jaws and between fossil groups, and to compare multivariate positions of individual fossil groups with those of the extant apes and humans.

All of these results emphasize once again the enormous complexity of the phenomenon of sexual dimorphism. They provide fascinating information in the comparison with living apes and humans from Chapter 2. They are especially interesting in the comparison with the fossils of Chapters 3 & 4. They have important implications in the understanding of the evolution of the hominoids.

Australopithecines and habilines

Those fossils that have been found mainly in Africa, australopithecines and habilines, date from as recently as 1 million years ago or less, to possibly 4 million years ago or even more. This is a period of time that almost matches the definition of the Pliocene that extends from 1.8 to 5 million years ago. We can fairly confidently expect that the range of these fossils will be extended, perhaps at both ends, by the fossil hunters and the date finders as investigations progress.

How many australopithecines are there? What are their characteristics? Which phylogenetic branches do they sustain? How, if at all, are the habilines involved with them?

The robust australopithecines are the ones about which there is less argument. The first evidence about them came from Kromdraai in southern Africa. Later the majority of the specimens came from Swartkrans and though given a different name, *Paranthropus crassidens*, by Broom and Robinson (1952) they eventually all became known as *Australopithecus robustus*.

As a group they share with other australopithecines the combination of a small cranium and well developed jaw. But they differ from them in several ways. The molar teeth are much larger, and the premolar teeth have extra cusps (molarization) so that they resemble molars. The anterior teeth in contrast are actually smaller than in the gracile forms.

Such few post-cranial bones as there are have been interpreted as demonstrating bipedalism and handiness (e.g. Napier, 1959). But both of these assessments have been challenged (e.g. Lewis, 1977; Oxnard, 1983a, 1984). They are generally believed nowadays to be separate from (although very close to) the direct human line.

More recently a fossil was found in Tanzania that was the first evidence from elsewhere in Africa of a form similar to *Australopithecus robustus*. Originally named *Zinjanthropus* by L. S. B. Leakey (1959) it was eventually reduced in rank to *Australopithecus* and given the specific name *boisei*.

It seems to be much closer, morphologically to the 'robust' rather than the 'gracile' australopithecines. The molar teeth are even more enlarged. The mandibular and cranial morphology seem to further reflect this. It is therefore described as 'hyper-robust' and is generally believed to be closely related to *A. robustus*.

The gracile australopithecines were first described by Raymond Dart (1925) from a specimen of a child found in southern Africa at Taung sixty years ago. Later Sterkfontein yielded specimens to Robert Broom that were first called *Plesianthropus* but that, eventually, came to be referred to as *Australopithecus africanus*. And in 1947 in Makapansgat cave were found more specimens that were referred to this genus.

These skulls are small (450–500 ccs) but, unlike the apes, spherical. The face is projecting, but unlike the apes, they do not have a 'muzzle'. The areas for the attachment of jaw and neck muscles are large and display crests, but these crests are thought to be unlike those in apes. The dental arcades are rounded like those of female apes, but in marked contrast to those of male apes (with which they are usually compared).

The post-cranial bones are few. But one extensive find includes parts of ribs, vertebrae, pelvic girdle and femora for one individual. These, and other fragments, have suggested to many workers that these creatures were bipedal.

The fossils, *Australopithecus afarensis*, (the name which they were eventually given) were found in 1973 and later in the valley of the Awash river near Hadar in Ethiopia (e.g. Johanson and Taieb, 1976). The most complete specimen consisted of many parts of the post-cranium as well as the cranial vault and mandible.

Most workers seem to think that they are like *A. africanus* in all the features just mentioned. Some have said that they seem more generalized, perhaps intermediate between *Ramapithecus* and *Australopithecus* (Wood, 1978). But that belief was held at a time when *Ramapithecus* was thought to be indisputably on a human line. And it was, in any case, based only upon the similarity in their v-shaped mandibles and the mandibular teeth. The Afar fossils are as much as two million years older than *Australopithecus africanus*.

The many post-cranial remains of *Australopithecus afarensis* seemed to indicate to the original discoverers that they walked on two legs. But many other workers (see later) think that in addition they had arboreal capabilities like *A. africanus*.

New finds from Olduvai prompted Leakey, Tobias and Napier (1964) to recognize a new form, *Homo habilis*. Though most of those original fragments are no longer thought to be *Homo habilis*, further finds at Olduvai and Laetoli in Tanzania, in the Omo and at Koobi Fora in Kenya, at Hadar in Ethiopia have been included as *Homo habilis*. Even some remains at Swartkrans and Sterkfontein in southern Africa may possibly be a similar but early *Homo* query *habilis* that is contemporaneus with australopithecines.

The range of size and morphology of all of these fossils is large. They span a considerable time range, 3.5 to 1.8 million years. They have features varying from vertical faces with large palates to projecting faces with small palates. All appear to have larger cranial capacities (700 to 800 ccs where they can be measured or estimated) than the australopithecines and most are referred unequivocally to *Homo habilis*.

Human ancestors?

The entire group although known from many specimens discovered over many years, and known especially from the extensive finds of recent years in Ethiopia and Kenya, remains curiously amongst the most problematical. There is great debate, not only about the possible phylogenetic linkages of the various individual fossils, but even about what and how many groups exist among the entire assemblage.

Some aver that the newly defined *Australopithecus afarensis*, also the oldest group, is the lineal progenitor of both humans and the other australopithecines (e.g. Johanson and White, 1979; White, Johanson and Kimbel, 1984).

Others believe that *Australopithecus afarensis* is only ancestral to the later robust australopithecines. *Australopithecus africanus*, previously the main candidate for a human lineal ancestor (e.g. Dart, 1925), is still that candidate (e.g. Broom, 1939; Le Gros Clark, 1940; Robinson, 1972, together with many other investigators in recent times).

No one now suggests the robust australopithecines as human ancestors, though that was also once believed to be the case (e.g. Broom, 1950). But even among the robust forms there is debate about the reality of their existence. Do they comprise one group or two: robust and hyper-robust?

There is even a similar discussion about the reality of the difference between *afarensis* and *africanus*. There are proponents for the view that they are virtually identical.

And there have even been, over the years, those who have believed that the links of the australopithecines with the human evolutionary story are so close that some of them (*Australopithecus africanus*) should be ascribed to the human genus: *Homo africanus* (Robinson, 1972). Certainly many of these specimens have been described as displaying striding bipedality 'of the human form' (Day and Wood, 1968).

The subgroup now known as *Homo habilis* is of particular interest. Although not all the specimens originally thought to be *Homo habilis* are still tagged with that name (e.g. the original foot and hand of *Homo habilis* are not now thought to belong to that species) sufficient other specimens have been found with somewhat higher cranial volumes (of about 800 ccs) that there is a reality to this cluster.

And when, finally, we understand that some of these species, the gracile and the robust, were suggested at one time as the two sexes of a single species (Brace, 1973), we realize just how complex and confused this whole group is. We have no certain idea just how many groups are represented in this assemblage of forms, extensive though the finds now are.

It should also be recorded that a small number of investigators do not see, in australopithecine anatomy, any group (except for *Homo habilis*) that is ancestral to humans at all. Earlier investigations (e.g. Zuckerman, 1950, 1955, 1966, 1970) suggest that the australopithecines are merely fossils whose ape-like features had been de-emphasized by most investigators as they made their human-like assessments.

Later investigations (Oxnard, 1968a, b, 1972a, 1973a; Zuckerman, Ashton, Flinn, Oxnard and Spence, 1973; Ashton, Flinn and Moore, 1975, 1976, Oxnard 1975a, b, 1979; Ashton, Flinn, Moore, Oxnard and Spence, 1981; Ashton, 1981; Oxnard, 1983a, 1984) have come to the further conclusion that the individual features of these creatures, whether like apes or humans individually, show, when aggregated into an overall pattern, anatomical systems that are unique.

Notwithstanding these various assessments, there is now general acceptance of the idea that there are five groups of these fossils: two gracile australopithecines (*afarensis* and *africanus*), two robust (*robustus* and *boisei*), and a single more human-like group (*Homo habilis*). There is also general acceptance of the view that all are very close to the human line. It is to these generally accepted groupings that we shall adhere in the descriptions that follow.

Sexual dimorphism in australopithecines: current views

The matter of sexual dimorphism in the australopithecines is complex and not clearly understood. One supposition is, that there is not only a size difference between the gracile and robust species groups but also, considerable size difference between their sexes. Thus, Krantz (1982) suggests figures of 55 kg and 21 kg for the two sexes of *A. robustus*, an absolutely enormous degree of body weight dimorphism. He also suggests 68 kg and 36 kg as the average weights for each sex of *A. africanus*, also an enormous difference. If these estimates are anywhere near correct they would represent sexual dimorphism unique among the primates. They would certainly be associated with major differences in the dimensions of the teeth.

Some attempts have been made to evaluate sexual dimorphism in the teeth, using the coefficient of variation for given groups. Initially this has been useful, because it certainly does discover if the relative amount of variation of a measure is greater in one group than another. Such increased variation could certainly be due to increased difference between the means for each component sex of the group.

But, as we have already seen, sexual dimorphism is much more complex. Differing variances for each sex combined with differences in means effects the values of this coefficient. Non-normal distributions, especially (**a**) the plateau-like, (**b**) plateau-like with a central peak, and (**c**) bimodal histograms, markedly affect the interpretation of the value of this coefficient. Especially do (**d**) unequal numbers of each sex, affect the coefficient. Thus, its use is not the best way to attempt to understand degrees and patterns in a phenomenon that is as complex as we now know sexual dimorphism to be.

In fact, this increased complexity of sexual dimorphism is far better detectable with the methods employed in this book.

New studies of individual measures of australopithecine teeth

Because of all these confusions, because my expertise is not in the taxonomy of fossils, and because of the small sizes of samples for different teeth for the different fossil groups, we look at the data using the most generally accepted definitions of groupings, making the fewest assumptions about them.

First, we study all australopithecines together as the subfamily. For it was carrying out this type of apparently naive investigation that made it clear that the ramapithecines comprised two distinct groups, rather than one group with marked sexual dimorphism. This is possible, of course, at every tooth locus because, for the entire subfamily, there are enough specimens to allow it.

Second, we investigate, separately, all gracile specimens and all robust specimens. This can be done for all tooth positions. The results are reported here, only for those positions where numbers of specimens are so small as to prevent investigation of the more detailed subgroups. Though all gracile and all robust specimens, each, almost certainly contain subgroups, there is nevertheless enough of a fundamental difference between gracile and robust forms for this to make biological sense. Of course, we have used the designations supplied by others as to which specimens are gracile and which robust.

Third, the most important and detailed studies are those, in which we study data from the specimens when grouped into the four australopithecine genera: *Australopithecus afarensis*, *A. africanus*, *A. robustus* and *A. boisei*.

Finally, we include, for the few teeth where the amount of material available allow it, *Homo habilis* as a fifth separate group. The earliest definition of *Homo habilis* specimens was based upon an assemblage of hand bones, an almost complete but disarticulated foot and a few cranial fragments (Leakey, Tobias and Napier, 1964). Most of these original specimens have now been discarded as not being from *Homo habilis*. The foot is clearly that of a bipedal animal that could climb well and is probably, therefore, the foot of a gracile australopithecine. The hand also shows arboreal climbing features, but has mostly been discarded as not *Homo habilis* but belonging to other non-hominoid climbing primates. The remaining elements of the hand are probably what would be expected in a tree climbing australopithecine. This leaves, for that first specimen, only the fragments of jaws and parietals that may provide evidence of an endocranial volume of 700 to 800 ccs. If this is so they could not be australopithecine but might truly represent *Homo habilis*.

But since those days the new specimens, mentioned previously, have more clearly determinable cranial capacities at around 700–800 ccs. They have now been more certainly named *Homo habilis*. It is also more certain that they have cranial capacities some half way between those of australopithecines proper and *Homo erectus*. On that ground it seems prudent to follow the idea of assigning them to a separate group. We have, therefore, distinguished them for analysis as *Homo habilis* according to the evaluations provided in the literature.

Figures 5:1 through to 5:5 show what some of the

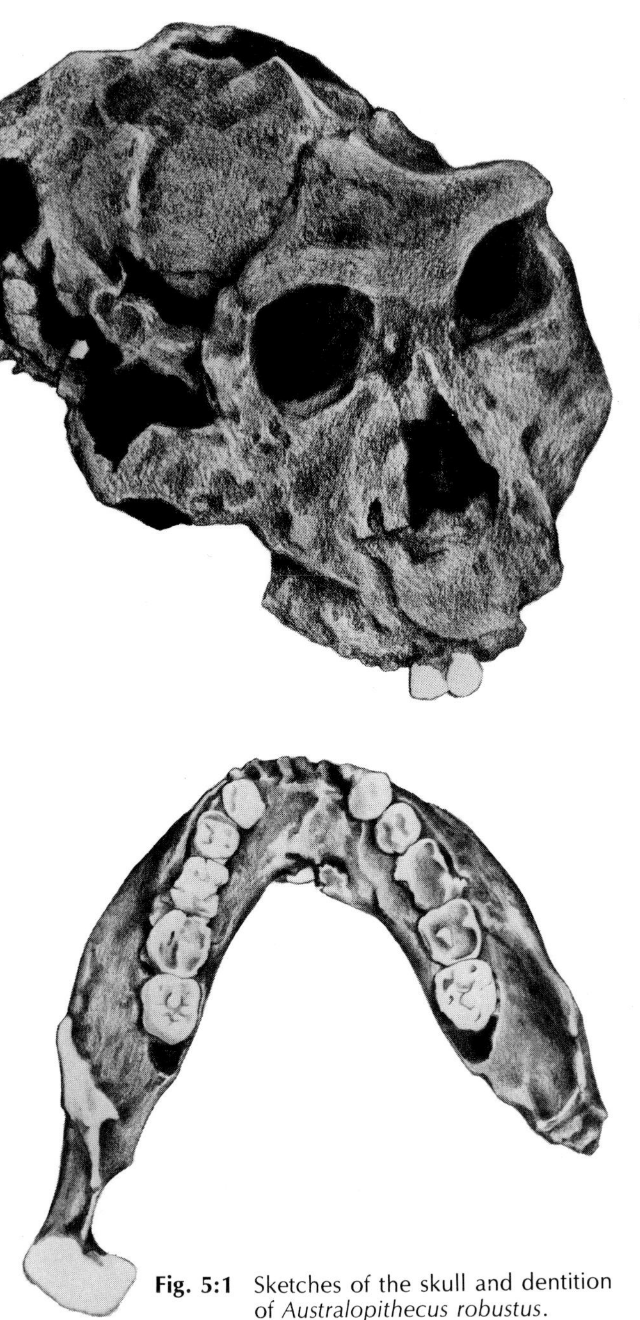

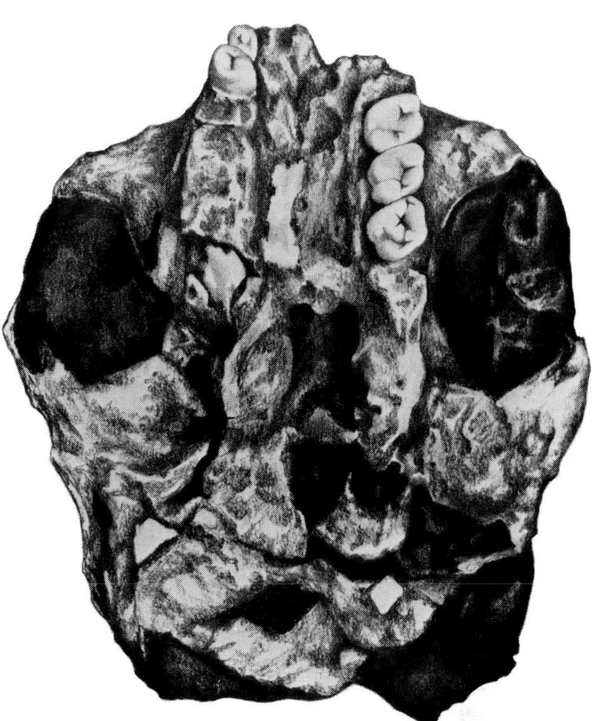

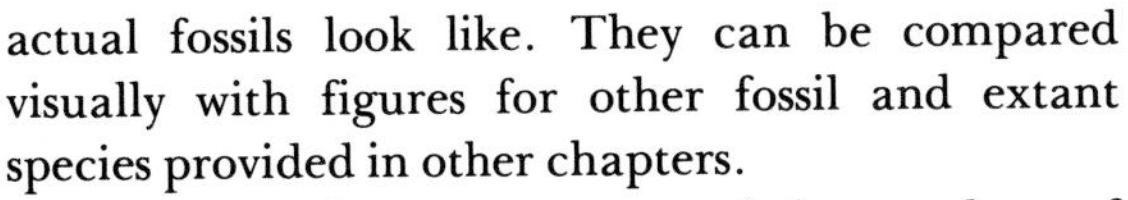

Fig. 5:1 Sketches of the skull and dentition of *Australopithecus robustus*.

actual fossils look like. They can be compared visually with figures for other fossil and extant species provided in other chapters.

Table 5:1 gives a summary of the numbers of measurements available for each tooth for each group. There are 750 teeth altogether, but, though some tooth positions are represented by less than 10 teeth and thus cannot be studied by our techniques, there are 20 or more teeth at most positions and they are, thus, susceptible to our investigations.

The data are from the studies of many investigators (Blumenberg and Lloyd, 1983; Boaz and Howell, 1977; Carny *et al*, 1971; Clark, 1977; Clark *et al*, 1970; Coppens, 1970, 1971, 1973a, 1973b; Frayer, 1973; Grine, 1981; Johanson, White and Coppens, 1982; Leakey *et al*, 1971; Leakey, Leakey and Behrensmyer, 1978; Leakey and Walker, 1973; Robinson, 1962; White, 1977, 1980; Wolpoff, 1971, 1973). Blumenberg and Lloyd (1983) and Wolpoff (1971) have provided most useful compendia and summaries.

Pooled group of all australopithecines

As a pooled group, the australopithecines do not provide any coherent picture such as results from looking at the pooled group of all ramapithecines. The histograms for the various dental dimensions range, from unimodal distributions that are not significantly different from normal, through heavily skewed distributions that are significantly different from normal, at levels even below those given by the computer programs with which we work (i.e. below 0.001) through various plateau-like and bimodal distributions, to various types of complex multimodal distributions with varying degrees of significance, in relation to fitted normal curves.

This complex picture is so different from what

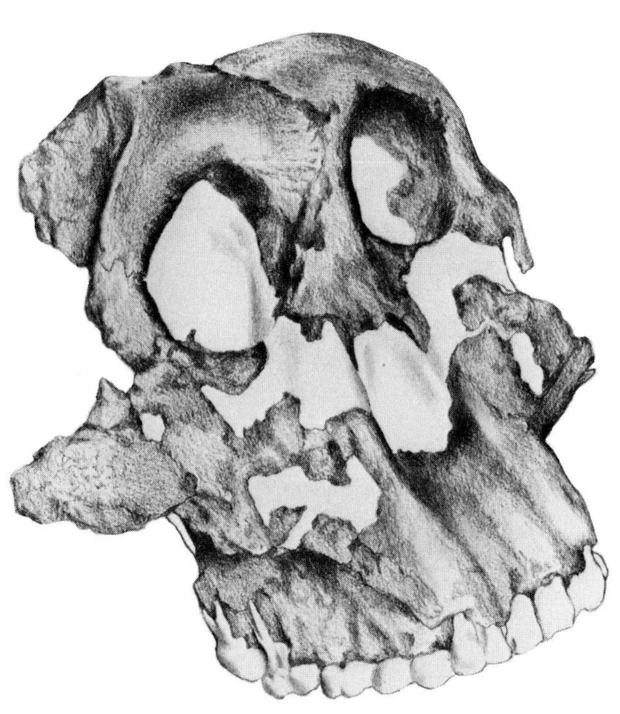

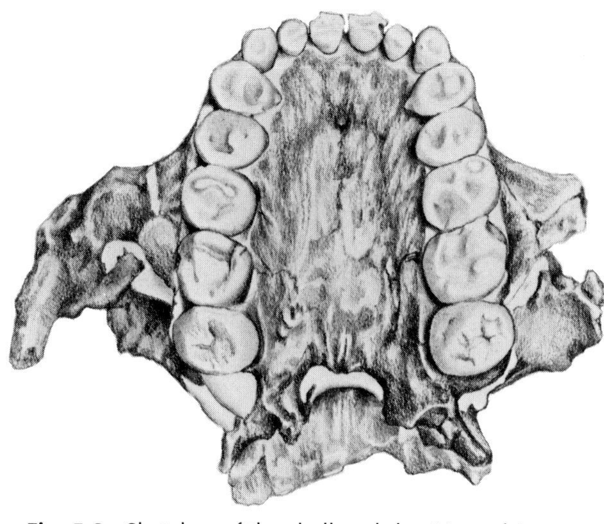

Fig. 5.2 Sketches of the skull and dentition of *Australopithecus boisei*.

Table 5:1

Materials available for study in australopithecines and *Homo habilis*

Lower teeth	*afarensis*	*africanus*	*robustus*	*boisei*	*habilis*
Incisors			insufficient data		
Canines			insufficient data		
P_3	18	15	14	6	9
P_4	16	14	15	11	7
M_1	18	19	20	9	14
M_2	18	17	10	14	10
M_3	14	18	13	14	8
Upper teeth					
Incisors			insufficient data		
C′	gracile specimens: 15		robust specimens: 13		
P^3	9	20	15	4	10
P^4	9	20	16	3	8
M^1	8	27	16	4	13
M^2			insufficient data		
M^3			insufficient data		

we have found in any other fossil group, that it undoubtedly means the obvious: that the pooled group of all australopithecines includes pooling of so many individual sub-groups that the analysis is futile. It may seem curious to the reader that we should have carried out such a cautious analysis. But our experience with other materials (e.g. ramapithecines, which, it had been confidently averred were merely males and females of a single group) make caution worthwhile. Suffice it to say that it supports the notion, held by almost everyone, that there are several species involved here.

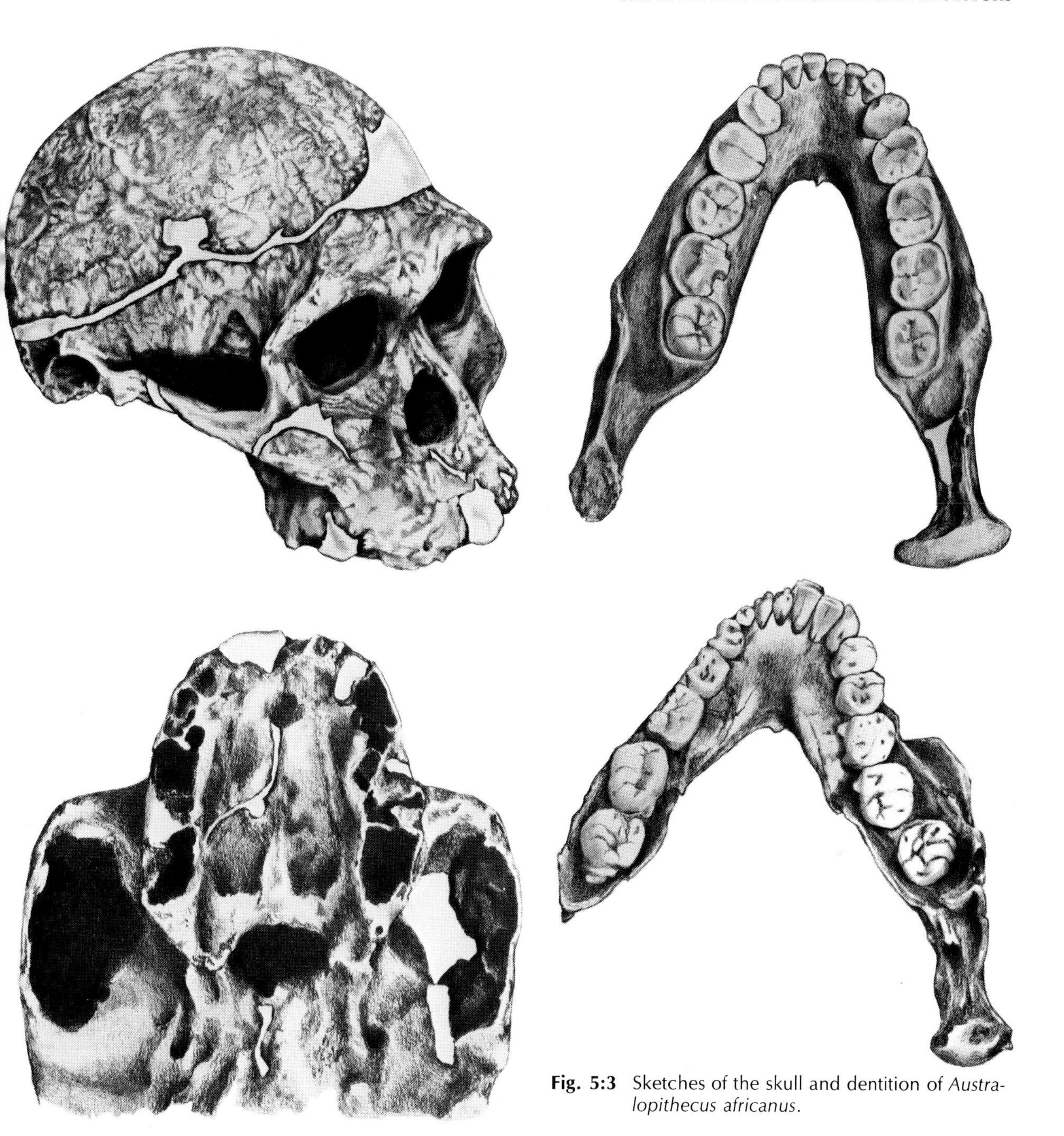

Fig. 5:3 Sketches of the skull and dentition of *Australopithecus africanus*.

Gracile and robust forms pooled separately

For the same reasons that we look at the pooled group of all australopithecines, it is useful to know what happens when we examine only two subgroups: all gracile and all robust species pooled separately.

For lengths and breadths of the lower canines the data are so deficient that no studies at all can be made upon them. But for the upper canines, although the data do not allow us to study the five main species groups, they do allow examination of the differences within each of gracile and robust forms. Because the canine is so important in dental sexual dimorphism, and because, at least in some species, such dimorphism may be large enough to be detectable, even with minimal numbers of specimens, it is worthwhile undertaking the study at this coarse level.

Data are available for 27 upper canines, 15 of the gracile type and 12 of the robust type. Notwith-

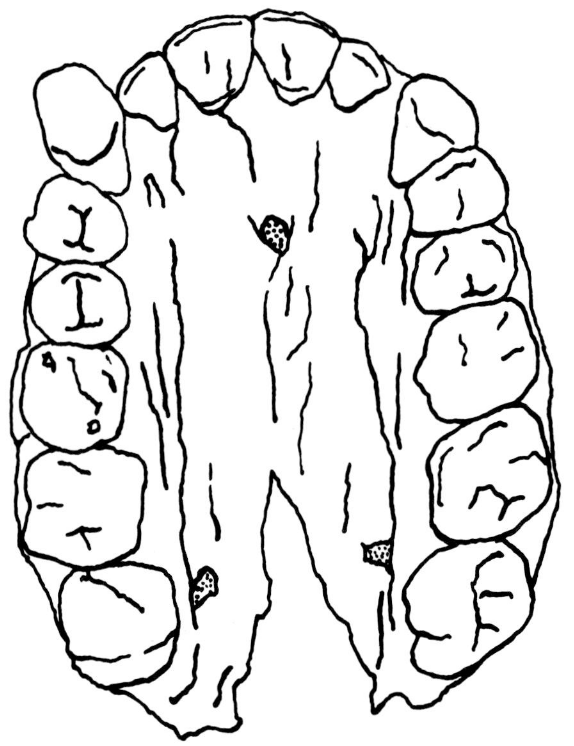

Fig. 5:4 Sketch of dentition of *Australopithecus afarensis*.

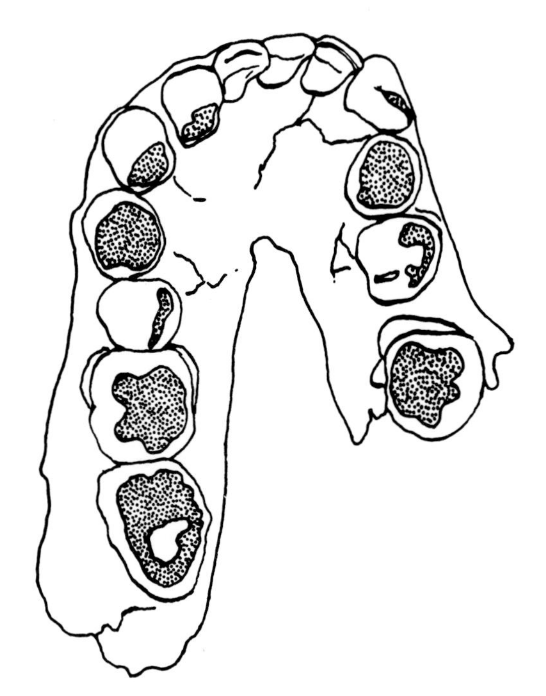

Fig. 5:5 Sketch of dentition of *Homo habilis*.

standing these very small sample sizes, dimorphism is evidently so marked in these species that the result of examining these data is unequivocal.

Though the length of the upper canine is not significantly different from normal, its breadth, in both gracile and robust species, has a bimodal distribution (Fig. 5:6). The distance between the two peaks is large (more than 2 mm) indicating a large difference between two means. The dispersions for each of the two peaks in the distribution for the gracile species cannot be judged because the number of cells permitted in the analysis is too small. However, the dispersions for each mode in the robust species are quite different, that for the peak of larger specimens being much greater than that for the peak of smaller specimens. Finally the number of specimens in the peak for the smaller dimensions is almost twice that for the larger measures in both species groups: gracile and robust.

This information from the canines, sparse though it may be, suggests (**a**) that, both gracile and robust species have two modes each; (**b**) that, if this is sexual dimorphism then it implies a large sexual dimorphism of means in both gracile and robust groups; (**c**) that, again, if this is sexual dimorphism, then in the robust species group there is evidence of a possibly larger dispersion for males than females, and (**d**) that, yet again, if this is sexual dimorphism then there is an approximately 2:1 ratio of females to males in both gracile and robust groups. The values for the individual measurements for each specimen make it unlikely that the two sets of double peaks are due to the four underlying species. This, together with the fact that the differences are greater in breadths than lengths, further implies that the results may be due to marked sexual dimorphism in all four subgroups.

It requires the results in the next two sections for us to see whether or not these suggestions hold up.

The gracile species: *afarensis* and *africanus*

Studies of anterior teeth: Data available for lengths and breadths of incisor teeth are so few that no studies can be undertaken upon them. There are, however, data from 33 lower third premolars, 30 lower fourth premolars, 29 upper third premolars and 29 upper fourth premolars spread among the two gracile species. Although somewhat marginal, these numbers are large enough to permit examination of histograms.

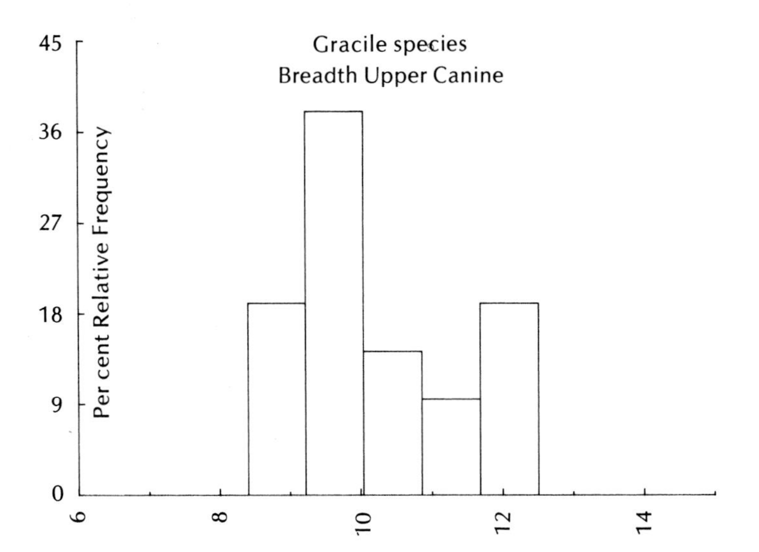

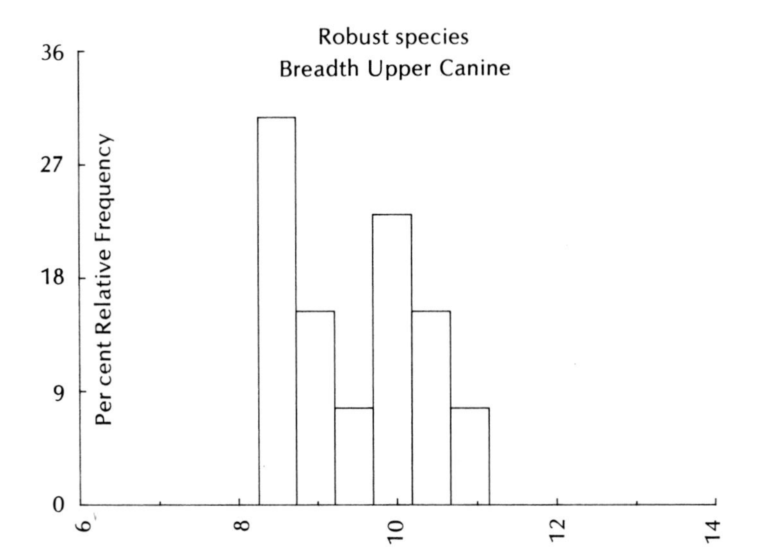

Fig. 5:6 Distributions of dimensions of canine teeth for the pooled groups of gracile and robust australopithecines respectively. Each shows a bimodal distribution with a difference between the modes of 2 mm or more that may represent large sexual dimorphism. Each shows, also, a ratio in size of the two peaks that suggests, if sexual dimorphism is represented here, that there is a ratio of more females to fewer males (at least 2:1 or greater). The dimension for the gracile pooled group does not give any indication of a different variance for males; but that for the robust group does suggest by the increased width of the smaller upper peak, that the variance for males (again if this is the cause of the bimodality) is greater than that for the females.

For each of the species: *A. afarensis* and *A. africanus* both lengths and breadths of the lower third premolars show marked bimodal distributions. There are considerable differences between the peaks of the modes (2 mm and more). The spreads for the upper modes are generally greater than those for the lower modes. The peaks for the larger teeth contain about half as many specimens as do those representing the smaller teeth.

For lower fourth premolar the picture is clearer in *A. afarensis* with bimodal histograms that are significantly different from fitted normal curves, with large differences between the modes, with larger spreads for the peak representing the larger specimens, and with fewer specimens in the peaks for the larger teeth than in those for the smaller teeth. In this tooth in *A. africanus* the picture is less clear, the length being unimodal and the breadth, though bimodal, insignificant statistically.

In contrast, in the upper premolars, it is *A. africanus* that shows the clearest results. The breadth of the upper third premolar is clearly bimodal though not statistically significant. Both lengths and breadths of the upper fourth premolar show distributions heavily and significantly skewed. There are too few specimens of *A. afarensis* for anything to be discerned.

For both upper and lower premolar teeth, therefore, two modes are present for each of *A. afarensis* (Fig. 5:7) and *A. africanus* (Fig. 5:8). The degree of

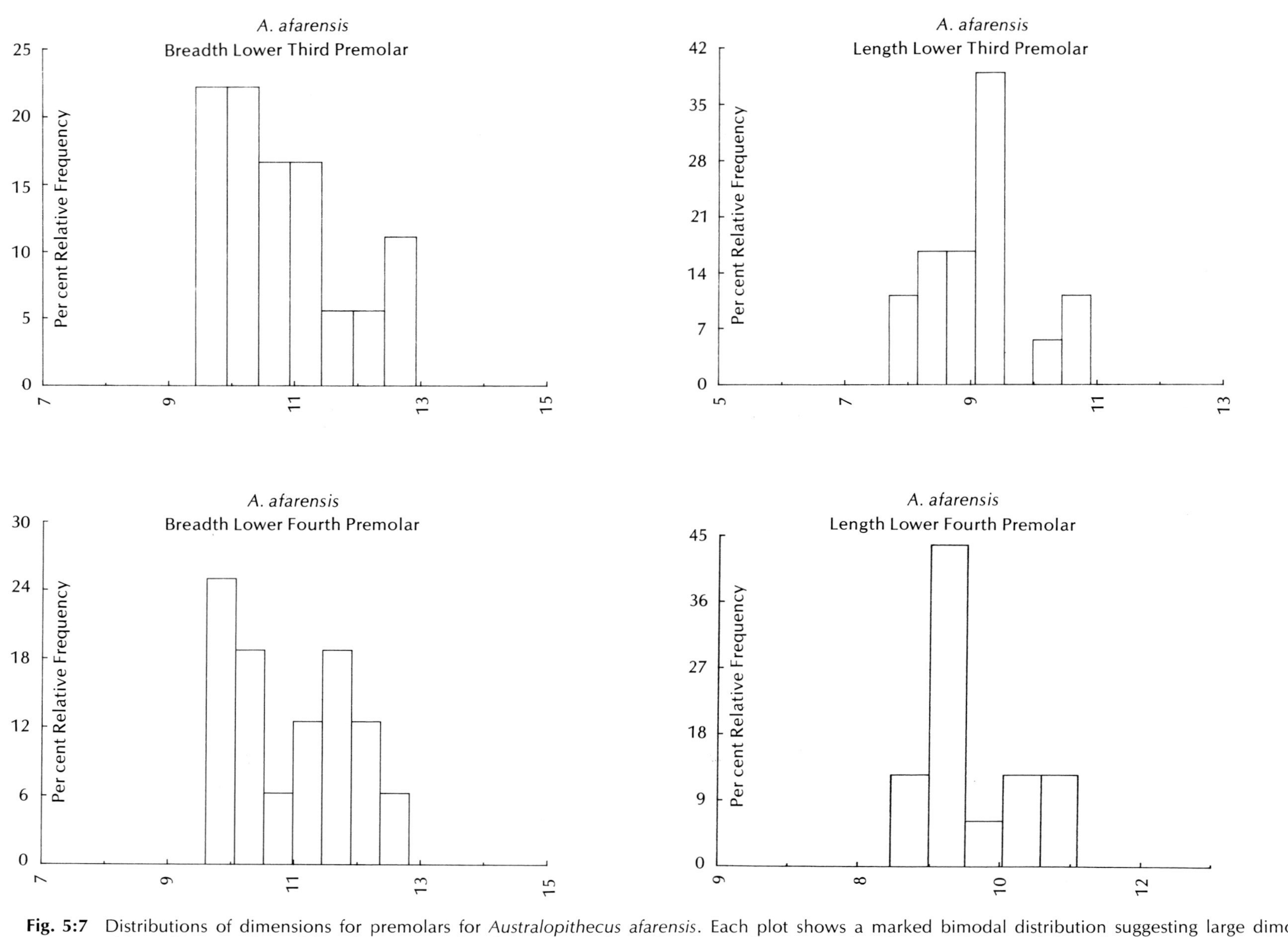

Fig. 5:7 Distributions of dimensions for premolars for *Australopithecus afarensis*. Each plot shows a marked bimodal distribution suggesting large dimorphism of means. Two of the plots suggest that the variances for males may be larger than females, two do not. All four plots show larger peaks of smaller specimens and smaller peaks of larger specimens suggesting that the ratio of the number of females to males is large, at least 2:1 or even greater.

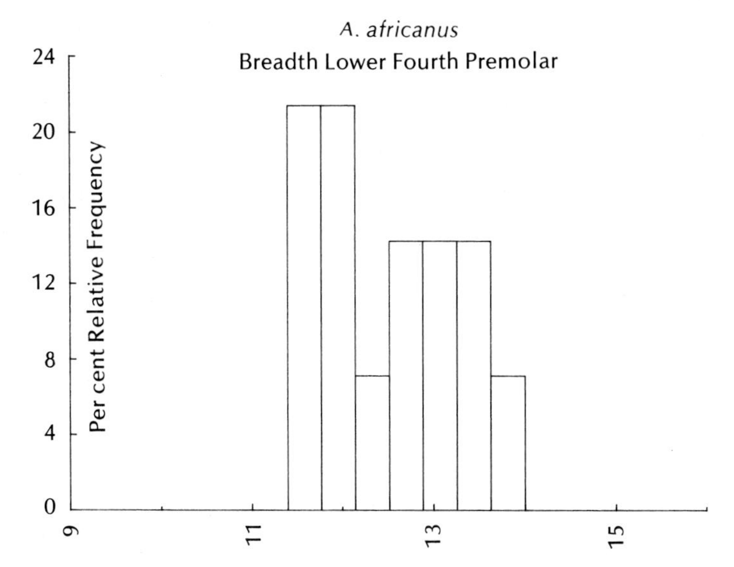

Fig. 5:8 Distributions of dimensions for premolars for *Australopithecus africanus*. Each plot shows a marked bimodal distribution suggesting large dimorphism of means. Again, one of the plots suggests that the variances for males may be larger than females, the others do not. All three plots show larger peaks of smaller specimens and smaller peaks of larger specimens suggesting that the ratio of the number of females to males is large, at least 2:1 or even greater.

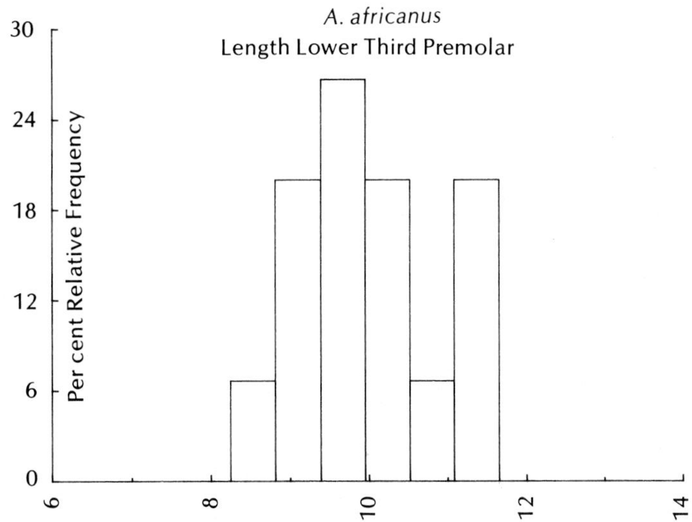

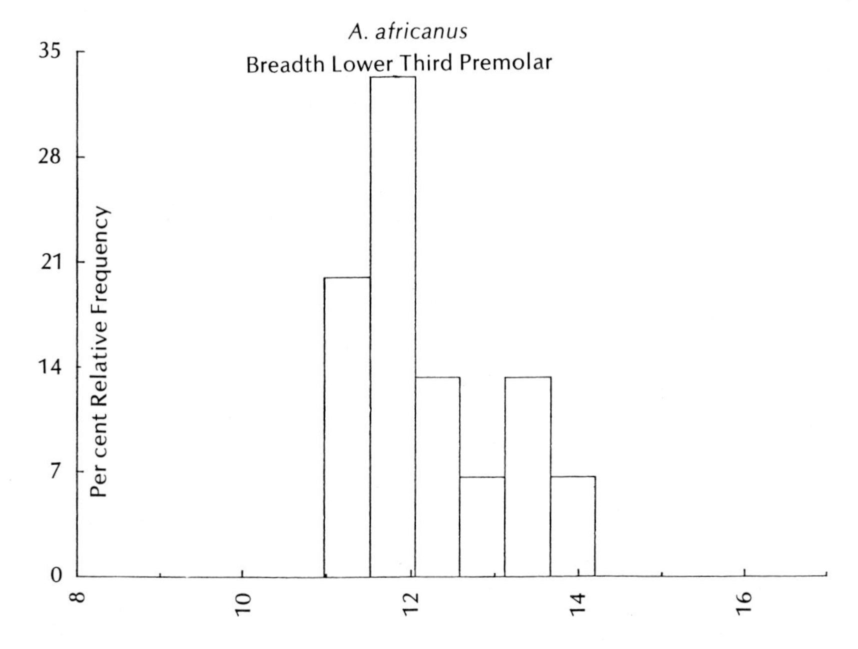

this dimorphism, as measured by the differences between the modes (when these exist) is large. The form of the dimorphism involves greater dispersions of the modes containing the larger specimens, and smaller dispersions for the modes containing the smaller specimens. The number of smaller specimens is about twice that of the larger specimens, as judged both from bigger peaks of smaller teeth and smaller peaks for larger teeth. Those measures that show distributions that are skewed (Fig. 5:9) may also be indicating both differential dispersions between the modes and smaller numbers of the bigger teeth (see, for example, the situation in *Pan*, Chapter 2). It is likely that all these findings are due to sexual dimorphism in each species.

The particular form of the sexual differences includes: (**a**) big sexual dimorphism of means in both gracile species, (**b**) big sexual dimorphism of dispersions in both gracile species, and (**c**) female/male ratios in each gracile species that are about 2:1 or greater. This is quite concordant with the more tentative results from the upper canine.

Studies of posterior teeth: The numbers of specimens available for these species for the molar teeth are 37, 35 and 32 for the lower first, second and third molars respectively, and 35 for the upper first molars. It is thus, possible, to examine many of the dimensions of these teeth for each separate species.

A. afarensis shows clear bimodal distributions for the lengths and breadths of the lower second and lower third molars. The peaks for each mode are separated by a considerable distance, of the order of 2.5 mm and more. Differences in dispersions between the two modes cannot be estimated, but visual inspection suggests that, the dispersions for the larger modes are greater than those for the smaller modes. The form of the bimodal distributions includes peaks for the smaller teeth, that contain twice as many or more specimens, than the peaks for the larger teeth.

All this is less evident in the lower first molar, its length and breadth showing only plateau-like distributions. The numbers of specimens of the upper first molar for *A. afarensis* are too few for analysis.

A somewhat similar picture is available for *A. africanus* although at different tooth positions. Thus, *A. africanus* shows bimodal distributions for the lengths and breadths of both lower and upper first molars, and the length only of the lower second molar. The other dimensions show only plateau-like distributions.

In each case the amount of dimorphism in *A. africanus* as measured by the distance between the modes is quite large, though not quite as large as in *A. afarensis*, being of the order of 1.5 mm. The dispersions of the parts of the distributions representing the larger specimens, are, as far as can be judged from visual examination, considerably greater than those for the smaller specimens. The numbers of specimens in the peaks representing the larger teeth are half or less than the numbers representing the smaller teeth.

For both upper and lower molars for both *A. afarensis* (Fig. 5:10) and *A. africanus* (Fig. 5:11), therefore, there is further corroborating informa-

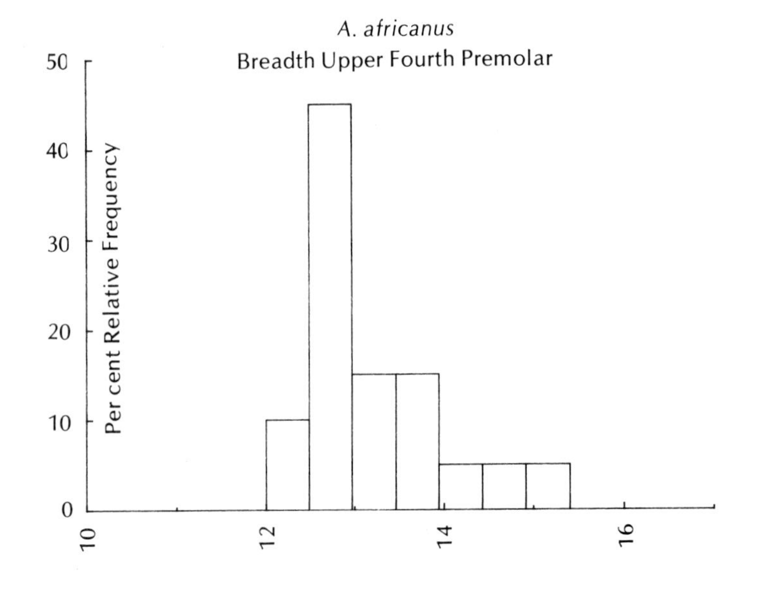

Fig. 5:9 A distribution of a dimension of a premolar for *Australopithecus africanus* that does not show a bimodal plot. It does however show marked skewing similar to what can be seen in some dimensions of *Gorilla* and *Pan* (see Chapter Two). One implication of this could well be a significant difference between females and males, with a larger variance for males, and a ratio of more females to males.

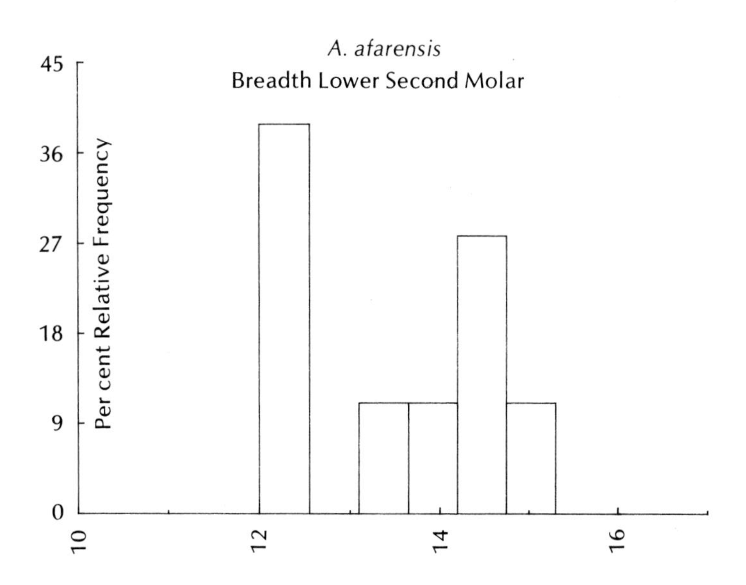

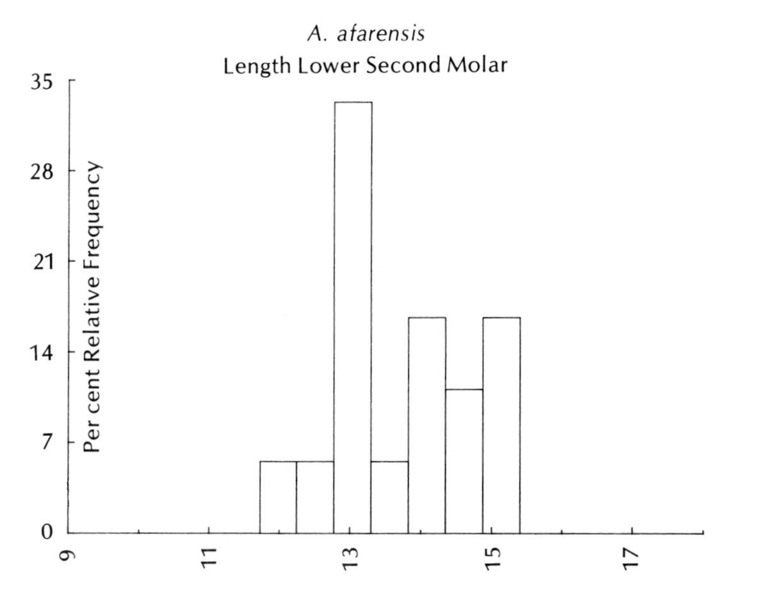

Fig. 5:10 Distributions of dimensions for molars for *Australopithecus afarensis*. Each plot shows a marked bimodal distribution suggesting large dimorphism of means. Two of the plots suggest that the variances for males may be larger than females, one does not. All three plots show larger peaks of smaller specimens and smaller peaks of larger specimens suggesting that the ratio of the number of females to males is large, at least 2:1 or even greater.

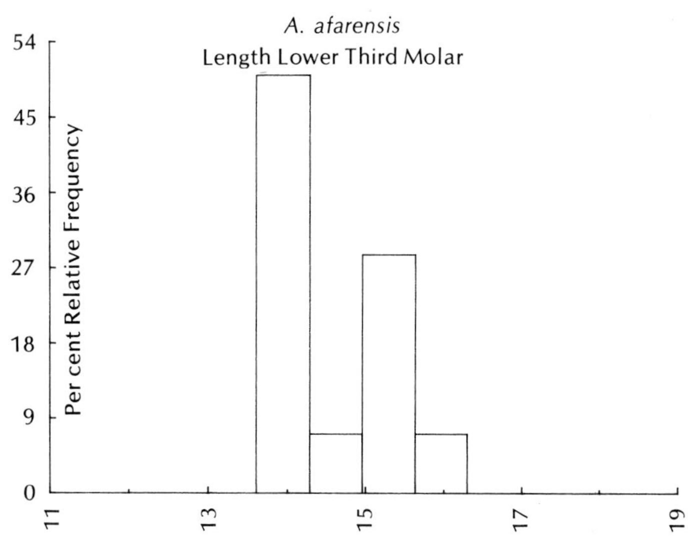

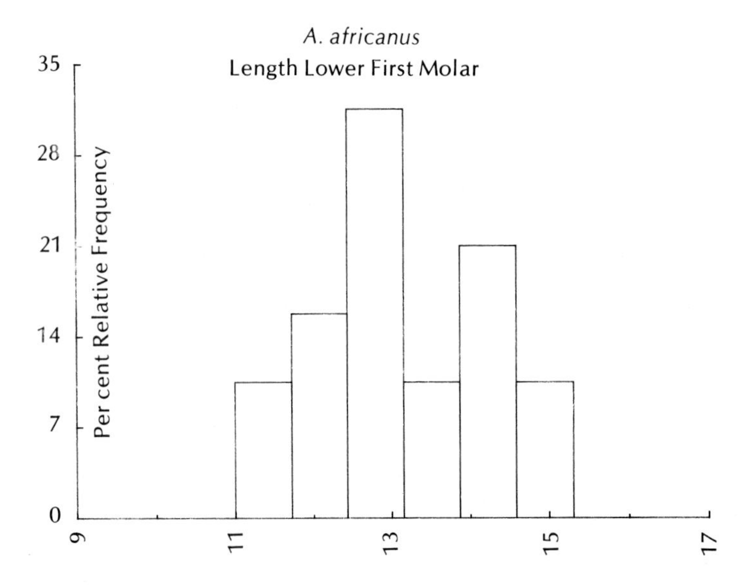

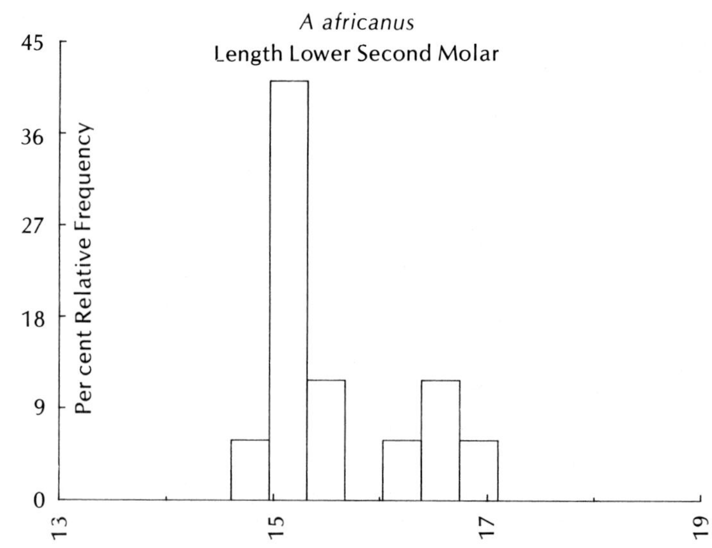

Fig. 5:11 Distributions of dimensions for molars for *Australopithecus africanus*. Each plot shows a marked bimodal distribution suggesting large dimorphism of means. In this case the plots do not suggest that the variances for males may be larger than females. All three plots show larger peaks of smaller specimens and smaller peaks of larger specimens suggesting that the ratio of the number of females to males is large, at least 2:1 or even greater.

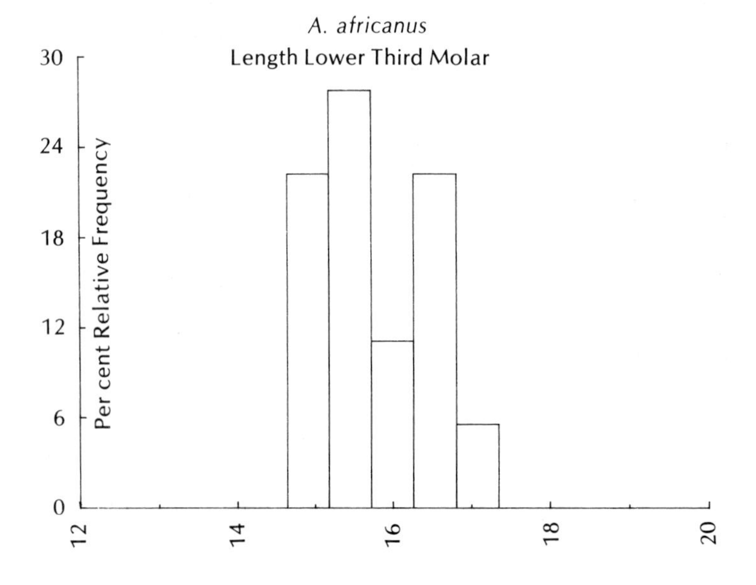

tion suggesting (**a**) large degrees of sexual dimorphism in means, (**b**) large sexual dimorphism in dispersions, and (**c**) female/male ratios of 2:1 or greater.

The robust species: *robustus* and *boisei*

Studies of anterior teeth: As for the various gracile species the data available, for lengths and breadths, of incisor teeth are so few that no studies can be undertaken upon them. But there are 19 lower third and 25 lower fourth premolars, together with 18 upper third and 18 upper fourth premolars. Although somewhat marginal, there are enough data from these teeth to permit examination of some dimensions of premolars in the groups *A. robustus* and *A. boisei*.

For *A. robustus* the lengths and breadths of the lower third premolar, the breadth of the lower fourth premolar, both lengths and breadths of the upper third premolar and upper fourth premolar all show bimodal distributions although sample sizes are too small to allow a statistical determination of the degree to which these do, or do not, fit a normal curve. In only one case, the breadth of the upper fourth premolar, is the number of specimens sufficient to determine that it is statistically significant. The distances between the modes are, in general, rather smaller than in the gracile species, being of the order of 1 mm. Visual examination suggests that, the dispersions are considerably greater for the peaks representing the larger teeth than the smaller. And there are about half as many specimens in the peaks representing the larger teeth, than in the peaks representing the smaller in each case.

For *A. boisei*, the numbers of specimens are even smaller so that only the breadth of the lower fourth premolar can be examined in this way. The results are, however, the same as for *A. robustus*.

For both upper and lower premolar teeth, therefore, there is strong evidence suggesting that two modes are present for *A. robustus* (Fig. 5:12) and weaker evidence for *A. boisei* (Fig. 5:13). The degree of dimorphism in *A. robustus* as measured by differences between the modes (when these exist) is small, generally about 1 mm. In *A. boisei*, the degree of dimorphism appears, from the single tooth position that can be examined in this way, to be considerably larger, 2 mm or more. The dispersions for the larger modes in both species appear, from visual examination, to be considerably greater than those for the smaller modes. (And it is possible that, this is also the explanation for those dimensions that are unimodal, but heavily skewed. Figure 5:14, as in *Pan*, Chapter 2). There are, finally, more specimens in the peaks representing the smaller specimens than in the peaks representing the larger ones in both species.

All this suggests that in both *A. robustus* and *A. boisei* there is (**a**) a fairly high degree of sexual dimorphism of means, (**b**) a high degree of sexual dimorphism of dispersions, and (**c**) a female/male ratio of about 2:1 or greater.

Studies of posterior teeth: The largest numbers of specimens are available for the molar loci, 30 each for each lower molar. There are data from 19 upper first molars. It was possible therefore to examine these teeth for each separate species of robust australopithecine.

The species *A. robustus* shows clear bimodal distributions for the lengths and breadths of the lower second molars, lower third molars and upper first molars. It is, however, the case that it is only for the upper first molar that there is sufficient data for us to see that the bimodality is significantly different from normal.

In each case the amount of dimorphism, as measured by the distance between the modes (when they exist), is quite large being of the order of 2 mm and more. The dispersions of the parts of the distributions representing the larger specimens, are, as far as can be judged from visual examination, greater than those for the smaller specimens. The numbers of specimens in the peaks, representing the larger specimens, are half or less than those representing the smaller specimens in every case.

A similar picture is available for the *A. boisei* specimens although at different and fewer loci (there are fewer specimens of *A. boisei*). Thus, *A. boisei* only shows bimodal distributions for the lengths and breadths of the lower second and third molars.

And in each case for *A. boisei* the amount of dimorphism, as measured by the distance between the modes, is larger than for *A. robustus*, being of the order of 3 mm and more. The dispersions for the peaks of larger specimens, are, as far as can be judged from visual examination, greater than those for the smaller specimens. The numbers of specimens in the peaks, representing the smaller specimens, are twice or more than those in the peaks, representing the larger specimens in every case.

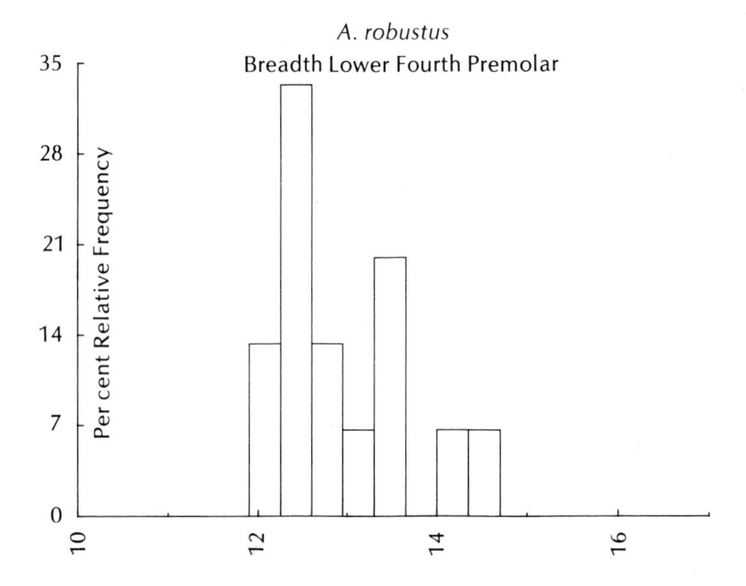

Fig. 5:12 Distributions of dimensions for premolars for *Australopithecus robustus*. Each plot shows a marked bimodal distribution suggesting large dimorphism of means. None of the plots especially implies that the variances for males is larger than that for females. All three plots show larger peaks of smaller specimens and smaller peaks of larger specimens suggesting that the ratio of the number of females to males is large, at least 2:1 or even greater.

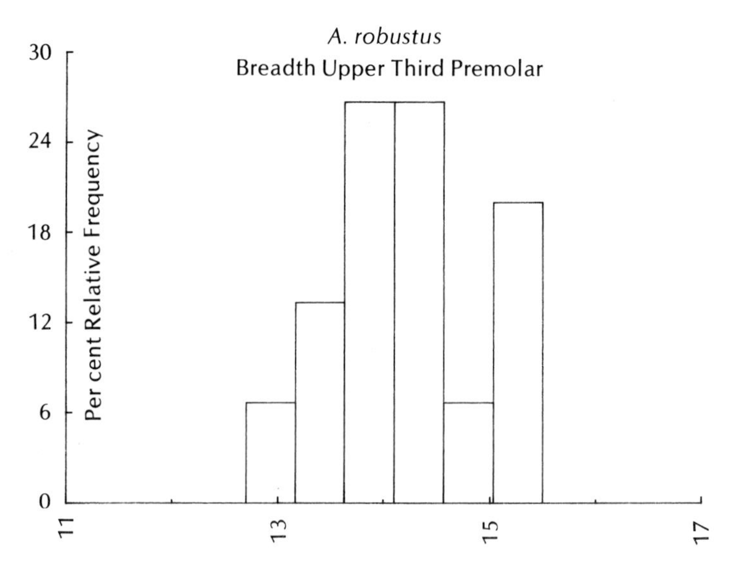

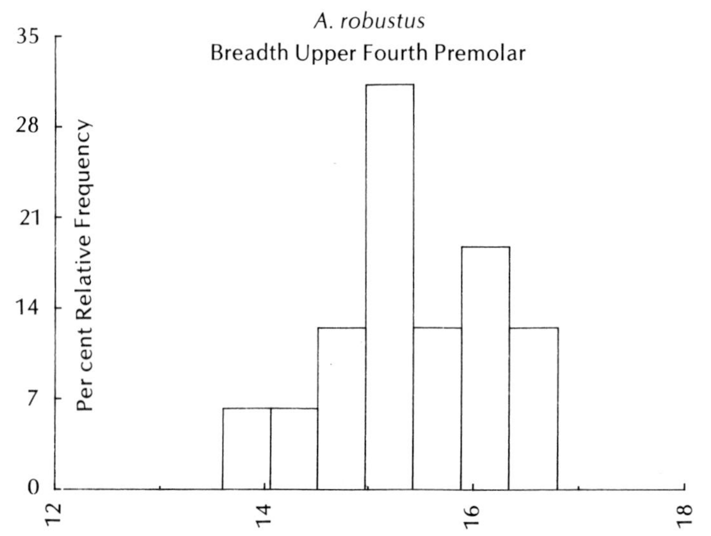

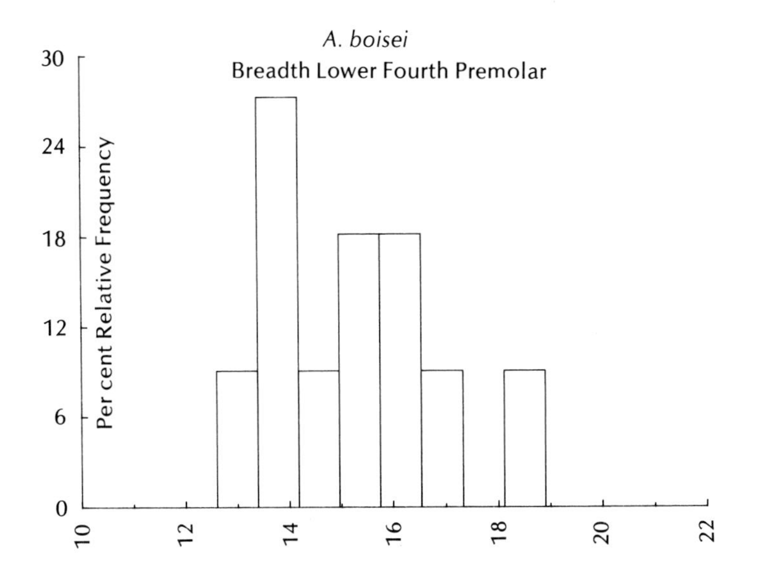

Fig. 5:13 A distribution of a dimension of a premolar for *Australopithecus boisei*. This plot shows a marked bimodal distribution suggesting large dimorphism of means. It also gives information suggesting that the variance of the males may be larger than that of the females. It shows a larger peak of smaller specimens and smaller peak of larger specimens that suggests that the ratio of the number of females to males is large, at least 2:1 or even greater.

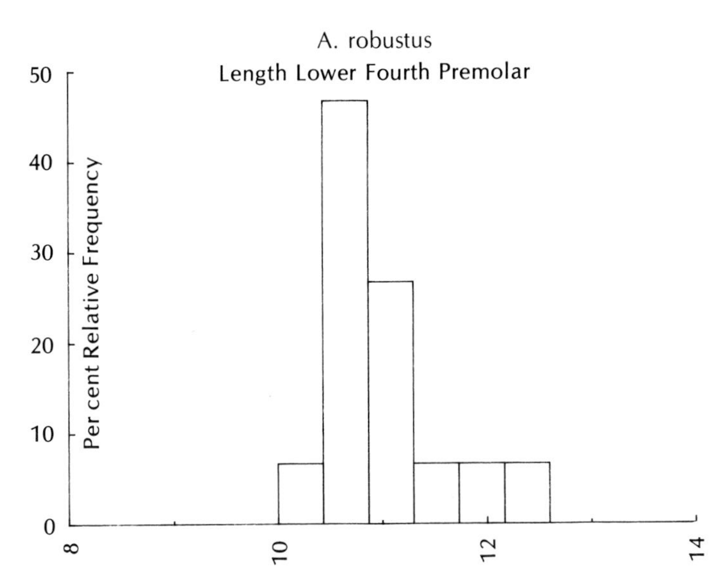

Fig. 5:14 A distribution of a dimension of a premolar for *Australopithecus robustus* that does not show a bimodal plot. It does however show marked skewing similar to what can be seen in some dimensions of *Gorilla* and *Pan* (see Chapter Two). One implication of this could well be significant difference between females and males, with a larger variance for males, and a ratio of more females to males.

For both upper and lower molars of both robust (Fig. 5:15) and hyper-robust (Fig. 5:16) species therefore, the data continue to corroborate the information from the other teeth that suggest (**a**) large degrees of sexual dimorphism of means, (**b**) large sexual dimorphism in dispersions, and (**c**) female/male ratios of about 2:1 or greater.

The data also suggest that, notwithstanding the smaller numbers of specimens of the hyper-robust form, it is in this form that there is the greater amount of sexual dimorphism in each of these categories.

The special case of *Homo habilis*

There are sufficient specimens to examine *Homo habilis* in this way for the dimensions of only the lower third premolar and the lower and upper first molar, together with the breadths only of the lower second and lower third molars. In none of these cases can statistical significance be determined. But in each of these measures bimodal distributions are apparent. In each case they possess (**a**) fairly large differences between the modes (although smaller than for the australopithecines), (**b**) similar dispersions for each mode, and (**c**) modes representing the smaller teeth containing an equal number of specimens as modes representing the larger (Fig. 5:17).

Even given the very small sample sizes for *Homo habilis*, it is evident that there is (**a**) considerable sexual dimorphism of means (although less than for australopithecines), (**b**) zero sexual dimorphism in dispersions, and (**c**) a female/male ratio of 1:1.

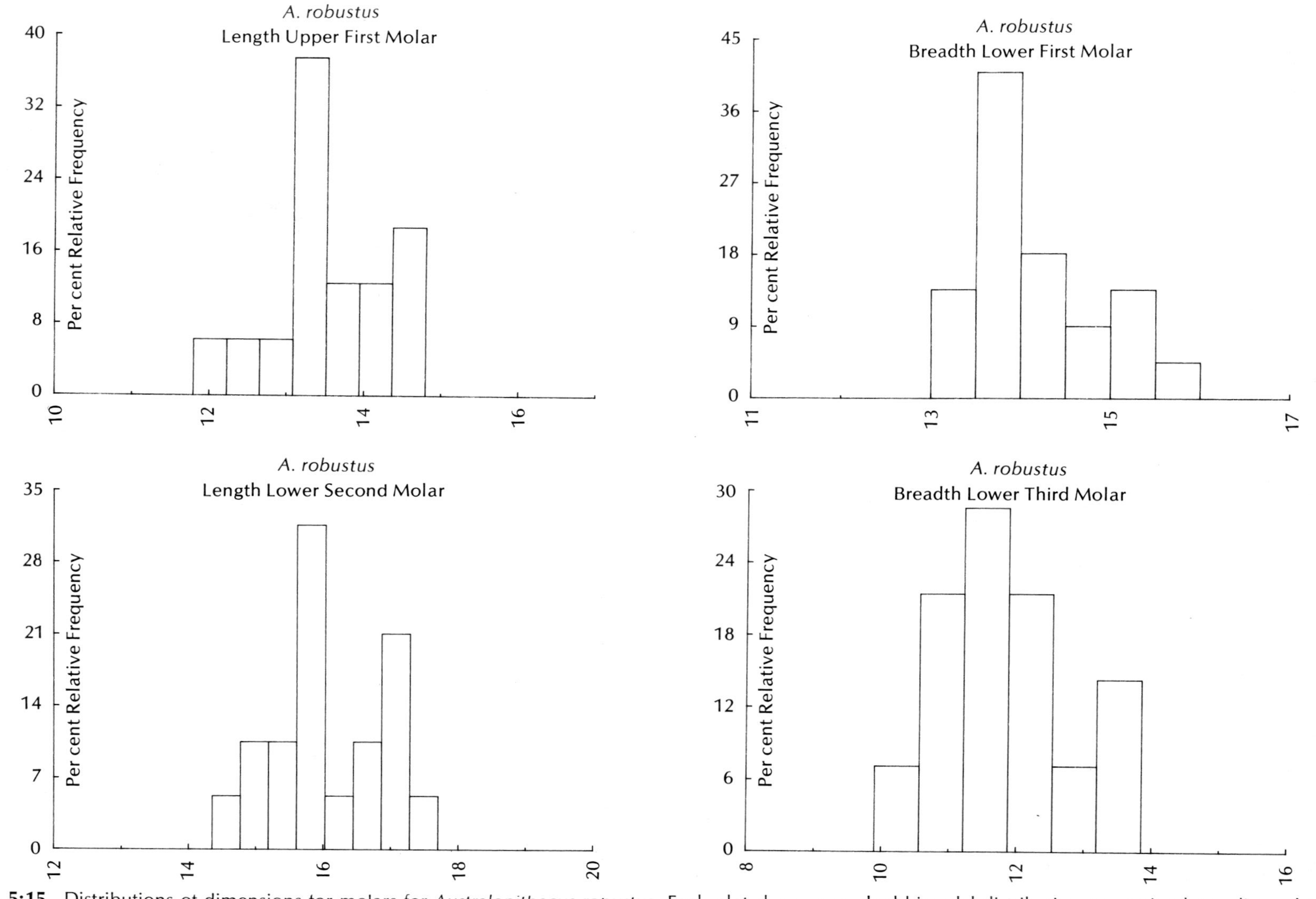

Fig. 5:15 Distributions of dimensions for molars for *Australopithecus robustus*. Each plot shows a marked bimodal distribution suggesting large dimorphism of means. None of the plots necessarily imply that the variances for males is larger than females. All four plots show larger peaks of smaller specimens and smaller peaks of larger specimens suggesting that the ratio of the number of females to males is large, at least 2:1 or even greater.

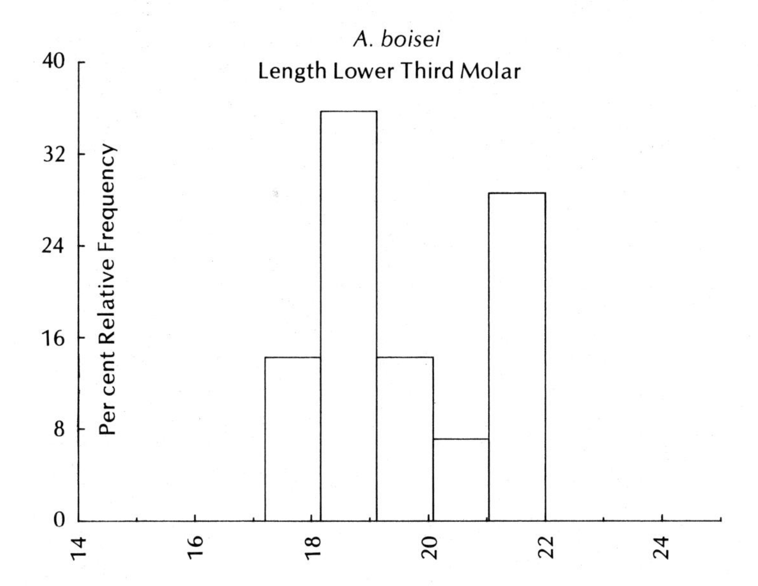

Fig. 5:16 Distributions of dimensions for molars for *Australopithecus boisei*. Each plot shows a marked bimodal distribution suggesting large dimorphism of means. Neither plot implies any especially larger variance for males than females. Both plots show larger peaks of smaller specimens and smaller peaks of larger specimens suggesting that the ratio of the number of females to males is large, at least 2:1 or even greater.

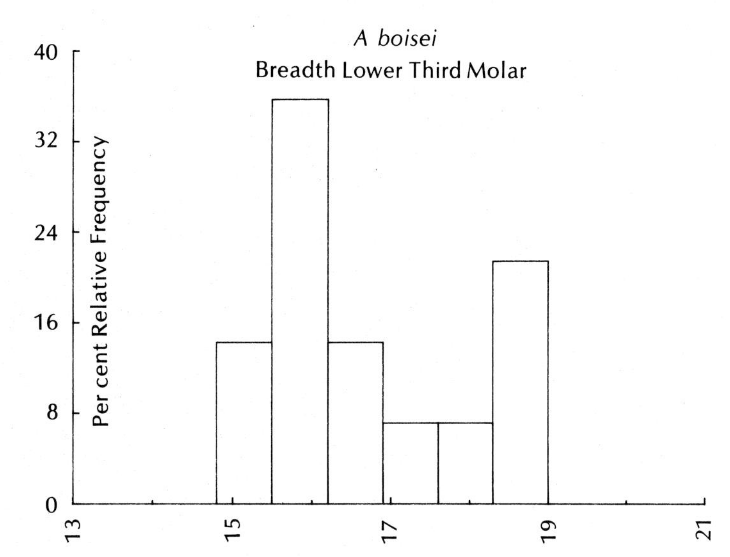

Regional differences along the tooth row in australopithecines

There are also considerable sexual dimorphisms of pattern in these teeth. This can be seen from consideration of the locations along the tooth row at which the most obvious differences occur. Table 5:2 demonstrates this, and further implies, if evidence were further needed at this point, that size dimorphism between mean values is not the only, not even the major difference between the sexes.

New studies of australopithecine teeth: all measures combined

Of course, the above data are taken from individual teeth from many different and incomplete specimens of *Australopithecus*. It is not, therefore, possible to say except to some limited extent which particular teeth at one locus, are from the same individual as which teeth at other loci. For this reason it is not possible to carry out a multivariate statistical study, which incorporates the data from the australopithecines in the same manner, as for the humans and extant apes examined in the second chapter. But it is possible to take the mean values for each unimodal dimension and the modal values for each bimodal dimension as the approximate means for the two sexes. These values can then be interpolated into the previously determined multivariate statistical analyses in the same way as was done for the fossils of *Homo*, *Ramapithecus* and *Sivapithecus* in previous chapters. Again, because of limitations to the original extant data this can only be done for the upper and lower jaws separately.

The goal of this part of the study is to expand the examination of the data from extant hominoids using multivariate statistical analyses. Several questions are addressed.

What are the natures of the sexual dimorphisms in the dentition of the various australopithecines?

What patterns are apparent in multivariate analyses of australopithecines that might not have appeared in univariate studies?

Which of the species so far examined do australopithecines most resemble?

What are the implications of the results for primate and more specifically human phylogeny?

The data on extant species used in this study are outlined in Chapter 2. The fossil data are the length and breadth measurements from the australopithecine specimens given earlier in this chapter.

The 750 teeth suitable for study in this way (adult, unbroken, undistorted and not badly worn) include representatives from every tooth position in both maxilla and mandible. Some tooth positions are not well represented, with means derived from less than 10 specimens. Others are represented by means and modes calculated from many more specimens. In all cases all available tooth dimensions have been included.

Four multivariate analyses are performed on the data. For the extant primates, mandibular and maxillary data are analyzed separately, using canonical variates analysis. In both cases the seven groups used are: *Gorilla* females, *Gorilla* males, *Pan* females, *Pan* males, *Pongo* females, *Pongo* males, and *Homo*, sex unknown. In each case, therefore, six canonical axes are generated.

The distributions for the fossil groups are already known, from earlier in this chapter, to be bimodal in most measurements. Where this was the case, the values for the centres of the lower and upper peak were taken as the values for the means for females and males respectively. In the case in which the distributions for given dimensions are unimodal, then the values for female and male are taken as equal even though, given complete information about sex for each specimen, there would still be significant separations between the sexes for at least an additional number of these variables. Our values determined as above for the modes for females and males of the fossils (and also for known females and males of modern *Homo*, Willcox materials) are then interpolated into the canonical variates analyses made on the extant species (Table 5:3).

Canonical variates analyses

Figures 5:18 and 5:19 are plots of canonical variates means for the seven groups described earlier for the mandibular analysis. The fossils are, additionally, interpolated into these diagrams. (Because the information for each jaw is basically similar — the

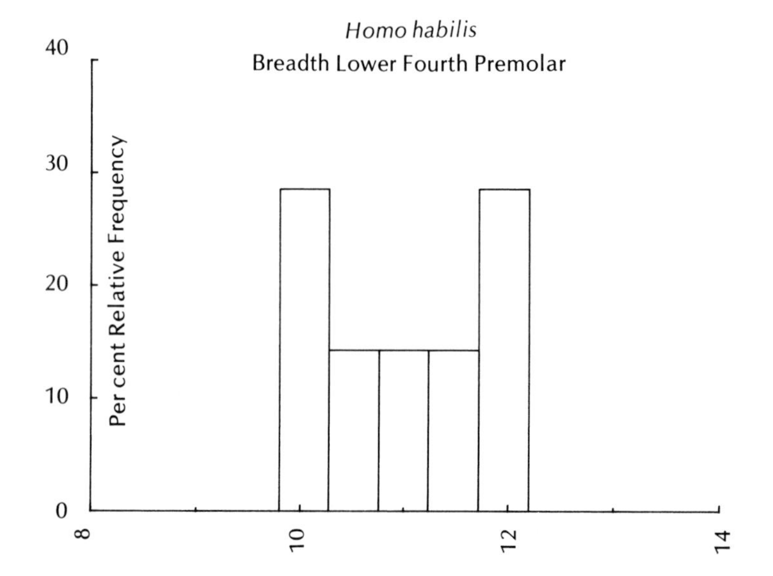

▷

Fig. 5:17 Examples of distributions of dimensions for premolars and molars for *Homo habilis*. Each plot shows a moderate bimodal distribution suggesting a moderate sexual dimorphism of means. The variances for males appear to be similar to females. All plots show equal peaks suggesting that the ratio of the number of females to males is equal.

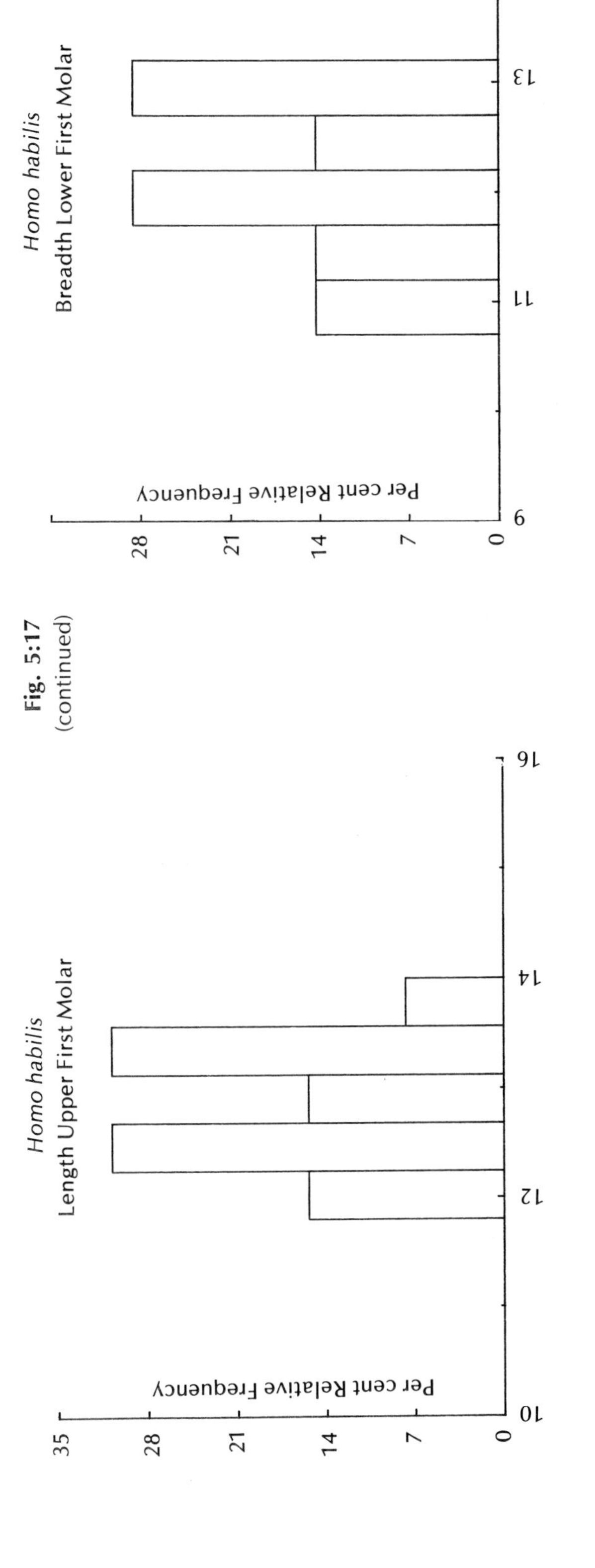

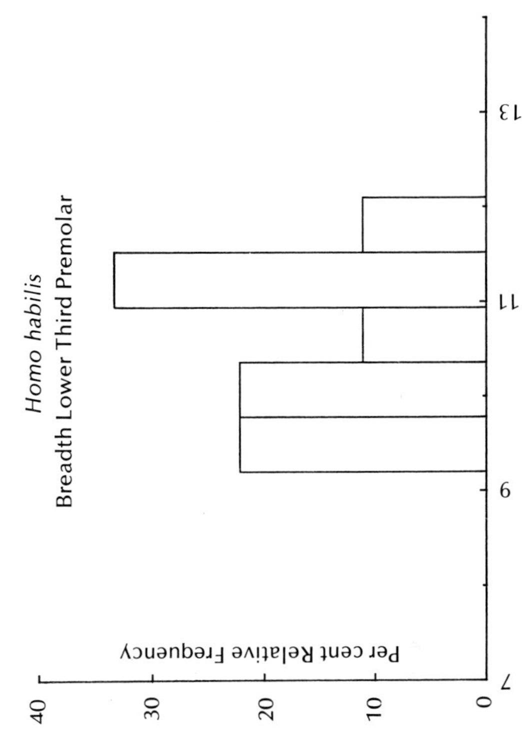

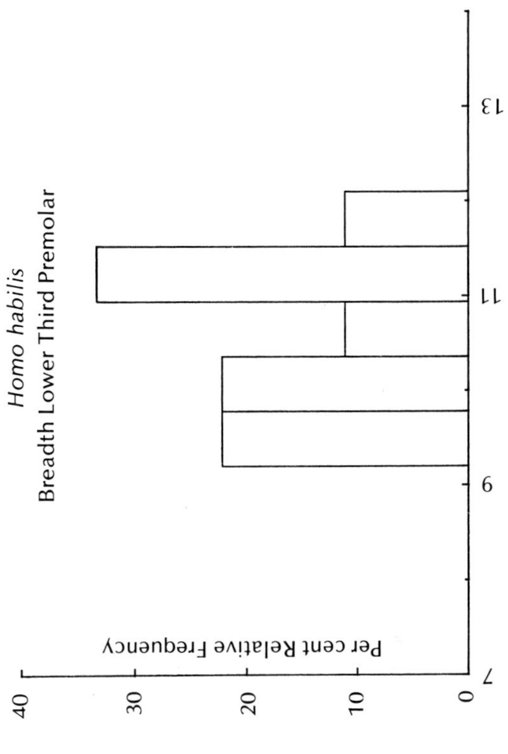

Homo habilis
Length Lower Second Molar

Per cent Relative Frequency

Fig. 5:17
(continued)

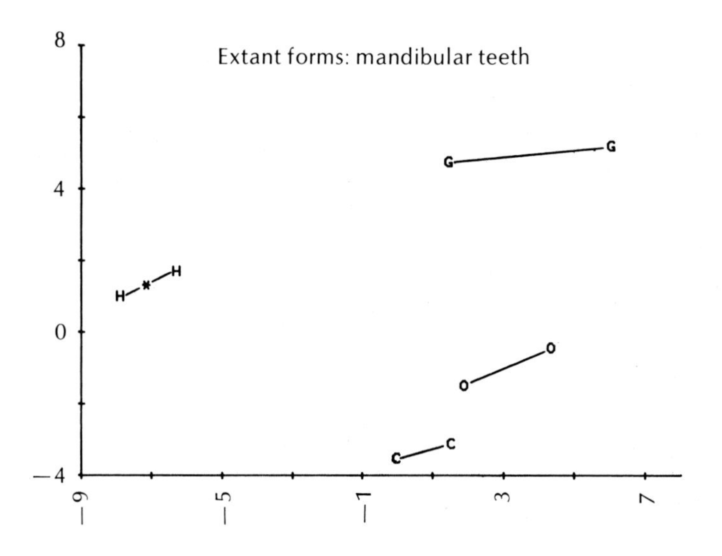

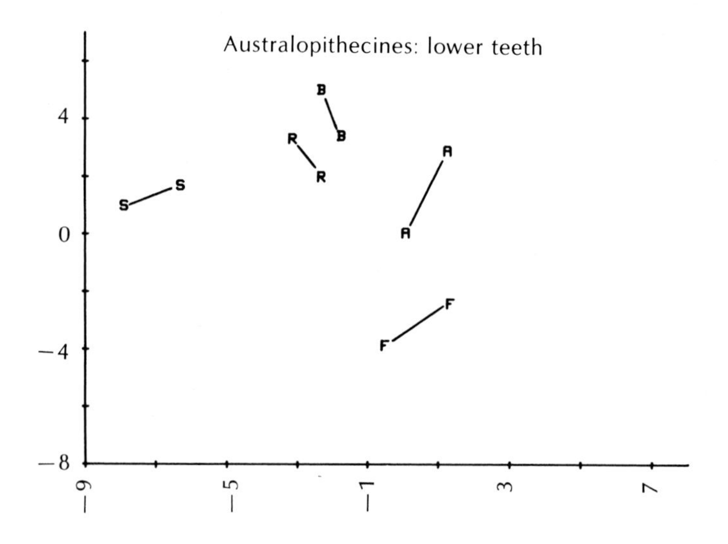

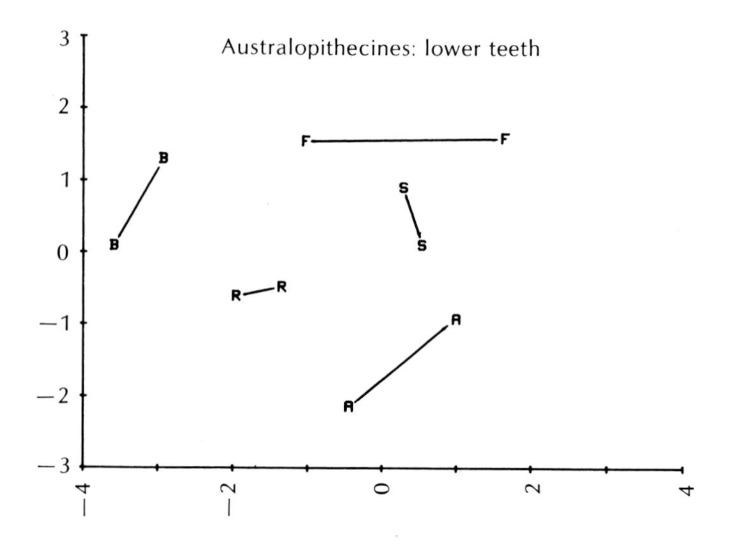

Fig. 5:18 The upper diagram shows a plot of the first two canonical axes for the extant species (H-H = *Homo*, C-C = *Pan*, 0-0 = *Pongo*, G-G = *Gorilla*, females are on the left in each case) for the original canonical variates analysis of the mandibular data.

This forms a reference for the examination of the middle diagram showing the interpolated positions of the fossils (S-S = *Homo* for reference, F-F = *Australopithecus afarensis*, A-A = *A. africanus*, R-R = *A. robustus*, B-B = *A. boisei*) in the same canonical variates analysis. The two gracile forms fall closest to *Pan* and *Pongo* and resemble them in having quite large dimorphism. But as seen from the different slope of the line joining female (always on the left) and male modes, they have a quite different multivariate pattern of sexual dimorphism. The two robust forms do not fall near any species; they have a considerably smaller dimorphism than the apes; they possess a multivariate pattern of dimorphism different from any form so far examined.

Examination, lowest diagram, of the plot of axes 3 and 4 for the fossils confirms that they truly do fall as two pairs, robust and gracile, each with a different multivariate pattern of sexual dimorphism from *Homo* and from each other.

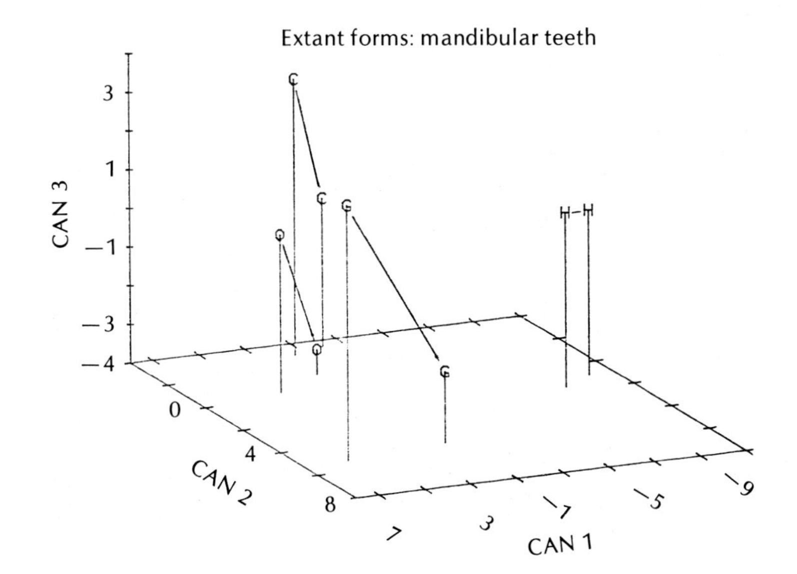

Fig. 5:19 This shows three-dimensional models of the first three canonical axes.

The upper plot is of the extant species for reference (H-H = *Homo*, C-C = *Pan*, O-O = *Pongo*, G-G = *Gorilla*, with the females on the right in each case). We can not only see the difference between the placement of humans and apes, but we can also see the completely different sexually dimorphic pattern in humans than in apes.

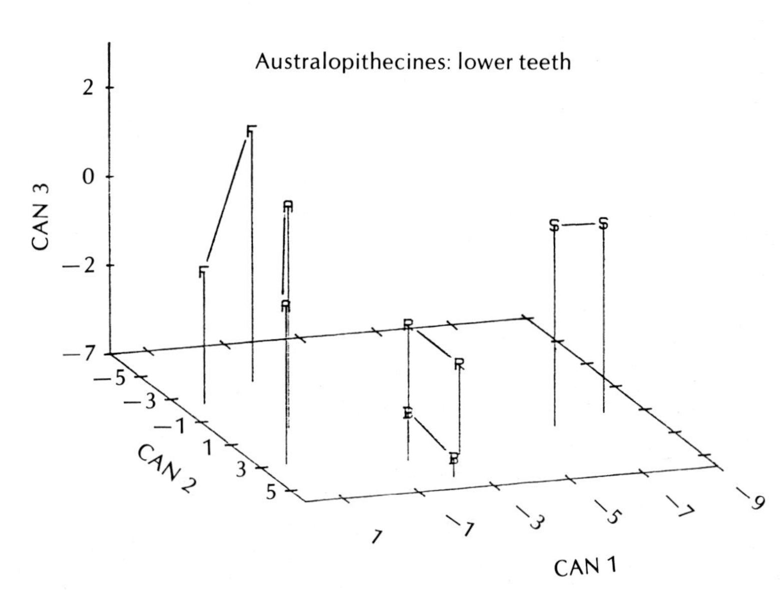

The lower plot shows the positions of the fossils when interpolated into this analysis (S-S = *Homo*, F-F = *Australopithecus afarensis*, A-A = *A. africanus*, R-R = *A. robustus*, B-B = *A. boisei*, females on the right in each case). It confirms that though the gracile species are near the positions of the *Pan* and *Pongo* sexes, they have an almost totally opposite pattern of sexual dimorphism. It is quite unlike that in any extant ape. It also confirms that though there are some similarities in pattern between sexual dimorphism in the robust forms and the apes, they are not at all close to one another in absolute terms. Neither fossil species is at all like humans.

mandible is somewhat more discriminating, as was also the case for the univariate data — only the mandibular plots are here described).

For the first two axes in the mandibular analysis (Fig. 5:18) the various species of *Australopithecus* are spread out in a crescent around the genus *Homo*. The two robust forms are at one end of that crescent closest (apparently) to *Homo*. The two gracile species are a good deal further away from *Homo* so that they appear closer to *Pan*. They also appear to be quite close to female *Pongo*, but sexual dimorphism is so great in *Pongo* that they are not at all close to male *Pongo*.

Homo habilis also falls on the crescent apparently between the two gracile forms. It is, therefore, apparently quite close to both *Pan* and female *Pongo*.

Consideration of the positions of the various groups in the second two axes (Fig. 5:18) makes it clear, however, that positions in the first two are merely apparent. Thus the second two axes demonstrate that the apparent closeness of both the robust species to *Homo* is spurious. They are actually separated from *Homo* by a considerable distance in the third and fourth axes. And the apparent similarity of *A. afarensis* and *A. africanus* to *Pan* in

Table 5:2

Pattern of differences in sexual dimorphism in australopithecines and *Homo habilis* along the tooth row

Lower teeth

		afarensis	*africanus*	*robustus*	*boisei*	*habilis*
Incisors		—	—	—	—	—
Canines		—	—	—	—	—
P_3	L	—	N	B=	—	—
	B	B—	B≠	B≠	B≠	—
P_4	L	—	S	B=	—	—
	B	B—	B	B≠ *	B≠	—
M_1	L	B	B≠ *	B≠	—	B=
	B	B	B≠	B≠ *	—	B= *
M_2	L	B≠ *	B≠ *	B≠ *	B≠	B=
	B	B≠ *	B≠	B≠	B≠	—
M_3	L	B≠	P	B≠	B≠	B=
	B	B=	B	B=	B≠	B=

Upper teeth

		afarensis	*africanus*	*robustus*	*boisei*	*habilis*
Incisors		—	—	—	—	—
C′	L	gracile: N		robust: B≠		—
	B	gracile: B≠ *		robust: B≠		—
P^3	L	B≠ *	B= *	B≠	N	B=
	B	B≠	B=	B≠	N	B=
P^4	L	B≠ *	P	S	N	—
	B	B≠ *	B≠	B≠ *	B	—
M^1	L	—	B≠	B≠ *	—	B≠
	B	—	B≠	B≠	—	B≠
Molars$^{2\&3}$		—	—	—	—	—

Notes: — = no information; N = unimodal distribution; S = skewed unimodal distribution; P = plateau-like distribution; B = bimodal distribution; "=" = equal peaks in bimodal distribution; ≠ = unequal peaks in bimodal distribution (larger peak containing fewer specimens); * = statistically significant (0.1 level).

the first two axes is also spurious. They are quite far from *Pan* in the third and fourth axes. Indeed, similarity with *Pan* is found for *A. robustus* and *A. boisei* in these two axes.

And in these two axes, *Homo habilis* is quite close to both *Pan* and *Homo* (which are not, themselves, greatly separated by these axes).

A good picture is also provided by the three-dimensional plot of the first three axes (Fig. 5:19). It confirms the idea that these forms fall in a three-dimensional crescent, one end of which is near *Pan* and the other end is far removed from any extant species. *Homo* is placed as though it were approximately at the centre of the ball of which the three-dimensional crescent might be thought of as an arc. This demonstrates that all the australopithecine species are approximately equidistant from *Homo* but in different directions in the canonical space.

These descriptions speak only to the relative positions of the fossil groups as species. When we observe how the sexes are separated by these axes (for that is also part of the separation that is achieved) then other information comes to the fore. This is also best displayed in the three-dimensional plot (Fig. 5:19). It shows that these species display three different kinds of sexual difference.

Table 5:3

Mean lengths and breadths of teeth for sex subgroups of australopithecines and *Homo habilis*

Lower teeth		*afarensis*		*africanus*		*robustus*		*boisei*		*habilis*	
		f	m	f	m	f	m	f	m	f	m
I_1	L	6.6	6.6	5.6	5.6	5.4	5.4	5.1	5.1	6.6	6.6
	B	7.5	7.5	6.6	6.6	6.3	6.3	6.4	6.4	6.6	6.6
I_2	L	6.4	6.4	6.4	6.4	6.2	6.2	6.0	6.0	7.5	7.5
	B	7.5	7.5	7.8	7.8	7.0	7.0	7.3	7.3	7.1	7.1
$C_,$	L	9.1	9.1	9.1	9.1	7.9	7.9	7.9	7.9	8.8	8.8
	B	10.4	10.4	10.0	10.0	8.4	8.4	8.8	8.8	9.0	9.0
P_3	L	9.0	10.7	9.7	11.4	9.5	10.0	10.8	10.8	9.3	9.3
	B	10.7	10.7	11.9	13.3	11.8	11.8	13.1	13.1	10.7	10.7
P_4	L	9.3	10.5	10.1	10.1	11.0	11.0	13.6	13.6	9.5	9.5
	B	10.0	11.7	11.8	13.2	12.5	13.8	13.9	16.0	10.8	10.8
M_1	L	12.6	12.6	12.8	14.2	14.4	14.4	16.0	16.0	13.0	13.0
	B	12.8	12.8	13.1	13.1	13.8	15.1	15.2	15.2	11.7	12.7
M_2	L	13.0	14.6	15.2	16.6	15.8	17.0	16.5	18.0	13.3	15.2
	B	12.3	14.2	14.5	14.5	14.8	14.8	16.5	16.5	13.1	13.1
M_3	L	14.0	15.3	15.5	16.5	16.0	18.1	18.5	21.5	9.1	10.4
	B	13.3	13.3	14.2	14.2	11.7	13.5	15.9	18.5	12.4	12.4
Upper teeth											
I^1	L	10.6	10.6	9.2	9.2	9.3	9.3	10.0	10.0	11.3	11.3
	B	8.2	8.2	8.3	8.3	7.5	7.5	7.8	7.8	7.9	7.9
I^2	L	7.7	7.7	6.6	6.6	6.9	6.9	7.0	7.0	7.1	7.1
	B	7.2	7.2	6.3	6.3	6.7	6.7	6.8	6.8	6.7	6.7
C'	L	9.9	9.9	9.6	9.6	8.6	8.6	8.5	8.5	9.5	9.5
	B	11.0	11.0	9.5	9.5	9.5	9.5	9.1	9.1	9.7	9.7
P^3	L	8.6	8.6	9.0	9.0	9.7	9.7	10.9	10.9	8.8	8.8
	B	12.5	12.5	12.5	12.5	14.0	15.6	15.2	15.2	12.6	12.6
P^4	L	8.9	8.9	9.5	9.5	10.7	10.7	11.6	11.6	9.3	9.3
	B	12.3	12.3	12.6	14.0	15.0	16.2	16.9	16.9	13.0	13.0
M^1	L	12.0	12.0	14.1	14.1	13.3	14.7	12.5	13.8	12.9	12.9
	B	13.3	13.3	14.2	14.2	14.7	14.7	16.2	16.2	13.3	13.3
M^2	L	12.7	12.7	14.0	14.0	14.7	14.7	16.5	16.5	13.0	13.0
	B	14.5	14.5	15.7	15.7	16.0	16.0	18.2	18.2	14.6	14.6
M^3	L	12.3	12.3	13.7	13.7	15.3	15.3	16.6	16.6	12.0	12.0
	B	14.1	14.1	15.9	15.9	16.8	16.8	18.8	18.8	14.3	14.3

One obvious pair of species is *A. robustus* and *A. boisei*. In both of these, the differences between males and females in terms of the first three axes is such that a line joining females to males slopes upwards and to the left (in the particular perspective in which the plot is drawn). This contrasts markedly with the situation in *Homo sapiens* where the difference between females and males is apparent as a horizontal line towards the left. Yet, though completely different from the absolute position for *Pan*, the multivariate form of sexual dimorphism in these fossils is quite similar to that in *Pan* where the line going from female to male also slopes upwards and to the left.

A second obvious pair of species is *A. africanus* and *A. afarensis*. In these, the difference from female to male is displayed by a line sloping downward and to the left. This sexual dimorphism is

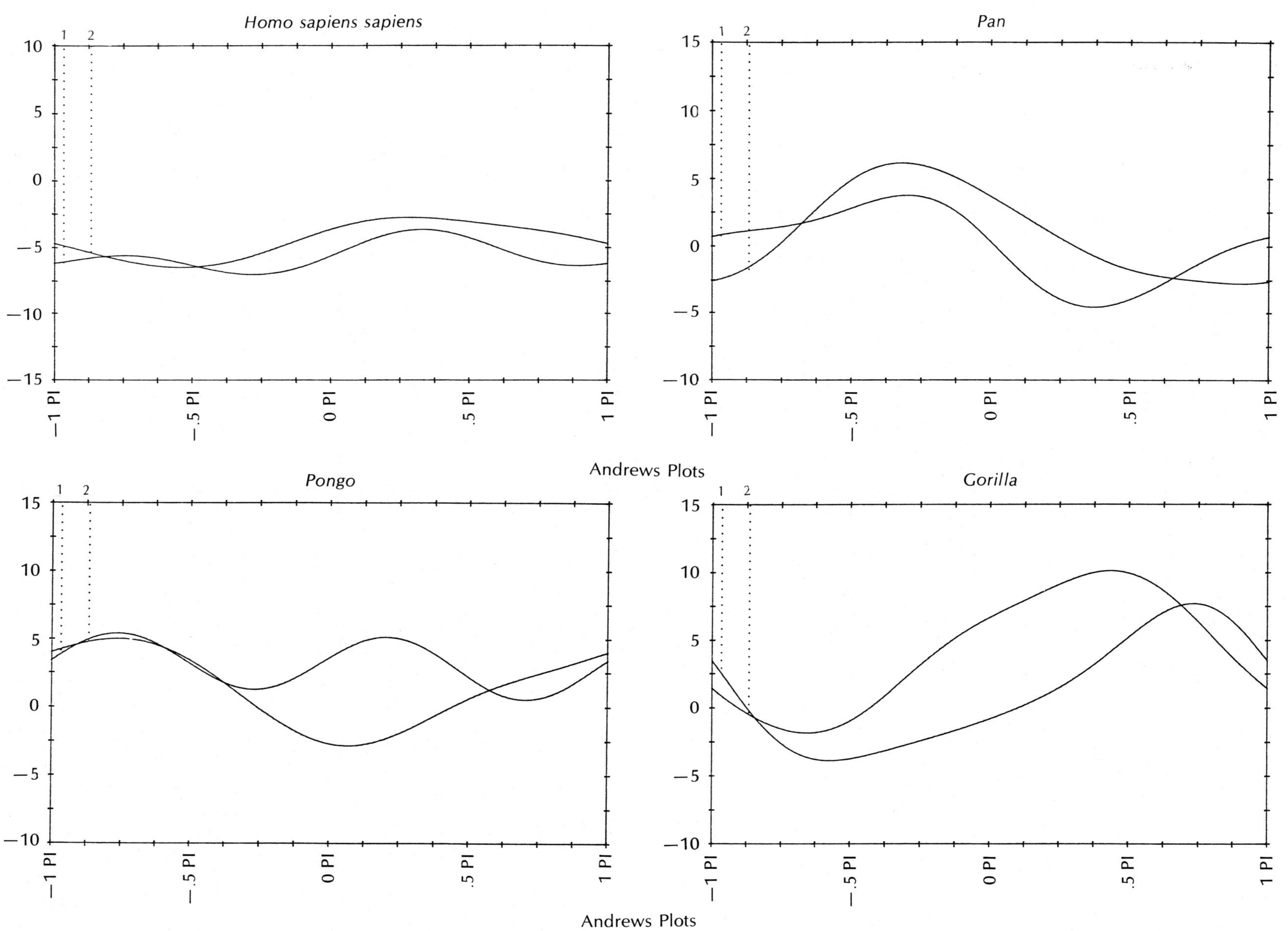

Fig. 5:20 High-dimensional display for the extant species for comparison with Fig. 5:21. Males (even numbers) are placed higher on the plots than females in each case. Note that *Homo* is placed at a different location on the vertical scale.

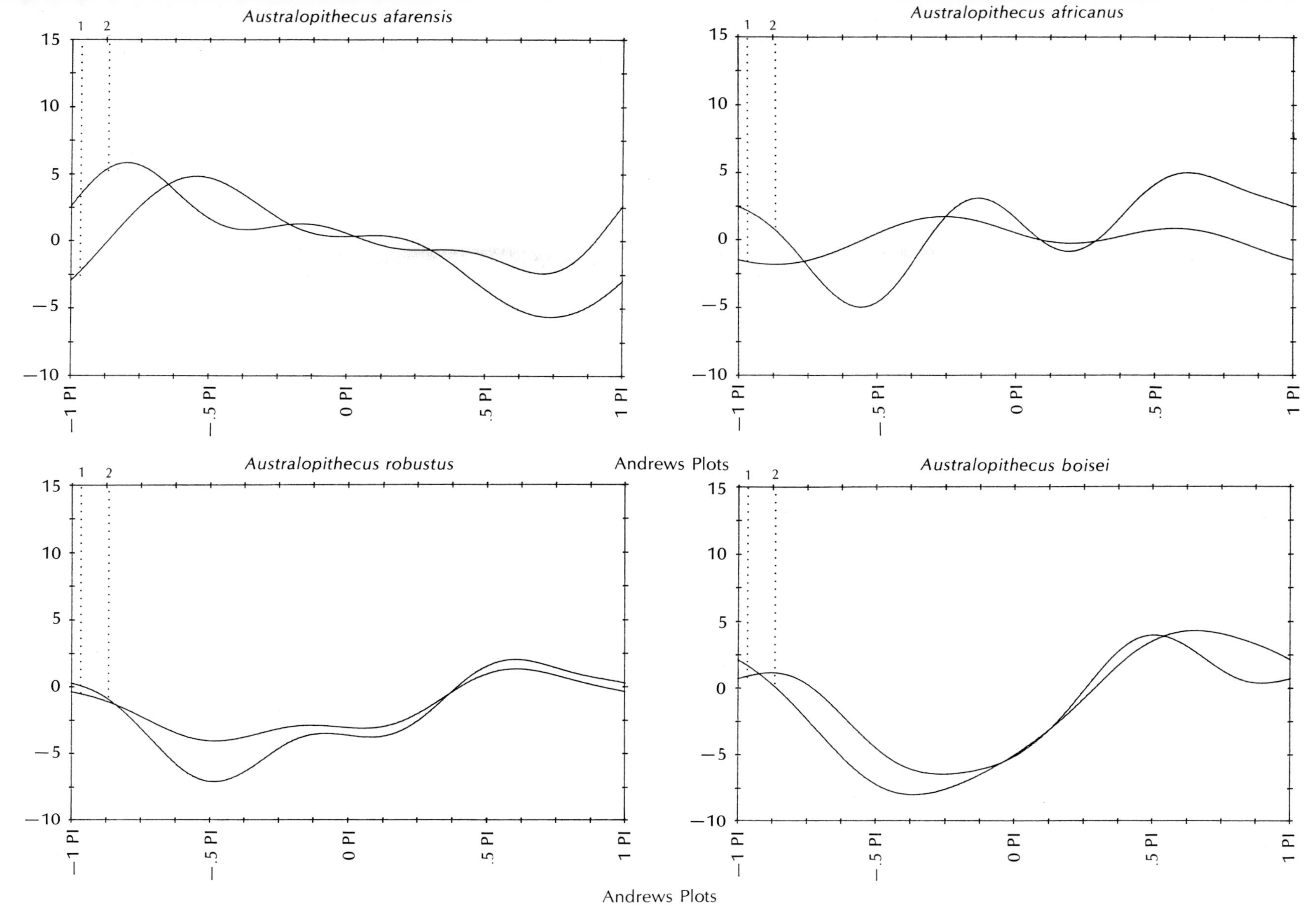

Fig. 5:21 High-dimensional displays for the fossils (males, even numbers, are placed higher in the plots in each case).

utterly unlike that in *Homo*, in either absolute position or in pattern. It can also be compared with the closest extant form *Pan*. In this case, though the fossils are located absolutely rather close to *Pan*, they possess a multivariate pattern between the sexes which is in almost the opposite direction.

Each group of australopithecines displays, therefore, a combination of overall species position and sexually dimorphic pattern, that renders them not only completely different from each other, but also completely different from each of the closest extant species.

Homo habilis, though differing in its absolute position from *Homo* as explicated above, possesses a difference between the sexes that is almost identical to that in *Homo sapiens*, a trend from female to male that is horizontal and to the left. And this goes with a sex ratio (approximately 1:1) that is also identical to that in *Homo*.

In summary *Homo habilis* is different from

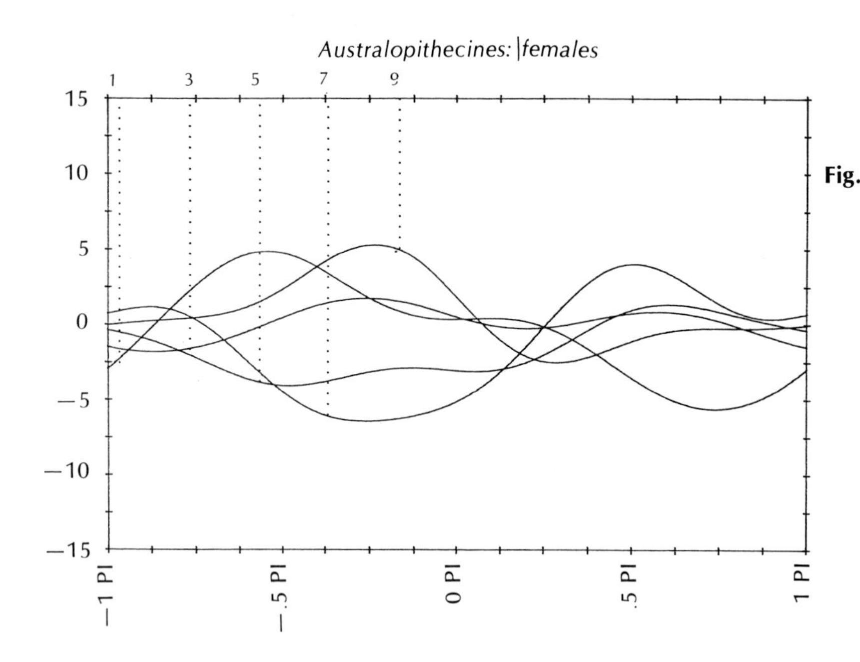

Fig. 5:22 High-dimensional plots for all fossil females (above) and all fossil males (below). The overall envelope for females is smaller than for males indicating that the females are generally more like each other. The males are more distinct in different directions in each genus.

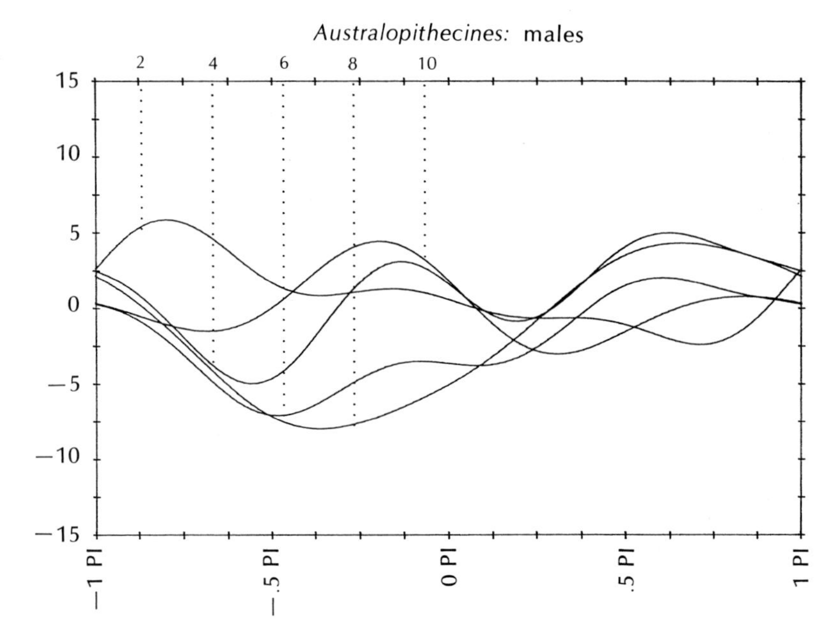

Homo sapiens in absolute terms but has similar patterns in each of its sexual dimorphisms. The various australopithecine genera fall into two pairs, both of which are quite different from any extant species.

High-dimensional displays

As for the extant genera, high-dimensional plots are generated in order to display information for the fossils in all axes together. This procedure allows us to view multi-dimensional information in a way denied us by the more usual two or three-dimensional methods. And, though the higher axes contain no big separations among the extant forms, this procedure allows us to see if big, important, and statistically significant information has been parlayed into the higher axes for the interpolated (fossil) groups.

Figures 5:20 and 5:21 show the high dimensional plot of the mandibular analyses for the putative female and male means alone. Total sexual dimorphism (represented by the area between the high-dimensional plots and how different the high-dimensional curves are from one another) in *Australopithecus* is greater than in *Homo* and about the same as in *Pan*.

The overall similarities of the pairs of genera, gracile on the one hand and robust on the other, is clear. So, too, is the fact that, appearances in early axes notwithstanding, none of these genera have major similarities with either *Pan* or *Homo* (Fig. 5:21).

The nature of the sexual dimorphism in each species, as shown by the pattern between the curves for each sex, is also different from that in the extant forms. It is even of interest that the females of all the species taken together are more similar to one another than are the males. The dimorphism is achieved, as it were, by peripheral males lying around more centrally located females (Fig. 5:22).

Conclusions: australopithecine fossils

The australopithecines have some similarities with living apes. Thus, univariately they show fairly high sexual dimorphism of means (and more so in the gracile species), high dimorphism of dispersions (and probably more so in the gracile species) and sex ratios of 2:1 or more (in both gracile and robust forms). Multivariately the australopithecines are closer to *Pan* although there are differences within the group. Thus the gracile forms are closer to *Pan* overall but the form of their dimorphism is such as to separate them rather sharply from *Pan*. The robust species are more distant from *Pan* but the form of their multivariate sexual dimorphism is rather similar to *Pan*. Multivariately, all four species bear some similarities with one another although they do lie as two quite clearly demarcated pairs of species.

Only *Homo habilis* among these fossils, has similarities with *Homo*. Its univariate sexual dimorphism displays an intermediate degree of dimorphism between that of *Homo* and *Pan*. But it shows the zero dispersion dimorphism typical of *Homo*, and it shows the 1:1 sex ratio of *Homo*. Its multivariate expression of sexual dimorphism also confirms that, although this genus is some way away from *Homo* and a little closer to *Pan*, the nature of the difference between the sexes is such that it has clear similarities with *Homo*. This association with *Homo* becomes even clearer as we make the final comparisons in Chapter 8 with the data for fossils from other chapters.

Summary: This review of sexual dimorphism in the dental dimensions of the australopithecines suggests to us that, in the one to perhaps four million years that they existed, they displayed a fairly marked degree of dental sexual dimorphism, both univariate and multivariate. Of far greater interest, however, is the fact that in the details of their sexual dimorphism, clearly enormously complex as we have found in each hominoid so far examined, they display a series of curious features. Some are similar to modern apes, some similar to modern and fossil humans, but most are different from both apes and humans. The overall evaluation must be that their sexual dimorphisms are uniquely different from those of either extant humans or apes.

Thus, their sexual dimorphisms of means are large like apes. Some of them display sexual dimorphisms of variance, also like apes (but for some groups samples are small enough that this cannot be properly determined). The multivariate sexual dimorphisms of the gracile species are large as also it is in apes. But the multivariate patterns of both fossil species are quite different from those of any extant form. The sex ratio in the various robust and gracile forms seems to be between two-to-one and three-to-one as in many primates that show marked sexual dimorphism.

In marked contrast to all robust and gracile forms, are the features of the group *Homo habilis*. Though examined briefly in Chapter 3 with other species of *Homo*, this fossil is also examined here, because of its presumed closer overall resemblance to australopithecines. Yet it turns out that *Homo habilis* presents sexual dimorphisms of means and variances, and univariate and multivariate sexually dimorphic patterns that are closer by far to those of *Homo* (especially, as we saw in Chapter 3, to *Homo erectus*) than to any australopithecine or to any ape. And, like various *Homo* species, it shows a one-to-one sex ratio.

The time span occupied by the gracile and robust fossils overlaps that occupied by the genus *Homo* especially when we include *Homo habilis*. Thus, if *Homo habilis* truly stems from an australopithecine source, the traditional view, then the new sexual dimorphism must have arisen very quickly indeed, and at a very specific time. In addition, it must have done so leaving behind many specimens and several species that did not change in their sexual dimorphism. This is problematical.

What is even more problematical for current views of australopithecine evolution, however, is the existence of sexual dimorphism in a much earlier form, *Ramapithecus*, that is not too dissimilar from that of fossil *Homo*, as explicated in Chapter 4.

This means that there are further complications in viewing the australopithecines as close to human ancestry. Let us leave them for the summary discussion of the final chapter.

CHAPTER 6

The Intervening Period: An Asian Relative!

The Enigma of *Gigantopithecus*!
Studies of Individual Measures — Sexual Dimorphisms in Canines
in Incisors — in Premolars — in Molars
Individual Dental Measures and Sexual Dimorphism — a Trap!
Combined Measures — Canonical Variates Analyses — High-dimensional Displays
Conclusions — Sexual Dimorphisms in *Gigantopithecus*

Abstract: We review, briefly, the previous studies of *Gigantopithecus*. They have assessed this genus as an aberrant giant ape, an aberrant giant prehuman, an aberrant giant *para*-human, or none of the above. Status as a giant Asian ape is the one most often accepted.

We then go on to examine the individual dimensions of the Chinese *Gigantopithecus* teeth using the methods described elsewhere in this book. The enormous and well-known bimodality that they display is obvious. They possess features that imply that truly enormous sexual dimorphism exists. But there is also, in the data, clear evidence as to how dangerous it can be to try to assess sex of individual specimens. The distributions also give information about sex ratio in the fossil sample, even though we do not know which specimens are from which sex.

We examine the dimensions multivariately using the data on extant forms from Chapter 2 as the reference population. Here, the sexual dimorphism is seen to be even greater and even more complex than in any other species so far examined. Elements of the multivariate sexual dimorphism show complex relationships with both living apes and living humans.

But what may be most interesting of all is the existence of a 'creature' with a combination of sexual dimorphism and sex ratio unique among mammals.

The enigma of *Gigantopithecus*

All the prior results in this book make it of considerable interest to study another enigmatic fossil from China: *Gigantopithecus*. The first fossil evidence of *Gigantopithecus* is in the romantic story of fossil teeth found in a Chinese drug store in Hong Kong by G. H. R. von Koenigswald in 1935. Among a collection of odd 'dragon' teeth he purchased was a single, worn, lower third molar of enormous size. He recognized it as obviously primate (von Koenigswald, 1952). It was later established that it (and others that he also purchased later) came from caves in southern China and were about 2 million years old.

A second species of *Gigantopithecus* was discovered in 1968 in the Siwalik hills in India. It was believed then to be between 5 and 9 million years old. It is clearly a different creature from the Chinese population.

The fossil materials for the Chinese *Gigantopithecus* (Figs. 6:1 and 6:2) eventually came to be very extensive, comprising three fairly complete mandibles and over one thousand teeth (Woo, 1962). The materials were discovered by continuous field work, carried out since 1956 by the Institute of Vertebrate Paleontology and Paleoanthropology, Academia Sinica, Beijing under the Directorship of Professor Wu Rukang.

The three mandibles are enormous and heavily buttressed. One mandible is especially larger than the other two. The molars are large and elongated; the anterior teeth are rather small. The canines do not project above the tooth row but contrast with human canines in being worn to a flat surface.

Extending back from perhaps 1 million years or more (the Chinese form *G. blackii*) to as much as 7 million years or more (the Indian form *G. bilaspurensis*), this group has been variously assigned as an aberrant pongid (e.g. Remane, 1960; Simons and Pilbeam, 1965; Corruccini, 1975; Simons and Pilbeam, 1978), as an extinct hominid side branch (e.g. Von Koenigswald, 1952, 1958; Woo, 1962), and as a hominid ancestor (e.g. Weidenreich, 1945; Heberer, 1959; Dart, 1960).

Most of the more recent investigations have

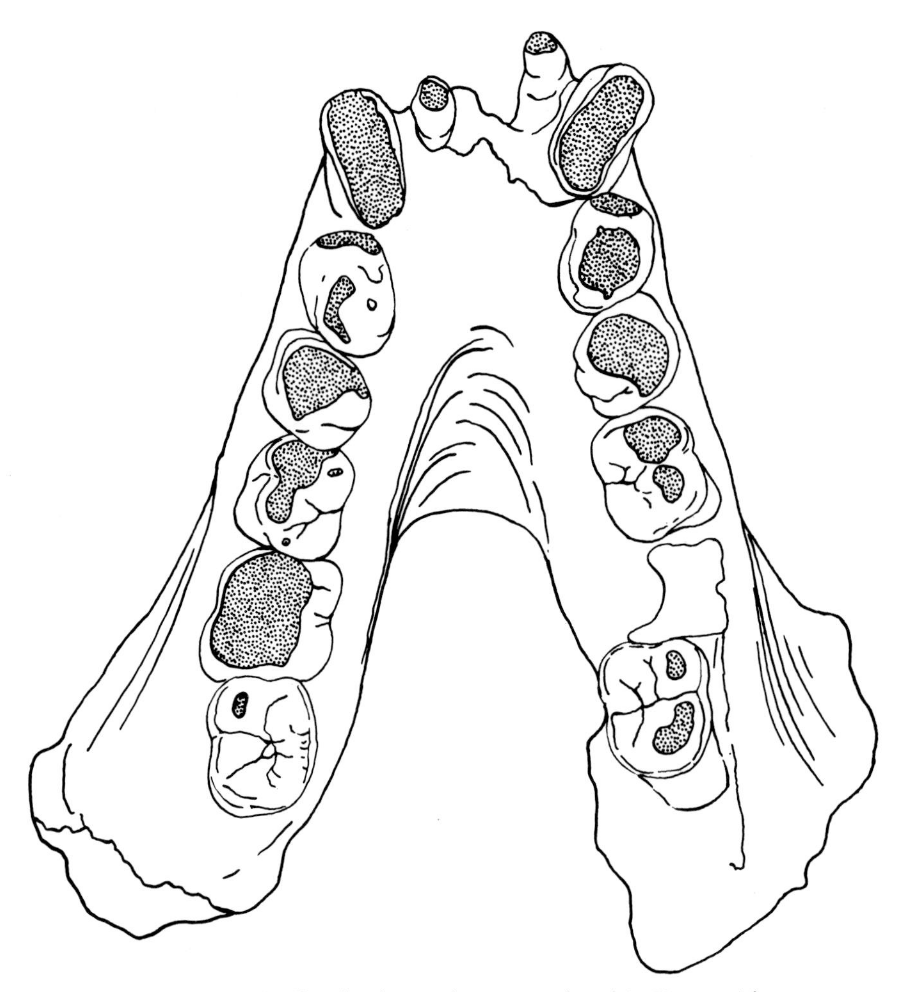

Fig. 6:1 Sketch of jaw of (presumed male) *Gigantopithecus*.

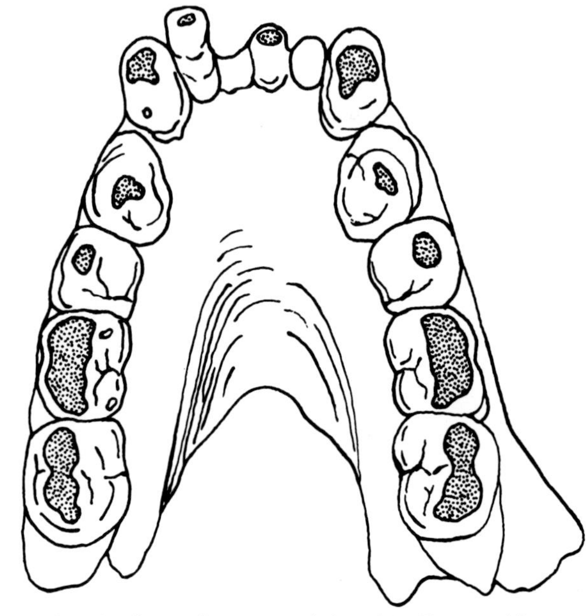

Fig. 6:2 Sketch of jaw of (presumed female) *Gigantopithecus*.

evaluated *Gigantopithecus* affinities in the context of fossil hominids and living apes. Only the study of Gelvin (1980) examines relationships in patterns that included fossil apes as well, and applies a multivariate statistical approach. Gelvin's results show that *Gigantopithecus* displays more affinities with hominids, particularly the Plio-Pleistocene hominids, than with any apes. His results support the earlier view that the best hypothesis at present is that *Gigantopithecus* is an extinct side-branch of the Hominidae.

Even Gelvin, however, did not consider the different patterns of sexual dimorphism that might exist, though he did test whether or not the existence of sexual dimorphism might have had some biasing effects upon his results (it turns out that it would not).

Professor Wu Rukang's original study (Woo, 1962) had assessed the two smaller (though still enormous) mandibles as female, the larger one as male. And he was easily able to separate the smaller pieces of jaws with a few related teeth and the many isolated teeth into small (female) and large (male) subsets. Thus Professor Wu readily recognized that *Gigantopithecus* had sexual dimorphism large enough for males and females to be identified for each single tooth. This is a remarkable situation for primates; but, of course, the overall size of these remains are also quite remarkable among primates. The fact that Professor Wu has kindly made these data available to me, presents a marvellous opportunity for statistical investigation of their overall dimensions.

Accordingly, then, the lengths and breadths of 1,094 individual teeth (1,057 isolated) of *Gigantopithecus* from the three caves in the Tahsin and Liucheng districts, Guanxi, China, are examined here using the same univariate (basic statistical data, computer derived histograms, fitted normal curves and 'Chi Square' tests) and multivariate (canonical variates analysis and high-dimensional displays) statistical methods as in prior chapters. Comparisons are made with similar study of equivalent data from extant humans and great apes, and other fossil hominoids (Lieberman, Gelvin and Oxnard, 1985). From such studies it may be possible to understand something of the numbers of groups represented in this collection of teeth, of their general variability, of their sexual dimorphism and, even, possibly, of their socio-sexual structure.

The materials include teeth from every position in both upper and lower jaws. The sizes of the samples range from as few as 8 for the upper first incisor through 91 for the upper third molar, to as many as 118 for upper first and second molars combined (the form of the first and second molars do not allow of them being separated). Maximum length and breadth were taken on each adult, unbroken and not too badly worn tooth. In addition, in order to increase the sizes of the samples as much as possible, a few lengths or breadths were included even when the condition of individual teeth prevented the other measure from being included. Thus the sample size for each dimension for a given tooth is not always quite the same. This was done especially for those teeth for which the sample size was marginal. Even with such supplementation, however, sample sizes for most of the incisor dimensions are too small for statistical examination, and those for canine dimensions are marginal. Table 6:1 gives details of the materials. The final answer for the sizes of these samples depends, of course, upon the amount of dimorphism. If sexual dimorphism turns out to be as small as in most teeth of humans then samples of at least 20 are the minimum. If dimorphism proves to be as great as in the canines of large apes, then even a sample as small as those available for the canines for *Gigantopithecus* may still be capable of divulging information. The latter situation is the case.

First, the values for each measurement (length or breadth) are pooled and examined without regard to the original designation of sex. Second, the data are examined grouped by sex as assigned by prior studies (Woo, 1962). The results suggest that attributions of sex are well made for those teeth in which sexual differences are truly marked (as seen from the bimodal distributions that we have discovered that are statistically significantly different from normal for the data pooled regardless of sex). Examples include the lengths of upper third premolars and upper third molars. But for other teeth where sex differences are much less marked (i.e. where study of the pooled dimensions show only

Table 6:1

Numbers of specimens available for study in *Gigantopithecus*

	Lower teeth	Upper teeth
First incisor	8	9
Second incisor	4	6
Canine	14	19
Third premolar	68	40
Fourth premolar	78	70
First & second molars	122	141
Third molar	65	91

unimodal distributions not significantly different from normal) it appears that the initial determination of sex was probably erroneus.

Let us first examine the results of univariate statistical analyses, basic statistical data, histograms, fitted normal curves, and Chi Square tests.

Studies of individual measures: sexual dimorphisms in canines

The numbers of upper and lower canines available are so small that it is almost impossible to do any definitive statistical tests. Nevertheless, as can be seen from Figure 6:3, there are, indeed, two 'groups' of *Gigantopithecus* that are so widely different that, even with these small samples, they are completely separated by the dimensions of the canines. This is especially so for the length and breadth of the lower canine and the length of the upper canine. There are absolute gaps between the lower and upper parts of these bimodal distributions. This accounts for why Wu (Woo, 1962) was able to be so certain in his designation of sex for this form.

For it seems most likely that this represents sexual dimorphism in the canines. It is always possible, of course, that these two peaks represent different subspecies of *Gigantopithecus*, and this should always be borne in mind. But other facts render that a suspect judgement.

The distances between the values that represent the peaks of the bimodal distributions is of the order of 4–6 mm, a dimorphism that is enormously greater than anything found in modern humans. It is an amount, indeed, that is greater even than that in *Gorilla*, the most dimorphic (in this regard) of the extant apes. This, together with the fact that three of the four canine measures are bimodal (even, again, with these small samples whereas in modern humans only one such measure is clearly bimodal even with samples of about 60) suggests that in the canines at least, *Gigantopithecus* actually shows very much greater sexual dimorphism than modern humans.

The equal width of each peak in those measures that have bimodal distributions suggests, again like modern humans but also, in this case, like orangutans, that the type of sexual dimorphism that is measured by a difference between the dispersions for each sex is absent. This is a major difference of this heavily dimorphic species from the also heavily dimorphic extant *Gorilla*, indeed from both the very heavily dimorphic (in this feature) African apes.

The fact that the peaks of those distributions that are bimodal show equal numbers of specimens suggests, that, again like modern humans, the female-to-male ratio was 1:1. This is rather surprising, when we realize that it goes with mean differences between the sexes that are even greater than those known for the most dimorphic extant apes (*Gorilla* and *Pongo*).

Individual measures again: sexual dimorphisms in incisors and premolars

There are too few incisor teeth for any significant information to be divulged. But it is of interest that the small number of measures that we do have show, for the length of the upper first incisor, (**a**) a bimodal distribution with a large gap between each mode, (**b**) an equal dispersion for each mode and (**c**) the same number of specimens in each mode.

There are considerably larger samples of premolars. Three dimensions, the length of the upper third premolar, the breadth of the lower third premolar and the length of the lower fourth premolar show very distinct bimodal distributions (Fig. 6:4).

The absolute distances between the modes in each of the significantly bimodal dimensions is 2 mm or greater. This, together with the fact that such differences exist in several more measures than is the case in modern forms with very much larger samples, suggests that sexual dimorphism, if this is what these bimodal distributions represent in *Gigantopithecus*, is actually considerably greater than in any extant species. It is evident, however, in a quite different mix of dimensions and tooth loci than in extant forms.

The equal dispersions of the two peaks in the significant bimodal distributions indicates, that there is no sexual dimorphism of dispersion. In this respect the fossil is similar to modern humans and the single extant ape, *Pongo*.

Likewise, the equal sizes of the two peaks in the bimodal distributions suggests that there are equal numbers of females and males in the available samples, as in modern humans, but in no living great ape.

Individual measures a third time: molar sexual dimorphisms

It is in the posterior dentition that samples are largest of all. The dimensions of the third molars

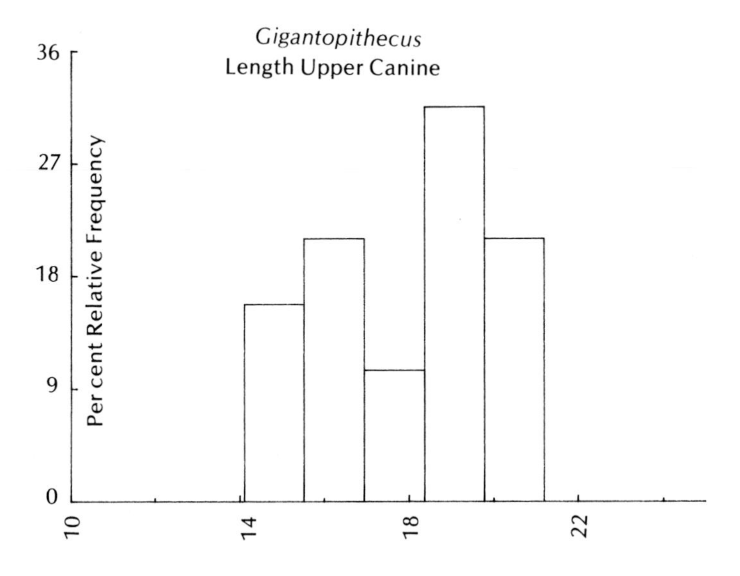

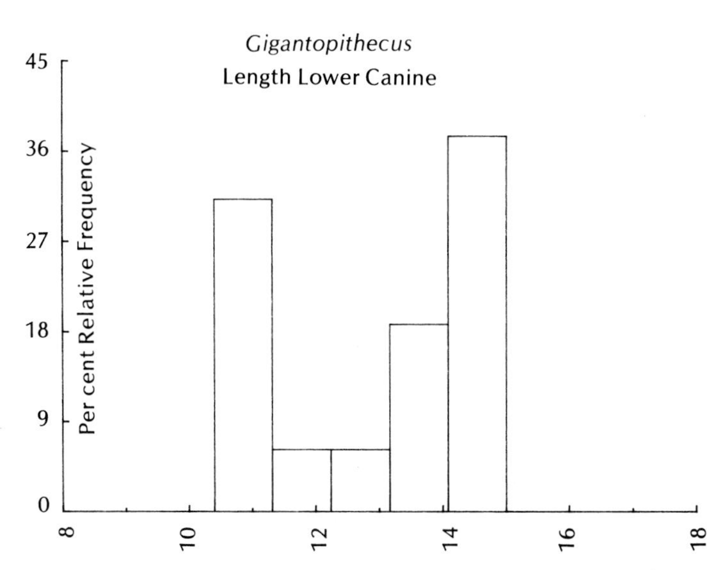

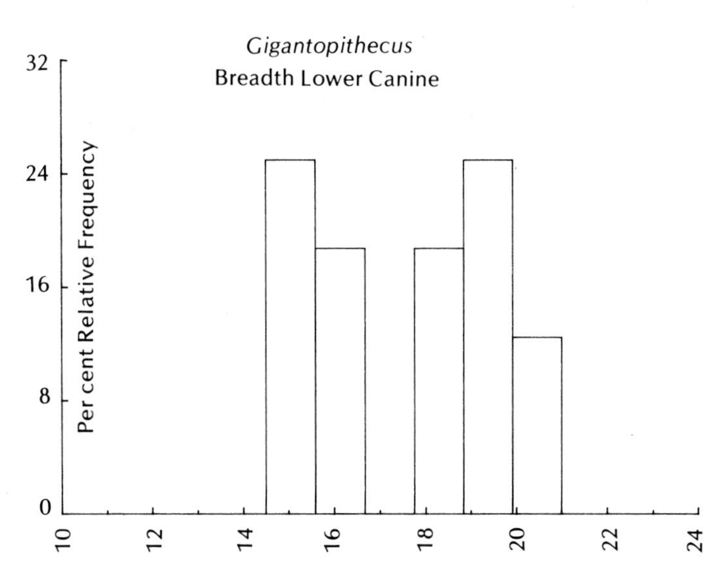

Fig. 6:3 The data for canines are very few. Nevertheless, because there is such large dimorphism in this species, it seems as though useful information has been obtained. The figures show bimodal distributions for various canine dimensions. In each case, there is a clear, in one case absolute, difference between the two modes. This demonstrates extremely large dimorphism compared with any living primate (but then, of course, compared with any living primate, these are by far the largest). The form of the bimodality suggests equal variance for each sex. The sizes of the peaks are approximately equal implying strongly that there is a one-to-one sex ratio in this species.

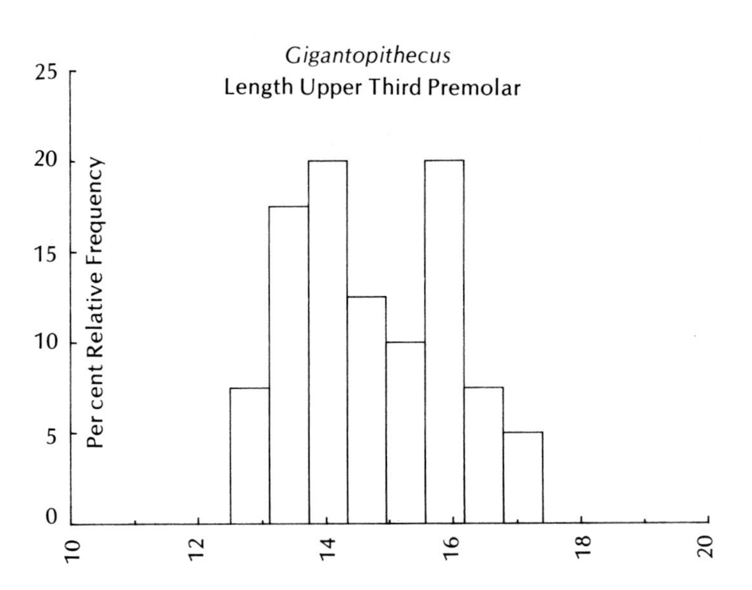

Fig. 6:4 The data for premolars are very numerous. Accordingly very good information has been obtained. The figures show bimodal distributions for two premolar dimensions. In each case, there is a clear difference between the two modes. This demonstrates extremely large dimorphism compared with any living primate (but then, of course, compared with any living primate, these are by far the largest). The form of the bimodality suggests equal variance for each sex. The sizes of the peaks are equal implying strongly that there is a one-to-one sex ratio in this species.

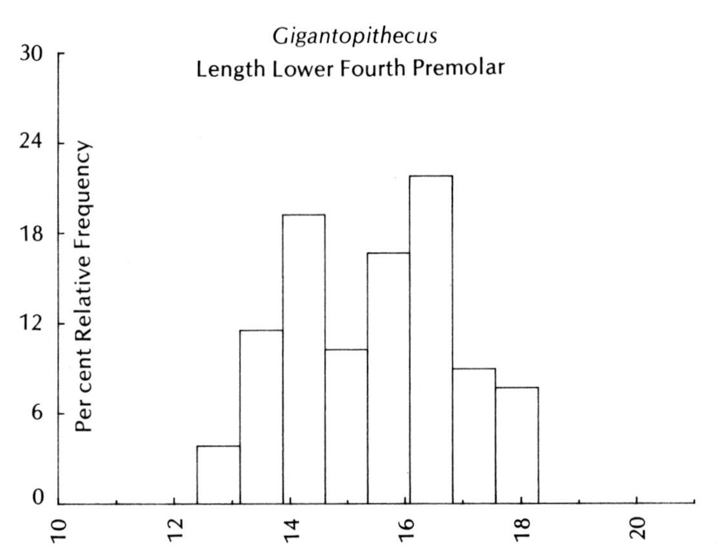

should be considered first because there is no doubt as to which teeth are third molars. Both lengths and breadths of upper third molars show significant bimodal distributions (Figs. 6:5 and 6:6). The same applies to the first and second molars pooled (Fig. 6:7).

The absolute distance between the modes is large for the breadth (over 2 mm) and extremely large for lengths (over 4 mm). The two peaks are equal in dispersion as far as can be judged visually. And the sizes of the two peaks are equal in both cases. All this replicates the findings for the other teeth for this genus, suggesting large dimorphism of mean difference, zero dimorphism of dispersion difference, and equal numbers of females and males in the sample.

The investigators in Beijing believed that the dimorphism of mean values was so large that they could actually identify which teeth were from males and females. Our examination of each sex subgroup as they were identified by Chinese investigators shows each to comprise a normal distribution in its own right. And although there can be no guarantee that these investigators identified intermediate teeth correctly, it would appear, because the dimorphism is truly so large and because the numbers in each sex are equal, that they succeeded in dividing the specimens in such a way that our later studies have obtained these normal distributions for each sex.

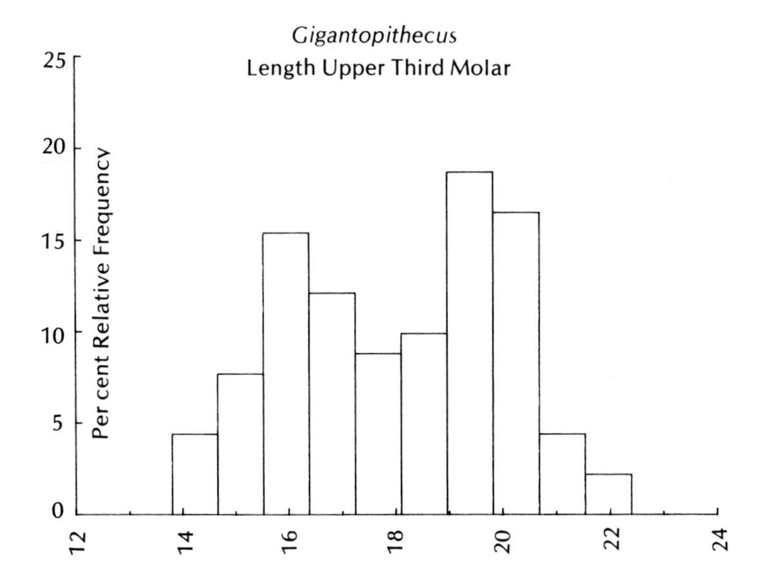

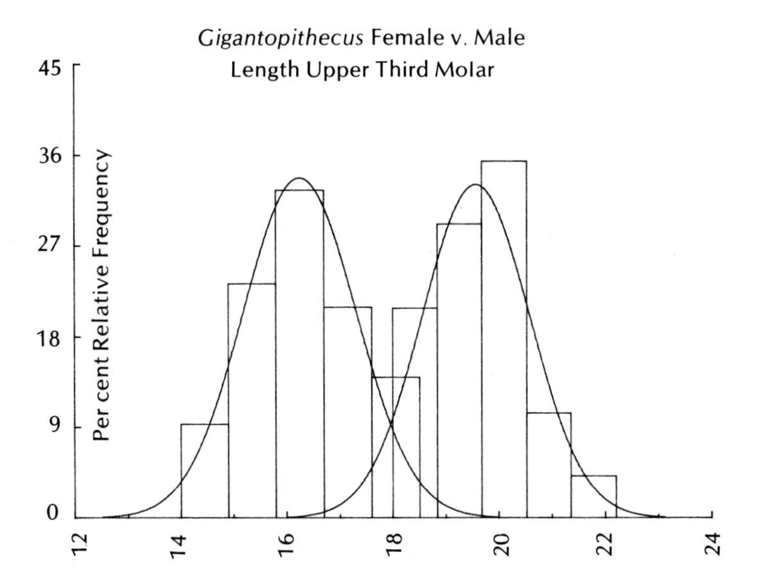

Fig. 6:5 The data for molars are very numerous indeed and provide the best information in this book.

The upper figure shows a very clear bimodal distribution for the length of the upper third molar. There is a clear difference between the two modes demonstrating extremely large dimorphism compared with any living primate (but then, of course, compared with any living primate, these are by far the largest). The form of the bimodality suggests equal variance for each sex. The sizes of the peaks are equal implying strongly that there is a one-to-one sex ratio in this species.

The difference between females and males for this tooth is so great that the original Chinese investigators believed that they could actually assign each tooth to its sex. The lower figure shows that when the data are examined on the basis of their judgment about sex, excellent normal distributions are indeed obtained for each sex.

Individual dental measures and sexual dimorphism: a trap!

The cases of the upper fourth premolar and the lower third molar are quite the opposite. Here the histograms for each dimension show unimodal distributions that are not significantly different from the fitted normal curve (Figs. 6:8 and 6:9). Sexual dimorphism must be much less in these teeth than in any so far discussed.

When, however, we examine the sexes separately (as determined by the Beijing investigators) we find that the distributions for each 'sex' are totally significantly different from normal. This is not, however, because they are bimodal but because they are enormously heavily skewed. So heavy is this skewing that it appears, as though each 'sex' comprised one half of a normal distribution. This is exactly what we might expect to find if there were very little sexual dimorphism in these particular dimensions, and if the attempt to 'find' the sexes had merely divided the sample artificially about its single mode into the smaller and larger specimens. This is one of the major traps in studies of sexual dimorphism.

Summary of study of individual dimensions

Gigantopithecus shows enormously greater mean

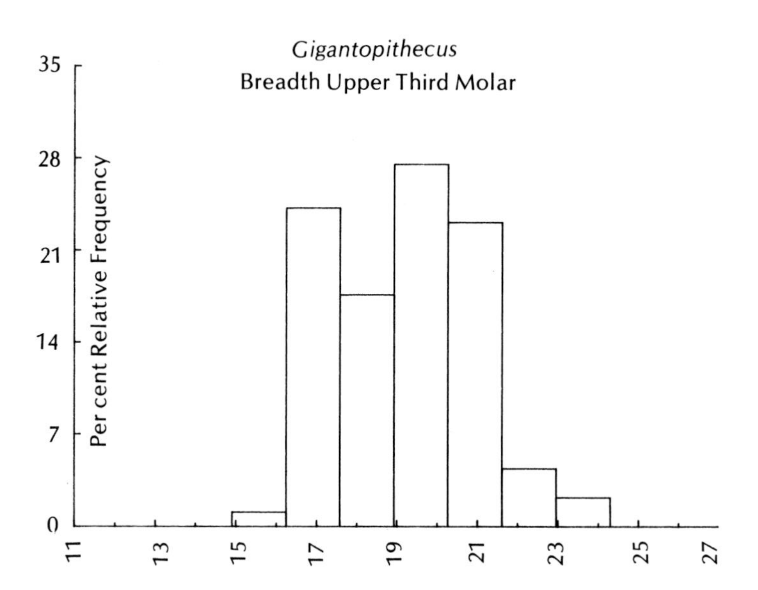

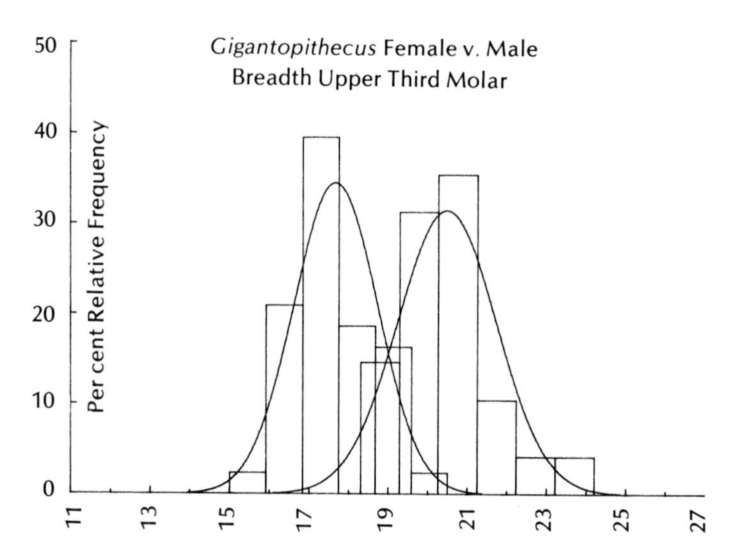

Fig. 6:6 A similar picture is seen for the breadth of the upper third molar. The upper figure shows a bimodal distribution for the breadth of the upper third molar. There is a clear difference between the two modes demonstrating extremely large dimorphism compared with any living primate (but then, of course, compared with any living primate, these are by far the largest). The form of the bimodality suggests equal variance for each sex. The sizes of the peaks are equal, implying strongly that there is a one-to-one sex ratio in this species.

The difference between females and males for this tooth is so great that the original Chinese investigators believed that they could actually assign each tooth to a specific sex. The lower figure shows that when the data are examined on the basis of their judgment about sex, excellent normal distributions are indeed obtained for each sex.

size sexual dimorphism almost everywhere along the tooth row, as compared with any living form, human or ape. However, *Gigantopithecus* shows the same, zero, dispersion difference between males and females as in modern *Homo*, a feature which is also shared with orang-utans. Finally *Gigantopithecus* shows evidence of a female-to-male ratio of 1:1 (Table 6:2) This is also as in modern *Homo* but contrasts, of course, with the situation in any extant ape.

Studies of dental measures taken in combination

Of course, these data are taken from individual teeth from many different and incomplete fossil *Gigantopithecus*. It is not therefore possible to say, except to some limited extent, which particular teeth at one locus are from the same individual as teeth at other loci. For this reason it is not possible to carry out a multivariate statistical study which incorporates the data from *Gigantopithecus* in the same manner as for the humans and extant apes, previously examined. But it is possible to take the mean values for each unimodal dimension, and the modal values for each bimodal dimension, as the approximate means for the two sexes. These can be interpolated into the previously determined multivariate statistical analysis, in the same way as has been done for the other fossils and for the known sexes of humans from Willcox' materials. Because of

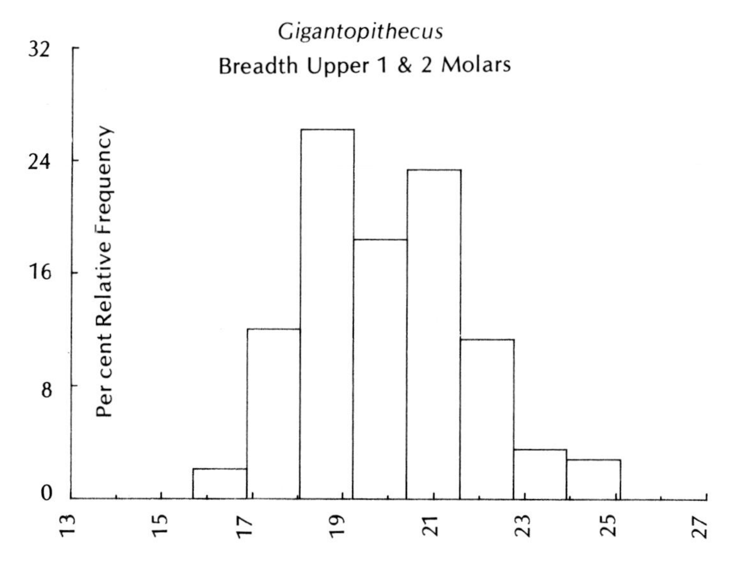

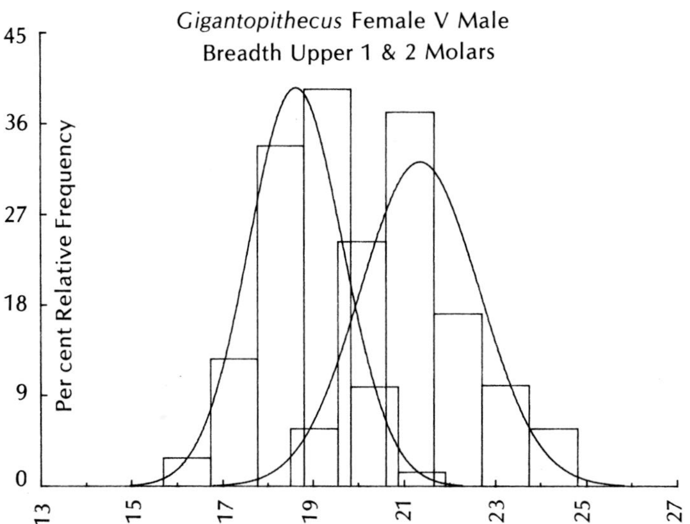

Fig. 6:7 A similar picture is seen for the pooled breadths of the upper first and second molars (these have to be pooled because a separate determination for the large number of isolated first and second molars cannot be made). The upper figure shows a bimodal distribution for the breadth of these two molars combined. There is a clear difference between the two modes demonstrating extremely large dimorphism compared with any living primate (but then, of course, compared with any living primate, these are by far the largest). The form of the bimodality suggests equal variance for each sex. The sizes of the peaks are equal, implying strongly that there is a one-to-one sex ratio in this species.

The difference between females and males for this tooth is so great that the original Chinese investigators believed that they could actually assign each tooth to a specific sex. The lower figure shows that when the data are examined on the basis of their judgment about sex, excellent normal distributions are indeed obtained for each sex.

limitations to the original extant data, this can only be done for the upper and lower jaws separately.

The goal of this study is to expand the studies of the data from extant hominoids, using multivariate statistical analyses. A similar set of questions are addressed as in previous chapters.

What is the nature of sexual dimorphism in the dentition of *Gigantopithecus*?

What patterns are apparent in multivariate analyses of *Gigantopithecus* that might not have appeared in univariate studies?

Which of the living species so far examined does *Gigantopithecus* most resemble?

What are the implications of the results for hominoid and, more specially, human phylogeny?

The data on extant primates used in this study are outlined in the second chapter. The fossil data are length and breadth measurements from those *Gigantopithecus* specimens given in the publication by Wu (Woo, 1962). The 736 teeth suitable for study in this way (adult, unbroken, undistorted and not badly worn) include representatives from every tooth position in both maxilla and mandible, with a maximum of 91 teeth and an average of 46 teeth for any given locus.

Four multivariate analyses are performed on the data. For the extant primates, mandibular and maxillary data are analyzed separately, using canonical variates analysis. In both cases the seven groups used are: *Gorilla* females, *Gorilla* males, *Pan* females, *Pan* males, *Pongo* females, *Pongo* males, and *Homo*, sex unknown. In each case, therefore, six canonical axes are generated.

The distributions for the fossil group,

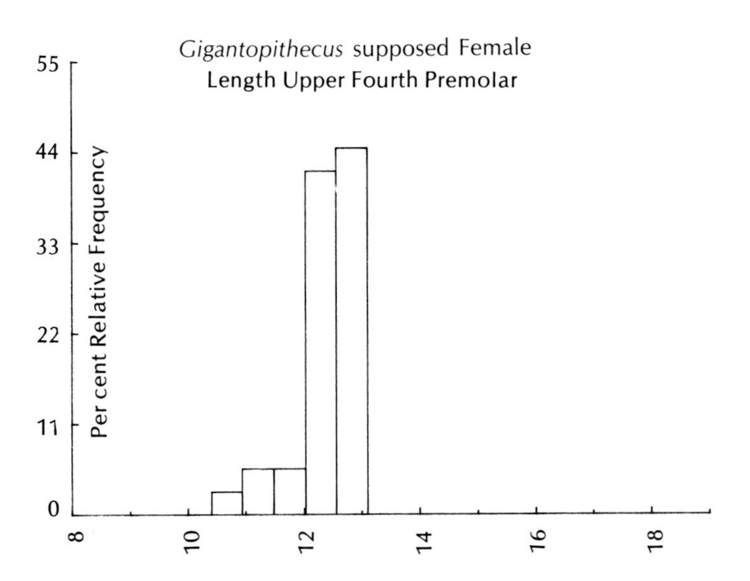

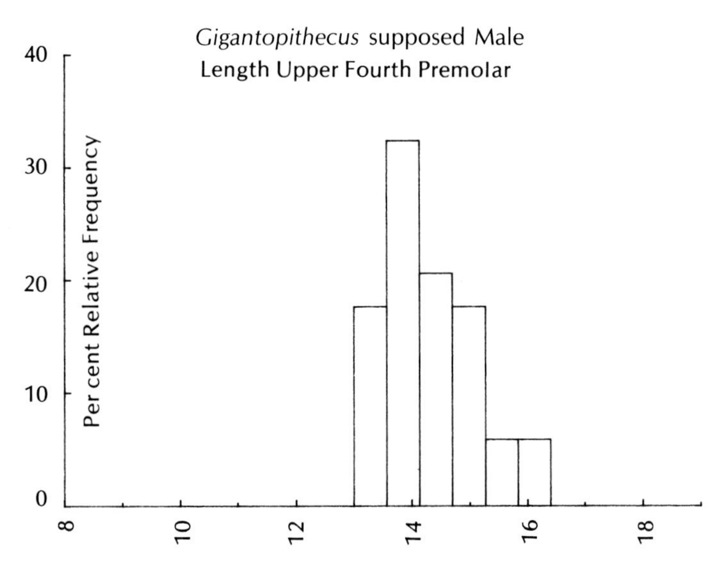

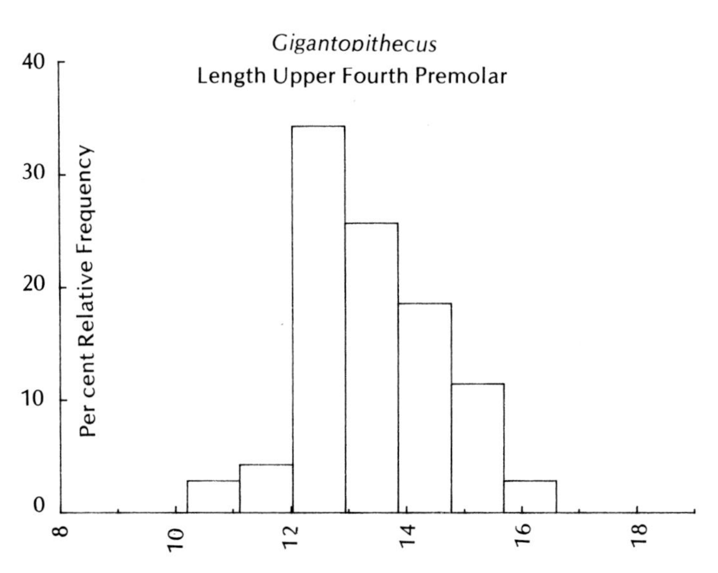

Fig. 6:8 In the case of the upper fourth premolar, the original assessments of sex may not have been so good. The lower frame shows that the distribution of the measurements of this tooth are unimodal. However dimorphic this species may have been, strong evidence does not exist for sexual dimorphism in this tooth.

The assessment of sex originally provided shows, when each 'sex' is examined in the same way, two distributions (middle and upper frames) that are unimodal and so completely skewed that they can only have been achieved by the unwitting splitting of the unimodal distribution shown below.

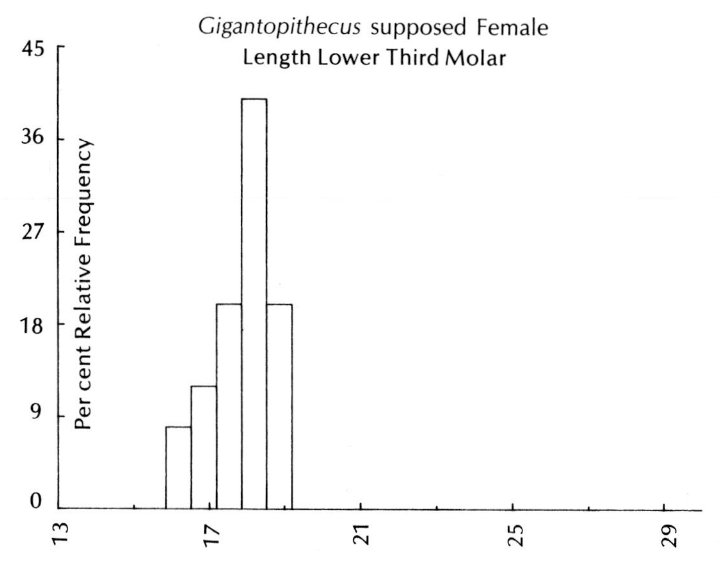

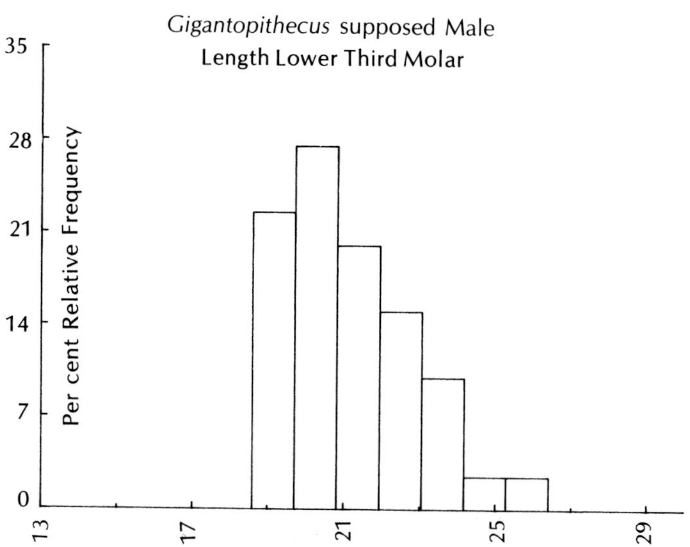

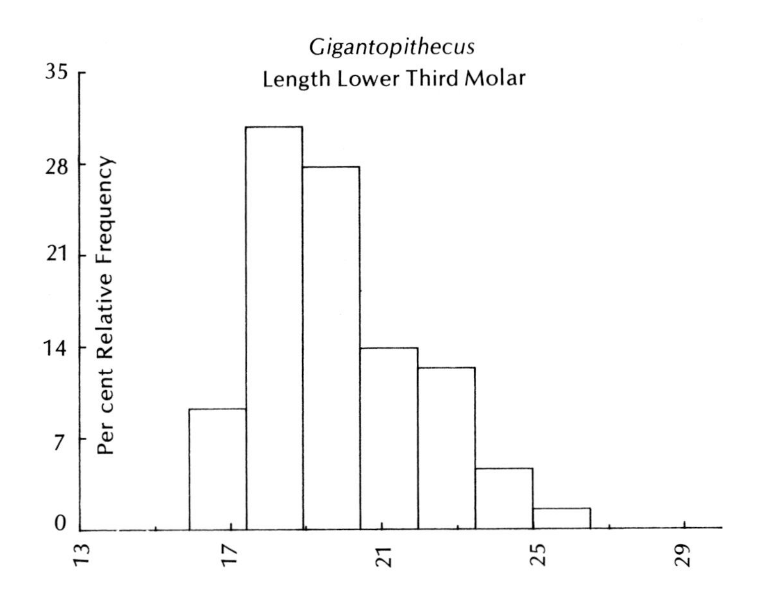

Fig. 6:9 In the case of the lower third molar, the original assessments of sex may have been even worse than in Fig. 6:8. The lower frame shows that the distribution of the measurements of this tooth are unimodal. However dimorphic this species may have been, strong evidence does not exist for sexual dimorphism in this tooth.

The assessment of sex originally provided shows, when each 'sex' is examined in the same way, two distributions (middle and upper frames) that are unimodal and so completely skewed that they can only have been achieved by the unwitting splitting of the unimodal distribution shown below.

Table 6:2

Pattern of differences in sexual dimorphism in *Gigantopithecus* along the tooth row.

Lower teeth	length	breadth
I_1	N	N
I_2	—	—
$C_,$	*B* = *	*B* = *
P_3	*B* = *	B =
P_4	*B* = *	N
$M_1 + M_2$	N	N
M_3	S *	S *
Upper teeth		
I^1	B	B
I^2	B	B
C'	*B* = *	*B* = *
P^3	B = *	N
P^4	S *	S *
$M^1 + M^2$	N	N
M^3	*B* = *	*B* = *

Notes: N = unimodal distribution; S = skewed unimodal distribution; B = bimodal distribution; "=" = approximately equal peaks in bimodal distribution; italics = slightly larger number of male specimens than females; * = statistically significantly different from normal; — = number of specimens too few for any determination.

Gigantopithecus, are already known to be bimodal in most measurements. The values for means for each sex are taken, as previously explained, from the peaks of both unimodal and bimodal distributions (Table 6:3). In no case were the values for males and females separately (as presented by Woo, 1962) utilized because of the problems posed by examination of the lower third molar and upper fourth premolar and the first and second molars combined (Figs. 6:7 through to 6:9).

Canonical variates analyses

Figures 6:10, 6:11 and 6:12 are plots of canonical variates means for the seven groups described earlier for both maxillary and mandibular analyses respectively. The fossils are, additionally, interpolated into these diagrams.

For the first two axes in the mandibular analysis *Gigantopithecus* putative females and males are closest to the same two sexes in *Gorilla*. The direction of difference between female and male *Gigantopithecus* is the same as that between female and male of each extant ape (but especially *Gorilla* Fig. 6:10).

Table 6:3

Mean lengths and breadths of teeth for sex subgroups of *Gigantopithecus*

	Length f	Length m	Breadth f	Breadth m
Lower teeth				
I_1	7.0	7.0	9.1	9.1
I_2	5.3	5.3	10.3	10.3
$C_,$	11.0	14.2	15.2	19.5
P_3	15.0	17.0	15.0	17.0
P_4	14.0	16.5	16.0	16.0
$M_1 + M_1$	19.8	19.8	16.9	16.9
M_3	20.2	20.2	16.8	16.8
Upper teeth				
I^1	12.4	15.8	14.0	14.0
I^2	9.0	9.0	11.2	11.2
C'	16.2	19.7	15.8	21.8
P^3	14.0	16.0	20.0	20.0
P^4	13.5	13.5	19.0	19.0
$M^1 + M^1$	19.4	19.4	19.9	19.9
M^3	16.0	19.8	17.0	20.2

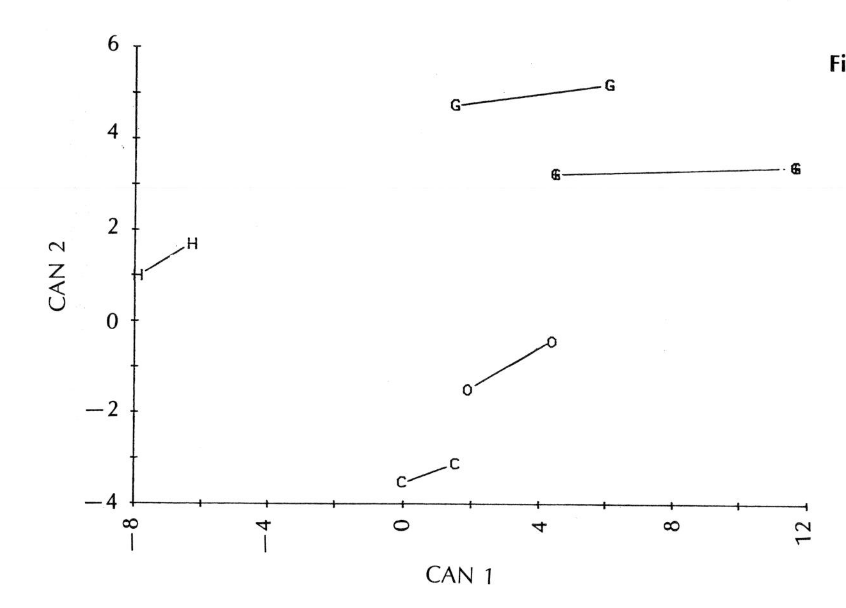

Fig. 6:10 Plot of the first two canonical variates of the study of the mandibular data (H-H = *Homo*, C-C = *Pan*, O-O = *Pongo*, G-G = *Gorilla*; the letter on the left indicates the female in each case). *Gigantopithecus* is interpolated into this study and in this plot shows very large multivariate sexual dimorphism at least as large as *Gorilla*. It also lies fairly close to *Gorilla* towards the *Pongo* side.

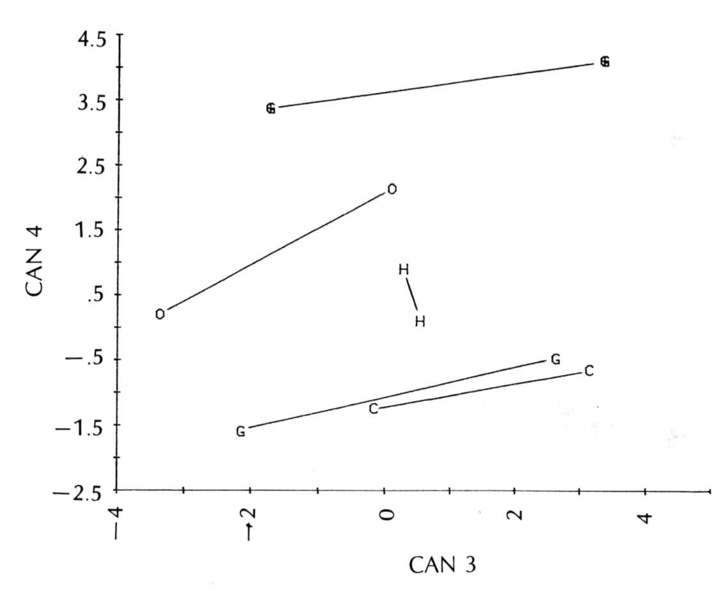

Fig. 6:11 Plot of the canonical variates analysis of the second two axes of the study of the mandibular data (H-H = *Homo*, C-C = *Pan*, O-O = *Pongo*, G-G = *Gorilla*; the letter on the left indicates the female in each case). *Gigantopithecus* is interpolated into this study and in this plot again shows very large multivariate sexual dimorphism at least as large as *Gorilla*. It lies fairly close to *Pongo* and the combination of this figure with Fig. 6:10 places it as being intermediate between *Gorilla* and *Pongo*.

For the second two axes in the mandibular analysis *Gigantopithecus* again shows a similar and very large directional difference between the sexes that is the same as in each of the other great apes. But in this case, *Gigantopithecus* is far removed from *Gorilla* and nearer to *Pongo* showing that its absolute location as a genus in all four axes is approximately equidistant from each of the large highly dimorphic living apes. In particular, the apparent similarity with *Gorilla* shown in axes one and two is spurious (Fig. 6:11).

These similarities and differences are rather clearly shown in the three-dimensional plot of the first three axes (Fig. 6:12).

But the plot of canonical axes five and six (which do not separate the living species — they form a neat single group in the middle of the plot) demonstrates that there is much additional data for *Gigantopithecus* (Fig. 6:13). Some of this additional difference clearly separates *Gigantopithecus* from all living species. And a good deal more of this difference goes towards producing a separation between the sexes, a multivariate sexual dimorphism, that is very large. This additional separation makes sexual dimorphism in *Gigantopithecus* utterly different from *Gorilla*, which it otherwise superficially resembles. These differences are not surprising, of course, for a creature dating from two million years ago. And they provide information, that would support a search for a new evolutionary mechanism for the existence of great sexual dimorphism in a species with equal numbers of males and

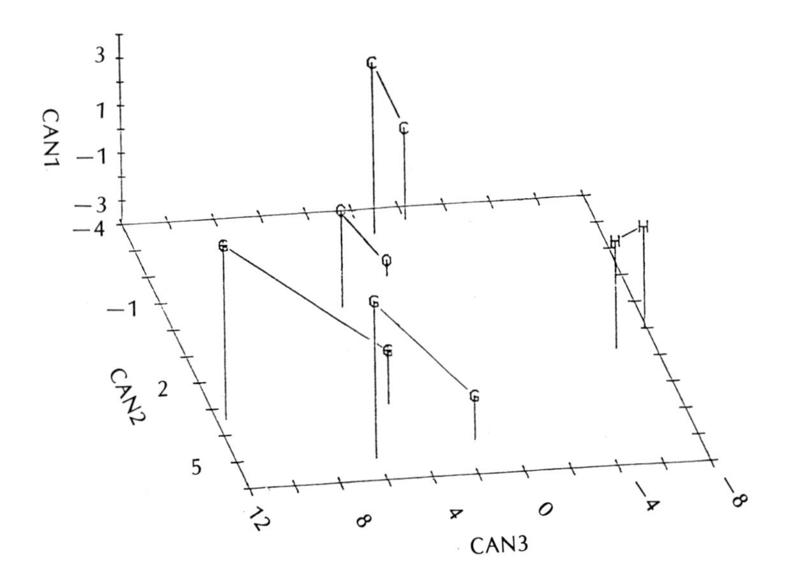

Fig: 6:12 Another view of the canonical variates analysis of the mandibular data is provided by this three-dimensional model (H-H = *Homo*, C-C = *Pan*, O-O = *Pongo*, G-G = *Gorilla*; the letter on the right indicates the female in each case). *Gigantopithecus* is interpolated into this study and this plot emphasizes the fact that taking several axes together, *Gigantopithecus* shows very much larger multivariate sexual dimorphism than any living hominoid.

Fig. 6:13 This shows the fifth and sixth canonical axes of the same multivariate statistical study with *Gigantopithecus* interpolated. It demonstrates that though these two axes do not separate the living forms at all, there are additional separations for *Gigantopithecus* that provide it with a form of sexual dimorphism that is not only larger than that in any hominoid, but is also totally different in its pattern. Indeed, this difference in pattern may be a greater difference than the mere size.

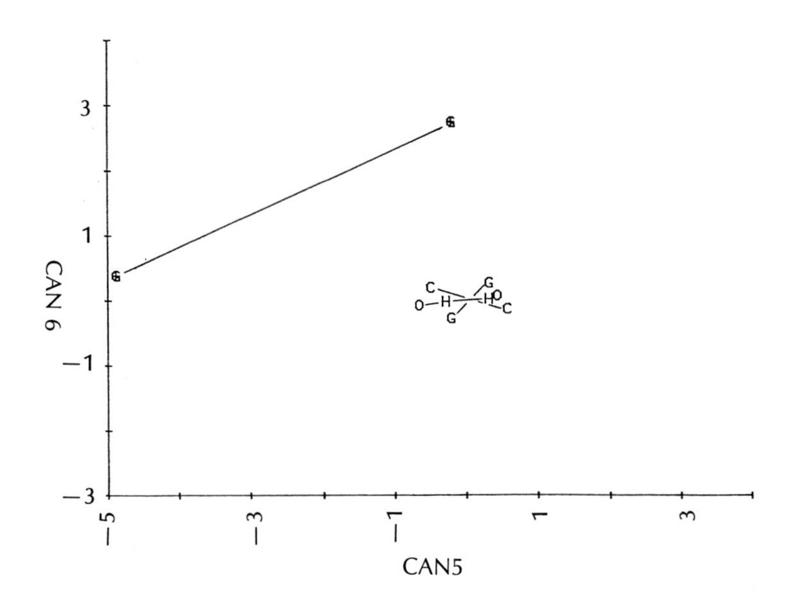

females. Such a mechanism must be something rather different from anything so far worked out.

Similar findings, though with lesser separations, are available from the maxillary studies.

High-dimensional displays

As was the case with the extant genera, high-dimensional plots were generated in order to include information in higher axes. In this case, however, the difference between *Gigantopithecus* and the living species is so great that the procedure is not necessary. It is presented in Figure 6:14 and this figure helps us further understand how the high-dimensional displays work. That *Gigantopithecus* truly is totally different from any living species is in no doubt.

Conclusions: sexual dimorphisms in *Gigantopithecus*

Gigantopithecus resembles no extant form closely. It is somewhat similar to *Pongo* in some features, both univariate and multivariate; and it is some-

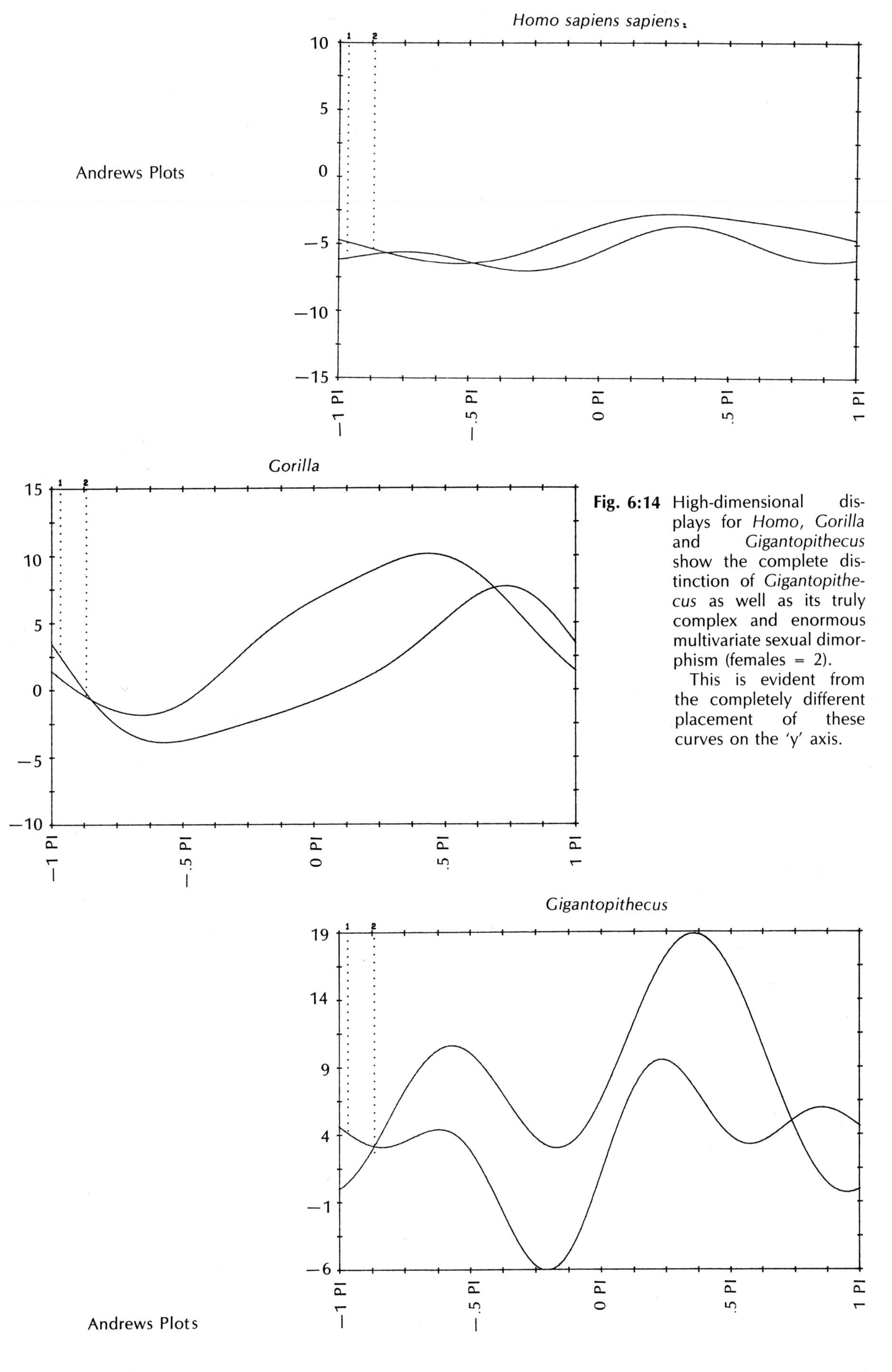

Fig. 6:14 High-dimensional displays for *Homo, Gorilla* and *Gigantopithecus* show the complete distinction of *Gigantopithecus* as well as its truly complex and enormous multivariate sexual dimorphism (females = 2).

This is evident from the completely different placement of these curves on the 'y' axis.

what similar to *Homo* in other features, again both univariate and multivariate. In a certain combination of these univariate and multivariate features it is similar to both *Homo* and *Pongo* because these are features shared by *Homo* and *Pongo*.

In most features *Gigantopithecus* is clearly totally different from all other living or fossil species.

In one special feature the sex ratio, *Gigantopithecus* is similar to all members of the genus *Homo* and the Chinese *Ramapithecus*.

Further discussions and conclusions of these matters clearly await the intercalations and comparisons of the information on all the other fossils, a matter for the final chapter.

Summary: This review of sexual dimorphism in *Gigantopithecus* shows that it has some features like those of living apes (especially the orang-utan). These are mainly features that are to do with the degree of dimorphism (large univariate dimorphism of means, large multivariate dimorphism).

It also shows that *Gigantopithecus* does not have the feature that is common to the African apes and australopithecines, large sexual dimorphism of dispersions.

Gigantopithecus shows a feature in which it is similar to both humans and orang-utans. That is, like both these creatures, it displays no difference in dispersions between putative males and females (in so far as this can be estimated from these data).

Most of all, however, *Gigantopithecus* shows a specific feature, a one-to-one sex ratio, that is confined, among all the hominoids examined in this book, to the species of the genera, *Homo* and the Chinese *Ramapithecus*.

Finally, in its overall multivariate pattern of sexual dimorphism, *Gigantopithecus* is totally different from any other form, even the most dimorphic of the large apes, *Gorilla*.

The evolutionary possibilities that stem from such a combination of features are multiple and tenuous. But the comparisons with the various other fossils in the final chapter, have implications for both the overall picture of hominoid evolution and the detail for *Gigantopithecus* that is painted by almost all the data in this book.

CHAPTER 7

Studying Sex In Fossils: Some Caveats

Abstract: The work outlined in previous chapters depends upon the use of particular types of data and particular statistical methods. The results seem clear; the methods, though somewhat complicated, have been worked out by statisticians and applied in many biological situations. Yet, in every investigation both data and methods are subject to constraints that need to be understood before discussions and conclusions can be broached. We must be appropriately self-critical and try to understand the qualifications to which this work, indeed all studies of this type, are subject. Of all things, this, self-criticism, is the most difficult to carry out.

Problems due to quality of measurements

All of these studies have been carried out using the overall lengths and breadths of teeth. Surely, says the percipient reader, something better than overall dimensions could have been measured. And this comment is indeed appropriate. There are many studies in the literature, wherein the complicated forms of teeth have been better captured through the use of other data.

Sometimes this has encompassed, through observation or measurement, the pattern of placement of the various complex cusps of the teeth. Study of these patterns has resulted in much of what we know about many fossil groups. They are often enormously complicated and contain a great deal of information about the relationships of animals. It has been shown many times that such patterns are somewhat akin to finger prints and reflect the underlying genetic make-up of animals. For instance, the incidence of 'Carabelli's cusp' is important in understanding human genealogies. Cusp patterns also tell us something about animal diets. We are all aware, for example, of the different cuspal patterns in carnivores and herbivores, and of the especial complexities of cusps in animals, such as elephants, reflecting masticatory processing of large amounts of very tough foods.

Sometimes, too, measures have been specifically aimed at defining the cutting, shearing and crushing edges and areas of the teeth. This is clearly related in part to the cusp patterns (though not completely, for cusp patterns may be eliminated by tooth wear during use, but shearing, cutting and grinding edges and surfaces remain; perhaps original cuspal patterns help determine eventual wear patterns). Such patterns, even more than those of the cusps, are related in a specific manner to different masticatory habits, and different food materials. We can look to carnivores and herbivores for extreme specializations along such lines.

Dental areas are also associated with other facets of the lives of animals. They are related to their overall physiological and metabolic requirements. They provide measures that can be seen in the light of overall amounts of food materials being triturated, overall energy requirements being met by the food, overall nutritional values of particular types of food materials, and so on.

And yet other measures of tooth areas, for example, cross-sectional areas of the main body of the tooth are related to the totality of stresses borne by the tooth, irrespective of the type of activity (cutting, crushing, grinding) in which it may be involved. In this sense, the changing cross-sectional area of the teeth along the tooth row are indicators, at least to some degree, of the changing resultant forces acting along the length of the entire dental apparatus during function. Such cross-sectional areas may be almost akin to a series of little 'average-force gauges' (if there were such things) placed upon the jaws at the positions of individual teeth.

And many of these measurements, especially perhaps, those of areas, may require manipulation in some useful way. For example, semi-logarithmic or logarithmic transformations may help us to deal with such complex matters as the relationships of areas to overall bodily weight, or the problems that may arise, statistically, when there is a positive and marked relationship between means and variances (larger means being sometimes associated with larger variances).

It seems evident then, that simple lengths and breadths of teeth may actually be by far the least useful of data to examine. Why, then, did we examine them? The answer is simple.

Important though all of these other measurements are, vastly greater though their information content may be, there are two obvious reasons for using simple lengths and breadths. First, they are all that are available to me at this time on all the fossils in which we are interested. Second, they are simple enough that inter-observer differences will be at a minimum. For logistical and other reasons, it has not so far proven possible for me to make comparable or better measurements upon every individual fossil specimen. We are forced to depend upon the measures of other investigators; simple lengths and breadths are all that are available in the literature for most of the fossils; and they are also all that it is reasonable to expect can be replicated by most investigators, without too much argument.

Even so, however, the eccentricities of individual investigators inevitably mean that slightly different results will be provided from different laboratories. When possible we have done tests to discover and account for such inter-observer biases. Undoubtedly we have not been able to get rid of them. The best that we can say is that this type of error is well known to be of the order of one or two tenths of a millimetre; the differences that we are reporting in our investigations are about five to ten times greater and are unlikely therefore to be excessively disturbed by such perturbations.

Problems due to quality of materials

These teeth are from creatures that had no access to dental care, that died at many different stages of adult life, that were undoubtedly affected in many different ways by the processes of predation, scavenging and decay after death, and that have been subjected to millions of years of fossilisation with all that that implies, before the callipers of today's scientists were placed upon them. Surely these many factors have altered or biased the measurements that we have studied.

Teeth are indeed available from the deciduous dentition of infants and children. But most of the teeth are from the permanent dentitions of pre-adolescents, adolescents and young, middle and old adults. Although study of the deciduous dentition would indeed be fascinating and give us a very important understanding of dental development, the absolute numbers of such teeth are very small. Accordingly, in the statistical studies, we have had to exclude them. At least we know that our results are not artificially biased by their accidental inclusion.

The teeth that are adult vary in size because of differential wear. A tooth that is just about to erupt (perhaps in a pre-adolescent or young adult) shows no wear at all. Teeth that have been active in the mouths of their owners for many years may be worn down to pegs. And everything in between may be observed. Study of such wear patterns could give us enormously interesting information related perhaps to diet, to masticatory habits and mechanics, to non-masticatory usages of teeth (chewing skins to make them soft, for instance), and so on. It would be most valuable to have such information about these fossils. However, to subdivide the teeth according to wear would be to convert near-marginal samples into samples so small as to be unviable for statistical studies. Therefore we have not done this.

But if we ignore wear patterns, then our measurements will be biased. Worn teeth are smaller than unworn teeth; not taking account of wear would give us wrong values for our measurements. Indeed, so important is the effect of wear known to be on the dimensions of teeth that mechanisms have been evolved to take account of the amount of wear in evaluating dental dimensions. And there is one particular form of force, approximal contact, that is due to the teeth bearing upon one-another along their length during growth and function. It produces interstitial wear that differentially reduces lengths of teeth as compared with breadths (e.g. Wolpoff, 1971, 1983b). As with the prior questions, however, the numbers of teeth available for study in each group just are not great enough to allow assessment of the effect of wear on tooth dimensions.

Accordingly, then, in dealing with wear we have been forced to be more simple. We have removed from the data analysed all dimensions from teeth that are heavily worn. But we have kept all other data. The measures that we have kept will not be affected by gross errors due to differences in wear. But we have not been able to eliminate all errors that could arise from this source.

The available teeth are in different conditions of completeness. Roots are usually missing. Chewing by predators or scavengers, as well as simple fossilisation breakage of a weaker part of the tooth are two of the reasons for incompleteness. Pieces of crown are sometimes broken off. This can obviously occur pre-mortem, during function. It can occur post-mortem during scavenging of the carcass. It is especially likely to occur during fossilisation as a result of a tooth lying against other hard objects such as stones, or during the deforming pressures, sometimes enormous, or even heat, all part of the geological mechanism of fossilisation. On occasion no part of the tooth may be missing, but shape distortions may result from the same geological processes. This may give especially dangerous (because somewhat less easily recognized) and spurious values for measurements.

It is possible for damage to the teeth to occur during preparation of the fossil by the museum curator. However careful the technical preparation may be, this effect upon our measurements cannot be discounted. Damage to teeth may even occur when no-one is looking, in the museum specimen box. Both extant and fossil teeth readily splinter with differences in temperature and humidity; small pieces are easily lost or crumble to dust. Suffice it to say that many other problems to do with the actual conditions of fossil teeth at the time of measurement may alter the values of measurements.

There is little that we can do about the majority of these problems. What we have done is to take careful note of the most gross of these matters. When individual teeth are broken (even though an investigator may have estimated the size of the missing piece), especially when individual teeth appear to be distorted, when individual teeth are heavily worn, we have simply eliminated data representing them from these analyses. This, too, is not a very good resolution, and it has made small samples even smaller. But it is the best, it is almost the only thing that we have been able to do.

Problems due to taxonomic status, geological site, and investigator

An absolutely fundamental problem in the analysis of data from samples of fossils is that the materials must be arranged in samples before analysis can be started. For example, it is necessary, even with extant forms, to give the sample a name and to make sure that it contains only materials that correctly share that name. Even with materials from extant species, this may be a problem. Just because a museum label says that a particular skull is that of a female mountain gorilla, does not mean that it really is so.

In fossils, the actual decision as to what taxonomic group the fossil belongs may be inconclusive. Mistakes of attribution are especially common because so little of the specimen may be available. It is well known how often the taxonomic status of fossils may change in the years subsequent to their initial discovery.

The effect of geographic locality is more subtle, but for that reason, even more important. Thus, if materials of a single species come from each of two geographic sites it is not impossible, indeed it is likely, that this would be be reflected in the distributions of any measurements that might be taken. For example, it is well known that samples from animals on islands may be both larger and more variable than those from mainland sites. Samples from species taken from areas with different humidity, or different heights above sea level, or at different latitudes may show differences in values. Such problems are evident for living species where we often know the environmental parameters and have the rest of the skeleton to verify anatomical facts (e.g. Ashton and Zuckerman, 1950a, b, 1951a, b, c; Ashton, 1960; and Ashton, Flinn, Griffiths and Moore, 1979 in a continuing study of the St. Kitts monkey, and Fooden, 1969; Albrecht, 1978, 1979 and 1980 in a continuing series of investigations of the Sulawesi macaques). How much worse is the situation in fossils where we know almost nothing?

The sites from which a given fossil sample is obtained may be scattered widely across the face of the earth. Is it really correct to pool the specimens of a particular species from localities that may vary by thousands of miles?

The geological ages of each specimen in a sample may differ by hundreds of thousands, even possibly by millions of years. Is it really appropriate to put such specimens into a single group?

And all these matters are rendered even more complex by the often extremely poor physical condition of the specimens, as compared with samples of living species that form reference populations. Is it really meaningful to compare materials of such differing condition?

In most instances nothing much can be done about these problems. They are what make anthropology an extremely difficult subject. However, recognizing that they may exist is most important because, by taking care, it is possible to study materials in ways that are more likely to reduce their effect, or, at the very least, to provide caution in the interpretation of results.

There are, in the materials studied in this book, several levels of uncertainty of this type. One even attaches to the materials from the living species.

For example, some of the materials from extant humans are of unknown sex because information about sexes was not recorded or not available. In the teeth of humans the amount of overlap between the sexes is so great that it is not possible to decide on the sex of any particular specimen. But some of the extant human materials are very well known because clinical records are available (through the kindness of Dr Clifford Willcox); we have used them to try to understand this problem.

Another example also relates to humans. Humans are a widespread, highly diverse species and it is almost impossible to represent the entire spread of human variability. For the dimensions of teeth, this variability is very large (e.g. Brace and Ryan, 1980). The data for humans, sexes undefined, are completely unknown in this respect. The data for humans, sexes defined, are known to be from three groups of individuals, Europeans, Hispanic Americans and Asians. Even so, our data do not encompass the total spread of human variability.

There is much uncertainty in the materials from the apes. For example, there are two types of gorilla, lowland and mountain. These are not equally represented in the samples. Similar problems exist for the other great apes.

But it is for the fossils that these matters loom very large indeed. At one end of the spectrum are the materials for *Gigantopithecus* which come from only three caves in Guangxi province in China. Perhaps these represent a single breeding population over a rather short period of time. The ramapithecine materials from Lufeng, though apparently clearly representing two species or species groups, are also all from a single site. Though they are dated at about 8 million years, that date is by no means yet strong. And it is not yet known how long was the period of time that they were being laid down there. It seems likely however, that it was rather short. For both these groups, the data come mainly from isolated teeth; only a few of the teeth are associated with a nearly full range of other teeth in almost complete jaws. Yet these Chinese materials are as good as we can expect to get from fossils representing groups at a single site and a single time. They have been measured, moreover, by the same individual, Professor Wu Rukang.

It is when we come to the various other fossils, the species of *Homo* and *Australopithecus*, that we have the greatest difficulties. For these species no single site yields the full sample of specimens. No single date represents an entire taxon. No single individual investigator has made all the measurements that we have used. No single taxonomy is totally agreed upon. These are all serious difficulties for the analysis of these data.

But these data are all that we have. They have been used, usually only in univariate studies, by many, many other investigators (but especially by Wolpoff, 1971, Blumenberg, 1983, 1985, Kay, 1984). The work of these three investigators has been of extra value. Yet, although these problems beset us no more than any other investigator, we must be cautious in our interpretations.

At least, even in these fossil groups we have been able to weed out (**a**) those specimens that are known to be heavily worn, (**b**) those specimens about which there is serious controversy regarding taxonomic identification, and, of course, (**c**) one of the two sides from those specimens in which both sides are known to be represented.

Perhaps most importantly of all, throughout this entire study we have made no taxonomic judgements of our own, preferring to depend only upon those judgements that have already been made by the experts, and where the experts do not disagree too strongly.

The problem of not knowing which sex is which

At the level of studying univariate data there are a series of problems, and possible misconceptions, that relate to the bimodal distributions that we have so frequently found. We have suggested that these distributions result from the existence of females and males in our samples, even though we do not know which specimen is of which sex. Thus, in the univariate histograms there are differing sizes of peaks in bimodal distributions and we suggest that this reflects differing numbers of small and large specimens. The ratios of such numbers may well imply a similar sex ratio. But such ratios may also give rise to some misconceptions.

First, it is necessary that we remind ourselves that it is only for the living species that we actually know the sexes. We can, therefore, truly say, using *Homo* and *Pongo* as examples, that in *Homo* and *Pongo* the distributions for each sex in each species are as given Figure 7:1.

This figure clearly shows that for *Homo* it is almost impossible to say from which sex a particular tooth comes. Even the largest male is only very little greater than the largest female, the smallest male only very little larger than the smallest female. Even although there is clear, statistically significant sexual dimorphism, sexing any individual specimen is most difficult for all but the very largest, or very smallest, specimens.

But this figure also shows that even for *Pongo* where the differences between the sexes is large, there is still some overlap. We can say that some of the smallest specimens must be female and that some of the largest must be male. But there are still quite a large number of specimens about which we cannot be certain.

Making the sexual determination for a particular specimen in *Pongo* or *Gorilla* can be considerably easier if we have data from the canines, because the sexual dimorphism is quantitatively much greater in that tooth. In general, however, there is almost always major overlap between the sexes in dental dimensions in even these highly dimorphic groups.

We must, therefore, be especially careful when we interpret the distributions, sexes undefined, for any given species. Figure 7:2 gives these distributions for the same two examples: *Homo* and *Pongo*. In this case the distributions for the sexes combined are clearly bimodal. But of course, although the presence of the two peaks indicates the presence of two sexes, although the mode for each peak is a measure of the mean for each sex, and although the ratio between the size of each peak is a measure of the ratio of the numbers of each sex, we must be very clear that we cannot identify individuals. *Members of both sexes are present in both peaks.* The peaks cannot be used to identify the sex of individual specimens, only to provide estimates of the mean for each sex.

Let us look at this in more detail first in *Homo*. Obviously, comparing Figures 7:1 and 7:2 for *Homo* shows us that the lower peak for *Homo* must contain both females and males. It is only because there are fewer small males and more females of those same sizes that they obtrude as a separate peak. Equally the upper peak also must contain both males and females. Again, it is only because there are fewer large females and more males of those same sizes that they, too, form a visible peak.

What about the value for each mode in *Homo*. Clearly this figure is not exactly the same as the mean for that sex. It does however approximately represent that mean if we assume, and it is a reasonable assumption, that the distributions for each sex are approximately symmetrical (Fig. 7:1). (That this is generally true is readily seen by examining many individual distributions for individual sexes as provided in Chapter 2).

What about the size (number of specimens) of each peak? Again, this does not represent the number of specimens for each sex. Given, however, that the same smaller number of each sex will appear in the peak mainly filled by the other sex, then the ratio of the numbers in the two peaks will approximate to the actual ratio present in the sample.

For the genus *Homo* all these facts are readily seen by comparing the distributions for each sex with the distribution for the sexes undefined. At every locus where the degree of dimorphism is large enough to produce bimodal distributions, this is what we find.

Let us now take the case of *Pongo*. Again, it must be obvious, from the separate distributions for each sex (Fig. 7:1) that bimodal distributions should result in such cases (Fig. 7:2). As for *Homo* the lower peak must contain both females and males. As for *Homo* this peak obtrudes because there are fewer small males and more females at those same small sizes. Equally, as for *Homo* the upper peak must also contain both males and females. In this case however, the absolute number of males is only half that of females. It is not, therefore, absolutely clear that this peak will obtrude. If it does so (and it does in most cases) this will be because the degree of dimorphism is so much greater than in *Homo*; the number of large females is much smaller than the number of males (lesser absolute numbers notwithstanding), at those same large sizes.

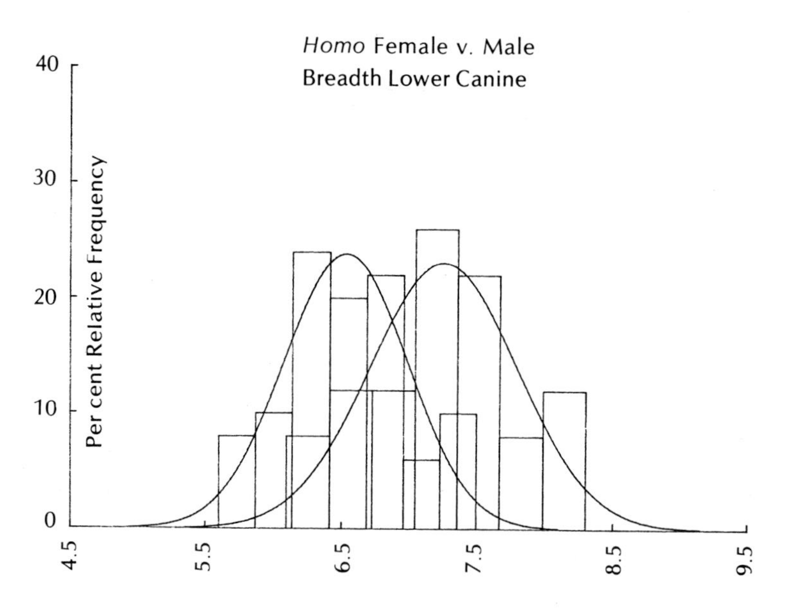

Fig. 7:1 Distributions, sexes defined, of individual dimensions of teeth for *Homo* and *Pongo*. These figures emphasize that there is no difference in variance for each sex in these two species. Small and large dimorphism, respectively, are easily observed.

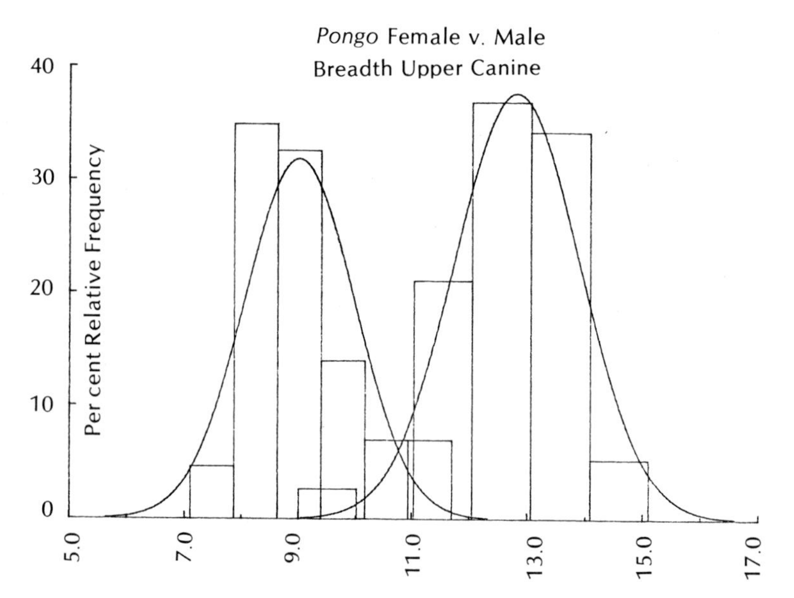

What about the value for each mode in *Pongo*. Again these figures are unlikely to be exactly the same as the means for each sex. They do, however, approximately represent those means if we assume, and it is again a reasonable assumption, that the distributions for each sex are approximately symmetrical (Fig. 7:2). (That this is true for *Pongo* indeed for all extant species, is readily seen by examining many individual distributions for individual sexes as provided in Chapter 2).

What about the ratio of the sizes of the peaks in *Pongo*. This case is more complex. As has been explained, the numbers of specimens of each known sex were chosen, using a random numbers program, so that there were actually twice as many females as males. This was to allow us to look at such actual ratios to see what would happen to the combined distributions. The result is that, even though each peak contains some specimens from the opposite sex, the total of most of the large number of females, plus a few of the smaller number of males that overlap with them at the smaller sizes, is approximately twice the total of most of the smaller number of males plus a few of the females that overlap with them at the upper sizes.

All this can be confirmed by doing theoretical studies where we 'add' together separate distributions. Figure 7:3 shows that adding two equal distributions that are reasonably widely separated

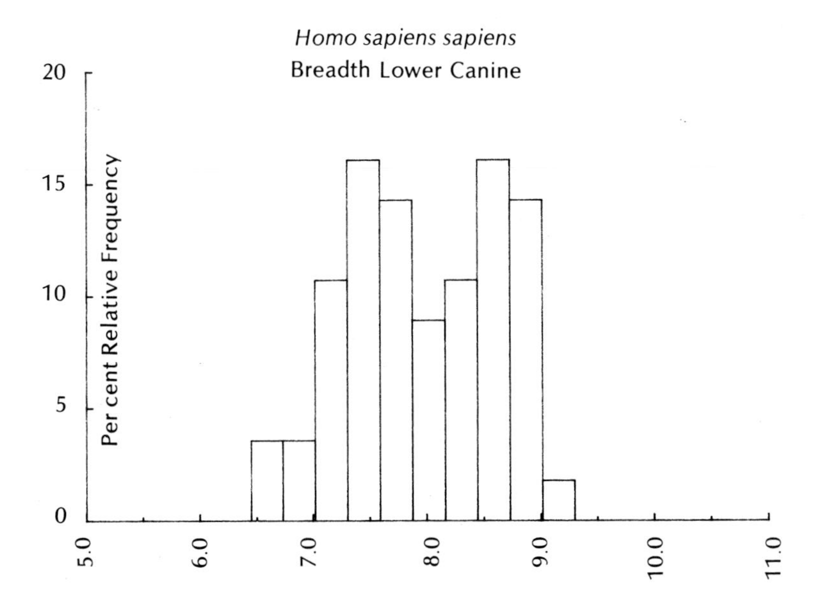

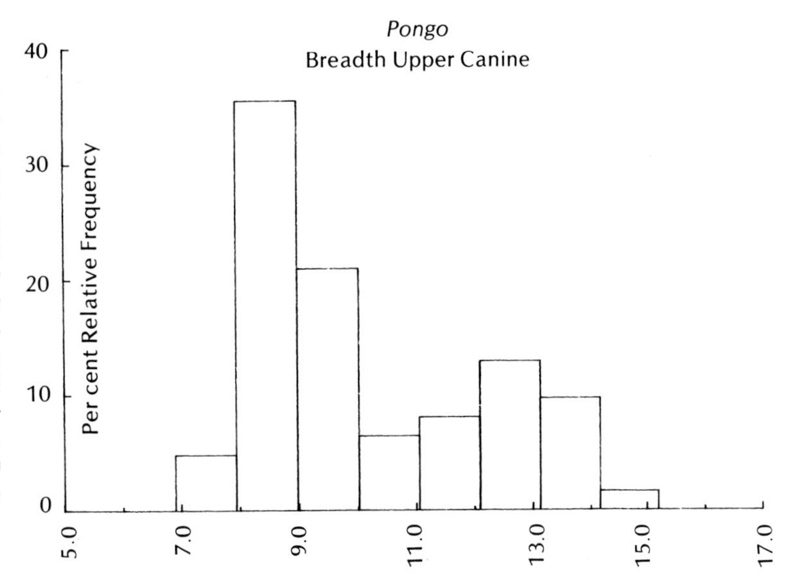

Fig. 7:2 Distributions, sexes undefined, of the same individual dimensions of teeth for *Homo* and *Pongo* as in Fig. 7:1. These figures show bimodality emphasizing the sexual dimorphism that is known from the prior figure to be present. They also show that zero variance difference between the sexes has no untoward effect upon the distributions, sexes undefined. And they show that when sex ratios are unbalanced, this can be clearly seen.

does give an equal bimodal distribution (as in *Homo*). Figure 7:4 shows that adding two equal distributions, where the number of specimens in the first is twice the number in the second, provides an unequal bimodal distribution (as in *Pongo*).

It is interesting to remember that adding two separate distributions that are close together gives a unimodal distribution. Thus, the presence of a unimodal distribution does not mean that two statistically separate distributions do not exist within it; merely that the degree of difference is not large enough for us to see it (Fig. 7:5). Thus, there are many examples in the living species where we 'know' that there are significant differences between the sexes but where we cannot see this from examining the distribution sexes undefined. It is necessary, therefore, to remember that this will also be the case on occasion for some of the fossil distributions. However, this 'plays against us' as it were; its existence strengthens our case rather than weakening it.

Finally, it is worth remembering that if our samples for each sex are small then they are likely to resemble more a 'square' distribution than a normal one. The numbers of specimens in the 'tails' of the distributions occur so rarely that they are likely not to occur at all in small samples. This means that the samples will tend more to the 'square' form. But this also means that when we add such small samples together then, even when

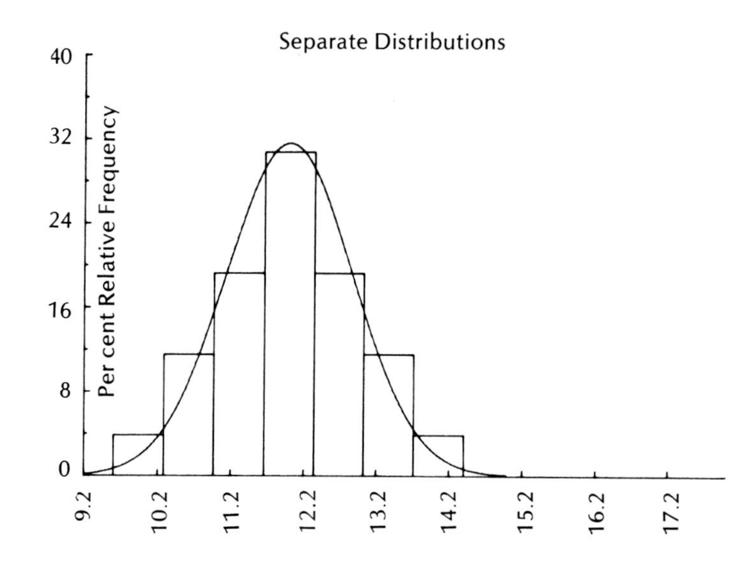

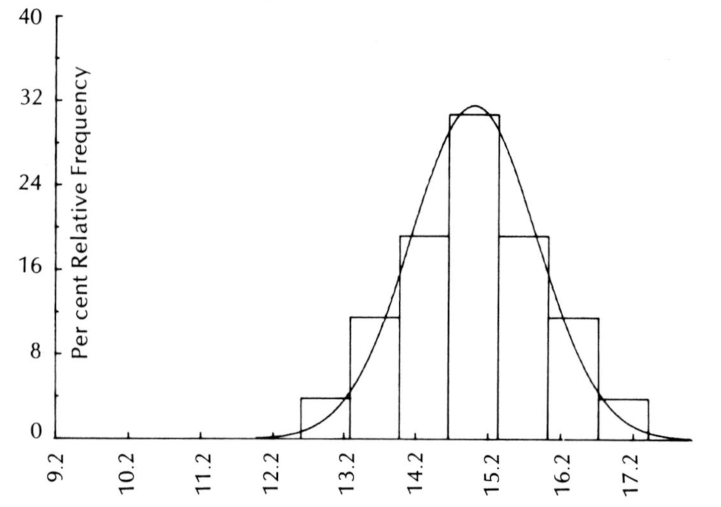

Fig. 7:3 This figure shows what we may think is rather obvious, that is: that adding together two normal histograms each containing equal numbers of specimens, the one being significantly different from the other, gives a total histogram that is bimodal. This models what happens when we add data like that presented here for humans.

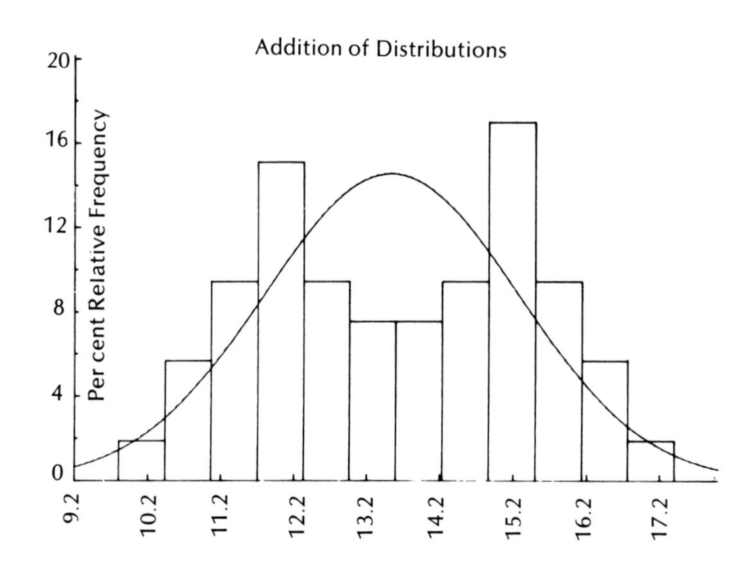

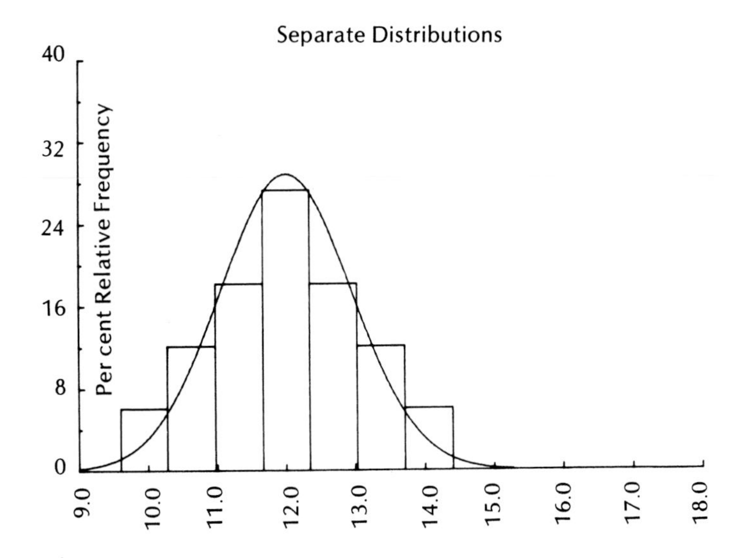

Fig. 7:4 This figure shows that adding together two normal histograms, one containing twice as many specimens as the other and the two being significantly different from one another, gives a total histogram that is bimodal with unequal peaks. This models what happens when we add the data for the orang-utan.

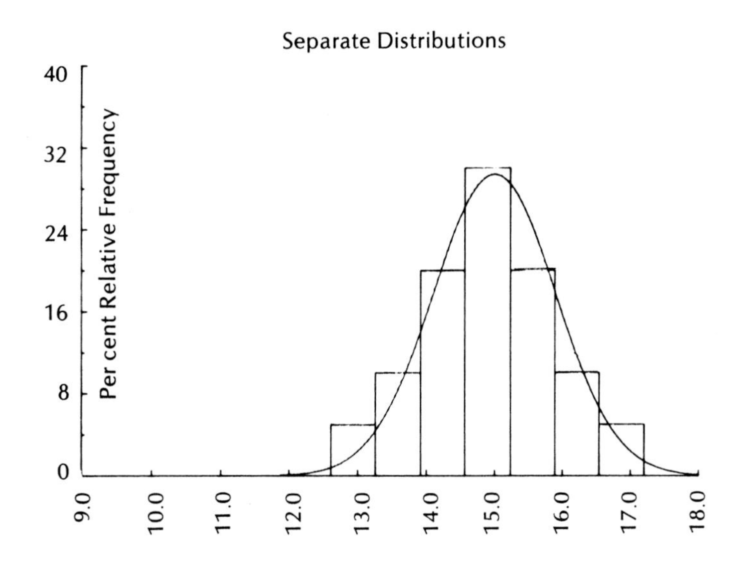

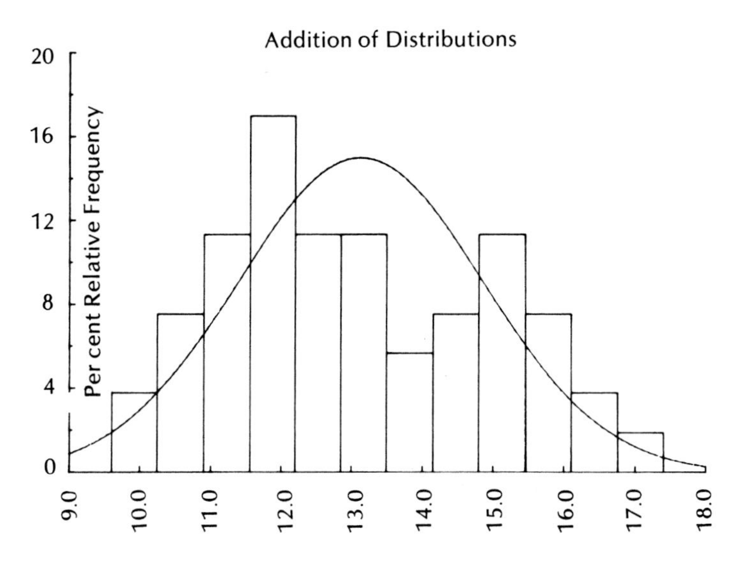

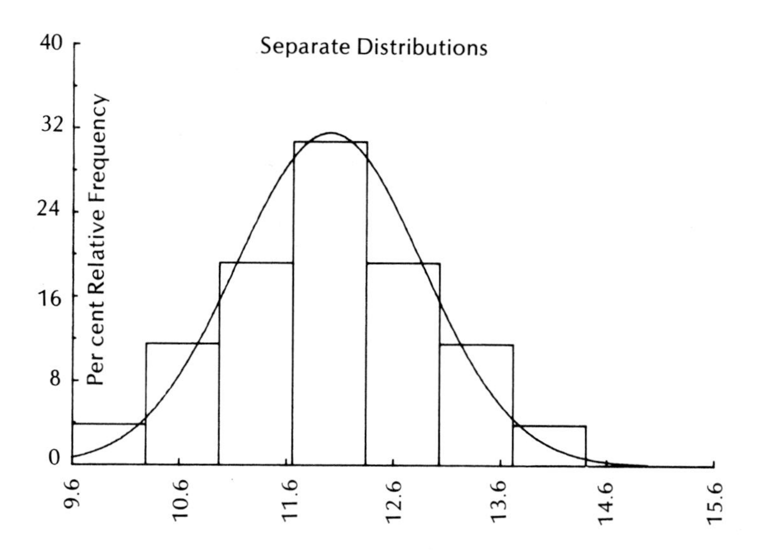

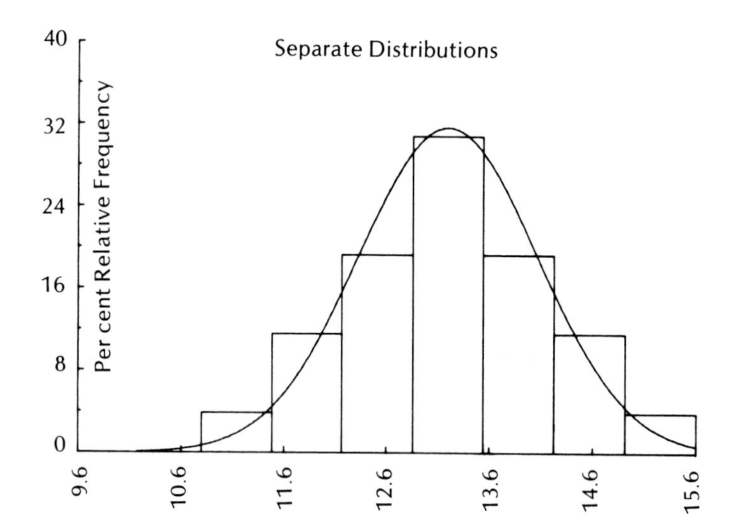

Fig. 7:5 This figure shows what is less obvious, that repeating the study of Fig. 7:3 when the original two groups are rather close to one another, even though statistically significantly different, may give an ultimate histogram that is normal. Thus a unimodal histogram does not rule out the existence of dimorphism; it merely indicates that even if significant, the amount is not sufficient to obtrude.

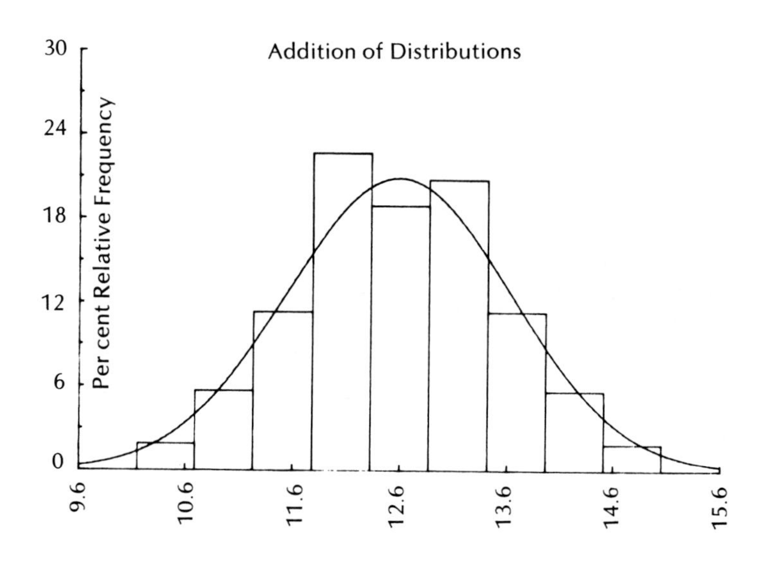

they are somewhat distant one from another, we may not see a bimodal distribution. Sometimes we may see a 'good' normal distribution (Fig. 7:6). But sometimes what we may see is a distribution in the form of a plateau with a single central peak. In other words, the combined distribution will be unimodal but kurtotic. A theoretical example of this is presented in Figure 7:7.

Normally when we see kurtosis in biology we tend to think that we have a single population with some minor effect causing kurtosis. We often deal with the situation by applying some transformation to rid us of the unwanted effect. This example reminds us that, though unimodal in form, kurtosis may result from a genuinely bimodal situation where the samples are small. There are several examples of this in the data presented in this book (see Figs. 7:8 and 7:9). Therefore, this particular form of unimodal distribution 'may' imply sexual dimorphism.

In *Pan* and *Gorilla*, these matters are even more complex. Figure 7:10 shows us two particular examples in *Pan* and *Gorilla* in which we can see the distributions for each sex. That the variances are different is immediately obvious. That the numbers in each sex are also different is not obvious because the vertical axes in the plots (as in all the plots in this book) are not absolute numbers, but percentage numbers.

Figure 7:11 shows the distributions, sexes undefined, for these two particular plots. The ratio of the sizes of the peaks in *Pan* and *Gorilla* are affected by the two features from the separate distributions for each sex. First is the fact, that (as for *Pongo*) there actually are twice as many females as males. Second is the fact, that the variances for each sex are radically different from one another. The final result is that, even though each mode contains some specimens from the opposite sex, the total of most of the large number of females, plus a few of the smaller number of males that overlap with them at the smaller sizes, is approximately twice the total of most of the smaller number of males plus a few of the females that overlap with them at the upper sizes.

But whether or not separate peaks are discernible depends upon the absolute sizes of the differences between them. In the case of those teeth in *Gorilla* and *Pan* where the differences are almost always large, two peaks of different size are seen. But in the case of the particular teeth we have chosen to examine in this example where the differences are smaller, the smaller peak is drawn into the larger peak. The result is a unimodal distribution that is assymetrical. Usually, in biology, when we see skewed distributions, we tend to think that they represent single samples but that there are minor disturbing factors that cause the skewness. We usually deal with the situation by using some transformation to rid us of the unwanted effect. With hindsight in this example, however, we can see that the skewness may result from the sample having both unequal numbers and unequal variances for each sex.

In our real data, we have found many examples of skewed distributions. It is only in the extant forms that we know it is due to significant differences between the sexes (of the type found in the African great apes). But finding it in many examples in the fossils, may give us further pause to realize that it may be due to sexual dimorphism, and especially to sexual dimorphism of the unequal variance and unequal sex ratio type like that in the apes. Almost all the examples of this skewness are to be found, in addition to extant *Pan* and *Gorilla*, among australopithecines (Fig. 7:12).

It is in this rather complex way that some idea, of sexual dimorphism and sex ratio, can be obtained although we do not actually know, and do not try to guess, which specimens (in the combined distributions) are from which sex. It is our ability to examine the data from living forms with sexes known that allows us to see all this. It is enormously important, for understanding the distributions and the ratios that we have found in the fossils where, of course, we cannot do the test with sexed samples to see if we are right.

The effects of taphonomy

Much emphasis has been placed in these studies on the question of bimodal distributions, on the ratios that can be discerned between their two peaks, and on the implications that this may have for sexual dimorphism. It should be immediately recorded that the inferences that have been drawn from such ratios must be viewed with taphonomic considerations in mind. I am much indebted to Alan Turner (and Turner, 1983, 1984a, b, c, d, and Fieller and Turner, 1982) for discussions of this subject.

There are at least two components that affect the ratios of specimens represented in any assemblage of bones or teeth. A first component is the number of specimens that are due to selection from the living population, to form the original dead population. A second component is the selection and

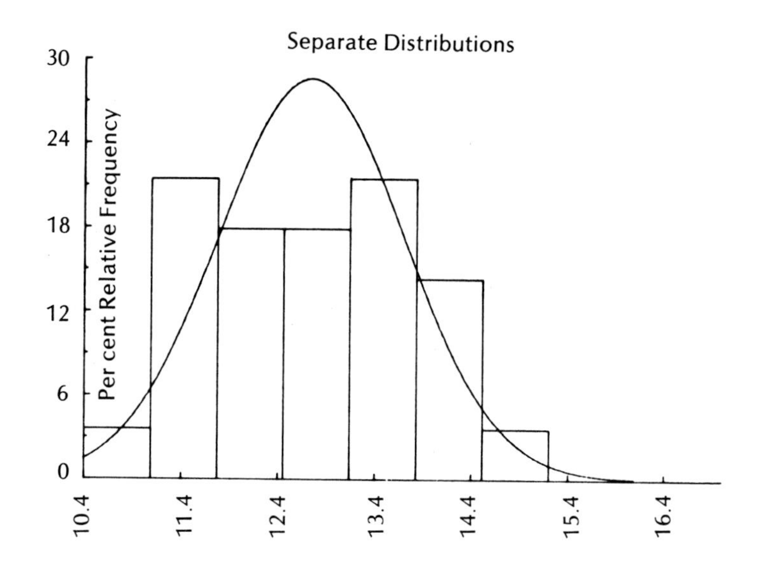

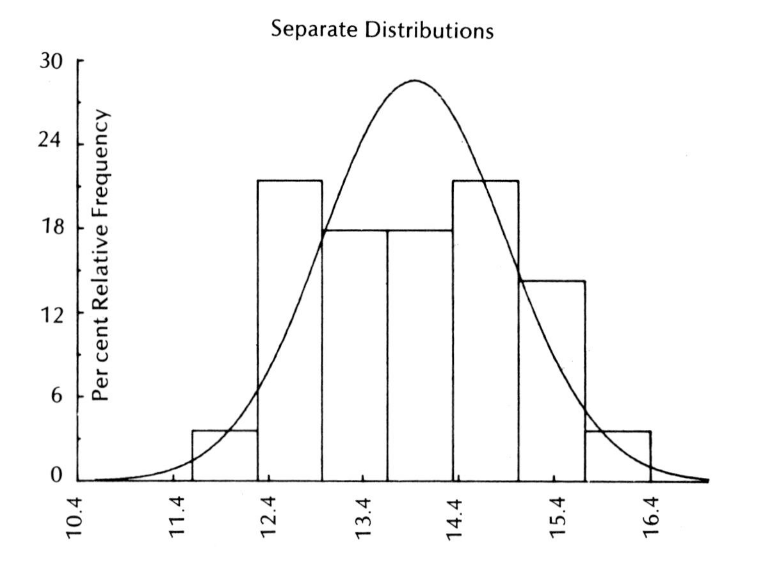

Fig. 7:6 This figure repeats the study of Fig. 7:5 but with small samples so that the original histograms are rather more 'square' in form than normal. Obviously the same answer results: an ultimate histogram that is normal.

Thus, again, a unimodal histogram does not rule out the existence of dimorphism; it merely indicates that even if significant, the amount is not sufficient to obtrude. This figure is necessary to understand Fig. 7:7.

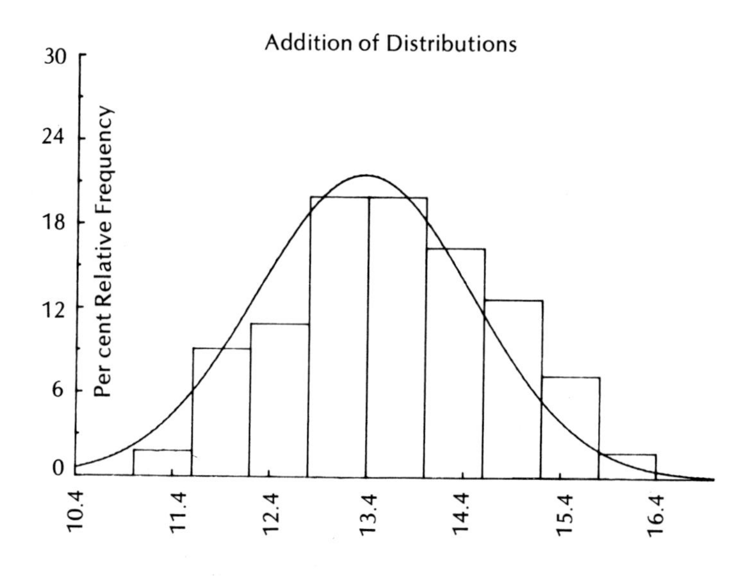

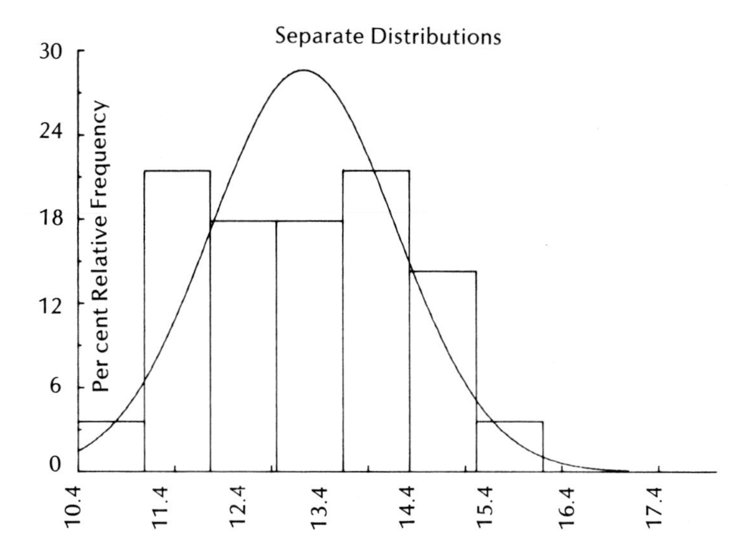

Fig. 7:7 This figure also repeats the study of Fig. 7:5 with small samples so that the original histograms are rather more 'square' in form than normal, but in a situation where the samples are rather more different from each other than in Fig. 7:6. The answer is not intuitively obvious. The addition of these samples results in a unimodal histogram, but one that has a plateau with a single high central peak. This might be observed as 'kurtosis' in the real situation.

Thus a unimodal histogram showing kurtosis may well indicate sexual dimorphism if the original samples of each sex were small.

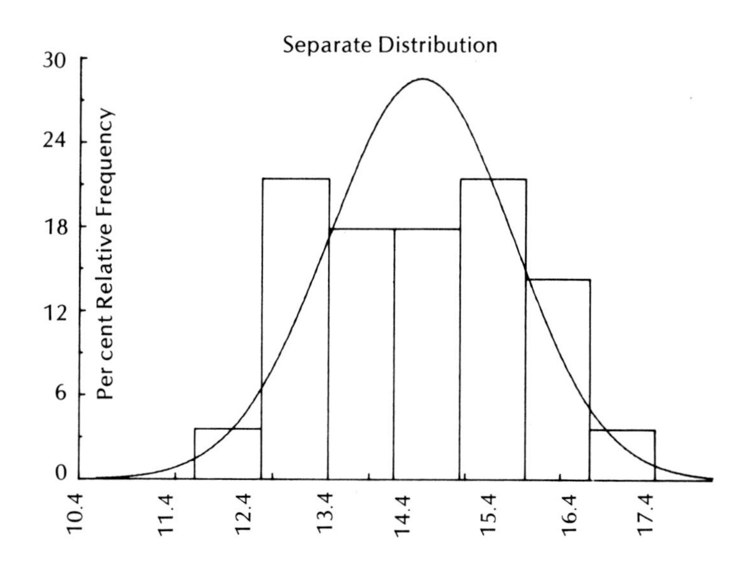

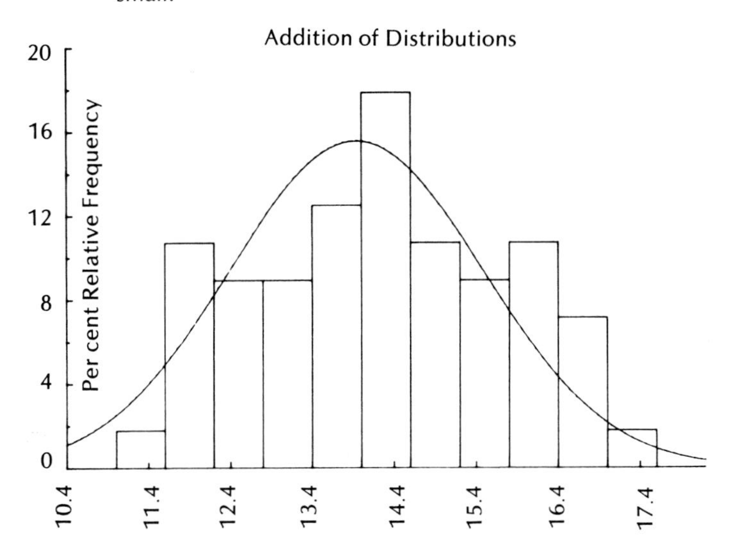

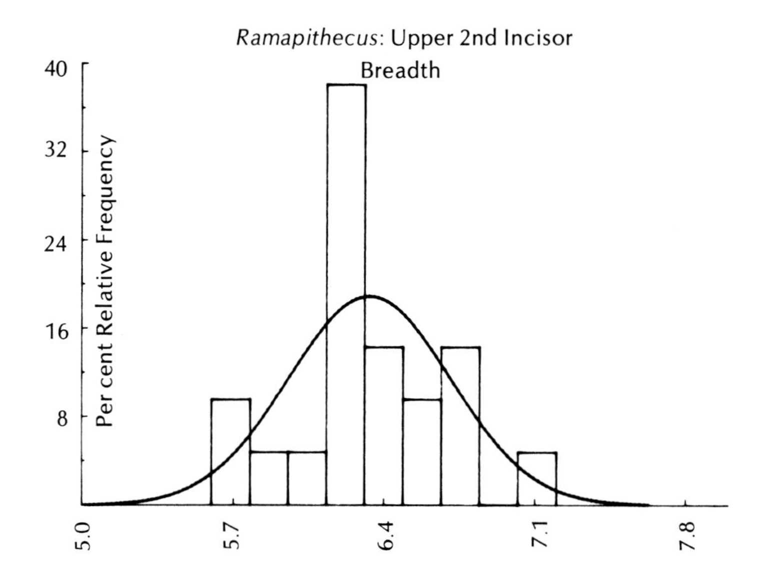

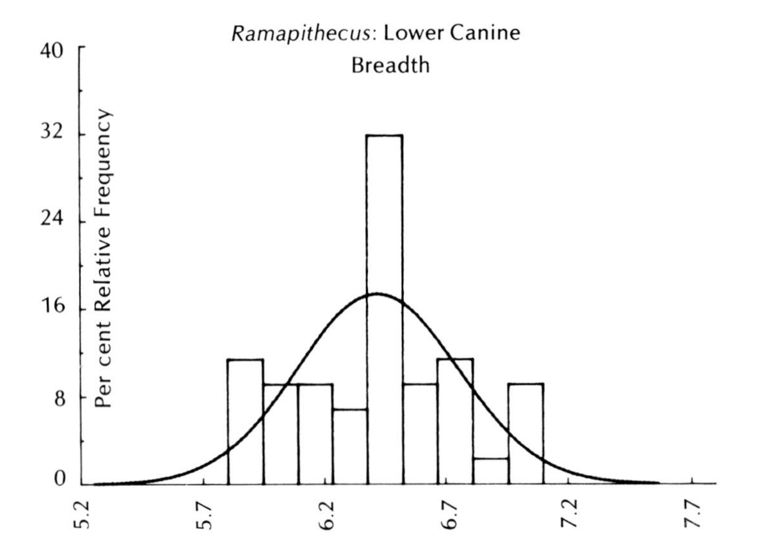

Fig. 7:8 This shows two actual examples of kurtotic histograms in *Ramapithecus* that may well be due to sexual dimorphism in the small sample situation.

treatment of the dead remains in the long period of deposition and fossilisation to form the ultimate number of fossils. These components are part of the subject of taphonomy.

Examples of the first, preferential selection from the living population, might include the following. A given sample of living forms with a certain sex ratio might produce a group of dead specimens that showed a different ratio in a human-like group because the dead of the two sexes were treated differently. For instance, with a single dead male of high estate, might be buried all his dead consorts providing a many-female-to-one-male ratio in the burial chamber. Yet the general ratio of females and males in that human population might be one-to-one. In animals, similar effects might occur for other behavioural reasons. For instance solitary males die alone, whereas family males and females might die together. Again, one can easily imagine how factors like these might give a different ratio of males to females, in the living species, as compared with the dead assemblage.

Examples of the second, differential treatment of the dead remains might include the following. Of the individuals that die, or are killed, predators and scavengers may alter the killed specimens. For instance, it would be possible that small specimens might be almost completely eaten even the bones. But large specimens might be less completely masticated. Again, small specimens might be

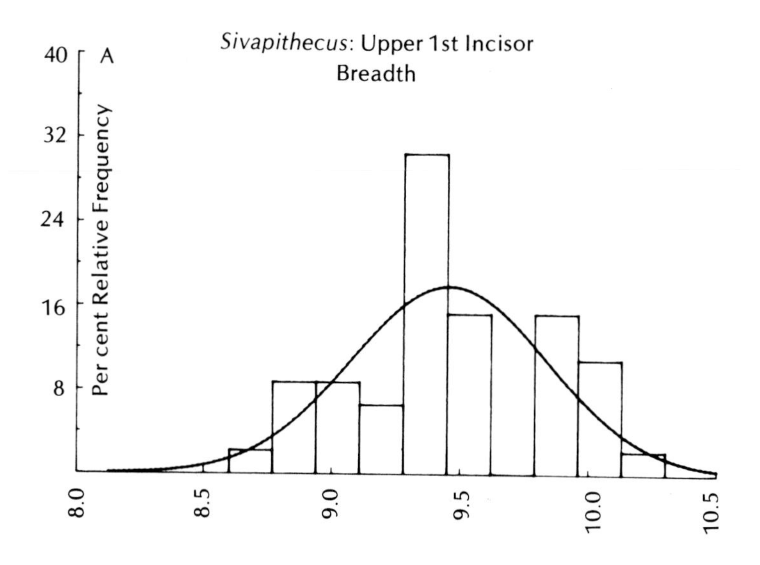

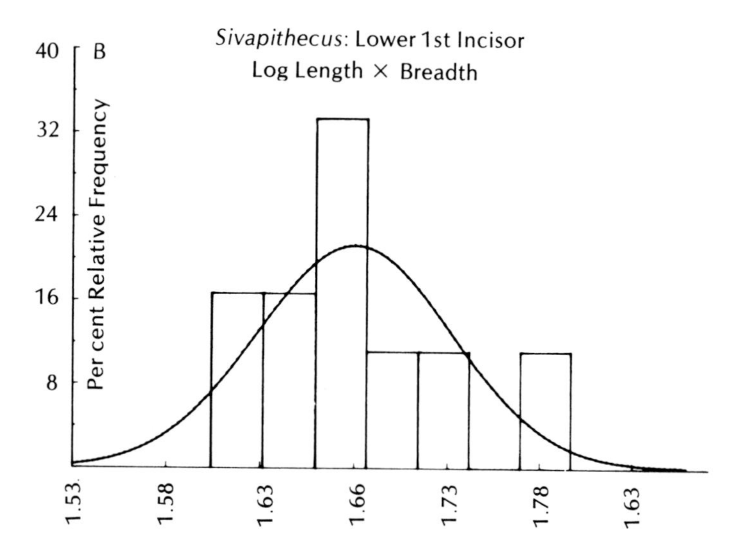

Fig. 7:9 This shows two actual examples of kurtotic histograms in *Sivapithecus* that may well be due to sexual dimorphism in the small sample situation.

dragged by a predator to a lair. Large specimens might not, and be dispersed much more widely by a succession of scavengers. Even rivers and floods might deal differentially with large and small specimens. One can think of all kinds of possible interferences with the recently dead carcass. These could, if there were marked differences in size between two sexes, result in the actual ratio in the living forms being represented by a different ratio in those remains left for ultimate fossilisation.

It is even possible that the process of fossilisation itself might affect such materials differentially. For instance small teeth (e.g. incisors) might be preferentially destroyed by some geological crushing process that did not affect large teeth (e.g. molars) to the same degree. Of course, this in itself does not change the ratio of females to males in the sample, rather only the ratio of incisors to molars (and it is a common occurrence that the number of molars that survive *is* greater than the number of incisors). However, to the degree that female teeth *are* smaller than male teeth, the effects that operate on incisors because they are smaller, could also act upon female teeth from whatever region because *they* are smaller.

There must be a host of factors like these that could affect the relative numbers of females and males as we come to see them in the collection of fossils that are available to us today. It would be foolish to deny that they exist.

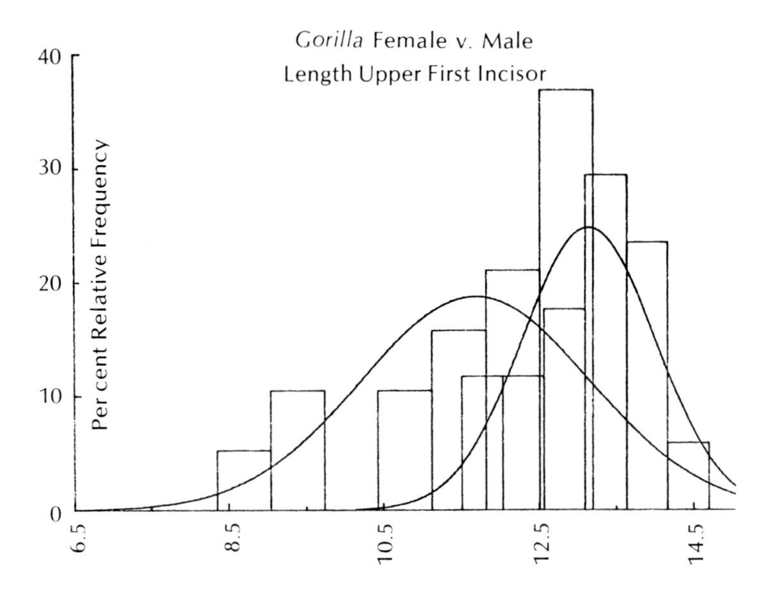

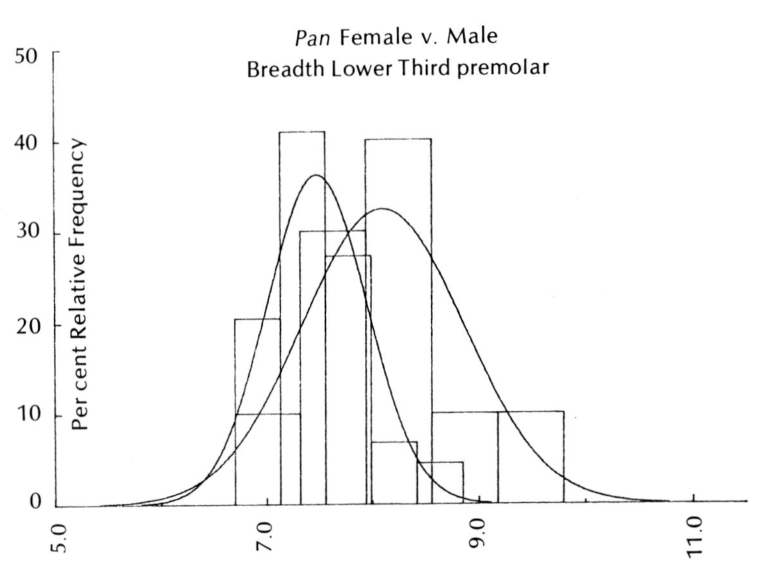

Fig. 7:10 This figure shows histograms where (a) there is a significant difference in mean between the known sexes, (b) there is a significant difference in variance between the known sexes and (c) there is a significantly different number of specimens in each sex (artificially adjusted 2:1 ratio of females to males).

Is it possible to make any estimates of the degree to which factors like these may have been active? The work of Turner (cited above) shows that it is possible to allow for them statistically. However, such calculations require the much larger samples that are often available for non-primate mammalian fossils. For primates, the samples are usually so small that corrections of this type are not possible.

There is however, one finding that helps us believe that these factors may not have been responsible for the ratios that we have found in the primate fossils, examined in this book. That is: the relative constancy of the findings. The ratios of the number of specimens in the peaks in the distributions for breadths especially, and for lengths on occasion, for a large number of different teeth for every australopithecine we have examined, provides the ratio of two or three times as many specimens in the smaller peaks as in the larger. In not a single bimodal distribution among the australopithecines was this found. Likewise in every fossil species of the genus *Homo* examined, for every tooth position, and for lengths as well as breaths (though less often for the former), a ratio of one-to-one exists between the two peaks. Indeed, in *Homo* there was only a single exception.

If these ratios had been due to the variety of factors mentioned above it would have been highly unlikely that, for different teeth, at different geological sites, and in different taxonomic groups, all

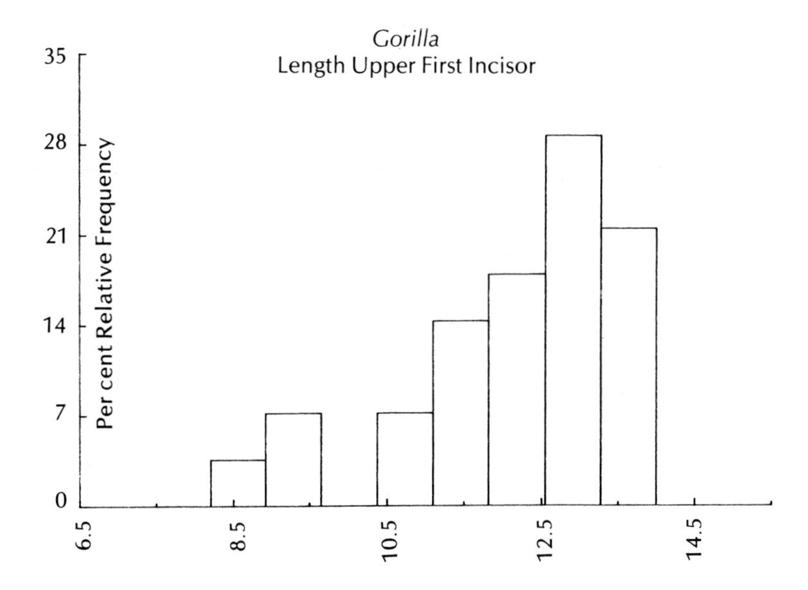

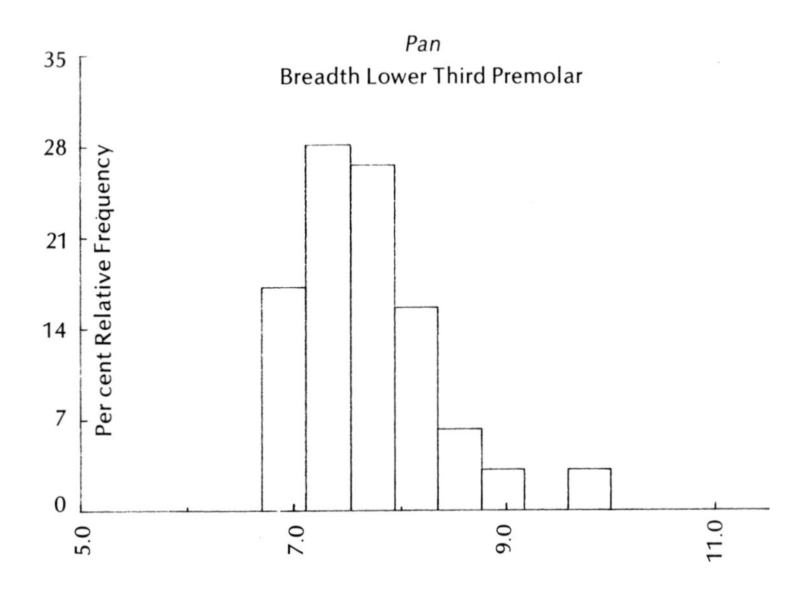

Fig. 7:11 This figure shows the histograms that result from the data in Fig. 7:10 if we add them together irrespective of sex. The combined histograms show no evidence of bimodality. The combined effects of the sex number difference and the variance difference has resulted in unimodal skewed distributions. Thus unimodal distributions, especially if they are skewed, may be prima facie evidence of sexual dimorphism of the 'variance different', 'sex ratio different' type.

australopithecines should always come out one way, and all *Homo* the other. This gives us real hope that, though these confounding factors undoubtedly exist in these data as in any other fossil data, the differences resulting from sexual dimorphism have been so great that they have overshadowed (at this sample size) these kinds of effects.

Special problems for fossils in multivariate statistical analyses

There is a special problem in the use of multivariate statistics with unknown (fossil) forms that differs from its usage in known (living) groups. This relates to the fact that in a study of groups, their separations by the statistic are due to the contributions that the means, variances and covariances of each group make to the calculation of the statistic (whether that be a canonical variate, a discriminant function or a principal component).

As a result, values for individual specimens, or the means of groups of specimens which, for special reasons to do with being unknown cannot be entered directly into the analyses, must be considered differently to those of the known forms upon which the underlying analysis depends. Much of this has been spelt out in other publications (e.g. Oxnard, 1972a, 1975a, 1978a, 1981a, 1983a, 1984). But repetition is nessary here because the multivariate

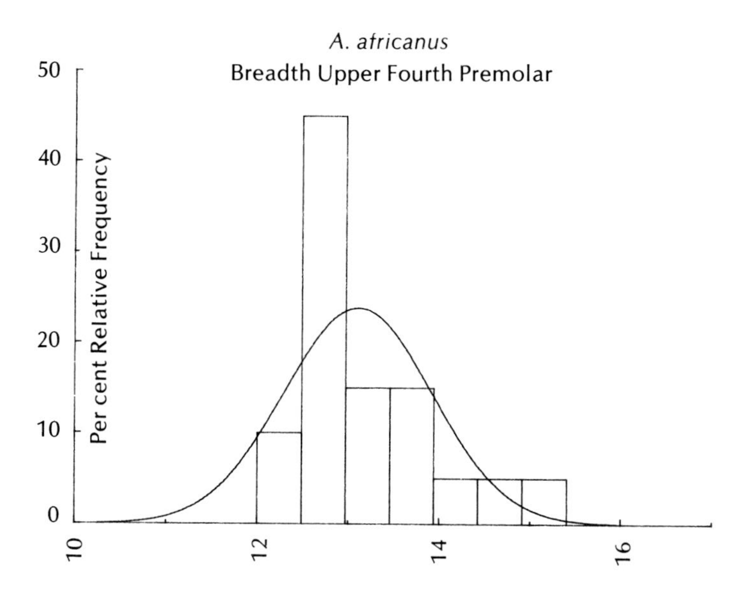

Fig. 7:12 This figure shows, that the theoretical example of Fig. 7:11, distributions that are heavily skewed can be found as practical examples, in some of the fossil data presented in this book. This may well be additional evidence for a sexual difference in variance and an unbalanced sex ratio in some of these fossils.

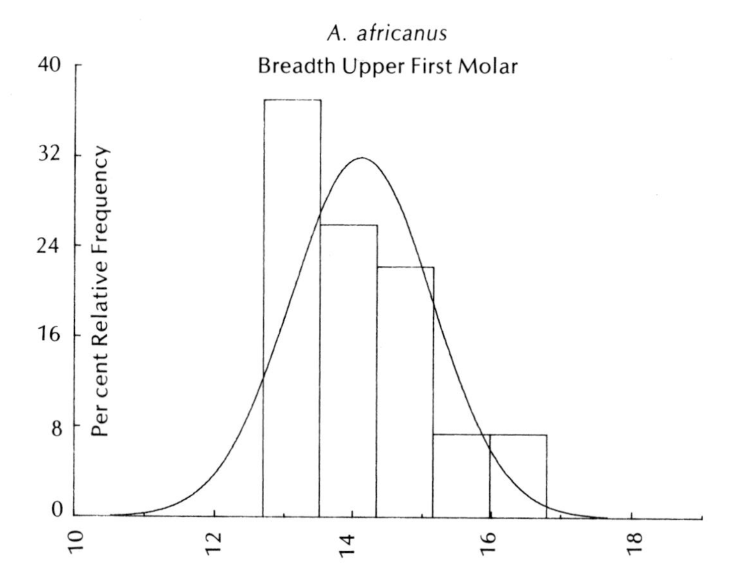

part of this particular book depends so heavily upon the interpolation of unknowns.

In a canonical variates analysis, the calculations produce separations in a first axis that are as large as possible. They then produce, in a second axis, separations that are again as large as possible but excluding those produced in the first. They next produce separations in a third axis that are as large as possible but excluding those already expressed in the prior two. And this process continues until all the separation among the groups has been used up. Obviously, the separations provided are of smaller and smaller degree in the higher and higher axes. And statistics can be calculated to show how significant such separations may be. They are often significant for the overall separation of the groups in quite high axes, even although the amount of the separation between the groups may be quite small. For the highest axes of all they may be statistically insignificant.

It is usual that only three or four axes show separations between groups that are of reasonable size (say more than ten per cent of the total). Several more axes (say five, six, seven and eight) may have separations of the order of five to ten percent, and they thus seem to be supplying less information of biological import, but they may, nevertheless still be statistically significant. Even higher axes (say, numbers 9, 10, and 11) may be statistically significant but contain only a few per cent of the separation between the groups. Though still statistically significant, we may judge that they are not of biological significance. And the highest axes of all will contain not only very little separation indeed (one or two per cent), but also separations that are not even statistically significant. (These numbers have been chosen as examples from a particular analysis actually carried out).

Obviously, using these criteria, one can make one's own judgements as to how far into the higher axes one is willing to go in making biological interpretations about the separations of the known groups.

What seems not always to be recognized is that *none of this applies to canonical variates values for unknown specimens or groups if (for technical reasons) they have not contributed directly to the analyses.* In the studies in this book, the 'technical reason' is that in the living forms each suite of teeth come from the same jaw but in the fossils most of the teeth are individual isolated specimens.

When unknown forms have to be intercalated in this way, all axes must be examined. Even an axis which is statistically insignificant for the known groups may provide important, even the most important, information about the unknown form. This is why higher axes must be examined individually. It is why several smaller separations in each of several higher axes may sum (in a Pythagorean sense) to a very large separation overall. And it is especially why the high-dimensional analyses, that allow all dimensions to be 'seen' at once, as it were, are especially important.

General problems of multivariate statistical analyses

The use and interpretation of multivariate statistics in studies of anatomical structure is one of the most vexing questions in physical anthropology today. This contrasts, interestingly enough, with its complete acceptance in other life science disciplines such as ecology, evolution, systematics, functional vertebrate morphology, and the biomedical sciences.

Multivariate statistical approaches stem from the discoveries of Hotelling, Fisher, Mahalanobis, Wilks, Bartlett and others in the thirties, and from the developments of Rao, Yates, Kendall and others in the forties and fifties. But though the antecedents of these methods came from before the present century (e.g., Galton, Pearson), it has only been in the late 1950's and 1960's that they have come to be applied to complex anthropological problems, at first by a small number of physical anthropologists (e.g. Trevor, Howells and Ashton and Oxnard) and almost always in collaboration with statisticians (e.g. Rao, Healy). Only in the last decade and a half has their use become widespread.

The values of multivariate statistical approaches have been seen by different commentators as lying anywhere from one end of a spectrum, implying that they can give major insight in anthropological problems (e.g. Oxnard, 1973a), to the other end of the spectrum suggesting that they provide only obfuscation and confusion (e.g. Day, 1977; Hershkovitz, 1977). That these opposite opinions can be held at the same time is partly because the difference between results, and interpretations stemming from results, has not always been clearly understood. It is also partly because it is not common, for published presentations to include full details of all the statistical testing necessary, before reliance can be placed upon results. It is due in part, to the fact, that it is not always recognised that multivariate statistical analysis is not a single method, but can be used in different ways for a variety of problems. The existence of these opposite opinions, is because the methods have been sometimes used in ways that result in other investigators being unable to replicate the results, even, sometimes, in ways that are palpably incorrect. Finally, it is because some investigators believe that multivariate statistics give conflicting results, when applied by different investigators. This last has been especially examined in our studies, because the accidents of the coincident activities of several workers, have resulted in approximate replication of investigations.

Biological interpretations of statistical descriptors: If a multivariate statistical study of the structure of a given anatomical region, supplies an interpretation involving the biology of that region, the finding is strengthened if similar information arises from other studies involving that same anatomical region. We have done this kind of hypothesis-testing of interpretations in all the anatomical regions that we have studied. But such testing has been taken furthest, naturally, in that anatomical area earliest examined: the primate shoulder (e.g. Ashton and Oxnard, 1963, 1964a, b; Ashton, Healy, Oxnard and Spence, 1965). Some of the testing of those studies was presented by Oxnard (1967, 1973a), and the entire matter is summarized in Oxnard (1983b).

In the original study of the primate shoulder,

measures of the bones were chosen based upon knowledge of (a) the field behaviours of primates, (b) the biomechanical function of the shoulder resulting from those behaviours, and (c) the identification and then measurement of apparently biomechanically related characteristics of shoulder muscles. The bony features that were defined by those studies were then measured and investigated using canonical variates analysis. The research resolved the relationships of 41 genera of primates, each genus being defined by 9 dimensions taken on the shoulder girdle, a total of 551 shoulder girdles in all.

The non-human primates were separated by the first two canonical axes. These axes placed the various primate genera in ways that made sense when seen in the light of their different locomotor styles. This could be expected, given the likelihood that the form of the shoulder is strongly related to its function. Thus, the first canonical axis separated the various non-human primates according to the degree to which the shoulder sustains tension in raised positions during locomotion. The second canonical axis separated the various non-human primates to the degree to which they are arboreal or terrestrial (Figure 7:13).

A third canonical axis performed no separation of interest among the non-human primates but distinguished humans from all other genera. Such a placement for humans coincides with the functional uniqueness of the human shoulder: the only shoulder, among the primates, that is not involved in locomotion in a weight-bearing manner. These interpretations were unusually clear. They depended, however, upon a very special set of 'coincidences' between statistical descriptors of structures (canonical variates) on the one hand, and summaries of function (locomotion) on the other. Corroborative tests of these 'coincidences' were, therefore, necessary.

One series of tests related to the data. These tests used the same multivariate statistical technique (canonical variates analysis) but applied it to different sets of data. The first of these was a set of new variables taken from the same anatomical region, the shoulder of primates. The second consisted of the original set of variables on the shoulder but comprising measurements from a new suite of animals — arboreal species of non-primate mammals. The results of the analysis of both were unequivocal. Irrespective of the set of variables or the suite of animals, the same associations between the statistical form of the shoulder and the summary of its function in arboreal locomotion were obtained (e.g. Figures 7:14 and 7:15).

A second series of tests related to the method. These used the same anatomical area, and in some cases the same actual data, but applied to them techniques that differed totally from multivariate statistics. Thus a cluster finding approach (neighbourhood limited classification), a biomechanical method (experimental stress analysis), and an imaging technique (optical data analysis) were applied. These studies, too, showed that the inferences drawn from the original statistics about functions were sound (e.g. Figure 7:16).

A third group of tests was made by examining related anatomical regions. Such parallels may demonstrate how widespread, or how narrow, are the interpretations stemming from the original investigations. For instance though shoulders, arms and forearms are different, each participates in common functions within locomotion. If studies of the shoulder provide statistical parameters that appear to contain certain functional information, then somewhat similar information should be seen in comparable studies of the arm, forearm and the entire upper limb. Such comparisons have been made, and they further confirm that the inferences drawn from the original statistics about function were sound (Figure 7:17).

Yet another way of testing whether or not there is reality in the 'biological meanings' attributed to statistical parameters is through study of how the original anatomical variables are clustered. For, if functional meaning can be derived from the clustering of the animals by measurements of individual anatomical parts such as the shoulder, then the way the shoulder measurements are themselves clustered should also be functionally interpretable. In the same way, in those studies in which the interpretations seem to be associated with the evolutionary relationships of the animals, we might expect to find the anatomical measurements clustered in ways more closely related to evolutionary concepts. Both of these would be a powerful test of the respective interpretations. Of course, we might also find that the clusters of variables for most of the studies were only random or meaningless. That finding would be a powerful negative test of the interpretations.

Such studies have been carried out (Oxnard, 1983a, 1984). Tests of functional interpretations of the shoulder, arm and forearm, pelvis and thigh, talus and foot show very clearly clusters of variables that make functional (biomechanical) sense, in

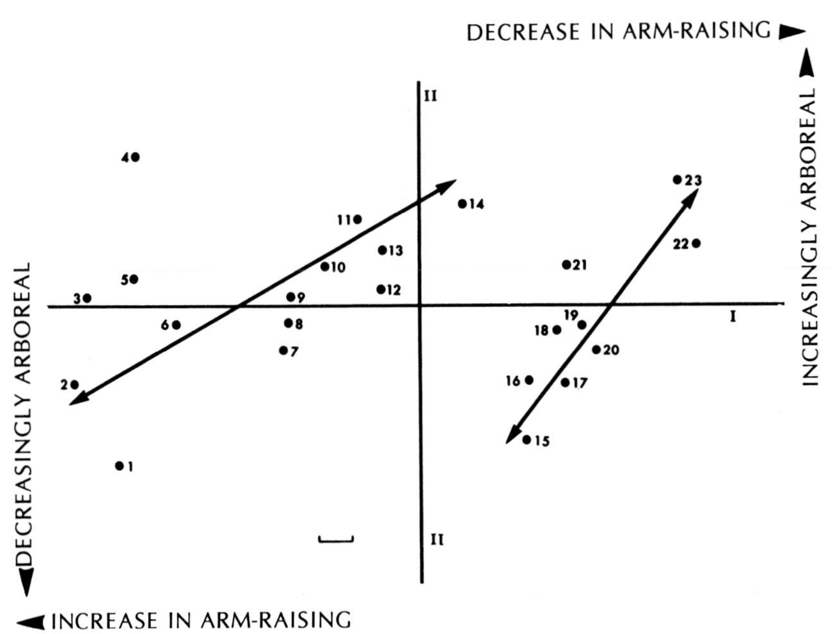

Fig. 7:13 This figure shows the separation given by the first two canonical variates of the original primate shoulder study. The marker indicates one standard deviation unit in all directions. The two double headed arrows provide a summary of the entire result. Axis one is related to increase in armraising and tension from left to right, axis two is related to increase in arboreality from top to bottom.

The actual positions of individual genera are given by the numbered points: 1 = *Pongo*. 2 = *Hylobates*, 3 = *Pan*, 4 = *Gorilla*, 5 = *Ateles*, 6 = *Brachyteles*, 7 = *Nasalis*, *Pygathrix*, 8 = *Lagothrix*, 9 = *Rhinopithecus*, 10 = *Alouatta*, 11 = *Colobus*, 12 = *Presbytis*, high canopy, 13 = *Presbytis kasi*, 14 = *Presbytis*, low canopy, 15 = *Pithecia*, 16 = *Cacajao*, 17 = *Aotus*, *Callicebus*, 18 = *Callithrix*, *Leontocebus*, *Callimico*, 19 = *Cercopithecus*, *Cebus*, 20 = *Saimiri*, 21 = *Macaca*, *Cercocebus*, 22 = *Erythrocebus*, 23 = *Papio*, *Mandrillus*.

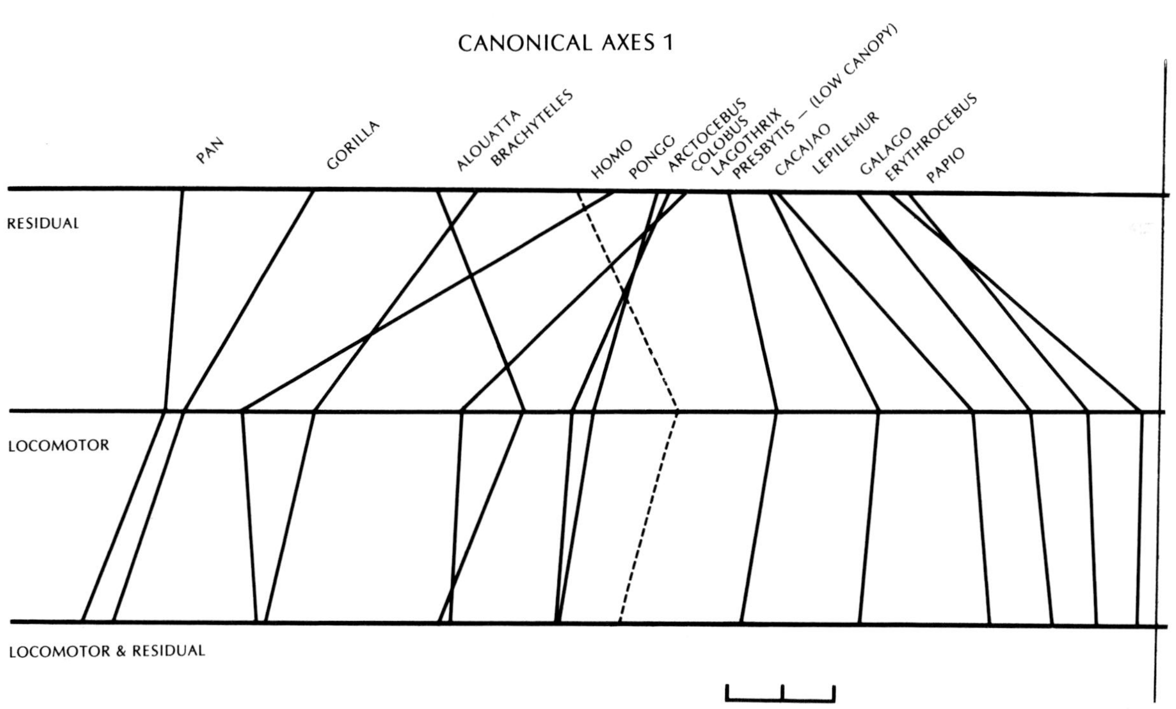

Fig. 7:14 This figure shows the replicate study of different suites of dimensions of the primate shoulder. They include the original 'locomotor' variables, the additional 'residual' dimensions, and both suites of data taken together: 'locomotor and residual dimensions'. The figure demonstrates that the same rank order of genera is provided by each study although with increasing sensitivity from residual, through locomotor to both combined. The scale has been adjusted for each study so that the standard deviation marker applies to all. Thus the basic separations of the locomotor dimensions are mirrored by residual and residual plus locomotor dimensions.

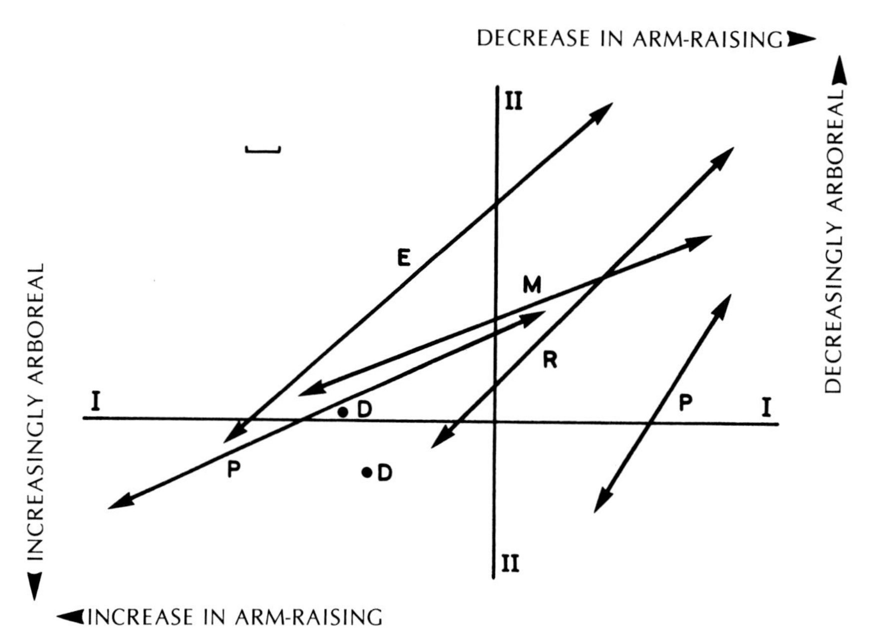

Fig. 7:15 This figure shows the replicate study of locomotor dimensions for a wide variety of arboreal mammals. Individual genera are not marked (for their positions see Oxnard, 1968). But the two arrows marked P represent primates. The other arrows are indicated by E = arboreal edentates, M = arboreal marsupials, R = arboreal rodents, and the two points marked D = the two arboreal (and gliding) dermopterans. The axes are interpretable in the same way as in Fig. 7:13 as indicated. Thus the basic separations of the arboreal primates are mirrored by separations of various arboreal mammals.

terms of the functions of the specific anatomical regions. These clusters were mostly related to features such as combinations of particular muscular pulls, and combinations of particular joint orientations (e.g. Table 7:1).

Tests of evolutionary interpretations were also carried out for those studies where these resulted: studies of overall bodily proportions, both for the primates as a whole and for the prosimians more specifically. These tests, too, provided clusters of variables that seemed to make good sense in relation to evolutionary ideas. These clusters were mostly related to phenomena like proximo-distal gradients, medio-lateral arrays, and serially homologous elements (e.g. Table 7:2).

Statistical validity. There is a different kind of testing, internal testing of the statistics themselves, that must be carried out in all statistical investigations. We have always performed such tests, but the customs of publication are such that full description of such tests tend to be confined to doctoral theses; most scientific papers refer to them in little more than a few terse phrases. As a result the detailed nature of such testing is not always understood. Implied disagreements as set out by Corruccini (1978), with the approaches that we have adopted would appear to stem, at least in part, from an incomplete appreciation of the tests we have used. Some applied multivariate statistical texts, however, do go into these matters (e.g. Gnanadesikan, 1977); nontechnical usages in anthropology are given by Oxnard (1983b). The catalogue (Table 7:3) of these internal tests is large and there are many equivalent ways of performing them.

Simple preliminary tests: Initially, then, we have routinely carried out a whole series of simple preliminary tests. These include tests for errors of replication (data cannot be gathered with total accuracy), tests for inter-observer errors (in at least two of our studies there were two observers), and tests of inter-instrument errors (in several of our studies measuring smaller specimens required different tools and, therefore, assessment of inter-instrument errors).

Such simple tests also involved studying differences existing as a result of known phenomena, not of direct interest to the investigation at hand. In this category were tests due to the existence of the two sexes, of differently aged specimens, of subspecific or geographic subgroups, even of pathological specimens. In some cases, e.g. sex and age,

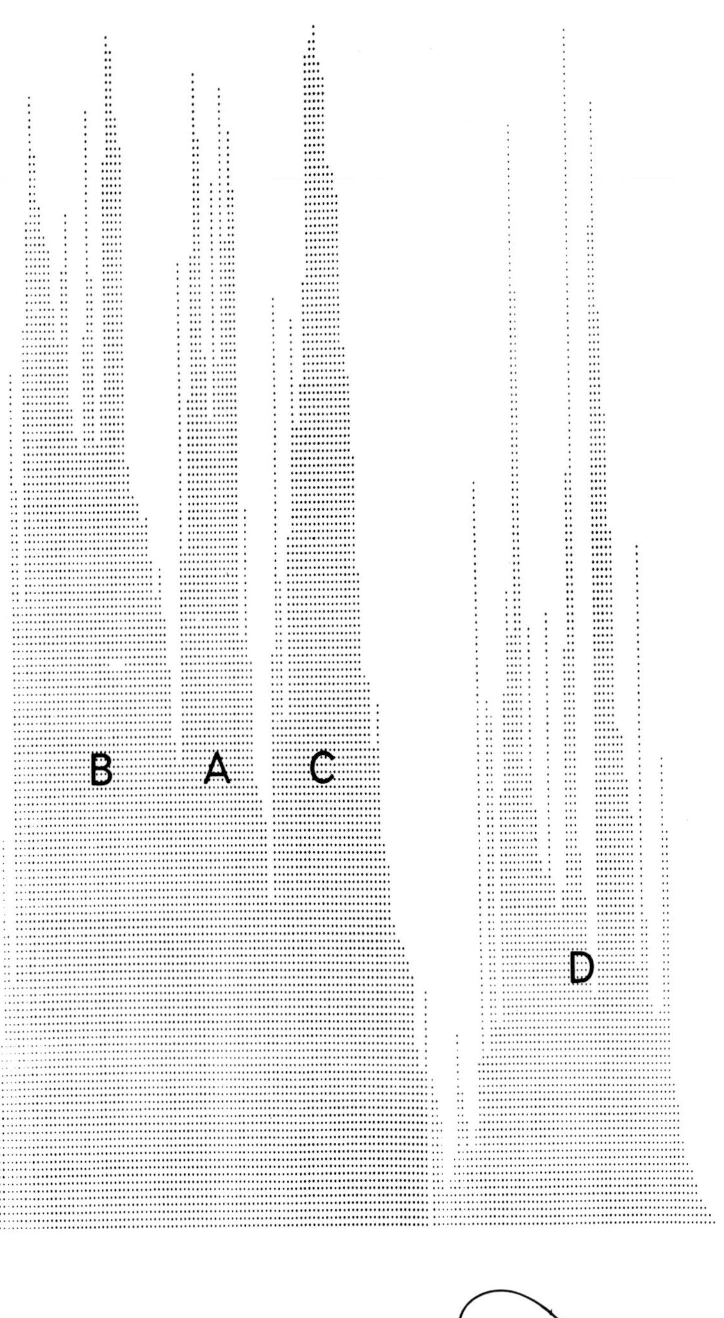

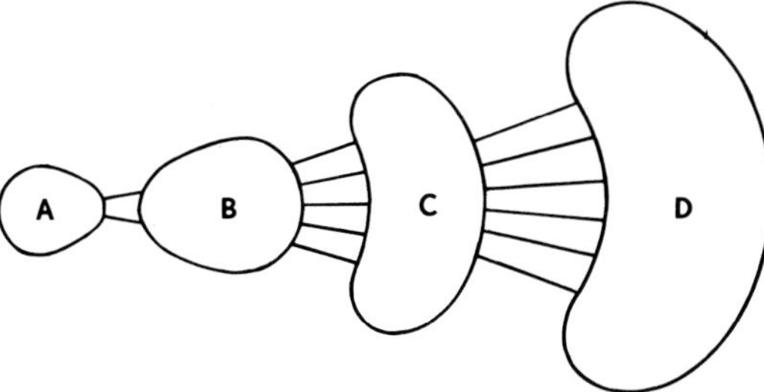

Fig. 7:16 A completely different study of the same data on the shoulder using neighbourhood limited classification (Oxnard and Neely, 1969). The first diagram gives the clusters of specimens as shown by the grouping diagram of the computer output. The second diagram gives the topological relationships of the clusters. Cluster A includes almost all specimens of terrestrial primates, cluster B almost all specimens of semiterrestrial semiarboreal primates, cluster C includes almost all specimens of generally arboreal primates, and cluster D includes all specimens of very highly arboreal primates capable of developed acrobatics and tension bearing in the upper limb. Though expressed in a completely different way from canonical analysis, and though based upon specimens rather than genera, this study mirrors the same functional information as the initial analysis of the shoulder, Fig. 7:13.

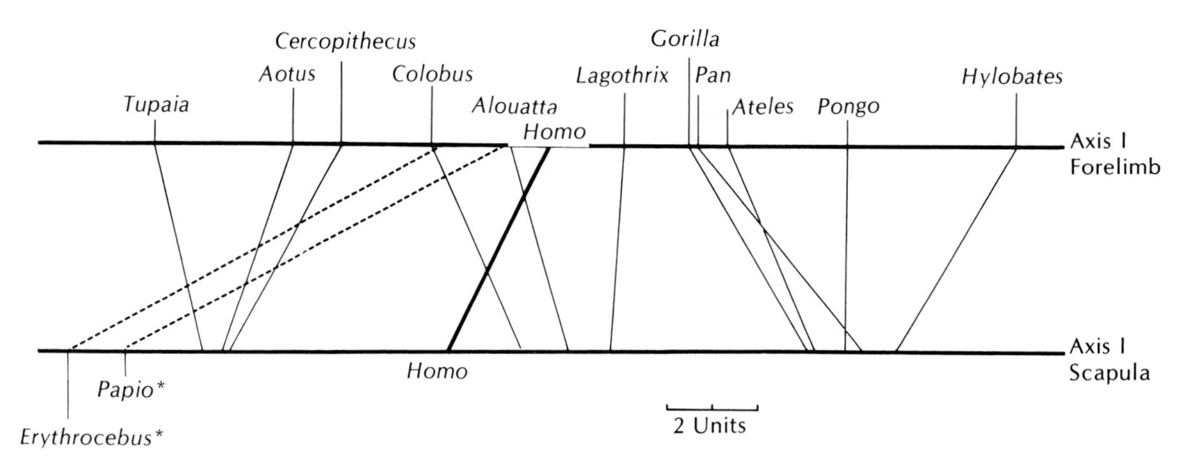

*Erythocebus and Papio are 5.6 and 6.8 units different from this position in higher axes of **FORELIMB** study.

Fig. 7:17 The rank order of selected genera in the study of the shoulder is closely mirrored by the rank order in the study of the entire forelimb. The picture is not changed by inclusion of more species (left out here in order to keep the picture uncluttered). The two main differences that do exist are included: the two highly terrestrial species have a markedly different position in the first canonical axis, but this apparent difference is resolved in the examination of higher axes (Oxnard, 1983a, 1984).

specific tests are required because it is not possible to eliminate these phenomena. In other cases, e.g. pathology, most problems were eliminated by restricting samples to those specimens not showing the confounding factor.

Such tests also included examinations for phenomena such as skewness and kurtosis. The normality of the data was determined when possible, likewise the equality of variance among groups. When necessary, but this was very rarely the case, correcting transformations were applied.

In a sense, routine examination of basic statistical data (means, variances, standard errors, fiducial limits, 't' tests, and so on), were also part of the testing process, even though their examination was also necessary in order to understand the univariate information contained within the data.

Finally, searches were made for outlying points in the data. In addition to the usual univariate and bivariate methods we also applied multivariate searches for outliers. What should be done about such outliers is another matter. Our own choice was to accept them, unless it was certainly and objectively shown that they resulted from measurement error, mislabelling of specimen, or some other identifiable and correctable problem.

Tests within the multivariate statistical analyses: We have also routinely carried out a series of more complex tests involving preliminary multivariate statistical studies. Principal components analysis may be useful for studying the normality and homogeneity of dispersion of those individual subgroups of the data, large enough to permit the procedure. This technique may also help to identify multivariate outliers (Figure 7:18). It may be further utilized to reveal subgroups within what may seem to be a single group (e.g. Lisowski, Albrecht and Oxnard, 1976). Multivariate probability plotting, based upon generalized distances, also proves useful in revealing non-normality and outliers in reasonably large samples.

But in addition to the prior testing described above, there are many tests related specifically to the ultimate multivariate statistical analyses themselves. These include (**a**) significance of latent roots, (**b**) per cent of information within individual statistical axes, (**c**) standard deviations and limits to individual multivariate groups, (**d**) standard errors of the positions of the means of individual multivariate groups, (**e**) homogeneity (or otherwise) of the dispersion matrices, and so on. Presumably because our studies were applied to groups of animals enormously different one from another, these tests never raised problems. For instance in our studies, canonical axes had statistical significance at a dimensionality far beyond that, which we described as possessing discernible biological significance.

However, it is easy to be mislead about this. For

Table 7:1

FACTOR ANALYSIS of DATA on ARM and FOREARM:
CLUSTERS of VARIABLES

Clusters	Anatomical features	Overall description
Shared factor pattern	Facet on humerus for ulna Facet on ulna for humerus Projection epicondyles Position radial tuberosity Insertion of triceps	Measures at elbow for flexion and extension
Factor axis 2	Projection of ulnar styloid Relative sizes, both styloids Projection of radial styloid Relative widths, radius and ulna	Measures at wrist for flexion and extension, adduction and abduction
Shared factor pattern	Distal insertion of pronator Distal insertion of biceps Lateral bowing of radius Angle of interosseous ridge Maximum bowing of radius	Measures between radius and ulna for pronation and supination

Table 7:2

FACTOR ANALYSIS of DATA on LIMB PROPORTIONS of PROSIMIANS:
CLUSTERS of VARIABLES

Clusters	Anatomical features	Overall description
Factor 1	Eighteen variables: Four upper limb lengths Four lower limb lengths Five hand lengths Five foot lengths	Proximo-distal dimensions of the limb
Factor 2	Length of fourth metacarpal Lengths of fourth phalanges Length of fourth digit	Variables pertaining to digit four
Factor 3	Length of forearm Length of leg (shin) Length of hand Length of foot	Mirror image serial elements (see factor 5)
Factor 4	Lengths of middle metacarpals Lengths of middle metatarsals Middle phalanges of hand Middle phalanges of foot	Pre-axial to post-axial in hand and foot
Factor 5	Length of upper arm Length of thigh Length of hand Length of foot	Mirror image serial elements (see factor 3)

Table 7:3

TESTS on MULTIVARIATE MORPHOMETRIC ANALYSES

Simple tests

Errors of replication
Inter-observer errors
Inter-instrument errors
Differences between sex, age, sub-specific, pathological and other confounding groupings.
Normality of data, and if not normal, appropriate transformation
Equality of variance, and if not equal, appropriate transformation
Univariate, bivariate and multivariate searches for outliers

More complex tests

Principal components analysis on individual groups to study normality and homogeneity of dispersion
Principal components analysis on individual groups to identify hidden sub-groups of specimens
Principal components analysis to summarize information from group means alone

Tests internal to ultimate analysis

Significance of latent roots
Variance co-variance tests
Homogeneity of dispersion matrices
Significance and per cent of information in individual axes
Tests of significance of positions of individual groups

Tests of ultimate analysis

Groupings of animals
- Based on all genera separately
- Based upon pooled groups from classifications, e.g. all Old World monkeys, all apes
- Based upon locomotion, e.g. all quadrupeds, all leapers
- Based upon combinations, e.g. all leaping prosimians

Groupings of anatomies
- Individual anatomical regions, e.g. pelvis, femur
- Idividual functional regions, e.g. lower end of humerus, upper ends of radius and ulna = elbow
- Individual anatomical form of variable, e.g. all transverse variables, all longitudinal variables
- Individual metrical form of variable, e.g. all angles, all indices, all measures

Sample size and numbers of variables
- Comparison of groups with large samples only and groups with large and small samples together
- Comparison without and with interpolated data from single specimens
- Comparison without and with particular peculiar variables (e.g. tail length different, so tested separately)

Tests relating to overall bodily size

Tests comparing analysis of measures with analysis of other variables
Test of extent to which individual discriminant axes represent animal size
Test of extent to which individual factor axes represent size
Tests of effect of manipulating size through regression adjustment (or other method)

Methods of display

Plots of single, paired or three (model) discriminant axes
Dendrograms of generalized distance connections
Minimum spanning trees of distance connections
Models, usually three-dimensional, of generalized distance connections
High-dimensional displays of patterns of discriminant or factor axes

Independent corroboration

Use of several appropriate multivariate methods
Use of methods with different axiomatic bases, e.g. neighbourhood limited classification
Combination of methods, e.g. neighbourhood limited classification and discriminant function analysis (Oxnard, 1967)

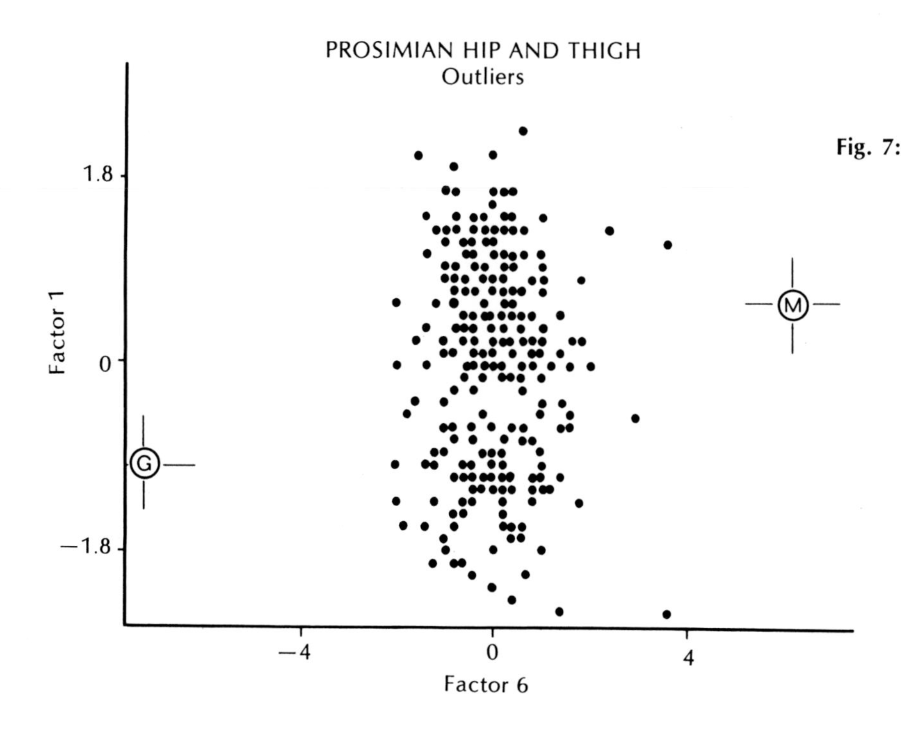

Fig. 7:18 The use of principal components analysis in searches for outliers. Principal component one (and also two through five — not shown) do not separate any individual specimens. But the sixth axis shows that two specimens (G = *Galago* and M = *Microcebus*) are markedly different from the rest. These were later found to be mistakes in the data.

example, in one study (Figure 7:19) the investigators believed (**first frame**) that their groups (species within the same genus) were separated by thirty standard deviation units or more! More complete study of those data by Albrecht demonstrated (**second frame**) that a mistake had been made. The true differences were very much less, so small, in fact that it was quite hard to separate the groups. The original result — thirty units separating species in the same genus — should have provided a warning in the original study. And there are a number of studies in the literature in which large separations between closely related groups should make us pause.

Other internal tests proved especially important in our studies. For instance, when the variances of individual groups were different among the different primates, transformations were applied to equalise variance. These were based, of course, upon only the larger groups in the analyses. There was then no reason to suppose that similar values of the variances did not also apply to those groups for which, by chance, only small samples were available. Even when only a single specimen was available to represent a group, there was no reason to assume that the standardized variance common among the many larger groups did not apply to the group from which it came.

In contrast, however, the positions of the means of the smaller groups were not equally determined even if common variance was assumed. For these groups the position of the means was clearly more equivocal. This was easily shown by the larger standard errors applying to the smaller groups (Figure 7:20).

Tests of statistical normality — a comment: A particular form of testing that is important, in certain usages of multivariate statistics, is the question of the normality of the basic data. Some basic data may be in the form of measurements; certainly that applies to most of the studies in this book; and as can be seen, normality testing of these measurements has yielded enormously important information.

But some measurements can also be compounded to express particular aspects of shape. Ratios are a simple and traditional way of doing this. When appropriately designed, ratios give a good overall reflection of particular aspects of shape and proportion. The problem is that ratios may show non-normal distributions and this may effect multivariate studies of them. Oxnard (1973a) certainly was well aware that ratios may show markedly non-normal distributions. He provided diagrams showing how bimodal distributions of ratios could result from combination of measurements that were, themselves, quite normal in distribution. Oxnard was also aware, however, that ratios could be, and in his studies generally were,

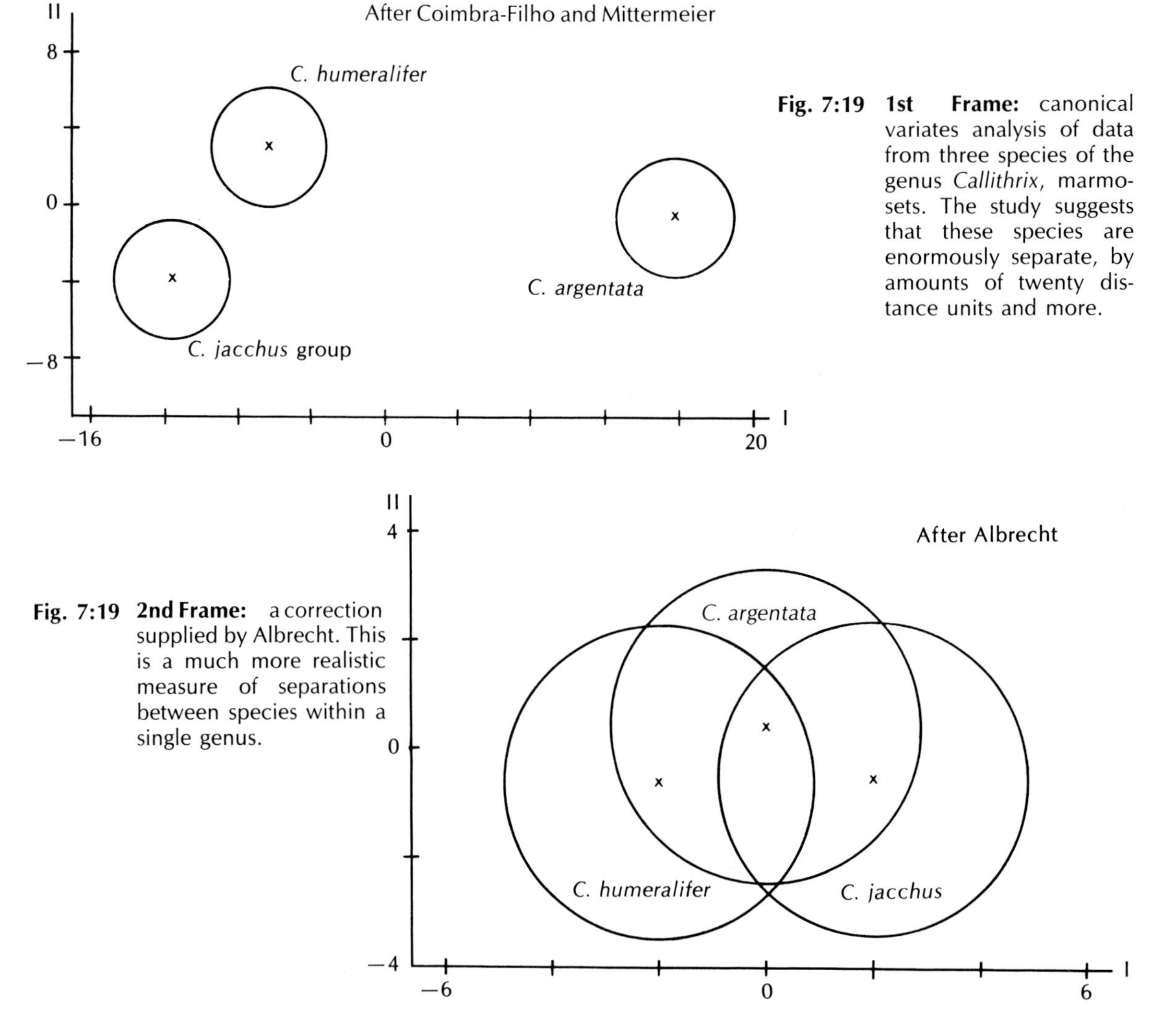

Fig. 7:19 1st Frame: canonical variates analysis of data from three species of the genus *Callithrix*, marmosets. The study suggests that these species are enormously separate, by amounts of twenty distance units and more.

Fig. 7:19 2nd Frame: a correction supplied by Albrecht. This is a much more realistic measure of separations between species within a single genus.

as entirely normal as any other data. Since then the problems raised by non-normality of ratios for multivariate statistical analysis have been particularly carefully studied by Atchley, Gaskins and Anderson (1976).

In most of our studies some sample sizes were so restricted, by matters outside our control, that their normality or non-normality were not determinable. But, as a practical matter, in those individual groups large enough to be tested for normality, we have found that even when we used ratios, departures from normality were usually very small. It is only in the case of ratios involving breadths that distributions were non-normal. But in this special case it is not because they are ratios, but because they more clearly demonstrate sexual dimorphism than most other dimensions. Thus these ratios show bimodal distributions. When sexes are separately identified, these dimensions are as normal as any others.

In any case, comparisons of multivariate studies of normal large groups (and excluding small groups whose normality cannot be determined) with studies of large and small groups together, showed no major differences. These comparisons demonstrate that the multivariate statistical methods used are sufficiently robust that they are relatively unaffected by this factor. This is probably because the differences that we are interested in charting are between animals that are enormously different from one another (e.g. gorillas and marmosets).

It is true, however, that this robusticity might well not obtain in studies of, for instance, geographic subgroups of a non-human species, or of so-called racial groups of humans, where the differences overall are very small, (e.g. Howells, 1973, who has carefully tested for this effect).

Much more importantly, however, is the fact that

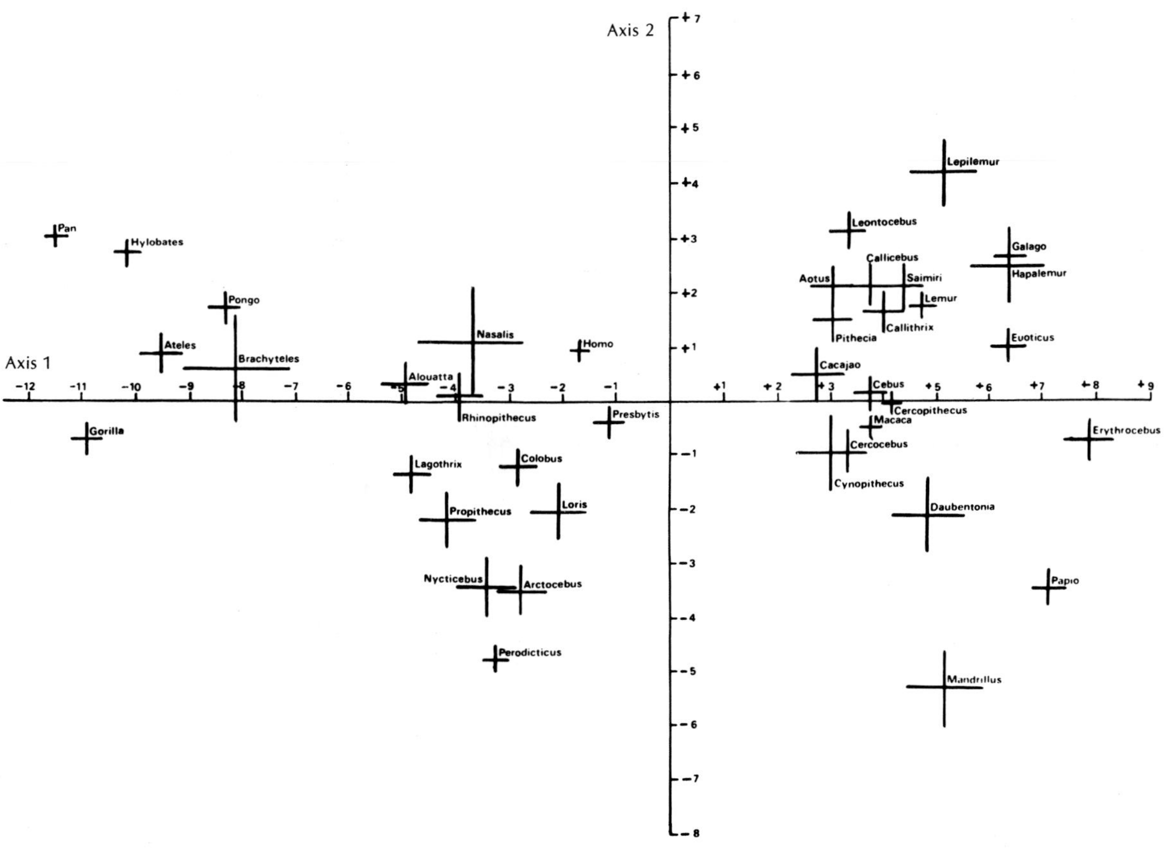

Fig. 7:20 A plot of the first two canonical axes for the full shoulder study of the primates. In this diagram the strength of the determination of the position of the mean of each group is shown by the length of the arms of the cross, the centre of which represents the mean. *Pan*, for instance, is represented by a large sample and the position of its mean is well determined as shown by the very small cross. *Nasalis* and *Brachyteles*, in contrast, are represented by very small samples; the positions of their means are correspondingly less well determined; their crosses are very large.

the criterion of normality is irrelevant in the hypothesis-free usage of multivariate statistics. That is, it is irrelevant in those situations where groups that are already known to be highly significantly different are being studied to discover the structure of relationships among them (see Albrecht, 1980). This is the usage in our investigations.

Our usage of ratios, and this general matter has been consistently misunderstood by Corruccini (1978), is 'hypothesis free'. Corruccini seems unaware of this difference between an 'hypothesis free' use of the statistics, where normality is a less important criterion, and other usages where normality is vital. He, furthermore, consistently ignores the fact that, in any case, examinations of our data have shown that they are normal. One suspects that though ratios can be non-normal, they are, in general, not much different in normality than most other types of data.

Curruccini (1978) further seems to think that the deployment of a dimension in more than a single ratio 'increases the danger of diluting informative measures with more variables or less meaningful ones.' In fact, the account taken of correlation between ratios when they are subsequently compounded by multivariate techniques removes the 'dilution' and ensures appropriate summation.

He also seems to believe that increased variability in a particular variable decreases its value in a multivariate statistic. It is certainly true that characters of higher than average variability do contribute less univariate discrimination than others. But the entire importance of the multivariate statistic is that it allows such highly variable characters to enhance discrimination, not because of the univariate separations that they contain (which is obviously less than that of less variable characters), but because of the multivariate intercorrelations that they may display in association with other characters (e.g. Blackith and Blackith, 1969). These intercorrelations may provide small or large discrimination; but this certainly cannot be judged ahead of performing the multivariate statistical examination.

An especially important consideration relating to the use of ratios not noted by Corruccini (1978) concerns function. Ratios may, if appropriately constructed, compound aspects of functionally significant biomechanical features. The absolute distance (measure) of a muscle attachment from, say, a joint axis, may be totally unimportant biomechanically. Its distance relative to that of another muscle from that same axis (ratio), providing a measure of lever arm, may be the key datum. The absolute radius (measure) of a joint surface may be of no importance biomechanically, but that radius relative to that of another joint surface may be the critical biomechanical advantage (ratio) that must be examined. Such ratios are mechanically dimensionless and are the appropriate features to be examined in both biomechanical analysis and biometrical examinations of biomechanically relevant data. I am most pleased to record here that this view is now clearly understood by those interested in biomechanics and that, specifically, Rayner (1985) is proposing a vehicle (the general structural relation) for dealing with this type of situation.

These spurious criticisms of Corruccini's are noted here because there is little doubt that an uncritical acceptance of his opinions has added to the current disenchantment with morphometrics of some physical anthropologists.

Tests of the research design: There are a series of further tests in most of our studies. Some relate to questions about the groupings of the animals.

Obviously, the ultimate analyses were based upon study of the multivariate separation of all groups (genera or species) taken individually. This prevents introduction of bias due to any prior ideas that we may have had about the groups (genera and species, of course, are groups whose reality depends upon a large body of prior information totally independent of the data of the study). But because taxonomic supergroupings (e.g. families, superfamilies) might impact upon the studies, analyses were performed where the genera were a priori grouped in this way. Thus, in most of our studies, useful insight into the data came from analyses in which pooling into larger groups, e.g. all Old World monkeys, all New World monkeys, all hominoids, all prosimians, etc, was carried out.

Such procedures supplied information relating to the reality of the clusterings that were 'discovered' by the descriptive use of the statistic as applied to all genera independently. In particular, they proved especially useful in revealing problems due to interpolation of specimens that were, in reality, widely different from all the rest (Oxnard, 1972a).

When the existence of groupings based upon biomechanical function was at issue, it proved useful to compare the patterns of clusterings that emerged from statistical study of genera with the relationships between groups defined by a priori functional determination. Thus genera were compared in groups arranged as leapers, climbers, acrobats and so on. Tests of this type provided evidence confirming the idea of continuous functional-structural spectra rather than of discrete functional-structural groups (Oxnard, 1975a).

Yet other groupings of anthropological significance were studied, and gave useful ancillary information. For example, study of sex subgroups was undertaken as a precaution against such subgroups overly distorting the distribution of the data. Those tests have resulted in the demonstration of a new view of sexual dimorphism: that not one, but several sexual dimorphisms exist among the primates, even among groups as closely related as the great apes and humans (Oxnard, 1983c). And they have been seminal in leading to the studies described in this book (Oxnard, 1984d).

Some tests examined subgroupings of the variables. For instance, the study of the pelvis and femur included dimensions from the bony pelvis and the proximal and distal femur. Study of each of these separately revealed that the result for the pelvis was similar to that for the proximal femur. This is sound because, after all, these are but two sides of a single joint. But the result for the distal femur was completely different (Fig. 7:21). This is not surprizing because the lower end of the femur is functionally more closely related to the other side of the knee joint, the proximal tibia and fibula. Accordingly, in the ultimate study of these data, attention was aimed first at the hip joint complex (Oxnard, German and McArdle, 1981), leaving the lower end of the femur to be examined with the knee.

There are yet other ways in which anatomical variables were grouped. For instance, multivariate statistical study of all transverse measures, presumably related to robusticity, proved important in defining the forms of sexual dimorphisms which the data suggest.

Likewise, study of subsets of variables comprising all those in a particular format (for example, all dimensions derived by a common calculation, or all measures expressed as angles) helped reveal errors within the results. Thus, in one study three dimensions were clustered so distinctly from the rest as to be rendered suspect. It turned out that the same mathematical error had been made in the calculation of each (Fig. 7:22).

Finally, subgroupings of the data were used to test the effects of sample size, interpolated specimens and highly variable variables. Analyses of large groups were compared with those including both large and small groups; this allowed assessment of the distortion produced by the inclusion of small groups. In no study that we have tackled, that involved separations of generic or higher groups, did the inclusion of small groups cause any marked perturbations. Where individual specimens were interpolated, the results of their inclusion and exclusion were compared. Again, in our studies at generic and higher levels, such interpolations produced no sizable distortions as long as all axes were examined. Where highly variable variables existed, insight was obtained by comparing analyses which included and excluded such variables. Sometimes highly variable variables nevertheless contribute markedly to a multivariate statistical analysis. Sometimes they do not. For example, tail length was a highly variable variable in one study and as a result of such tests we excluded it as adding little information (Ashton, Flinn and Oxnard, 1975).

Interpretations of individual multivariate statistical axes

Functional interpretations: In many studies biological meaning has been attached to axes resulting from multivariate statistical treatments. One of the earliest was a study of the painted turtle (Jolicoeur and Mosimann, 1960). In that investigation one principal component axis reflected size. In much the same way, investigations using canonical variates analysis provided apparent meaning for canonical axes. For example, in a study of mirid bugs, Waloff (1966) identified a canonical axis as related to geographical distribution. In these cases, however, the biological problems themselves were not complicated, involving study of a few variables taken on a small number of similar organisms. The first complex study that provided such meaning in individual canonical axes was our work on the primate shoulder. This was noted by Blackith and Reyment (1971) and Marriot 1974), and is continued in the second edition of the former text: Reyment, Blackith and Cambell (1984).

Further studies of complex situations, whether by ourselves (e.g. arm and forearm, Ashton, Flinn, Oxnard and Spence, 1976; pelvis, Zuckerman, Ashton, Flinn, Oxnard and Spence, 1973) or by others, (e.g. pelvis, McHenry and Corruccini, 1975 and 1978) were, at first sight, not as successful as the work on the shoulder, in providing interpretations for individual canonical axes. Indeed, it may be that these findings turned some authors away from multivariate statistical analysis.

Hindsight leads me to believe that the direct relationship between particular canonical axes and specific anthropological concepts in the investigation of the shoulder was a happy accident, perhaps the result of the special nature of the shoulder. The scapula is one of the few regions of the body where a bone is almost completely suspended by muscles. Thus, to a degree greater than in any other region, muscular forces are mainly responsible for its form. This simplicity could well result in the form of the scapula being determined by a small number of independent biomechanical features. Such independence would be easily picked up by the multivariate statistic in its search for independent statistical parameters. Hence the canonical axes themselves might the more readily mirror the biomechanical situation. This is unlikely to be the case in most anatomical regions.

In the pelvis, for instance, though muscular forces do, indeed, shape that bone, so also do forces due (**a**) to weight-bearing, (**b**) to the functions of the body cavities (e.g. especially pregnancy and parturition), and in some primates (**c**) to the function of a very powerful tail. These are bound to be highly correlated phenomena. It is unlikely, therefore, that specific orthogonal axes chosen by a multivariate statistic, would be directly aligned along any one of the above biological phenomena. This may explain the lack of success in interpreting specific canonical axes in these other studies in the same way as was possible for the shoulder. But that does not mean that the analyses do not contain information of anthropological import. It only means that such information does not, in most cases, lie directly in the canonical directions. Almost all our more complex studies demonstrate arrangements where major separations are along axes lying at angles to the canonical ones (e.g. Figure 7:23).

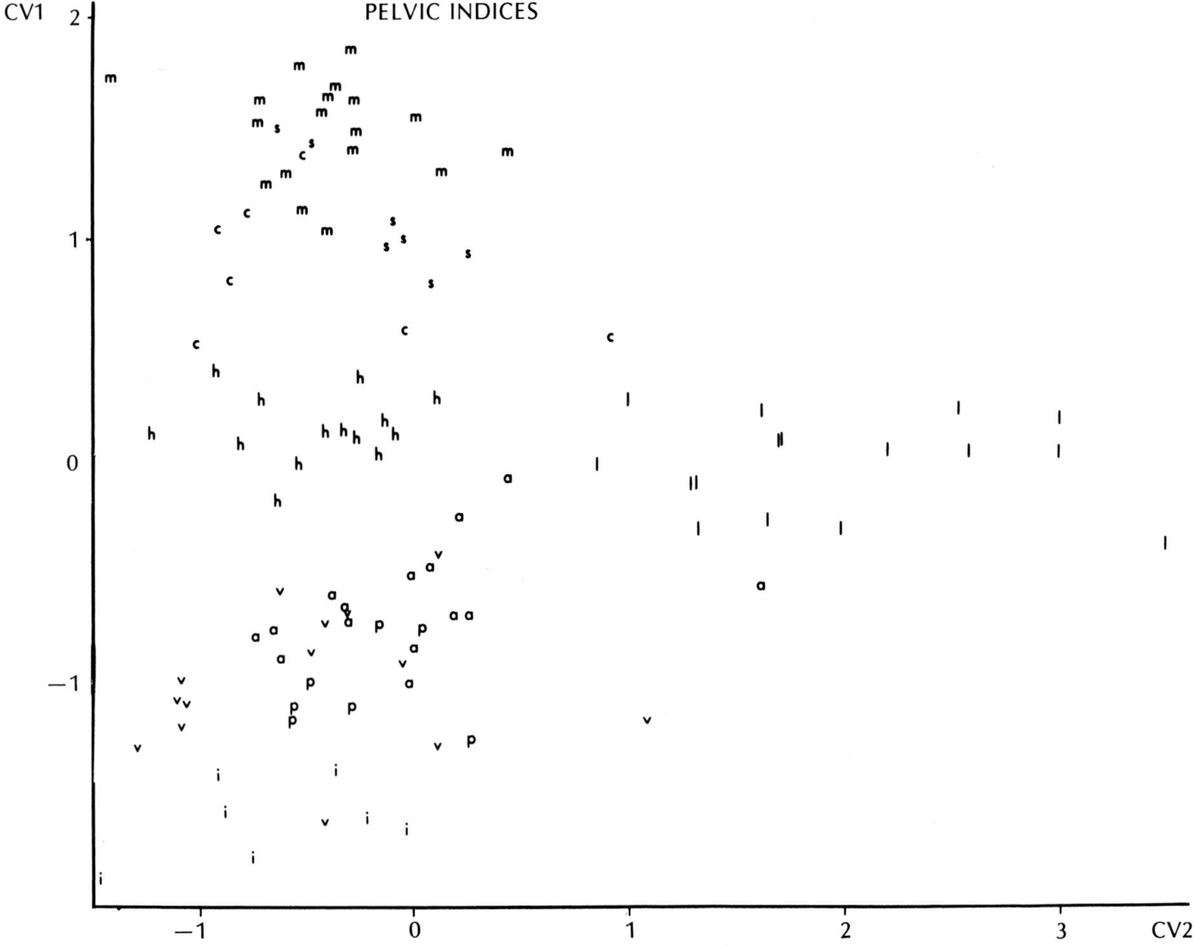

Fig. 7:21 Four preliminary studies of data from the hip and thigh for prosimians. The first three plots show that the pattern of individual specimens of each species (labelled by letters) are basically similar. These are plots for the hip alone, the upper end of the thigh alone, and the hip and upper end of the thigh taken together. This similarity is related at least in part to the fact that each study is of the same functional complex — the hip joint.

The fourth plot is of the same specimens for the lower end of the thigh. It shows a completely different arrangement, related, undoubtedly, to the function of the knee joint.

Because of this, the interpretations were not directly along canonical axes but (**a**) in axes oblique to the canonical directions, or (**b**) in combinations of two or more canonical axes, or (**c**) in the total generalised distances, or even, (**d**) in the overall pattern of contribution of canonical axes (as displayed using the high-dimensional technique). These possibilities have resulted in the anthropological interpretations of our more recent studies. They are especially important in the studies of teeth, outlined in this book; it is these interpretations that the tests are especially able to confirm or deny (Oxnard, 1983c).

Interpretations of first axes as size: During recent years, first multivariate axes have often been interpreted as size. It is well known that in the analyses of measurements of specimens from small numbers of groups of closely related animals (especially the kinds of animals that continue to grow throughout life), a first principal component is indeed likely to be more closely allied with differences in size than with anything else. How could it be otherwise? In a similar way, in most simple situations (few closely related groups, variables in the form of measurements), a first canonical axis is more likely to reflect size (but also everything correlated with size) than anything else.

Such observations have been used to criticize the interpretations we made about the first canonical axes in the studies of the shoulder. Surely, goes the criticism, the first axis in those studies, too, must be

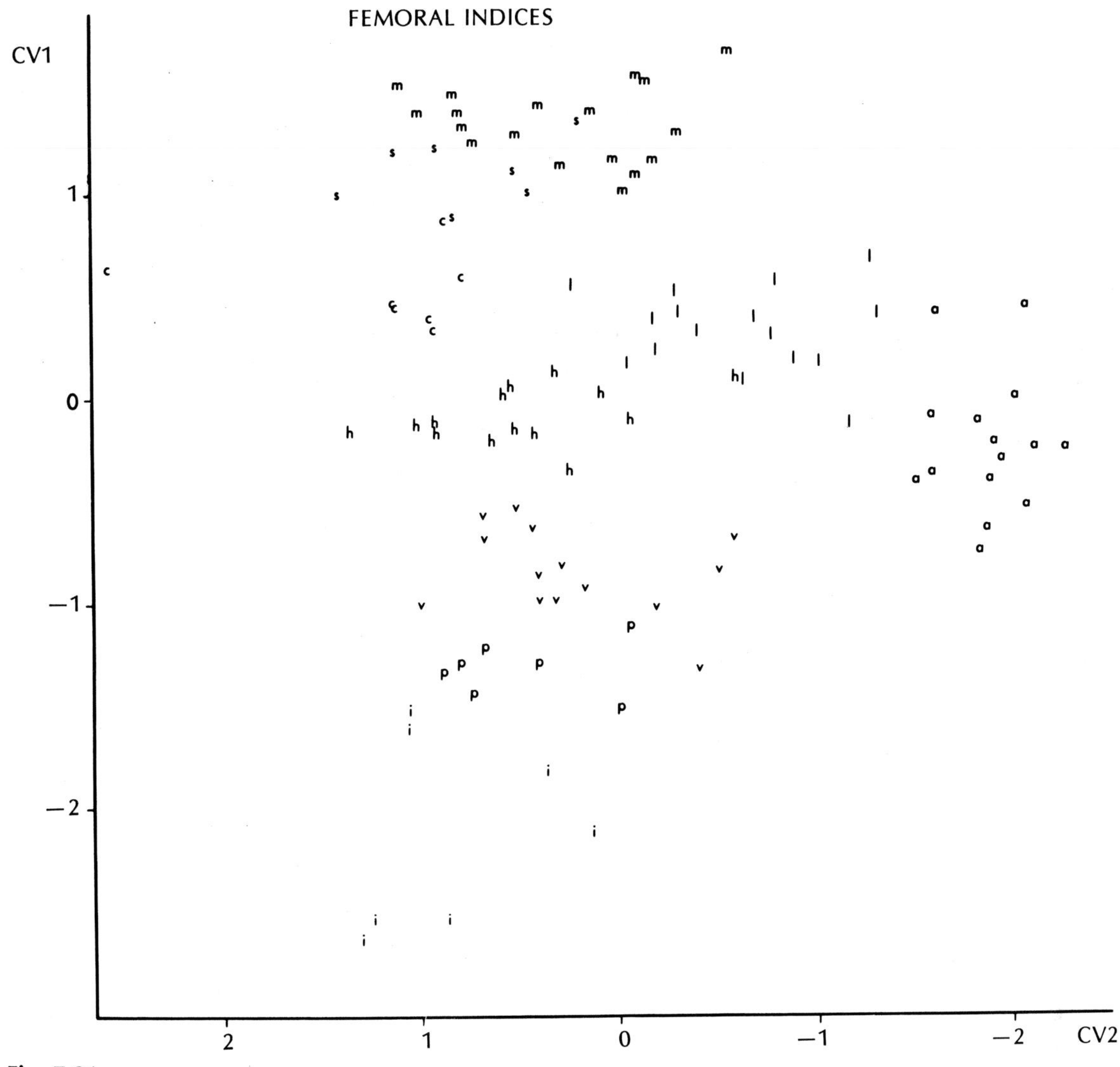

Fig. 7:21

size (Corruccini and Ciochon, 1976). Thus, Corruccini and Ciochon pointed out that the largest primates, gorillas, lay at one end of the first canonical axis, and the smallest primates, tarsiers, lay at the other. That this observation is spurious is clearly seen when the rank order of all the genera based upon size is compared with their rank order in the first canonical axis (Figure 7:24). A similar criticism was applied to our investigations of prosimians. Once again, comparison of the two sets of rank orders makes it clear that it is spurious (Figure 7:25).

In the studies in this book, despite the fact that the raw data are measurements rather than indices, the first axis is clearly not size. Size is implicated, but differently in the different species, and in several different axes. Thus, size would would seem to be somewhere involved in the first two axes in the genera *Homo* and *Ramapithecus*, but in the first three axes in all apes, all australopithecines and the genus *Sivapithecus*. In *Gigantopithecus* size may be carried over even further into the fourth and fifth axes.

It is worth asking why size does not fall out in the first axes in these more complicated studies. The answer seems to be complex. In some studies it may have been because the largest portion of size, the isometric portion common to all of the animals under investigation, was removed in an approximate manner by the use of ratios. Such size as remained in those data was presumably the smaller, supra-isometric portion, and because it was small, it did not fall out first. It would even be surprizing, given the complexity of our studies (large numbers of

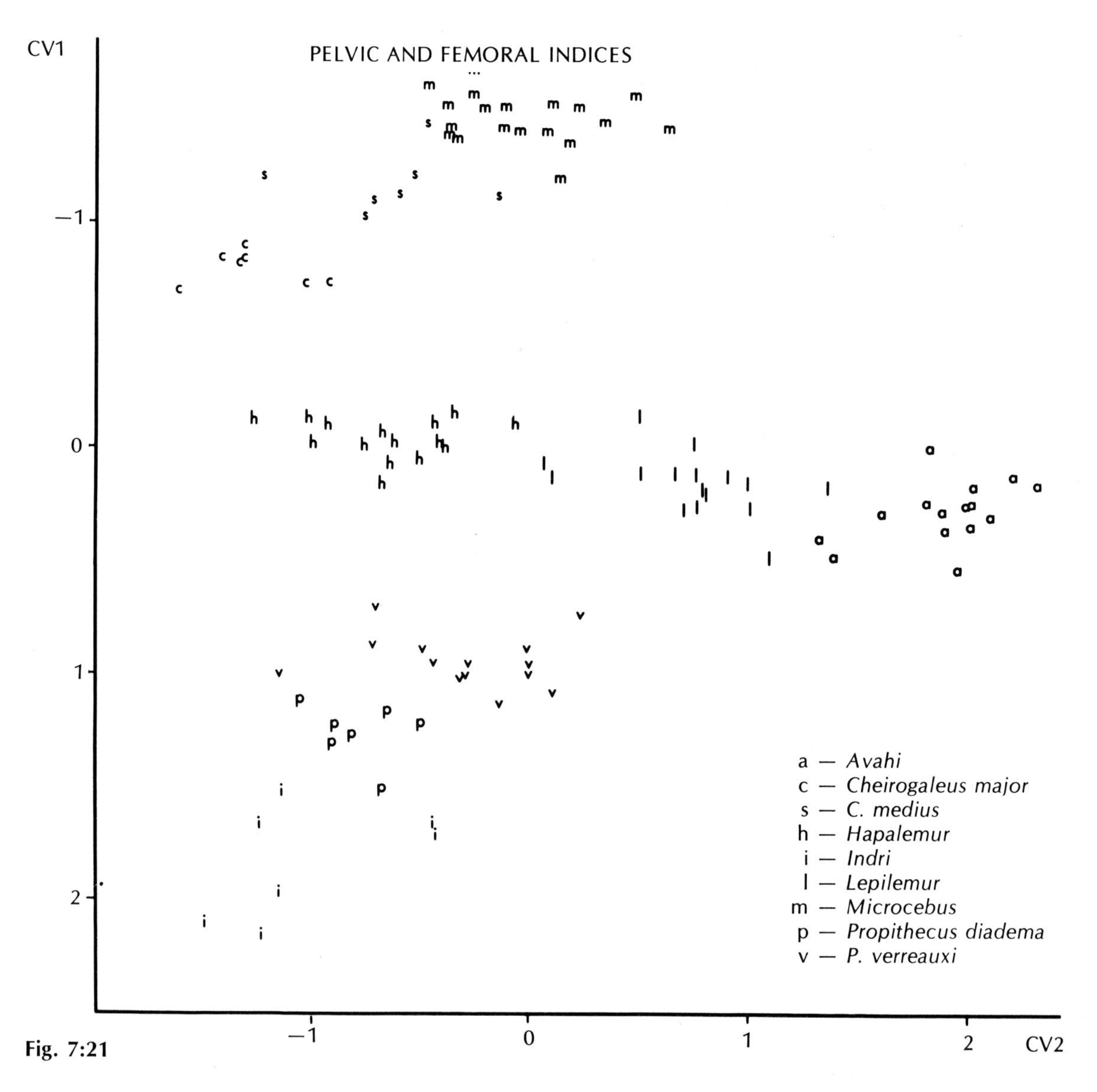

Fig. 7:21

groups of distantly related animals), however, if the remaining size effects were to appear within a single axis for all primate groups. In studies which utilize measurement rather than ratios (such as the studies in this book) size is clearly differently arranged in the different species under investigation. This would suppy the complex result that we have noted above: that size seems to be expressed in the first two axes in *Homo* and *Ramapithecus*, the first three axes in all apes, all australopithecines and the genus *Sivapithecus*, and even higher axes in *Gigantopithecus*. It is encouraging to report that an understanding of this complexity of size, especially the fact that size and shape are interdependent, is now being recognized (e.g. Wood, 1978; Shea, 1985).

It is also worth asking: is there, in fact, any value in attempting to remove 'size' in studies such as these? The answer to our question must clearly be no. Many attempts have been made in the past to do this. In my own laboratory (e.g. Manaster, 1975) an attempt to do this resulted in almost no difference in the ultimate results (Figure 7:26). Presumably this was because the animals examined, individual species of cercopitheque, are all so similar that size affects them all in almost precisely the same way. And this is an interesting finding in itself.

But a few investigators (e.g. Corruccini, 1978, 1983) continue to perform manipulations that they claim 'remove size'. And as they do this they denigrate studies where 'size' has not been 'removed'.

First, size is inextricably tied up in function (the

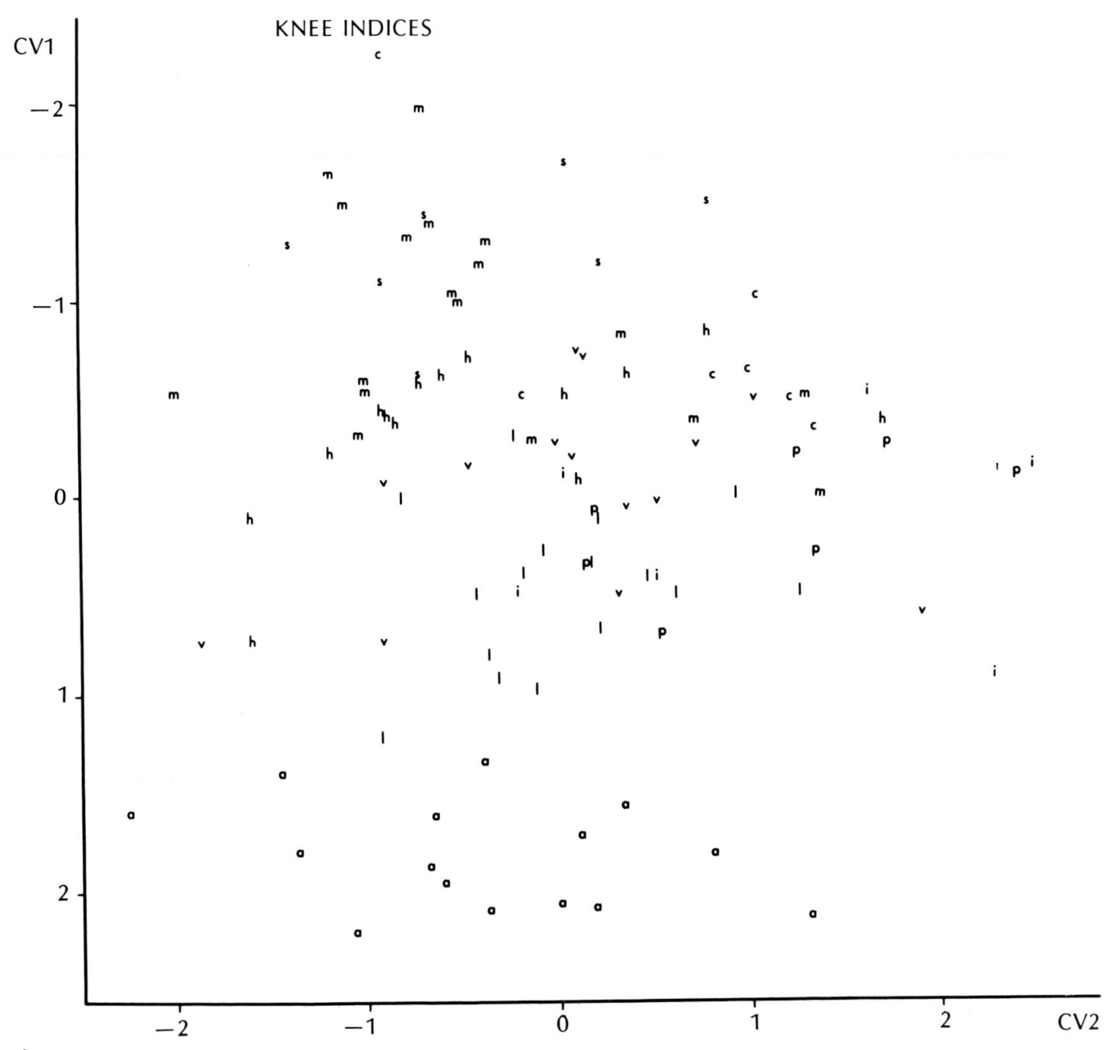

Fig. 7:21

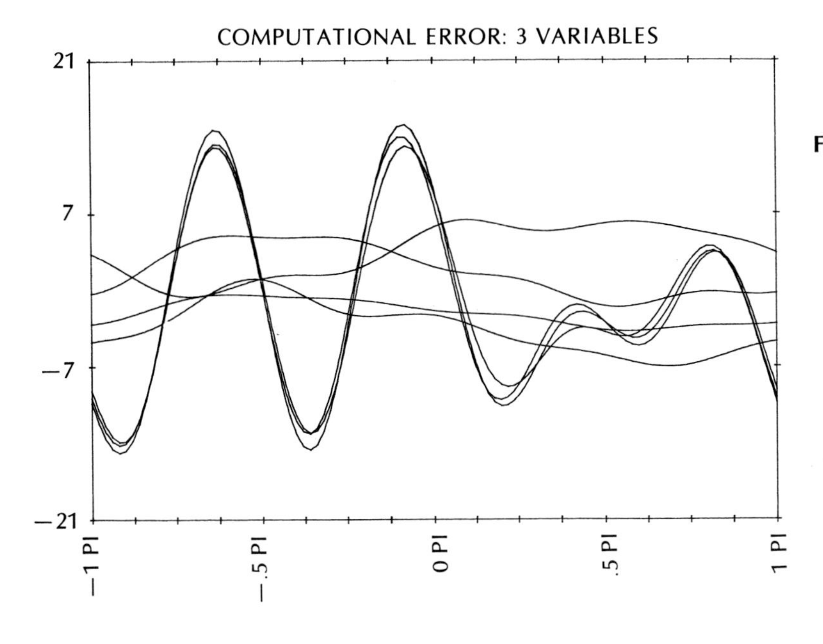

Fig. 7:22 A high-dimensional plot of a series of variables. Three of the curves are separated most peculiarly in a very high canonical axis — their plots show extreme waviness. This similarity was because the same computational error had been made in the calculation of each. This is an excellent way to check for such errors.

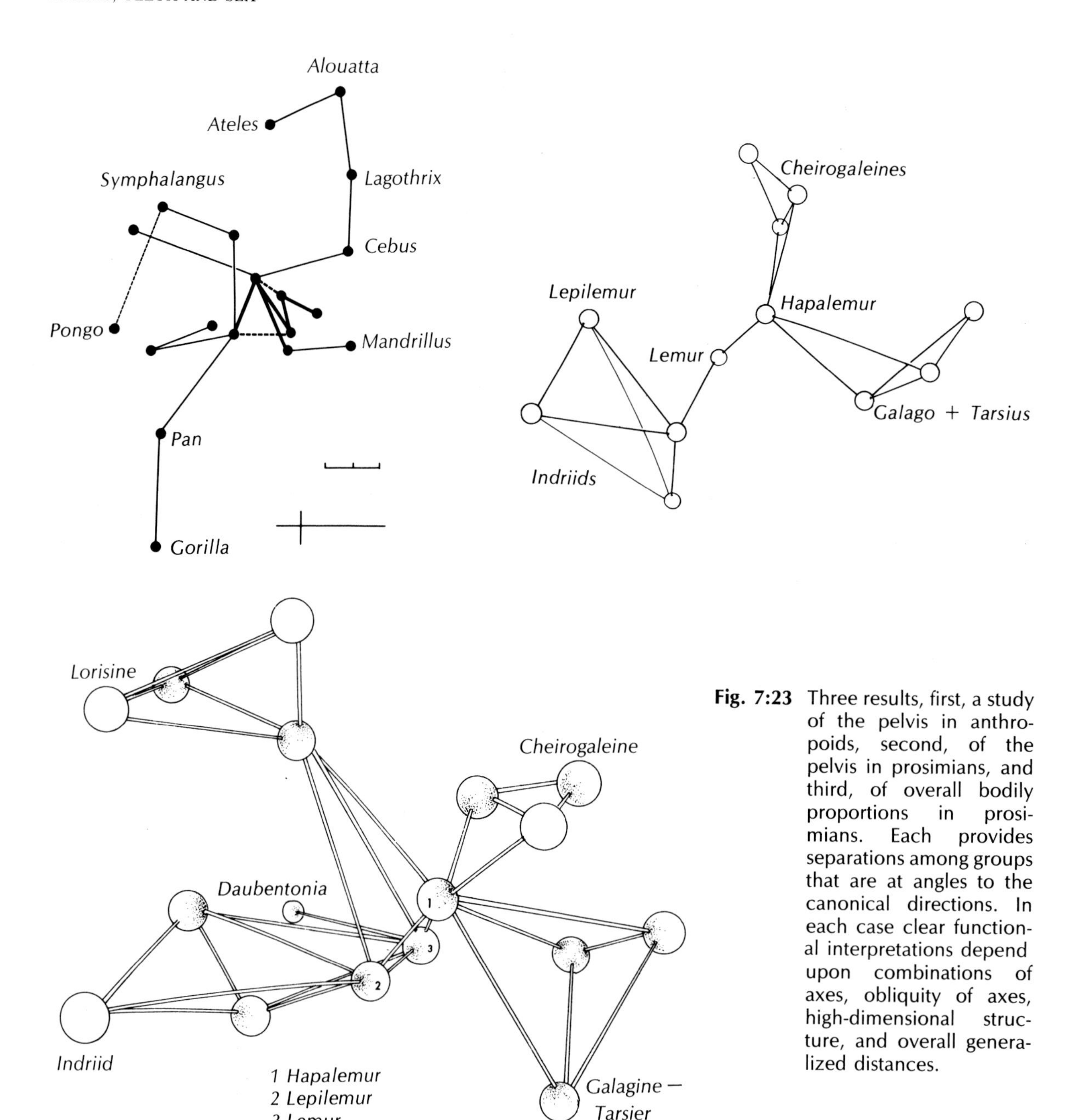

Fig. 7:23 Three results, first, a study of the pelvis in anthropoids, second, of the pelvis in prosimians, and third, of overall bodily proportions in prosimians. Each provides separations among groups that are at angles to the canonical directions. In each case clear functional interpretations depend upon combinations of axes, obliquity of axes, high-dimensional structure, and overall generalized distances.

very element that we hope to be reflected in our statistical parameters). **Second** it is now well established that there are marked differences between intra-specific size relationships (often call ontogenetic) and inter-specific size differences (often called phylogenetic). In fact, it is highly likely that a series of different 'phylogenetic size' relationships can be discerned depending upon the particular evolutionary levels with which we might be concerned. **Third**, attempts to remove 'size' totally (e.g. using multivariate regression techniques — McHenry, Corruccini and Howell, 1976) remove not only effects that are truly size, but also everything else that merely happens to be correlated with it. As a result, in those studies (e.g. Figure 7:27) what remains after 'size removal' shows, once the diagrams have had a scale introduced into them, separations that are of almost no significance at all.

Not everything that happens to be correlated with a thing is that thing.

Thus, investigating the way that shape depends upon size (in terms of phylogenetic scaling, ontogenetic scaling or biomechanical scaling) is the

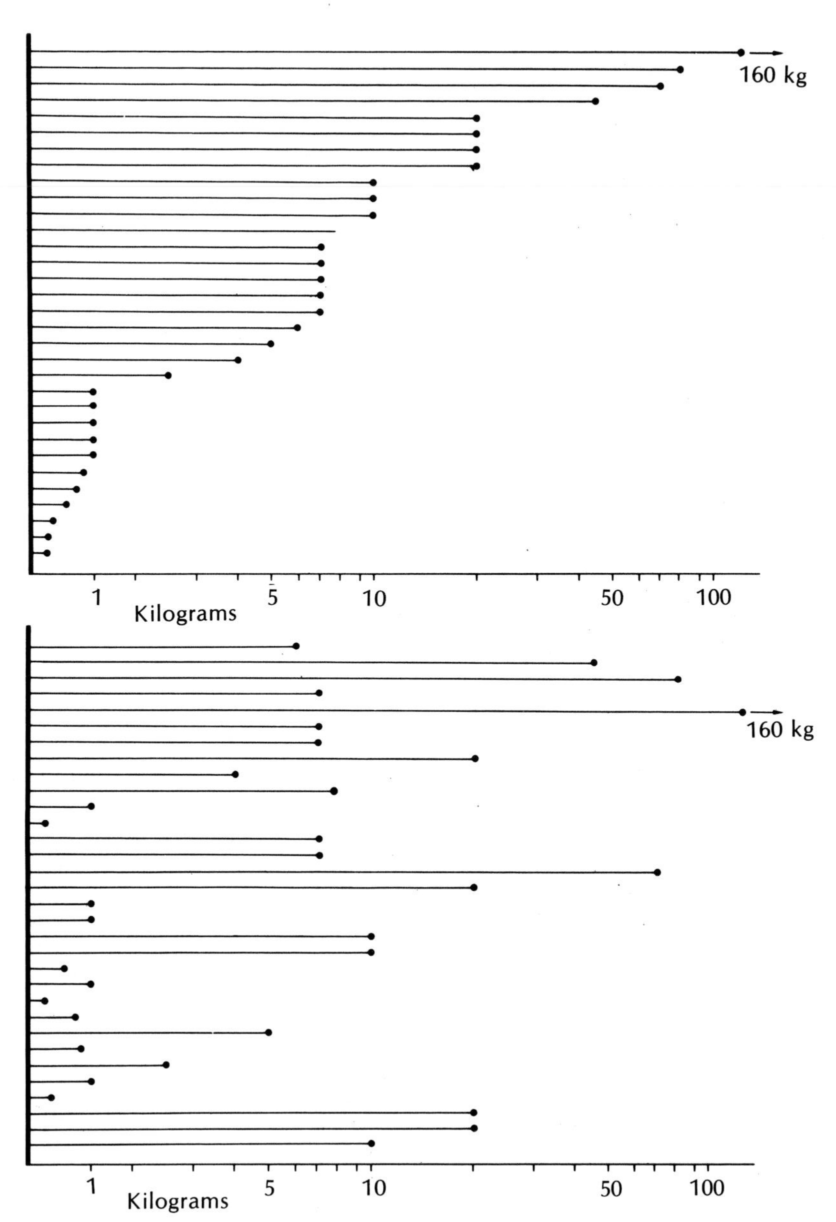

Fig. 7:24 **1st Frame:** rank order based upon overall size, of the series of primates for the shoulder study. **2nd Frame:** rank order actually discovered in the first canonical axis of shoulder data for these genera. It is apparent that there is no relationship between size and first canonical axis in this study.

key problem. This cannot be done if it is assumed a priori that these factors are independent (Shea, 1985). What are required in such multivariate procedures are ways to incorporate and interpret accurately the many different but undoubtedly correlated factors of size. These include phylogenetic size difference, relative growth of the individual within the breeding population, interspecific biomechanical scaling, size independent adaptative changes, and whatever other factors should obtrude into our consciousnesses as we take these extra steps. An artificial statistical separation of 'size' from 'shape' is spurious.

These can all be seen from the problems exhibited by those studies where removal of size was attempted. The separations that remained were so small that (when correctly calibrated) they clearly provide almost no information (McHenry, Corruccini and Howell, 1976). Most of the groups were indistinguishable one from another. In other words, the manipulation that was intended to remove size also removed almost everything else of interest. This contrasts with investigations in which size was not removed. Here separations among groups are

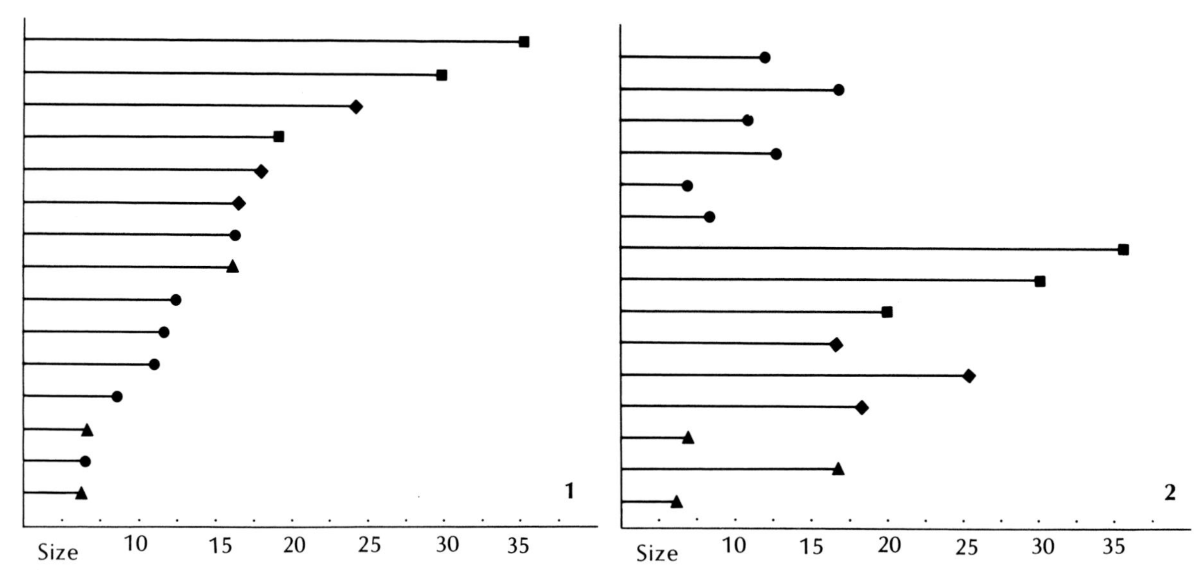

Fig. 7:25 **1st Frame:** rank order based upon overall size, of the series of prosimians in the pelvis study. **2nd Frame:** rank order actually discovered in the first canonical axis of pelvic data for these species. It is apparent, again, that there is almost no relationship between size and first canonical axis.

four or five times greater, with appropriately increased sensitivity. And this example reminds us that dendrograms should not be 'read' purely from the tree diagram. Determinations of the branching points in dendrograms have, themselves, their own inherent error of determination (Figure 7:28).

Replicability of multivariate statistical results

As expressed earlier, one of the main reasons for some of the current disenchantment with multivariate statistical approaches to morphological assessments in anthropology, is the perceived instability of their results. If two different studies provide totally different results, how can we believe that this is a useful method (Day, 1977)? I am not here speaking of replicability within the laboratories of a single group of investigators, but rather, the ability of other laboratories to make similar findings.

In fact, this criticism is not true; the reverse is the case. In those few cases where replicate studies have been carried out results are remarkably similar from one laboratory to another. A first example is our study of the arm and forearm (Ashton, Flinn, Oxnard and Spence 1976). At the same time that the work was being carried out, Feldesman (also 1976) was working independently on the same problem. Although these two investigations used different measurements taken on different specimens, and with different representation of genera throughout the primates, the overall result was almost identical (Figure 7:29).

A second example, the result of a study of the hominoid pelvis carried out by McHenry and Corruccini (1975), confirmed the comparable part of an earlier study by Zuckerman and colleagues. McHenry and Corruccini examined only those pelvic parts in which the fossil resembled humans. When that part of Zuckerman and colleagues study is compared, the results are almost identical (Figure 7:30). When the various other elements of the pelvis are also included, then the complete result obtained by Zuckerman, Ashton, Flinn, Oxnard and Spence (1973) and now confirmed and elaborated by Ashton, Flinn, Moore, Oxnard and Spence (1981) demonstrates the remarkable difference of the australopithecine pelvis from the human.

Yet a third example is the study of the primate talus by Day and Wood (1968) as compared with those by Lisowski, Albrecht and Oxnard (1974, 1976). Here, comparisons of rank orders in first canonical axes are virtually identical in the two studies (Figure 7:31). The controversy that arises is not due to the result being different, but to a different interpretation being applied to a similar result. Day and Wood interpreted their first canonical axis as measuring degree of bipedality, and surmized, therefore, that the australopithecines, which fell part way along that axis, were part way along the path to bipedality. In our studies orang-utans were also included. Though the relationships between humans and African apes in the two first

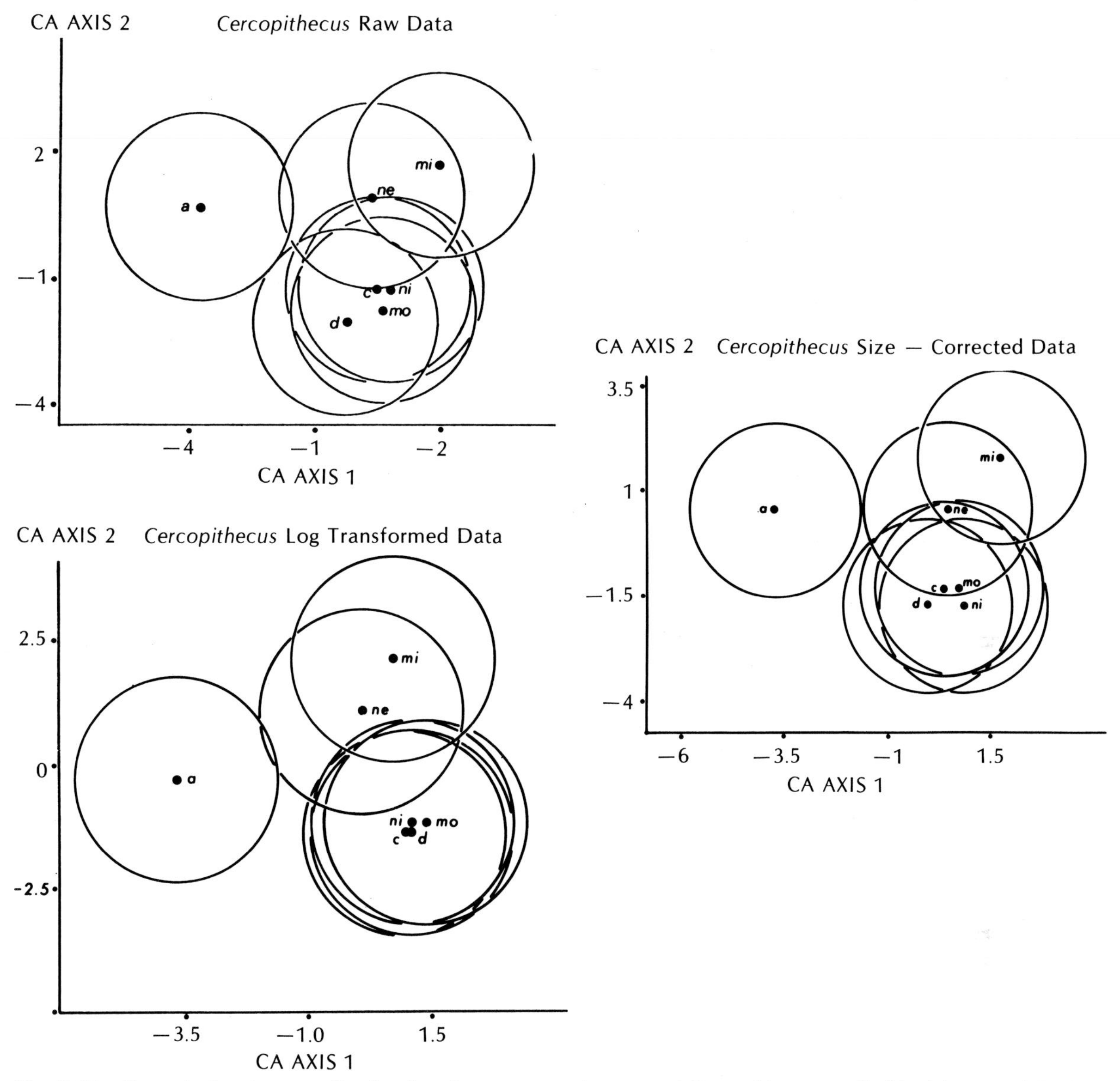

Fig. 7:26 Canonical variates studies for data from seven subgroups of *Cercopithecus* studied by Manaster (1976). The first plot shows the analysis of the raw data, the second of data log transformed, and the third of 'multivariate size corrected' data. There is almost no difference between the patterns of symbols representing each subgroup in these studies. In this case, presumably because the animals being investigated are enormously similar, manipulations aimed at 'allowing' for size had almost no effect. Possibly such size related effects as are present in this genus, and there must be some, were similar for each species.

canonical axes were indeed similar to what Day and Wood had found, the placement of the australopithecines together with the orang-utan denies the interpretation of Day and Wood.

Even other examples exist (e.g. similarities between two investigators in as many as three canonical axes in studies of the shoulder by Ashton, Flinn, Oxnard and Spence, 1971 and Corruccini and Ciochon, 1976). In this last case, careful inspection demonstrates that, notwithstanding different measurements, specimens, observers, and even a different multivariate technique, the results are basically the same (Figure 7:32).

Indeed, if one thing is remarkable about the multivariate, statistical approach it is exactly that it can be replicated by different investigators far more easily than the older technique of visual assessment.

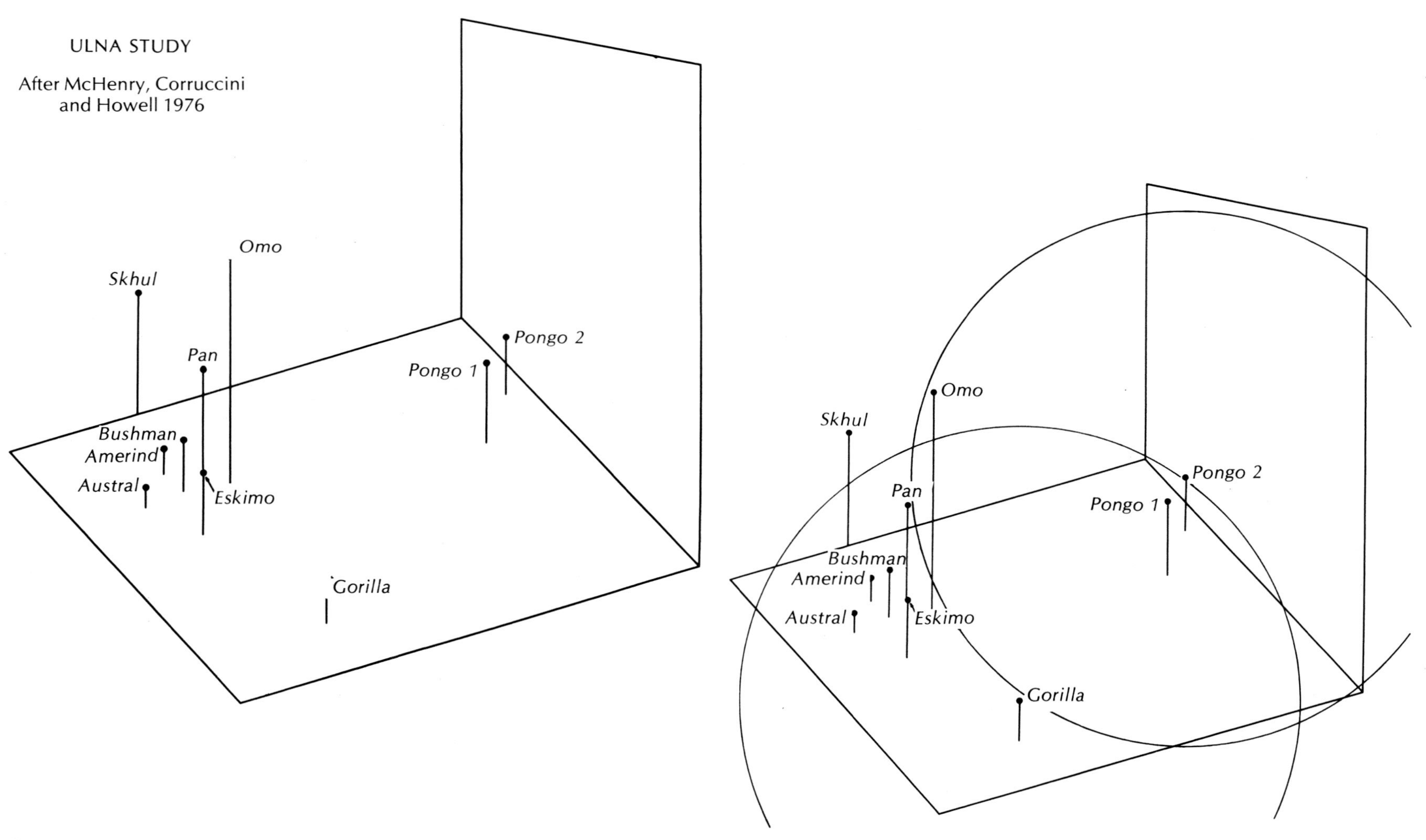

Fig. 7:27 A multivariate statistical study of the ulna. In this study an allometric 'size correcting' manipulation was introduced. This first frame shows the separations of the genera that were produced in the three-dimensional plot of the first three axes. Note that there is no scale in this diagram. Interpretations were made based upon how close certain species were to other species.

The second frame shows the picture when approximate (because of perspective problems) 95 percent limit circles are drawn around representative species. In fact the sensitivity of this analysis can be seen to be so low that the model contains almost no information. The reason for this is that most of the information was removed along with 'size' by the 'allometric size correcting' manipulation.

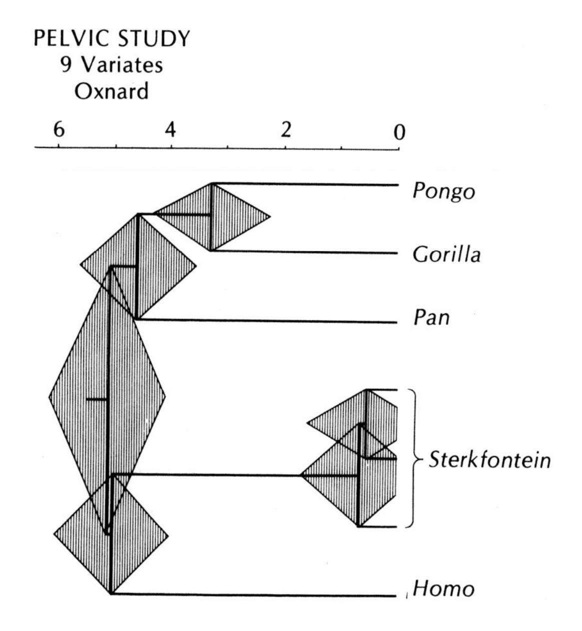

Fig. 7:28 1st Frame: A morphometric study of the pelvis in which the relationships are portrayed as a dendrogram (the thick lines). The fact that links in the dendrogram are only approximately determined is shown by the additional vertical shaded diamond-shaped areas. These indicate the 95 per cent limits that should be placed upon the dendrogram links. Therefore the actual dendrogram presented is only one of a number that could have been formed from the same data. Nevertheless the links are fairly well determined. In any of the possible dendrograms, the various extant species and the Sterkfontein fossil (three replicates are closely similar) are approximately equidistant from one another.

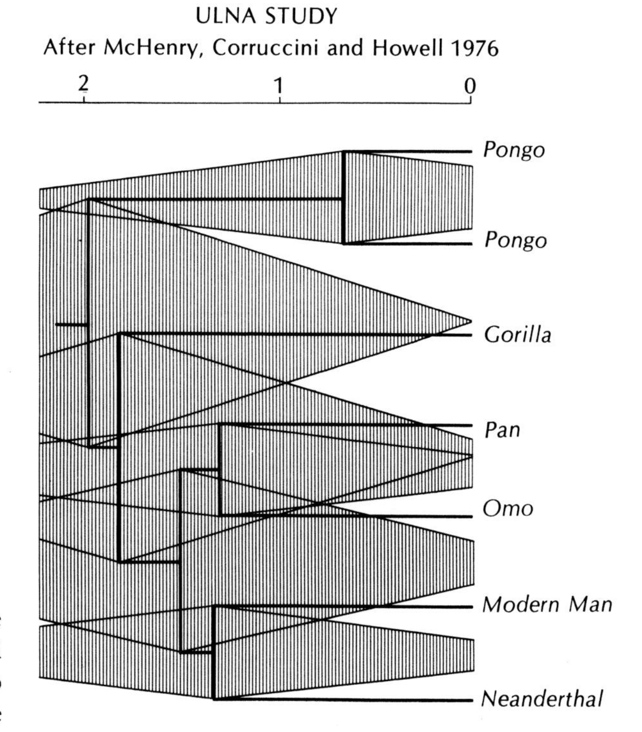

2nd Frame: The morphometric study of the ulna in which the relationships are also portrayed as a dendrogram (the thick lines). Using the same conventions as above. In contrast with the first frame, the great extent of these limits indicates that the dendrogram contains scarcely any information at all. This is, again, because the 'allometric size removal' technique has removed not only size but also almost everything else from this study.

All the foregoing demonstrates that multivariate statistical analyses of structure may yield useful interpretations. Many tests are necessary in order to make certain that such interpretations are not the romancing of an uncritical mind. Especial care is required to prevent a particular subset of such interpretations from being specially selected as 'correct' over and above others for little good reason. Especially, also, is it necessary not to 'reject' certain parts of the multivariate information just because they do not 'fit' with a priori views of the biology of the situation.

The 'design of observations': These patterns of testing also suggest a process whereby some interpretations can be rendered even more rigorous. We might call this process: 'the design of observations' — parallel to the 'design of experiments' so long known in other areas of biological science.

For instance, naive comparative studies often compare two animal types. Though some useful information may come from such a study it is often not a particularly useful exercise. Morphological differences can almost always be found between two groups. It is too easy to assume that such differences are related to the functional differences being investigated, rather than to other, perhaps unrecognised, factors. This is especially the case in studies that look for differences associated with sex; such differences can almost always be found simply by increasing sample size. They may not necessarily be biologically important at all. This type of problem can be avoided in several ways.

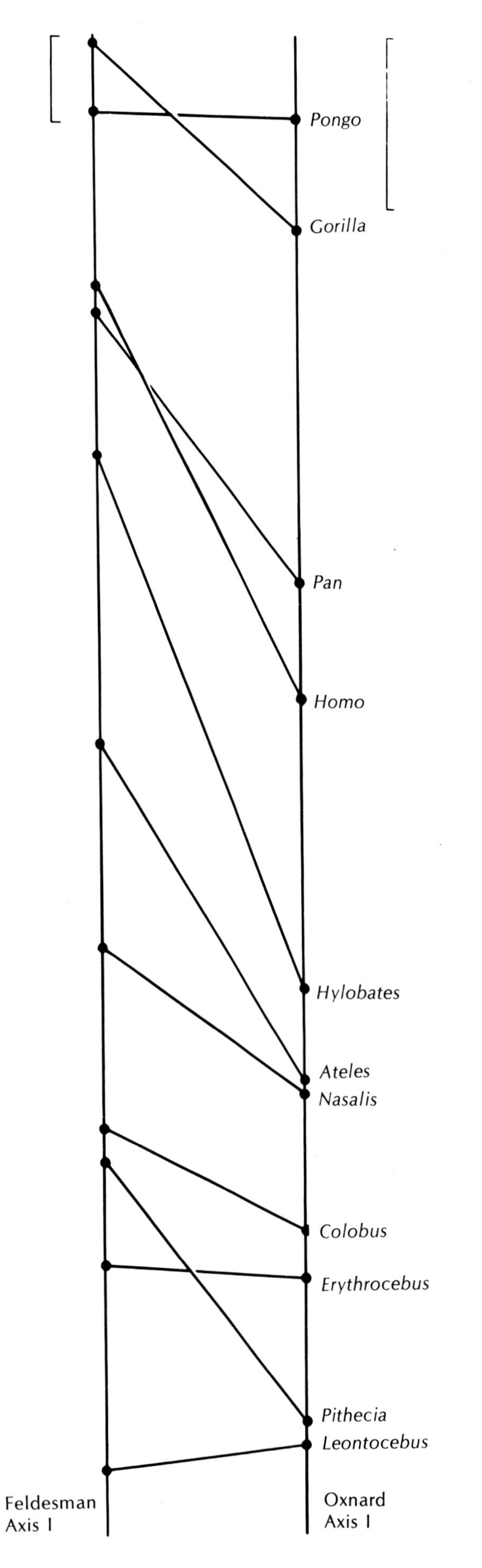

Fig. 7:29 ◁ Arm-forearm studies. Replication of rank orders in first canonical axis by two different investigators. Both investigators found the same result and made the same interpretations.

Fig. 7:30 ▽ Pelvic studies. Replications of plots in first two canonical axes of iliac variables by two different sets of investigators. Additional studies incorporating many more dimensions from the ischium and pubis make the final interpretations of the second investigators more complete and totally different. Note, there was no scale available for the upper graph. Δ = apes, ⊙ = humans, □ = fossils.

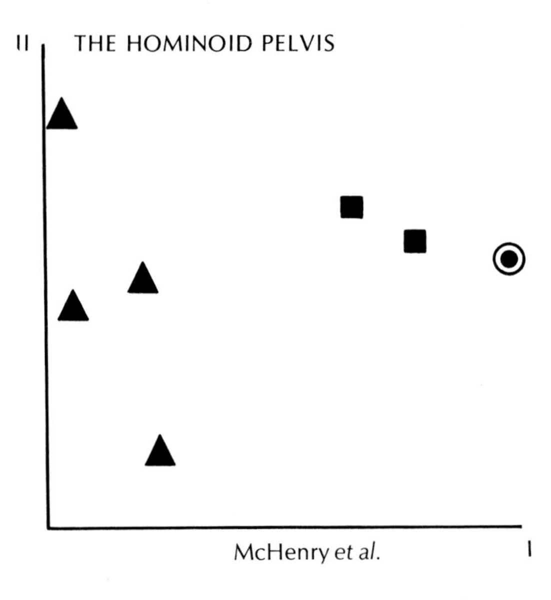

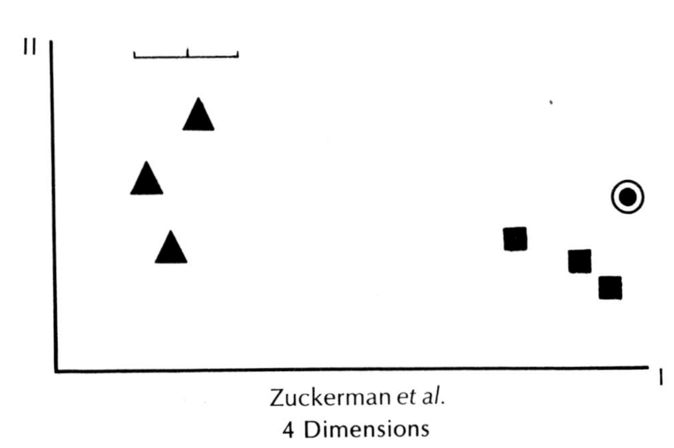

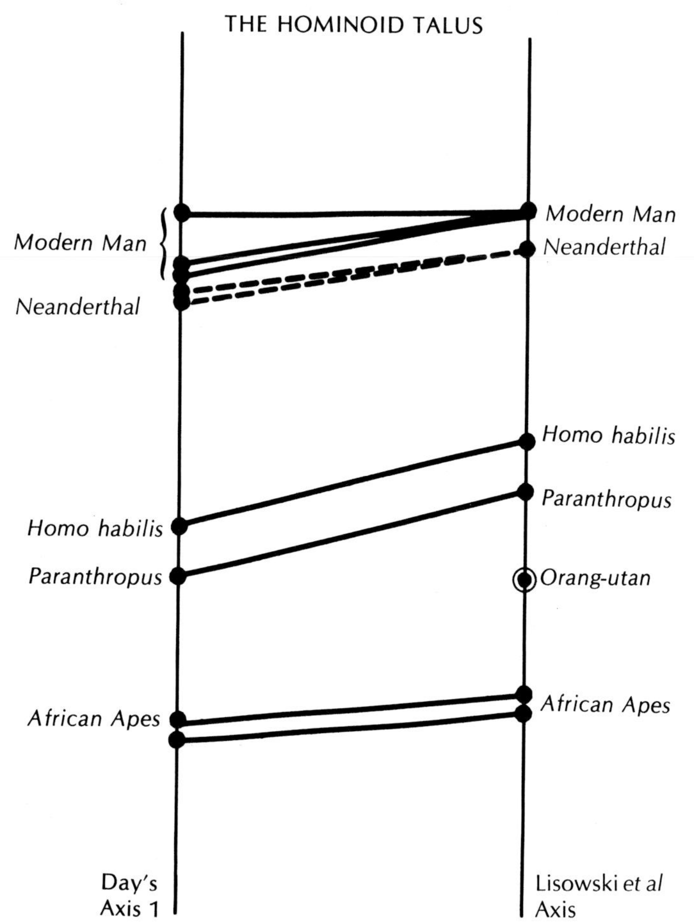

Fig. 7:31 Ankle bone studies. Replications of rank orders in first canonical axes by two different sets of investigators. The additional presence of the orang-utan in the second study makes the interpretations of the second investigators completely different.

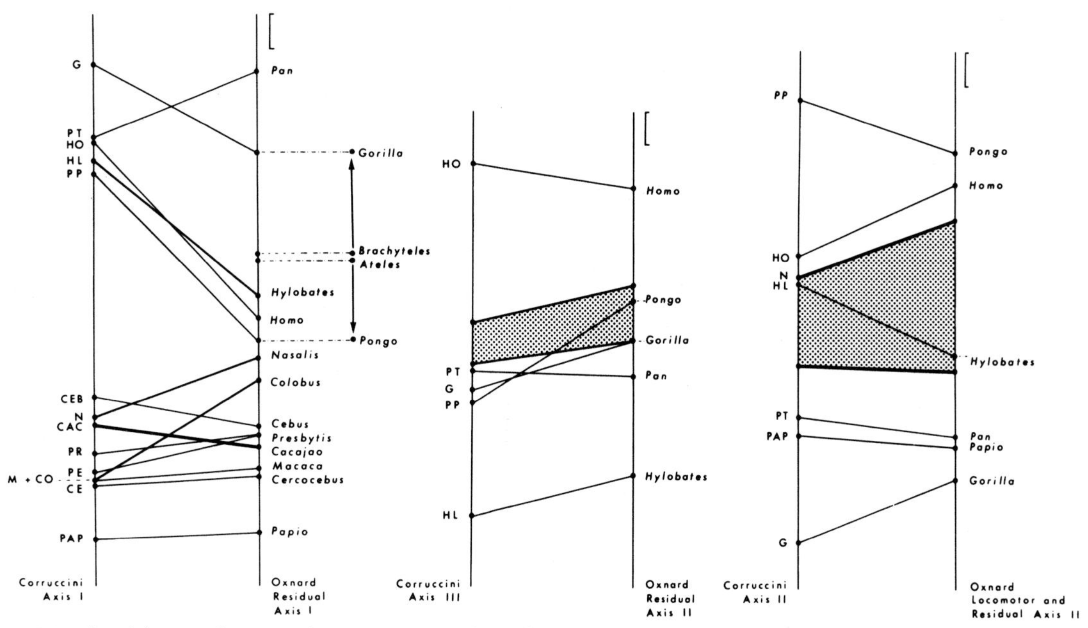

Fig. 7:32 Shoulder studies. Replications or rank orders in several different axes show that, notwithstanding different variables, different specimens and even a somewhat different multivariate statistical technique, the overall results are remarkably similar even though this was not recognized by Corruccini (1978). The shaded areas represent a number of closely placed species.

First, comparisons can be made among several sequential groups of animals displaying a consistent functional difference, or several pairs of sexes displaying a consistent sexual pattern (e.g. polygyny) rather than between a single pair. A similar spectrum of difference over several groups helps prevent spurious or accidental associations from wrongly channelling our ideas.

Second, comparisons may include several pairs of animals or several pairs of sexes displaying parallel situations in different taxonomic groups. This further increases the likelihood that the associations eventually drawn will be real. Considerations such as these can have a profound effect upon comparative anatomical studies.

Thus, from being merely a comparison of two organisms or two sexes of a single organism, such studies have a detailed internal design exactly aimed at increasing the information flowing from them, and especially designed to detect spurious results. In order to make these designs clear, let us look at some examples.

The simple attempt to discover the association between, say, climbing and upper limb structure might compare two animals, say *Cercopithecus aethiops*, which being more terrestrial climbs less, and *Cercopithecus diana*, which being more arboreal, climbs more. In the same way, a simple study designed to elucidate the nature of sexual dimorphism in a polygynous situation might look at the two sexes within a particular species known to be polygynous.

But how much more powerful are the kinds of studies (Oxnard, 1967; Manaster, 1975) which examined the linear series within the *Cercopithecus* group:

(a_1) terrestrial forms (e.g. *Erythrocebus patas*),
(a_2) semi-terrestrial (e.g. *C. aethiops*),
(a_3) arboreal main branch (e.g. *C. mitis*) and
(a_4) arboreal fine branch (e.g. *C. diana*)?

Any morphological or morphometric finding consistent within such a detailed linear series was considerably more likely to be related to the functional difference posited in the descriptions of habitat.

A similar linear design in studies of sexual dimorphism examined sexual dimorphism in a whole series of polygynous Old World monkeys (Oxnard, 1983c). Any findings made within such a serial design would be far more likely to discover a set of structural correlates underlying polygyny in general. This design would also allow the discovery of whether or not several different polygynous patterns existed. This, indeed, seems to be the finding of these investigations.

The second, even more powerful, observational design involves parallel studies. Thus a design to discover associations between more and less terrestrial forms (Oxnard, 1968) involved five parallel sequences as:

(a_1) more and
(a_2) less arboreal squirrels,
(b_1) more and
(b_2) less arboreal carnivores,
(c_1) more and
(c_2) less arboreal edentates,
(d_1) more and
(d_2) less arboreal marsupials,
(e_1) more and
(e_2) less arboreal primates.

Any morphological findings consistent within these parallel sequences is highly likely to be related to the functional descriptions implied in the descriptions of habitat of the animals.

A similar design to discover differences in structure possibly related to climbing (Oxnard, 1967; Manaster, 1979) included comparison of:

(a_1) more and
(a_2) less arboreal cercopitheques,
(b_1) more and
(b_2) less arboreal mangabeys,
(c_1) more and
(c_2) less arboreal macaques,
(d_1) more and
(d_2) less arboreal langurs.

Again, these four parallel sequences allowed the detection of differences in structure associated with the functional differences implied in the descriptions of habitat.

Such design in studies of sexual dimorphism examines sexual dimorphism in parallel sets of polygynous hominoids, Old World monkeys, New World monkeys, and prosimians. An additional element of design is introduced in those studies by examination of further parallel sets of monogamous hominoids, Old World monkeys, New World monkeys and prosimians (Oxnard, 1983c). Any findings made within such a parallel or multiple parallel design may be even more likely to discover a set, or several sets, of structural correlates underlying sexual dimorphism. The plurality of the situation seems to be one major finding of these investigations.

In each of these examples, the 'design of observations' holds constant, or constantly varying, biological features unrelated to the elements under discussion. It is in this sense that these designs mirror the design of experiments.

Although the earliest of our studies did not show

such explicit design, at least part of our success in multivariate statistical interpretation may be due to the implicit existence of such design (e.g. Oxnard 1967). In our more recent studies the designs are quite overt (e.g. Oxnard, German and McArdle, 1981; Oxnard, German, Jouffroy and Lessertisseur, 1981; Oxnard, 1983a, 1984, and this book).

It is not common for attention to be drawn to this type of design in morphological studies. It is, however, my opinion, that as we come to study in greater and greater detail more refined groupings of animals, differences will become of so fine a grade that design of this type will be necessary to reveal clear information. Certainly such designs are essential in studies of sexual dimorphism in closely related species. They can be expected to refine yet further the interpretations that can be obtained from multivariate statistical studies.

Conclusions on Multivariate Statistical Problems

A certain reluctance to utilize the findings of much multivariate statistical work in the study of fossils seems to be due to lack of appreciation of the amount of testing that these methods have undergone. The foregoing outlines the many ways in which the methods have been tested. These tests are all the more important when, as not uncommonly occurs, multivariate statistical studies provide results that question conventional ideas and suggest new concepts.

Thus, the interpretations resulting from individual studies were tested by serial investigations that attempted to examine the same hypotheses from several different aspects.

Further, the interpretations resulting from individual studies were tested through parallel sets of investigations designed to see if the hypotheses spread themselves appropriately into neighbouring anatomical regions.

Individual multivariate studies also contain their own series of internal statistical tests. Such tests are usually only very briefly described in scientific publications. The tests we have used are here categorized and drawn together.

Of especial importance in the acceptance of multivariate statistical results is their repeatability. This has been questioned, especially by those who do not use the methods themselves. In fact, repeatability is easily obtained within the same laboratory. And contrary to common belief, repeatability is also easily obtained even by competing laboratories.

Many of these tests have led to an appreciation that multivariate statistical studies can be conducted within a 'design of observations' that is somewhat reminiscent of the design of experiments.

All these concepts have been used in our studies of the postcranial skeleton of primates over many years. They have been particularly applied in these new studies of the hominoid dentition.

Summary: In this chapter we have been concerned to examine our data and our methods as critically as possible. For the data and the methods are not perfect; they cannot be perfect. We have taken account of such factors as we could. But we are left with a certain bulk of uncertainty that is irreducible at the present time. Understanding such technical uncertainty is essential in arriving at judgements to be applied to the final discussion and conclusions of Chapter 8.

CHAPTER 8

A New Perspective On Human Evolution

The living primates: morphological, molecular and morphometric agreement

Thinking about a new perspective on human evolution requires that we first know the old. The old story can be told at a number of different levels. A first level is the entire Order Primates. There is remarkable unanimity among almost all investigators in the broad picture of primate relationships.

Since the time of Charles Darwin it has been well established that humans evolved from tree-living animal ancestors. We know this mainly from studies of classical morphology. Comparison of our anatomy with those of lower primates (creatures such as pottos, tarsiers and bushbabies), of monkeys (from both the New and Old Worlds) and, of course, of apes has resulted in a single broad view. It is one that sees all these animals belonging with us in the same zoological Order: the Primates.

A second level relates to us and our closest relatives. This is the idea that within the entire order, there is a natural alliance: humans and apes forming the superfamily Hominoidea.

These were the opinions of the older comparative anatomists such as the first Huxley (1895, see also Elliott, 1913). And they are also the consensus judgements of most of the primate biologists of the present century (e.g. Zuckerman, 1933; Le Gros Clark, 1959; Schultz, 1969).

In the last twenty years that broad picture has been confirmed by new studies of molecules. They corroborate the major groupings of the primates: prosimians, New World monkeys, Old World monkeys and hominoids. They especially confirm the link of humans with apes in the Hominoidea (Fig. 8:1).

Most recently of all, this broad picture has been further corroborated by morphometric studies of the type described in this book. They encompass multivariate statistical studies of measurements describing most regions of the anatomy of the body taken from more than fifty per cent of the genera of the Order (Oxnard, 1981a, 1983a, b, 1984).

These agreements are most gratifying.

A third level of relationship is to do with associations among the various apes and humans. Thus most morphologists (e.g. Elliott, 1913; Simpson, 1945; Le Gros Clark, 1959 agreed that there was a major subdivision within the living Hominoidea. This was believed to be a subdivision between, on the one hand, **all apes (gibbons, siamangs, orang-utans, chimpanzees and gorillas)** and on the other, **humans (including, of course, prehuman fossils)**.

This dichotomy is thought to be so strong that it remains, even today, formalized into classification through the taxonomic terms 'Pongidae' meaning the family of ape-like forms, and 'Hominidae' the family of human-like forms (Hershkovitz, 1977). This view also implies that the phylogenetic division

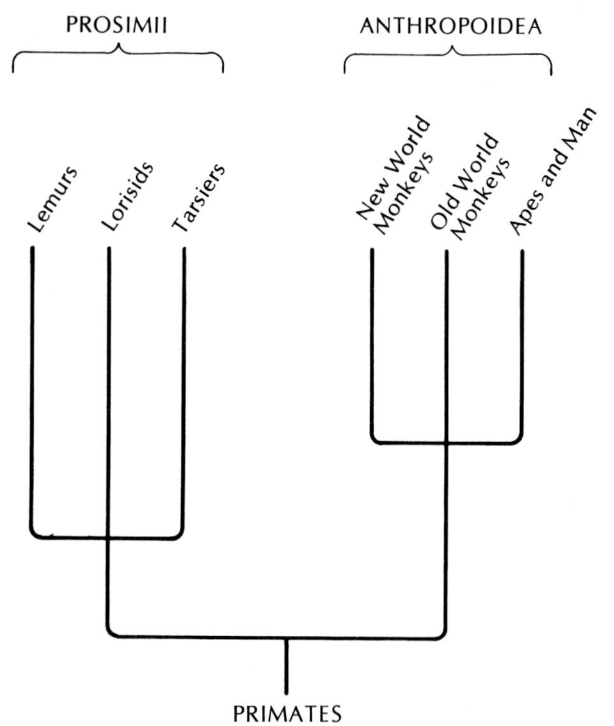

Fig. 8:1 A somewhat simplistic, but at a broad level not necessarily completely incorrect, view of the relationships of the primates. (Tarsiers may be more completely intermediate between prosimians and anthropoids, or even distantly but more closely related to anthropoids). A view not unlike this is seen whatever methods, morphological, molecular, or morphometric, are used for studying the primates at the broad level.

is between all apes and all humans and though an old idea, this, too, has been maintained by some almost to the present day (e.g. Tuttle, 1977).

But this third idea is not confirmed by studies of molecules or morphometrics.

The living hominoids: molecular disagreement

Although, as described above, the new molecular studies generally confirm the broad arrangements of the primates that stem from classical morphology, this is not the case when we look in detail at smaller subdivisions of the primates. The older morphological view of the subdivision within the hominoids is now challenged by the new molecular evolution. Within the Hominoidea study of the molecules finds two different subgroupings. One of these comprises **humans together with gorillas and chimpanzees**; the other consists of **orang-utans alone**, or possibly, **orang-utans together with the lesser apes, gibbons and siamangs**. This link, between ourselves and the African apes, is now believed to be so close that it has become almost a truism. Humans and chimpanzees may hold in common as much as 98% of their genetic materials.

The results from the molecules, though by no means as extensive as the centuries of data from classical morphology, do now depend upon the studies of large numbers of investigators, using techniques as widely different as those of cytogenetics, immunodiffusion, radioimmunoassay, electrophoresis, microcomplement fixation, nucleic acid hybridisation, restriction endonuclease mapping and DNA-DNA hybridization.

At this juncture we should remind ourselves that both classical morphology and biomolecular methods are much older than we generally realize.

The use of morphology as a way to understand animal relationships stems from long before any confident understanding of evolution itself. Belon in 1555 figures a comparison of the skeletons of a human and a bird, clearly recognizing homologies, for instance, between wings and arms. Aristotle knew some of this even in a prior millenium. Knowledge of equivalent similarities between human and simian structures (e.g. by Galen of Pergamum) is indeed old.

Molecular evolution is likewise far older than we usually assume. Such studies exploded as a result of the biomolecular revolution of two decades ago. It is usual to credit Zuckerkandl and Pauling, in the early sixties, with the idea that evolutionary relationship might be read directly through a measure of molecular distance. But a seminal review by Zuckerman more than fifty years ago (1933) pinpointed very clearly the use of biochemical and related phenomena for understanding the relationships of primates. Works on topics such as, primate blood reactions and the understanding that this could speak to matters of phylogeny, were abroad as early as the turn of the century in England (Nuttall, 1904) and in Germany (Friedenthal, 1900). Half a century before that, however, Darwin himself had glimpsed the possibility:

> 'Nevertheless all living things have much in common, in their chemical

composition, their cellular structure, . . . and their liability to injurious influences.'

How much closer could Darwin have come, given the language of his day, to the concepts of molecular, ultrastructural and immunological evolution of our times?

Morphometrics and the relationships of apes and humans

With the advent of computers morphometrics has become available to help in the study of the relationships of animals. It depends, like classical morphology, upon investigations of structure at the organ and organismal level. But it is carried out, like molecular evolution, using modern ideas, techniques and equipment. Morphometrics allows the enormous and diverse complexity of animal form to be rendered quantitatively. It analyses the resulting morphological quantities using methods that can eliminate the redundant information they contain. It reveals elements of animal form and pattern that are not available to the naked eye.

There are many individual ways of applying morphometrics to the problems of animal complexity (cluster finding procedures, image analysis and pattern recognition, mathematical transformations, and so on, Oxnard, 1978a). But the best known and the most widely used at present are various methods often known generally as multivariate statistical analysis. The development of these statistics is rather old depending upon the work of such masters as Fisher (1936), Hotelling (1936), Mahalanobis (1936) in the thirties, and with roots that extend back into the last century through Pearson (1901), Galton (1889) and others. But until the computer developments of recent decades, these techniques had not been especially valuable for tackling complex problems of biological structures. They are now, however, being used rather extensively to help us understand the tangled relationships of many groups of organisms and the complex structures of many detailed anatomies.

Almost from the beginning of my research career, and with the support and collaboration of Professor Lord Zuckerman and Professor E. H. Ashton of the University of Birmingham, U.K., I have participated in the use of morphometric tools for studying the structures of prosimians, monkeys, apes and humans. In the beginning, the morphometric investigations tried mainly to understand the functional anatomy of particular regions of the body. At later stages, the morphometric studies were additionally aimed at investigating phylogenetic relationships of particular species among the primates (both living and fossils). Most recently still the investigations have become extensive enough that they impact upon our understanding of the internal complexities of the anatomies of the whole organism, and of the primates as an Order.

Thus, early studies allowed us to understand something of the structure and function of the primate shoulder and pelvis (e.g. Ashton, Healy, Oxnard and Spence, 1965; Zuckerman, Ashton, Flinn, Oxnard and Spence, 1973). Later studies were aimed at evaluating individual fossil fragments such as *Australopithecus* (e.g. Oxnard 1968a, b, 1973a, b, 1975a, b) and individual living species such as *Tarsius* (e.g. Oxnard 1973c, 1976, 1978b). The most recent studies of all are complex morphometrical analyses of most of the anatomy of almost all the genera representing the entire Order (e.g. Oxnard, 1981a, 1983a, d, 1984).

These investigations are based upon the voluminous data of some dozen investigators, united in my collaborations. They include not only continued collaboration with the original Birmingham group, but also, at different times, with students and colleagues in, successively, Chicago and Los Angeles, with transplanted Birmingham workers (Hong Kong, Hobart, Leeds), and with collaborators from other laboratories (Stony Brook, Paris, Hong Kong [University of Hong Kong and Chinese University of Hong Kong], Beijing [Institute of Vertebrate Paleontology and Paleoanthropology, Academia Sinica], Lawrence [Kansas] and Northridge [California]).

The methods used include personal dissection of many hundreds of primate cadavers, observations made upon many thousands of bones, and analyses of many tens of thousands of measurements taken upon them. The investigations represent almost every region of the primate body (upper and lower limbs, trunk, and head and neck), and almost a complete array of the genera (and in some subdivisions, even species) of the Order Primates. They have been carried out using a battery of techniques ranging from simple dissection and osteological examination, through osteometry, simple and multivariate statistics, cluster analyses, and studies of stress and strain in anatomical situations, to image and pattern recognition culminating in Fourier transforms of bone sections and radiographic patterns using lasers. They span a period of continuous investigation of almost thirty years and are summarized in *THE ORDER OF MAN: A Biomathematical Anatomy of the Primates* (Hong Kong University Press, 1983 and Yale University Press, 1984).

What are the most recent results of this entire programme of morphometric research on the Primates as an Order?

One result is confirmatory, but almost inconsequential.

It is that, like morphologies and molecules before them, it has confirmed the broad view: a pattern of clustering that separates the major groups, prosimians, New World monkeys, Old World monkeys, and hominoids, and places all within a single Order, the Primates (Fig. 8:1).

But a second result is startling.

It speaks to the new molecular perception: that the largest primates of all are subdivided into two groups. The first consists of **orang-utans** (or perhaps **orang-utans rather distantly linked with lesser apes, gibbons and siamangs**). The second comprises **gorillas, chimpanzees and humans** very closely linked indeed. In this matter of clustering humans and African apes morphometrics mirrors molecules rather than morphologies (Fig. 8:2).

Lest we think that such a finding is only accidental it should be recorded that it has been corroborated in two ways. The **first** depends upon the same morphometric result being obtained from two quite different analyses: one from the addition of a series of rather broad measurements of the overall proportions of the primates (Oxnard, 1981a), and another from the summation of many detailed dimensions of smaller anatomical regions (Oxnard, 1983d). The **second** corroboration rests upon the finding that a similar series of discordances between classical morphology and molecular evolution exists in each of the other segments of the Order (Old World monkeys, New World monkeys, prosimians) and in each case, it is the molecular side that is supported by morphometrics (Oxnard, 1981a, 1983a, d, 1984).

Surely the molecular view is likely to reflect more correctly the evolutionary story, dealing as it does with molecules, the very stuff of evolution. The molecular methods confirm, absolutely, that gorillas, chimpanzees and humans are as close in time, evolutionarily speaking, as the blinking of an eye. **This new corroboration from morphometrics is the first time that information at the organismal level has reinforced the idea of the molecular propinquity of African apes and humans.**

Even within this last decade some primate morphologists were still publishing evolutionary diagrams that placed African apes with orang-utans and separated them as all great apes from humans (e.g. Tuttle, 1977). But the last few years have actually seen a major acceptance by most morphologists that the biomolecular viewpoint represents the likely truth of the matter.

The only major exception to this modern consensus arises from those who view certain special similarities between humans and orang-utans as measures of evolutionary closeness between these two species (e.g. Schwartz, 1984). This is clearly controversial, however, as there are several different possibilities. For instance, Walker (1984) searches for an explanation in the idea of the orang-utan as a 'living fossil'. Our own studies (Oxnard, 1969, 1973b, 1975a) have long noticed such similarities but relied on functional explanations. The combination of both these latter seems to make most biological sense.

The view of a special relationship between orang-utans and humans depends heavily upon the notions of cladistics as applied to similarities and differences in observable anatomical features.

Some types of resemblances between such features ('characters') are well recognized in cladistics.

For example, some similarities between orang-utans and humans may be due to the possession by both species of ancient characteristics that have not changed in either lineage (though they have changed in the later evolution of the African apes from a pre-human/pre-African ape line). To make this judgement we would have to know that orang-utans and humans were anciently connected. Some similarities may also be due to the possession by both species of novel characteristics that have changed after the separation of their conjoint lineage from that of the African apes. To make this judgement we have to know that orang-utans and humans were recently connected. It would appear that such designations cannot then be used to discover if the relationships between the species are ancient or modern without invoking circular reasoning.

Other types of resemblances between observable features are not recognised so readily by cladistics.

Some resemblances, for instance, may result from both orang-utans and humans displaying special features that arise from their present (orang-utan) and past (presumably both orang-utan and pre-human) abilities at climbing in trees. More detailed functional-structural study (not

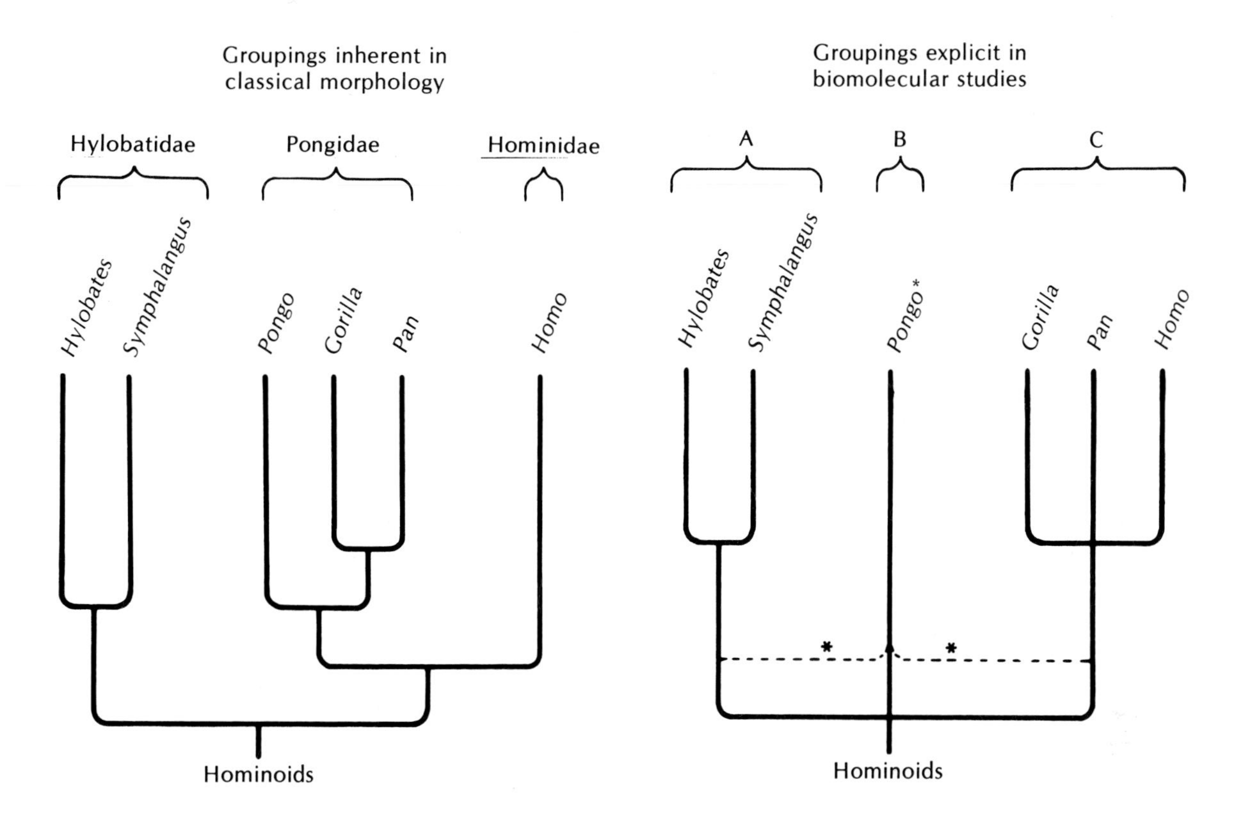

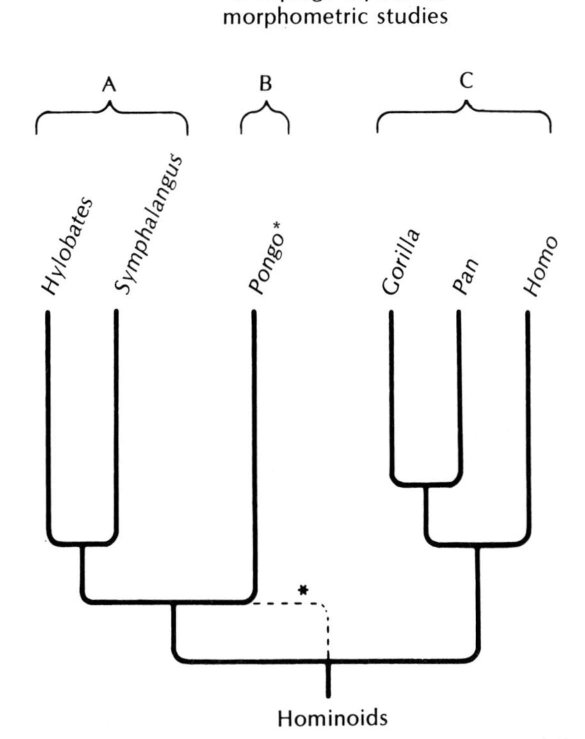

Fig. 8:2 A more detailed view of the relationships of the hominoids when different kinds of evidence are used. It shows that there is a clash between the morphological (first frame) and molecular (second frame) views. This latter is the one generally accepted today, even by morphologists. This figure also shows that the even newer morphometric (third frame) view aligns itself with the molecular information.

cladistic investigation) may be able to tell us whether these similar abilities (and hence similar anatomical features) are single retentions of primitive features or independently evolved parallel acquisitions.

Other resemblances, for example, may be due to the absence in both humans and orang-utans of functional features related to similarities in the functional histories of other, also closely related, species, the African apes. For instance neither humans nor orang-utans display the special features of the African apes that arise from their acquisition (whether early or late — let us not prejudge that issue) of special quadrupedal (knuckle-walking) behaviours. Again, only more detailed study may be able to tell us whether such functional resemblances are due to non-acquisition or loss after acquisition.

Yet other reasons may cause resemblances. Thus features that stem from the possession by orang-utans, of an arboreal habitus, may seem similar to those springing from an arboreal habitus of humans (past) but that, at the same time, proved useful without obvious modification for the human bipedal terrestrialism (present). Only more detailed studies of functional anatomy can suggest whether similarities may be due to the double functional potential of anatomical features.

Most of all, however, each anatomical resemblance is likely to include a combination of these various possibilities, a combination, that is to say, of both primitive and derived observable features ('characters'). These cannot, in our present phase of understanding, be disentangled by cladistics. Any assessment that evaluates a given observable feature as either primitive or derived (the decision that has to be made in cladistics) can only be wrong. For any observable feature must be made up of several underlying characters that truly may be primitive or derived.

We may not know what the combination of true underlying characters is (25% primitive and 75% percent derived or the reverse, or 50%-50%, or any other). We may not know the actual split. But we can know in the great majority of cases, indeed we can know almost with certainty, that the assessment of any split between primitive or derived for any given observable feature as 0%-100% or 100%-0%, the only assessment that can be made by cladistics, is wrong. Indeed, this may be the only thing about cladistics of which we can be certain.

It is true that the cladistic assessment may come close to being correct, in those cases where the contribution differential of underlying characters to any observable feature is, say, 80% or more of the same polarity. And it is also the case that in such a situation, what the cladistic method is doing, is assessing the observable feature as zero or one hundred per cent primitive or derived. Under this circumstance cladistics is taking a crude account of correlation and thus, acting as a crude multivariate statistics. This may be why it sometimes seems to give results that are similar to those of multivariate statistics. For example, the cladistic analyses of hominoid fossils by Wood (1985) provides a similar result (that currently known gracile australopithecines are not on the direct human lineage) as the multivariate statistical analyses of this volume.

But to return to the issue of orang-utan relationships, there is much reason to doubt the cladistic assertion that orang-utans and humans are more closely related to one another than is either to the African apes.

Into this new framework of the relationships of the living hominoids, we can now attempt to place those fossils that are best known. However, there are two ways in which we can do this. One represents the general consensus resulting from the views of most anthropologists until recently. The second is a challenge to the conventional view that has recently received remarkable new confirmation.

The relationships of the fossils: current consensus, current controversy

The general consensus about most of the fossils (all from Africa) has not, of course, remained static over the years. Figure 8:3 shows the basic plan that is generally accepted, and Figure 8:4 shows some of the variations on the theme that are currently being argued. The arguments revolve around which African fossils are seminal to the human line and which are on a parallel line, leading to the extinctions of the robust species. In the main, the discoverers (and their associates) of a particular fossil favour the lineage that places 'their' fossil on the main line towards humans and removes the fossils of 'others' from that favoured position. Despite such argument, however, there is an overall consensus. It is that all African finds, all australopithecines, now numbering many hundreds of specimens, are on or very close to the human lineage.

It follows, then, that there is also a second overall consensus. It is the idea that no African fossils (of

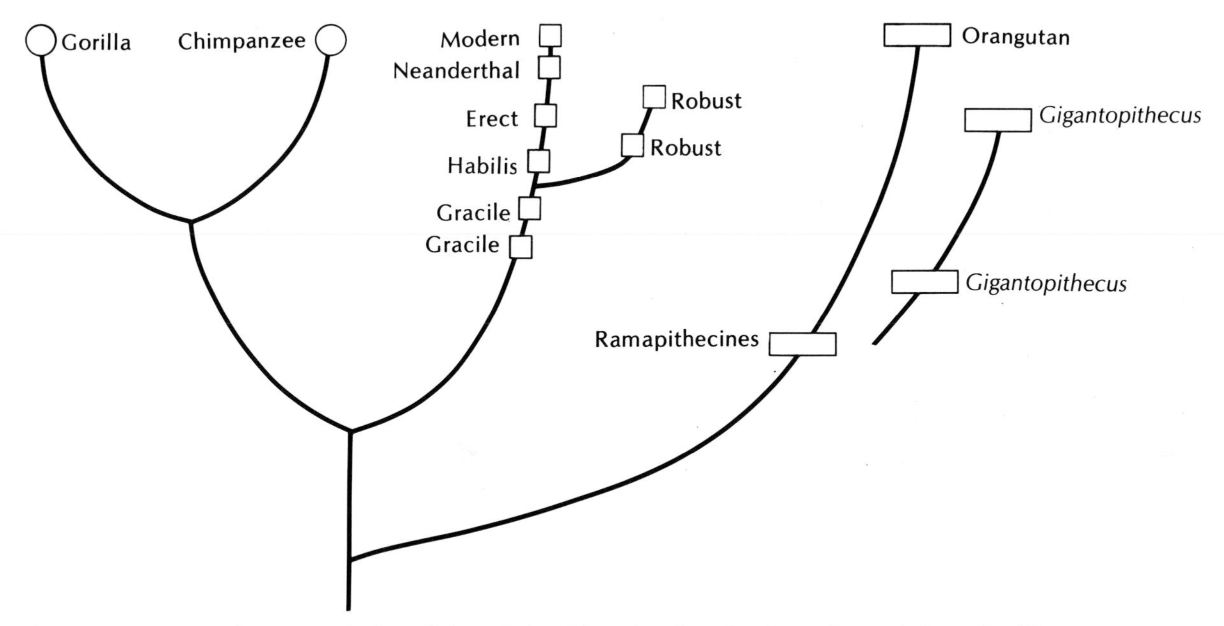

Fig. 8:3 A commonly accepted plan of the relationships of various fossils to those of about 8 million years ago. All African fossils (*Homo habilis*, early gracile: *Australopithecus afarensis*, late gracile, *A. africanus*, early robust, *A. robustus* and late robust, *A. boisei*) are on or close to the human lineage. All non-human Asian fossils (ramapithecines, *Gigantopithecus*) are on or close to ape lineages. There is plenty of disagreement within such a picture (for example: whether one of the great apes is closer to the human lineage than the other great ape, what is the timing of this phylogenetic tree, and so on) but the broad view is a general consensus.

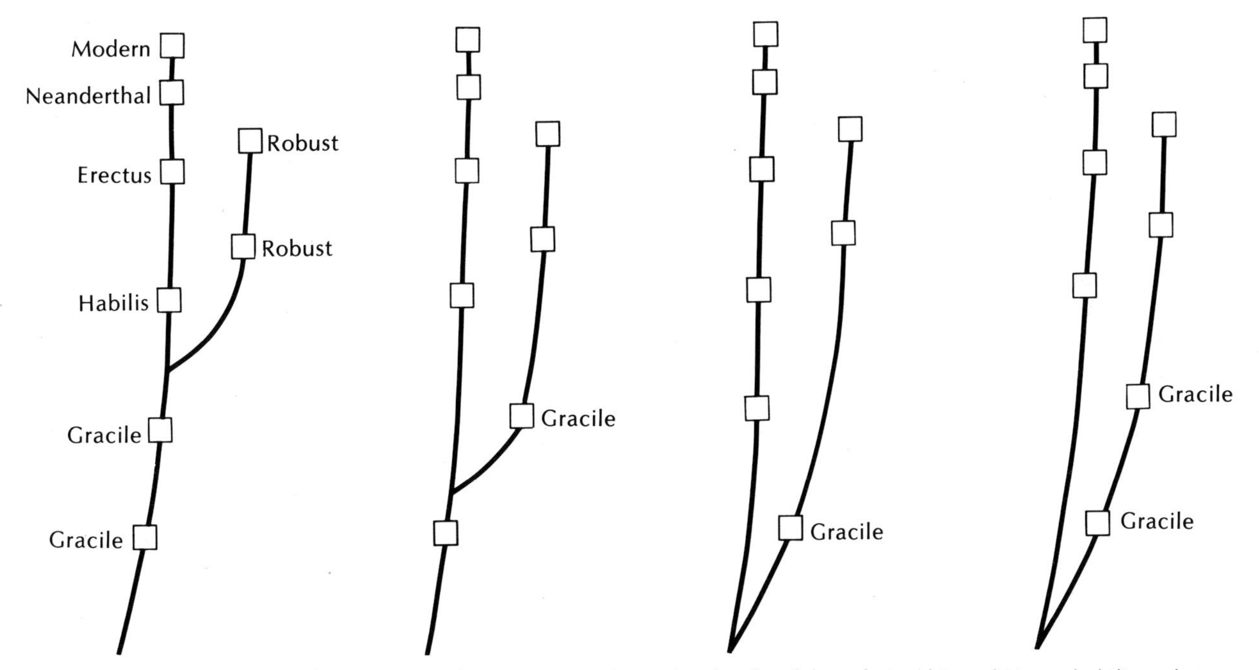

Fig. 8:4 The main points of argument with Fig. 8:3 are about the details of the relationships of *Homo habilis* and the various australopithecines to the human lineage. The first tree here gives the view held by many. Robust forms (*Australopithecus robustus* and *A. boisei*) are the side issue, all other are ancestral. The second tree is the view held by some discoverers of *A. afarensis*. It is that *A. afarensis* is the stem form; other australopithecines are off the main line. The third tree is the view held by some discoverers of *A. africanus*. It is that *A. africanus* is on the main line, *A. afarensis* leading to the side issue of the robust species. And finally the fourth tree is held by some of the discoverers of *Homo habilis*. It is that all the australopithecines are on the side lines; *Homo habilis* is the true one.

However, these are rather minor differences. All these possibilities are subsumed under the general verdict that the australopithecines are on or very close to the human lineage.

(First lineage fully labelled, subsequent lineages show only new positions labelled).

this time period) are on ape lineages.

Isn't this remarkable?

Yet a third point of consensus is the notion that none of these African fossils are clearly distinct from both extant ape and extant human lineages. Not one fossil represents, in other words, a clearly parallel or sibling form to both African apes and humans.

Isn't this, too, remarkable?

What, we may ask are the positions of Chinese fossils? There are at least two answers.

Those Chinese fossils that are clearly human, modern *Homo sapiens*, archaic *H. sapiens*, *H. erectus*, are well represented on the human lineage. Indeed the well preserved specimens (though now lost) from Zhoukoudian (Peking man) are amongst the earlier known. And the new archaeology in China is now yielding such large numbers of human fossils that a map of China with a spot for each newly discovered human fossil site looks as if it had measles (Fig. 8:5). Though these many human remains have been by no means fully studied, there can be no conclusion but that they represent early man in China, just as early man is represented almost everywhere else in the Old World. A casual glance shows that they are human in form (Fig. 8:6).

But what of Chinese fossils that are older than obviously human?

There are a few teeth that could possibly represent *Australopithecus* in China. They are, however, so few that a cautious approach denies that they can tell us anything until more are found (Fig. 8:7). Indeed, one recent investigator (Zhang Yinyun, 1984) believes that these may really be the teeth of very early *Homo erectus*. Any opinion biased by the notion that all important parts of human evolution occurred in Africa easily rejects any major importance attaching to these few teeth.

There are also a few teeth believed to represent *Dryopithecus* in China (Fig. 8:8). These are very few, very hard to assess without associated remains, and again, therefore, best left as problematical until more finds become available.

In addition, however there are the very extensive finds described earlier in this book that have also been made in different parts of China.

There are the several jaws and skulls, and many teeth of *Gigantopithecus* described in earlier chapters (Fig 8:9). Though early investigators perceived the possibility that this form was an aberrant giant human (e.g. Weidenreich, 1945; von Koenigswald, 1952), most workers now place it as an aberrant giant ape (Corrucini, 1975; Delson and Andrews, 1975; Simons and Pilbeam, 1978; Chopra, 1978).

And there are several jaws and skulls, and many teeth available for ramapithecines from China, also described in earlier chapters (Fig. 8:10). Again, the current consensus is that these forms are ape (probably pre-orang-utan, and probably female and male) ancestors (e.g. Smith and Pilbeam, 1980; Lipson and Pilbeam, 1982; Andrews and Cronin, 1982; Todd, 1982; Wu, Xu and Lu, 1983).

We thus perceive yet another interesting, but unlikely, element to the current pattern. Every African fossil is included as close to the human lineage, every Chinese fossil (except for those obviously *Homo*) is excluded (Fig. 8:3).

Isn't this most remarkable of all?

A new view of the relationships of the fossils

What are the challenges to these current views?

The current views as described take no account of a series of investigations into the structure of australopithecine fossils from Africa, studies that have been going on for many years now. At first these studies, mainly of cranial and dental features, seemed to show that in addition to possessing some human-like features, these creatures also have many ape-like features (e.g. Zuckerman, 1928; Ashton, 1950; Ashton and Zuckerman, 1950a, 1951, 1952, 1956, 1958; Ashton, Healy and Lipton, 1957). The ape-like characteristics had generally been overlooked or even denied by most investigators.

Later, the investigations came to include studies of primate postcranial anatomy. These included the shoulder (Ashton and Oxnard, 1963, 1964a, b; Ashton, Oxnard and Spence, 1965; Ashton, Healy, Oxnard and Spence, 1965; Ashton, Flinn, Oxnard and Spence, 1971; Oxnard, 1963, 1968c, 1969, 1972a, 1973a, 1977; Oxnard and Neely, 1969), the hip (Zuckerman, Ashton, Flinn, Oxnard and Spence, 1973; Ashton, Flinn, Moore, Oxnard and Spence, 1981: Oxnard, German and McArdle, 1981), the talus and foot (Lisowski, Albrecht and Oxnard, 1974, 1976; Oxnard 1980), overall bodily proportions (Ashton, Flinn and Oxnard, 1975; Oxnard, 1983a, 1984), the forelimb and hindlimb both separately and together (Oxnard, 1983a, 1984), limb proportions in prosimians (Oxnard, German, Jouffroy and Lessertisseur, 1981; Jouffroy,

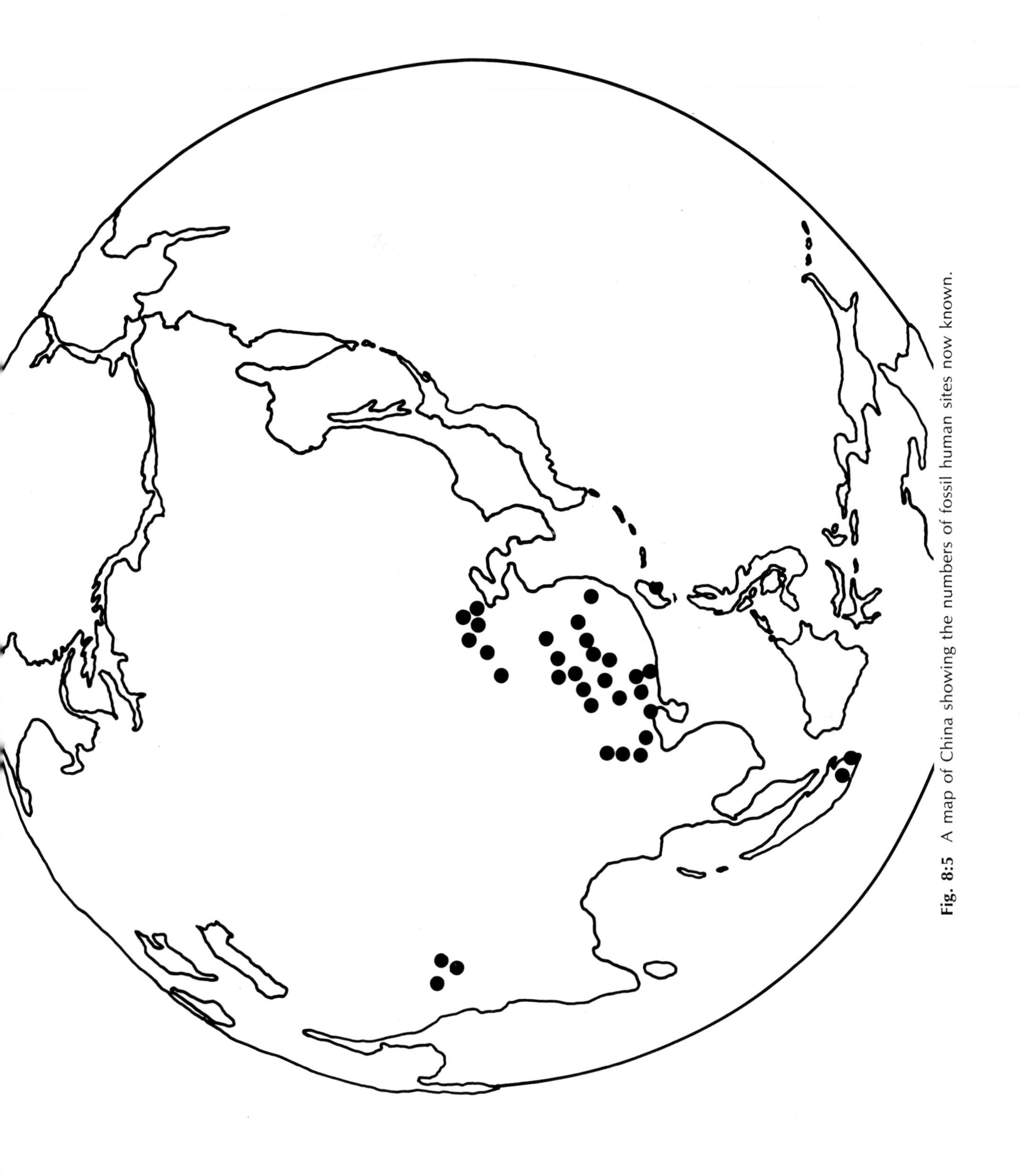

Fig. 8:5 A map of China showing the numbers of fossil human sites now known.

Fig. 8:6 ▷

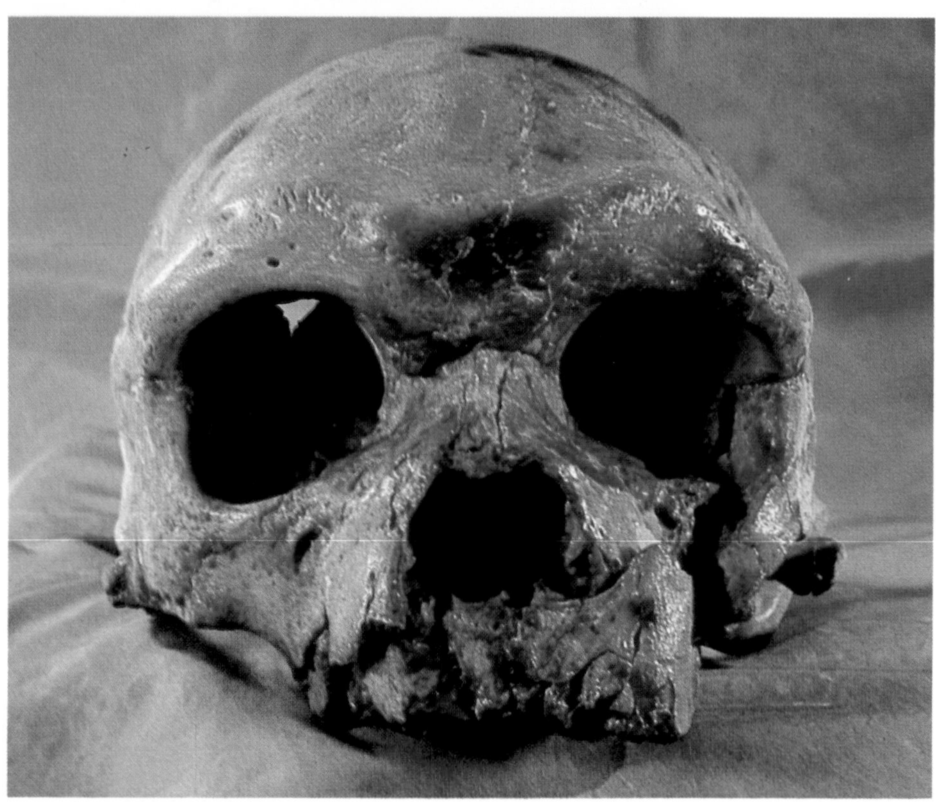

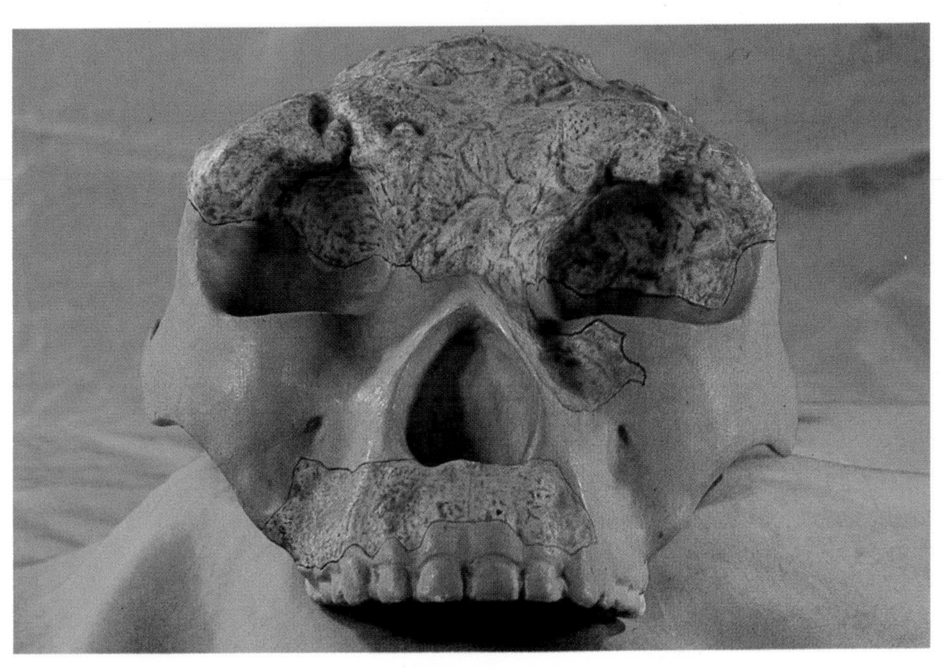

Fig. 8:6 Some of the human fossils unearthed in China: *Homo sapiens* and *Homo erectus* are both well represented (courtesy Professor Wu Rukang).

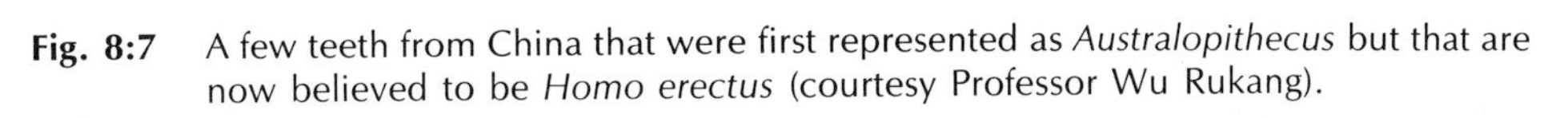

Fig. 8:7 A few teeth from China that were first represented as *Australopithecus* but that are now believed to be *Homo erectus* (courtesy Professor Wu Rukang).

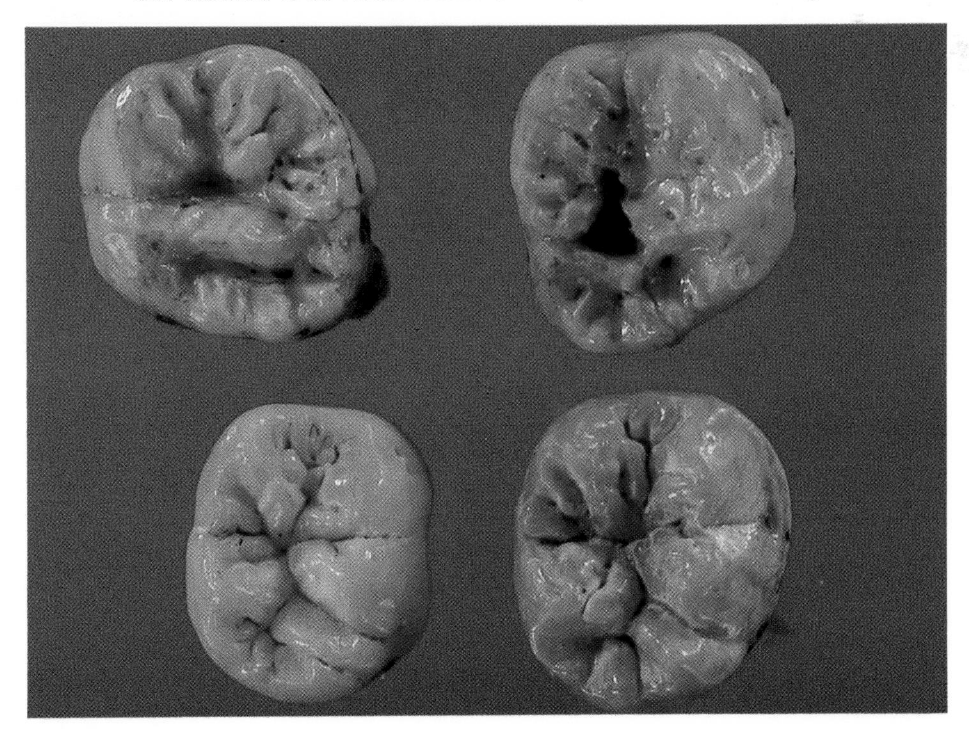

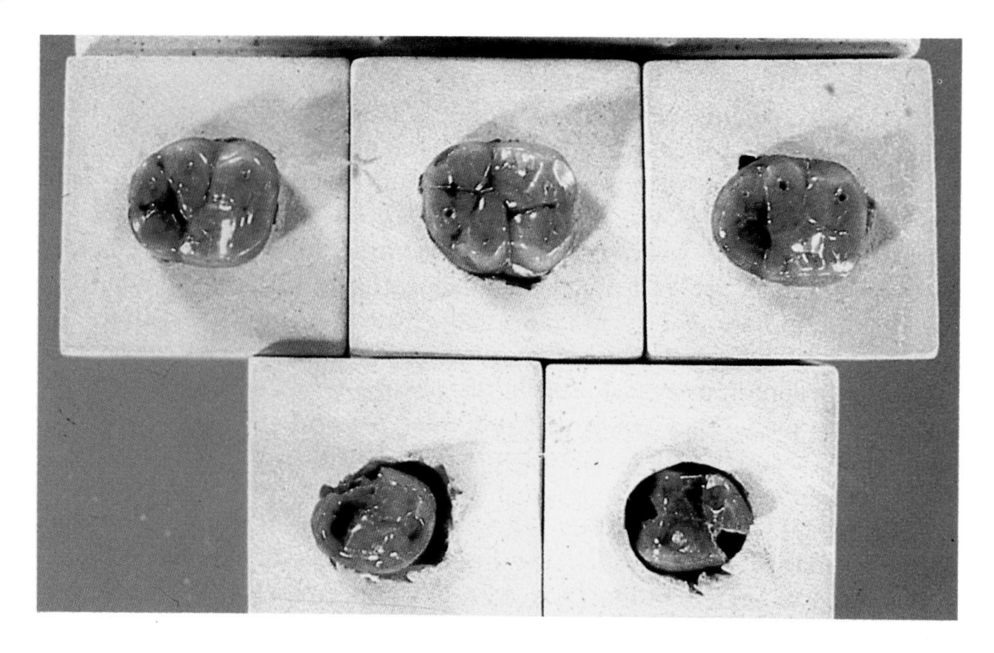

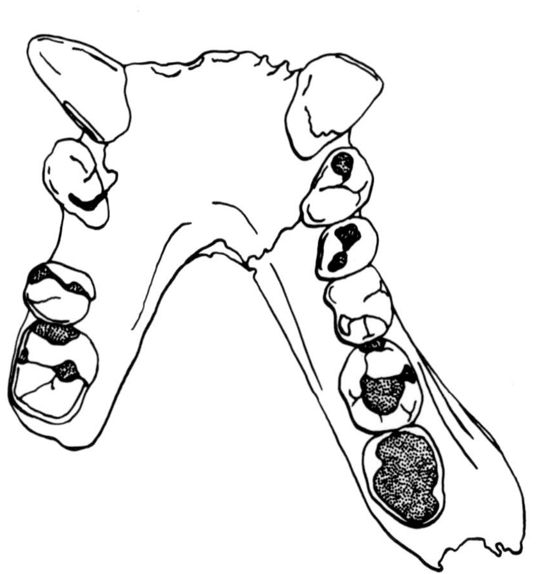

Fig. 8:8 A few teeth from China that may be *Dryopithecus* (courtesy Professor Wu Rukang) together with sketches of dryopithecine material from elsewhere.

Oxnard and German, 1981), vertebrae (Oxnard, 1972c; Oxnard and Yang, 1981; Oxnard, 1982), together with many other, more restricted investigations. These regional studies of the living primates are the basic materials against which can be compared such fossil postcranial fragments as become available.

As a result of these studies, it became possible to provide some new evaluations of various postcranial parts for the australopithecinae. These included new assessments for fossil clavicles, scapulae and shoulders in general (Oxnard, 1968b, 1968c, 1969), for fossil ankles and feet (Oxnard, 1972a; Lisowski, Albrecht and Oxnard, 1974,

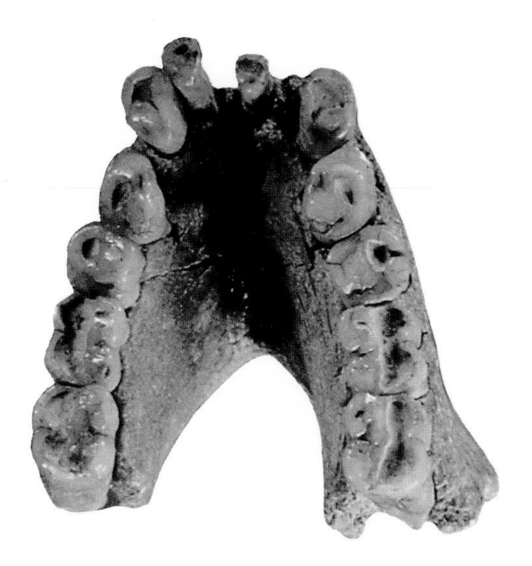

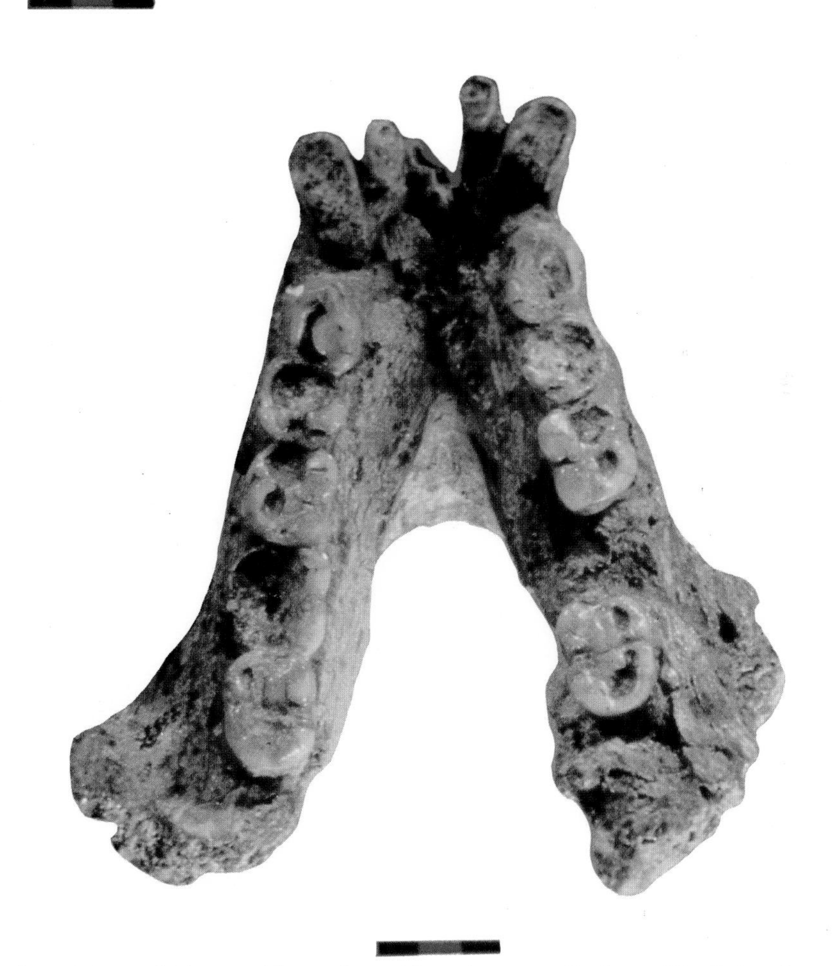

Fig. 8:9 Teeth and jaws of *Gigantopithecus* from China (courtesy Professor Wu Rukang).

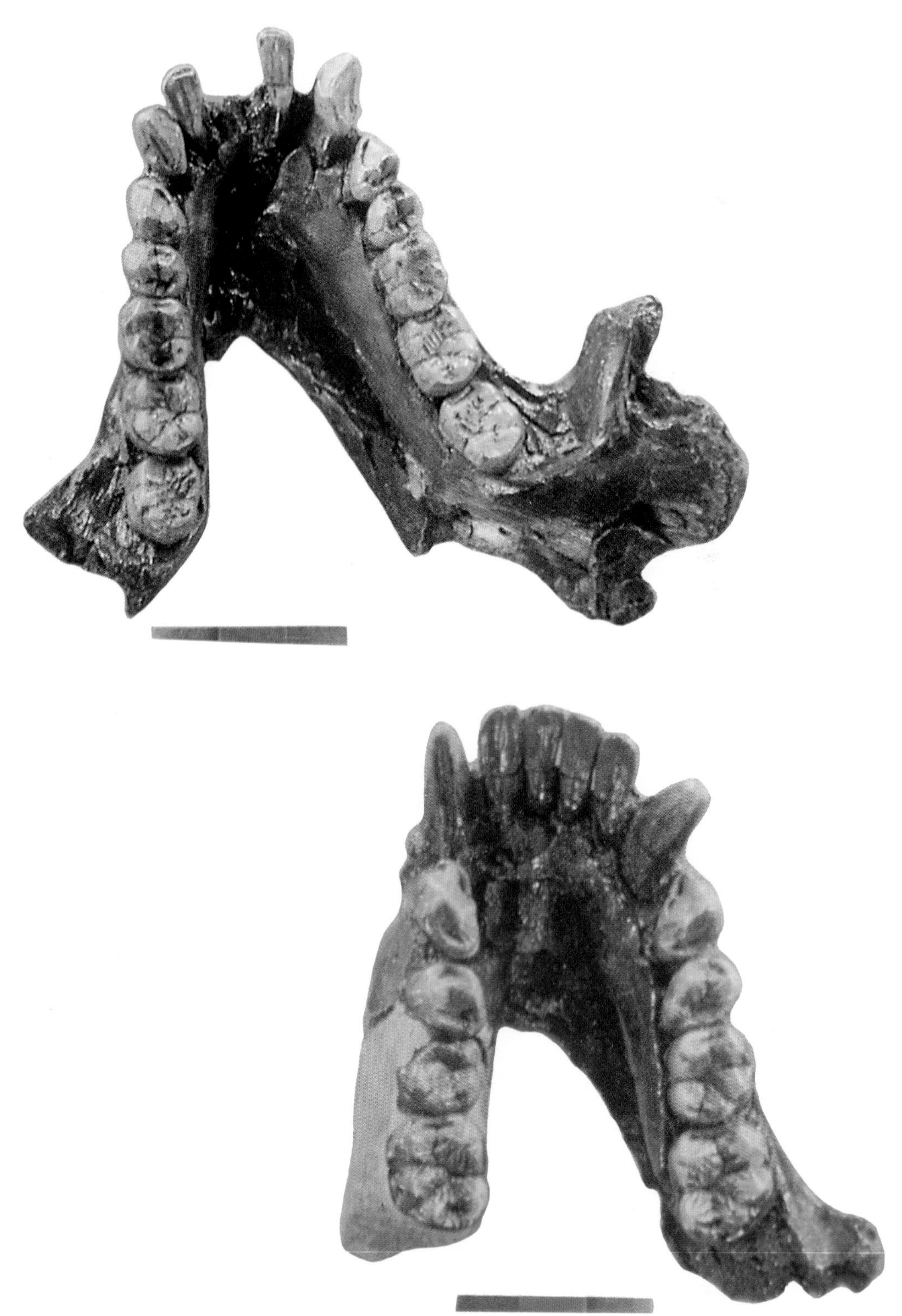

Fig. 8:10 Jaws of ramapithecines from China (courtesy Professor Wu Rukang).

1976; Oxnard, 1980), for fossil pelves (Zuckerman, Ashton, Flinn, Oxnard and Spence, 1973; Ashton, Flinn, Moore, Oxnard and Spence, 1981) and for many other individual anatomical regions of fossils including humerus, hand, and knee as well as regions already mentioned (Oxnard, 1973a, b, 1975a, b, 1979, 1983a, 1984). In addition, a series of further studies on different regions of fossil crania were progressing and providing similar findings (e.g. Adams and Moore, 1975, Ashton, Flinn and Moore, 1975; Ashton, Moore and Spence, 1976).

Eventually, as a result of all these studies, a new descriptive idea can be added to the prior concept that australopithecines possessed both human-like and African ape-like features. This is, that the australopithecines also possessed some features in which they were specifically orang-utan-like, and many features in which they were markedly different from both humans and apes. This has lead to the recognition that they were not like humans or apes, or midway between them, but actually completely different from any living forms. This new view of the uniqueness of the australopithecines was first suggested by Oxnard (1967). As our many individual studies have progressed it has become clearer and clearer (Oxnard, 1969, 1972a, 1973a, 1975a, 1978a, 1980; Adams and Moore, 1975; Ashton, Flinn and Moore, 1975; Ashton, Moore and Spence, 1976; Ashton, 1981; Ashton, Flinn, Moore, Oxnard and Spence, 1981).

A recent summary of all these results and discussion has now expounded this conclusion as three levels or orders (Oxnard, 1983a, 1984).

First Order Conclusion: The first order of conclusion is simply to do with the resemblance or otherwise of the fossils to humans. It states that these fossils are not closely similar to humans.

Figures 8.11, 8:12 and 8:13 show three examples of the evidence (in ankle bones, metacarpals and humeri, and in both gracile and robust australopithecines). In each case although initial studies suggest that the fossils are similar to humans, or at the worst intermediate between humans and African apes, study of the complete evidence readily shows that the reality is otherwise. These fossils clearly differ more from both humans and African apes, than do these two living groups from each other. The australopithecines are unique.

Though for many years this first order conclusion met with resistance, there were always a few investigators who made findings similar to those of the extended Birmingham group. Indeed, Straus (1948) and Kern and Straus (1949) actually antedated those findings in showing that the distal ends of a particular australopithecine humerus and femur were no more ape-like than they were human-like, and that they specifically were not intermediate between the two.

The last decade has now, however, seen this notion become generally accepted. The various australopithecines are, indeed, more different from both African apes and humans in most features than these latter are from each other. Part of the basis of this acceptance has been the fact that even opposing investigators have found these large differences as they too, used techniques and research designs that were less biased by prior notions as to what the fossils might have been (e.g. McHenry and Corruccini, pelvis, 1975; femur, 1978).

The Second Order Conclusion: The second order conclusion stems from the more recent functional morphometric studies of the postcranial bones cited above. It states that the unique difference from humans that has been defined is most consonant with unique assessments about function.

For instance, though bipedal, it is likely that their bipedality was mechanically different from that of humans. Though terrestrial, it is further likely that these fossils were accomplished arborealists. The combination of the two functions within the same set of creatures is certainly unique among hominoids. However good a human acrobat may appear with training, arboreal activity as a human life style is not the regular scene, and would certainly be a total liability in escaping from predators. Likewise, however able most apes (indeed most non-human primates) may be as terrestrial bipeds, the habitual use of bipedality is not a major component of their life styles, and certainly not the way that they survive.

This second order conclusion, too, was disputed or ignored for many years. But again, this time within the last five years, it has come to be accepted by many investigators (although not by all). In this case the bases of acceptance have been new functional studies, both of living primates and of the larger number and better preserved fossil specimens, that have become available in recent years. In this case, also, most of the new studies have come from laboratories independent of those representing individuals who have found the fossils (e.g. Feldesman, 1982a, b; Senut, 1981; Stern and Susman, 1983a, b; Schmidt, 1984; Susman, Stern

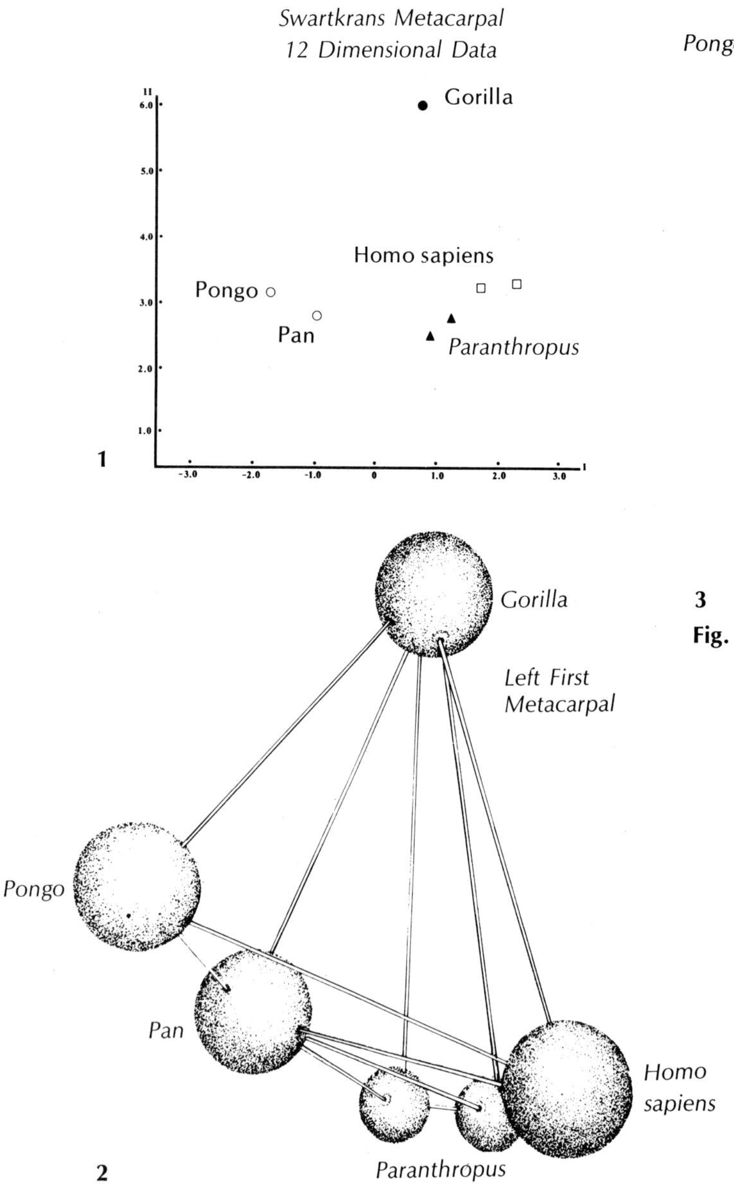

Fig. 8:11 **1st Frame:** shows a multivariate statistical analysis of metacarpals of extant large hominoids with materials representing two specimens of *Australopithecus robustus* interpolated. In this plot of the first two axes of that study the Australopithecines seem to be closest to *Homo*. But the original investigator (Rightmire) knew that his results implied more than this figure shows; thus he noted in his text that there was some evidence that these robust fossils had similarities with *Pan* even though this could not be seen from his plot.

◁ **2nd Frame:** shows that when we made a three-dimensional model of the results of Rightmire's study, one particular view indeed coincided with the information in the first two canonical axes provided in the first frame.

Δ **3rd Frame:** demonstrates well, however, that when we rotated the model the robust fossils were actually not only not at all like *Homo*, but also not especially more closely related to *Pan*. They are just different from any of these extant forms, and by an amount that is far greater than any difference between modern apes and humans. These fossils are actually uniquely different from any of these living forms.

The general scale of this model is some ten standard deviation units in greatest dimension.

and Rose, 1983; Tardieu, 1981; Cook *et al* 1983; Prost, 1980; 1983; Jungers and Stern, 1983; Zonnenveld, 1985). Most of them suggest clearly that the australopithecines had abilities in the trees not possessed by humans. A smaller number suggest that the bipedality that the australopithecines probably did have was not the same as that possessed by humans.

The Third Order Conclusion: The third order conclusion relates to possible phylogenetic assessments that can be made once the degree of resemblance and its functional association has been accepted. And it contains two possibilities. The first is the possibility that the unique morphology and the unique function are unique because they represent some curious mosaic situation in a linear evolutionary scheme. The second is the possibility that the unique morphology and the unique

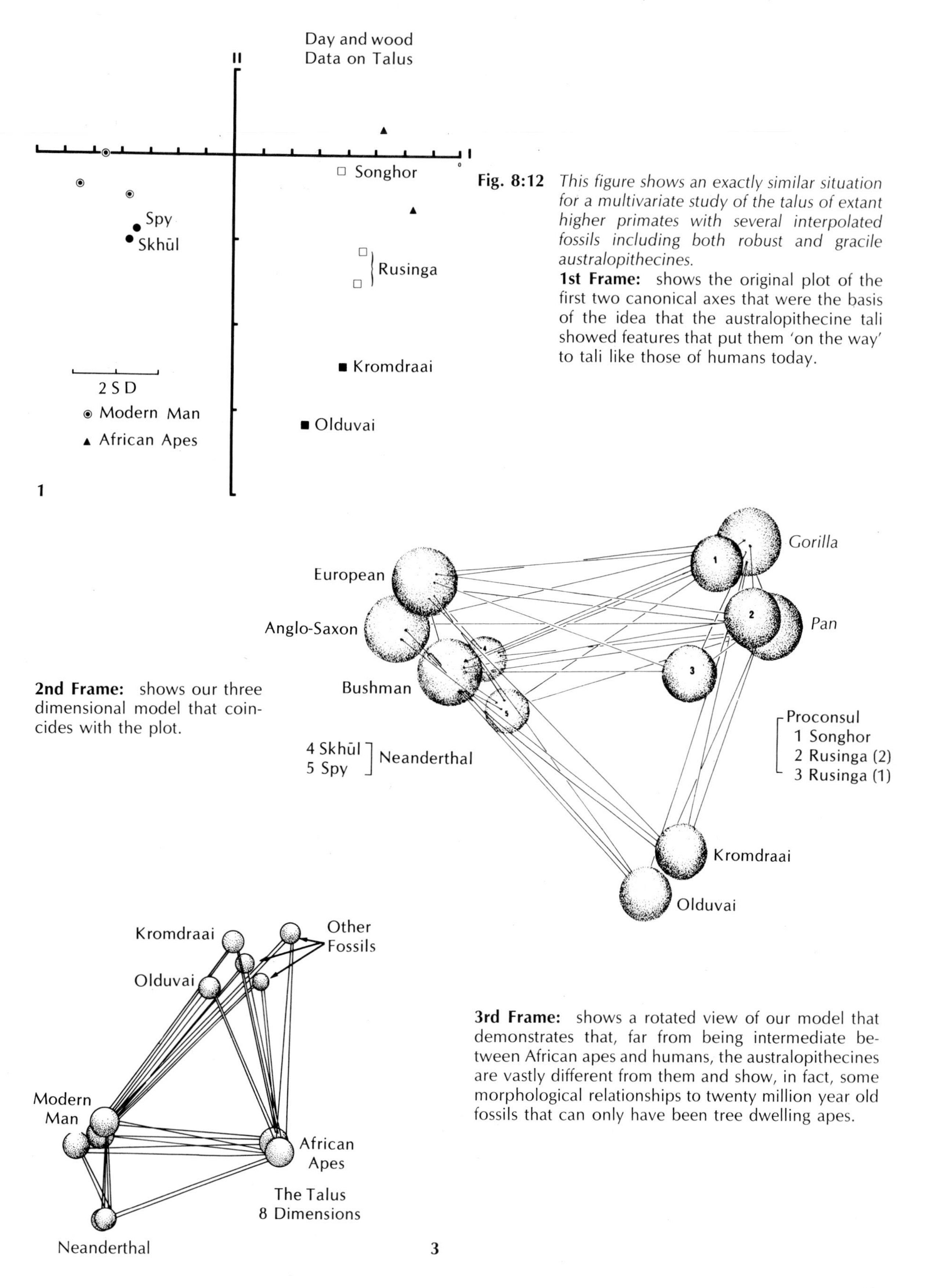

Fig. 8:12 *This figure shows an exactly similar situation for a multivariate study of the talus of extant higher primates with several interpolated fossils including both robust and gracile australopithecines.*

1st Frame: shows the original plot of the first two canonical axes that were the basis of the idea that the australopithecine tali showed features that put them 'on the way' to tali like those of humans today.

2nd Frame: shows our three dimensional model that coincides with the plot.

3rd Frame: shows a rotated view of our model that demonstrates that, far from being intermediate between African apes and humans, the australopithecines are vastly different from them and show, in fact, some morphological relationships to twenty million year old fossils that can only have been tree dwelling apes.

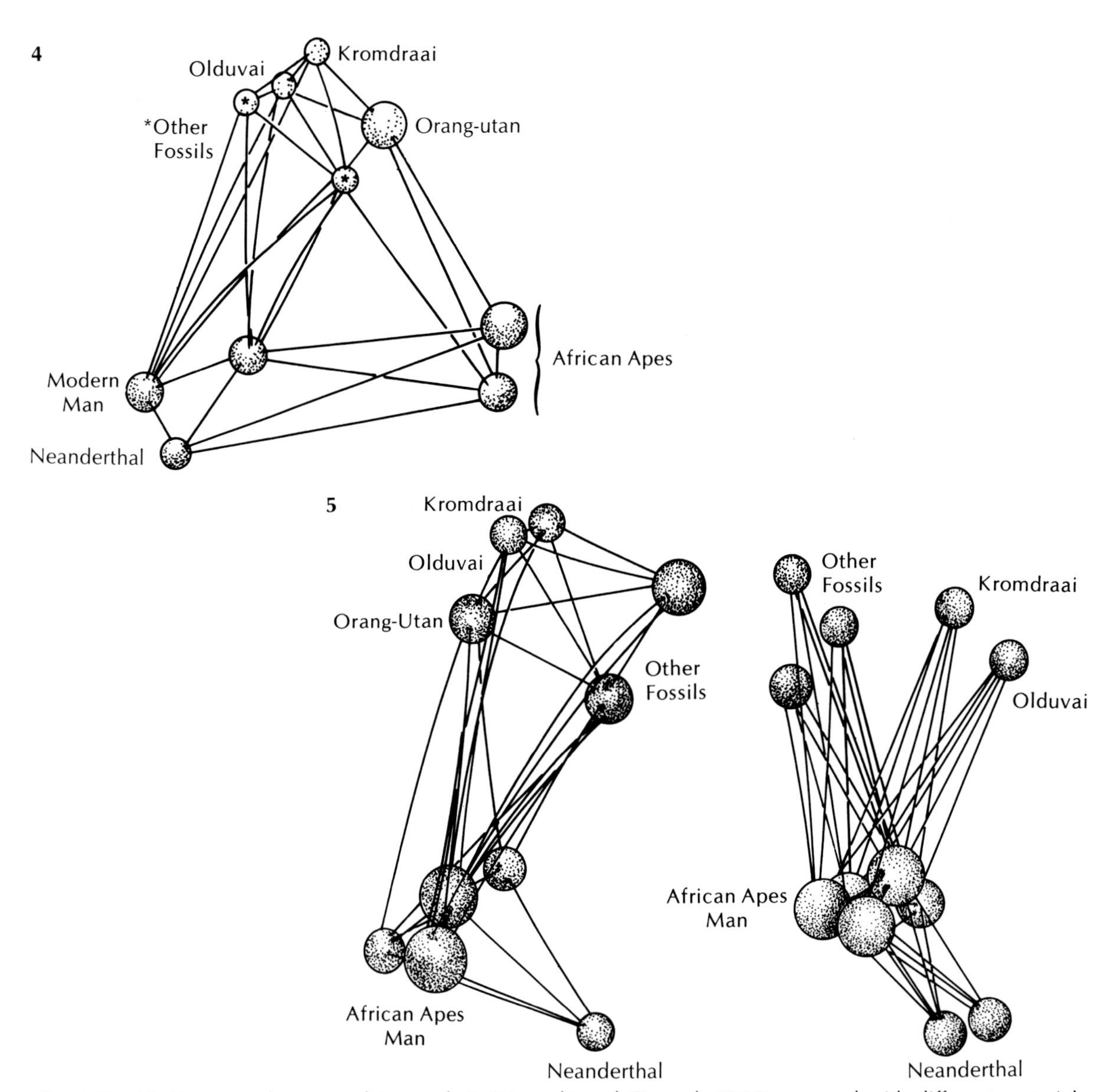

Fig. 8:12 **4th Frame:** shows our later analysis (Lisowski and Oxnard, 1974) prepared with different materials, different data for extant species, different measures of the talus, different fossils (but including the same australopithecines), and including, especially, a known modern arboreal form, the orang-utan. This picture (a) confirms the overall similarity with our reinterpretation of the original study, and (b) further shows that the australopithecines and the twenty million year old fossils share similarities with the orang-utan. As the orang-utan is known to be arboreal and the twenty million year old ape fossils are unlikely not to have been arboreal, this suggests that in the australopithecines tali we are seeing the hallmarks of a basically arboreal foot.
5th Frame: shows further rotated views of these two models to make it quite clear that additional information is not being hidden. This view confirms both the similarity of the original two studies and the new interpretations for the australopithecines.

function are unique because they represent a parallel situation in a radiating evolutionary scheme.

The idea of mosaicism as an evolutionary mechanism is quite old, and as an evolutionary event, is perhaps more likely than any simple minded idea of an easy intermediate on a straight pathway. It would imply that the evolution of the new bipedality and the loss of the old arboreal ability had not proceeded hand in hand. It is in this way that the process may have given rise to a functionally and morphologically unique descendent.

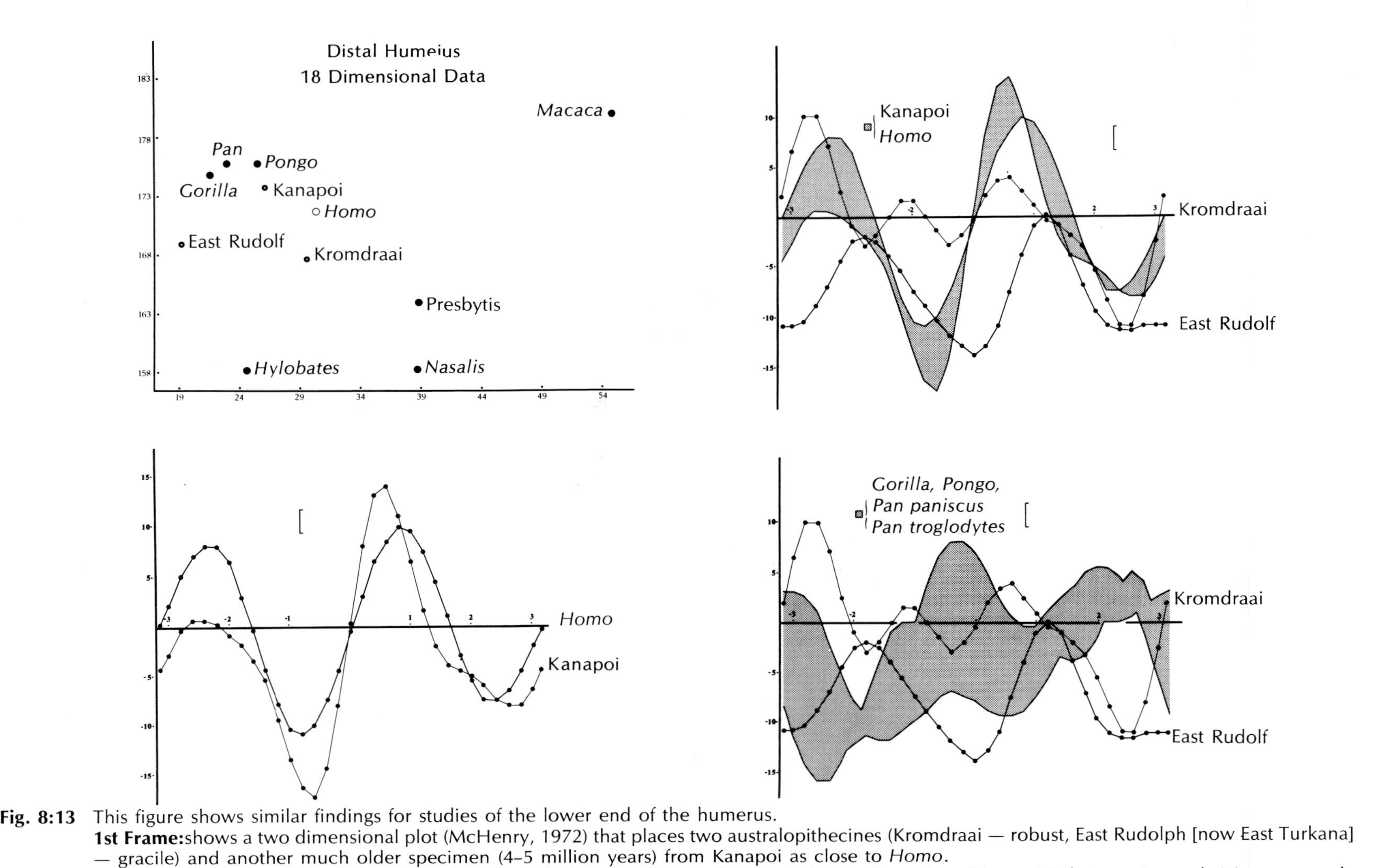

Fig. 8:13 This figure shows similar findings for studies of the lower end of the humerus.
1st Frame:shows a two dimensional plot (McHenry, 1972) that places two australopithecines (Kromdraai — robust, East Rudolph [now East Turkana] — gracile) and another much older specimen (4–5 million years) from Kanapoi as close to *Homo*.
2nd Frame: shows our high-dimensional display of this result that confirms that the specimen from Kanapoi (whatever it may be) is enormously similar to *Homo*. This reflects the much earlier results of Patterson and Howells.
3rd Frame:shows that our high-dimensional displays demonstrate that the australopithecine specimens (both from Kromdraai and East Turkana) are quite different from *Homo* and Kanapoi.
4th Frame:shows that our high-dimensional display actually places the australopithecine humeri as not too different from the apes. This may have been because, like the apes, the australopithecines were capable climbers.

The idea of parallelism is an even older evolutionary concept, and is probably an even more likely phenomenon within evolution. It involves the following. If a different form of bipedalism was extant several million years ago, and if this different form of bipedalism was linked, in the same creatures, with arboreal activity, then it is quite possible, indeed even rather likely, that this special bipedalism, and therefore the creatures that displayed it, arose independently. Because it is likely that there are at least two forms of bipedality among australopithecines, in hominoids as a group bipedality may have arisen three times or even more. Such multiple origins of a novel function in an evolutionary radiation is a general phenomenon in biology.

Mosaicism implies a unique event in the evolution of a single human lineage with bipedality appearing only once. Parallelism implies a non-unique event in which the large hominoids may have been part of an evolutionary radiation within which bipedality arose a number of times.

The australopithecines may well have been sibling groups to both the African apes and humans. This is an idea that would remove the australopithecines from being closely related to the human lineage and would place them unequivocally within an evolutionary radiation. Of these lineages, some, australopithecines, became extinct; some African apes, are almost extinct; only one genus, *Homo*, survives strongly at the present time.

At this time it is difficult to say which of the above possibilities represents what the actuality may have been. But one thing is certain: both should be discussed and examined. And this is not the present custom in anthropology.

The third level conclusions are obviously the least strong because any third level conclusion must be weaker than the second and first level conclusions, from which they derive. However, whatever their possible strength or weakness, they are scarcely accepted, as an alternative couplet, by anyone. Indeed, it seems that the parallel idea is so extreme that some workers (e.g. Wood, 1984) are not even able to accept it as worthy of examination. Yet the general acceptance of the conclusions of the first and second order now make it a possibility that must be tested.

The problem of numbers

Now that we have reminded ourselves about the current consensus of human evolution and the new challenges to it, it is of interest to see how the studies of teeth outlined in this book do, or do not, fit. In particular we may be especially interested to see the degree to which they support the one, or the other, of the third level conclusions just outlined.

As we start to do this we need to be aware of one of the criticisms that has been put forward about our studies of the postcranial bones. It is a criticism that has to do with numbers. There are very few individual postcranial fragments. It can scarcely be expected, suggests one critique (McHenry, 1976), that studies of a few individual bones will change the minds of many anthropologists.

Of course, the background to our studies is based, as previously explained, upon very large numbers, upon personal dissection of hundreds of primate cadavers, upon voluminous investigations of thousands of primate bones, and upon analyses of tens of thousands of individual measurements. But it is true that the number of postcranial fossil fragments that have been studied is a mere handful. This is not a deficiency of our studies alone. It is a deficiency of all studies of fossil postcrania, because it is a reflection of the rarity of postcranial fossil fragments in general.

There are only two good fossil australopithecine pelves known — we studied the only one that was available to us at the time (Zuckerman, Ashton, Flinn, Oxnard and Spence, 1973; Ashton, Flinn, Moore, Oxnard and Spence, 1981). There are only two good australopithecine feet known today — again, we studied the only one that existed at the time (Oxnard, 1972a; Lisowski, Albrecht and Oxnard, 1974, 1976; Oxnard, 1975a, 1980). Though almost complete finds (such as Lucy for australopithecines and the recent skeleton found by Walker and Leakey for *Homo erectus*) are known, the great majority of hominoid fossils are available only from the neck up.

To make these postcranial studies any more certain requires that we have reasonable samples of postcranial bones for each anatomical region, and for each fossil group. It will be a long wait before that is the case, however active the fossil hunters may be.

Yet the criticism has a validity. Studies of populations of fossils are clearly the best way to make evolutionary evaluations. This is, in part, why we have come to investigate dental measurements. The dentition may be only a small portion of the skeleton. And it may not give very good information about the relationships of animals overall. But at least large samples are available. Is it possible to examine dimensions of teeth, not only to learn about the dentition, but also to learn about other aspects of the lives of the fossils?

Many prior studies suggest that it is. And many prior studies imply that one of the powerful things that we can learn in population studies of dentitions (apart from learning about the dentitions themselves) is about sexual dimorphism. Before we can start to meld the information in the earlier chapters of this book, we need to summarize some notions about sexual differences in relation to evolutionary studies.

The problem of sex

The history of the place of sex in evolutionary studies is short and poor.

In our scientific culture, as McCown (1982) has pointed out, it has been usual to regard the male as best exemplifying the species. In Elliot's review of the monkeys and apes, the number of type specimens that are adult females can be counted on the fingers of one hand. In the museums of the world the specimens available for study that are female are totally outnumbered by the specimens from males. This can be seen in our own studies, a bias that is most assuredly not due to our data collecting habits but to limitations in materials available in almost all the major collections. Even sexual differences, when they have been studied, are usually expressed by most investigators using female form as a percentage of a 'standard' form — the male.

There have been recent attempts to correct biases like this. Of course, nothing can be done about the type specimens of the past, or about the numbers of specimens available as a result of past collecting habits. But even what can be done about bias towards the male, in the expression of data, tends to fall into an opposite, but equal error, that of regarding female form as the more useful guide to the anatomy of the species (Nowak, 1980; McCown, 1982).

Some studies have attempted to use a sex-less phantom as the standard (Ross and Wilson, 1974; Ross and Ward, 1982). Even this is being questioned today (Shephard *et al*, 1985). It is somewhat equivalent to what has been most usual in biological studies, using the midway position between female and male as representative of the species. As long as we believe that male-female differences can be explained primarily on a single quantitative (size) axis it seems not too unreasonable a procedure. Mean position on that axis could characterize the position of a given species, dispersion around the mean along that axis could describe the amount of variation in the species that results from sexual dimorphism.

It is generally true that studies of growth and development, suggest that male form is often an elaboration of female form due to such phenomena as longer growth, later maturity, larger size, and so on. And it is certainly true, as can be seen most explicitly in the studies in this book, that female forms of different species tend to be more similar to each other than are male forms to each other. But it is also clear that the comparison of species is much more complex than has previously been thought. It should certainly not just be a comparison of means for each species, whether of male mean or female mean, or even mean of females and males pooled. It is certainly, also, not adequate to compare species through these various means together with the addition of measures of the dispersion of the pooled group of both (e.g. coefficients of variation).

The studies in this book imply that comparisons of species require comparing such scalar quantities as the differences in (**a**) means and (**b**) dispersions for each sex, (**c**) ratio quantities such as the relative numbers of males and females, and (**d**) vector quantities such as the amounts and directions of difference between the sexes. And the studies in this book further suggest that the comparisons should also include (**e**) the complex patterns that result when we look at differences in many different individual features, and (**f**) the even more complex associations that result when interactions among many individual features are included. Such a descriptive list is much more complex. But it presumably does give a far better picture of a species and its sexes.

All this requires that we must know these amounts, ratios, vectors, univariate patterns, and multivariate associations. For measures of teeth, these have been, at least partially, revealed in the work described in the previous chapters.

The whole matter has especial importance for human evolution. Sexual dimorphism in humans at the present time is described as being small in populations with approximately the same numbers of females as males. It is generally assumed that sexual dimorphism was much larger in many-female few-male arrangements in the recent past.

Now, however, that we know that sexual dimorphism is a complex pattern, rather than merely a large or small amount, and now that we can discover some evidences as to female/male ratios a long way back in time, then it is likely that human evolution has taken a different evolutionary path than the one generally accepted.

A new question can, therefore, be posed.

Was large dimorphism and a polygynous social sexual arrangement necessarily characteristic of our recent ancestors? As long as we look to ape-like models we must surely think so (e.g. Brace and Ryan 1980; Hrdy, 1981). But as soon as we realise that even within the living apes there are several different sexual dimorphisms of sizes, shapes, patterns and ratios, and that among the fossils there are even more, the whole matter must be completely reopened. Especially as soon as we realize that sexual dimorphism of size alone is a complex feature that demands many levels of explanation then we must be prepared to reject the simple idea.

The whole matter is of especial interest for ape evolution. Though orang-utans (and modern humans, for that matter) display equal variances for male and females, the African apes do not. In particular, the African apes demonstrate two different patterns. At almost every tooth position, where a significant difference is observed between the means for each sex, there is also a significant difference in variance. The pattern in gorillas is such that gorillas have some teeth in which the female variance is much the largest encompassing the male variance, and other teeth in which the situation is the reverse. In chimpanzees, too, almost all teeth that show significant differences between the means for each sex also show significant differences in variance but, in contrast to gorillas, this is with the male variance always being greater than the female.

Professor Wesley Whitten of the University of Tasmania, and to whom I am indebted for this discussion, has suggested that this might possibly be related to specific genetic mechanisms. Thus, the larger variances of particular features in males, may be associated with at least a portion of the genetic materials that control those features, being found on autosomes but dependent upon teststerone and thus, on the y chromosome. Larger variances in particular features in females, may be due to genes or gene complexes on their double x chromosomes.

Of course, the explanations may not be due to such factors. But the findings are a most interesting difference between the African apes and other hominoids. They are especially interesting in that they indicate one element of sexual dimorphism (difference in variance), in which chimpanzees are actually larger than any other extant hominoid. And they are of yet further interest, because some of the australopithecine materials provide hints of similar differences in variance between the sexes. The human and orang-utan stocks do not.

The impact of the new studies of teeth: the genus *Homo*

The studies of teeth reported group by group in earlier chapters of this book speak to some of these possibilities.

First, these new studies demonstrate the basic similarity of sexual dimorphism in all those species, recent and early *Homo sapiens*, *H. sapiens neandertalensis* and *H. erectus*, that have long been accepted as closely related to the last million years of the human lineage. They all share a complex pattern at many of the individual tooth positions: small sexual dimorphism of means, small sexual dimorphism of variances, similar less complex univariate patterns of sexual dimorphism, small multivariate sexual dimorphism, similar patterns of multivariate sexual dimorphism, similar multivariate positions for the species as a whole, and one-to-one sex ratios. This is a happy, if, perhaps, unnecessary confirmation of a long held position: that all are, indeed, members of the genus of *Homo* (Fig. 8:14; Table 8:1).

Because of the newly determined extreme age of some recent *Homo erectus* finds even this summary provides new information. For rather than being merely some few hundred thousand years old (as of, perhaps, three decades ago), or some half a million years old (two decades ago), or even nearly one million years old (one decade ago), the genus *Homo* from modern humans through the species group *H. erectus* is now clearly at least two million years old. This may mean that a single consistent pattern of sexual dimorphism including several relatively small sexual dimorphisms and one-to-one sex ratio, is also at least two million years old.

Almost inevitably new finds will be made that will be older yet. For it is unlikely that we have seen the last of this process of extension of the recognized groups of *Homo* back through time. The several species of the genus *Homo*, together with their

Table 8:1

Patterns of 1:1 Ratios of Lower and Upper Peaks

	I1	I2	C	P3	P4	M1	M2	M3
H. sapiens sapiens								
Lower Jaw	=		=				=	
Upper Jaw				=	=			
H. s. neandertalensis								
Lower Jaw	=	=	=	=				
Upper Jaw		=	=	=	≠			=
H. erectus								
Lower Jaw		=	=	=	=	=	=	=
Upper Jaw				=		=		
H. habilis								
Lower Jaw				=	=	=	=	
Upper Jaw				=	=			
Ramapithecus								
Lower Jaw	=			=		=		=
Upper Jaw	=		=	=	=		=	=
Gigantopithecus								
Lower Jaw			=	=	=			
Upper Jaw			=	=				=

common pattern of sexual dimorphism and one-to-one sex ratio, are, on this ground, older, even, than two million years.

Our findings go yet further, however. The basic similarity between the aforementioned genus *Homo* (modern through erect) with the special forms, *Homo habilis* and Lufeng *Ramapithecus* is noteworthy. In this book we have generally kept *H. habilis* separate from the genus *Homo* because it is just possible that *Homo habilis* is really only an australopithecine. Certainly we have kept *Ramapithecus* from Lufeng separate from *Homo* because it clearly is a much earlier species.

It is certainly the case that some of the earlier postcranial fragments assigned to *Homo habilis* (e.g. the hand and foot from Olduvai) were indeed likely australopithecine. But newer cranial finds, possessing cranial capacities of the order of 700 and 800 ccs (well above those typical for extant apes and australopithecines) mean that *Homo habilis* is indeed likely not to be *Australopithecus*. The dentitions that are associated with this order of cranial volume are what we have examined here; it is these dentitions that are markedly similar to other *Homo* specimens, both in their sex ratio and in all the features of their sexual dimorphism just outlined. Thus, *Homo habilis*, too, has relatively small sexual dimorphism of means, small sexual dimorphism of variances, similar and small univariate pattern of sexual dimorphism, small multivariate sexual dimorphism, similar pattern of multivariate sexual dimorphism, similar multivariate position and one-to-one sex ratio, as in other *Homo* finds (Fig. 8:14; Table 8:1).

But *Homo habilis* is even older than *Homo erectus*. Individual finds are dated at well beyond two and a half million years ago. This in turn means that we can expect *habilis* finds eventually to turn up from, say, three million years ago or even more.

If, furthermore, the talus from East Turkana and the humerus from Kanapoi (both clearly vastly different from various australopithecine tali and humeri, but not very different from tali and humeri of the genus *Homo* — Figs. 8:15 and 8:16) should eventually be confirmed as from early members of the genus *Homo*, we would be back to four or four and a half million years. Add a component to allow for fossils that have not yet been found (the 'error' component, if you like) and we may be back as far as five million years.

If, yet again, the findings for *Ramapithecus* from Lufeng, which has relatively small sexual dimorphism of means, small sexual dimorphism of variances, similar and small univariate patterns of sexual dimorphism, small multivariate sexual dimorphism, and one-to-one sex ratios, also as in all *Homo* finds to date, then these features may stem from even earlier (Fig: 8:14; Table 8:1). The genus *Homo* and its relatives, with their special small sexual dimorphisms and one-to-one sex ratios may be truly older than we now think.

The genus: *Australopithecus*

The data assembled here for the various australopithecine species, not including the *habilis* specimens, seem to show unequivocally that there are fundamental differences between all australopithecines and all *Homo* groups. Thus the australopithecines show, at many tooth positions, larger sexual dimorphisms of means, larger sexual dimorphisms of variances, different univariate patterns of sexual dimorphism, different multivariate sexual dimorphisms, different multivariate positions, and two-to-one to three-to-one sex ratios (Fig. 8:17; Table 8:2).

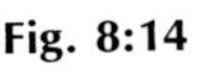
Fig. 8:14

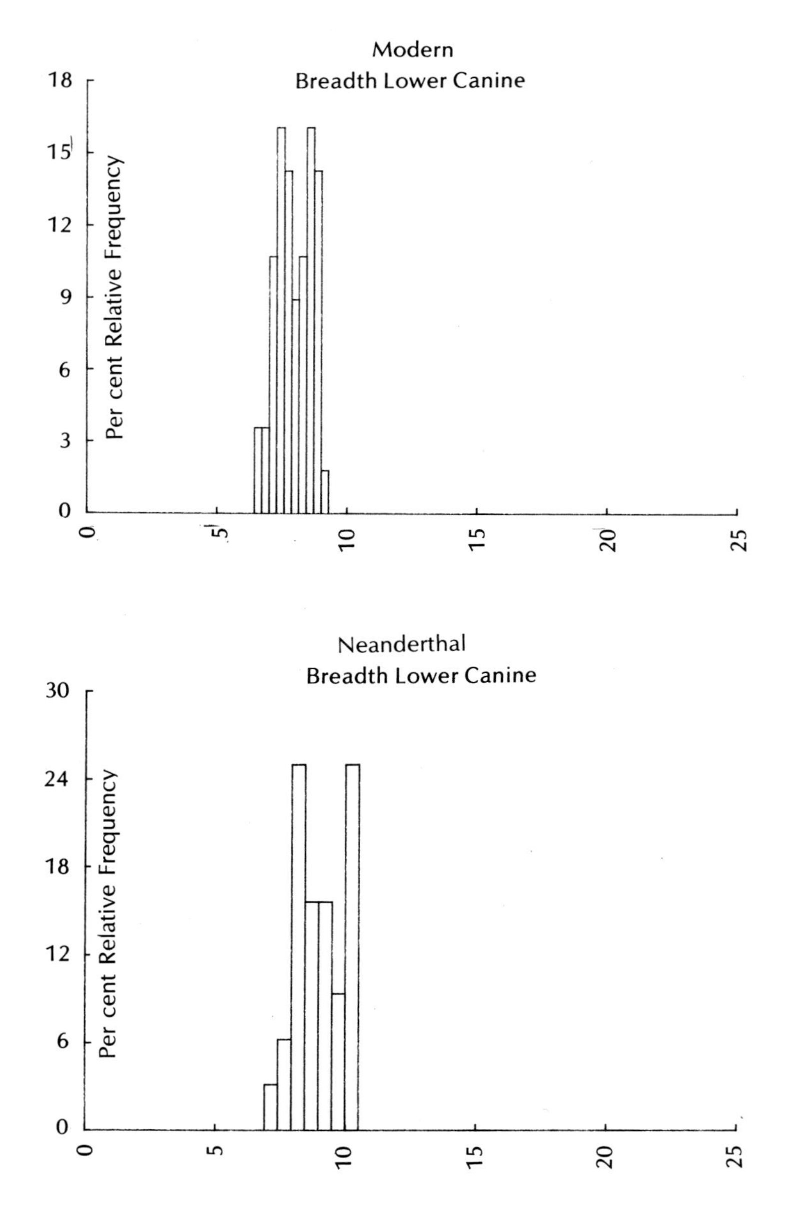
Modern
Breadth Lower Canine
Per cent Relative Frequency
Neanderthal
Breadth Lower Canine
Per cent Relative Frequency

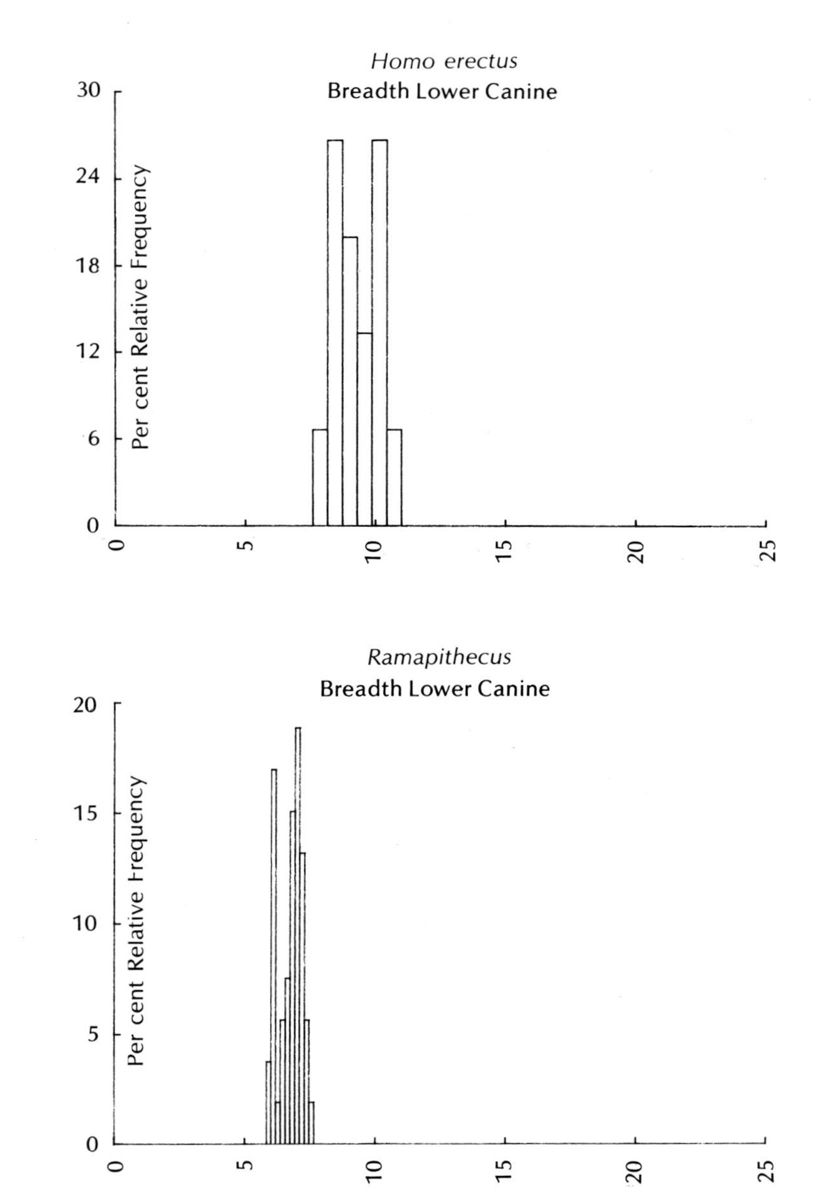
Homo erectus
Breadth Lower Canine
Per cent Relative Frequency
Ramapithecus
Breadth Lower Canine
Per cent Relative Frequency

Fig. 8:14 This figure repeats the univariate and multivariate results for those forms that show 1:1 sex ratios.
1st Frame: shows, at the same scale for each, the histograms for the breadth of the lower canine. It reminds us of the bimodality of distribution with equal peaks in each of these species, *Homo sapiens sapiens*, *Homo sapiens neandertalensis*, *Homo erectus*, *Ramapithecus* and *Gigantopithecus*. *Homo habilis* shares this same pattern but data are not available for that species for this particular tooth.

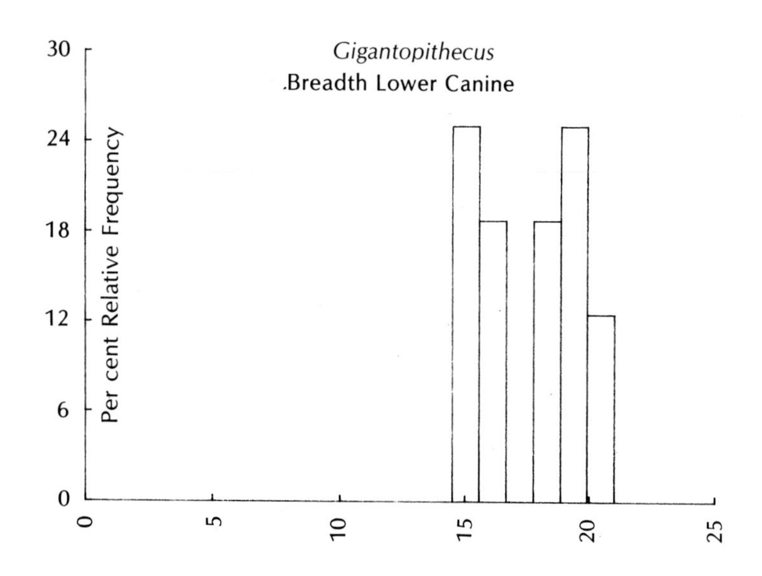

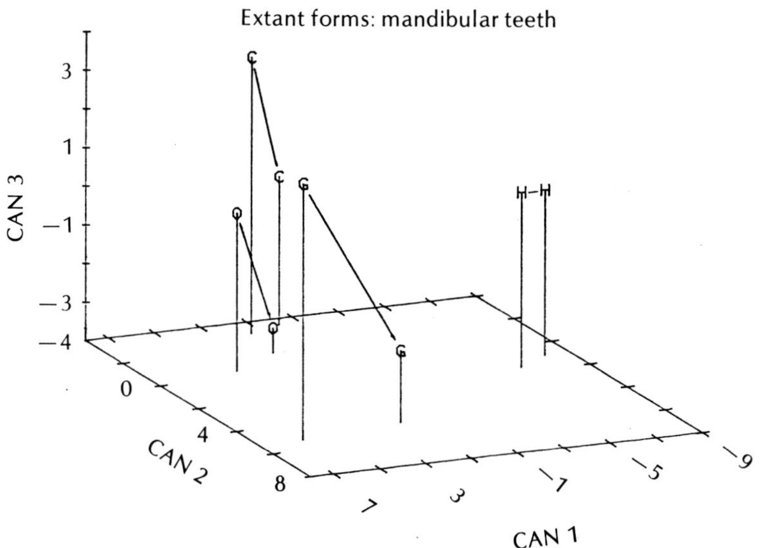

2nd Frame: shows first the multivariate result for the extant forms (H-H = *Homo*, C-C = *Pan*, O-O = *Pongo* and G-G = *Gorilla*, females always on the right). It also shows the relationship to the extant forms of the fossils that show small dimorphism and 1:1 ratios (S-S = *Homo sapiens sapiens*, N-N = *Homo sapiens neandertalensis*, E-E = *Homo erectus*, R-R = *Ramapithecus*, again females to the right). The multivariate similarity in both general position and especially sexual dimorphism between all fossils and modern *Homo*, and their overall dissimilarity from all extant apes is clear.

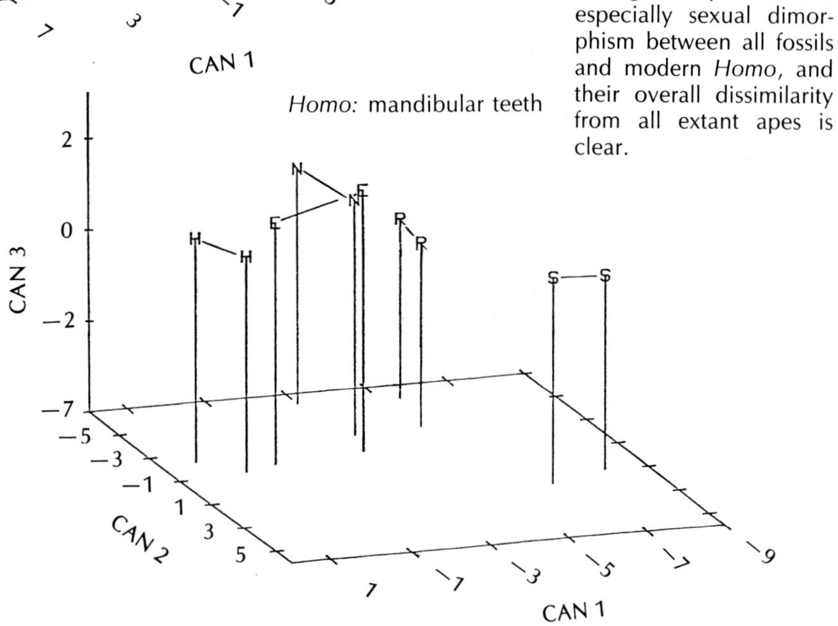

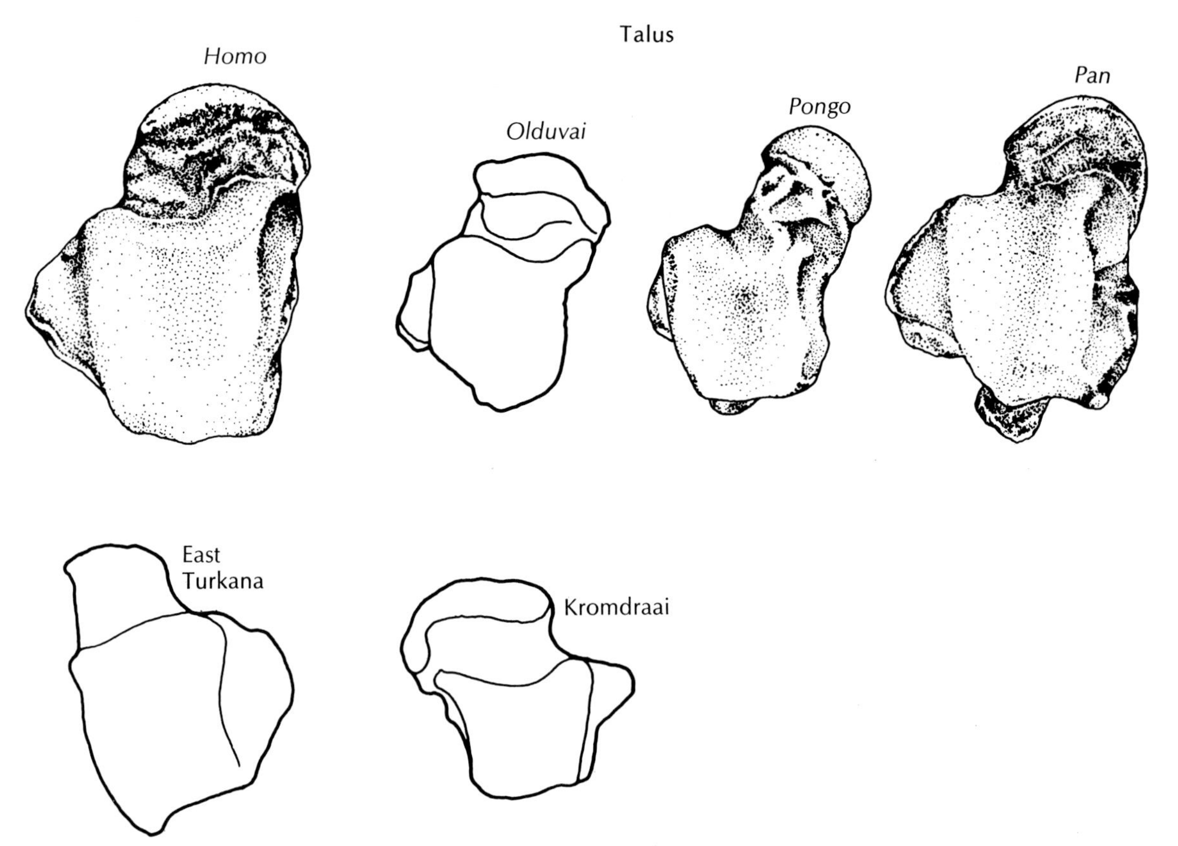

Fig. 8:15 This figure reminds us that there is a talus from East Turkana that is more human-like than are the tali of both gracile and robust australopithecines. Yet this talus is at least as old, if not older, than these australopithecine tali.

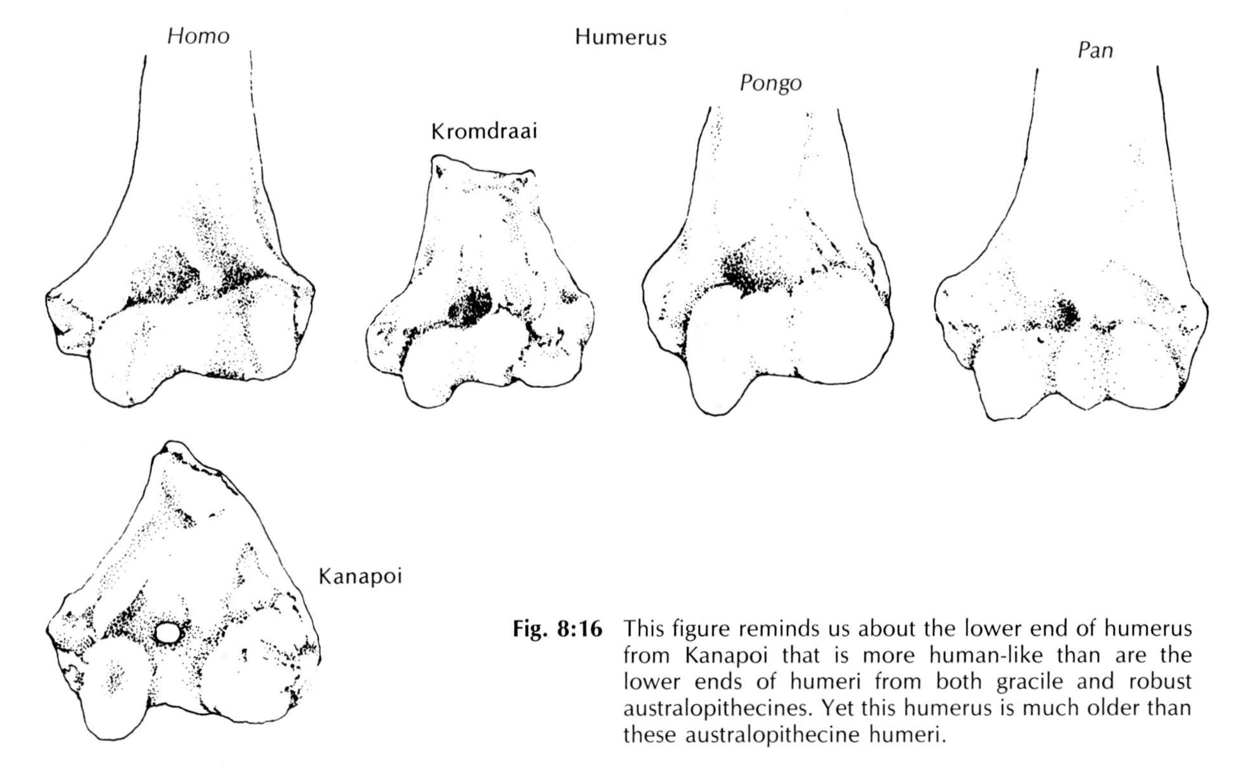

Fig. 8:16 This figure reminds us about the lower end of humerus from Kanapoi that is more human-like than are the lower ends of humeri from both gracile and robust australopithecines. Yet this humerus is much older than these australopithecine humeri.

Table 8:2

Patterns of 2:1 Ratios of Lower and Upper Peaks

	I1	I2	C	P3	P4	M1	M2	M3
afarensis								
Lower Jaw				≠	≠	≠	≠	≠
Upper Jaw			≠		≠	≠		
africanus								
Lower Jaw				≠	≠	≠	≠	≠
Upper Jaw				≠	≠	≠		
robustus								
Lower Jaw				≠	≠	≠	≠	≠
Upper Jaw				≠	≠	≠		
boisei								
Lower Jaw				≠	≠		≠	≠
Upper Jaw				≠	≠	≠		
sivapithecus								
Lower Jaw	≠	≠		≠		≠		≠
Upper Jaw	≠	≠	≠	≠	≠		≠	≠

And though apparently similar to extant apes in sex ratio, the australopithecines show considerable differences, from the extant African apes, in having different univariate and different multivariate patterns of sexual dimorphism.

There appear to be, furthermore, marked differences within the australopithecines. Thus, the robust (*Australopithecus robustus* and *A. boisei*) species group forms a pair of species that differ consistently from the gracile (*A. africanus* and *A. afarensis*) species group. The robust species pair, though located multivariately far distant from extant African apes, possess a multivariate form of sexual dimorphism that is somewhat similar in its pattern to that of extant African apes. The gracile species pair, though similar in multivariate position to some of the extant African apes, possesses a multivariate form of sexual dimorphism that is, so far at least, unique among hominoids. These data taken together show that the two species pairs are quite different from extant African apes, and also that they are as different from each other than either is from any ape. This combination of characteristics further assesses both pairs of australopithecines as utterly different from modern or fossil *Homo* (Fig. 8:17, Table 8:2).

All australopithecines that are younger than the newly extended genus *Homo* have to be placed outside the human lineage. This could be anywhere from three million years to almost five million years depending upon how we assess *Homo*.

If we take the five million year date as at least possible, this would remove all known australopithecines from being close to the genus *Homo*.

Even if we assess the genus *Homo* as starting at any of the more recent dates suggested above, then other possibilities exist that are even more unlikely. One is that we must accept only those australopithecines older than that date (whatever it may be) as possibly within the lineage leading to *Homo*. A second is that we must accept a very sudden change from the pattern of sexual dimorphisms evident in *Australopithecus* to that evident in *Homo*. And a third is that we must accept that the pattern evident in australopithecines before the evolution of the pattern in *Homo* also continued in an unchanged fashion for a further two million years or more in the later australopithecines.

These are complex and unlikely possibilities. The notion that the australopithecines form one, or more likely, two sub-groups that are sibling in relationship to both *Homo* and African apes, is far simpler and far more likely.

The Chinese ramapithecines

The data in these studies further complicate the conventional situation when we come to take into account the fossils of eight million years ago that were found in China.

In parentheses, we should remind ourselves that discussing the Chinese ramapithecines is something quite different from discussing ramapithecines from the rest of the world. The latter are mostly well over ten million years old; some of them are as much as eighteen million years old; they are quite few in number compared with the richness of the Chinese situation; they are from many different sites, indeed from sites separated by many thousands of miles not only from each other, but also from the single Chinese site. Whatever is found about the Chinese ramapithecines does not automatically apply to any of the others, indeed, probably does not apply to the others at all.

With this caveat in mind, we can first discount the possibility that there was a single species or species group of ape-like ramapithecine fossils at Lufeng. We can likewise firmly discount the idea that these fossils represent very small females and

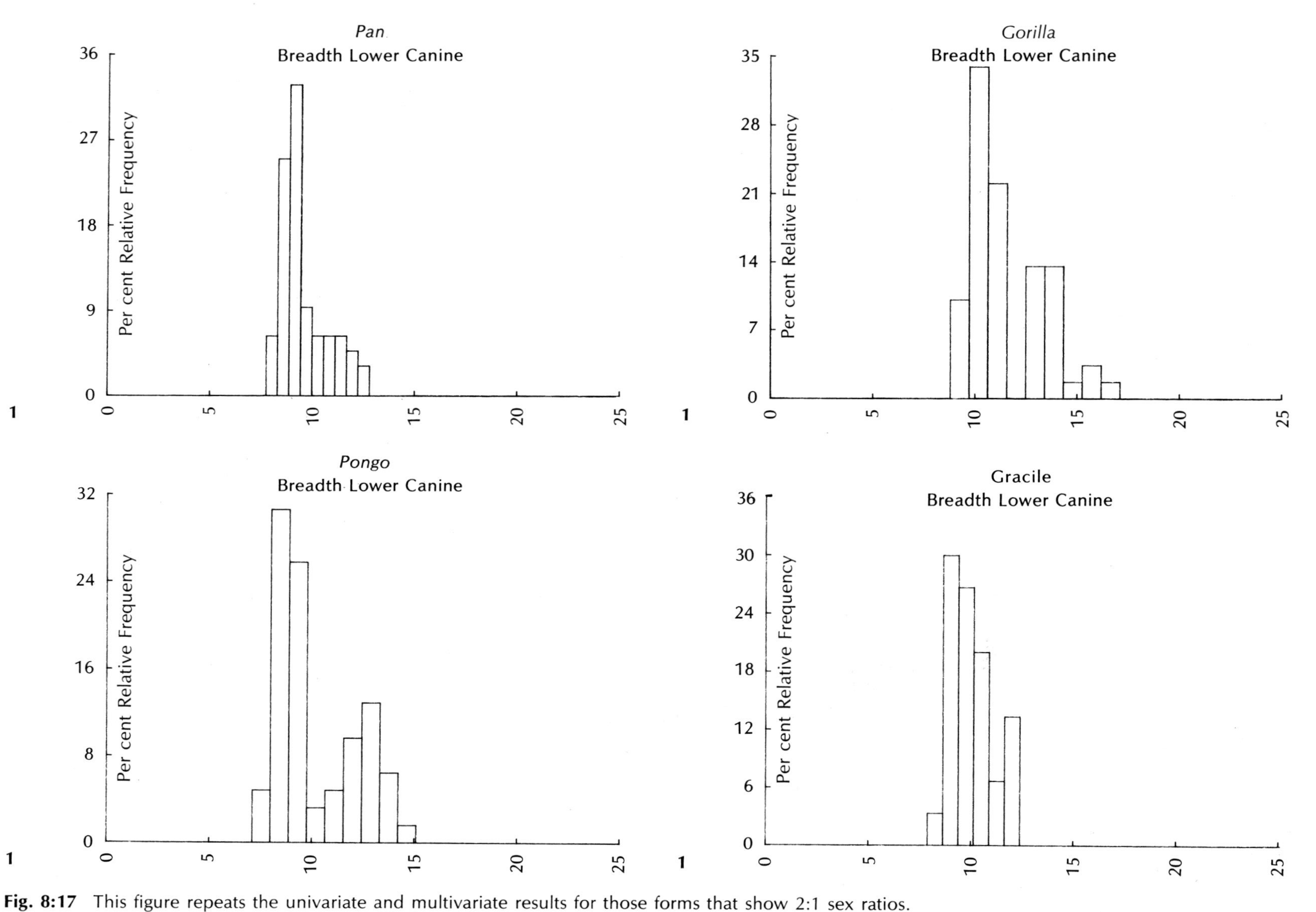

Fig. 8:17 This figure repeats the univariate and multivariate results for those forms that show 2:1 sex ratios.
1st Frame: shows, at the same scale for each, the histograms for the breadth of the lower canine. It reminds us of the bimodality of distribution with unequal peaks in each of these species, *Pan, Gorilla, Pongo*, gracile australopithecines, robust australopithecines, and *Sivapithecus*. (The australopithecines are not examined in greater detail because, for this tooth, sufficient data is not available. As we have seen, however, the results for other teeth confirm this summary for each individual australopithecine species).

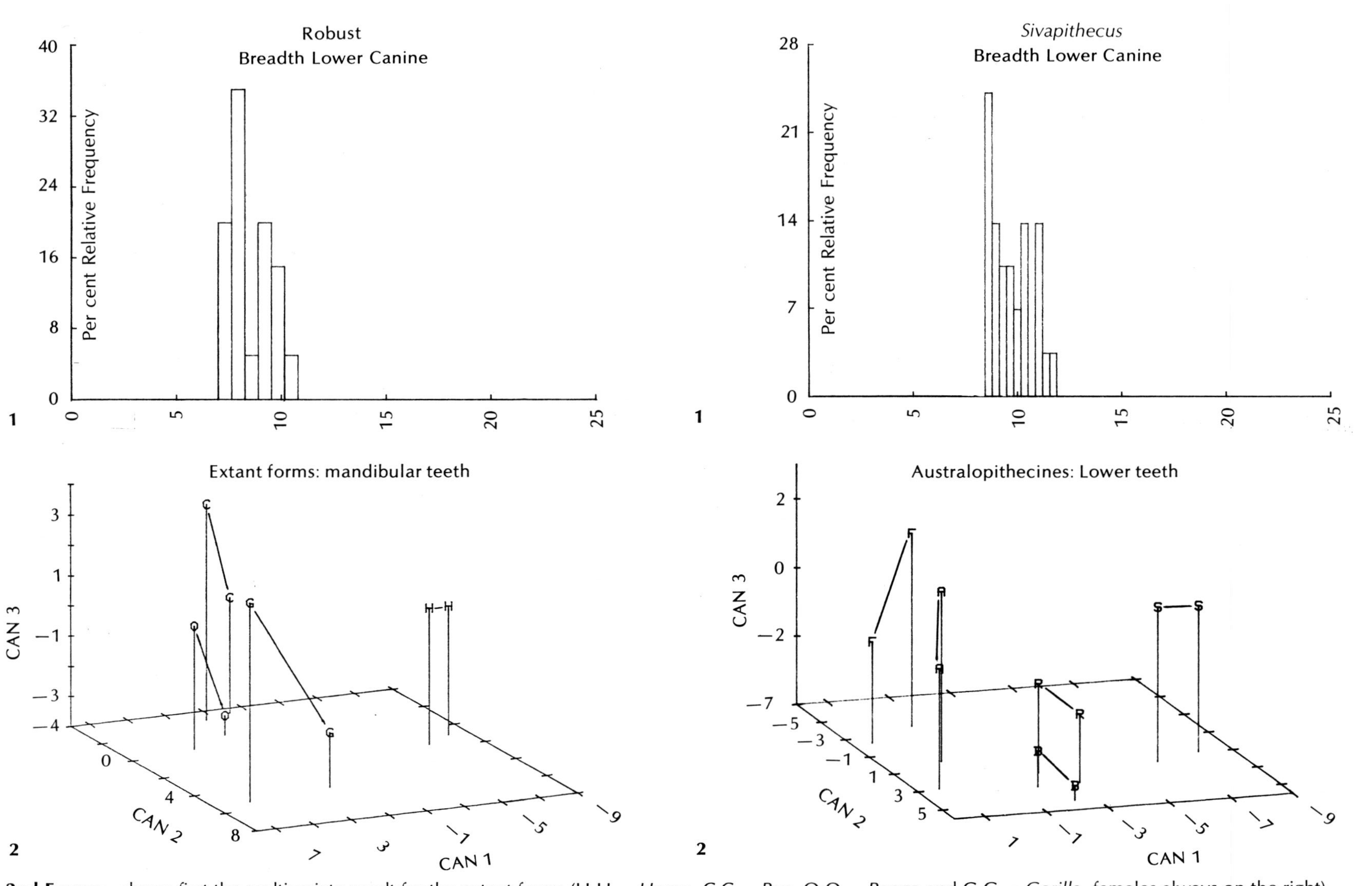

2nd Frame: shows first the multivariate result for the extant forms (H-H = *Homo*, C-C = *Pan*, O-O = *Pongo* and G-G = *Gorilla*, females always on the right). It shows, second, the relationship to the extant forms of the fossils that demonstrate large dimorphism and 2:1 or greater sex ratios (S-S = *Homo sapiens sapiens*, R-R = *Australopithecus robustus*, B-B = *Australopithecus boisei*, A-A = *Australopithecus africanus*, F-F = *Australopithecus afarensis*, again females to the right). The multivariate difference in both general position and especially sexual dimorphism between all these fossils and modern *Homo*, is clear. Their general dissimilarity from the living apes, especially in their multivariate pattern of sexual dimorphism is also clear.

very large males, and display, therefore, sexual dimorphism so large that it was greater than that known in any primate, living or fossil. These are all characteristics that have been claimed for non-Chinese ramapithecines and suggested for the Chinese fossils by a number of workers.

These studies show, in contrast, that the group of larger fossil teeth from Lufeng that have been labelled *Sivapithecus* have all the characteristics of a single species or species group in their own right. They really are rather similar, in all the features of their sexual dimorphism to the genus *Pongo*. This is seen from their possession, at many individual tooth positions, of large sexual dimorphism of means, small (zero) sexual dimorphism of variances, particular form of univariate pattern of sexual dimorphism, larger multivariate sexual dimorphism, similar pattern of multivariate sexual dimorphism, similar multivariate position, and two-to-one to three-to-one sex ratios. And they existed as long ago as eight million years (Fig. 8:17 and 8:18; Table 8:3).

But these studies also demonstrate, unequivocally, that eight million years ago there was another species group at Lufeng labelled *Ramapithecus* that had many dental similarities with both fossil and extant *Homo*. *Ramapithecus* possessed, at many individual tooth loci, small sexual dimorphism of means, small (zero) sexual dimorphism of variances, similar univariate sexually dimorphic patterns, small multivariate sexual dimorphisms, similar patterns of multivariate sexual dimorphism, similar multivariate positions, and one-to-one sex ratios as are found in all groups of *Homo* (Fig. 8:14 and 8:18; Table 8:3).

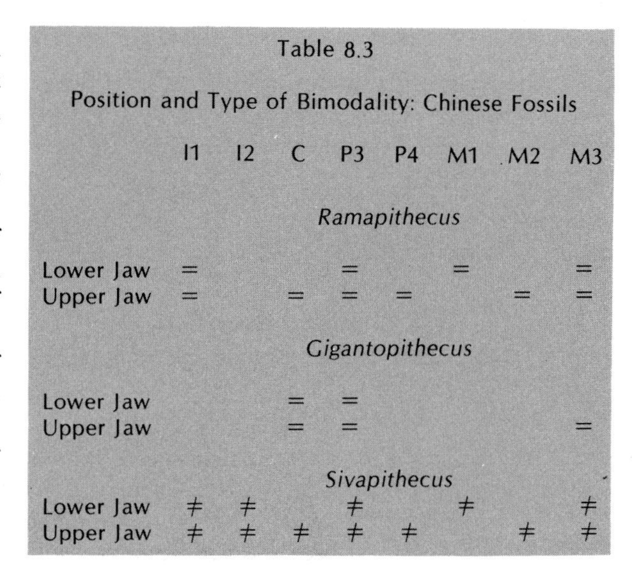

Table 8.3

Position and Type of Bimodality: Chinese Fossils

	I1	I2	C	P3	P4	M1	M2	M3
Ramapithecus								
Lower Jaw	=			=		=		=
Upper Jaw	=		=	=	=		=	=
Gigantopithecus								
Lower Jaw			=	=				
Upper Jaw			=	=				=
Sivapithecus								
Lower Jaw	≠	≠		≠		≠		≠
Upper Jaw	≠	≠	≠	≠	≠		≠	≠

The discovery of the *Sivapithecus* patterns at eight million years suggests something that might be part of an orang-utan radiation. This fits reasonably closely to the present suggestion that the sivapithecines are likely on or close to the orang-utan lineage. But the discovery of the *Ramapithecus* design at eight million years demonstrates not one but a whole package of features that resembles, among all of these groups, only the genus *Homo*. If we are to maintain in any way the idea that any of the australopithecines had anything special to do with human evolution, this finding forces us to accept either several remarkable evolutionary parallels if we exclude this ramapithecine, or several remarkable evolutionary reversals if we include it.

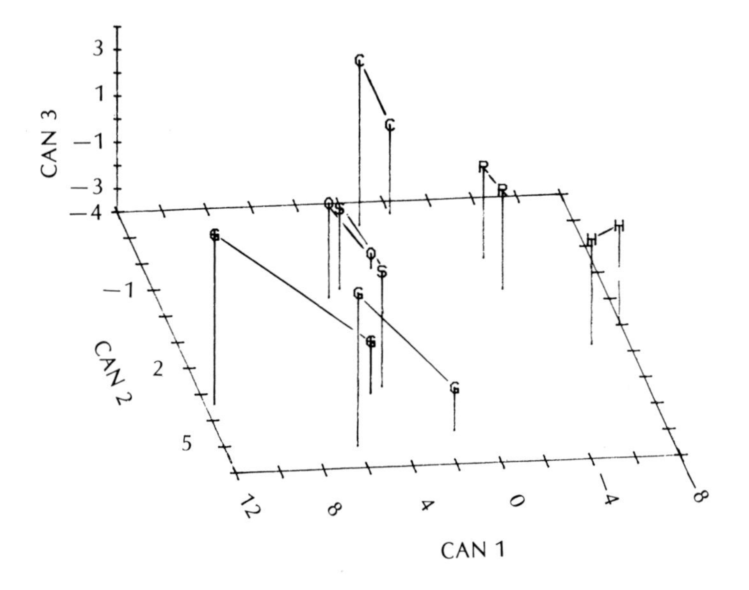

Fig. 8:18 This figure shows the multivariate result for Chinese fossils (H-H = *Homo*, C-C = *Pan*, O-O = *Pongo* and G-G = *Gorilla*, R-R = *Ramapithecus*, S-S = *Sivapithecus* and Ǥ-Ǥ = *Gigantopithecus*, females always on the right). This shows that some of the similarity of *Sivapithecus* to the extant apes, of *Ramapithecus* to extant humans, and to a degree the unique position of *Gigantopithecus*.

Excluding this ramapithecine from an australopithecine/human lineage would require parallel evolution of the system of sexual dimorphism that is common to *Homo sapiens*, *H. neandertalensis*, *H. erectus*, *H. habilis*, and *Ramapithecus*. That would be somewhat remarkable because of the large number of internal features that would have had to have evolved at least twice. These include: small sexual dimorphism of means, small (zero) sexual dimorphism of variances, univariate sexually dimorphic patterns, multivariate sexually dimorphic patterns, multivariate positions, and one-to-one sex ratios. Though one can readily see parallel evolution of one or two such features, it seems to be stretching it somewhat to see parallel evolution of such a large and complex series of features.

Including this ramapithecine form as a preliminary to an australopithecine/human lineage would require a set of evolutionary reversals. This would also be somewhat remarkable because it would have to involve not only one but several reversals in a complex series of features. The reversals would consist of going from one pattern characterized by a two-to-one sex ratio of a pre-ramapithecine form (presumably more like an early ape), through a pattern characterized by a one-to-one sex ratio as in *Ramapithecus*, back through a two-to-one sex ratio, as in one or other australopithecines, and back again to the one-to-one sex ratio as in *Homo*. In addition, these reversals would have to apply not only to the sex ratio that I have cited as an example, but also to most of the other features in which *Ramapithecus* and *Homo* on the one hand differ from australopithecines and presumed early apes on the other.

It makes the clearest sense and provides the simplest picture if we assume that in *Ramapithecus*, *Homo habilis*, *Homo erectus* and *Homo sapiens* we have various members of a radiation of human-like forms that shared similar sexual dimorphisms of means and dispersions, similar patterns of univariate and multivariate sexual dimorphisms and similar one-to-one sex ratios. It means that we can expect, in the future, to find evidence of this type of sexual dimorphism and one-to-one sex ratios at some intermediate time, say, six million years.

There are no data examined here for the far older ramapithecines (ten to eighteen million years ago) from Africa, Europe and India. And there are no data examined here for any of the twenty or more million year old dryopithecines (also possibly from all three continents). Consideration, however, of dating alone would suggest that these species might consist of early great ape-like forms showing great ape-like sex ratios and great ape-like sexual dimorphisms. This will be something to be corroborated or denied as further specimens are examined for these groups from those earlier times.

The Chinese genus: *Gigantopithecus*

Finally, the data examined here for *Gigantopithecus* at two million years in China remain complex and difficult to assess. The individual data from many of the tooth loci suggest that in their great sexual dimorphism of means this species resembles the largest apes. But in their very small sexual dimorphism of variances, however, this species resembles both a particular ape (orang-utans) and all members of the genus *Homo*. In their one-to-one sex ratio the genus resembles humans alone. And in their multivariate sexual dimorphism and multivariate position, the genus is rendered widely different from everything else so far considered.

Whether all this means that *Gigantopithecus* is just completely different from everything else phylogenetically, or whether it means that it is a markedly aberrant species *that is nevertheless related to the human part of the radiation* is a matter for conjecture. Our ultimate evaluation must await more detailed study of these materials. But a proximate evaluation should probably be biased towards the latter, given the finding of a one-to-one sex ratio as being otherwise solely associated with *Homo*.

We have discovered here an evolutionary novelty: extremely strong sexual dimorphism, but in a species with approximately equal numbers of males and females. A new mechanism is needed to account for such a finding (Figs. 8:14 and 8:18).

The usual causal agents suggested for strong sexual dimorphism relate to inter- and intra-sexual competition and are associated with harem mating patterns, marked polygyny, and, as we have seen, two- or three-to-one (or even much greater) sex ratios. In the case of this particular genus, if there was strong inter- and intra-sexual dimorphism it was operating within a social system where the numbers of the sexes were approximately equal. It would seem possible that there could be strong inter- and intra-sexual competition in such a sociosexual arrangement if pair bonding were entirely absent and mating among all possible pairs the norm. That would mean both a polyandrous and polygynous mating system, though not polygyny in the harem sense, recognized in so many animal societies.

Such an arrangement is unusual. In mammals large sexual dimorphism is almost always associated with strong intra-sexual competition and markedly polygynous mating systems. But a special situation is found in certain of the mustelids (and I am indebted to Professor Michael Stoddard of the University of Tasmania for drawing my attention to this). In these species there is marked size sexual dimorphism (males up to twice the size of females) coexisting with a monogamous mating system and no marked intra-sexual competition. The increased size of the males seems to be related to their ability to switch prey during periods when normal prey are in short supply. Both sexes eat creatures such as mice and voles, but when these are in short supply the females take what few mice and voles come their way and the males switch to considerably larger prey such as rabbits (e.g. Lockie, 1976). It would appear most unlikely that 'prey switching' is the reason for equal numbers of males and females being coincident with very marked dimorphism in *Gigantopithecus*.

In *Gigantopithecus*, therefore, we may be looking at a very rare situation. Given their relationships as certainly hominoid, and possibly hominid, it seems to make most sense to look for non-animal, 'para-human', reasons for this curiosity. It is entirely possible that the strong sexual dimorphism, though occurring in a society with equal numbers of females and males and multiple mating pairings, might be due, not to inter- or intra-sexual biological selection, but to strong social role differences between the sexes. If this strong social role were associated with harsh environmental conditions, such as may have existed for small populations of *Gigantopithecus* in earlier times, then marked physical differences might have resulted.

What could be a more likely situation is a combination of the above two factors: equal numbers of each sex, but without pair-bonding and with matings resulting between any and all receptive adults of each sex. The resultant increased proportion of females pregnant at any one time under such a system (perhaps almost all of them), together with harsh environmental conditions, including fierce predator pressures and the relative safety of cave dwelling, could all combine to produce small inter- or intra-sexual selection but strong sex-role differences and therefore strong sexual dimorphism.

Of course, we must be aware that this is speculation. But some set of factors, other than the usual intra- and inter-sexual competition in a society with equal numbers of males and females, does seem to be called for to explain what we have found. It is certainly easier to see such an explanation within the context of a human or para-human behavioural milieu, rather than in a simpler animal social milieu.

It is also possible that the relationship between *Gigantopithecus* and *Homo* is somewhat similar to that between the 'giant' and 'regular' forms of other evolutionary couples, such as seem to be not uncommon among primates and other mammals. Giant subfossil orang-utans and regular orang-utans, giant subfossil gibbons and regular gibbons, perhaps even giant chimpanzees (gorillas) and regular chimpanzees (both almost subfossil), are examples of other such couplets.

There are no data examined here for the much older *Gigantopithecus* specimens (*bilaspurensis*) that are known at six million years from regions outside of China. What they might display can only be conjecture at this point.

A question of pattern: lineage or radiation?

It is possible for these findings to be painted into the current evolutionary picture for the hominoidea, one that includes australopithecines as a part of, or close to, the human lineage (Fig. 8:19). Such a picture requires, however, (**a**) the parallel evolution indicated above, (**b**) the evolutionary reversals indicated above, (**c**) a very definitively located time and a very high speed for the switch between australopithecines and the genus *Homo*, and (**d**) many otherwise indistinguishable members of the australopithecine species to have remained unchanged after the evolutionary switch. All of this seems unreasonable.

It seems far more reasonable to interpolate these findings into the, so far, unacceptable system which does not place the australopithecines as close to human. This is shown in Figure 8:20. It is remarkably simple. It requires only that the relative position, type of sexual dimorphism, and sex ratio characteristic of humans today, be features also found in a pre-human radiation. Under this scheme the Chinese *Ramapithecus* is an early radiating branch and the various species of the genus *Homo*, including *Homo habilis*, are later radiating branches. The Chinese genus *Gigantopithecus* is, under this scheme, a highly aberrant form, but one

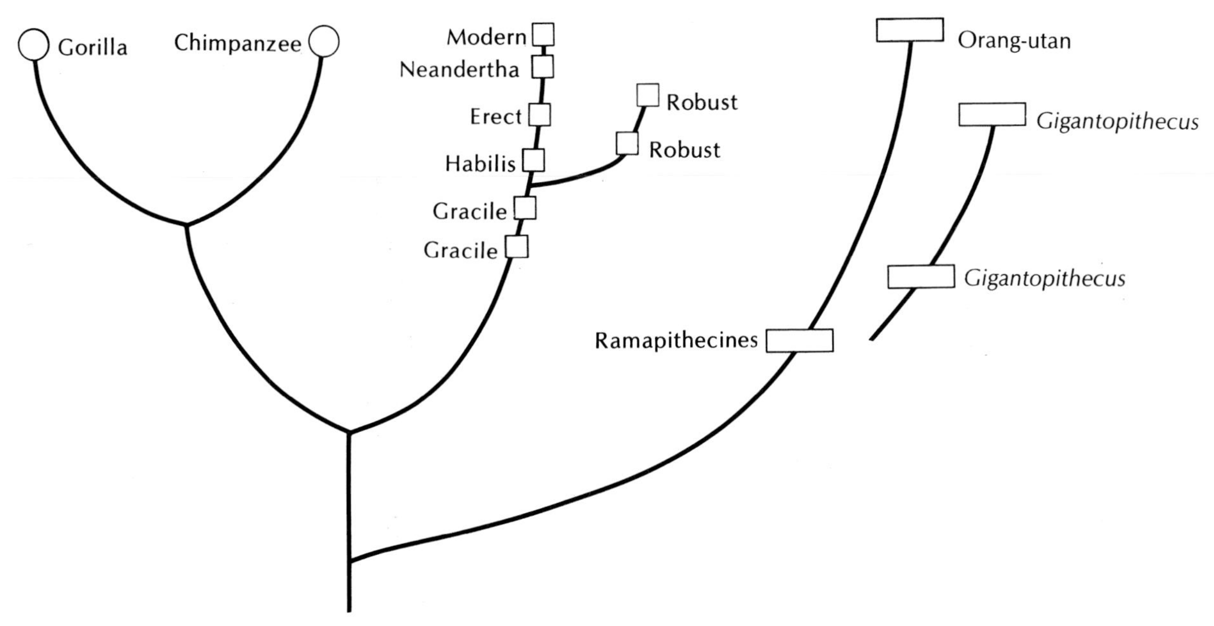

Fig. 8:19 The general thrust of the current idea of the relationships of the extant and fossil hominoids at the present time. A repeat of Fig. 8:3.

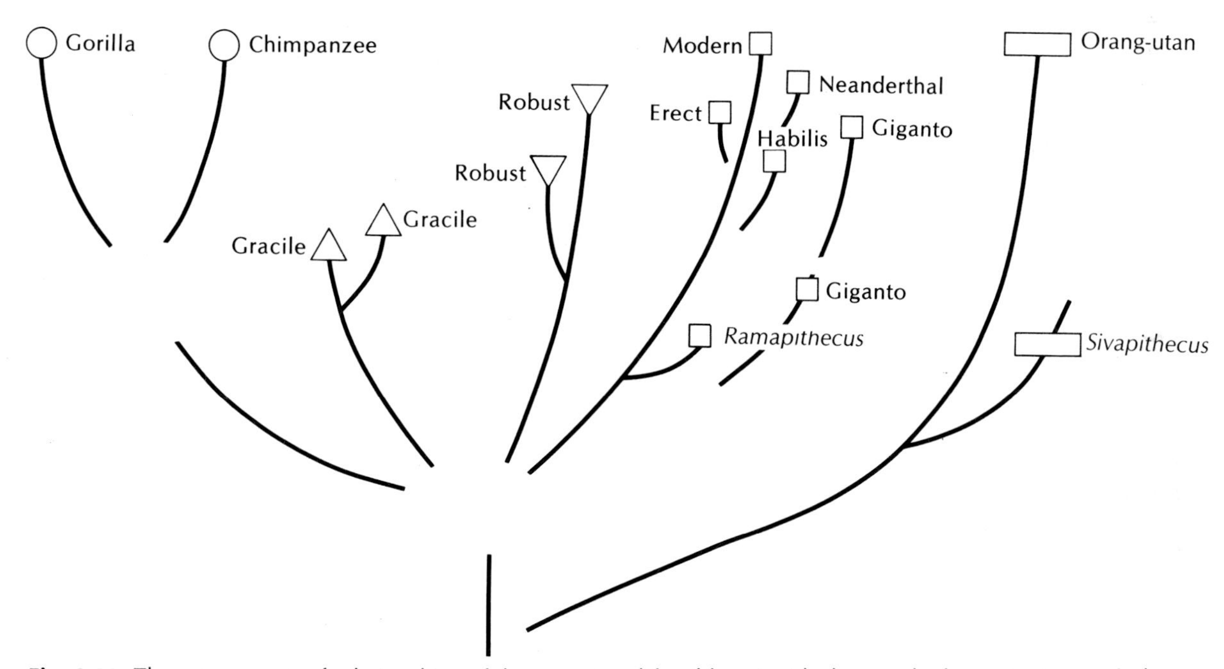

Fig. 8:20 The new system of relationships of the extant and fossil hominoids that results from the data and ideas presented in this book.

displaying enough special pre-human-like or para-human-like features of its socio-sexual structure that it is best linked with the pre-human radiation.

For the australopithecines and the African great apes, the scheme shown in Figure 8:20 is also remarkably simple. It merely suggests that, in addition to the radiation leading towards *Homo* in its various forms, there were other radiating branches leading to a number of other sister groups (African apes, robust australopithecines, gracile australopithecines, perhaps indeed yet others depending upon new discoveries and how palaeontologists eventually agree to split the complex of australopithecines).

This system requires no especial reversals in evolutionary directions, no games with time implying highly specifically dated changes, no marked changes in speed and direction of evolution, and no splitting of australopithecines into those that were prior to the origin of the human lineage and those, otherwise almost indistinguishable, that existed after the origin of the human lineage. It seems altogether more satisfactory.

Perhaps, most of all, this scheme is flexible. It allows future discovery ot australopithecines that are older or younger than those presently known without there having to be a major change in the scheme. It allows the discovery of members of the genus *Homo* that are older than those previously found without doing irreparable damage. It allows prehuman-like forms to be found in the 'gap' between the two and a half million years of the oldest *Homo habilis* and the eight million years of *Ramapithecus*. Such forms are likely to be unearthed as explorations continue. Indeed, in the talus from East Turkana and the humerus from Kanapoi, both more like humans than any australopithecine, these pre-human but non-australopithecine forms may already be represented (again, see Figs. 8:15 and 8:16).

This system does have two major problems and one fascinating implication. One of the problems relates to what is generally believed about the times of hominoid evolution based upon the molecular data. The second problem relates to what is generally believed about the place of human evolution based upon where most of the fossils have been discovered. The fascinating implication involves what we generally think about the evolution of sexual differences. We will take up these matters in subsequent sections.

A question of time: five million years or ten?

All of the possibilities discussed previously are preempted by the general acceptance of 'molecular clock' studies, studies that link humans and African apes as recently as the last five million years (Gribbin and Cherfas, 1983). Indeed, this five million year date for the common ancestor had the palaeontologists urgently fussing and fuming over the fossils for some ten years. There is no doubt in my mind that the principal reason for evicting *Ramapithecus* from the pre-human lineage has been this 'molecular' date. The literature hints that this was the more powerful reason for this change of mind, more so, at any rate, than the re-evaluation of the morphological evidence that went with it.

It is, therefore, necessary to look at the molecular timing rather critically. It turns out that the various molecular clock studies do not all give the same answer. It turns out, also, that there are many problems with the underlying axioms involved in using molecular data to estimate time of divergence. It turns out, furthermore, that the results of the molecular studies have been progressively increasing the length of time since divergence, during the length of time that such studies have been prosecuted. It turns out, finally, that the most recent estimates of 1984 between them cover the entire spectrum of possibilities that have been suggested. Let us examine the findings in more detail.

The most generally accepted molecular estimate about the splitting time for humans and chimpanzees suggests a link between humans and African apes of about five million years. But as various investigators have worked on the problem, the splitting time has been set as low as one million years (Hasegawa, Yano and Kishino, 1984). In between are estimates at three million years (reported in Cronin, 1983). And there were early studies suggesting estimates as high as ten million years (e.g. Bauer, 1972; Read, 1975). So the matter was never fully settled. But it seems as though the five million year estimate (modified to read four to six million years to take account of difficulties in the analyses) might well represent a final assessment. And it is certainly the case that acceptance of that time makes inadmissable any scheme that includes ramapithecines as being linked to humans and not African apes.

One single possibility, however, a resetting of the molecular clock so that the ape-human common ancestor stemmed from some earlier time, say eight million years ago, ten million years ago, or even longer ago would remove all objections to those ideas.

It is, therefore, interesting that some recent findings (e.g. one based upon a specific method: carbonic anhydrase sequences, Goodman *et al.*, 1982, and another based upon a summation of many methods, Cronin 1983) suggest upper limits for the human ape common ancestor as far back as seven and a half, and even eight million years respectively.

It is likewise interesting that yet newer findings from DNA-DNA hybridization studies of Sibley and Ahlquist (1984, also summarized in Lewin, 1983 and Pilbeam, 1984; and see Oxnard, 1983d) suggest an upper limit of as much as eight and ten million years for that common ancestor.

And it is finally interesting that by discounting the notion of linear molecular evolution, Gingerich (1984, 1985) recalculates dates of divergence times from the molecular literature to be as early as eleven to thirteen million years.

With all these recent increases in estimating the date of that common ancestor, the findings of a Japanese laboratory, that the link between humans and African apes might have been as recent as one million years (Hasegawa, Yano and Kishino, 1984) looms especially important.

One million years to thirteen million years in the one year 1984. This surely makes us realize just how problematical these calculations are.

And the even more recent results of Lee and Friedman (1985) and of Wu and Li (1985) remind us of the old idea that 'using the primary structure of a single gene or protein to time evolutionary events...is potentially fraught with error' and that 'there is no such thing as *the* molecular clock' (Lewin, 1985).

Certainly the new estimates of 1984 provide (**a**) enough leeway to allow us easily to include the Chinese *Ramapithecus* as being close to humans and not apes, and (**b**) enough courage to suggest that we are not yet at a time when molecular evolutionary assessments of time mean anything much at all. (Molecular assessments of patterns of clustering, of relationships, are another matter, and are very strong).

A question of place: Asia as well as Africa

In the scientific generation before ours, anthropologists were making most of their findings in Asia. It was not surprising, therefore, that Asia ranked very high upon their list of the places, where events significant to human evolution occurred. Many workers (for instance, Weidenreich, 1940) put forward schemes that included Asia and Asian fossils as important in human evolution.

In our own generation, however, the fact that the most active fossil hunting has taken place in southern and eastern Africa, the fact that dating during this time has been much more accurate, the fact that better comparative studies were being undertaken, these and a whole host of other facts have meant that there has been a very heavy emphasis upon Africa as the place of human origins. This has even been made evident in the titles of books written during this period. The best known of these to the lay public is Ardrey's *African Genesis*, (1963). 'Not in innocence, nor in Asia, was mankind born' is his first sentence. Though Ardrey's idea of killer apes ('not in innocence', Ardrey's first point) has long been known to be wrong (but see later), the new data that we have found may mean that Ardrey was also most likely wrong on the second.

China has now embarked on a much larger scale of fossil studies. And such studies could also be carried out in Malaysia, Vietnam, Thailand, Pakistan, India, Burma, Nepal, Indonesia, and other countries if present economic, political and international situations did not make them extremely difficult. All this suggests that a wealth of pre-human and human fossils remain to be found in Asia. The large numbers of *Gigantopithecus* and *Ramapithecus* specimens, larger by far than finds at single sites in most other parts of the world, given especially the few years that Chinese colleagues have been working in this arena, may be the first evidence of that evidence.

However, looking towards one place on earth for human origins may be as hazardous an exercise as looking for one missing link. Not too long ago *Homo erectus* existed in Africa, Europe and Asia. At an earlier time, ramapithecines of various kinds existed in Africa, Europe and Asia. Even as early as twenty million years ago, we have to recognize that dryopithecine apes existed in Africa, Europe and Asia (Fig. 8:21).

Given the extremely wide dispersion of all these species (and many others, e.g. elephants, large cats, many ungulates), how likely is it that the genus *Homo* can be shown to have arisen specifically in a given place? A specific place may have existed; but presumably finding an ancestor at a specific place is even more statistically unlikely than just finding an ancestor (see the beginning of Chapter 1). Presumably for *Homo* as for any other genus, spread of the new form occurred quickly enough that, given the sampling problems inherent in palaeontology, it may be ludicrous to suggest that all the critical stages of human evolution occurred in one place. And a truly multifocal origin for *Homo* surely cannot be ruled out.

There is now clear evidence that critical events occurred in China about eight million years ago. Others may have occurred there about two million years ago. We do not yet know what may have happened in between. Certainly other events critical in early pre-human evolution (e.g. *Homo habilis*) are known from Africa. But that genesis of *Homo* in Africa represents the whole story, is unlikely in the extreme.

Fig. 8:21a World distribution of fossil *Homo*.

Fig. 8:21b World distribution of ramapithecines.

Fig. 8:21c World distribution of dryopithecines.

A Question of Sex: Similarity and Difference

The findings in this book mean that we need to re-evaluate some aspects of similarities and differences between the sexes in human evolution. Many prior studies of sexual dimorphism may have been interpreted too simply in the past. It is unlikely that small sexual dimorphism always means monogamy, big sexual dimorphism, polygyny.

One part of the new complexity relates to the fact that sex ratios may change a great deal, or only a little, during the life histories of the different species. Primates are usually believed to show approximately one-to-one sex ratios at birth (e.g. Austin, Edwards and Mittwoch, 1981). Professor Wesley Whitten has drawn my attention to the fact that in adults the matter of sex ratios is far more problematical. In monogamous species one-to-one sex ratios are almost always recorded. But in polygynous species very different sex ratios may be seen in specific local populations. And this can change rapidly over relatively small periods of time as groups coalesce or break up. Though there are usually more females than males, individual troupes can be seen with more males at specific times.

Thus the sex ratio, with which we must be concerned, is not what is seen in small spatial and temporal situations, but what exists as the global average over a longer time and in a larger geographical space. Under this circumstance it is likely that true adult sex ratios in polygynous apes are such that there are more adult females than adult males. Actual documentation of this is difficult. But Colin Groves, of the Australian National University, has drawn my attention to the work of Smith and Lee (1984) who were able to write of some other species that "in general, phalangeroids are characterized by a disproportionately high mortality in the juvenile age group, and this effect is more severe on males than females in species with polygynous mating systems". Such information suggests that infant and juvenile mortality is likewise large in polygynous primates and preferentially greater in males than females.

A second, larger part of the complexity includes the fact that polygyny and monogamy strictly defined are by no means the only possibilities (Hrdy, 1981). Primates live in pairs, as solitary individuals, in small unisex bands, in large multimale troupes, as small subunits that can on occasion link up into large associations, and as flexible individuals and communities that can move over from any of these to any other. Virtually every known social system exists except polyandry (one female several males). Thus, adult sex ratio cannot be indisputably linked with any single one of these. It is true, however, that many-to-one female-to-male ratios exclude consistent living in pairs. Many of these features are evident among the large apes.

A third part of the complexity relates to the fact that the idea of simple male dominance, especially when related to smaller females, is not necessarily correct. 'Females can be dominant, subordinate, equal, or not interested' (Hrdy, 1981). And this greatly affects social sexual relationships between the sexes. It is true that there are frequently dominance relationships among males that result in certain males temporarily gaining most (but not all) of the access to breeding females.

But it is now well documented that females are often accorded high or even the highest status. Even in polygynous situations females may take priority at feeding. They may control access to other group members. Females, with their infants, are, in such cases, often the central members of the groups, chasing some male members to the periphery. And females sometimes even form networks that have the effect of protecting female offspring more than male offspring. All this is relatively new information that stands in marked contrast to the conventional view of 'central male hierarchies' and 'dominant male leaders' (e.g. as reviewed in Liebowitz, 1978; Nowak, 1980; Hrdy, 1981).

All this has implications for the new features that we have observed in the dental anatomies: the major differences in patterns of structural sexual dimorphism, and the major differences in female/male ratios. They can be set against what we have found here for the living species. And they have special implications for what we have found in the fossils.

Sex ratio and sexual dimorphism in humans

Let us first look at humans. The sex ratio in adult humans is approximately one female to one male. It is true that there is a slight imbalance in this ratio at birth because of slight differences in viability of female as compared with male foetuses. In all probability this is a result of a marked imbalance at conception (perhaps as many as 140 males are conceived to each 100 females). This is reduced through spontaneous abortion and miscarriage to the approximately 106 males to every 100 females at birth, (Austin, Edwards and Mittwoch, 1981).

The changing balance towards fewer males continues throughout life. Perinatal male mortality is slightly greater than that of females, presumably to do at least in part with constitutional differences between the sexes. Infant, child, adolescent and young-adult male mortalities are slightly greater than those of equivalent females for many reasons. But the main one seems to be greater accidental death in males than in females. Even in mature adult life and with great age the differential mortality continues. In these cohorts it is more to do with disease than accident. Thus, the numbers of males falls more quickly, the ratio of females to males continues to rise, throughout life.

New data suggest that recent changes for females, such as increased contact with the accidents of a wider world (as more women work than ever before) and increased contact with carcinogens (as more women smoke than ever before) are starting to affect these ratios.

Having said all this however, the numbers of sexually mature males and females in most human populations are approximately even. The slight modifications of the approximately one-to-one ratio implied by these possibilities can only be seen when large samples are studied. The sizes of samples that have been available in the investigations in this book are small enough that they are only capable of providing an approximate estimate of one-to-one. They are not capable of revealing the more subtle variations on the one-to-one theme.

With this approximately one-to-one ratio go rather small sexual dimorphisms of the various kinds (means, dispersions, univariate patterns, multivariate patterns and so on) as compared, as we have seen, with large dimorphisms in our closest extant relatives. And these small dimorphisms are associated with sexual social arrangements in humans that are generally thought of as monogamous. Certainly that would be the conclusion that we would draw if we used the same arguments for humans as we use for non-human primates that have reduced sexual dimorphism.

Of course, we know that this is only true in a general sense. There is approximately a one-to-one adult sex ratio. There is generally a monogamous situation with a nuclear family structure. But we are all aware that when factors are suitable (i.e. when power, resources or money are markedly inequitable) a degree of polygyny may result. However, this type of polygyny does not imply imbalance in numbers. It exists alongside equal numbers of each sex. It is clearly different from what is observed in primates with large sexual dimorphism, where there truly is a larger number of adult females to each adult male. In these species, polygyny is obligatory, as it were. In humans it is merely facultative (that is: allowed or permitted, but not obligatory).

It may be less well-known that facultative polygyny is also true of some of the other lesser dimorphic primates. Thus most gibbons show small sexual dimorphism. And gibbons are basically monogamous. But it is recorded that, in fact, when food resources are especially abundant and especially easily defended, then some gibbons may form some polygynous groups. As in humans, however, this occurs within the general milieu of a one-of-one sex ratio.

This probably also applies to some of the other so-called monogamous primates. My example for gibbons does not include particular gibbons such as *Hylobates concolor* which truly is more sexually dimorphic than other gibbons, and which actually is somewhat more polygynous (Hrdy, 1981; Haimoff, personal communication).

The point of all this is to say that one-to-one ratios and monogamy do not go strictly together. But in some general sense they do. What this may imply will become clearer later.

Sex ratios and sexual dimorphisms in great apes

Let us now look at the great apes. Although it has not been well studied, it is likely the approximate sex ratio at birth is also one-to-one. There are probably minor variations in this figure for reasons somewhat similar to those in humans. However, in marked contrast with humans, it would appear that there really is a sex ratio in adult life that is of the order of two, three or four females to each male.

Some of the unbalancing factors for the apes may be the same as in humans. This would include increased death rates in male infant, child, adolescent and young adult groups, as compared with females, for reasons that are to do mainly with the increased susceptibility of the male to accident. But presumably such a factor would tamper only a little with the adult sex ratio as it does in humans. It is unlikely to be the main cause of the markedly unbalanced adult sex ratios in the apes.

It is possible that the main causes are now

known, thanks to studies in recent years by investigators such as Hrdy (e.g. 1979, 1981, 1983), Butynski (1982), Meickle, Tilford and Vessey (1984) and many others, see also reviews by McKenna (1983) and Hausfater and Hrdy (1984). They need to be seen, however, within the complexly different social arrangements of these several female/few male ratios in each ape. We therefore examine these arrangements first.

Orang-utans live in peculiar 'asocial' arrangements whereby individual solitary males have large (say twenty mile) territories with little overlap to those of other males. Each female, together with several of her immature young of different ages, has a smaller (say five mile) territory. The single solitary male services several adult females. Such an arrangement presumably means that there genuinely is a smaller number of adult males than females. However, we cannot be absolutely certain of that because there likely exist solitary younger males who do not participate (or participate less) in sexual activity than the small number of primary males.

In gorillas somewhat similar two-to-one or three-to-one adult female-to-male ratios exist as in adult orang-utans. The social structure is, however, quite different. Social groups ('family' groups) consist, usually, of one adult breeding male and two or three adult females and their offspring living in the same territory. This is more obviously a polygynous situation. And it does, therefore, seem that the adult female-to-male ratio will be several-to-one. Again, however, there may be some immature or young adult males living either solitarily or in small two- or three-male bands. Whether these are numerous enough to restore the adult female-male ratio to one-to-one is possible, but problematical to say the least.

Finally, chimpanzees also have similar ratios of several females to fewer males. However, the details are different. Chimpanzees display a third socio-sexual arrangement. They live in social groups with several males and a somewhat greater number of females. Rather than being a simple polygynous situation (one male to two or three females) there seems to be considerably more promiscuity than is generally observed in orang-utans and gorillas. That is: the larger numbers of females copulate with each of the smaller number of males. Whether this is random, indiscriminate or in some other pattern is not yet totally clear. This is a more complex situation. Yet it is associated with a final ratio of more females to males.

In the case of chimpanzees, it is well known that solitary males, usually younger adults, live unassociated with the breeding groups until such changes occur as may draw them into a group. And it is also well known that some younger adult males do actually form all-male bands that have little to do with family units until one or more are drawn into such a unit (sometimes by the death of the main male). Again, not enough is known about the vital statistics of chimpanzees to be certain, if these peripheral males are sufficiently numerous, to bring the female-male ratio down to one-to-one or not. But factors like those discussed hereafter suggest that it is unlikely that they are.

In all probability, peripheral males notwithstanding, the real ratio of adult females to males is two- or three-to-one in each of the great apes.

What could possibly be the cause of this?

This is where we must intercalate the recent work of Hrdy (1979, 1981, 1983), Butinsky (1982), Meickle, Tilford and Vessey (1984) and many others, see also reviews by McKenna (1983) and Hausfater and Hrdy (1984). These studies have shown, in a number of groups of polygynous primates, that there is a special differential male mortality. This is not due to the ordinary kinds of accidents that might affect infants, young, or immature adults of either sex.

First, in infant life and young childhood, death is likely to occur at the hands of adult males within the group. This is especially the case when there has just been a change of breeding male, but is apparently also a propensity at other times in the life of a group. This affects male offspring more than female in part because male offspring trespass further from their mothers and are more likely to come within the purview of the infanticidal male. It is also, in part because there is some considerable tendency for the mother to proffer extra preferential protection to her female offspring.

Second, into subadult and young adulthood, the young males are likely to be challenged and attacked by adult breeding males, so that they are 'chased off' into solitariness or into all-male bands. During such challenges some are likely to be injured and this will have a not inconsiderable associated mortality. Even if injury does not result, a significant proportion of these males, younger and less experienced, less well able to protect themselves, are forced into the solitary state where they are more likely to be killed through predation, or through the attacks of bands of other all-male groups. Young males may even, on occasion, be forced into the more dangerous solitary periphery by groups of females acting in concert. The all-male groups are not stable protective entities, as there is often replacement of some members into breeding groups that is likely to leave others in the solitary and less defensible situation.

Finally, there is a reverse effect, differential protection of younger females living with the family groups, that has its own reciprocal effect in enhancing the ratio of females to males. This is the existence of a 'network' among most, or all, of the females of individual family groups that result in female offspring being more closely looked after, and therefore more protected, by co-operating groups of adult females, than are equivalent males of the same age.

This information is not available in a detailed manner for orang-utans, gorillas and chimpanzees. But detailed studies do exist for many polygynous forms such as rhesus monkeys, *Macaca mulatta* (Meickle, Tilford and Vessey, 1984), blue monkeys, *Gercopithecus mitis stuhlmanni* (Butynski, 1982), langurs, *Presbytis entellus* (Hrdy, 1981) red howler monkeys, *Alouatta seniculus* (Crockett and Sekulic, 1984) and baboons, *Papio* (Collins, Busse and Goodall, 1984). Such activities have certainly been reported, but in a more anecdotal manner, in apes. Thus the work of Fossey (1976, 1984) among gorillas and Goodall (1977) among chimpanzees showed that these species have a record of infanticide that is impressive, given their smaller numbers of births. And infanticide has also been reported for the orang-utan (Hrdy, 1981, Hausfater and Hrdy, 1984).

It must immediately be recorded that not all infanticides result in changes in female-to-male adult ratios. Some must affect infants of both sexes equally. Nor, indeed, do all infanticides occur within the breeding groups. The circumstances vary widely. Some relate to killings by new males of many infants at the time of their original establishment within a group. Some are not even aimed at infants at all, but at females who may be merely carrying an infant (which may be damaged or killed in the altercation). Some may be related to the 'stealing' of adult females by another group. Many seem to be related to inter-group conflicts and the introduction of new members into groups. Probably there are many others factors involved. But one end result of all of this, whatever else it may be related to, is likely to be a final adult female-to-male ratio that is markedly greater than one.

These factors do not operate, or operate to much lesser degrees, in species which, irrespective of whether or not polygyny exists, usually display monogamy, have equal numbers of relatively similar males and females, and display more co-operative arrangements between them.

We cannot, thus, directly relate many-female/few-male ratios to polygyny alone, because polygyny does occur in equal female/male ratio groups. But what we perhaps can equate with many-female/few-male ratios is (**a**) high competition between males (with killing of males), (**b**) high co-operation between females (with differential protection of females), and (**c**) high aggression between one male and another, and between males and females (often with groups of females banding together against individual males). All these factors contribute to the imbalance in adult sex ratio in the types of polygynous groups found in the great apes. All these factors are, presumably, much less in equal female-to-male ratio groups.

Conversely, in equal female-to-male ratio groups it is known that the equal ratio is not only the result of the absence of these three features (**a**), (**b**) and (**c**) above, but also due to the presence of yet others: (**d**) a more equal caring for offspring of both sexes by both parents, and (**e**) a more equal sharing and co-operation by adults of both sexes in foraging, in territory maintenance, in defence against predators, and so on.

It thus seems, that it is not polygyny or monogamy *per se* that is the important difference. It is, rather, the existence of many-to-one or one-to-one adult sex ratios that tells us about the differences between these two sets of social systems.

Sex ratios and sexual dimorphisms in the fossils

How do the various fossils appear when we apply these ideas to them?

There have been two attempts to look at these matters in fossils in recent years. One is the idea that humans have evolved from a markedly dimorphic, strongly polygynous species (like modern apes) into the category of a 'lesser dimorphic' and 'mildly polygynous' species with 'female promiscuity' (Hrdy, 1981). This idea leans heavily upon matters in the great apes as models of what may have been prior pre-human behaviours. It is dependent upon the view that the australopithecines have large sexual dimorphism and presumed obligatory polygyny (*my presumption*) and that these have become reduced to smaller dimorphism and 'mild' polygyny as evolution proceeded towards modern humans.

The second is the older, and directly contrary notion that humans are basically monogamous. It has received a recent boost through the idea that pair bonding was crucial to the emergence of early humans (Lovejoy, 1981). But because Lovejoy is also wedded to the idea that australopithecines were direct human ancestors, he is forced, as Hrdy (1981) points out, to play down the evidence for large dimorphism in australopithecines and, as he believes, in other early pre-humans. He has to provide special pleading, to argue that 'human sexual dimorphism is clearly not typical'.

Both these concepts are affected by our new findings for the fossils. The first idea would seem to be denied by the findings in this book, that imply that small dimorphism and one-to-one sex ratios are ancient in the human lineage. The second is denied by the recognition that there need be no special pleading for pair bonding and general monogamy in pre-humans, because that system did not arise from, but rather bypassed, the large dimorphism and the (as we now know from our results) several-to-one female to male ratios of the australopithecines.

Our data show that the highly dimorphic and truly several-female-to-each-male ratios of the living apes are also evident in all species of australopithecines and in the Chinese *Sivapithecus*. Although there are also major differences between all these species, they must have shared obligatory polgyny.

This suggests that special protection of female offspring and lack of protection of male offspring through (**a**) unequal protection of adult females with unequal killing by adult males, through (**b**) competition between adult males, and through (**c**) aggression against adult females, with co-operation between adult females against adult males may, as in the living apes, have characterized all four australopithecines species and the Chinese *Sivapithecus*. (It is in this sense, a sense different from what he originally intended, that Ardrey's term 'killer apes' may, in fact, have a modicum of truth within it).

We must, of course, be most cautious in suggesting hypotheses as to social structure based upon the sex ratio findings alone. However, when several-female to few-male sex ratios are associated with large sexual dimorphism and, separately, a considerable degree of canine dimorphism, as is the case in all these groups, then strong morphological sexual selection can probably be assumed, and either obligatory polygyny and other modes evident in the polygynous apes and monkeys are not unlikely.

Our data also show that, as in *Homo sapiens*, there is small dimorphism and a one-to-one ratio in *Homo sapiens neandertalensis*, *Homo erectus*, *Homo habilis* and the Chinese *Ramapithecus*. It would seem likely that obligatory polygyny could not have operated in those forms. Such polygyny as did exist need be no different from that found in any monogamous species on occasion.

This suggests, first, that the factors associated with several-to-one sex ratios and, therefore, obligatory polygyny: (**a**) high competition between males (with differential loss of younger males), (**b**) high co-operation between females (with differential protection of younger females), and (**c**) high aggression among males and between males and females, did not exist in *Homo sapiens*, *H. s. neandertalensis*, *H. erectus*, *H. habilis*, and *Ramapithecus*.

It suggests, second, that what may have existed in these fossils, extending back certainly to three and a half million years, perhaps even to eight million years, is the absence of features (**a**), (**b**) and (**c**), together with the presence of (**d**) a more equal caring for offspring of both sexes by both parents, and (**e**) a more equal sharing by adults of both sexes in foraging, in territory maintenance and in defence against predators.

Of course, we must be most cautious in suggesting hypotheses as to social structure based upon the sex ratio findings alone. However, when equal sex ratios are associated with reduced sexual dimorphism overall and, separately, reduced canine dimorphism, as is the case in all these groups, then strong morphological sexual selection can probably be discounted, and either general monogamy or social groups of equal numbers are likely.

We can see that the evolution of a large brain may have been only a late character of the human lineage (Fig. 8:22). After all, that feature only goes back perhaps three million years (with the brain of *Homo habilis* being the earliest brain known that is significantly larger than that of other hominoids.

We can even see that the evolution of bipedality may have been only an intermediate character of the pre-human radiation. Bipedality, presumably, does not go back beyond, say, some four million years as bipedality evolved, whether twice or several times, in this entire assemblage of hominoid fossils (Fig. 8:23).

No, the key difference may have been the fact

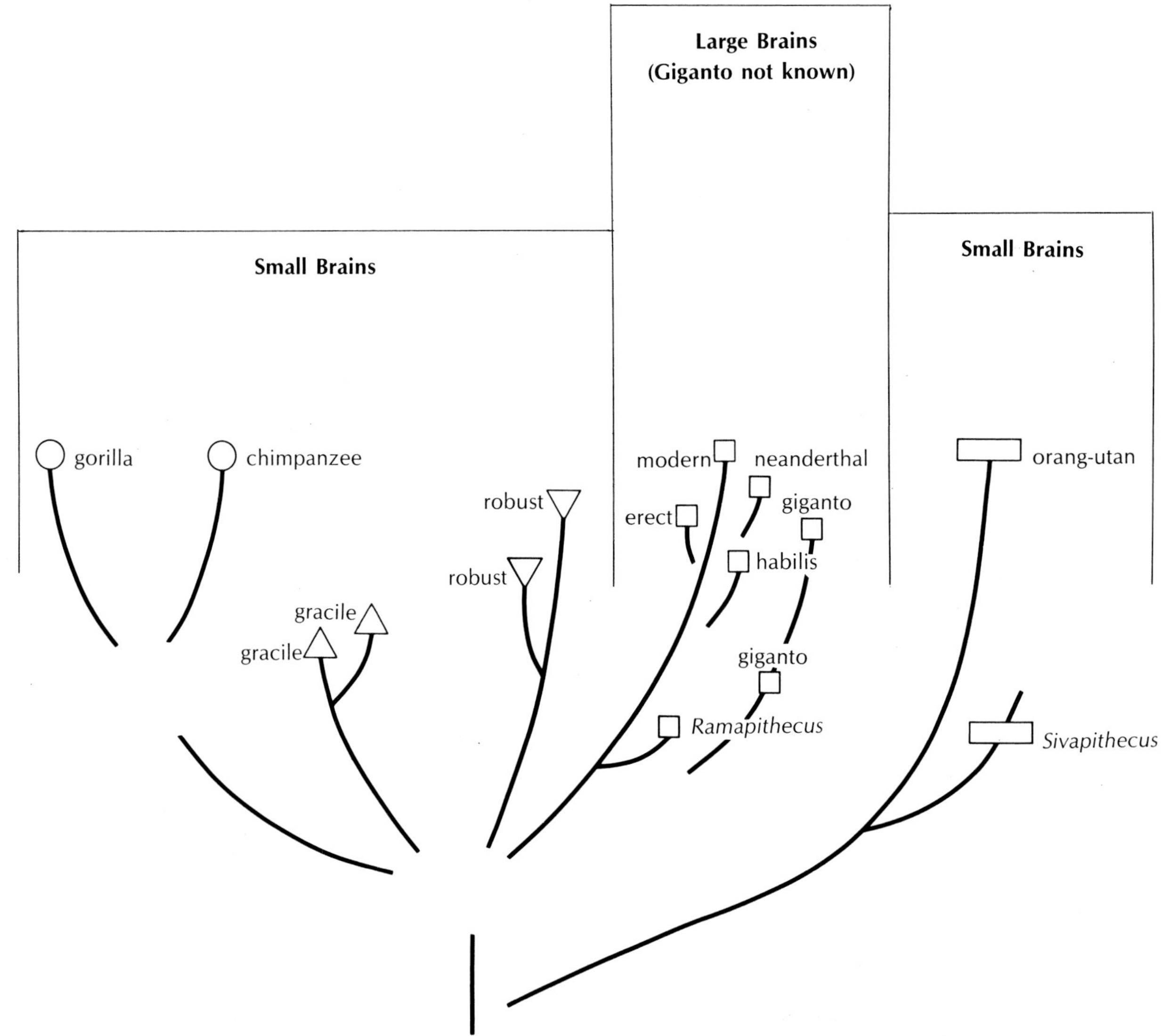

Fig. 8:22 The new system seen in the light of data about skull capacity.

that the basic background in the human lineage and related forms was small sexual dimorphism and one-to-one sex ratios. This would compare with large sexual dimorphism and several-to-one sex ratios not only in the various evolving apes of the day, but also in the radiations involving the four australopithecines species (Fig. 8:24).

The paradoxes that Hrdy (1981) causes in positing an originally polygynous system in pre-humans may not be necessary. And the contortions that Lovejoy (1981) enjoys because he has to have both monogamy and the australopithecines in the same cake may be unnecessary. Much of the data in this book suggest that monogamy in pre-humans could have existed for a very long time, and that this could well have been parallel to polygyny in relatives, but not ancestors, the Australopithecinae.

The key adaptation may have been the development, in an already essentially monogamous species with pair bonding and a nuclear family structure, of small social communities of equal numbers of adults of each sex and small role differences between the sexes. Presumably this could have lead to the 'mild' polygyny (and even the 'mild promiscuity') that seems to exist not infrequently in our species today. This adaptation may have been possible only in a species with small biological role differences between the sexes (as in monogamous non-human primates).

This key adaptation may involve the role of

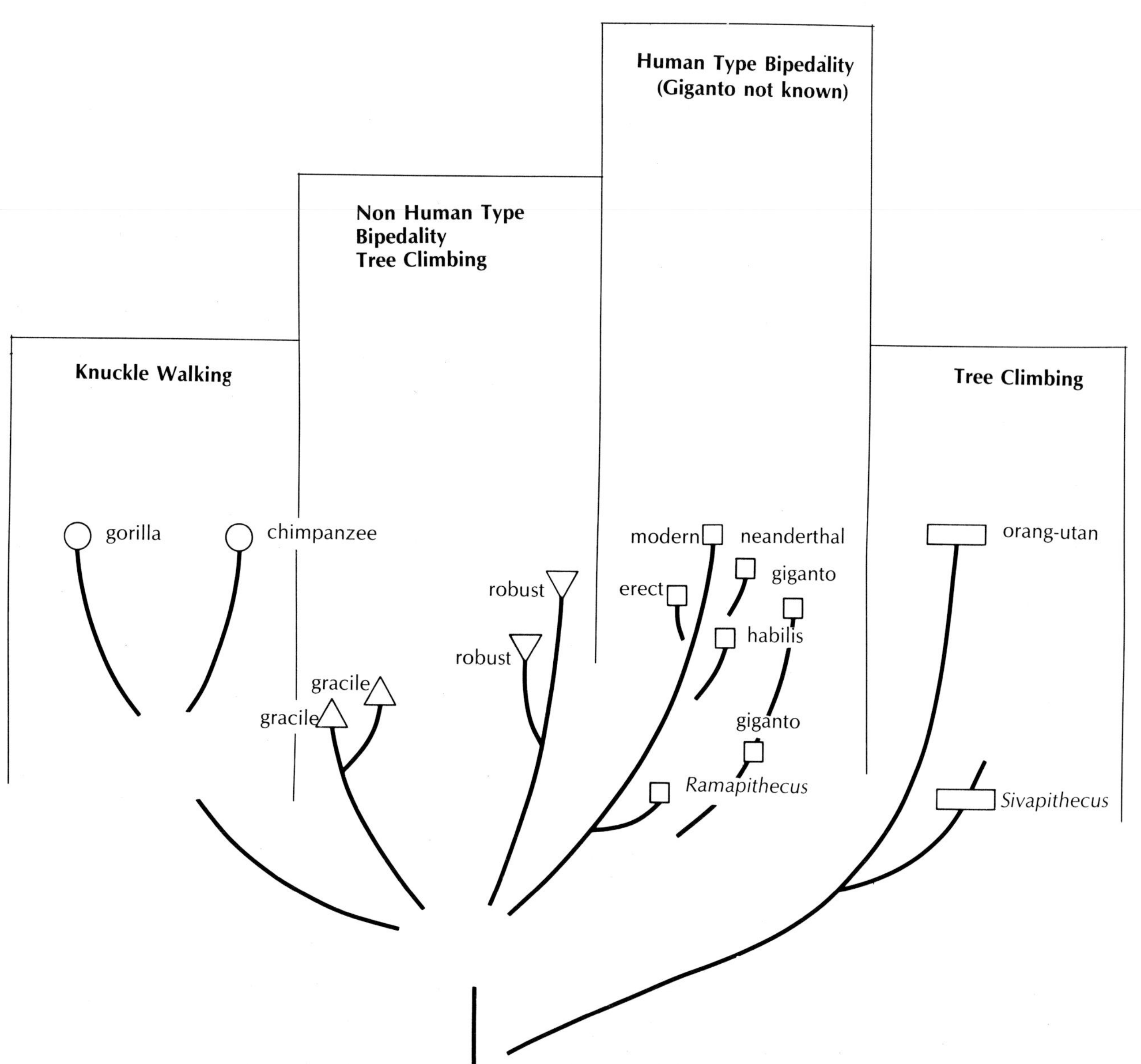

Fig. 8:23 The new system seen in the light of data about locomotion.

olfaction in the evolution of specifically human sexual biology. The idea has been proposed by Professor Michael Stoddard, and I am indebted to him for the following discussion resulting from a recent visit that I made to the University of Tasmania.

Most primates (but not all) do not provide externally recognizable visual signals advertising ovulation. But the importance of covert olfactory signals of ovulation has been generally ignored by anthropologists discussing the evolution of the sexual history of humans. In fact, marked olfactory signals of ovulation are now well recognized in many primates (e.g. Doty, 1976; Gautier and Gautier, 1977; Vandenburgh, 1983; Albone, 1984). But the involvement of olfactory signals in human reproduction, if any, is a matter of dispute.

When the very early pre-human stock first became gregarious with co-operation, and if that stock (whether *Homo habilis* at nearly three million years or *Ramapithecus* at almost eight) were monogamous, as is clearly suggested by the data in this book, then it would be necessary for pre-existing olfactory signals of ovulation to be repressed. Such a repression would prevent non-bonded females from being pursued by males other than her bonded mate while he was absent during co-operative endeavours. And it would, therefore, prevent the development of polgynous situations that have actually evolved in australopithecines and the

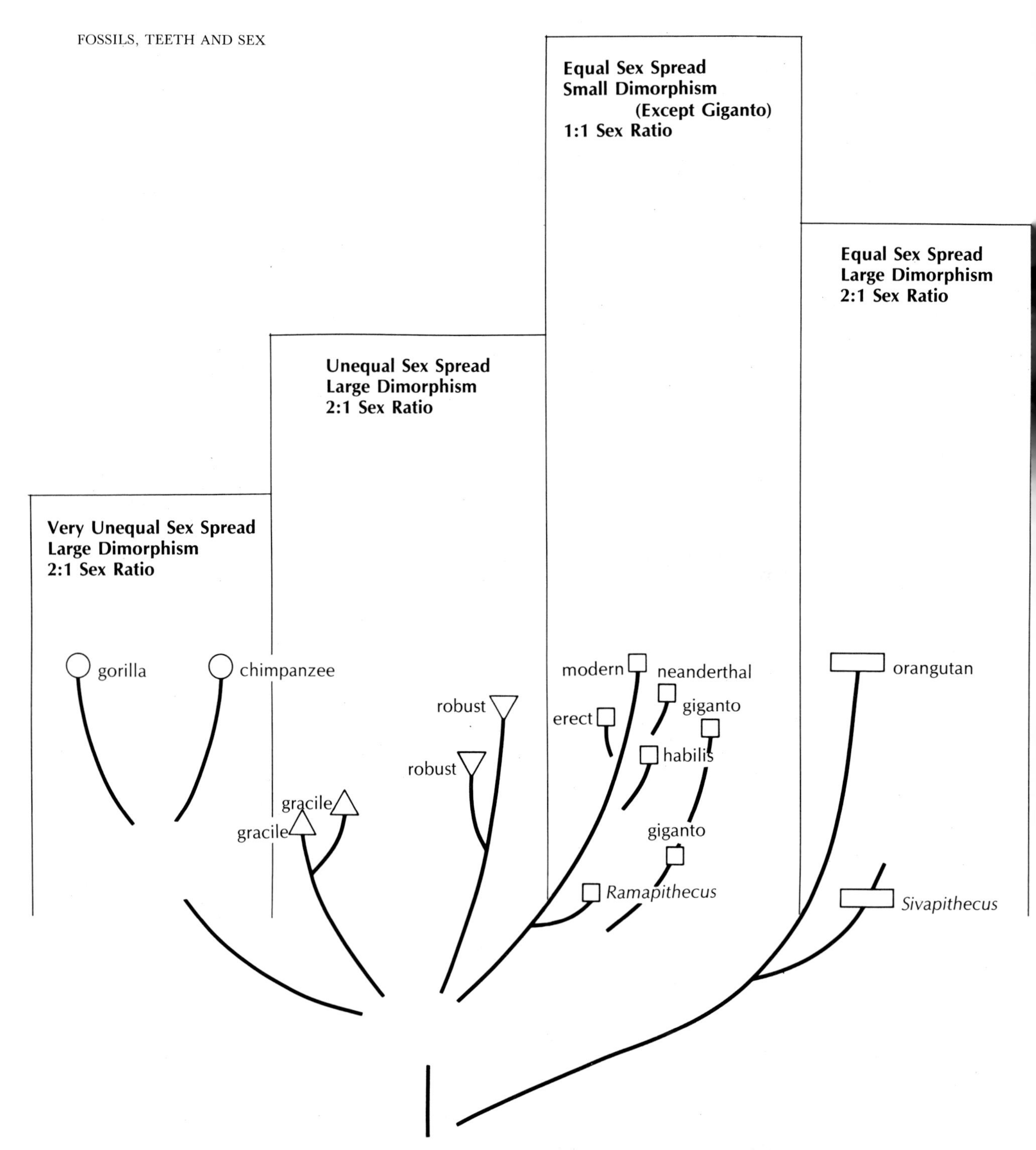

Fig. 8:24 The new system seen in the light of data about sexual dimorphism.

extant great apes. Certainly, as far as modern humans are concerned, there is, as yet, little evidence that odours play much part in the identification of ovulation.

This change probably did not occur through repression of the production of the olfactory compounds. Humans are as 'smelly', actually much more so, than most other primates. They produce glandular and urinary metabolites with strong scents. And it appears that all races and cultures place great importance upon artificial 'body odour' suggesting a deep seated psychological awareness that bodies should smell.

Nor did this change likely occur through the

olfactory inability of humans to sense these compounds. For though some humans today cannot 'smell' such substances, many others can. And the use of artificial scents is ubiquitous in both sexes of humans today.

It is most likely that the changes were initially due to alterations in the central nervous system mechanism so that, though both 'produced', and 'smelled', the neurological signals induced were 'scrambled' so that they did not retain their original meaning of ovulation. Such a mechanism may have been a most important part of a system, allowing monogamous early pre-humans to become gregarious, without intrasexual competition leading to the evolution of polygyny and unbalanced sex ratios as in australopithecines and modern apes (Stoddard, 1985).

Thus, the competitive and aggressive habits of many-to-one sex ratios, and the large sexual dimorphisms associated with large biological role differences between the sexes, may have been what prevented the humanization of both apes and australopithecines. Conversely, the co-operative habits of one-to-one sex ratios, and the small sexual dimorphisms associated with small biological role differences between the sexes, may have been what allowed monogamous groups of 'non-australopithecines' to band together in small communities. This may have produced initially only small differences in social role in each sex. Thus, may have occurred the gradual humanization of those fossils that were sibling both to the australopithecines and to the progenitors of the African apes.

These new evolutionary possibilities may fit well with the idea of relatively equal sex roles in 'prehumans, the scavengers', rather than the markedly unequal sex themes implied by 'men, the hunters'. A possible scavenging origin of human foraging has been put forward most clearly by Shipman (1985) as she describes for us new work in taphonomy.

Scavenging of all kinds may well have been the original break from the primarily vegetarian diets, with only little animal protein, that characterize so many non-human primates of the present day. Truly omnivorous diets, with reasonably large volumes of animal products, may have stemmed originally from scavenging. This may well have been most easily achieved in the small group situation, with the sexes operating in a co-operative mode. Though Shipman sees some evidence of scavenging in australopithecines, this may not have developed anywhere near as far in them, as in the one-to-one sexually balanced non-australopithecines.

What are we to make of *Gigantopithecus*? This peculiar species has enormous sexual dimorphism as judged, both by the skulls, and certainly by our analyses of the teeth. Yet it clearly has one-to-one sex ratios. I have not heard of this combination in any part of the primate world. And even among mammals this exists rarely, for instance in some mustelids monogamous but highly dimorphic, for reasons other than intrasexual competition. One can only assume, therefore, that the causal factors were not those that could exist in a primate or mammalian world. Could they be factors that existed only in some special, non-animal, situation existing within *Gigantopithecus* alone? This may be the species for which special pleading is required.

What could this special pleading be but something different from animals, something stemming, perhaps, from social and cultural factors related to an aberrant human-like situation? It is of particular interest that in *Gigantopithecus* there is actually evidence of a slight bias towards more males than females. One can readily imagine that factors such as: (**a**) obstetric complications coexisting with (**b**) extremely harsh environmental conditions acting upon a small cave dwelling community, and (**c**) a series of social role differences in relation to both the foregoing, could be associated with the curious combination, of very large dimorphism and approximately one-to-one ratios, and a bias towards more males. The one-to-one ratios might imply a human type of co-operative endeavour, without marked aggression and competition. The large sexual dimorphism might imply, that the marked social role differentiation described above, was associated with a physical difference between the sexes. The slightly greater number of males than females may even have been related to the additional reproductive fragility of females in harsh conditions, and from 'social and sexual promiscuity' in these communities. These are not features such as might be operative in most animal societies.

Last words, new thoughts

These new thoughts, about structural sexual dimorphism have implications, it seems to me for other non-structural differences between the sexes.

As long as a single pattern of structural sexual difference, in hominoids, is thought to be part of a consistent arrangement that might be as old as twenty million years (if of hominoid origin) or forty million years (if of anthropoid origin) or seventy million years (if confined to primates) or even one hundred and twenty million years (if broadened to include all mammals), then the genetic basis of that dimorphism might be supposed to be equally old. This could be interpreted as implying truly ancient, and perhaps very rigid, biological constraints within which the new human structural sexual dimorphism must have appeared very recently, and to which it must be very firmly attached.

If, instead, the various patterns of structural differences between the sexes are different in each hominoid, then structural sexual dimorphism has changed several times very recently in parallel within the hominoid radiation. Hereditary components in its causality, would therefore, also be much more recent. And would have changed more frequently than is usually thought. The biological basis of hominoid structural sexual dimorphisms would then be very new and malleable.

To the degree that findings, about biological structure, suggest ideas about non-structural aspects of organisms then they also suggest that we should re-evaluate some of our ideas about non-biological sexual dimorphism in humans.

If the biological constraints, on structural sexual dimorphisms, are so much more relaxed than we have ever thought, then the biological constraints that may act on any non-structural, social, cultural, psychological, intellectual or other sexual dimorphisms, may be even smaller, even newer, even more plastic and more modifiable by epigenetic, environmental and psycho-social factors. Certainly these biological constraining factors may be much less than recent work in sociobiology leads us to suspect.

If biological causal factors are less necessary then non-biological causal factors may be correspondingly more important. The non-biological factors that affect similarities and differences between the sexes include (**a**) the equal existence, or not, of mentally enriched environments during development in both sexes, (**b**) the encouragement, or not, of individual decision-making, of new family arrangements between adults and in child raising for both sexes, (**c**) change, or no change, in individual and societal expectations for education and legislation, in economics and power for both sexes, and so on. These non-biological factors may all be much less constrained, much faster acting, and much more available to condition the non-structural similarities and differences between the sexes, than many of us may think.

All this provides exciting possibilities for improving the relationships of the sexes in different societies. It also places us in danger of worsening conditions in ways that may be difficult to foresee.

References

Adams, L. M., and Moore, J. W. 1975 A biomechanical appraisal of some skeletal features associated with head balance and posture in the Hominoidea. *Acta Anatomica*, **92**: 580-594.

Albone, E. S. 1984 *MAMMALIAN SEMIOCHEMISTRY*. Chichester, Wiley.

Albrecht, G. H. 1978 *THE CRANIOFACIAL MORPHOLOGY OF THE SULAWESI MACAQUES*. Karger, Basel.

Albrecht, G. H. 1979 The study of biological versus statistical variation in multivariate morphometrics: the descriptive use of multiple regression analysis. *Systematic Zoology*. **28**: 338-344.

Albrecht, G. H. 1980 Multivariate analysis and the study of form, with special reference to canonical variates analysis. *American Zoologist*. **20**: 679-693.

Alexander, R. D. 1976 Evolution, human behavior, and determinism. *Proceedings of the 1976 Biennial Meeting of the Philosophy of Science Association*. **2**: 3-21.

Andrews, D. F. 1972 Plots of high dimensional data *Biometrics*. **28**: 125-136.

Andrews, D. F. 1973 Graphical techniques for high dimensional data. In *DISCRIMINANT ANALYSIS AND APPLICATION* (edited by T. Cacoullos). New York, Academic Press, pp. 37-59.

Andrews, P. and Cronin, J.E. 1982 The relationship of *Sivapithecus* and *Ramapithecus* and the evolution of the orang-utan. *Nature*, **297**: 541-546.

Andrews, P. and Tobien, H. 1977 New Miocene localities in Turkey and evidence on the origin of *Ramapithecus* and *Sivapithecus*. *Nature*. **268**: 699-701.

Ardrey, R. 1963 *AFRICAN GENESIS*. London, Collins.

Ashton, E. H. 1950 The endocranial capacities of the Australopithecinae. *Proceedings of the Zoological Society*, London, **120**: 715-721.

Ashton, E. H. 1960 The influence of geographic isolation on the skull of the green monkey (*Cercopithecus aethiops sabaeus*). V. The degree and pattern of differentiation in the cranial dimensions of the St. Kitts green monkey. *Proceedings of the Royal Society* (**B**) **151**: 563-583.

Ashton, E. H. 1981 The australopithecinae: their biometrical study. In *PERSPECTIVES IN PRIMATE BIOLOGY*. (edited by E. H. Ashton and R. L. Holmes). London, Academic Press, pp. 67-126.

Ashton, E. H. 1984 Review of *The Order of Man*, by Charles E. Oxnard. *Annals of Human Biology*. **11**: 590-592.

Ashton, E. H., Flinn, R. M., Griffiths, R. and Moore, J. W. 1979 The results of geographic isolation on the teeth and skull of the Green monkey (*Cercopithecus aethiops sabaeus*) in St. Kitts — a multivariate retrospect. *Journal of Zoology*, London. **188**: 533-555.

Ashton, E. H., Flinn, R. M. and Moore J. W. 1975 The basicranial axis in certain fossil hominoids. *Journal of Zoology*, London. **176**: 577-591.

Ashton, E. H., Flinn, R. M. and Moore J. W. 1976 The articular surface of the temporal bone in certain fossil hominoids. *Journal of Zoology*, London. **179**: 561-578.

Ashton, E. H., Flinn, R. M., Moore, J. W., Oxnard, C. E. and Spence, T. F. 1981 Further quantitative studies of form and function in the primate pelvis with special reference to *Australopithecus*. *Transactions of the Zoological Society*, London, **86**: 1-98.

Ashton, E. H., Flinn, R. M. and Oxnard, C. E. 1975 The taxonomic and functional significance of overall bodily proportions in the primates. *Journal of Zoology*, London. **175**: 73-105.

Ashton, E. H., Flinn, R. M., Oxnard, C. E. and Spence, T. F. 1971 The functional and classificatory significance of combined metrical features of the shoulder girdle. *Journal of Zoology*, London. **163**: 319-350.

Ashton, E. H., Flinn, R. M., Oxnard, C. E. and

Spence T. F. 1976 The adaptive and classificatory significance of certain quantitative features of the forelimb in primates. *Journal of Zoology*, London. **179**: 515-556.

Ashton, E. H., Healy M. J. R. and Lipton S. 1957 The descriptive use of discriminant functions in physical anthropology. *Proceedings of the Royal Society*, **(B) 146**: 552-572.

Ashton, E. H., Healy, M. J. R., Oxnard C. E., and Spence, T. F. 1965 The combination of locomotor features of the primate shoulder girdle by canonical analysis. *Journal of Zoology*, London, **147**: 406-429.

Ashton, E. H., Moore, J. W. and Spence, T. F. 1976 Growth changes in the endocranial capacity in the Cercopithecoidea and Hominoidea. *Journal of Zoology*, London. **180**: 355-365.

Ashton, E. H., and Oxnard C. E. 1963 The musculature of the primate shoulder. *Transactions of the Zoological Society*, London. **29**: 553-650.

Ashton, E. H., and Oxnard C. E. 1964a Locomotor patterns in primates. *Proceedings of the Zoological Society*, London. **142**: 1-28.

Ashton, E. H., and Oxnard C. E. 1964b Functional adaptations in the primate shoulder girdle. *Proceedings of the Zoological Society*, London. **142**: 49-66.

Ashton, E. H., Oxnard, C. E. and Spence, T. F. 1965 Scapular shape and primate classification. *Proceedings of the Zoological Society*, London. **145**: 125-142.

Ashton, E. H. and Zuckerman, S. 1950a Some quantitative dental characteristics of the chimpanzee, gorilla and orang-utan. *Philosophical Transactions of the Royal Society*. **(B) 234**: 471-484.

Ashton, E. H. and Zuckerman, S. 1950b Some quantitative dental characters of fossil anthropoids. *Philosophical Transactions of the Royal Society*. **(B) 234**: 485-520.

Ashton, E. H. and Zuckerman, S. 1951 Some cranial indices of *Plesianthropus* and other primates. *American Journal of Physical Anthropology*. **9**: 283-296.

Ashton, E. H. and Zuckerman, S. 1952 Age changes in the position of the occipital condyles in the chimpanzee and gorilla. *American Journal of Physical Anthropology*. **10**: 277-288.

Ashton, E. H. and Zuckerman, S. 1956 Age changes in the position of the foramen magnum in hominoids. *Proceedings of the Zoological Society*, London, **126**: 315-325.

Ashton, E. H. and Zuckerman, S. 1958 The infraorbital foramen in the Hominoidea. *Proceedings of the Zoological Society*, London, **131**: 471-485.

Atchley, W. R., Gaskins, C. T. and Anderson, D. 1976 Statistical properties of ratios, I. Empirical results. *Systematic Zoology*. **25**: 137-148.

Austin, C. R., Edwards, R. G. and Mittwoch, U. 1981 Introduction. In *MECHANISMS OF SEX DIFFERENTIATION IN ANIMALS AND MAN*. (Edited by C. R. Austin and R. G. Edwards). London, Academic. pp. 1-54.

Bailey, D. W. 1984 Genes that shape the mandible, and: Genes affect sex difference in mandible shape. *The Jackson Laboratory*, Maine. 55th. *Annual Report*. pp. 24 and 35.

Bartlett, M. S. 1935 Contingency table interactions. *Supplement to the Journal of the Royal Statistical Society*. **9**: 248-252.

Bauer, K. 1973 Age determination by immunological techniques of the last common ancestor of man and chimpanzee. *Humangenetik*. **17**: 253-265.

Biggerstaff, R. H. 1979 The biology of dental genetics. *Yearbook of Physical Anthropology*. **22**: 215-227.

Billy, G. and Vallois, H. V. 1977 La mandibule pre-Rissienne de Montmaurin. *L'Anthropologie*. **81**: 411-458.

Bilsborough, A. 1973 A multivariate study of evolutionary change in the hominid cranial vault and some evolutionary rates. *Journal of Human Evolution*, **2**: 387-403.

Blackith, R. E. and Blackith, R. M. 1969 Variation of shape and of discrete anatomical characters in the morabine grasshoppers. *Australian Journal of Zoology*. **17**: 697-718.

Blackith, R. E. and Reyment, R. A. 1971 *MULTIVARIATE MORPHOMETRICS*. London, Academic.

Blumenberg, B. 1985 Biometrical studies upon hominoid teeth: the coefficient of variation, sexual dimorphism and questions of phylogenetic relationship. Unpublished manuscript and personal communication.

Blumenberg, B. and Lloyd, A. T. 1983 *Australopithecus* and the origin of the genus *Homo*: aspects of biometry and systematics with accompanying catalogue of tooth metric data. *Biosystems*. **16**: 127-167.

Boaz, N. T. and Howell, F. C. 1977 A gracile cranium from the Upper Member G of the Shingura Formation, Ethiopia. *American Journal of Physical Anthropology*. **46**: 93-108.

Brace, C. L. 1967 Environment, tooth form, and size in the Pleistocene. *Journal of Dental Research*. **46**: 809-816.

Brace, C. L. 1973 Sexual dimorphism in human evolution. *Yearbook of Physical Anthropology*. **16**: 31-49.

Brace, C. L. 1980 Biological parameters and Pleistocene hominid life-ways. In *ECOLOGICAL INFLUENCES ON SOCIAL ORGANIZATION: EVOLUTION AND ADAPTATION*. (Edited by I.S. Bernstein). New York, Garland. pp. 263-289.

Brace, C. L. and Ryan, A. S. 1980 Sexual dimorphism and human tooth size differences. *Journal of Human Evolution*. **9**: 417-435.

Broom, R. 1939 A restoration of the Kromdraai skull. *Annals of the Transvaal Museum* (Pretoria). **6**: 1-124.

Broom, R. and Robinson, J. 1952 Swartkrans ape man, *Paranthropus crassidens*. *Memoirs of the Transvaal Museum* (Pretoria), **6**: 1-123.

Brose, D. S. and Wolpoff, M. H. 1971 Early upper paleolithic man and late middle paleolithic tools. *American Anthropologist*, **73**: 1156-1194.

Butler, P. M. 1939 Studies of the mammalian dentition. Differentiation of the postcanine dentition. *Proceedings of the Zoological Society*, London. **109**: 1-36.

Butynski, T. M. 1982 Harem-male replacement and infanticide in the blue monkey (*Cercopithecus mitis stuhlmanni*) in the Kibale forest, Uganda. *American Journal of Primatology*. **3**: 1-22.

Campbell, B. 1972 *SEXUAL SELECTION AND THE DESCENT OF MAN*. Chicago, Aldine.

Carny, J., Hill, A., Miller, J. A. and Walker A. 1971 Late australopithecine from Baringo District, Kenya. *Nature*, London. **230**: 509-514.

Chopra, S. R. K. 1978 New fossil evidence on the evolution of the hominoidea in the Siwaliks and its bearing upon the evolution of early man in India. *Journal of Human Evolution*. **7**: 3-9.

Clark, W. E. Le Gros. 1940 Palaeontological evidence bearing on human evolution. *Biological Reviews*. **15**: 202-230.

Clark, W. E. Le Gros 1959 *THE ANTECEDENTS OF MAN*. Edinburgh: University Press.

Clarke, R. J. 1977 A juvenile cranium and some adult teeth of early *Homo* from Swartkrans, Transvaal. *South African Journal of Science*. **73**: 46-49.

Clarke, R. J., Howell, F. C. and Brain, C. K. 1970 More evidence of an advanced hominid at Swartkrans. *Nature*, London. **225**: 1219-1222.

Clutton-Brock, T. H., Harvey, P. H. and Rudder, B. 1977 Sexual dimorphism, socioeconomic sex ratio, and body weight in primates. *Nature*, London. **269**: 797-800.

Clutton-Brock, T. H. and Harvey, P. H. 1977 Primate ecology and social organization. *Journal of Zoology*, London. **183**: 1-39.

Clutton Brock, T. H. and Harvey, P. H. 1978 Mammals, resources and reproductive strategies. *Nature*, London. **273**: 191-195.

Coimbra-Filho, A. F. and Mittermeier, R. A. 1973. New data on the taxonomy of the Brazilian marmosets of the genus *Callithrix* Erxleben, 1877. *Folia Primatologia*, **20**, 241-264.

Collins, D. A., Busse, C. D., and Goodall, J. 1984, Infanticide in two populations of savanna baboons. In *INFANTICIDE* (edited by G. Hausfater and B. S. Hrdy). New York, Aldine.

Cook, D. C., Buikstra, J. E., DeRousseau, C. J. and Johanson, D. C. 1983 Vertebral pathology in the Afar australopithecines. *American Journal of Physical Anthropology*. **60**: 83-101.

Coon, C. S. 1967 *THE ORIGIN OF RACES*. New York, Knopf.

Coppens, Y. 1970 Les restes d'Hominidés des séries inférieures et moyennes des formations pliovillafranchiennes de l'Omo en Ethiope. *Compte Rendu de la Academie des Sciences* **D**. 2286-2289.

Coppens, Y. 1971 Les restes d'Hominidés des séries inférieures et moyennes des formations plio-villafranchiennes de l'Omo en Ethiope. *Compte Rendu de la Academie des Sciences* **D**. 36-39.

Coppens, Y. 1973a Les restes d'Hominidés des séries inférieures et moyennes des formations plio-villafranchiennes de l'Omo en Ethiope (recoltes 1970, 1971 et 1972). *Compte Rendu de la Academie des Sciences* **D**. **276**: 1823-1826.

Coppens, Y. 1973b Les restes d'Hominidés des séries inférieures et moyennes des formations plio-villafranchiennes de l'Omo en Ethiope (recoltes 1970, 1971 et 1972). *Compte Rendu de La Academie des Sciences* **D**. **276**: 1981-1984.

Corruccini, R. S. 1975 *Gigantopithecus* and hominids. *Anthropologischer Anzeiger*, **35**: 55-57.

Corruccini, R. S. 1978 Morphometric analysis: uses and abuses. *Yearbook of Physical Anthropology*. **21**: 134-150.

Corruccini, R. S. and Ciochon, R. L. 1976 Morphometric affinities of the human shoulder. *American Journal of Physical Anthropology*. **45**: 19-38.

Corruccini, R. S. and Ciochon, R. L. 1983 Overview of ape and human ancestry: phyletic relationships of Miocene and later Hominoidea. In *INTERPRETATIONS OF APE AND HUMAN ANCESTRY*. (Edited by R. L. Ciochon and R. S. Corruccini). New York, Plenum, pp. 3-20.

Crockett, C. M. and Sekulic, R. 1984 Infanticide in red howler monkeys (*Alouatta seniculus*). In *INFANTICIDE*. (Edited by G. Hausfater and B. S. Hrdy). New York, Aldine.

Cronin, J. E. 1983 Apes, humans and the molecular clock. In *INTERPRETATIONS OF APE AND HUMAN ANCESTRY*. (Edited by R. L. Ciochon and R. S. Corruccini). New York, Plenum. pp. 115-149.

Crook, J. H. 1972 Sexual selection, dimorphism, and social organization. In *SEXUAL SELECTION AND THE DESCENT OF MAN*. (Edited by B. Campbell). Chicago, Aldine. pp. 231-281.

Dart, R. 1925 *Australopithecus africanus*: the Man Ape of South Africa. *Nature*, London. **115**: 195-199.

Dart, R. 1960 The status of *Gigantopithecus*. *Anthropologischer Anzeiger*. **24**: 139-145.

Darwin, C. 1859 *ON THE ORIGIN OF THE SPECIES BY MEANS OF NATURAL SELECTION, OR PRESERVATION OF FAVOURED RACES IN THE STRUGGLE FOR LIFE*. London, Murray.

Day, M. H. 1977 *GUIDE TO FOSSIL MAN: A HANDBOOK OF HUMAN PALAEONTOLOGY*. London, Cassell.

Day, M. H., and Wood, B. A. 1968 Functional affinities of the Olduvai hominid 8 talus. *Man*, **3**: 440-455.

Delson, E. and Andrews, P. 1975 Evolution and interrelationships of the catarrhine primates. In *PHYLOGENY OF THE PRIMATES: A MULTIDISCIPLINARY APPROACH*. (Edited by W. P. Luckett and F. S. Szalay). New York, Plenum, pp. 405-446.

Doty, R. L.1976 *MAMMALIAN OLFACTION, REPRODUCTIVE PROCESSES AND BEHAVIOR*. New York, Academic.

Elliot, D. G. 1913 A REVIEW OF THE PRIMATES. New York, Monographs of the American Museum of Natural History.

Ettler, D. 1983 The Lufeng fossil ape site and the place of the Chinese sivapithecines in hominoid phylogeny. M.Sc. dissertation, University of Wisconsin-Milwaukee.

Fedigan, M. L. and Baxter, M. J. 1984 Sex differences and social organization in free-ranging spider monkeys (*Ateles geoffroyi*). *Primates*. **25**: 279-294.

Feldesman, M. R. 1976 The primate forelimb: morphometric study of locomotor diversity. *University of Oregon Anthropological Papers* **10**: 1-154.

Feldesman, M. R. 1979 Further morphometric studies of the ulna from the Omo Basin, Ethiopia, *American Journal of Physical Anthropology*. **51**: 409-416.

Feldesman, M. R. 1982a Morphometric analysis of the distal humerus of some cenozoic catarrhines: the late divergence hypothesis revisited. *American Journal of Physical Anthropology*, **59**: 73-76.

Feldesman, M. R. 1982b Morphometrics of the ulna of some cenozoic 'hominoids'. *American Journal of Physical Anthropology*, **57**: 187-196.

Fieller, N. R. J. and Turner, A. 1982 Number estimation in vertebrate samples. *Journal of Archaeological Science*. **9**: 49-62.

Fisher, R. A. 1936 The use of multiple measurements in taxonomic problems. *Annals of Eugenics*. **7**: 179-188.

Fleagle, J. G. 1984 The master of multiple dimensions. *American Journal of Primatology*, **7**: 151-153.

Fleagle, J. G., Kay, R. F. and Simons, E. L. 1980 Sexual dimorphism in early anthropoids. *Nature*. **287**: 328-330.

Fooden, J. 1969 Taxonomy and evolution of the monkeys of the Celebes (Primates: Cercopithecidae). *Bibliotheca Primatologica*. **10**: 1-148.

Fossey, D. 1976 The behaviour of the mountain gorilla. Ph.D. Thesis. University of Cambridge.

Fossey, D. 1984 Infanticide in Mountain Gorillas (*Gorilla gorilla beringei*) with comparative notes on Chimpanzees. In *INFANTICIDE* (edited by G. Hausfater and S. B. Hrdy). New York, Aldine.

Frayer, D. W. 1973 *Gigantopithecus* and its relationship to *Australopithecus*. *American Journal of Physical Anthropology*. **39**: 413-429.

Frayer, D. W. 1978 Evolution of dentition in Upper Paleolithic and Mesolithic Europe. *University of Kansas Publications in Anthropology*. **10**: 1-201.

Friedenthal, H. 1900 Ueber einen experimentellen Nachweis von Blutsverwantschaft. *Archives of Anatomy and Physiology*, Leipzig, **Physiology Volume**, 494-508.

Friedman, R. C., Richart, R. M. and Vande Wiele, R. L. 1974 *SEX DIFFERENCES IN BEHAVIOR*. London, Wiley.

Galton, F. 1899 *NATURAL INHERITANCE*. London, Macmillan.

Garn, S. M. Lewis, A. B., Swindler, D. R. and Karevsky, R. 1967 Genetic control of sexual dimorphism in tooth size. *Journal of Dental Research*. **46**: 963-972.

Garn, S. M., Lewis, A. B. and Walenga, A. J. 1968 Two-generation confirmation of crown-size body-size relationships in human beings. *Journal of Dental Research*. **47**: 1197.

Gautier, J. P. and Gautier, A. 1977 Communication in Old World monkeys. In *HOW ANIMALS COMMUNICATE*. (Edited by T. A. Seboek). Bloomington, University of Indiana Press. pp. 890-986.

Gautier-Hion, A. 1975 Dimorphisme sexuel et organisation sociale chez les cercopithecine forestiers africains. *Mammalia*. **39**: 365-374.

Geist, V. 1974 On the relationship of social evolution and ecology in ungulates. *American Zoologist*. **14**: 205-220.

Gelvin, B. R. 1980 Morphometric affinities of *Gigantopithecus*. *American Journal of Physical Anthropology*, **53**: 541-568.

Gingerich, P. D. 1981 Cranial morphology and adaptations in eocene Adapidae. I. Sexual dimorphism in *Adapis magnus* and *Adapis parisiensis*. *American Journal of Physical Anthropology*. **56**: 217-234.

Gingerich P. D. 1984. Rates of evolution; effects of time and temporal scaling. *American Journal Physical Anthropology*, **63**: 163.

Gingerich, P. D. 1985 Nonlinear molecular clocks and ape-human divergence times. In *PAST, PRESENT AND FUTURE OF HOMINID EVOLUTIONARY STUDIES*. (Edited by P. V. Tobias). New York, Liss. pp. 411-416.

Gingerich, P. D. and Martin, R. D. 1981 Cranial morphology and adaptations in Eocene Adapidae. II. The Cambridge skull of *Adapis parisiensis*. *American Journal of Physical Anthropology*. **56**: 235-257.

Gnanadesikan, R. 1977 *METHODS FOR STATISTICAL DATA ANALYSIS OF MULTIVARIATE OBSERVATIONS*. New York, Wiley.

Goodall, J. 1977 Infant killing and cannibalism in free-living chimpanzees. *Folia Primatologia*. **28**: 259-282.

Goodman, M. 1982 *MACROMOLECULAR SEQUENCES IN SYSTEMATIC AND EVOLUTIONARY BIOLOGY*. New York, Plenum.

Goodman, M., Romero-Herrera, A. E., Dene, H., Czelusniak, J. and Tashian, R. 1983 Amino acid sequence evidence on the phylogeny of primates and other Eutherians. In *MACROMOLECULAR SEQUENCES IN SYSTEMATIC AND EVOLUTIONARY BIOLOGY*. (Edited by M. Goodman). New York, Plenum, pp. 115-192.

Gregory, W. K. and Hellman, M. 1926 The dentition of *Dryopithecus* and the origins of man. *American Museum of Natural History Anthropological Papers.* **28**: 1-123.

Gregory, W. K. Hellman, M. and Lewis, G. 1938 Fossil anthropoids of the Yale-Cambridge Indian Expedition of 1935. *Carnegie Institute of Washington Publications.* **495**: 1-27.

Gribbin J and Cherfas, J. 1983 *THE MONKEY PUZZLE.* New York, Pantheon.

Grine, F. E. 1981 Description of some juvenile hominid specimens from Swartkrans, Transvaal. *Annals of the South African Museum.* **86**: 43-71.

Hall, R. L. 1982 *SEXUAL DIMORPHISM IN Homo sapiens: A QUESTION OF SIZE.* New York, Praeger.

Harvey, P. M., Kavanagh, M. and Clutton-Brock, T. H. 1978 Sexual dimorphism in primate teeth. *Journal of Zoology,* London. **186**: 475-485.

Hasegawa M., Yano, T. and Kishino, H. 1984 A new molecular clock of mitochondrial DNA and the evolution of the hominoids. *Proceedings of the Japanese Academy,* **60**: 95-105.

Hausfater, G. and Hrdy, S. B. 1984 *INFANTICIDE.* New York, Aldine.

Healey, M. J. R. 1968 Disciplining of medical data. *British Medical Bulletin.* **24**: 210-214.

Heberer, G. 1959 The descent of man and the present fossil record. *Cold Spring Harbor Symposium on Quantitative Biology.* **24**: 235-244.

Hershkovitz, P. 1977 *LIVING NEW WORLD MONKEYS (PLATYRRHINI).* Chicago, University of Chicago Press.

Hotelling, H. 1936 The generalization of 'Students' ratio. *Annals of Mathematics and Statistics.* **2**: 360-378.

Howell, F. C. 1951 The place of neanderthal man in human evolution. *American Journal of Physical Anthropology,* **9**: 379-416.

Howells, W. W. 1973 *CRANIAL VARIATION IN MAN: A STUDY BY MULTIVARIATE ANALYSIS OF PATTERNS OF DIFFERENCE AMONG RECENT HUMAN POPULATIONS.* Harvard, Peabody Museum of Archaeology and Ethnology.

Hrdy, S. B. 1979 Infanticide among animals: a review, classification and examination of the implications for reproductive strategies of females. *Ethology and Sociobiology,* **1**: 13-40.

Hrdy, S. B. 1981 *THE WOMAN THAT NEVER EVOLVED.* Harvard, Cambridge.

Hrdy, S. B. 1983 Behavioral biology and the double standard. In *THE SOCIAL BEHAVIOR OF FEMALE VERTEBRATES.* (Edited by S. K. Wasser). New York, Academic Press. pp. 3-17.

Huxley, T. H. 1895 MAN'S PLACE IN NATURE. London, Macmillan.

Jacklin, C. N. 1981 Methodological issues in the study of sex-related differences. *Developmental Review.* **1**: 266-273.

Jacob, T. 1973 Paleaeoanthropological discoveries in Indonesia with special reference to the finds of the last two decades. *Journal of Human Evolution.* **2**: 474-485.

Johanson, D. and Edey, M. 1980 *Lucy: the beginnings of human kind.* New York, Simon and Schuster.

Johanson, D.C. and Taieb, M. 1976 Plio-pleistocene hominid discoveries in Hadar, Ethiopia, *Nature,* London. **260**: 293-297.

Johanson, D. C. and White, T.D. 1979 A systematic assessment of early African hominids. *Science.* **203**: 321-330.

Johanson, D., White, T. D. and Coppens, Y. 1982 Dental remains from Hadar Formation, Ethiopia: 1974-1977 collections. *American Journal of Physical Anthropology.* **57**: 545-604.

Jolicoeur, P. and Mosimann, J. E. 1960 Size and shape variation in the painted turtle: a principal component analysis. *Growth.* **24**: 339-354.

Jungers, W. L. and Stern, J. T. Jr. 1983 Body proportions, skeletal allometry and locomotion in the Hadar hominids: a reply to Wolpoff. *Journal of Human Evolution.* **12**: 673-684.

Kay, R. F. 1981 The nutcrackers — a new theory of the adaptations of the Ramapithecinae. *American Journal of Physical Anthropology.* **55**: 141-151.

Kay, R. F. 1982a. *Sivapithecus simonesi*, a new species of Miocene hominoid with comments on the phylogenetic status of the Ramapithecinae. *International Journal of Primatology* 3: 113–174.

Kay, R. F. 1982b. Sexual dimorphism in Ramapithecinae. *Proceedings of the National Academy* **79**: 209–212.

Kay, R. F. and Simons, E. L. 1983 A reassessment of the relationship between later Miocene and subsequent Hominoidea. In *INTERPRETATIONS OF APE AND HUMAN ANCESTRY*. (Edited by R. L. Ciochon and R. S. Corruccini). New York, Plenum. pp. 577-624.

Kendall, M. G. 1957 *A COURSE IN MULTIVARIATE ANALYSIS*. London, Griffin.

Kern, H. M. Jr. and Straus, W. L. Jr. 1949 The femur of *Plesianthropus transvaalensis*. *American Journal of Physical Anthropology*. **7**: 53-78.

Krantz, G. S. 1982 The fossil record of sex. In *SEXUAL DIMORPHISM IN Homo sapiens A QUESTION OF SIZE*. (Edited by R. L. Hall). New York, Praeger. pp. 85-106.

Kretzoi, M. 1975 New ramapithecines and *Pliopithecus* from the lower Pliocene of Rudabanya in North Eastern Hungary. *Nature*, London. **257**: 578-581.

Lavelle, C. L. B. 1968 Anglosaxon and modern British teeth. *Journal of Dental Research*. **47**: 811-815.

Leakey, L. S. B. 1959 A new fossil skull from Olduvai. *Nature*, London, **184**: 491-493.

Leakey, L. S. B. 1962 A new lower Pliocene fossil primate from Kenya. *Annals and Magazine of Natural History*. **4**: 689-696.

Leakey, L. S. B. 1966 *Nature*, London. **209**: 1279-1281.

Leakey, L. S. B., Tobias, P. V., and Napier, J. R. 1964 A new species of the genus *Homo* from Olduvai Gorge. *Nature*, London, **202**: 7-9.

Leakey, M. D., Clarke R. J. and Leakey, L. S. B. 1971 New hominid skull from Bed I, Olduvai Gorge, Tanzania. *Nature*, London. **232**: 308-312.

Leakey, R. E. F., Leakey, M. D. and Behrensmeyer, A. K. 1978 The hominid catalogue. In *KOOBI FORA RESEARCH PROJECT, VOLUME I: THE FOSSIL HOMINIDS AND AN INTRODUCTION TO THEIR CONTEXT*, 1968-1974. (Edited by M. G. Leakey and R. E. F. Leakey). Oxford, Clarendon. pp. 86-182.

Leakey, R. E. F. and Walker, A. 1973 New australopithecines from East Rudolf, Kenya (III). *American Journal of Physical Anthropology*. **39**: 205-222.

Lee, Y. M., Friedman, D. J. and Ayala, F. 1985 *Proceedings of the National Academy of Sciences*, U.S.A. **82**: 824.

Leutenegger, W. 1977 Sociobiological correlates of sexual dimorphism in body weight in South African australopithecines. *South African Journal of Science*. **73**: 143-144.

Leutenegger, W. 1982 Scaling of sexual dimorphism of body weight and canine size in primates. *Folia Primatologia*. **37**: 163-176.

Leutenegger, W. and Cheverud, J. 1982 Correlates of sexual dimorphism in primates: ecological and size variables. *International Journal of Primatology* **37**: 387-402.

Leutenegger, W. and Kelly, J. T. 1977 Relationships of sexual dimorphism in canine size and body size to social, behavioral, and ecological correlates in anthropoid primates. *Primates*. **18**: 177-186.

Lewin, R. 1983 Is the orang-utan a living fossil? *Science*. **222**: 122-123.

Lewin, R. 1985 Molecular clocks scrutinized. *Science*. **228**: 571.

Lewis, G. E. 1934 Preliminary notice of new man-like apes from India. *American Journal of Science*. **27**: 161-181.

Lewis, O. J. 1980 The joints of the evolving foot. Part I. The ankle joint. Part II. The intrinsic joints. Part III. The fossil evidence. *Journal of Anatomy*, London. **130**: 527-543; **130**: 833-857; **131**: 275-298.

Lieberman, S. S., Gelvin, B. R., and Oxnard, C. E. 1985 Dental sexual dimorphisms in some extant hominoids and ramapithecines from China: a quantitative approach. *American Journal of Primatology*. **9**: 305-326.

Liebowitz, L. 1978 *FEMALES, MALES, FAMILIES: A BIOSOCIAL APPROACH*. Massachusetts, Duxbury.

Lipson, S. and Pilbeam, D. 1982 *Ramapithecus* and hominoid evolution. *Journal of Human Evolution*. **11**: 545-555.

Lisowski, F. P. 1982 An overview of hominoid history and early humans in China. *Homo*. **33**: 248-261.

Lisowski, F. P., Albrecht, G. H., and Oxnard, C. E. 1974 The form of the talus in some higher primates: a multivariate study. *American Journal of Physical Anthropology*. **41**: 191-215.

Lisowski, F. P., Albrecht, G. H. and Oxnard, C. E. 1976 African fossil tali: further multivariate morphometric studies. *American Journal of Physical Anthropology*. **45**: 5-18.

Lockie, J. D. 1976 Territory in small carnivores. *Symposia of the Zoological Society*, London. **18**: 143-165.

Lovejoy, C. O. 1981 The origin of man. *Science*. **211**: 341-350.

Lovejoy, C. O., Meindl, R. S., Pryzbeck, T. R., Barton, T. S., Heiple K. G. and Kotting, D. 1977 Paleodemography of the Libben site, Ottawa County, Ohio. *Science*. **198**: 291-293.

Mahalanobis, P. C. 1936 On the generalised distance in statistics. *Proceedings of the National Institute of Science of India*. **2**: 49-55.

Mahler, P. E. 1973 Metric variation in the pongid dentition. PhD Thesis, University of Michigan, Ann Arbor.

Manaster, B. J. M. 1975 Locomotor adaptations within the *Cercopithecus*, *Cercocebus*, and *Presbytis* genera: a multivariate approach. PhD Thesis, University of Chicago, Chicago.

Manaster, B. J. M. 1979 Locomotor adaptations within the *Cercopithecus* genus: a multivariate approach. *American Journal of Physical Anthropology*. **50**: 169-182.

Marriott, F. H. C. 1974 *THE INTERPRETATION OF MULTIPLE OBSERVATIONS*. New York, Academic.

McArdle, J. E. 1978 Functional morphology of the hip and thigh of the Lorisiformes. PhD Thesis. University of Chicago, Chicago.

McCown, E. R. 1982 Sex differences: the female as baseline for species descriptions. In *SEXUAL DIMORPHISMS IN Homo sapiens A QUESTION OF SIZE*. (Edited by R. L. Hall). New York, Praeger, pp. 37-84.

McHenry, H. M. 1973 Early hominid humerus from East Rudolf, Kenya. *Science*. **180**: 739-741.

McHenry, H. M. 1976 A view of the hominid lineage. A review of Uniqueness and Diversity in Human Evolution: multivariate studies of australopithecines. By Charles E. Oxnard. *Science*. **189**: 988-989.

McHenry, H. M. 1982 The pattern of human evolution: studies on bipedalism, mastication, and encephalization. *Annual Reviews of Anthropology*. **11**: 151-173.

McHenry, H. M., and Corruccini, R. S. 1975 Multivariate analysis of early hominid pelvic bones. *American Journal of Physical Anthropology*. **43**: 263-270.

McHenry H. M., and Corruccini, R. S. 1978 The femur in human evolution. *American Journal of Physical Anthropology*. **49**: 473-488.

McHenry, H. M., Corruccini, R. S. and Howell, F. C. 1976 Analysis of an early hominid ulna from the Omo Basin, Ethiopia. *American Journal of Physical Anthropology*. **44**: 295-304.

McKenna, J. J. 1983 Primate aggression and evolution: an overview of sociobiological and anthropological perspectives. *Bulletin of the American Academy of Psychiatry and the Law*. **11**: 105-130.

Meickle, D. B., Tilford, B. L. and Vessey, S. H. 1984 Dominance rank, secondary sex ratio, and reproduction of offspring in polygynous primates. *American Naturalist*. **124**: 173-188.

Montagu, A. 1974 *THE NATURAL SUPERIORITY OF WOMEN*. New York, Colliers.

Moore, W. J. 1984 Review of *The Order of Man*, by C. E. Oxnard. *Journal of Anatomy*, London. **139**: 584-585.

Mukherjee, R., Rao, C. R. and Trevor, J. C. 1955 *THE ANCIENT INHABITANTS OF THE JEBEL MOYA*. Cambridge, Cambridge University Press.

Murrill, R. I. 1975 A comparison of the Rhodesian and Petralona upper jaws in relation to other Pleistocene hominids. *Zeitschrift fur Morphologie und Anthropologie*. **66**: 176-187.

Napier, J. R. 1959 Fossil metacarpals from Swartkrans. *Fossil mammals of Africa*. **17**: 1-18.

Napier, J. R. 1962 Fossil hand bones from Olduvai Gorge. *Nature*, London. **196**: 400-411.

Napier J. R. and Napier, P. R. 1967 *A HANDBOOK OF THE LIVING PRIMATES*. London, Academic.

Nowak, M. 1980 *EVE'S RIB: A REVOLUTIONARY NEW VIEW OF FEMALE SEX ROLES*. New York, St Martins.

Nuttall, G. H. F. 1904 *BLOOD IMMUNITY AND BLOOD RELATIONSHIPS*. Cambridge, University Press.

Oxnard, C. E. 1963 Locomotor adaptations of the primate forelimb. *Symposia of the Zoological Society*, London, **10**: 165-182.

Oxnard, C. E. 1967 The functional morphology of the primate shoulder as revealed by comparative anatomical, osteometric and discriminant function techniques. *American Journal of Physical Anthropology*, **26**: 219-240.

Oxnard, C. E. 1968a A note on the fragmentary Sterkfontein scapula. *American Journal of Physical Anthropology*. **28**: 213-217.

Oxnard, C. E. 1968b A note on the Olduvai clavicular fragment. *American Journal of Physical Anthropology*. **29**: 429-431.

Oxnard, C. E. 1968c The architecture of the shoulder in some mammals. *Journal of Morphology*. **126**: 249-290.

Oxnard, C. E. 1969 Evolution of the human shoulder: some possible pathways. *American Journal of Physical Anthropology*. **30**: 319-331.

Oxnard, C. E. 1972a Some African fossil foot bones: a note on the interpolation of fossils into a matrix of extant species. *American Journal of Physical Anthropology*. **37**: 3-12.

Oxnard, C. E. 1972b The use of optical data analysis in functional morphology: investigation of vertebral trabecular patterns. In *THE FUNCTIONAL AND EVOLUTIONARY BIOLOGY OF THE PRIMATES*. (Edited by R. H. Tuttle). Aldine Atherton, Chicago. pp. 337-347.

Oxnard, C. E. 1973a *FORM AND PATTERN IN HUMAN EVOLUTION: SOME MATHEMATICAL, PHYSICAL AND ENGINEERING APPROACHES*. Chicago, University Press.

Oxnard, C. E. 1973b Functional inferences from morphometrics: problems posed by uniqueness and diversity among the primates. *Systematic Zoology*, **22**: 409-424.

Oxnard, C. E. 1973c Some locomotor adaptations among lower primates. *Symposia of the Zoological Society*, London. **33**: 255-299.

Oxnard, C. E. 1975a *UNIQUENESS AND DIVERSITY IN HUMAN EVOLUTION: MORPHOMETRIC STUDIES OF AUSTRALOPITHECINES*. Chicago, University Press.

Oxnard, C. E. 1975b The place of the australopithecines in human evolution: grounds for doubt? *Nature*, London **258**: 389-395.

Oxnard, C. E. 1977 Human Fossils: the new revolution. In *THE GREAT IDEAS TODAY*. (Edited by J. Van Doren). Chicago, Britannica Press. pp. 92-153.

Oxnard, C. E. 1978a One biologist's view of morphometrics. *Annual Reviews of Systematics and Ecology*. **9**: 219-241.

Oxnard, C. E. 1978b The problem of convergence and the place of *Tarsius* in primate phylogeny. In *RECENT ADVANCES IN PRIMATOLOGY, Volume 3, EVOLUTION*. (Edited by D. J. Chivers and K. A. Joysey). London, Academic Press. pp. 239-247.

Oxnard, C. E. 1980 Convention and controversy in human evolution. *Homo*, **30**: 225-246.

Oxnard, C. E. 1981a The place of man among the primates: anatomical, molecular and morphometric evidence. *Homo*. **32**: 149-176.

Oxnard, C. E. 1981b The uniqueness of *Daubentonia*. *American Journal of Physical Anthropology*. **54**: 1-22.

Oxnard, C. E. 1982 The association between cancellous architecture and loading in bone: an optical data analytic view. *The Physiologist*. **5**: 37-40.

Oxnard, C. E. 1983a and 1984 *THE ORDER OF MAN: A BIOMATHEMATICAL ANATOMY OF THE PRIMATES*. Hong Kong, Hong Kong University Press (1983); New Haven, Yale University Press (1984).

Oxnard, C. E. 1983b Multivariate statistics in physical anthropology: testing and interpretation. *Zeitschrift fur Morphologie und Anthropologie*. **73**: 237-278.

Oxnard, C. E. 1983c Sexual dimorphisms in the overall proportions of primates. *American Journal of Primatology*, **4**: 1-22.

Oxnard, C. E. 1983d Anatomical, biomolecular and morphometric views of the living primates. In *PROGRESS IN ANATOMY*. (Edited by R. J. Harrison and V. Navaratnam). Cambridge, University Press. pp. 113-142.

Oxnard, C. E. 1985a Hominids and hominoids, lineages and radiations. In *THE PAST PRESENT AND FUTURE OF HOMINID EVOLUTIONARY STUDIES*. (Edited by P. V. Tobias). New York, Liss. pp. 271–278.

Oxnard, C. E. 1985b *HUMANS, APES AND CHINESE FOSSILS*. Hong Kong, Hong Kong University Press.

Oxnard, C. E., German, R. Z., Jouffroy, F-K. and Lessertisseur, J. 1981 A morphometric study of limb proportions in leaping prosimians. *American Journal of Physical Anthropology*. **54**: 421-430.

Oxnard, C. E., German, R. Z. and McArdle, J. H. 1981 The functional morphometrics of the hip and thigh in leaping prosimians. *American Journal of Physical Anthropology*. **54**: 484-498.

Oxnard, C. E., Lieberman, S. S. and Gelvin, B. R. 1985 Sexual dimorphisms in dental dimensions of higher primates. *American Journal of Primatology*, **8**: 127-152.

Oxnard, C. E. and Neely, P. 1969 The descriptive use of neighborhood limited classification in functional morphology: an analysis of the shoulder in primates. *Journal of Morphology*. **129**: 117-148.

Oxnard, C. E. and Yang, H. L. C. 1981 Beyond biometrics: studies of complex biological patterns. *Symposia of the Zoological Society*, London. **46**: 127-167.

Patterson, B., and Howells, W. W. 1967 Hominid humeral fragment from the early pleistocene of northwestern Kenya. *Science*. **156**: 64-66.

Pearson, K. 1901 On lines and planes of closest fit to systems of points in space. *Philosophical Magazine*. **2**: 559-572.

Pilbeam, D. R. 1969 Tertiary Pongidae of East Africa: Evolutionary relationships and taxonomy. Peabody Museum of Natural History, *Yale University Bulletin*, **31**: 1-185.

Pilbeam, D. R. 1972. *THE ASCENT OF MAN*. New York, MacMillan.

Pilbeam, D. R. 1984. The descent of Hominoids and Hominids. *Scientific American* **250**: 84-96.

Pilgrim, G. E. 1910 Notices of new mammalian genera and species from the Tertiary of India. *Records of the Geological Survey of India*. **40**: 63-71.

Pilgrim, G. E. 1915 New Siwalik primates and their bearing on the questions of the evolution of man and the Anthropoidea. *Records of the Geological Survey of India* **45**: 1-74.

Prost, J. H. 1980 The origin of bipedalism. *American Journal of Physical Anthropology*. **52**: 175-190.

Prost, J. H. 1983 *Australopithecus*: arboreal or terrestrial? *American Anthropological Association Abstracts*, November, 1983: **36**.

Rao, C. R. 1948 The utilisation of multiple measurements in problems of biological classification. *Journal of the Royal Statistical Society* **B**. **10**: 159-203.

Rayner, J. M. V. 1985 Linear relations in biomechanics: the statistics of scaling functions. *Journal of Zoology*, London. **206**: 415-440.

Read, D. W. 1975 Primate phylogeny, neutral mutations, and "molecular clocks". *Systematic Zoology*. **24**: 209-221.

Remane, A. 1960 Die Stellung von *Gigantopithecus*. *Anthropologische Anzeiger*. **24**: 146-159.

Reyment R. A., Blackith, R. E., and Campbell, N. A. 1984 *MULTIVARIATE MORPHOMETRICS*. London, Academic Press.

Rightmire, G. P. 1980 Middle Pleistocene hominids from Olduvai Gorge, northern Tanzania. *American Journal of Physical Anthropology*. **53**: 225-241.

Rhoads, J. G. and Trinkhaus, E. 1977 *American Journal of Physical Anthropology*. **46**: 29-43.

Robinson, J. T. 1962 Australopithecines and artefacts at Sterkfontein. Part I. Sterkfontein stratigraphy and the importance of the extension site. *South African Archaeological Bulletin*. **17**: 87-107.

Robinson, J. T. 1972 *EARLY HOMINID POSTURE AND LOCOMOTION*. Chicago, University of Chicago Press.

Ross, W. D., and Ward, R. 1982 Human proportionality and sexual dimorphism. In *SEXUAL DIMORPHISM IN Homo sapiens A QUESTION OF SIZE* (Edited by R. L. Hall). New York, Praeger. pp. 317-362.

Ross, W. D., and Wilson, N. C. 1974 A stratagem for proportional growth assessment. *Acta Paediatrica Belgica*. **28**: 169-182.

Sartono, S. 1973 Observations on a newly discovered jaw of *Pithecanthropus modjokotensis* from the lower Pleistocene of Sangiran, central Java. Proceedings: *Koninklijke nederlandse Akademie van Wetenschappen* (Amsterdam). **B**. **76**: 25-31.

Sausse, F. 1975 La mandibule atlantothropienne de la carriére Thomas I (Casablanca). *L'Anthropologie*. **79**: 81-112.

Schmidt, P. 1984 Eine rekonstruktion des skellettes von A. L. 288-1 und deren konsequenzen. *Folia Primatologia*. **40**: 283-306.

Schultz, A. H. 1929 The technique of measuring the outer body of human foetuses and of primates in general. *Contributions to Embryology* **213**-257.

Schultz, A. H. 1936 Characters common to higher primates and characters specific for man. *Quarterly Review of Biology*. **11**: 259-283.

Schultz, A. H. 1956 Post embryonic age changes. *Primatologia*. **1**: 886-964.

Schultz, A. H. 1969 *THE LIFE OF PRIMATES*. New York, Universe Books.

Schwartz, J. H. 1984 The evolutionary relationships of man and orang-utans. *Nature*, London. **308**: 501-505.

Selander, R. K. 1966 Sexual dimorphism and differential niche utilization in birds. *The Condor*. **68**: 133-151.

Senut, B. 1981 Humeral outlines in some hominoid primates and plio-Pleistocene hominids. *American Journal of Physical Anthropology*. **56**: 275-284.

Shea, B. T. 1984 Primate Morphometrics. A review of *The Order of Man*. by Charles E. Oxnard. *Science*. **224**: 148-149.

Shea, B. T. 1985 Bivariate and multivariate growth allometry, statistical and biological considerations. *Journal of Zoology*. **206**: 367-390.

Shephard, R. J. LaBarre, R., Jécquier, J.-C., Lavallée, H., Rakic, M. and Volle, M. 1985 The "unisex phantom", sexual dimorphism, and proportional growth assessment. *American Journal of Physical Anthropology*. **67**: 403-412.

Shipman, P. 1985 The ancestor that wasn't. *The Sciences*. March, 1985, 43-48.

Sibley, A. G., and Ahlquist, J. E. 1984 The phylogeny of the hominoids as indicated by DNA-DNA hybridization. *Journal of Molecular Evolution*. **20**: 2-22.

Simons, E. 1964 On the mandible of *Ramapithecus*. *Proceedings of the National Academy of Science*. **51**: 528-535.

Simons, E. 1974 Diversity among the early hominids: a vertebrate paleontologist's viewpoint. Paper delivered at the Wenner Gren Conference, January 1974. (Later re-published in 1978 in *EARLY HOMINIDS OF AFRICA*. Edited by C. Jolly). London, Duckworth. pp. 543-566.

Simons, E. 1977 *Ramapithecus*. *Scientific American*. **236**: 28-35.

Simons, E. 1978 Diversity among the early hominids: a vertebrate paleontologists's viewpoint. In *EARLY HOMINIDS OF AFRICA*. (Edited by C. Jolly). London, Duckworth. pp. 543-566.

Simons, E. and Pilbeam, D. 1965 Preliminary revision of the Dryopithecinae (Pongidae, Anthropoidea). *Folia Primatologia*. **3**: 81-152.

Simons, E. and Pilbeam, D. R. 1978 *Ramapithecus* (Hominidae, Hominoidea). In *EVOLUTION OF AFRICAN MAMMALS* (Edited by V. J. Maglio and H. B. S. Cooke). Harvard University Press, Cambridge. pp. 147-153.

Simpson, G. G. 1945 The principles of classification and a classification of mammals. *Bulletin of the American Museum of Natural History*. **85**: 1-350.

Smith, A. and Lee, A. 1984 The evolution of strategies for survival and reproduction in possums and gliders. In *POSSUMS AND GLIDERS*. (Edited by A. Smith and I. Home). New South Wales, Beatty. Chapter. 3.

Smith, R. J. and Pilbeam, D. 1980 Evolution of the orang-utan. *Nature*, London. **284**: 447-448.

Stern, J. T. Jr. 1984 Book Review: *The Order of Man*. By Charles Oxnard. *American Journal of Physical Anthropology*. **65**: 329-331.

Stern, J. T. Jr., and Susman, R. L. 1983a The locomotor anatomy of *Australopithecus afarensis*. *American Journal of Physical Anthropology*, **60**: 279-318.

Stern, J. T. Jr. and Susman, R. L. 1983b Functions of peroneus longus and brevis during locomotion in apes and humans. *American Journal of Physical Anthropology*. **60**: 256.

Steudel, K. 1984 Allometric perspectives on fossil catarrhine morphology. In *SIZE AND SCALING IN PRIMATE BIOLOGY* (Edited by W. L. Jungers). Plenum, New York. pp. 449-475.

Stini, W. A. 1969 Nutritional stress and growth: sex differences in adaptive response. *American Journal of Physical Anthropology*. **31**: 417-426.

Stoddard, D. M. 1985 The role of olfaction in the evolution of human sexual biology. Unpublished manuscript. 18 pp.

Straus, W. L. Jr. 1948 The humerus of *Paranthropus robustus*. *American Journal of Physical Anthropology*. **60**: 285-312.

Susman, R. L., Stern, J. T. Jr., and Rose, M. D. 1983 Morphology of KNM-ER 3228 and OH 28 innominates from East Africa. *American Journal of Physical Anthropology*. **60**: 256.

Swindler, D. R. 1976 *DENTITION OF LIVING PRIMATES*. London, Academic.

Tardieu, C. 1981 Morpho-functional analysis of the articular surfaces of the knee-joint in primates. In *PRIMATE EVOLUTIONARY BIOLOGY* (Edited by A. B. Chiarelli and R. S. Corruccini). Berlin, Springer Verlag. pp. 68-80.

Templeton, A. R. 1983 Phylogenetic inference from restriction endonuclease cleavage site maps with particular reference to the evolution of humans and apes. *Evolution*. **37**: 221-224.

Tobias, P. V. 1972 'Dished faces', brain-size and early hominids. *Nature*, London. **239**: 468-469.

Todd, M. P. 1982 The face of *Sivapithecus indicus*: description of a new, relatively complete specimen from the Siwaliks of Pakistan. *Folia Primatologia*, **38**: 141-157.

Trivers, R. L. 1972 Parental investment and sexual selection. In *SEXUAL SELECTION AND THE DESCENT OF MAN*. (Edited by B. G. Campbell). Chicago, Aldine. pp. 1871-1971.

Turner, A. 1983 The quantification of relative abundances in fossil and subfossil bone assemblages. *Annals of the Transvaal Museum*. **33**: 311-321.

Turner, A. 1984a Dental sexual dimorphism in European lions (*Panthera leo* L.) of the upper Pleistocene: palaeoecological and palaeoethological implications. *Annals of Zoology*, Fennici. **21**: 1-8.

Turner, A. 1984b Subsampling animal bone assemblages: reducing the work-load or reducing the information? *Circaea*. **2**: 69-76.

Turner, A. 1984c Identifying bone accumulating agents. In *FRONTIERS: SOUTHERN AFRICAN ARCHAEOLOGY TODAY*. (Edited by M. Hall, G. Avery, D. M. Avery, M. L. Wilson and A. J. B. Humphreys). Cambridge monographs in African Archaeology. pp. 334-339.

Turner, A. 1984d Behavioural inferences based on frequencies in bone assemblages from archaeological sites. In *FRONTIERS: SOUTHERN AFRICAN ARCHAEOLOGY TODAY*. (Edited by M. Hall, G. Avery, D. M. Avery, M. L. Wilson and A. J. B. Humphreys). Cambridge monographs in African Archaeology. pp. 363-366.

Tuttle, R. H. 1977 Naturalistic positional behavior of apes and models of hominid evolution, 1929-1976. In *PROGRESS IN APE RESEARCH*. (Edited by G. H. Bourne). New York, Academic. pp. 277-296.

van Vark, G. N. and Howells, W. W. 1984 *MULTIVARIATE STATISTICAL METHODS IN PHYSICAL ANTHROPOLOGY*. Amsterdam, Reidel.

Vandeburgh, J. G. 1984 *PHEROMONES AND REPRODUCTION IN MAMMALS*. New York, Academic.

von Koenigswald, G. H. R. 1952 *Gigantopithecus blackii* von Koenigswald, a giant fossil hominoid from the Pleistocene in southern China. *Anthropological Papers of the American Museum of Natural History*. **43**: 295-325.

von Koenigswald, G. H. R. 1968 Observations upon two *Pithecanthropus* mandibles from Sangiran, central Java. *Proceedings, Koninklijke nederlandse Akademie van Wettenschappen* (Amsterdam). **B 71**: 99-107.

von Koenigswald, G. H. R. 1972 Ein unterkiefer einesfossilen Hominoiden aus dem Unterpliozen Griechlands. *Proceedings: Koninklijke nederlandse akademie Wetenschappen* (Amsterdam), **B. 75**: 385-394.

von Koenigswald, G. H. R. 1981 A possible ancestral form of *Gigantopithecus* (Mammalia, Hominoidea) from the Chinji layers of Pakistan. *Journal of Human Evolution*. **10**: 511-515.

Waloff, N. 1966 Scotch broom (*Sarothamnus scoparius* (L.) Wimmer) and its insect fauna introduced into the Pacific Northwest of America. *Journal of Applied Ecology*. **3**: 239-311.

Ward, S. C. and Kimball, D. R. 1983 Maxillofacial morphology of Miocene hominids from Africa and Indo-pakistan. In *INTERPRETATIONS OF APE AND HUMAN ANCESTRY*. (Edited by R. L. Ciochon and R. S. Corruccini). New York, Plenum. pp. 211-238.

Weidenreich, F. 1945 Giant early man from Java and South China. *Anthropological Papers, American Museum of Natural History*. **40**: 1-134.

Weiner, J. and Campbell, B. C. G. 1964 The taxonomic status of the Swanscombe skull. In *THE SWANSCOMBE SKULL: A SURVEY OF RESEARCH ON A PLEISTOCENE SITE*. (Edited by C. D. Ovey). Occasional Papers of the Royal Anthropological Institute, London. pp. 175-209.

White, T. D. 1977 New fossils hominids from Laetoli, Tanzania. *American Journal of Physical Anthropology*. **46**: 197-230.

White, T. D. 1980 Additional fossil hominids from Laetoli, Tanzania: 1976-1979 specimens. *American Journal of Physical Anthropology*. **53**: 487-504.

White, T. D. Johanson, D. C. and Kimball, W. H. 1981 *Australopithecus africanus*: its phyletic position reconsidered. *South African Journal of Science*. **77**: 445-470.

Wilson, S. 1984 Towards an understanding of data in physical anthropology. In *MULTIVARIATE STATISTICAL METHODS IN PHYSICAL ANTHROPOLOGY*. (Edited by G. N. van Vark and W. W. Howells). Amsterdam, Riedel. pp. 261-282.

Wilks, S. S. 1935 On the independence of k sets of normally distributed variables. *Econometrica*. **3**: 309-326.

Wolpoff, M. H. 1971 Metric trends in hominid dental evolution. *CASE WESTERN RESERVE UNIVERSITY, Studies in Anthropology*, **2**: 1-244.

Wolpoff, M. H. 1973a Posterior tooth size, body size and diet in South African gracile australopithecines. *American Journal of Physical Anthropology*. **39**: 375-393.

Wolpoff, M. H. 1973b Interstitial Wear. *American Journal of Physical Anthropology*. **34**: 205-228.

Wolpoff, M. H. 1980 *PALEOANTHROPOLOGY*. New York, Knopf.

Wolpoff, M. H. 1982 *Ramapithecus* and hominid origins. *Current Anthropology*. **23**: 501-522.

Woo, J. K.: see Wu R.

Wood, B. A. 1975 An analysis of sexual dimorphism in primates. PhD Thesis, University of London.

Wood, B. A. 1976 The nature and basis of sexual dimorphism in the primate skeleton. *Journal of Zoology*, London. **180**: 15-34.

Wood, B. A. 1978 *HUMAN EVOLUTION*. London, Chapman and Hall.

Wood, B. A. 1984 Primatology by numbers. A review of *The Order of Man: a Biomathematical Anatomy of the Primates*. By Charles Oxnard. *Nature*, London. **309**: 289-290.

Wood, B. A. 1985 A review of the definition, distribution and relationships of *Australopithecus africanus*. *Proceedings of the Taung Diamond Jubilee International Symposium*. Johannesburg. p. 41.

Wu, C. and Li, W. 1985 *Proceedings of the National Academy of Sciences*, U.S.A. **82**: 824.

Wu R. (Woo, J. K.) 1957 *Dryopithecus* teeth from Keiyuan, Yunnan Province. *Vertebrata Palasiatica*. **1**: 25-29.

Wu R. (Woo, J. K.) 1962 The mandibles and dentition of *Gigantopithecus*. *Palaeontologica Sinica*, **146**: 1-94.

Wu R. 1982 *RECENT ADVANCES OF CHINESE PALAEONTOLOGY*. Hong Kong, Hong Kong University Press.

Wu, R., Han, D., Xu, Q., Lu, Q., Pan, Y., Zhang, H., Zheng, L., and Xiao, M. 1981 *Ramapithecus* skulls found first time in the world. *Kexue Tongbao*. **26**: 1018-1021.

Wu, R. Han, D., Xu, Q., Qui, G., Lu, Q., Pan, Y., and Chen, W. 1982 More *Ramapithecus* skulls from the Lufeng, Yunnan — Report on the excavation at the site in 1981. *Acta Anthropologica Sinica*. **2**: 101-108.

Wu, R. and Olsen, J. 1985 *PALEOANTHROPOLOGY AND PALEOLITHIC ARCHAEOLOGY IN CHINA*, San Francisco. Academic Press.

Wu, R. and Oxnard, C. E. 1983a Ramapithecines from China: evidence from tooth dimensions. *Nature*, London. **306**: 258-260.

Wu, R., and Oxnard, C. E. 1983b *Ramapithecus* and *Sivapithecus* from China: some implications for higher primate evolution. *American Journal of Primatology*. **5**: 303-344.

Wu, R. and Wu, X. 1983 Hominid fossils from China and their relation to neighbouring regions. In *PALAEOENVIRONMENT OF EAST ASIA FROM THE MID TERTIARY*. Hong Kong, Centre for Asian Studies, University of Hong Kong.

Wu, R., Xu, Q., Lu, Q. 1983 Morphological features of *Ramapithecus* and *Sivapithecus* and their phylogenetic relationships. *Acta Anthropologica Sinica* **2**: 1-14.

Xu, Q. and Lu, Q. 1979 The mandibles of *Ramathecus* and *Sivapithecus* from Lufeng, China. *Vertebrata Palasiatica*. **17**: 1-13.

Xu, Q. and Lu, Q. 1980 The Lufeng ape skull and its significance. *China Reconstructs*. **29**: 56-57.

Yates, F. 1950 The place of statistics in the study of growth and form. *Proceedings of the Royal Society of London*. **B**. **137**: 479-489.

Yates, F. and Healy, M. J. R. 1951 Statistical methods in anthropology. *Nature*, London. **168**: 1116-1117.

Yip, C. 1983 *FOSSIL MAN IN CHINA*. Hong Kong, Hong Kong Museum of Natural History.

Zhang, Y. 1982 Variability and evolutionary trends in tooth size of *Gigantopithecus blackii*. *American Journal of Physical Anthropology*. **59**: 21-32.

Zhang, Y. 1985 *Gigantopithecus* and *"Australopithecus"* in China. In *PALAEOANTHROPOLOGY AND PALAEOLITHIC ARCHAEOLOGY IN THE PEOPLE'S REPUBLIC OF CHINA*. (Edited by Wu Rukang and J. W. Olsen). London, Academic. pp. 69-78.

Zihlman, A. L. 1985 *Australopithecus afarensis*: two sexes or two species. *Proceedings of the Taung Diamond Jubilee International Symposium* Johannesburg, **31**.

Zonnenveld, F. W. 1985 A new method for high resolution computed tomography of hominid fossils. *Proceedings of the Taung Diamond Jubilee International Symposium*, Johannesburg, **32**.

Zuckerman, S. 1928 Age changes in the chimpanzee, with special reference to growth of brain, eruption of teeth and estimation of age; with a note on the Taungs ape. *Proceedings of the Zoological Society*, London. **1**-42.

Zuckerman, S. 1933 *FUNCTIONAL AFFINITIES OF MAN, MONKEYS AND APES*. London, Kegan Paul.

Zuckerman, S. 1950 Taxonomy and human evolution. *Biological Reviews*. **25**: 435-485.

Zuckerman, S. 1955 Age changes in the basicranial axis of the human skull. *American Journal of Physical Anthropology*. **13**: 521-539.

Zuckerman, S. 1966 Myths and methods in anatomy. *Journal of the Royal College of Surgeons of Edinburgh*. **11**: 87-114.

Zuckerman, S. 1970 *BEYOND THE IVORY TOWER*. New York, Taplinger.

Zuckerman, S., Ashton, E. H., Flinn, R. M., Oxnard C. E., and Spence, T. F. 1973 Some locomotor features of the pelvic girdle in primates. *Symposia of the Zoological Society*, London. **33**: 71-165.

General Index

Index Of Species

Index Of Authors